MW01493533

EDITORIAL BOARD

ROBERT C. CLARK
DIRECTING EDITOR
Distinguished Service Professor and Austin Wakeman Scott
Professor of Law and Former Dean of the Law School
Harvard University

DANIEL A. FARBER
Sho Sato Professor of Law
University of California at Berkeley

HEATHER K. GERKEN
Dean and the Sol & Lillian Goldman Professor of Law
Yale University

SAMUEL ISSACHAROFF
Bonnie and Richard Reiss Professor of Constitutional Law
New York University

HAROLD HONGJU KOH
Sterling Professor of International Law and
Former Dean of the Law School
Yale University

SAUL LEVMORE
William B. Graham Distinguished Service Professor of Law and
Former Dean of the Law School
University of Chicago

THOMAS W. MERRILL
Charles Evans Hughes Professor of Law
Columbia University

ROBERT L. RABIN
A. Calder Mackay Professor of Law
Stanford University

UNIVERSITY CASEBOOK SERIES®

SECURITIES REGULATION

NINTH EDITION

LARRY D. SODERQUIST
Late Professor of Law
Vanderbilt University

THERESA A. GABALDON
Lyle T. Alverson Professor of Law
George Washington University School of Law

FOUNDATION
PRESS

The publisher is not engaged in rendering legal or other professional advice, and this publication is not a substitute for the advice of an attorney. If you require legal or other expert advice, you should seek the services of a competent attorney or other professional.

University Casebook Series is a trademark registered in the U.S. Patent and Trademark Office.

© 1982, 1988, 1994, 1999, 2003 FOUNDATION PRESS
© 2006, 2010 THOMSON REUTERS/FOUNDATION PRESS
© 2014 by LEG, Inc. d/b/a West Academic
© 2018 LEG, Inc. d/b/a West Academic
     444 Cedar Street, Suite 700
     St. Paul, MN 55101
     1-877-888-1330

Printed in the United States of America

ISBN: 978-1-68328-712-4

In Memorium

Larry D. Soderquist

———————

For Bob and Will, with thanks.

PREFACE

Each chapter save the first features one or more situations involving a hypothetical client. These situations are designed to place the chapter's materials in a context that students can understand and to stimulate students' thought as they prepare assignments. Teachers who wish to use the situations in class will find they provide substantial raw material for discussion. The book does not force a particular teaching method, however, and the situations can be left to the students' own consideration if a teacher desires.

One basic idea behind the book is that securities law is inextricably bound up with business transactions, making it difficult to learn securities law outside the context of these transactions. For example, to understand the concept of "offer" one must first understand the kinds of activities that issuers, underwriters, and dealers engage in when doing an offering. This may be obvious. Less obvious, but also true, is that unless students are presented with a discrete context, those without a business background are likely to feel undue anxiety about their ability to handle the securities law course. The situations included in the book are designed to provide a sufficient and understandable context that will give students confidence.

A second idea behind the book is that the various areas of securities law tend to be practiced from one of two viewpoints: prospective or retrospective. For example, in the securities registration area, the lawyer usually works as a planner, viewing transactions prospectively. He or she takes the law as a given and structures transactions around it. On the other hand, the liability areas tend to be more the bailiwick of the litigator. Transactions the litigator is concerned with are in the past, so his or her job is to structure the law, by analysis and argument, so as to fit facts that are viewed retrospectively. Depending on which mode the securities lawyer is operating in, he or she will view the law in different ways. For instance, whether a particular statement by a court is dictum may be important to the litigator, but virtually irrelevant to the planner. The litigator does not mind working in the vanguard, but the lawyer operating as planner wishes to take no avoidable chance of running afoul of the law. With these differences in mind, it seems helpful to have students approach various areas of the securities law course from one or the other of these viewpoints. The situations accomplish this by placing students, before they have begun studying a particular area, in the midst of a factual situation that encourages them to approach the area in one or the other of the two modes.

The book is organized in a straightforward way. After a general introductory chapter, the beginning chapters focus on the Securities Act of 1933 (the " '33 Act") and later chapters on the Securities Exchange Act of 1934 (the '34 Act), with additional chapters on issues in securities law litigation, on the special responsibilities of securities lawyers, on the state regulation of securities, and on international aspects of securities regulation.

Larry Soderquist, the founding author of this book, and I tried to present material in a sequence that has later materials building on earlier. By this sequencing, and by the choice of materials and their editing, we attempted to avoid throwing students in over their heads. Also, we included a fair amount of explanatory material. This material is along the lines of what might be called written tutorials. It is designed to take the students through a particular area, for example Section 5 of the Securities Act, in the same sort of way one might in a tutorial or, for that matter, in the same way an experienced lawyer might in the course of training a new lawyer.

Citations of authority and references of various sorts, along with footnotes, have been omitted from the readings in the book, except where inclusion, or partial inclusion, has served a specific purpose, and the footnotes that have been included have been renumbered. These deletions, the modification of some descriptive headings of Securities and Exchange Commission releases, the correction of typographical errors, and a few miscellaneous deletions and revisions of a minor nature have not been indicated, but other editorial changes in the readings have been. Readers should be aware that there have been many re-numberings of various provisions of the Securities and Exchange Act. The book utilizes the most current numbering system, indicating with brackets when this represents a change from quoted sources.

SECURITIES LAW: A WORK IN PROGRESS

Users of the *Ninth Edition* should know that securities law is very much a work in progress. Corporate scandals in the early 2000s, a credit crisis and accompanying financial panic that began to sweep the globe in 2008, and a subsequent financial recession led to a patchwork of regulatory responses. Some of those are being rethought or have inspired ostensibly compensatory exemptions and the result is complexity, to say the least.

What does this mean for those who would master the field of securities regulation? It should be mildly reassuring to know that securities regulation has undergone many alterations since its basic contours were established in the 1930s. Those who already are familiar with those contours and experienced in navigating the details of the terrain probably are the best equipped to deal with whatever changes transpire. It may be even more reassuring, however, to ponder the distinction between *financial* regulation and *securities* regulation, and to recognize that many of the regulatory shortcomings contributing to shifting economic and financial conditions had little to do with what is studied in the ordinary course for which this book is used.

Securities regulation is a subset of financial regulation. Thus, financial regulation comprehends regulation of specific transactions in securities, as well as the markets in which those transactions occur. Financial regulation also extends to the regulation of commodities, commercial banking, and insurance, and, in a larger sense, regulation of the money supply. Whether each of these elements *should* be separately regulated is debatable; the fact, however, is that financial regulation has been balkanized among a number of federal and state authorities. Certainly, many reform proposals focus on this state of affairs and call for change. Neither centralization nor co-ordination of regulation automatically means abandonment of workable regulatory schemes.

The message, then, is two-fold. Users of this or any book providing an overview of securities regulation should proceed with some confidence that what they are studying will be of use in the future. They should be equally confident, however, that what they are studying is only a part of the larger picture of financial regulation, and that the larger picture is in a state of flux.

OTHER MATTERS

Thanks are owed to Elizabeth R. Flint and her firm, Wilson Sonsini Goodrich & Rosati, as well as Morgan Stanley Dean Witter, for providing the tombstone advertisement appearing in Chapter 3. I am grateful also to the various copyright holders who have allowed us to reprint material by other authors. I want to thank the Practising Law Institute for allowing the use of material from Larry Soderquist's book, *Understanding the Securities Laws*, and to express appreciation to the many students who in diverse ways provided helpful assistance, including a number of very able research assistants. Most recently, the input of Xiaoyang (Winnie) Ma was invaluable. I also wish to acknowledge and thank Ms. Toni Foncette for going above and beyond in the preparation of the manuscript. I appreciate the efforts and insights of Robert Palmer, and the inspiration of Will Palmer.

Most importantly, I want to express my deep gratitude to Larry Soderquist, who generously involved me in the authorship of this book, and without whom the book would never have existed. Larry's death in 2005 has left a void that cannot be filled. I hope, however, to be joined on the next and later editions by new co-authors.

Please feel free to contact me with any questions or comments you may have, either by phone at (202)994–6995 or by email at tgabaldon@ law.gwu.edu. I'll look forward to hearing from you.

THERESA A. GABALDON

August 2017

SUMMARY OF CONTENTS

PART 4. SECURITIES LAW LITIGATION

PART 5. SPECIAL RESPONSIBILITIES OF SECURITIES LAWYERS

PART 6. STATE REGULATION OF SECURITIES

PART 7. INTERNATIONAL ASPECTS OF SECURITIES LAW

TABLE OF CONTENTS

PART 3. SECURITIES EXCHANGE ACT OF 1934

PART 5. SPECIAL RESPONSIBILITIES
OF SECURITIES LAWYERS

PART 6. STATE REGULATION OF SECURITIES

PART 7. INTERNATIONAL ASPECTS OF SECURITIES LAW

TABLE OF CASES

The principal cases are in bold type.

UNIVERSITY CASEBOOK SERIES®

SECURITIES REGULATION

NINTH EDITION

PART 1

INTRODUCTION

CHAPTER 1

APPROACHING SECURITIES LAW

A. HISTORICAL AND CULTURAL PERSPECTIVE

Securities law, and the Securities Act of 1933 especially, is tricky— it is a puzzle that can be put together in many ways, only one of them right. It will help in approaching this puzzle to understand something of the beginnings of the federal securities statutes, for it is there that the trickiness finds its roots.

The Securities Act of 1933 is quintessential New Deal legislation that grew out of the 1929 stock market crash and Franklin Roosevelt's 1932 campaign. Within weeks of his inauguration, Roosevelt moved to begin the securities reform that had been promised in the Democratic platform. A former Federal Trade Commissioner named Huston Thompson was given the task of drafting the Securities Act. His bill went to Congress in March of 1933, accompanied by a message from the President stating his desires as to the thrust of the legislation. It quickly became apparent that the Thompson bill was not consistent with these desires. The President agreed with Brandeis that "sunshine is said to be the best of disinfectants; electric light the most efficient policeman,"[1] and he wanted regulation through disclosure requirements. Although this philosophy was embodied in a 1932 campaign plank, the Thompson bill went in another direction. It mandated what has become known as "merit regulation." This scheme, much used in state securities law, gives a governmental body the power to pass upon the merits of securities offerings and to prevent unworthy offerings.

In early April, a new drafting team was formed. The members' identities, their intellect, and the constraints on them as they worked are important parts of the tale. The group, which was assembled by Felix Frankfurter, consisted of James M. Landis, a Harvard Law School professor; Thomas G. Corcoran, a government lawyer recently out of a securities law practice; and Benjamin V. Cohen, a practicing lawyer. Each was brilliant, and from the statute they created it is apparent that they delighted in mental challenges involving interwoven complexities and neatly hidden traps.

The team set to work on a Friday. For political reasons, they did not scrap the Thompson bill. They used it as a base for amendment, while drawing heavily on the English Companies Act of 1929. By late Saturday they had a draft that, more than fifty years later, still constitutes the

---

[1] L. Brandeis, Other People's Money 92 (1914).

main body of the Securities Act. The Act is a masterpiece, an intellectual tour de force. It is fun to work with—once you know how. For now, realize that when one works with the Securities Act, one plays a complex mental game devised by three exceptional minds, over a weekend, more than a half century ago.

The Securities Exchange Act of 1934, the other statute dealt with in this book in some detail, is the second part of the securities regulatory scheme that was contemplated as early as the 1932 Democratic campaign. It is substantially longer than the Securities Act, and its coverage is much more diverse. It is also more straightforward, making it easier to work with than the Securities Act. Although the two acts shared Benjamin Cohen as a draftsman, the Exchange Act lacks the idiosyncratic sparkle that makes the Securities Act at once more interesting and difficult.

Since the early 1980s, the Securities and Exchange Commission ("SEC"), described immediately below, has done much to integrate disclosure under the Securities and Exchange Acts. This has simplified practical compliance for many companies but has complicated the job of the securities lawyer.

B. FEDERAL REGULATORY SCHEME

I.   THE SEC: WHAT IT IS AND WHAT IT DOES

What We Do

Securities and Exchange Commission, 2017.

INTRODUCTION

The mission of the U.S. Securities and Exchange Commission is to protect investors, maintain fair, orderly, and efficient markets, and facilitate capital formation. As more and more first-time investors turn to the markets to help secure their futures, pay for homes, and send children to college, our investor protection mission is more compelling than ever. As our nation's securities exchanges mature into global for-profit competitors, there is even greater need for sound market regulation. And the common interest of all Americans in a growing economy that produces jobs, improves our standard of living, and protects the value of our savings means that all of the SEC's actions must be taken with an eye toward promoting the capital formation that is necessary to sustain economic growth.

The world of investing is fascinating and complex, and it can be very fruitful. But unlike the banking world, where deposits are guaranteed by the federal government, stocks, bonds and other securities can lose value. There are no guarantees. That's why investing is not a spectator sport. By far the best way for investors to protect the money they put into the securities markets is to do research and ask questions.

The laws and rules that govern the securities industry in the United States derive from a simple and straightforward concept: all investors, whether large institutions or private individuals, should have access to certain basic facts about an investment prior to buying it, and so long as they hold it. To achieve this, the SEC requires public companies to disclose meaningful financial and other information to the public. This provides a common pool of knowledge for all investors to use to judge for themselves whether to buy, sell, or hold a particular security. Only through the steady flow of timely, comprehensive, and accurate information can people make sound investment decisions.

The result of this information flow is a far more active, efficient, and transparent capital market that facilitates the capital formation so important to our nation's economy. To insure that this objective is always being met, the SEC continually works with all major market participants, including especially the investors in our securities markets, to listen to their concerns and to learn from their experience.

The SEC oversees the key participants in the securities world, including securities exchanges, securities brokers and dealers, investment advisors, and mutual funds. Here the SEC is concerned primarily with promoting the disclosure of important market-related information, maintaining fair dealing, and protecting against fraud.

Crucial to the SEC's effectiveness in each of these areas is its enforcement authority. Each year the SEC brings hundreds of civil enforcement actions against individuals and companies for violation of the securities laws. Typical infractions include insider trading, accounting fraud, and providing false or misleading information about securities and the companies that issue them.

One of the major sources of information on which the SEC relies to bring enforcement action is investors themselves—another reason that educated and careful investors are so critical to the functioning of efficient markets. To help support investor education, the SEC offers the public a wealth of educational information on [its] Internet website, which also includes the EDGAR database of disclosure documents that public companies are required to file with the Commission.

Though it is the primary overseer and regulator of the U.S. securities markets, the SEC works closely with many other institutions, including Congress, other federal departments and agencies, the self-regulatory organizations (e.g. the stock exchanges), state securities regulators, and various private sector organizations. In addition, the Chairman of the SEC represents the agency as a member of the Financial Stability Oversight Council (FSOC).

* * *

ORGANIZATION OF THE SEC

The SEC consists of five presidentially-appointed Commissioners, with staggered five-year terms * * * . One of them is designated by the

President as Chairman of the Commission—the agency's chief executive. By law, no more than three of the Commissioners may belong to the same political party, ensuring non-partisanship. The agency's functional responsibilities are organized into five Divisions and 23 Offices, each of which is headquartered in Washington, DC. The Commission's approximately 4,600 staff are located in Washington and in 11 Regional Offices throughout the country.

It is the responsibility of the Commission to:

- interpret federal securities laws;
- issue new rules and amend existing rules;
- oversee the inspection of securities firms, brokers, investment advisers, and ratings agencies;
- oversee private regulatory organizations in the securities, accounting, and auditing fields; and
- coordinate U.S. securities regulation with federal, state, and foreign authorities.

The Commission convenes regularly at meetings that are open to the public and the news media unless the discussion pertains to confidential subjects, such as whether to begin an enforcement action.

[The SEC's staff is organized into divisions and offices with specific areas of responsibility for various segments of the federal securities laws. Divisions serving under the Commission include the Division of Corporation Finance, the Division of Trading and Markets, the Division of Investment Management, the Division of Enforcement, and the Division of Economic and Risk Analysis.

Offices serving under the Commission include, among others, the Office of General Counsel, the Office of the Chief Accountant, the Office of Compliance Inspections and Examinations, the Office of Credit Ratings, the Office of International Affairs, the Office of Investor Education and Advocacy, the Office of Municipal Securities, the Office of Ethics Council, The Office of the Investor Advocate, the Office of Women and Minority Inclusion, the Office of Legislative and Intergovernmental Affairs, the Office of Public Affairs, and the Office of Administrative Law Judges.]

DIVISION OF CORPORATION FINANCE

The Division of Corporation Finance assists the Commission in executing its responsibility to oversee corporate disclosure of important information to the investing public. Corporations are required to comply with regulations pertaining to disclosure that must be made when stock is initially sold and then on a continuing and periodic basis. The Division's staff routinely reviews the disclosure documents filed by companies. The staff also provides companies with assistance interpreting the Commission's rules and recommends to the Commission new rules for adoption.

The Division of Corporation Finance reviews documents that publicly-held companies are required to file with the Commission. The documents include:

- registration statements for newly-offered securities;

- annual and quarterly filings (Forms 10–K and 10–Q);

- proxy materials sent to shareholders before an annual meeting;

- annual reports to shareholders;

- documents concerning tender offers (a tender offer is an offer to buy a large number of shares of a corporation, usually at a premium above the current market price); and

- filings related to mergers and acquisitions.

These documents disclose information about the companies' financial condition and business practices to help investors make informed investment decisions. Through the Division's review process, the staff monitors compliance with disclosure requirements and seeks to improve the quality of the disclosure. To meet the SEC's requirements for disclosure, a company issuing securities or whose securities are publicly traded must make available all information, whether it is positive or negative, that might be relevant to an investor's decision to buy, sell, or hold the security.

* * *

The Division's staff provides guidance and counseling to registrants, prospective registrants, and the public to help them comply with the law. For example, a company might ask whether the offering of a particular security requires registration with the SEC. Corporation Finance would share its interpretation of the relevant securities regulations with the company and give it advice on compliance with the appropriate disclosure requirement.

The Division uses no-action letters to issue guidance in a more formal manner. A company seeks a no-action letter from the staff of the SEC when it plans to enter uncharted legal territory in the securities industry. For example, if a company wants to try a new marketing or financial technique, it can ask the staff to write a letter indicating whether it would or would not recommend that the Commission take action against the company for engaging in its new practice.

DIVISION OF TRADING AND MARKETS

The Division of Trading and Markets assists the Commission in executing its responsibility for maintaining fair, orderly, and efficient markets. The staff of the Division provide day-to-day oversight of the major securities market participants: the securities exchanges; securities firms; self-regulatory organizations (SROs) including the Financial Industry Regulatory Authority (FINRA), the Municipal Securities

Rulemaking Board (MSRB), clearing agencies that help facilitate trade settlement; transfer agents (parties that maintain records of securities owners); securities information processors; and credit rating agencies.

* * *

The Division's additional responsibilities include:

- carrying out the Commission's financial integrity program for broker-dealers;

- reviewing (and in some cases approving, under authority delegated from the Commission) proposed new rules and proposed changes to existing rules filed by the SROs;

- assisting the Commission in establishing rules and issuing interpretations on matters affecting the operation of the securities markets; and

- surveilling the markets.

DIVISION OF INVESTMENT MANAGEMENT

The Division of Investment Management assists the Commission in executing its responsibility for investor protection and for promoting capital formation through oversight and regulation of America's $66.8 trillion investment management industry. This important part of the U.S. capital markets includes mutual funds and the professional fund managers who advise them; analysts who research individual assets and asset classes; and investment advisers to individual customers. Because of the high concentration of individual investors in the mutual funds, exchange-traded funds, and other investments that fall within the Division's purview, the Division of Investment Management is focused on ensuring that disclosures about these investments are useful to retail customers, and that the regulatory costs which consumers must bear are not excessive.

* * *

DIVISION OF ENFORCEMENT

First and foremost, the SEC is a law enforcement agency. The Division of Enforcement assists the Commission in executing its law enforcement function by recommending the commencement of investigations of securities law violations, by recommending that the Commission bring civil actions in federal court or before an administrative law judge, and by prosecuting these cases on behalf of the Commission. As an adjunct to the SEC's civil enforcement authority, the Division works closely with law enforcement agencies in the U.S. and around the world to bring criminal cases when appropriate.

The Division obtains evidence of possible violations of the securities laws from many sources, including market surveillance activities, investor tips and complaints, other Divisions and Offices of the SEC, the self-regulatory organizations and other securities industry sources, and media reports.

All SEC investigations are conducted privately. Facts are developed to the fullest extent possible through informal inquiry, interviewing witnesses, examining brokerage records, reviewing trading data, and other methods. With a formal order of investigation, the Division's staff may compel witnesses by subpoena to testify and produce books, records, and other relevant documents. Following an investigation, SEC staff present their findings to the Commission for its review. The Commission can authorize the staff to file a case in federal court or bring an administrative action. In many cases, the Commission and the party charged decide to settle a matter without trial.

Whether the Commission decides to bring a case in federal court or within the SEC before an administrative law judge may depend upon the type of sanction or relief that is being sought. For example, the Commission may bar someone from the brokerage industry in an administrative proceeding, but an order barring someone from acting as a corporate officer or director must be obtained in federal court. Often, when the misconduct warrants it, the Commission will bring both proceedings.

* * *

DIVISION OF ECONOMIC AND RISK ANALYSIS

The Division of Economic and Risk Analysis assists the Commission in executing its mission to protect investors, maintain fair, orderly, and efficient markets, and facilitate capital formation by integrating robust economic analysis and rigorous data analytics into the work of the SEC. The Division has a broad role in Commission activities, interacting with nearly every Division and Office, providing sophisticated and data-driven economic and risk analyses to help inform the agency's policymaking, rulemaking, enforcement, and examinations.

There are two main functions for the Division. First, DERA staff provide vital support in the form of economic analyses in support of Commission rulemaking and policy development. Second, the Division also provides economic analysis and research, risk assessment, and data analytics to critically support the agency's resources on matters presenting the greatest perceived risks in litigation, examinations, and registrant reviews, as well as providing economic support for enforcement matters.

* * *

THE LAWS THAT GOVERN THE SECURITIES INDUSTRY

SECURITIES ACT OF 1933

Often referred to as the "truth in securities" law, the Securities Act of 1933 has two basic objectives:

- require that investors receive financial and other significant information concerning securities being offered for public sale; and

- prohibit deceit, misrepresentations, and other fraud in the sale of securities.

The full text of this Act is available at: http://www.sec.gov/about/laws/sa33.pdf.

PURPOSE OF REGISTRATION

A primary means of accomplishing these goals is the disclosure of important financial information through the registration of securities. This information enables investors, not the government, to make informed judgments about whether to purchase a company's securities. While the SEC requires that the information provided be accurate, it does not guarantee it. Investors who purchase securities and suffer losses have important recovery rights if they can prove that there was incomplete or inaccurate disclosure of important information.

THE REGISTRATION PROCESS

In general, securities sold in the U.S. must be registered. The registration forms companies file provide essential facts while minimizing the burden and expense of complying with the law. In general, registration forms call for:

- a description of the company's properties and business;

- a description of the security to be offered for sale;

- information about the management of the company; and

- financial statements certified by independent accountants.

All companies, both domestic and foreign, must file their registration statements electronically. These statements and the accompanying prospectuses become public shortly after filing, and investors can access them using EDGAR. Registration statements are subject to examination for compliance with disclosure requirements.

Not all offerings of securities must be registered with the Commission. Some exemptions from the registration requirement include:

- private offerings to a limited number of persons or institutions;

- offerings of limited size;

- intrastate offerings; and

- securities of municipal, state, and federal governments.

By exempting many small offerings from the registration process, the SEC seeks to foster capital formation by lowering the cost of offering securities to the public.

SECURITIES EXCHANGE ACT OF 1934

With this Act, Congress created the Securities and Exchange Commission. The Act empowers the SEC with broad authority over all aspects of the securities industry. This includes the power to register, regulate, and oversee brokerage firms, transfer agents, and clearing agencies as well as the nation's securities self regulatory organizations (SROs). The various stock exchanges, such as the New York Stock Exchange, and The Nasdaq Stock Market are SROs. The Financial Industry Regulatory Authority (FINRA) is also an SRO.

The [Exchange] Act also identifies and prohibits certain types of conduct in the markets and provides the Commission with disciplinary powers over regulated entities and persons associated with them.

The [Exchange] Act also empowers the SEC to require periodic reporting of information by companies with publicly traded securities.

CORPORATE REPORTING

Companies with more than $10 million in assets whose securities are held by more than a specified number of holders must file annual and other periodic reports. These reports are available to the public through the SEC's EDGAR database.

PROXY SOLICITATIONS

The Securities Exchange Act also governs the disclosure in materials used to solicit shareholders' votes in annual or special meetings held for the election of directors and the approval of other corporate action. This information, contained in proxy materials, must be filed with the Commission in advance of any solicitation to ensure compliance with the disclosure rules. Solicitations, whether by management or shareholder groups, must disclose all important facts concerning the issues on which holders are asked to vote.

TENDER OFFERS

The Securities Exchange Act requires disclosure of important information by anyone seeking to acquire more than 5 percent of a company's securities by direct purchase or tender offer. Such an offer often is extended in an effort to gain control of the company. As with the proxy rules, this allows shareholders to make informed decisions on these critical corporate events.

INSIDER TRADING

The securities laws broadly prohibit fraudulent activities of any kind in connection with the offer, purchase, or sale of securities. These provisions are the basis for many types of disciplinary actions, including actions against fraudulent insider trading. Insider trading is illegal when a person trades a security while in possession of material nonpublic information in violation of a duty to withhold the information or refrain from trading.

REGISTRATION OF EXCHANGES, ASSOCIATIONS, AND OTHERS

The [Exchange] Act requires a variety of market participants to register with the Commission, including exchanges, brokers and dealers, transfer agents, and clearing agencies. Registration for these organizations involves filing disclosure documents that are updated on a regular basis.

The exchanges and FINRA are identified as self-regulatory organizations (SROs). SROs must create rules that allow for disciplining members for improper conduct and for establishing measures to ensure market integrity and investor protection. SRO proposed rules are published for comment before final SEC review and approval.

The full text of this Act can be read at: http://www.sec.gov/about/laws/sea34.pdf.

* * *

II. SECURITIES ACT AND EXCHANGE ACT INTEGRATION

Owing largely to technological advances, information filed with the SEC becomes quickly and widely available. The interest of market participants in information relating to the largest issuers of securities is thought to lead to particularly efficient dissemination. In recognition of these linked phenomena, the SEC has adopted a number of rules effectively resulting in different tiers of *Securities* Act regulation for different types of issuers. The most important determinants have to do with the issuer's *Exchange* Act filing status and its size. This integration of the two regulatory schemes has complicated the study of securities law and is a matter that frequently will be revisited in this book.

III. OTHER FEDERAL SECURITIES STATUTES

The Securities Act and the Exchange Act constitute the foundation of general federal securities regulation. Most securities lawyers deal primarily with these two acts. There are, however, a number of other federal securities statutes, each of which deals with a specialized area. The most important of these statutes are: (1) the Trust Indenture Act of 1939, (2) the Investment Company Act of 1940, and (3) the Investment Advisers Act of 1940.

As the title suggests, the Trust Indenture Act of 1939 relates to trust indentures, which are contracts between the issuer of debt securities and a trustee. The Trust Indenture Act contains a variety of provisions designed to protect the holders of debt securities covered by an indenture. Included in the Act are provisions establishing requirements for trust indentures and relating to who may serve as a trustee, along with provisions governing the conduct of trustees. The Act applies to most indentures relating to securities that are required to be registered under the Securities Act.

The Investment Company Act of 1940, which regulates mutual funds, and the Investment Advisers Act of 1940, which regulates certain investment advisers, are aggressive statutes aimed at specific groups within the securities industry. Like the Trust Indenture Acts, each of these statutes is the main preserve of a small percentage of securities lawyers. These three specialized acts share one important attribute—each is best approached by someone who understands the Securities Act and the Exchange Act.

Each of the statutes discussed above essentially creates a comprehensive regulatory scheme. Over the years, acts of Congress have amended and supplemented these schemes many times. Of particular note are three Acts passed in the present century: The Sarbanes-Oxley Act of 2002 ("Sarbanes-Oxley"), the Dodd-Frank Wall Street Reform and Consumer Protection Act of 2010 ("Dodd-Frank"), and the Jumpstart Our Business Startups Act of 2012 ("JOBS").

Sarbanes-Oxley was a response to a wave of corporate scandals largely involving accounting irregularities. In the words of the SEC, it "mandated a number of reforms to enhance corporate responsibility, enhance financial disclosures and combat corporate and accounting fraud, and created the "Public Company Accounting Oversight Board," also known as the PCAOB, to oversee the activities of the auditing profession." Some of Sarbanes-Oxley's changes directly affected the Exchange Act.

Dodd-Frank reacted to the financial crisis that arguably began in 2008. It swept more broadly than Sarbanes-Oxley, attempting a systemic overhaul of financial regulation and aiming at increasing stability and transparency. Although a number of its provisions do not affect the work of the SEC or the general study of securities regulation, some do. For instance, several changes were made in the area of proxy regulation. Dodd-Frank also made it clear that the SEC has authority to bring enforcement actions against those who aid or abet violations of the Securities Act and clarified the SEC's jurisdiction with respect to certain types of financial instruments.

The financial crisis dragged on in the form of the worst recession since the Great Depression. One of its results was the JOBS Act. In contrast to Sarbanes-Oxley and Dodd-Frank, the thrust of the JOBS Act is deregulatory. Among other things, the JOBS Act requires the SEC to study capital formation, disclosure, and registration requirements, and to implement liberalizing rules.

C. SOURCES OF FEDERAL SECURITIES LAW

I. THE FORCE OF LAW AND OTHER TYPES OF AUTHORITY

The various federal securities statutes are, of course, the primary source of federal securities law. Congress, however, has given the Securities and Exchange Commission the power to supplement the securities statutes by rules, as indicated in the preceding section. Congress also has granted the Commission the authority to exempt any person, security or transaction from any provision of the Securities Act and from most of the provisions of the Exchange Act.

The delegating grants are sometimes general, sometimes specific, and sometimes in-between. For instance, Section 19(a) of the Securities Act provides a general, or catchall, grant of rulemaking power: "The Commission shall have authority from time to time to make * * * such rules and regulations[2] as may be necessary to carry out the provisions of this title * * * " Similarly, Section 28 of the Securities Act, added in 1996, permits the Commission to "conditionally or unconditionally exempt any person, security or transaction * * * [from any provision of the Act] to the extent that such exemption is necessary or appropriate in the public interest,[3] and is consistent with the protection of investors." On the other hand, Section 2(a)(15) of the Securities Act specifies that the term "accredited investor" includes both the persons listed in the statute and "* * * any person who, on the basis of such factors as financial sophistication, net worth, knowledge, and experience in financial matters or amount of assets under management qualifies * * * under rules and regulations which the Commission shall prescribe."

Notice that, with respect to the definition of an accredited investor, Congress in Section 2(a)(15) both makes its own law and gives the Commission guidance for rulemaking. In other situations, Congress has chosen simply to turn everything in a particular area over to the Commission. Section 14(a) of the Exchange Act provides a good example: "It shall be unlawful for any person * * * , in contravention of such rules and regulations as the Commission may prescribe * * * , to solicit * * * any proxy * * * in respect of any security * * * registered pursuant to section 12 of this title."

Congress has given the Commission's rules under Exchange Act Section 14(a) the force of law by use of the phrase "It shall be unlawful * * * ." This is the basic way giving rules the force of law is handled in

---

[2] In Commission usage, regulations are compendiums of rules or "items" covering a particular topic or purpose. For example, Regulation D is a series of rules relating to three exemptions from the Securities Act's registration requirements and Regulation S–K is the general repository of disclosure requirements under the Securities Act and the Exchange Act. Regulation S–K's components are called items, with item 102, for example, relating to disclosures concerning a company's properties.

[3] Under Securities Act Section 2(b), also added in 1996, the "public interest" specifically includes both the protection of investors and the promotion of efficiency, competition and capital formation.

the Exchange Act, since Section 32(a), as amended by the Sarbanes-Oxley Act of 2002, provides:

> Any person who willfully violates any provision of this title, * * * or any rule or regulation thereunder *the violation of which is made unlawful or the observance of which is required under the terms of this title,* * * * shall upon conviction be fined not more than $5,000,000, or imprisoned not more than 20 years, or both, except that when such a person is a person other than a natural person, a fine not exceeding $25,000,000 may be imposed * * * . (Emphasis added.)

Rules are also given the force of law in Section 24 of the Securities Act:

> Any person who willfully violates any of the provisions of this title, or the rules and regulations promulgated by the Commission under authority thereof * * *, shall upon conviction be fined not more than $10,000 or imprisoned not more than five years, or both.

Although, as the foregoing may suggest, Congress historically has been quite deferential to the SEC's expertise, its attitude may have changed a bit in recent years. Sarbanes-Oxley, Dodd-Frank and the JOBS Act all had specific mandates for SEC rule-making activity, in some cases including deadlines—not all of which have been met.

In any event, in administering the securities statutes, the Commission does issue a large number of rules, along with many pronouncements that are not rules, at least in the usual sense of the term. Some of these pronouncements have the force of law. For example, Securities Act registration statement forms are given the force of law by Securities Act Rules 130 and 401(a), the latter of which says "a registration statement * * * shall conform to the applicable * * * forms" and the former of which provides that the term "rules and regulations," as used in certain sections of the Securities Act, includes the registration statement forms.

The bulk of the Commission's pronouncements, which usually take the form of a release, do not have the force of law. Under the Securities Act the Commission has issued over 10,200 releases, and it has issued more than 79,600 under the Exchange Act. In many of these releases, the Commission promulgated a rule or made an announcement with respect to a rule, a registration statement form, or some other matter. In others, however, the Commission, or a division of the Commission, announced a policy or an interpretation of a statute or rule. Although these policies and interpretations do not have the force of law, as a practical matter they are often given almost that effect by a securities lawyer. A litigator can expect a court to pay substantial deference to the Commission's interpretations and policies, and so he or she must consider them not far below the rules in the real world hierarchy of securities regulation. The lawyer working as a planner, which describes securities lawyers most of the time, typically moves Commission policies and interpretations even closer to rules in the lawyer's own hierarchy. First, the planner wishes to take no avoidable chance of running afoul of the law. Second, congruence with the Commission's policies and interpretations is often the best way efficiently to accomplish a client's transaction.

Also of substantial importance to the securities lawyer are the interpretive letters and so-called no-action letters that are issued, upon request, by the staff of a division of the Commission. In certain instances, the Commission's staff interprets a provision of law for an interested person. In other cases, the no-action letter procedure is used. The process of issuing a no-action letter begins when an interested person, or more usually his or her lawyer, writes a letter outlining a proposed transaction. If the staff is amenable, it responds by indicating that if the transaction is entered into, it will not recommend enforcement action to the Commission. In some areas of the law, the Division of Corporation Finance has issued Staff Legal Bulletins, which the director of the division described as "super no-action letters." Until 1970 no-action letters were not made public, constituting in a sense a private body of "law" known only to a small group of securities experts. Now all are published, except for cases in which confidential treatment is sought and approved.

Lawyers sometimes call the Chief Counsel's office in the Division of Corporation Finance for an informal interpretation of some aspects of securities law. Helpfully, the Commission has published a manual of telephone responses given by the Division of Corporation Finance, and this manual may answer a lawyer's question. The manual is available online but is not updated frequently and may, with respect to some matters, be out-of-date.

Beginning in 2005, the Commission has made the staff's subsequently issued comment letters with respect to filed documents, as well as the responses to these letters by issuer's counsel, available on the Commission's website. These letters provide extremely helpful information about the current issues being focused on by the staff, although they are not made available until forty-five days after the staff has completed its review of a filing.

Court decisions, of course, are as important in interpreting securities statutes and rules as they are in other areas. Coverage by case law is, however, far from uniform among the various securities statutes. Some provisions have come under continual judicial scrutiny, while others have received virtually no attention from the courts. In addition to giving the Commission the power to make rules, Congress has also given the Commission the power to sit in a quasi-judicial capacity and adjudicate with respect to the statutes it administers. The adjudication process starts with a hearing before an administrative law judge,[4] whose decision

---

[4]   It is worth noting that, as of 2017, there was active controversy among the lower federal courts with respect to whether the Commission's method of appointing its administrative law

is appealable to the Commissioners. The Commissioners' decisions look very much like those of courts and serve the same interpretive—and, in a real world sense, lawmaking—function. Decisions of the Commission may be appealed to a United States Court of Appeals.

Adding the Constitution at the top, and remembering the interpretive function of courts and the Commission in its quasi-judicial capacity, one finds then the following hierarchy:

Constitution

Securities statutes

Rules and other pronouncements given the force of law

Policy and interpretive releases

Staff Legal Bulletins

Interpretive and no-action letters

Manual of telephone interpretations

Telephone interpretations

Staff comments on filed documents[5]

There is one other item that must be considered—what securities lawyers sometimes call "lore." Much of the knowledge it takes to deal with the Commission, and otherwise practice in the field, is not the subject of an official pronouncement. If, for example, a lawyer were to prepare and file a Securities Act registration statement following only the statute, rules, and registration statement form, the Commission would likely reject it on the basis that it is so far afield that the staff does not know how to deal with it.

II. FINDING THE VARIOUS TYPES AUTHORITY

Lore aside, where does one find the various statutes, rules, forms, releases, and no-action and interpretive letters? There are at least two ways to break down the publications containing these materials: (1) official and unofficial,[6] and (2) government and private. There are official and unofficial government publications, but all private publications are unofficial. One should refer to the official publications when needed, but unofficial publications, and especially private ones, are generally more useful.

Ask the average lawyer where to find the most authoritative text of the federal securities statutes, and you likely will be told United States Code ("Code"), or perhaps even United States Code Annotated. Actually,

---

judges is constitutional. *See, e.g.,* Bandimere v. SEC, 844 F.3d 1168 (10th Cir.2016); Lucia v. SEC, 832 F.3d 277 (D.C.C.2016).

　　[5]　This hierarchy is not completely set. For example, for the person to whom a no-action letter is addressed, its place is higher on the list than releases of general applicability.

　　[6]　"Official" is used in the sense of there being a legal recognition, to some degree or other, of the authoritativeness of the publication.

the first of these publications is quite far removed from being the most authoritative, and the second is published by a private company and has no authority at all. The most authoritative text is actually found in the bills that contain the original statutes and amendments as passed by Congress. The next most authoritative sources are Statutes at Large, which are "legal evidence" of laws, and slip laws, which are "competent evidence" of laws (there being no apparent difference between "legal" and "competent" evidence). It is, however, generally easier to deal with the Code.

The securities statutes are codified in Title 15 of the Code. Some titles of the Code have been enacted into what is called "positive law," making them also legal evidence of the laws they contain. Title 15 has not been so enacted, and therefore it is merely prima facie evidence of the law. Courts have made it clear that if a section of the Code that is not enacted into positive law is in conflict with Statutes at Large, the latter governs. Some text is changed systematically to enable statutes to fit into the Code. For example, the Securities Act begins, "This act may be cited * * * ," but the Code reads, "This subchapter may be cited * * * ." The greatest difference is in the area of numbering. The Securities Act, for instance, appears as Title 15, beginning with Section 77a; Section 77a corresponds to Section 1 of the Act, Section 77b to Section 2, and so on. The United States Code, like Statutes at Large, is difficult to track through government sources.

The most authoritative, practically available government sources of Commission rules are the Federal Register, published daily, and the codification known as the Code of Federal Regulations, which is published annually (there is, however, an unofficial online version that is updated daily). The Code of Federal Regulations is divided into numbered titles, parts, and sections. The rules under the securities statutes are found in Title 17, beginning at Part 200. In CFR, rules are not referred to as rules, but as sections of the Code. For example, Securities Act Rule 144 appears as 17 C.F.R. § 230.144. Not only is this the CFR form for rules, but Commission action with respect to rules is often phrased in terms of CFR. For example, in a release amending Rule 144, the Commission might begin: "17 C.F.R. § 230.144 is amended to read as follows * * * ." When discussing rules, however, securities lawyers and the Commission's staff invariably use rule numbers, specifying the governing statute when there is any question.

The Commission's website gives access to a number of materials. Thus, the most important securities laws, along with their implementing regulations and forms, are available at www.sec.gov. They are a bit hard to find, as they are in a section called "About the SEC." The website also gives constantly expanding access to letters, Staff Legal Bulletins and administrative law decisions. It is not, however, a particularly user-friendly research destination and generally is not as complete as many private commercial sources.

D. STATE SECURITIES LAW

By the time Congress passed the Securities Act, most states had been in the business of securities regulation for many years. The New Deal securities statutes preserved the ability of the states to engage in securities regulation, and they continued vigorous activity in this area. The result was fairly comprehensive, albeit widely divergent, state regulatory schemes. In 1996, however, Congress amended federal law to reduce state jurisdiction substantially. It still is not unusual for a state to exercise jurisdiction in many of the major areas covered by the Securities Act and the Exchange Act, as well as to regulate small investment advisers. Thus, like the Securities Act (but subject to its preemption for a number of issuers and transactions), the typical state statute requires that securities be registered before sale, unless an exemption is available. It also regulates brokers and dealers to some extent, overlapping here with the Exchange Act. The typical state statute also prohibits various kinds of fraud. Although fraud is proscribed by both the Securities Act and the Exchange Act, state anti-fraud regulation generally has not been pre-empted, and assertions of anti-fraud enforcement authority by state regulators have achieved both notoriety and high-stakes settlements.

Like the more specialized of the federal statutes, state securities laws are more easily understood when they are approached by someone who knows the federal scheme. Partially for this reason, a more thorough introduction to state securities regulation is saved until Part VI of this book.

D. STATE SECURITIES LAW.

SECURITIES ACT OF 1933

PART 2

SECURITIES ACT OF
1933

CHAPTER 2

Business Context of Securities Act Registration

SITUATION 2

Your firm represents Microtec Computer Corp., a very successful, though small, computer manufacturer. Its major products are specialized microcomputers and microcomputer software. The company sells, through dealers, mainly to computer hobbyists and research laboratories. It fabricates the cases for its computers in its own shop, but purchases the components from others. Microtec employees develop some of its software, but much of the software is created by others working under contract.

Microtec has been in business just over four years. After a first year of losses, it has increased its net income each year, to a current level of $2 million. Its success is attributable to many factors. Main among them is the fact that it offers carefully integrated systems of special purpose hardware, matched by some of the industry's most creative software. Microtec is, however, currently limited by a lack of production capacity. For the last year it has advertised very little, since it could not handle an increased volume of orders. Even without substantial advertising, it currently has a three-month order backlog.

The company is owned 50% each by James Moore and Ann Simpson. Neither has been named chief executive officer, but rather they operate essentially as "equal partners." Both are convinced that Microtec could at least double its sales if it increased its production capacity. Also, each realizes that the company must spend increased amounts on development of both hard and software if it is to remain competitive. In addition, each wants to do more software development in-house. All this will require substantial additional funds. Moore and Simpson started the company with limited capital, and they currently have no funds to contribute. The company has always borrowed heavily from banks and probably cannot borrow more unless further equity is brought into the company. Simpson and Moore believe a sale of stock to the public may be the answer to Microtec's capital needs, and also that it may offer some personal advantages.

The registration of securities is at the core of the Securities Act, and most of the Act's provisions are built around the registration framework. Before examining the registration provisions, however, it will be helpful to focus briefly on the business context of an initial public offering ("IPO").

In 2004–2007, the SEC was receiving filings for approximately 20 IPOs per month. A precipitous decline during the financial crisis commencing in 2008 was followed by a rebound to a peak of 363 filings in 2014. Uncertainty relating to foreign economies and the U.S. Presidential election are credited with the drop to only 128 IPOs in 2016. In any event, IPOs have gone through ebbs and flows for decades, and understanding the IPO process and its consequences is a necessary step in understanding the federal securities laws.

A. TAKING A COMPANY PUBLIC

What Makes a Company a Good Candidate for Going Public? Criteria, Advantages, and Disadvantages Related to Going Public

John F. Olson and Daniel W. Nelson.[*]
SG 022 ALI–ABA 231.

* * *

Investment bankers typically do not consider a company to be a good candidate for going public unless that company possesses the size, product lines, markets, and management sufficient to achieve at least $75 to $100 million in annual sales in the near future. Although there are no hard and fast rules as to how large a company must be to satisfy the financial community's expectations, five factors provide valuable guidance: (1) the company's size; (2) the company's financial ratios and historic performance; (3) current company management; (4) public appeal of the company's business; and (5) present market conditions.

A.   Company Size

Except in "hot" areas, such as biotechnology stocks recently and Internet-based "dot com" stocks in the late 1990s, most companies considering going public should have annual sales of at least $20 million and net income of $1 million or more in the current fiscal year. Few companies with annual sales of less than $10 million have had successful [IPOs].

Economies of scale work against small companies. A major reason that smaller companies often do not have successful IPOs is that the cost per dollar of equity raised generally decreases marginally as the size of the offering increases, and smaller companies typically have smaller IPOs than larger companies. This decreasing marginal cost occurs because expenses associated with an IPO are, to a large extent, fixed. For this reason, many IPO costs are similar whether an offering is $5 million

    *   Copyright © 2001 John F. Olson and Daniel W. Nelson. Reprinted with permission.

or $500 million. Smaller companies are also hit with reverse economies of scale with respect to the continuing expenses of being public, such as public filings and investor relations. Because many of these costs are also fixed, smaller companies must dedicate a greater percentage of their revenues to the continuing expense of being publicly owned.

* * *

Owners of small companies must typically sell a larger percentage of their companies in IPOs. Selling 50 percent or more is not uncommon for such companies. The founding owners may also have only a limited opportunity to obtain liquidity for their own investments. Underwriters often require founding owners to "lock up" their holdings for some time in order to allay investor concerns that the founders are cashing out and lack commitment to the business.

B.   Growth Potential and Financial Performance to Date

In order to attract public investors, a company's financial ratios (including debt-to-equity, liquidity, and debt coverage) should be comparable or superior to industry averages. The company should also have a history of solid revenues and earnings from continuing operations that have consistently grown over the last three to five years and will continue to grow in the future. At least three years of financial statements that a recognized accounting firm has audited can provide documentation of this historical performance.

Public investors generally expect a company's earnings to grow from 12 to 15 percent or more per year. Companies with aging product lines or small markets may not be able to sustain this level of growth.

Although public investors usually prefer companies with proven operating results, there have also been cases in which start-up companies with little or no operating history have completed successful IPOs. Such companies typically have new, unique products that have generated significant public interest or are in "hot" fields. Even companies in hot fields, however, must present credible business plans that explain how they will employ IPO capital to create growth in value for investors. This is particularly true in times of economic downturn, when investors are increasingly risk-averse.

C.   Quality of Current Management

Perhaps the most important characteristic that a company hoping to go public must possess is a sound management team. Although a single energetic entrepreneur may be capable of running a private business, public investors will demand that the company's management contain a number of high-quality executives with broad experience. * * *

The addition of three or more independent directors with proven records can also enhance a company's management group and is required for admission to trading on major securities markets.

D.   Public Appeal

The company's business must be one in which the public would *like* to invest. There should be a growing demand for the company's products and a sufficiently large market for those products to sustain strong, healthy growth for the next several years. The company should be an industry leader or should occupy an identifiable, promising niche in its industry, with a strong competitive position that will protect it from attack by others in the market.

E.   Market Timing

* * * [M]arket conditions often have as much impact on the success or failure of an IPO as the intrinsic value of the company. In short, the stock market is fickle. Industries that were in vogue last year or last month can quickly fall out of favor with investors. Furthermore, the IPO market as a whole experiences upturns and downturns based on public confidence and the returns available from other investments. Many promising IPOs have failed due to rapidly changing market conditions.

For this reason, it is very important for a company that is considering a public offering to have experienced investment bankers. Accomplished investment bankers have a good feel for the pulse of the market and can help a company to match the timing of its IPO with a "window" in the market when investors will be most receptive to the company's stock.

II.   ADVANTAGES AND DISADVANTAGES OF GOING PUBLIC

A.   Advantages

Every year, the owners of hundreds of private companies decide to fundamentally alter their enterprises by selling company stock to the public. There are many advantages to be gained by taking a company public, including financial flexibility and personal wealth realization, as well as prestige and other intangibles.

1.   Increased Financial Flexibility Through the Ability to Raise Capital

A lack of funds is almost always an impediment to a private company's growth. Small companies with rapidly expanding businesses need cash to finance their growth. The most obvious benefit of an IPO is the infusion of capital, which the company can use to develop new products, expand existing facilities, increase advertising, establish new markets, retire existing debt, and establish an equity base for future borrowings.

In addition, because the company's stock is now publicly traded, it may be easier to expand the company through acquisitions of related businesses. Once a company's stock becomes established and relatively stable in the public equity markets, the company can acquire other businesses with its own stock rather than with cash.

If a company's stock performs well in the market after its IPO, the company may also find it easier to raise additional equity capital through a secondary public offering or through a private placement with institutional investors. The cost of capital from either of these alternatives will ordinarily be lower after a successful IPO due to higher liquidity and lower risk associated with the company's stock.

2. Liquidity of Owners' Investments

It is difficult for owners of private companies to value—let alone realize—the wealth in their businesses. Going public creates instant valuation and establishes a market for the newly-public company's stock. It may also allow the company's owners to enjoy the fruits of their labor by selling stock in the IPO or in the subsequently created market (subject to whatever lock-up arrangements the company's underwriters require and to the limits of market absorption) without relinquishing complete control of the enterprise.

* * *

Even when there is an established market for the stock of a newly-public company, federal law imposes significant restrictions on the formerly private owners' ability to sell stock in the public market. * * *

* * *

In addition to the resale restrictions imposed by the [federal securities laws], underwriters often require the existing shareholders of a company that is going public to agree not to sell any of their stock for a specified period of time after the IPO (usually 90 to 180 days, sometimes longer). This period is called a "lock-up" or "holdback" period. Underwriters require lock-up or holdback periods to ensure that the price of a company's stock is not driven down immediately after its IPO by a flood of sales by the company's existing shareholders.

Many analysts believe that the expiration of lock-up periods can lead to volatility in the market for the newly-public company's stock. When lock-up periods expire, formerly restricted shareholders often rush to sell their shares, flooding the market and causing stock prices to fall.

* * *

3. Prestige and Other Intangibles

The ultimate personal achievement for many entrepreneurs is successfully taking their businesses public.

Apart from the psychological benefits, bringing a company public can be beneficial to the company's business as well. Public companies receive a great deal of "free" public relations. In addition to the fanfare that surrounds going public, the media regularly reports the stock prices, business prospects, and other information about public companies. Furthermore, a company that is publicly traded is arguably viewed by its customers as being more prestigious (with higher quality products) than a private enterprise.

The process of going public is usually very exciting to a company's employees as well. In many instances, this excitement alone may increase worker productivity as the company strives to increase the price of its stock. Most companies have an employee stock option plan of some sort in place before an IPO because such plans are often very effective in recruiting, retaining, and motivating employees. Employee stock option plans become even more desirable once a company's stock is publicly traded because employees have a ready valuation and market for the stock they accumulate.

B. Disadvantages

1. High Initial Expenses

One of the largest deterrents to going public is the cost to the company. The expenses associated with the IPO alone can be prohibitive for many small companies. For example, the cost of even a very small IPO of $10 million can be several hundred thousand dollars—more if the company's house is not in order or other difficulties arise.

The lion's share of this cost goes to underwriters. Underwriters typically demand six to nine percent of the proceeds (the "underwriting discount") as a fee for placing a company's securities.[1] The percentage charged depends primarily on the size of the offering and investor interest in the offering. In a hypothetical $10 million IPO, the underwriting discount would amount to approximately $800,000. Attorneys' fees associated with the offering would probably total about $150,000. Depending on the nature of the selling effort and the number of preliminary prospectuses to be distributed, printing costs might add another $150,000. Accountants' fees could amount to $75,000 or more. There would also be various miscellaneous expenses for fees charged by the [Securities Exchange Commission], the [Financial Industry Regulatory Authority (an organization that assists in the regulation of the conduct of brokers and dealers)], the relevant stock market, and the transfer agent.[2] In addition, company executives would likely spend numerous hours negotiating the IPO process—time that could have gone toward some other aspect of the company's business.

2. Continuing Reporting Obligations; Dealing with Analysts and Financial Press

Much of the cost of being a public company is incurred after the IPO has closed. Once a company is public, it becomes subject to various federal securities laws and regulations. These laws require the company to file a number of public reports * * * . The reporting requirements are

---

[1] The commission charged on debt typically is less than that charged on stock. The Financial Industry Regulatory Authority caps allowable commissions at 10%. [Eds.]

[2] Moreover, states still may require filings and payment of fees notwithstanding federal preemption of other types of regulation for some offerings. [Eds.]

designed to ensure that the public is kept informed of material developments affecting the company since the filing of its IPO registration statement.

The company will be obligated, among other responsibilities, to: (a) comply with complex rules relating to the solicitation of proxies; (b) distribute an annual report to its shareholders describing company performance during the last fiscal year; (c) publicly disclose any material developments through press releases and other channels; and (d) establish a system of internal financial controls in satisfaction of the Foreign Corrupt Practices Act. In addition, the company's officers, directors, and major shareholders must file reports detailing their holdings of company stock * * * [and certain executives personally must certify the company's financial statements].

Additional regulatory requirements imposed in the last [few] years have added further expense and risk for public companies. * * * [For instance, a public disclosure requirement] is triggered when a senior company official or investor relations or public relations representative privately discloses material non-public corporate information to an "enumerated person," which includes any analyst, investment manager, or shareholder who could reasonably be expected to trade in the company's securities. [If this occurs], a company must promptly disclose any such information to the public. Disclosure must be simultaneous with respect to intentionally leaked information; inadvertently leaked information must be publicly disclosed within 24 hours.

* * *

3.   Increased Exposure to Securities Law Actions

* * * Suffice it to say that a public company, its officers, its directors, and its major shareholders could all face civil and/or criminal consequences for (among other things):

- any material misstatement or failure to disclose a material fact regarding the company in a registration statement or periodic report filed with the [Commission or, in the case of executives, any defrauding of shareholders];

- trading by the company, its insiders, or their "tippees" in the company's stock during a time when all material information about the company is not available to the public;

- any purchase or sale made within six months of another purchase or sale;

- a short sale of the company's stock by an insider; and

- any failure to comply with the periodic reporting and other requirements set forth above.

4.   Decreased Flexibility

* * *

Board approval may become more formalized because new directors are often added after the IPO and because the board is responsible to all shareholders (rather than to the wishes of the founding entrepreneur). The company's broadened shareholder base renders it impractical to obtain written shareholder consents to corporate transactions that require shareholder approval. A public company is generally subject to the [Commission's] rules regarding solicitation of shareholders' proxies.[3]

Moreover, public shareholders' interests may not always be consistent with the long-term interests of the company. Public shareholders typically want management to maximize the price of the company's stock in the short term; however, short-term maximization of stock price may not always be consistent with the company's long-term interests. On the contrary, it may be in the company's long-term interest to increase funding for research and development, which could result in a loss in the current fiscal quarter or year. Public shareholders are not always receptive to reducing earnings today in exchange for the possibility of increased earnings five (or even two or three) years in the future.

5.   Loss of Privacy

The owner of a recently public company must be able to adjust to life in the public eye. Because the business is now owned by members of the public, management is obligated to keep the public informed about matters that materially affect the company.

One particularly difficult adjustment for the management of a newly public company is the fact that salaries, significant benefits, and "perks" of each of the company's executives must be disclosed to the public. Owners and senior executives of newly public companies must accept that their neighbors, employees, and scores of people they have never met will know how much money they have been making over the past several years.

* * *

Finally, a public company's competitors can have access to financial statements and other information about the company's business simply by reading its registration statement and periodic SEC filings.

6.   Takeover Exposure

As discussed above, the owner of a newly public company necessarily loses some degree of control over the business after an IPO because the company's board of directors is responsible to each of its new public owners. Nevertheless, an owner is often well-advised to retain a large

---

[3]   In addition, the ability to enter transactions with insiders may be constrained by disclosure requirements; loans to officers are prohibited. [Eds.]

enough interest in the company to allow the owner, in conjunction with supportive management and shareholders, to exercise control over the company. In addition, takeover deterrents, such as staggered board terms and the issuance of lower vote shares to the public, can be introduced at the time of a company's IPO. Such provisions are not easily added later, but if they are in place when the company first offers its shares to the public, they may help to protect the company from a hostile takeover and improve the company's bargaining position if a takeover is proposed.

* * *

In addition to the disadvantages of going public mentioned in the foregoing reading, a number of very costly requirements impacting corporate management and decision-making were added by the Sarbanes-Oxley Act of 2002. These are described in subsequent Chapters, particularly Chapter 9. The Jumpstart Our Business Startups Act of 2012 has, however, ameliorated some of these requirements for many issuers during the first five years after registering under the Securities Act.

B. FUNCTIONS OF SECURITIES FIRMS AND THE EFFECTS OF FINANCIAL UNREST

Securities firms perform a number of different functions, both in connection with registered offerings and otherwise. When they perform these functions, the firms are referred to by various descriptions that relate to the function that is performed. The major aspects of these functions are outlined below.

I. UNDERWRITING

Underwriting generally refers to the function of helping a company, or one or more of its major shareholders, sell securities to the public through an offering registered under the Securities Act. This function is accomplished in one of three ways:

    1. *Firm Commitment Underwriting.* In the firm commitment underwriting, the underwriter purchases securities from a company, or one or more major shareholders, at an agreed price. It then attempts to resell these securities to the public at a profit. In this and the other forms of underwriting, a group of underwriters usually acts together under the leadership of a managing underwriter. In practice, the managing underwriter makes all the arrangements with the issuer, and during the course of the work on the offering it puts together the group of underwriters, which is called a syndicate. Each underwriter in the group agrees to underwrite a specific percentage of the total

amount of securities being offered, and its profit or loss is based on this percentage. The managing underwriter receives a fee for its efforts, paid out of the proceeds of sale.

2.   *Best Efforts Underwriting.* In the best efforts underwriting, an underwriter or group of underwriters agrees to use its best efforts to sell an agreed amount of securities to the public. The underwriters may simply agree to sell whatever portion of the total they can. On the other hand, their agreement may be on an all or none, or an agreed minimum percentage, basis. This form of underwriting obviously offers less risk to underwriters than does the firm commitment. It is used almost exclusively by smaller underwriters.

3.   *Standby Underwriting.* The standby form of underwriting is typically used in so-called rights offerings. In such an offering, a company directly offers its existing security holders the right to purchase additional securities at a given price, and underwriters agree to purchase from the company any securities that are offered to the security holders but not purchased by them. This form of underwriting, in a sense, is a variation of the firm commitment underwriting.

For business reasons, basically relating to the volatility of securities prices, underwriters in a firm commitment underwriting wish to dispose of an entire issue almost immediately. To accomplish this quick sale, the underwriters often sell a portion of the securities, at a discount from the public offering price, to other securities firms, which in turn attempt to resell them to the public. As discussed below, these other firms function as dealers, since they take title to the securities. Underwriters with a large sales force and an ability to sell securities quickly may sell all or most of the securities they are underwriting. Others may sell few or even none themselves.

The financial arrangements in an underwriting of stock might work like this for each share sold (assuming the maximum allowable commission):

Public offering price	$10.00
Price to underwriter	9.00
Gross profit to underwriter	$ 1.00
Fee to managing underwriter	.20
Profit to underwriter if it sells the share to the public	$ .80
Discount to dealer	.50
Profit to underwriter if it sells the share to a dealer	$ .30

Considerations in Selecting the Managing Underwriter(s) for an Initial Public Offering

Laird H. Simons III.*
1328 PLI/Corp 73.

I.   Objectively analyze your company from the underwriters' point of view.

* * *

II.   Know the various underwriters' standard requirements.

* * *

III.   Further reasons for selection after the field of potential underwriters has been narrowed.

(a)   Reputation. What is the underwriter's reputation generally and in doing offerings for your industry or in your geographical area. * * *

(b)   Quality of underwriting group. The managing underwriter(s) typically will put together a group (syndicate) of other investment bankers to sell the offering. Some underwriters develop stronger syndicates (investment banking houses with greater abilities and reputations) than others.

(c)   Distribution strength. The lead manager must control and influence the channels of distribution. It is important that the underwriters sell out the offering and do so swiftly. In certain "go-go" markets, this concern may be minimal; however, when the overall market is poor and the IPO "window" is largely closed (or the screen through which companies are filtered is extremely fine), the ability to do an offering at all, or at least at a price that you consider reasonable, may be in jeopardy.

(d)   Personal chemistry between company management and the underwriter's personnel.

(1)   Relationships are not built in a day. It is important to begin getting to know underwriters at least six months and possibly a year or more before the offering is anticipated. Interview reasonably broadly at first, not just a smattering of underwriters—perhaps four to nine firms.

(2)   During the offering process you will work eyeball-to-eyeball with the underwriters. You need to be able to trust their judgment, competence, commitment, credibility and honesty.

(3)   As the final choice of underwriters gets closer, make sure you meet the key people in the organization—the head of the syndicate department, the head of institutional sales, the individual who will trade your company's stock, the head of the office and the underwriter's corporate finance team that would work on your offering. Get a feeling for their philosophy.

---

*   Copyright © 2004. Reprinted with permission.

(4) Venture capital investors may try to influence your choice of underwriters, but you have to live with the choice. Make sure you have a philosophical fit.

(e) Mix of retail/institutional customers. Some investment bankers sell primarily to institutions (e.g., Robertson Stephens) and others (like Prudential Securities or UBS PaineWebber) have large retail sales organizations. Many of the traditional high technology underwriters have focused primarily on institutions and large customers and do not have large retail sales organizations. The types of customers to which the underwriter primarily directs its marketing activities may have some impact on its ability to sell an offering (or to sell it quickly) in particular types of markets.

(1) Institutions, by and large, have led the pricing of all large offerings during the last several years. They are very important in the first weeks after the offering. However, prone to a "herd" instinct, they can move in packs and may not hold shares as long as retail customers. Institutions can understand a complex company or technology more easily.

(2) Retail purchasers tend to be more stable. They hold stock longer and, since more fragmented, do not buy and sell as a group. They are not subject to the quarterly performance reviews of the big institutions. They can help to stabilize the after-market.

(3) Disagreement between retail and institutionally-oriented underwriters. Retail firms say institutional firms have problems if their institutional "herd" backs away from a deal (although the institutional firm might still be able to reach retail customers through the syndicate it forms). Institutional firms maintain that 60–75% of deals (at least technology deals) end in the hands of institutions, so why not place them there immediately? Retail firms believe that too high a percentage of institutional ownership is risky and that analysts do not like to follow firms that are exclusively held by institutions. Institutional firms say that ownership by the "right" institutions will cause more analysts to follow a company's stock.

* * *

(f) Post-offering market support ("after-market support"). The underwriter's role is not finished once the offering is completed. Underwriters provide a variety of after-offering services including performing as a market maker (i.e., facilitating over-the-counter trading by standing ready to buy and sell the company's stock), purchasing shares for their own accounts, bringing the stock to the attention of analysts and investors (including its own customers) and facilitating the bringing of information about the company to the marketplace as a whole. All of this has a direct impact on performance of the company's stock after the offering is completed. A company needs a strong, deep, liquid, orderly market for its shares. This requires a number of well-capitalized market makers, starting with the managing underwriter(s) and the syndicate it (they) assemble(s). The underwriter should also provide ongoing support in getting the company's story to the public (e.g., by taking management on periodic trips to visit key institutions or groups of investors in important geographic areas).

(g)   Quality of analysts. There is a benefit to selecting an underwriter with analysts who are well known in and who know the company's industry and who are widely read in the investment community. Analyze the nature of the underwriter's commitment to research in your industry.
* * *

(h)   Additional capital. Once your company is public, in most instances it will have increased opportunities to raise additional capital. You may wish to choose an underwriter that has the capacity to grow with your company and to be able to perform larger offerings in the future. * * *

(i)   Continuing advice. In the future, your company may require advice and assistance on investment banking, mergers and acquisitions, corporate cash management, corporate strategy, private placements, investor relations, research and development partnerships, leasing and so forth. An investment banker with which the company has an ongoing relationship is the logical place to seek such advice, and some underwriters offer a much broader array of such services.

* * *

IV.   Some further considerations.

(a)   The role of price. Smaller underwriters may fix the price of an offering before a letter of intent or letter of understanding is reached. Larger underwriters usually provide no more than an indication of range of price until the evening before the offering is actually commenced. In one sense, early indications and promises are not worth the paper on which they are written. Ultimately "the market" prices the issue, not the underwriter, and once you have spent $1,500,000 or more in up-front costs, you are often stuck with what the underwriter determines the market to be (earlier promises notwithstanding). The highest price is not necessarily the most appropriate choice. In fact, in most instances, good underwriters will reach fairly similar conclusions on company valuation and stock price. It is important for companies to satisfy future investors in the marketplace, and a fully-priced offering runs a greater risk of the price declining, thereby rendering investors immediately unhappy. Most investment bankers will deliberately price an issue somewhat below the maximum amount for which it could be sold in order to permit a small increase in price immediately after the offering. This creates immediate goodwill with investors, provides a cushion should the company or the overall market do poorly in the near future and enhances the opportunities for the company to raise capital at a later time. Remember, however, that the underwriter serves two clients, the company and its usual (and other) investors. It must satisfy both and therefore is not solely on the company's side.

(b) Sole manager or co-managers. There is an advantage to underwriters in sole-managing a deal because of the economic rewards to them. There may also be an advantage to the company from a sole-managed deal because of the reduced need for coordination between two or more investment banks. Nevertheless, dual or multiple managers are the norm on all but the smallest deals. The use of dual or multiple managers (assuming that they work well together) can easily provide a balance between strength on the East Coast and strength on the West Coast, retail customers and institutional customers, a large investment bank and a regional investment bank, a well-known New York firm and a specialty technology firm, etc. However, for deals under $15,000,000, many underwriters may find it uneconomic and may decline to co-manage an offering.

* * *

II. ACTING AS DEALER, BROKER, AND MARKET MAKER

In industry parlance, the term "dealer" refers to a firm when it buys and sells securities for its own account (except the term is not used when the firm does this as an underwriter). A dealer takes title to securities when it buys and gives title when it sells. As indicated above, some firms operate as dealers in registered offerings by purchasing securities from the underwriters and then reselling them. Some firms that operate as dealers never function as underwriters in any transaction, but others may be an underwriter in some offerings and a dealer in others. In addition to operating as dealers in registered offerings, securities firms also function as dealers in the trading markets. The term "broker" refers to a firm when it buys or sells as an intermediary for a customer, rather than taking or giving title itself. Some confusion of these terms is created by the Securities Act, which in Section 2(a)(12) includes brokers within the definition of "dealer." Industry practice, however, is to use these terms with specificity. Further confusion is created by the use of the term "market maker" to describe a dealer that functions in the trading market by maintaining an inventory of a particular company's securities and holding itself open, on a continuing basis, as willing to buy and sell these securities.

III. INVESTMENT BANKING

The term "investment banking" can be used to encompass any of the above functions, and any person in a firm performing any of these functions could be called an investment banker. By convention, however, these terms usually are used less broadly. In large securities firms, for example, there are a number of departments. The one most visible to the public handles trades for individuals. The technical term for the persons working with customers in this department is "registered representative," but these persons are often called brokers or stockbrokers. Insiders would not call them investment bankers. A department almost invisible to the public handles underwritings and performs a wide range of services primarily for client companies. Among these are: (1) assisting companies in the sale of securities, almost always in large amounts, to private purchasers such as insurance companies, (2) finding acquisition partners for companies that wish to acquire or be acquired by others, and (3) giving financial advice of various sorts to client companies. This department is likely to be called the investment banking department. In any case, its functions are at the heart of the insiders' conception of investment banking. When referring generally to firms that perform investment banking functions, the term "investment banking firm" or, less commonly, "investment bank" is used.

Depression-era legislation for decades precluded commercial banks—those accepting depositor funds—from any involvement in investment banking functions. This preclusion was relaxed during the 1980s and 1990s and was repealed in 1999, permitting the formation of holding companies engaging in both commercial and investment banking activities.

IV. EFFECTS OF CHANGING MARKETS

Certainly, as IPOs dwindled in the wake of the panic beginning in 2008, it stood to reason that underwriters would be forced into increased competition. In some instances, this led to the involvement of multiple firms to perform the functions described in Part BI of this chapter (without any concomitant increase in the fee to the issuer). More significant, however, was the exit from the field of a number of "investment banks" meeting the description in Part BIII. Many of these entities had lost gambles undertaken in the heated financial markets of 2004–2007 (basically finding that they had over-leveraged themselves to acquire risky mortgage-backed securities.) When the housing market collapsed and credit sources became short, some established entities as Bear Stearns and Lehman Brothers went bankrupt, while others were acquired by or converted themselves into bank holding companies. In this form, they have access to customer deposits as well as to credit facilities made available by the federal reserve. The price was to subject themselves to an additional layer of regulation (by bank authorities).

This does not mean that the functions of securities firms described above have ceased to exist. A more dire threat (from the standpoint of those performing those functions) is posed by the internet. Brokerage and underwriting services presently are offered online, but the nature of the services themselves may change as savvy investors and issuers find ways of doing for themselves the things they used to rely on well-connected financial intermediaries to do.

Interestingly, as a further change to the landscape, the JOBS Act created a new type of financial intermediary known as a "funding portal," discussed more extensively in Chapters Six and Sixteen. Funding portals play a role in a type of offering exempt from Securities Act registration and are required to refrain from a variety of activities open to more traditional financial intermediaries.

C. STEPS IN A REGISTERED INITIAL PUBLIC OFFERING

In approaching the material that follows in the next chapter, it is helpful to have as background a conception of the broad sweep of events in a registered public offering. Here are the steps in a typical initial public offering by an issuer that does not file reports under the Securities Exchange Act of 1934:

1.   A company wishing to sell securities gets together with a firm that wishes to serve as its managing underwriter. The initial contact can be by either party, and often it is by an investment banking firm seeking underwriting business. At this point, the parties do not enter into a binding agreement, but they may sign a letter of intent.

2.   Counsel for the company begins drafting the registration statement. The managing underwriter engages a law firm to represent it and the underwriting syndicate that is to be formed. This counsel begins drafting the underwriting agreements. Typically, there are three types of agreements relating to the underwriting. First, there is an agreement among the underwriters in which the underwriters agree to act together in the underwriting and agree on which firm is to be the managing underwriter. Second, there is an agreement between the company and the underwriters in which the company agrees to sell and the underwriters agree to buy a specified amount of securities at an agreed price. Third, there are a series of agreements between the underwriters and the dealers relating to the sale of securities to the dealers at a discount from the public offering price. These agreements may informally be agreed to early on, but they are not executed until much later.

3.   Company counsel does any "housekeeping" work that is needed. This often involves clean-up work. For example, company counsel may find that the board of directors has not authorized certain actions of corporation officers that were beyond the officers' authority. In this case, a directors' meeting may need to be held to ratify past actions. Also, in the usual first public offering, the issuer's capital structure has to be changed. For example, a small private company that wishes to offer 500,000 shares, representing a 25 percent interest in the

company, must have authorized in its charter at least 2,000,000 shares, and 1,500,000 of these must be outstanding in the hands of the current owners. It is highly unlikely that this situation will exist by chance. Counsel can accomplish the required change in capital structure by a charter amendment that provides for an increase in authorized capital and a stock split.

4. The managing underwriter begins putting together the underwriting syndicate. This effort usually involves meetings and other communications with investment bankers in other firms. Any agreements reached are informal and nonbinding.

5. When the company and its counsel, and the managing underwriter and the underwriters' counsel, are satisfied with the draft of the registration statement, the company files it with the Commission. Although the Commission's staff may review it immediately, in some instances the staff review is delayed. Historically, the staff has almost always provided comment on the registration statement in 30 days. The Commission recently determined that issuers may submit their registration statements for comment before formally filing them. (The effect of this on the timing of staff comment remains to be seen.)

6. The managing underwriter continues to work on forming the underwriting syndicate and begins tentatively to form a prospective dealer group.

7. The prospective underwriters and dealers begin sending copies of a preliminary prospectus, which is an offering document that makes up the bulk of the registration statement, to customers and begin telephoning and emailing customers in an attempt to create interest in the offering.

8. The company files one or more amendments to the registration statement in preparation for its effectiveness. A company may file an amendment because material events have occurred since the filing of the registration statement. In the past, amendments often were required because the Commission's staff found what it considered problems in the registration statement as originally filed. At other times, a company files an amendment simply to fill in blanks that originally appeared in the registration statement.

9. When the registration statement is ready to become effective, the parties make a final decision as to whether to proceed with the offering, and under what terms. Typically, they complete final negotiations after the close of the securities markets on the day before expected effectiveness. This day is one agreed to by all parties and the Commission's staff, and so it does not come as a surprise. On the morning of effectiveness, the underwriters sign the agreement among underwriters and

the company and the underwriters enter into the underwriting agreement.

10. On the morning of effectiveness, the company might file a so-called price amendment to the registration statement, making final corrections and changes and adding previously unknown information such as the price to the underwriters, the price to the public, the discount to dealers, and the names of all the underwriters. More usually, if substantial final corrections and changes are not necessary, the issuer will forego filing a price amendment. Certain limited corrections and changes may simply be made, and information about pricing and the underwriting arrangements included, in the so-called "final" prospectus, which in this case will be filed shortly after effectiveness.

11. The registration statement becomes effective.

12. The underwriters and the dealers, after signing a dealer agreement, begin making sales to the public.

13. The closing, at which securities and money change hands, takes place. If the sale has gone well, by the closing the underwriters will have had time not only to sell all the securities, but to have collected the sales price from their customers.

14. The managing underwriter closes the books on the offering and either distributes profits to the underwriters or calls on them to pay their share of the loss.

CHAPTER 3

REGULATORY FRAMEWORK OF SECURITIES ACT REGISTRATION

A. TYPES OF ISSUERS

In 2005, the Commission adopted a number of new rules designed to ease compliance with the regulatory framework of Securities Act regulation. Without a doubt, it succeeded both in easing practical compliance and in vastly complicating legal analysis. Both of these effects were amplified in 2012 when the Jumpstart Our Business Startups (JOBS) Act was signed into law. Many of the changes related to the creation of different categories of issuers. Thus, as one approaches the succeeding materials, it is helpful to know in advance that different kinds of issuers are subject to different requirements. The basic types of issuer are described below.[1] A general description of each category is set out in the text; more technical definitions of some of the types may be found in the accompanying footnotes.

Non-Reporting Issuers—These are issuers that are not required to file reports under the Exchange Act, nor voluntarily doing so. Most commonly, they are first time registrants under the Securities Act. "Non-reporting issuer" is not actually a term defined in the Act or in the Commission's rules, although it is a discernible and useful concept.

Unseasoned Issuers—These are issuers that are required to file reports under the Exchange Act, or are voluntarily doing so, but that do not qualify as seasoned issuers (described immediately below). In general, issuers are required to report under the Exchange Act if they (a) have a class of security traded on a national exchange, or (b) have in excess of $10,000,000 in assets and a class of equity security in the hands of a specified number of security holders.[2] Once again, "unseasoned issuer" is not actually a term defined in the Commission's rules.

---

[1] In Chapter 4 reference will be made to a type of issuer known as a "small reporting company." This designation is not of significance for purposes of the analysis in Chapter 3.

[2] More specifically and as further discussed in Chapter 9, issuers are required to report under the Exchange Act if they (a) have a class of security traded on a national exchange, (b) have in excess of $10,000,000 in assets and a class of equity security held of record by either 2,000 or more persons or 500 or more "unaccredited investors," (c) have registered securities under the Securities Act within the last year, or (d) have registered securities under the Securities Act that are in the hands of more than 299 holders. The term "unaccredited investor" is not defined, but is understood as the opposite of "accredited investor," which is defined and further discussed in Chapter 6. The calculation in (b) excludes those purchasers acquiring their securities pursuant to an exemption from Securities Act registration known as "crowdfunding," which also is discussed in Chapter 6; moreover, certain issuers are exempt notwithstanding their satisfaction of that calculation.

Seasoned Issuers—In general terms, these are issuers that have filed reports under the Exchange Act for at least twelve months and either (a) have at least $75 million of common equity held by non-affiliates, or (b) meet certain other tests and are offering non-convertible debt. This group is identified, although not defined, in Rule 433(b).[3]

Well-known Seasoned Issuers—In general terms, these are seasoned issuers that have either (a) $700 million of common equity held by non-affiliates or (b) issued for cash more than $1 billion of registered non-convertible securities other than common equity in the last three years.[4] The technical definition of this class of issuer is contained in Securities Act Rule 405, which incorporates by reference portions of the Instructions to Securities Act Form S–3.

Emerging Growth Companies—An emerging growth company is an issuer, other than a well-known seasoned issuer, whose initial public offering is completed after December 8, 2011 and had annual gross revenue of less than $1.07 billion during its most recent fiscal year.[5] Qualifying for this category, which is defined in Section 2(a)(19), permits certain types of solicitational activity that otherwise would be prohibited.

The material that follows will clearly reveal that, as far as the first four categories are concerned, the more information that is publicly available about an issuer, and the more likelihood that the available information is being actively considered by the market, the more relaxed Securities Act compliance becomes. The clarity of this picture is, however, fuzzied a bit by the invention of the emerging growth company concept in 2012.

Section E of this Chapter contains a chart summarizing the relevant practical differences between the various types of issuers. Approach this chart with caution, however: the real challenge (and the real fun) of the job of a securities lawyer is to understand how the puzzle fits together.

---

[3] Rule 433 actually uses the term "seasoned issuers" only in a heading. The text of the rule simply refers to the issuer's qualifications to rely on specified Instructions permitting the use of Securities Act Form S–3 to register securities. (Form S–3 is dealt with in more detail in Chapter 4). Issuers registering non-convertible debt qualify as "seasoned issuers" if they both satisfy the twelve-month Exchange Act reporting requirement and satisfy one of four requirements relating either to past issuance of non-convertible securities registered under the Securities Act or to specified relationships with a "well-known seasoned issuer" (as defined in the text).

[4] Somewhat confusingly, issuers qualifying as well-known seasoned issuers under the second test must be registering non-convertible securities unless they also have at least $75 million of common equity in the hands of non-affiliates.

[5] The gross revenue cut-off was, as called for by the JOBS ACT, inflation adjusted in 2017 from the original $1 billion figure. Status as an emerging growth company terminates the last day of the fiscal year following the fifth anniversary of the date of the issuer's initial public offering or on the last day of the first fiscal year during which the issuer had annual gross revenues of $1.07 billion or more, as well as upon satisfaction of certain other conditions. Qualifying as an emerging growth company has benefits as far as the Securities Act registration process itself is concerned; these benefits are discussed in Chapter 4. It also eases compliance with various Exchange Act requirements discussed in Chapter 9.

B. PRE-FILING PERIOD

SITUATION 3B(1)

After discussions with you, Moore and Simpson decide to pursue the idea of a public offering. They first approach one of the leading investment banking firms. Officers of the firm are impressed with Microtec, but indicate that their firm simply does not underwrite issues for companies this size. They do, however, introduce Moore and Simpson to officers of Nielson Securities Co., a well respected regional underwriter. After several meetings between officers of Microtec and Nielson, the following events occur and come to your attention as counsel for Microtec:

1. In an attempt to determine if a Microtec offering is feasible, Nielson officers telephone other investment bankers in the region and discuss the possibility of working together on the offering.

2. Nielson officers also call several large financial institutions that are not investment banks in an effort to further assess the level of enthusiasm for Microtec's stock.

3. Microtec and Nielson sign a letter of intent for a firm commitment underwriting to be managed by Nielson. The offering is to be 1,000,000 shares of common stock at a projected price to the public of $10 a share. The offering is to be made in the states in the region.

4. Moore writes a letter to a financial reporter for the local newspaper. He announces the proposed offering through Nielson and states that Microtec expects to be able at least to double its sales as a result. The newspaper publishes a short item incorporating these statements.

5. Moore writes a letter to Microtec retailers in the region discussing the company's plans for expansion of production and increased product development activities. The letter does not mention the proposed offering. The letter is sent in hard copy and its text is posted on Microtec's internet website.

6. Nielson employees telephone prospective underwriters and dealers to offer them a place in the deal. Other Nielson employees correspond by e-mail for the same purpose.

7. Simpson participates in a forum discussion at a trade meeting attended by competitors and customers. She mentions Microtec's plans for increased production. When questioned about how Microtec would manage this, she mentions the possibility of a sale of securities, but gives no specifics.

8. Nielson distributes to its customers reprints of a securities research firm's report on the microcomputer industry.

The report describes the industry as "worthy of the investor's attention."

9. Microtec substantially increases its product advertising.

SITUATION 3B(2)

Assume that Mictrotec is, rather than a non-reporting issuer, an unseasoned issuer qualifying as an emerging capital growth company. How would your advice differ as to the events described in Situation 3B(1)?

SITUATION 3B(3)

Assume that Mictrotec is, rather than a non-reporting issuer, a seasoned issuer that does not qualify as an emerging capital growth company. How would your advice differ as to the events described in Situation 3B(1)?

SITUATION 3B(4)

Assume that Mictrotec is, rather than a non-reporting issuer, a well-known seasoned issuer. How would your advice differ as to the events described in Situation 3B(1)?

In considering these situations, refer to the following, in addition to the materials in this section: Securities Act Sections 2(a)(3), 2(a)(11), 2(a)(12), 2(a)(19), 5(a), 5(c) and 5(d), and Securities Act Rules 135, 139, 163, 163A, 168, and 169. Note that when securities are offered and sold in connection with certain business combinations, such as mergers and tender offers, the Commission's rules permit somewhat more and different communications with securities holders and the securities markets than are discussed here. These rules will easily be understood by anyone who has a good grasp of the material in this chapter.

I. STATUTORY SCHEME: PRE-FILING PERIOD

Consideration of the regulatory framework of registration must obviously begin with the Securities Act. This is one case, however, where one cannot profitably begin at the beginning. Because of the way the Act is structured, it is essential to begin by considering the prohibitions of Section 5. In doing so, it is most helpful to examine the various subsections not in the order in which they appear, but rather as they relate to the three time periods in an offering: (1) the period before a registration statement is filed (the pre-filing period), (2) the period after filing but before the registration statement becomes effective (the waiting period), and (3) the period after effectiveness (the post-effective period). The following table shows the basic applicability of the various subsections.

Pre-filing   **Waiting**   **Post-effective**

§§ 5(a) and (c)   §§ 5(a) and (b)(1)   § 5(b)

At this point we are concerned only with the pre-filing period and will, therefore, limit discussion to Sections 5(a) and (c). They provide:

PROHIBITIONS RELATING TO INTERSTATE COMMERCE AND THE MAILS

Section 5. (a) Unless a registration statement is in effect as to a security, it shall be unlawful for any person, directly or indirectly—

(1) to make use of any means or instruments of transportation or communication in interstate commerce or of the mails to sell such security through the use or medium of any prospectus or otherwise; or

(2) to carry or cause to be carried through the mails or in interstate commerce, by any means or instruments of transportation, any such security for the purpose of sale or for delivery after sale.

* * *

(c) It shall be unlawful for any person, directly or indirectly, to make use of any means or instruments of transportation or communication in interstate commerce or of the mails to offer to sell or offer to buy through the use or medium of any prospectus or otherwise any security, unless a registration statement has been filed as to such security, or while the registration statement is the subject of a refusal order or stop order or (prior to the effective date of the registration statement) any public proceeding or examination under section 8.

It is best to begin an analysis with Section 5(c), since it relates to offers and is applicable in its entirety to the pre-filing period (except for its provision on registration statements that are the subject of a refusal order, stop order, public proceeding, or examination under Section 8, which are rare occurrences that will be taken up later). Section 5(a), on the other hand, deals with sales (which chronologically follow offers) and is applicable to the waiting period as well as the pre-filing period.

The most helpful first step in understanding Section 5(c) is the culling of language that does not aid comprehension. For example, "directly or indirectly" adds very little to understanding, and "through the use or medium of any prospectus or otherwise" adds nothing. The provision relating to "means or instruments of transportation or communication in interstate commerce or of the mails" is a bit trickier. It is a practical impossibility to complete the usual securities offering without using one of the named "jurisdictional means." Of course, it is possible that a particular act, such as the making of a specific offer, might be done without use of these means. The jurisdictional means concept, however, is broad. Any use of the telephone or email by the offeror almost certainly satisfies the requirement, and it can be met in much more abstruse ways. For example, when the president of an issuer by chance encounters a friend at the country club and offers to sell the friend securities, the president probably has not used any jurisdictional means. But if the friend telephones for more information, a court would probably find that jurisdictional means had been used to "offer" the securities because the offeror reasonably could have foreseen the use of the telephone by the offeree. Lawyers litigating securities cases may sometimes find "no jurisdictional means" arguments helpful. Others will find such arguments too dangerous to rely on, and they can virtually ignore the jurisdictional means language of Section 5. This is what will generally be done in this book. After culling all this language, and setting aside language relating to refusal orders, stop orders, public proceedings, and examinations, one is left in Section 5(c) with this: "It shall be unlawful for any person * * * to offer to sell or offer to buy * * * any security * * * unless a registration statement has been filed as to such security * * * ."

All that remains, then, for understanding Section 5(c) is an understanding of what its various words and phrases mean. This is not as simple as it may seem. An examination of the Securities Act's definitions, contained in Section 2(a), shows that some of these terms have special meanings. After a reading of definitions, one is ready to consider rules, releases, cases, and so on in an attempt more fully to understand these terms.

After considering offers under Section 5(c), one should turn to Section 5(a). Taken to its essentials, Section 5(a)(1) prohibits the sale of securities unless a registration statement has become effective (that is, at the end of the waiting period). The major problem here is in determining what constitutes a sale. A look at Section 2(a)(3) shows that the word has special meanings, which are discussed below. Section 5(a)(2) contains a rather straightforward prohibition against transmitting unregistered securities through the mail, or by means of interstate commerce, for purposes of sale or delivery after sale. This provision is an important enforcement tool of the Commission, but one that relates to problems a securities lawyer rarely encounters while working as a planner.

Reading the basic portions of Sections 5(c) and 5(a)(1) together, the rule for the pre-filing period is: no offers, no sales. Whether an activity constitutes a sale may be an issue in the pre-filing period, but this issue is typically of more concern in the waiting period. For this reason, the treatment of sales appears in the context of the waiting period. Offers present the main problem of the pre-filing period, and they are handled here.

II. WHAT IS AN OFFER?

a. SECTION 2(a)(3)

The starting point for understanding the concept of an offer under the Securities Act is the definition contained in Section 2(a)(3), which in its basic part provides: "The term 'offer to sell,' 'offer for sale,' or 'offer' shall include every attempt or offer to dispose of, or solicitation of an offer to buy, a security or interest in a security, for value." The provision does not purport to be a complete definition because it speaks only in terms of what an offer "shall include." Presumably the drafters intended to take the common law definition of "offer" as a beginning and modify it. The modification immediately apparent is that the solicitation of an offer to buy is considered an offer to sell. As a result, it is not possible to avoid the "no offer to sell" prohibition of Section 5(c) by phrasing an offer in terms of a solicitation of an offer to buy.

The language of Section 2(a)(3) may have been meant to modify the common law definition of "offer" in a more significant way. It can be argued that the intent of the phraseology "shall include *every* attempt or offer to dispose of" (emphasis added) was to push the perimeters of the ordinary definition outward, so as to encompass activities that otherwise would not constitute offers. The full intent of the drafters is not clear, but a desire for expansiveness is not unlikely. In any case, the Commission has read the definition broadly, particularly in terms of pre-filing activities that, while falling far short of common law offers, condition the market for the securities to be sold.

b. CONDITIONING THE MARKET

The concept of conditioning the market first was articulated by the Commission in Securities Act Release No. 3844 (October 8, 1957). After referring to the definition of "offer" in Section 2(a)(3), the Commission stated without analysis that, in the pre-filing period, it is not legally possible to begin a public offering *or* "initiate a public sales campaign." The use of the connector "or" causes confusion. A public sales campaign is only unlawful when it involves an offer as defined in the Act. When it does, the campaign should be encompassed in the term "public offering." Presumably, the Commission used this latter term in the more restrictive sense of a formal offering, but it is difficult to be sure. What is clear in this release, and in later pronouncements on the subject, is that the Commission has not been precise or analytical in fitting its ideas into the statutory scheme.

As detailed in subsection c, there are now a number of activities that are specifically permitted notwithstanding the fact that they otherwise might constitute market conditioning (or outright offers under any definition). The concept of market conditioning still is of concern, however, particularly for first-time registrants. Moreover, attempted reliance on any new rule does not preclude reliance on the argument that a communication is not an offer under earlier interpretive guidelines. The following pronouncements by the Commission on the subject of what constitutes conditioning the market thus continue to be important.

Securities Act Release No. 3844

Securities and Exchange Commission, October 8, 1957.

PUBLICATION OF INFORMATION PRIOR TO OR AFTER THE EFFECTIVE DATE OF A REGISTRATION STATEMENT

Questions frequently are presented to the Securities and Exchange Commission and its staff with respect to the impact of the registration and prospectus requirements of section 5 of the Securities Act of 1933 on publication of information concerning an issuer and its affairs by the issuer, its management, underwriters and dealers. Some of the more common problems which have arisen in this connection and the nature of the advice given by the Commission and its staff are outlined herein for the guidance of industry, underwriters, dealers and counsel.

* * *

* * * It is necessary * * * that corporate management, counsel, underwriters, dealers and public relations firms recognize that the Securities Acts impose certain responsibilities and limitations upon persons engaged in the sale of securities and that publicity and public relations activities under certain circumstances may involve violations of the securities laws and cause serious embarrassment to issuers and underwriters in connection with the timing and marketing of an issue of securities. These violations not only pose enforcement and administrative problems for the Commission, they may also give rise to civil liabilities by the seller of securities to the purchaser.

* * *

It follows from the express language and the legislative history of the Securities Act that an issuer, underwriter or dealer may not legally begin a public offering or initiate a public sales campaign prior to the filing of a registration statement. It apparently is not generally understood, however, that the publication of information and statements, and publicity efforts, generally, made in advance of a proposed financing, although not couched in terms of an express offer, may in fact contribute to conditioning the public mind or arousing public interest in the issuer or in the securities of an issuer in a manner which raises a serious question whether the publicity is not in fact part of the selling effort.

* * *

Instances have come to the attention of the Commission in which information of a misleading character, gross exaggeration and outright falsehood have been published by various means for the purpose of conveying to the public a message designed to stimulate an appetite for securities—a message which could not properly have been included in a statutory prospectus in conformity with the standards of integrity demanded by the statute.

* * *

Example No. 1

An underwriter-promoter is engaged in arranging for the public financing of a mining venture to explore for a mineral which has certain possible potentialities for use in atomic research and power. While preparing a registration statement for a public offering, the underwriter-promoter distributed several thousand copies of a brochure which described in glowing generalities the future possibilities for use of the mineral and the profit potential to investors who would share in the growth prospects of a new industry. The brochure made no reference to any issuer or any security nor to any particular financing. It was sent out, however, bearing the name of the underwriting firm and obviously was designed to awaken an interest which later would be focused on the specific financing to be presented in the prospectus shortly to be sent to the same mailing list.

The distribution of the brochure under these circumstances clearly was the first step in a sales campaign to effect a public sale of the securities and as such, in the view of the Commission, violated section 5 of the Securities Act.

* * *

Example No. 6

In recognition of the problems presented, the Commission's staff frequently receives inquiries from company officials or their counsel with respect to circumstances such as the following:

The president of a company accepted in August, an invitation to address a meeting of a security analysts' society to be held in February of the following year for the purpose of informing the membership concerning the company, its plans, its record and problems. By January a speech had been prepared together with supplemental information and data, all of which was designed to give a fairly comprehensive picture of the company, the industry in which it operates and various factors affecting its future growth. Projections of demand, operations and profits for future periods were included. The speech and the other data had been printed and it was intended that several hundred copies would be available for distribution at the meeting. In addition, since it was believed that stockholders, creditors, and perhaps customers might be interested in the talk, it was intended to mail to such persons and to a list of other selected firms and institutions copies of the material to be used at the analysts' meeting.

Later in January, a public financing by the company was authorized, preparation of a registration statement was begun and negotiation with underwriters was commenced. It soon appeared that the coming meeting of analysts, scheduled many months earlier, would be at or about the time the registration statement was to be filed. This presented the question whether, in the circumstances, delivery and distribution of the speech and the supporting data to the various persons mentioned above would contravene provisions of the Securities Act.

It seemed clear that the scheduling of the speech had not been arranged in contemplation of a public offering by the issuer at or about the time of its delivery. In the circumstances, no objection was raised to the delivery of the speech at the analysts' meeting. However, since printed copies of the speech might be received by a wider audience, it was suggested that printed copies of the speech and the supporting data not be made available at the meeting nor be transmitted to other persons.

Example No. 7

Two weeks prior to the filing of a registration statement the president of the issuer had delivered, before a society of security analysts, a prepared address which had been booked several months previously. In his speech the president discussed the company's operations and expansion program, its sales and earnings. The speech contained a forecast of sales and referred to the issuer's proposal to file with the Commission later in the month a registration statement with respect to a proposed offering of convertible subordinated debentures. Copies of the speech had been distributed to approximately 4,000 security analysts.

The Commission denied acceleration of the registration statement and requested that the registrant distribute copies of its final prospectus to each member of the group which had received a copy of the speech.

* * *

In re Carl M. Loeb, Rhoades & Co.

Securities and Exchange Commission, 1959.
38 S.E.C. 843.

These are consolidated proceedings pursuant to Sections 15(b) and 15A(l)(2) of the Securities Exchange Act of 1934 ("Exchange Act") to determine whether to revoke the registration as a broker and dealer of Carl M. Loeb, Rhoades & Co. ("Loeb Rhoades") and of Dominick & Dominick ("Dominick"), whether to suspend or expel registrants from membership in the National Association of Securities Dealers, Inc. ("NASD"), a registered securities association, and whether, under Section 15A(b)(4) of the Exchange Act, Stanley R. Grant, a partner in Loeb Rhoades, is a cause of any order of revocation, suspension or expulsion which may be issued as to that firm.

The orders for proceedings allege that commencing on September 17, 1958, registrants and Grant offered to sell shares of stock of Arvida Corporation ("Arvida") when no registration statement had been filed as to such securities, in willful violation of Section 5(c) of the Securities Act of 1933 ("Securities Act").

* * *

THE OFFERING OF ARVIDA STOCK

Arvida was incorporated in Florida on July 30, 1958, pursuant to plans developed over the preceding 4 or 5 months to provide for the financing and development of the extensive real estate holdings of Arthur Vining Davis ("Davis") in southeastern Florida. In April 1958 each of the registrants was approached by representatives of Davis, and thereafter, in May and June 1958, as a result of discussions a plan was developed under which certain of Davis' properties would be placed in a new corporation to be financed in large part through a public offering of securities by an underwriting group proposed to be managed by registrants.

On July 8, 1958 a meeting was held in Miami to work out various aspects of the contemplated offering. At this meeting it was noted there was some concern in Florida real estate circles as to the ultimate disposition of the Davis properties and the possible effect thereof on real estate values, and it was decided to issue a press release. Grant prepared a draft release which included some description of the "great spread" of Davis' lands and mention of a proposed underwriting of the offering through Loeb Rhoades. This draft was revised by representatives of Davis so as to state merely that the major portion of the Davis land holdings was to be transferred to Arvida which would proceed with orderly development and arrange to obtain a large amount of new capital for that purpose. No mention was made of a public offering or of an underwriting or underwriters.[6] The substance of this release appeared during the next few days in various Florida newspapers.

On September 16 and 17, 1958, meetings were held in New York at which the proposals of registrants for the financing were placed in final form and submitted to representatives of Davis for transmission to him. At this time it was decided to issue an additional press release. Grant drafted such a release * * * . * * *

The release, which was issued on the letterhead of Loeb Rhoades, stated that Arvida, to which Davis was transferring his real estate, would be provided with $25 million to $30 million of additional capital through an offering of stock to the public, and that Arvida would have assets of over $100,000,000 "reflecting Mr. Davis' investment" and the public investment. It referred to a public offering scheduled within 60 days through a nationwide investment banking group headed by registrants

---

[6]   This release, and the September 18 release referred to below, are set out following this case. [Eds.]

and to the transfer from Davis to Arvida of over 100,000 acres "in an area of the Gold Coast" in 3 named Florida counties and contained a brief description of these properties including reference to undeveloped lands and to "operating properties."

* * *

Officers of Arvida were anxious to have the release issued promptly. Public relations counsel advised Loeb Rhoades that, in order to make sure that the story appeared in 3 prominent New York newspapers, which coverage Loeb Rhoades wanted, it would be advisable, in view of newspaper deadlines, to call reporters from these papers to Loeb Rhoades' office. This was done on the afternoon of Thursday, September 18. * * *

Copies of the release were also delivered to other New York newspapers and to the principal wire services. The substance of the release and the information supplied by Grant appeared in the 3 New York newspapers on September 19, 1958, and in numerous other news media throughout the country.

* * *

On September 22, 1958, we commenced an action in the United States District Court for the Southern District of New York against Arvida, registrants, Grant and others, seeking an injunction against further violations of Section 5(c) of the Securities Act. * * * On December 12, 1958, the Court entered a decree permanently enjoining violation of Section 5(c) by the defendants. * * * The Court concluded that, although the defendants appeared to have acted in good faith and to have had no intention to violate the Securities Act, and although they continued to deny that their activities violated the statute, their activities nevertheless constituted a violation of Section 5(c) of that Act.

* * *

THE IMPACT OF SECTION 5(c) OF THE SECURITIES ACT

Section 5(c) of the Securities Act, as here pertinent, prohibits offers to sell any security, through the medium of a prospectus or otherwise, unless a registration statement has been filed. Section [2(a)(3)] defines "offer to sell" to include "every attempt or offer to dispose of, or solicitation of an offer to buy, a security or interest in a security for value." Section [2(a)(10)] defines a "prospectus" to mean "any prospectus, notice, circular, advertisement, letter, or communication * * * which offers any security for sale * * * ." These are broad definitions, and designedly so. It is apparent that they are not limited to communications which constitute an offer in the common law contract sense, or which on their face purport to offer a security. Rather, as stated by our General Counsel in 1941, they include "any document which is designed to procure orders for a security."

The broad sweep of these definitions is necessary to accomplish the statutory purposes in the light of the process of securities distribution as it exists in the United States. Securities are distributed in this country by a complex and sensitive machinery geared to accomplish nationwide distribution of large quantities of securities with great speed. Multi-million dollar issues are often oversubscribed on the day the securities are made available for sale. This result is accomplished by a network of prior informal indications of interest or offers to buy between underwriters and dealers and between dealers and investors based upon mutual expectations that, at the moment when sales may legally be made, many prior indications will immediately materialize as purchases. It is wholly unrealistic to assume in this context that "offers" must take any particular legal form. Legal formalities come at the end to record prior understandings, but it is the procedures by which these prior understandings, embodying investment decisions, are obtained or generated which the Securities Act was intended to reform.

One of the cardinal purposes of the Securities Act is to slow down this process of rapid distribution of corporate securities, at least in its earlier and crucial stages, in order that dealers and investors might have access to, and an opportunity to consider, the disclosures of the material business and financial facts of the issuer provided in registration statements and prospectuses. Under the practices existing prior to the enactment of the statute in 1933, dealers made blind commitments to purchase securities without adequate information, and in turn, resold the securities to an equally uninformed investing public. The entire distribution process was often stimulated by sales literature designed solely to arouse interest in the securities and not to disclose material facts about the issuer and its securities. * * *

* * *

[P]ublicity, prior to the filing of a registration statement by means of public media of communication, with respect to an issuer or its securities, emanating from broker-dealer firms who as underwriters or prospective underwriters have negotiated or are negotiating for a public offering of the securities of such issuer, must be presumed to set in motion or to be a part of the distribution process and therefore to involve an offer to sell or a solicitation of an offer to buy such securities prohibited by Section 5(c). * * *

Turning to the facts of this case, we find that the September 19, 1958, press release and resultant publicity concerning Arvida and its securities emanated from managing underwriters contemplating a distribution of such securities in the near future as to which a registration statement had not yet been filed. We also find that the mails and instrumentalities of interstate commerce were used in the dissemination of this publicity. We further find that such release and publicity was of a character calculated, by arousing and stimulating investor and dealer interest in Arvida securities and by eliciting indications of interest from customers to dealers and from dealer to underwriters, to set in motion the processes of distribution. * * * Reporters were furnished with price data, and registrants were named as the managing underwriters thus permitting, if not inviting, dealers to register their interest with them. We find that such activities constituted part of a selling effort by the managing underwriters.

* * *

The principal justification advanced for the September 19 release and publicity was the claim that the activities of Mr. Davis, and specifically his interests in Florida real estate, are "news" and that accordingly Section 5(c) should not be construed to restrict the freedom of the managing underwriters to release such publicity. We reject this contention. Section 5(c) is equally applicable whether or not the issuer or the surrounding circumstances have, or by astute public relations activities may be made to appear to have, news value.[7]

* * *

However, we have taken into account a number of mitigating factors. Registrants bear an excellent general reputation in the securities business and have never before been the subject of disciplinary proceedings by us. The Court has found that they acted in good faith and in reliance upon the opinion of counsel. These proceedings and the judgment of the Court in the injunctive action we commenced have served to place registrants and the securities industry upon unmistakable notice of their obligations in the field of publicity and forcibly to direct the attention of registrants to the consequences of improper practices in this area. * * * We therefore conclude that the public interest and the protection of investors do not require that the registrations of registrants as brokers and dealers be revoked or that they be suspended or expelled from membership in the NASD.

* * *

Arvida Press Releases

The following are the press releases, relating to Arvida Corporation, that are referred to in the preceding case.

---

[7] It should be clear that our interpretation of Section 5(c) in no way restricts the freedom of news media to seek out and publish financial news. Reporters presumably have no securities to sell and, absent collusion with sellers, Section 5(c) has no application to them. Underwriters such as registrants are in a different position; they are in the business of distributing securities, not news. Failure to appreciate this distinction between reporters and securities distributors has given rise to a further misconception. Instances have arisen in which a proposed financing is of sufficient public interest that journalists on their own initiative have sought out and published information concerning it. Since such journalistic enterprise does not violate Section 5, our failure to question resulting publicity should not have been taken as any indication that Section 5 is inapplicable to publicity by underwriters about newsworthy offerings. Similar considerations apply to publicity by issuers.

July 8, 1958 release:

Arthur V. Davis Planning Development of Real Estate Holdings

Arthur Vining Davis, noted industrialist, who for many years has been accumulating real estate holdings in Southeast Florida announced today that he is entering into a new phase of his program for his Florida real estate. This new phase will emphasize planning and developing new communities and additions to existing communities for industrial, commercial, residential and recreation use. A primary objective of the program will be to attract new industry to Southeast Florida.

Mr. Davis is organizing a new company to which he will transfer a major portion of his land holdings, including approximately 100,000 acres of undeveloped land in Dade, Broward and Palm Beach Counties. This company, to be known as Arvida Corporation, will launch a full scale program for the orderly development of the lands. Arrangements are being made to provide a large amount of new capital to implement the program. Mr. Davis said that his new program will not affect the operation of his various business enterprises in Florida.

September 18, 1958 release:

Carl M. Loeb, Rhoades & Co.

42 Wall Street New York, 5 N.Y.

For Release

Friday, September 19, 1958

Arthur V. Davis Planning Multimillion Financing of Florida Gold Coast Properties

Arthur Vining Davis announced today that Arvida Corporation, to which he is transferring virtually all of his land and operating real estate in Dade, Broward, and Palm Beach counties Florida, will be provided with $25 to $30 million of additional capital through an offering of part of its new common stock to the public. Arvida Corporation will have assets in excess of $100 million reflecting Mr. Davis' investment in these properties over the past twelve years and the contemplated public investment.

The public offering, scheduled for some time in the next 60 days, will be conducted through a nationwide group of investment banking firms to be headed by Carl M. Loeb, Rhoades & Co. and Dominick & Dominick, both of New York. A registration statement to be filed with the Securities and Exchange Commission is now in preparation.

Mr. Davis is transferring to Arvida Corporation over 100,000 acres of land, more than 155 square miles, in an area of the Gold Coast extending from Delray Beach in Palm Beach county to Homestead in Dade county south of Miami. Mr. Davis began his selection of these lands as far back as 1946. Arvida Corporation will own in Delray and Boca Raton, Palm Beach county, over 6,500 acres of land, including property with approximately 7,500 feet of ocean frontage. Also included are the Boca Raton hotel and club and ten other operating properties. In Broward county, west of Fort Lauderdale and Hollywood, Arvida will own 23,000 acres of land. In Dade county, south of Miami, it will hold 72,000 acres of land, by far the largest block of privately held property in the county. The lands in Broward and Dade counties are largely undeveloped but sizable tracts of acreage are suitable for immediate use as residential and commercial sites.

Mr. Milton N. Weir, who has been active in Mr. Davis' real estate affairs for several years, will become president of Arvida Corporation and will be responsible for the planning and execution of its future program. Mr. Davis, who will be Chairman of the Board, emphasized that it will be Arvida's primary objective to treat each parcel of its property in the manner best suited to bring forth its highest economic value through a comprehensive program of orderly and timely development. Some property will be developed immediately into residential communities, with regional shopping areas, industrial parks, utility installations and public service and recreational facilities. Much of the land in so large a holding will, of course, be held for investment and future development as the area expands. The attraction of new industry will be an essential feature of the program. In this manner Arvida may be expected to be a potent force in the further growth of Southeastern Florida bringing benefit to the citizens, communities and businesses of that region.

After *Loeb, Rhoades,* securities lawyers have counseled caution in the release of any publicity about the issuer or its industry that might fall under Release No. 3844 or *Loeb, Rhoades.* However, since issuers usually depend on publicity to sell their products and services, it is impractical to suggest that all publicity be stopped. The Commission has long recognized, in fact, that publicly held companies should keep their security holders informed about company affairs, and in the years since *Loeb, Rhoades* there has been an increasing recognition of the obligation of such companies to do so. These conflicting duties have led to the fear that publicity may get a company in trouble under the Securities Act, and the lack of it may result in violations of the Exchange Act.

In response, the Commission in 1971 issued Securities Act Release No. 5180, which is the next reading below. Directly following this release is an interpretive letter request relating to corporate publicity, directed to members of the Commission's staff, along with the staff's response.

Securities Act Release No. 5180

Securities and Exchange Commission, August 16, 1971.

GUIDELINES FOR THE RELEASE OF INFORMATION BY ISSUERS WHOSE SECURITIES ARE IN REGISTRATION

The Commission today took note of situations when issuers whose securities are "in registration"[8] may have refused to answer legitimate inquiries from stockholders, financial analysts, the press or other persons concerning the company or some aspect of its business. The Commission hereby emphasizes that there is no basis in the securities acts or in any policy of the Commission which would justify the practice of non-disclosure of *factual* information by a publicly held company on the grounds that it has securities in registration under the Securities Act of 1933 ("Act"). Neither a company in registration nor its representatives should instigate publicity for the purpose of facilitating the sale of securities in a proposed offering. Further, any publication of information by a company in registration other than by means of a statutory prospectus should be limited to factual information and should not include such things as predictions, projections, forecasts or opinions with respect to value.

* * *

Guidelines

The Commission strongly suggests that all issuers establish internal procedures designed to avoid problems relating to the release of corporate information when in registration. As stated above, issuers and their representatives should not initiate publicity when in registration, but should nevertheless respond to legitimate inquiries for factual information about the company's financial condition and business operations. Further, care should be exercised so that, for example, predictions, projections, forecasts, estimates and opinions concerning value are not given with respect to such things, among others, as sales and earnings and value of the issuer's securities.

It has been suggested that the Commission promulgate an all inclusive list of permissible and prohibited activities in this area. This is not feasible for the reason that determinations are based upon the particular facts of each case. However, the Commission as a matter of policy encourages the flow of factual information to shareholders and the investing public. Issuers in this regard should:

1. Continue to advertise products and services.

2. Continue to send out customary quarterly, annual and other periodic reports to stockholders.

---

[8] "In registration" is used herein to refer to the entire process of registration, at least from the time an issuer reaches an understanding with the broker-dealer which is to act as managing underwriter prior to the filing of a registration statement and the period of * * * during which dealers must deliver a prospectus.

3.   Continue to publish proxy statements and send out dividend notices.

4.   Continue to make announcements to the press with respect to factual business and financial developments; *i.e.,* receipt of a contract, the settlement of a strike, the opening of a plant, or similar events of interest to the community in which the business operates.

5.   Answer unsolicited telephone inquiries from stockholders, financial analysts, the press and others concerning factual information.

6.   Observe an "open door" policy in responding to unsolicited inquiries concerning factual matters from securities analysts, financial analysts, security holders, and participants in the communications field who have a legitimate interest in the corporation's affairs.

7.   Continue to hold stockholder meetings as scheduled and to answer shareholders' inquiries at stockholder meetings relating to factual matters.

In order to curtail problems in this area, issuers in this regard should avoid:

1.   Issuance of forecasts, projections, or predictions relating but not limited to revenues, income, or earnings per share.

2.   Publishing opinions concerning values.

* * *

The determination of whether an item of information or publicity could be deemed to constitute an offer "a step in the selling effort" in violation of Section 5 must be made by the issuer in the light of all the facts and circumstances surrounding each case. The Commission recognizes that questions may arise from time to time with respect to the release of information by companies in registration and, while the statutory obligation always rests with the company and can never be shifted to the staff, the staff will be available for consultation concerning such questions. It is not the function of the staff to draft corporate press releases. If a company, however, desires to consult with the staff as to the application of the statutory requirements to a particular case, the staff will continue to be available, and in this regard the pertinent facts should be set forth in written form and submitted in sufficient time to allow due consideration.

* * *

———————

The Internet presented new opportunities for marketing both products and securities, as well as new challenges for the Commission.

These are addressed in Securities Act Release No. 7856, excerpted immediately below.

Securities Act Release No. 7856

Securities and Exchange Commission, April 28, 2000.

USE OF ELECTRONIC MEDIA

* * *

I.   Introduction

By facilitating rapid and widespread information dissemination, the Internet has had a significant impact on capital-raising techniques and, more broadly, on the structure of the securities industry. Today, almost seven million people invest in the U.S. securities markets through online brokerage accounts. * * * To serve this increasing interest in online trading, there has been a surge in online brokerage firms offering an array of financial services. * * * Additionally, many publicly traded companies are incorporating Internet-based technology into their routine business operations, including setting up their own web sites to furnish company and industry information. Some provide information about their securities and the markets in which their securities trade. Investment companies use the Internet to provide investors with fund-related information, as well as shareholder services and educational materials. Issuers of municipal securities also are beginning to use the Internet to provide information about themselves and their outstanding bonds, as well as new offerings of their securities. The increased availability of information through the Internet has helped to promote transparency, liquidity and efficiency in our capital markets.

* * *

Today's interpretive guidance will do the following:

* * *

- Reduce uncertainty regarding permissible web site content to encourage more * * * widespread information dissemination to all investors by clarifying some of the facts and circumstances that may result in an issuer having adopted information on a third-party web site to which the issuer has established a hyperlink for purposes of the anti-fraud provisions of the federal securities laws; and

- [Set forth] general legal principles that govern permissible web site communications by issuers when in registration. * * *

* * *

II. Interpretive Guidance

* * *

B. Web Site Content

* * *

2. Issuer Communications During a Registered Offering

Because of the increasing use by issuers of web sites to communicate in the ordinary course of business with their security holders, customers, suppliers and others, issuers have asked us for guidance on the permissible content of their Internet communications when they are in registration. * * * An issuer in registration must consider the application of Section 5 of the Securities Act * * * to all of its communications with the public. * * * In our view, this includes information on an issuer's web site as well as information on a third-party web site to which the issuer has established a hyperlink. * * * Thus, information on a third-party web-site to which an issuer has established a hyperlink that meets the definition of an "offer to sell," "offer for sale" or "offer" under Section 2(a)(3) of the Securities Act raises a strong inference that the hyperlinked information is attributable to the issuer for purposes of a Section 5 analysis. * * * To ensure compliance with Section 5, an issuer in registration should carefully review its web site and any information on third-party web sites to which it hyperlinks.

* * *

Although our original guidance was directed at communications by reporting issuers when in registration, it also should be observed by non-reporting issuers preparing to offer securities to the public for the first time. A non-reporting issuer that has established a history of ordinary course business communications through its web site should be able to continue to provide business and financial information on its site consistent with our original guidance. A non-reporting issuer preparing for its first registered public offering that contemporaneously establishes a web site, however, may need to apply this guidance more strictly when evaluating its web site content because it may not have established a history of ordinary-course business communications with the marketplace. Thus, its web site content may condition the market for the offering and, due to the unfamiliarity of the marketplace with the issuer or its business, investors may be unable to view the issuer's communications in an appropriate context while the issuer is in registration. In other words, investors may be less able to distinguish offers to sell an issuer's securities in a registered offering from product or service promotional activities or other business or financial information.

* * *

Rule 433, added in 2005, provides additional guidance. Historical issuer information identified as such and located in a separate section of the issuer's website is not considered an offer of the issuer's securities unless it is used or identified in connection with the offering.

c.   GENERAL EXCEPTIONS TO THE DEFINITION OF "OFFER"

There are now several generally applicable exceptions to the definition of "offer." The first is found in Section 2(a)(3) itself:

> The terms defined in this paragraph and the term "offer to buy" as used in subsection (c) of section 5 shall not include preliminary negotiations or agreements between an issuer (or any person directly or indirectly controlling or controlled by an issuer, or under direct or indirect common control with an issuer) and any underwriter or among underwriters who are or are to be in privity of contract with an issuer (or any person directly or indirectly controlling or controlled by an issuer, or under direct or indirect common control with an issuer).

It is important to note that, so far as securities firms go, the exception is limited to underwriters and therefore does not cover dealers. During the pre-filing period, then, the company can find a managing underwriter, or a prospective managing underwriter can find a company interested in doing a public offering, and the managing underwriter can work with other securities firms to gauge their interest in joining the underwriting syndicate. However, the managing underwriter cannot begin to assemble the dealer group, even tentatively (unless, as discussed below, the company is a well-known seasoned issuer).

The second generally applicable exception is contained in Securities Act Rule 135, which begins:

> For the purposes of section 5 of the Act only, an issuer or a selling securities holder (and any person acting on behalf of either of them) that publishes through any medium a notice of a proposed offering to be registered under the Act will not be deemed to offer its securities for sale through that notice if * * * [t]he notice includes a statement to the effect that it does not constitute an offer of any securities for sale; and * * * [t]he notice otherwise includes no more than the following information: * * * .

The information that may be included is very basic, and does not go much beyond the type, amount, and basic terms of the securities to be offered, the anticipated timing of the offering, and a brief statement of the manner and of the purpose of the offering, without naming the underwriters. In specialized situations, including rights offerings and offerings to employees, more (but still very basic) information may be included.

A third exception is applicable to all issuers that are not disqualified. (Basically, the most common categories of disqualified issuers are blank check companies, shell companies, and penny stock issuers. These companies are not permitted to take advantage of most of the Commission's liberalizing reforms.) It is expressed in Rule 163A, which provides that any communication made by or on behalf of an issuer more than 30 days prior to the filing of a registration statement will not be deemed to be an offer if that communication does not refer to the offering of securities. The issuer must, however, take reasonable steps to control further distribution or publication of the communication within 30 days before such a filing.

The Commission also has devised safe harbors that, though intended for use by different classes of issuers, have broad effects. One of these, contained in Rule 169, permits non-reporting issuers of all types to continue to communicate factual business information regularly released to persons other than in their capacity as investors or potential investors. Another, set out in Rule 168, permits companies reporting under the Exchange Act (as well as certain others) to continue to communicate regularly released factual business and forward-looking information, notwithstanding the type of recipient. Finally, Rule 163 permits a great deal of flexibility to well-known seasoned issuers. These issuers may make oral or written offers at any time. Written offers, however, must bear certain legends and be filed with the Commission. Written offers meeting these conditions are referred to as "free writing prospectuses."

It is important to note that Rules 163A, 168 and 169 all provide that the communications they permit will not constitute offers (and thus will have no consequences under other provisions of the Securities Act making use of that term). By contrast, Rule 163, for well-known seasoned issuers, provides that the offers made are exempt from Section 5(c), but nonetheless are offers for other purposes of the Securities Act.

Rules 163 and 168 clearly were geared toward easing Securities Act compliance for larger issuers. In 2012, however, Congress decided to help out the "little guy"—that is, the emerging capital growth company. Perhaps not everyone would agree with the chosen line of demarcation; nonetheless, as set out at the beginning of this chapter, any issuer that is not a well-known seasoned issuer and that has less than $1.07 billion in annual revenue generally may qualify for various exemptions from otherwise applicable Securities and Exchange Act requirements.[9] For the purpose of defining what is and what is not an offer, there are two exemptions available to emerging growth companies. One of these is fairly straightforward: Section 5(d) provides that the issuer or someone (including an underwriter) acting on its behalf may "test the water" for market interest by communicating with institutions meeting certain size

---

[9] By 2014, approximately 85% of companies registering IPOs claimed emerging growth company status.

or deemed sophistication tests.[10] In addition, Section 2(a)(3) now excludes from the definition of "offer" any research report on an emerging growth company by a broker or dealer (whether or not such broker or dealer is participating in the offering). A "research report" is defined broadly as a written, electronic, or oral communication "that includes information, opinions, or recommendations with respect to securities of an issuer or an analysis of a security or an issuer, whether or not it provides information reasonably sufficient upon which to base an investment decision." The Commission has indicated, however, that it views the Section 2(a)(3) exclusion as applying only to research reports that are issued by individuals within broker-dealer firms who function as research analysts rather than sales or trading personnel. Previously, the issuance of research reports with respect to any issuer was subject to fairly strict regulation under Rules 137 through 139.

d. SPECIAL SITUATIONS

Section 2(a)(3) contains two provisions relating to special situations. The first provision serves as an example of the drafters' skill at anticipating possible loopholes:

> Any security given or delivered with, or as a bonus on account of, any purchase of securities or any other thing, shall be conclusively presumed to constitute a part of the subject of such purchase and to have been offered and sold for value.

Actually, this exception is not necessary because neither the Commission nor a court was likely to accept any other interpretation.

The other exception provides:

> The issue or transfer of a right or privilege, when originally issued or transferred with a security, giving the holder of such security the right to convert such security into another security of the same issuer or of another person, or giving a right to subscribe to another security of the same issuer or of another person, which right cannot be exercised until some future date, shall not be deemed to be an offer or sale of such other security; but the issue or transfer of such other security upon the exercise of such right of conversion or subscription shall be deemed a sale of such other security.

This exception usually applies to a convertible security or an option (often called a warrant). Examples are preferred stock convertible into common stock, and a warrant to purchase additional common stock that is sold along with common stock. Under this provision, the underlying security does not have to be registered originally when the conversion or exercise cannot occur immediately, but rather can only take place at some point in the future. Although Section 2(a)(3) does not specifically address the

---

[10] The investors must be either "qualified institutional buyers" (described in Chapter 7) or institutional "accredited investors" (described in Chapter 6).

issue, at the time the conversion or exercise can occur, an offer exists, and the filing of a registration statement, or the availability of a registration exemption, is required. This conclusion is logical because the "no offer" exception speaks only to the time of original "issue or transfer," and the requirement of later registration is dealt with in the legislative history.

A number of Securities Act rules contain exceptions to the definition of "offer" that relate to special situations. These include situations involving general advertising concerning investment companies (Rule 135a), the use of certain materials concerning options trading (Rule 135b), offshore press activities conducted by foreign issuers (Rule 135e), and publication by securities firms of research reports in the ordinary course of business (Rules 137, 138 and 139).

C. WAITING PERIOD

SITUATION 3C(1)

After Microtec and Nielson sign the letter of intent, you and Nielson's counsel begin preparing the registration statement and related documents. After a few weeks' work, the registration statement is filed with the Securities and Exchange Commission. While waiting for the registration statement to become effective, you learn the following.

     1.   Nielson puts out a press release announcing the filing of the Microtec registration statement. The release excerpts information from the preliminary prospectus that is included in the registration statement. This information consists of the amount and type of stock to be sold, a short description of Microtec's business, and a statement about Microtec's plans for the future.

     2.   Nielson employees telephone, write and e-mail prospective underwriters and dealers attempting to line up support for the offering. Many respond positively, with a typical response being, "Put me down for _____ shares."

     3.   Several prospective buyers call their local securities firms asking to buy Microtec stock. A typical response is, "We'll be glad to sell it to you if we can get it." A few of these prospective buyers then send checks in various amounts, $1,000 being typical, to these securities firms, indicating that they want the funds held in their accounts pending the effective date of the Microtec registration statement. By one means or another, the customers indicate that they are making "good faith" deposits in the hope of being given priority over other customers in the event there is a shortage of Microtec stock.

     4.   Nielson mails to prospective underwriters and dealers, for their review, copies of the preliminary prospectus and a draft of underwriting agreements to be entered into by Microtec,

Nielson, and the other underwriters and dealers. Nielson includes in the mailing a memorandum on the microcomputer industry, and on Microtec specifically, that was written by an employee of Nielson. In some instances, the materials are all provided electronically.

5.   Nielson mails a total of several thousand copies of the preliminary prospectus to prospective underwriters and dealers, for their distribution to salespeople and customers.

6.   Some prospective underwriters and dealers send a copy of the preliminary prospectus to all customers who are solicited on the telephone and who show any interest in buying Microtec stock. Others are more selective, sending a copy only to those prospective customers the salespeople believe might want to read it. Still others simply invite prospective customers to access the preliminary prospectus that Microtec has posted on its website.

7.   Nielson places advertisements in several newspapers in the region, briefly describing the offering and asking readers to call or write for a prospectus. Specifically, the following information is given: Microtec's name; Nielson's name, address and telephone number; that Microtec is a manufacturer of microcomputers; and that 1,000,000 shares of common stock will be offered through Nielson and other underwriters.

8.   Moore and Simpson speak to Microtec employees, in a group meeting and privately, offering to arrange purchases of Microtec stock for them. A few days after the meeting, Simpson distributes a letter confirming this offer.

9.   A financial reporter from a newspaper in a large city in the region interviews Moore and Simpson. The interview is wide-ranging, covering Microtec's history, current place in the industry and plans for the future, including the stock sale. The newspaper publishes a fairly long article on Microtec, including information on the offering.

10. Moore and Simpson travel with representatives of Nielson to three cities to speak to securities analysts and institutional investors. Their prepared comments include financial projections. One of the sessions is videotaped and made generally available on Microtec's website.

11. Microtec and Nielson, for itself and the underwriting syndicate, sign the underwriting agreement, binding the syndicate to purchase the Microtec stock under certain conditions (foremost among them, that the registration statement will become effective by a certain date).

SITUATION 3C(2)

Assume that Mictrotec is, rather than a non-reporting issuer, an unseasoned issuer that is also an emerging growth company. How would your advice differ as to the events described in Situation 3C(1)?

SITUATION 3C(3)

Assume that Mictrotec is, rather than a non-reporting issuer, a seasoned issuer that is not an emerging growth company. How would your advice differ as to the events described in Situation 3C(1)?

SITUATION 3C(4)

Assume that Mictrotec is, rather than a non-reporting issuer, a well-known seasoned issuer. How would your advice differ as to the events described in Situation 3C(1)?

In considering this situation, refer to the following, in addition to the materials in this section: Securities Act Sections 2(a)(3), 2(a)(10)–(12), 5(a), 5(b)(1), 5(c), 5(d), 10(a), and 10(b), Securities Act Rules 134,163, 164, 430, 433, and 460, and Exchange Act Rule 15c2–8.

I.   STATUTORY SCHEME: WAITING PERIOD

During the waiting period, Section 5(a) continues to apply, prohibiting all sales and all transportation, by the mails or in interstate commerce, of securities for the purpose of sale or delivery after sale, and Section 5(b)(1)[11] becomes applicable also. It provides:

> (b) It shall be unlawful for any person, directly or indirectly—

> (1) to make use of any means or instruments of transportation or communication in interstate commerce or of the mails to carry or transmit any prospectus relating to any security with respect to which a registration statement has been filed under this title, unless such prospectus meets the requirements of section 10;

When the language concerning interstate commerce and the mails is ignored, the section provides that it is unlawful to use any prospectus unless it satisfies the requirements of Section 10. The definition of "prospectus" is found in Section 2(a)(10), which reads:

> The term "prospectus" means any prospectus, notice, circular, advertisement, letter, or communication, written or by radio or television, which offers any security for sale or confirms the sale of any security; except * * * .

---

[11] Section 5(b)(2) also applies as a technical matter, but the chances are slim that the situation it contemplates would occur during the waiting period. It is really a post-effective period provision, and it will be discussed in that connection.

Stripped of its detail, Section 2(a)(10) defines a prospectus as a written offer or a confirmation of sale (setting aside the exceptions and the concepts of radio or television offers). Exception (a) in Section 2(a)(10) relates to the post-effective period and is not considered here. Exception (b) is a typical administrative law provision. It sets out the law regarding which communications are not deemed a prospectus, and then gives the Commission power to supplement it:

> (b) a notice, circular, advertisement, letter, or communication in respect of a security shall not be deemed to be a prospectus if it states from whom a written prospectus meeting the requirements of section 10 may be obtained and, in addition, does no more than identify the security, state the price thereof, state by whom orders will be executed, and contain such other information as the Commission, by rules or regulations deemed necessary or appropriate in the public interest and for the protection of investors, and subject to such terms and conditions as may be prescribed therein, may permit.

To supplement this provision, the Commission adopted Rule 134, which is discussed below.

Section 10, entitled "Information Required in Prospectus," is too long to reproduce here, but it should be examined at this point. Section 10(a) provides that a prospectus "shall contain the information contained in the registration statement," with some exceptions. This requirement may lead to two misconceptions. First, it may seem that a registration statement is filed and a prospectus subsequently is drafted based on the filed document. Actually, a prospectus is drafted for inclusion in a registration statement. Practicality dictates this, and this is what is contemplated by the Commission's registration statement forms and rules. Second, the statute's language may make it appear that any prospectus included as part of a registration statement necessarily must satisfy the requirements of Section 10(a), whether or not the registration statement actually contains the information it is supposed to contain. This is not the case. Although the exact requirements of the section are somewhat unclear, at least it can be said that a prospectus does not comply with Section 10(a) when it contains blanks where required information is to be added.

It may be possible for the prospectus as originally filed to comply with the requirements of Section 10(a). Usually, however, certain required information is unknown at the time of filing. For example, the underwriting syndicate is seldom established at this time, and the names of the underwriters must usually be added by an amendment just before the registration statement becomes effective. The price of the securities to be offered is also typically left blank originally, along with miscellaneous other information. In the usual case, then, a Section 10(a) prospectus is not available in the waiting period. A prospectus that meets the requirements of Section 10(b) is available. This section gives the

Commission authority to permit the use of a prospectus, for the purpose of Section 5(b)(1), that omits or summarizes information required by Section 10(a). The Commission has exercised this authority in Rules 430 and 431. The first of these rules allows the use, during the waiting period, of what is called variously a "preliminary prospectus" or "prospectus subject to completion." This prospectus may contain omissions and any of its contents may later be changed. The second covers "summary prospectuses" and allows their use in certain circumstances.

The Commission also has exercised its Section 10(b) authority to adopt Rule 433, which (together with Rule 164) permits the use, after a registration statement is filed, of something called a "free writing prospectus." Free writing prospectuses generally must bear a prescribed form of legend and, in many cases, must be filed with the Commission. Though filed, they do not become part of the registration statement. If a free writing prospectus is prepared by or on behalf of an issuer, or by or on behalf of a participant in an offering by an issuer, it must be accompanied or preceded by a Section 10 prospectus other than a summary prospectus or another free writing prospectus—in other words, during the waiting period, it must be accompanied or preceded by the preliminary prospectus authorized under Rule 430. If the free writing prospectus is electronic and contains a hyperlink to the preliminary prospectus, the preliminary prospectus is deemed to accompany it.

Even more lenient treatment applies, however, to some classes of issuers. Seasoned (including well-known seasoned issuers "seasoned") are permitted by Rule 433 to use free writing prospectuses without regard to whether they are accompanied or preceded by any other prospectus. (This was privilege also was afforded, by Rule 163, to well-known seasoned issuers in the pre-filing period).

In their essentials, then, Sections 2(a)(10) and 5(b)(1) provide that, during the waiting period, no offer, in writing or by radio or television, may be made except by a Section 10 prospectus or a communication meeting the requirements of exception (b) to Section 2(a)(10).[12] Additionally, these sections prohibit confirmations of sale. During the waiting period, the prohibition on oral offers, included in Section 5(c)'s general pre-filing period prohibition of offers, is lifted.[13] As mentioned above, Section 5(a) continues to apply during the waiting period, prohibiting all sales and all transportation, by the mails or in interstate commerce, of securities for the purpose of sale or delivery after sale.

---

[12] Rule 134 supplements exception (b) to Section 2(a)(10). Rule 134a creates an additional exception in very specialized circumstances. These rules are discussed below.

[13] The prohibition on oral offers continues, however, if the registration statement is the subject of a refusal or stop order, or a public proceeding or examination. These exceptions are discussed in the next chapter.

II. WHAT IS A SALE?

The definition of "sale" contained in Section 2(a)(3) does not purport to be complete. Its basic provision is: "The term 'sale' or 'sell' shall include every contract of sale or disposition of a security or interest in a security, for value." Similar to its treatment of offers, the Securities Act takes the common law meaning of the term "sale" as its base and then expands it. The most striking thing about Section 2(a)(3) is its inclusion of contracts of sale within the ambit of "sale." This inclusion is a drafters' technique that allows provisions such as Section 5(a) to be written a little more cleanly, but at a price, for by this technique the drafters laid a little trap. In the waiting period, certain offers may be made. The trick is that when an offer is accepted and a contract is created, Section 5(a)(1) has been violated because a sale has occurred. As a practical matter, then, ordinary offers should not be made in the waiting period, but rather offerors should condition their offers in such a way that they cannot be accepted until the registration statement is effective. Partly for this reason, during the waiting period, securities firms make conditional offers and collect responses called "indications of interest," with the hope of turning these indications of interest into sales shortly after effectiveness.

As with offers, the Commission reads the Section 2(a)(3) definition of "sale" liberally, leading to an expansive application of an already expanded concept. By including in the definition not only contracts of sale, but "*every* * * * disposition of a security * * * for value*" (emphasis added), the drafters of Section 2(a)(3) provided the Commission a reasonable basis for this. An example of the Commission's expansive reading is found in the following case.

In re Franklin, Meyer & Barnett

Securities and Exchange Commission, 1956.
37 S.E.C. 47.

These are proceedings pursuant to Sections 15(b) and 15A(*l*)(2) of the Securities Exchange Act of 1934 ("Exchange Act") to determine whether to revoke the registration as a broker and dealer of Franklin, Meyer & Barnett ("registrant"), a partnership, or to suspend or expel registrant from membership in the National Association of Securities Dealers, Inc. ("NASD") and whether, under Section 15A(b)(4) of the Act, Albert W. Franklin, Jr. and Joseph H. Meyer, general partners, and Joseph A. Costa, Stephen Lustig, Edward Thompson, Jerome Schnur, Sol Frank, E. Steven Hickey and Seymour Radow, salesmen, are each a cause of any order of revocation, suspension, or expulsion which might be entered against registrant.

The order for proceedings alleges that between April 1 and 22, 1955, registrant and the persons named sold unregistered securities of Holly

Uranium Corporation ("Holly") in violation of Section 5(a)(1) of the Securities Act of 1933 ("Securities Act").

* * *

THE TRANSACTIONS IN HOLLY STOCK

On February 10, 1955, Holly filed a registration statement with this Commission covering a proposed public offering of 900,000 shares of its common stock at $3.50 per share. Registrant, as a co-underwriter, was to participate to the extent of 250,000 shares, and about March 30, 1955, it mailed to approximately 1,400 persons a preliminary prospectus together with a covering letter which stated that orders could not be solicited and accepted until the registration statement became effective and included a tear-off coupon to be signed and returned to registrant by those interested in receiving a copy of the final prospectus. The registration statement became effective on Friday, April 22, 1955, and thereafter confirmations and the final prospectus were mailed to purchasers.

The stipulation [of facts] sets forth the circumstances surrounding 23 sales of Holly stock by the salesmen named in the order for proceedings. It appears that 19 of these sales were clearly effected by these salesmen, with the exception of Radow, during the period prior to the effective date of the registration statement. * * *

Costa enclosed with the preliminary prospectus and covering letter sent to 4 customers, his business card upon which he wrote, "Phone me as soon as possible as my allotment is almost complete on this issue." Six of his customers sold securities owned by them prior to the effective date of registration in order to pay for the Holly stock in whole or in part, and such dispositions were suggested by Costa to 3 of these customers who did not have the money to pay for the Holly stock. Five of his customers mailed checks or postal money orders to registrant prior to effective registration, either for the full amount of the purchase price or for the balance due after crediting the proceeds of their dispositions. One of these checks bore the notation that it was for "200 shs. of Holly Uranium", and another that it was for "100 Holly." One of his customers sent a letter dated April 7 to registrant enclosing stock owned by him and confirming his instructions to Costa to sell that stock and apply the proceeds in partial payment for the Holly stock purchased by him.

Five of Lustig's customers sold securities at his suggestion in order to pay in whole or in part for the Holly stock they purchased prior to the effective date of registration, and one of these customers mailed a postal money order to registrant prior to the effective date for the balance due. Another customer sent a check to registrant in full payment during the same period. One purchaser did not receive a preliminary prospectus, and another received it after making the purchase.

Thompson and Hickey also suggested securities dispositions by their customers in order to pay for the Holly stock, and such dispositions were made during the pre-effective period. Frank's customers also sold securities during such period in order to pay for Holly stock, but it does not appear whether such dispositions were suggested by him. Schnur's customer, at his suggestion, mailed to registrant a check for $350 dated April 4 in full payment for his purchase of Holly stock.

PARTNERS' SUPERVISION OF SALESMEN

Of registrant's partners, only Meyer, Barnett and Zoref had supervisory functions in connection with the Holly offering during the period involved in these proceedings. Meyer was in charge of the underwriting, and instructed the salesmen at a number of meetings attended by Barnett and Zoref as to the proper procedure to follow during the pre-effective period in order to comply with the registration provisions of the Securities Act. Meyer stated at these meetings that only indications of interest and not orders could be accepted from prospective purchasers, and that after the effective date of registration such indications of interest had to be "firmed up" before a confirmation of sale could be sent to the customer. He also advised the salesmen who assisted in sending out the preliminary prospectus and covering letter that no other material could be enclosed in the envelopes. * * *

As previously stated, a number of checks in payment of Holly stock were sent to registrant prior to the effective date of registration and two of them indicated their purpose. * * *

According to Meyer it is customary for customers to send checks to the * * * firm merely for the purpose of having funds in their accounts, but no explanation was offered with respect to the partners' failure to instruct the records clerk to show them any checks expressly indicating their purpose as payment for Holly stock, nor did the partners make any attempt to ascertain whether any prospective purchasers appearing on the salesmen's lists of indications of interest had sent in any checks or whether any of the checks were in fact in payment for Holly stock. * * *

CONCLUSIONS AS TO VIOLATIONS

The record shows that, notwithstanding the partners' instructions, all of registrant's salesmen named in the order for proceedings, with the exception of Radow, accepted orders for Holly stock prior to the effective date of registration. Although they initially invited indications of interest, they accepted payments for Holly stock during the pre-effective period in the form of checks and the proceeds of the sale of other securities owned by the customers, and thereby went beyond the permissible scope of the Act. In addition, the business card which Costa enclosed with the preliminary prospectus and covering letter solicited an offer to buy and was therefore a prospectus within the meaning of Section [2(a)(10)] of the Securities Act. Obviously the card did not comply with the detailed requirements for a preliminary prospectus prescribed in Rule [430].

On the basis of the foregoing we find that Costa, Lustig, Schnur, and Thompson willfully violated Section 5(a)(1) of the Securities Act. While we make no similar findings with respect to Hickey and Frank, we note that these salesmen have joined in stipulating that the record in this proceeding and the findings of fact in this opinion may be used against them in any future proceeding concerning any other matter which may be instituted by us against either of them.

It is clear that registrant, Meyer, Barnett, and Zoref failed to exercise adequate supervision over the salesmen's activities. * * * We conclude that registrant, Meyer, Barnett and Zoref willfully violated Section 5(a)(1) of the Securities Act.

THE PUBLIC INTEREST

Registrant has undertaken to put into effect immediately all necessary measures of control and supervision required to prevent a recurrence of the violations found or similar violations. As we have seen, the three partners connected with the Holly underwriting did not directly participate in the violations, and they have asserted that this is the first disciplinary proceeding involving them. Under these circumstances we do not think that revocation of registrant's registration is required, and we conclude that suspension of registrant from membership in the NASD for a period of 10 days as provided in the offer of settlement is in the public interest. We further conclude that Meyer, Barnett, Zoref, Costa, and Lustig are each a cause of such suspension, but that Schnur and Thompson, in view of the fact that the record indicates that each of them participated in only one transaction which violated the Securities Act, are not such causes.

* * *

In contrast to the general expansiveness of the concept of "sale" is the exception in Section 2(a)(3), introduced in connection with the pre-filing period, that relates to "preliminary negotiations or agreements" between an issuer and underwriters, or among underwriters. This exception provides that all the terms in Section 2(a)(3), including "sale," do not include these agreements. On its face, the exception is ambiguous because it cannot be determined from the words themselves whether "preliminary" modifies only "negotiations" or whether it also modifies "agreements." If the latter were the case, neither the agreement among underwriters nor the underwriting agreement could be entered into during the waiting period, since these are not "preliminary" agreements. Everyone—including the Commission—wants the underwriting arrangements finalized prior to effectiveness. Perhaps because of this, a problem has never existed with interpretation: "preliminary" modifies "negotiations" only. It is then unclear how negotiations are so limited. It seems that there is no limitation, because the parties must finalize negotiations before they can sign agreements. It may be argued that by adding the word "preliminary," the drafters attempted to make clearer the distinction between negotiations and agreements: negotiations are preliminary to agreements, and agreements are not part of negotiations.

III. WHAT IS A PROSPECTUS?

Under Section 2(a)(10), without the exceptions, any written offer, offer by radio or television, or confirmation of sale is a prospectus. An understanding of the concept of "offer" provides a foundation for understanding what makes up a prospectus, because a determination of what constitutes an offer is much more complex than a determination of whether something is written or transmitted by radio or television. The most difficult part of the task, therefore, has been accomplished in the discussion of the pre-filing period. It is worth pausing, however, to review this discussion, and especially to note that some regularly released factual and (in the case of companies registered under the Exchange Act) forward-looking information will not be regarded as an offer, whether or not it is in writing. Moreover, a communication (including a written communication) made more than 30 days before a registration statement is filed will not be considered an offer unless the proposed offering is referenced. With respect to emerging growth companies, neither brokers' or dealers' research reports nor communications with certain institutions will be regarded as offers.

What remains is to discuss the "written or by radio or television" aspects of prospectuses, to cover the exceptions to the definition of the term "prospectus," and to discuss the possible application of a 1995 Supreme Court case.

a. "WRITTEN OR BY RADIO OR TELEVISION"

Garden variety written offers are spotted easily enough. It is indirect offers that cause a problem. Written publicity concerning the issuer or its industry that conditions the market for a security is the most common example of an indirect offer. The discussion of publicity in connection with the pre-filing period is equally applicable here. For instance, Release No. 3844 and the *Loeb, Rhoades* case involved press releases and a brochure. These publicity items were in writing and, therefore, constituted prospectuses because they made offers. Rules 164 and 433, adopted in 2005, specifically address statements to the media which lead to articles, resulting in prospectuses.

The "written or by radio or television" aspects of publicity can be subtle. Take, for instance, an oral announcement by the president of an issuer at a press conference that, if in writing, would constitute a prospectus under the section 2(a)(10) definition. There is probably little doubt that, when a reporter incorporates the announcement in an article, the president has made an offer that is "written." Analytically, it can be said that the president caused the writing, and that that is enough to make the offer one that is by means of a prospectus. Clearly, the statute does not speak in terms of who the scrivener is. Harder questions are presented by responses to press inquiries. Upon analysis, however, it becomes clear that the hardest questions relate to whether a particular statement involves an offer, rather than to whether the offer was "written or by radio or television." But that is not to say, for example, that a newspaper article including a puffing answer to a reporter's unsolicited question about a company's product would be as likely to constitute a section 5 problem as would prepared statements at a called press conference. The newspaper article would be less dangerous, but primarily because a court would not be as likely to decide that the answer involved an offer, written or otherwise.

Written publicity is not, of course, the only way indirect written offers can be made. In re Franklin, Meyer & Barnett, included above in this section, offers the example of a securities salesman sending to a customer a preliminary prospectus and also enclosing his business card, on which he wrote, "Phone me as soon as possible as my allotment is almost complete on this issue." The Commission's conclusion that the business card solicited an offer to buy, and was therefore a prospectus, seems clear enough. A different situation would be presented if the salesman had called the customer and, finding him not in, had left the above message, which was reduced to writing. One way to approach that situation is to begin with the above analysis relating to press inquiries. Would the idea of "causing" a writing be extended to encompass the salesman's acts? It is hard to say. Considering the flexibility inherent in the concepts discussed above, it might depend on how badly the Commission or a court wanted to expand the concept.

Factual permutations would make an affirmative answer to the question more or less likely. For example, it would be important to know if the salesman specifically asked that the message be put in writing or that it not be. Agency concepts should help the salesman in an argument along these lines: (1) that in the one situation the press is the agent of the issuer, whereas in the other whoever answered the customer's telephone is the customer's agent, not the salesman's; (2) that the oral statement to the agent was the equivalent of an oral statement to the customer directly; and (3) that the note-taking by the agent was therefore analytically indistinguishable from note-taking by the customer.

Technology has presented new challenges for those seeking to define "writing." For instance, practitioners grappled for several years with whether e-mail is more like a substitute for a telephone conversation or (given its ability to be forwarded, downloaded, etc.) more like a mailed document. In 2005, in an amendment to Rule 405, the Commission specified that "written communication" includes any "graphic communication." "Graphic communications" include Internet communications, e-mails, electronic postings on websites, and broadly disseminated or "blast" voice mail messages. Specifically excluded, however, are live communications carried in real time to a live audience, unless they are radio or television broadcasts. Special treatment for electronic road shows is set out in Rule 433.

b. EXCEPTIONS

Exception (b) to Section 2(a)(10), which is quoted above, allows certain written offers in the waiting period by deeming them not to be prospectuses. In supplementation of this provision, the Commission has adopted Rule 134. This rule offers a great deal more leeway than the statute. The rule is complex, following this form: (a) can be done if (b) is done, but (b) does not have to be done if either (c)(i) or (c)(ii) is done, and if its terms are followed, (d) can be done. Any type of communication that is written or by radio or television can meet the requirements of Rule 134. Press releases and letters are typical examples. Also common, although used more in the post-effective than in the waiting period, is the so-called tombstone advertisement, which gets its name from its stylized format. These are found most often in the financial section of newspapers, with *The Wall Street Journal* often including a number of them.

In addition to Rule 134, the Commission has adopted Rule 134a, which is a highly specialized rule providing that certain written material relating to standardized options, as defined in Exchange Act Rule 9b–1, is not deemed a prospectus. Unlike Rule 134, which takes exception (b) to Section 2(a)(10) as its starting point, Rule 134a's real foundation is the Commission's general rulemaking power found in Section 19(a).

The applicability of Rule 135, discussed in connection with the pre-filing period, is uncertain in the waiting period. Rule 135 provides that "an issuer or a selling securities holder * * * that publishes, through any medium, a notice of a proposed offering to be registered under the Act will not be deemed to offer its securities for sale * * * ." Its thrust clearly is toward the pre-filing period. Everything supports this conclusion, including the rule's focus on offers rather than on prospectuses as in Rules 134 and 134a, and statements by the Commission in the adopting release. None of this means, however, that Rule 135 could not apply during the waiting period. The important phrases in the rule to consider are "proposed offering" and "to be registered." In the usual situation, securities firms begin a public offering immediately after a registration statement is filed. In this situation, Rule 135 clearly could not continue to be used, because the offering no longer merely is "proposed." However, an offering may be delayed until later, for example until the registration statement becomes effective. (Note, however, that there is a theory that the offering begins either on the filing of the registration statement or on its being made public by the Commission, which occurs almost immediately.) The phrase "to be registered" is more problematical. In a technical sense, securities are still "to be registered" during the waiting period, since they are not "registered" until the registration statement is effective. But the term may be used in a somewhat looser sense, similar to the phrase "to be the subject of a registration statement." Usually, of course, it does not matter whether Rule 135 applies during the waiting period, because of the availability of Rule 134. But the question may be important to the occasional issuer that has published a notice meeting the information requirements of Rule 135 but not those of Rule 134. (This typically would happen when someone marked up a notice from a prior transaction without realizing that the notice was a Rule 135 notice.)

c.   THE POSSIBLE IMPACT OF *GUSTAFSON V. ALLOYD*

In connection with the waiting period issue of what constitutes a prospectus, *Gustafson v. Alloyd Co.,*[14] which is discussed in chapter 8, needs to be considered. This case deals with litigation under Securities Act Section 12(a)(2), which provides a civil remedy in the case of offers or sales "by means of a prospectus or oral communication" that contains a materially false or misleading statement. In reaching its decision, the Court discussed the meaning of the term "prospectus." For example, the Court indicated that the definition of the term in Section 2(a)(10) "refers to documents of wide dissemination." The Court also indicated that it could not "accept the conclusion that [the term 'prospectus'] means one thing in one section of the Act and something quite different in another." These statements, however, along with other broad language in the opinion, are merely dicta with respect to matters outside the holding of the case. As discussed in Chapter 8, the decision was based on an exceedingly flawed understanding of the Securities Act, and it generally is regarded as inapplicable in determining what constitutes a prospectus in a registered offering.

In fact, the Commission never has permitted *Gustafson* to affect its construction of the term "prospectus" for purposes of Section 5. Moreover, when it created the category of "free writing prospectuses," which may be used without violating Section 5, it specifically stated that they would be regarded as prospectuses for purposes of Section 12(a)(2).

IV. PRELIMINARY PROSPECTUS DELIVERY REQUIREMENTS

The Commission has perceived a shortcoming in Section 5 of the Securities Act, which allows, but does not require, that preliminary prospectuses be distributed during the waiting period. It views this as a shortcoming because securities firms direct much of their sales effort at customers during this period. The Commission has corrected this shortcoming by two roundabout means. The first relates to what is called "acceleration" of the effective date of a registration statement. Acceleration is discussed more fully in the next chapter, but for present purposes it is necessary to appreciate the importance of acceleration in most offerings. Section 8 of the Securities Act provides that a registration statement becomes effective twenty days after filing, or after the filing of any amendment. It also provides that a registration statement may

---

[14]   513 U.S. 561 (1995).

become effective on "such earlier date as the Commission may determine" or, in securities parlance, that its effective date may be "accelerated." The problem for issuers is that a registration statement can rarely be complete at the time it is filed. Certain information, such as the name of each underwriter in the syndicate, usually cannot be supplied until just prior to effectiveness. Thus, acceleration is typically required as a practical matter. How the Commission forces the distribution of preliminary prospectuses by means of its control over acceleration is outlined in the next reading.

The second means by which the Commission forces the distribution of preliminary prospectuses is even more roundabout than the first. Exchange Act Section 15(c)(2) prohibits securities firms from engaging "in any fraudulent, deceptive, or manipulative act or practice" and gives the Commission power to determine what acts and practices fit within this prohibition. In Exchange Act Rule 15c2–8, the Commission requires underwriters and dealers to take reasonable steps to furnish copies of the preliminary prospectus to any person who makes a written request for a copy. It also requires underwriters and dealers to furnish copies of the preliminary prospectus to their salesmen, and the managing underwriter to provide the underwriters and dealers with sufficient quantities of the prospectus to meet their delivery requirements. Further, in the case of offerings by non-reporting issuers (which includes many first-time registrants under the Securities Act), the rule requires underwriters and dealers to "deliver a copy of the preliminary prospectus to any person who is expected to receive a confirmation of sale at least 48 hours prior to the sending of such confirmation." The teeth behind these requirements is the Commission's determination, in Rule 15c2–8, that a failure to make these deliveries constitutes a deceptive act or practice under Exchange Act Section 15(c)(2).

Securities Act Release No. 4968
Securities and Exchange Commission, April 24, 1969.

PRIOR DELIVERY OF PRELIMINARY PROSPECTUS

* * *

The Commission has declared its policy in Rule 460 that it will not accelerate the effective date of a registration statement unless the preliminary prospectus contained in the registration statement is distributed to underwriters and dealers who it is reasonably anticipated will be invited to participate in the distribution of the security to be offered or sold. The purpose of this requirement is to afford all persons effecting the distribution a means of being informed with respect to the offering so that they can advise their customers of the investment merits of the security. Particularly in the case of a first offering by a nonreporting company, salesmen should obtain and read the current preliminary or final prospectus before offering the security to their clients.

The Commission also announced, in the exercise of its responsibilities in accelerating the effective date of a registration statement under section 8(a) of the Securities Act of 1933, and particularly the statutory requirement that it have due regard to the adequacy of the information respecting the issuer theretofore available to the public, that it will consider whether the persons making an offering of securities of an issuer which is not subject to the reporting requirements of section 13 or 15(d) of the Securities Exchange Act of 1934, have taken reasonable steps to furnish preliminary prospectuses to those persons who may reasonably be expected to be purchasers of the securities. The Commission will ordinarily be satisfied by a written statement from the managing underwriter to the effect that it has been informed by participating underwriters and dealers that copies of the preliminary prospectus * * * have been or are being distributed to all persons to whom it is then expected to mail confirmations of sale not less than 48 hours prior to the time it is expected to mail such confirmations. * * * Of course, if the form of preliminary prospectus so distributed was inadequate or inaccurate in material respects, acceleration will be deferred until the Commission has received satisfactory assurances that appropriate correcting material (including a memorandum of changes) has been so distributed.

* * *

The Commission has issued several releases addressing electronic delivery of prospectuses. One of these, Securities Act Release No. 7856 (April 28, 2000), set out in part in Section BIIb, provides that electronic delivery is permissible if the recipient gives informed consent, and that such consent can be given telephonically if a record is kept. Release No. 7856 also gives guidance as to what other electronic materials will be considered part of the prospectus, what materials will be considered delivered concurrently, and what the issuer's responsibility is for the content of its web site and hyperlinked materials. In addition, the Release sets out basic principles to be observed in conducting offerings entirely online. These releases have been augmented by the adoption in 2005 of Rule 433, which provides that an electronic preliminary prospectus that is hyperlinked to a free writing prospectus is deemed to accompany or precede it.

D. POST-EFFECTIVE PERIOD

SITUATION 3D(1)

Shortly after Microtec and Nielson sign the underwriting agreement, the registration statement becomes effective. After this, the following events occur and come to your attention:

1.   Employees of Nielson telephone and e-mail prospective dealers and attempt to get their commitments to buy specific amounts of Microtec stock. Some hesitate, but many agree to buy.

2.   Salespeople working for underwriters and dealers telephone and e-mail customers they have called during the waiting period and attempt to sell Microtec stock. Typical statements are: "I'd like to confirm your order" or "I'd like to firm-up your order."

3.   Before copies of the final prospectus arrive at their offices, some salespeople give copies of the preliminary prospectus to customers. In some cases, salespeople fill-in on the cover of the prospectus the public offering price.

4.   The final prospectus is posted on Microtec's website. Some salespeople, at the time they seek order confirmations, advise customers that it is available through this medium.

5.   Nielson publishes a "tombstone" advertisement in several newspapers. This advertisement contains the name of Microtec and of all underwriters, but it gives no URL or other addresses. It otherwise simply states that 1,000,000 shares of common stock are being offered at $10 per share.

6.   Nielson provides to its salespeople a short memorandum that summarizes information from the final prospectus. A number of salespeople give this memorandum to customers, either by itself or along with a copy of the final prospectus.

7.   Underwriters and dealers send bills to customers for the Microtec shares they have bought.

8.   Microtec provides stock certificates to the underwriters and dealers, in the names they have requested. In accordance with customers' requests, underwriters and dealers send certificates to customers.

9.   One dealer decides to keep a few hundred shares of Microtec stock indefinitely, hoping its price will rise. A few months after the registration statement becomes effective, this dealer sells this stock to customers for $12 a share, which is the prevailing market price. No prospectus is delivered.

SITUATION 3D(2)

Assume that Mictrotec is, rather than a non-reporting issuer, an unseasoned issuer that is also an emerging growth company. How would your advice differ as to the events described in Situation 3D(1)?

SITUATION 3D(3)

Assume that Mictrotec is, rather than a non-reporting issuer, a seasoned issuer that is not an emerging growth company. How would your advice differ as to the events described in Situation 3D(1)?

SITUATION 3D(4)

Assume that Mictrotec is, rather than a non-reporting issuer, a well-known seasoned issuer. How would your advice differ as to the events described in Situation 3D(1)?

In considering this situation, refer to the following, in addition to the materials in this section: Securities Act Sections 2(a)(3), 2(a)(10)–(12), 4(3), 5(a)(1), 5(b), 5(c), 5(d) and 10(a)–(b), Securities Act Rules 134, 172,173, and 174, and Exchange Act Rule 10b–10.

I.   STATUTORY SCHEME: POST-EFFECTIVE PERIOD

Section 5(b)(1), discussed in connection with the waiting period, continues to apply during the post-effective period. This section proscribes the use of any prospectus, unless it satisfies the requirements of Section 10. During the waiting period, rules adopted pursuant to the Commission's Section 10(b) authority permit use of preliminary prospectuses (Rule 430), summary prospectuses (Rule 431), and free writing prospectuses (Rule 433). Summary prospectuses may be used after effectiveness, in certain circumstances. Free writing prospectuses also may be used, although, in the case of issuers that are not seasoned or well-known seasoned issuers, the free writing must be accompanied (including by hyperlink) or preceded by the "final prospectus" called for by Section 10(a). For reasons that soon will become apparent, a writing that is accompanied or preceded by the final prospectus is not technically a prospectus at all.

Once the registration statement becomes effective, a few additional rules come into play under Section 10(b). These are Rules 430A, 430B and 430C (the last two of which were adopted in 2005). These rules permit, in the case of certain types of offerings and/or certain types of issuers, the use of prospectuses lacking specific items of information.

Usually, the only prospectus that complies with the requirements of Section 10(a) is the prospectus that is included in the registration statement just before it becomes effective (the registration statement having in many cases been amended shortly before effectiveness to include information, such as the names of all the underwriters, that was left blank in the preliminary prospectus). Also, during this period a new exception is applicable to the definition of "prospectus." This is exception (a) in Section 2(a)(10), which provides that a communication is not deemed a prospectus when it is accompanied or preceded by a prospectus that meets the requirements of Section 10(a). The term traditionally used to describe communications allowed by this exception is "free writing." Because, in the post-effective period, many of the free writing prospectuses now allowed must be accompanied or preceded by a Section 10(a) prospectus, they technically cease to be free writing "prospectuses" and become merely free writing.

After effectiveness, Section 5(a)(1) ceases to apply and Section 5(b)(2) comes into play. It provides:

> (b) It shall be unlawful for any person, directly or indirectly—

> (2) to carry or cause to be carried through the mails or in interstate commerce any such security for the purpose of sale or for delivery after sale, unless accompanied or preceded by a prospectus that meets the requirements of subsection (a) of section 10.

As a practical matter, this section provides that a security may not be delivered to a buyer unless the buyer simultaneously receives, or has received, a copy of the final prospectus. Rule 172(b), however, provides that for purposes of Section 5(b)(2) the final prospectus is deemed, in most instances, to be delivered when the registration statement becomes effective. This largesse (known as the "access equals delivery" model), does not apply for purposes of exception (a) of Section 2(a)(10), discussed above. Rule 173 requires (though not as a condition of reliance on 172) that issuers, underwriters and dealers provide their purchasers either final prospectuses or a prescribed form of notice within two business days of completing the sale. Non-participating dealers may be exempt from this requirement as described at the end of this chapter.

The final piece to the post-effective statutory puzzle lies in understanding the treatment of confirmations of sale, which generally are not sent until the post-effective period, the first time at which the sale itself lawfully may occur. Under Section 2(a)(10), confirmations of sale are included in the definition of "prospectus." Section 2(a)(10) then provides, in exception (a), that a communication sent during the post-effective period and accompanied or preceded by a final prospectus will not be considered a prospectus after all. Because business practice essentially requires that confirmations be delivered, and Rule 10b–10 under the Exchange Act explicitly requires such delivery, the statute would demand delivery of a final prospectus as well. Under Rule 172, however, most confirmations limited to the information necessary to comply with Rule 10b–10 (and notices of allocations) are exempt from the provisions of Section 5(b)(1).

During the post-effective period, then, oral offers may be made, since Section 5(c) does not apply during this period (except in the case of a registration statement that is the subject of a stop order or of a public proceeding instituted before the effective date). Written offers may be made by means of the final prospectus, as contemplated by Section 5(b)(1) and, in some cases, by summary, Rule 430A, 430B or 430C prospectuses. They may also be made by free writing, when accompanied or preceded by a final prospectus, as provided in Section 2(a)(10). Seasoned (including well-known seasoned) issuers may continue to use free writing prospectuses that are not accompanied or preceded by any other prospectus. Offers may continue to be made under exception (b) to Section 2(a)(10) and under Rules 134 and 134a. Sales may be made, since the prohibition on sales contained in Section 5(a)(1) no longer applies. Section 5(a)(2)'s prohibition of pre-effective deliveries ceases to pertain, and Section 5(b)(2)'s requirement that security delivery must be accompanied or preceded by a final prospectuses generally will be deemed satisfied, thanks to Rule 172(b). Nonetheless, issuers, underwriters and some dealers must deliver either the final prospectuses or the notice prescribed by Rule 173.

II. TOMBSTONE ADVERTISEMENTS

The following is an advertisement, of the type allowed by Securities Act Rule 134, that appeared in *The Wall Street Journal* in connection with the initial registration of securities under the Securities Act by Conoco. As is traditional, this advertisement appeared on the next business day after the registration statement became effective. Because of their format, advertisements such as this are called "tombstones." Under rule 134 as most recently revised, the information that could be presented exceeds that which appears below.

III. SECTION 5(b) AND DEFECTIVE PROSPECTUSES

As indicated above, during the post-effective period, Section 5(b)(1) allows the use of a prospectus that meets the requirements of Section 10, and Section 5(b)(2) requires that a Section 10(a) prospectus accompany or precede the delivery of a security. So much is clear. But what if a final prospectus is defective because it is materially false or misleading? Does such a defect prevent the prospectus from meeting the requirements of Section 10(a)?

The place to start to answer this question is Section 10(a) itself, which provides that "a prospectus * * * shall contain the information contained in the registration statement * * * ." On its face, this language seems to require only that the prospectus track the registration statement, defective or otherwise, although as the prior discussion of Section 10(a) has indicated, to comply with this section the prospectus must at least be complete. The language of the section itself, then, provides no help in answering questions concerning materially false or misleading prospectuses. The Commission and the Second Circuit have provided their answer in the following case.

SEC v. Manor Nursing Centers, Inc.

United States Court of Appeals, Second Circuit, 1972.
458 F.2d 1082.

■ Before ANDERSON, OAKES and TIMBERS, CIRCUIT JUDGES.

■ TIMBERS, CIRCUIT JUDGE:

* * *

The Securities and Exchange Commission brought this action pursuant to Section 22(a) of the Securities Act of 1933 * * *. The complaint alleged violations of the * * * prospectus-delivery requirement of Section 5(b)(2) of the 1933 Act. [The district court held that the defendants (appellants here) had violated this requirement, and it enjoined further violations.]

* * *

The Manor [Nursing Centers] prospectus purported to disclose the information required by [§ 10(a)]. The evidence adduced at trial showed, however, that developments subsequent to the effective date of the registration statement made this information false and misleading. * * * We hold that implicit in the statutory provision that the prospectus contain certain information is the requirement that such information be true and correct. A prospectus does not meet the requirements of § 10(a), therefore, if information required to be disclosed is materially false or misleading. Appellants violated § 5(b)(2) by delivering Manor securities for sale accompanied by a prospectus which did not meet the requirements of § 10(a) in that the prospectus contained materially false and misleading statements with respect to information required by § 10(a) to be disclosed.

* * *

Although the First Circuit has followed *Manor Nursing*,[15] it has done so without analysis. The Fifth Circuit has criticized the case strongly. In SEC v. Southwest Coal & Energy Co.,[16] the court was faced with a situation in which *Manor Nursing* was relevant by analogy. In rejecting

---

[15] 556 F.2d 619, 622 (1st Cir.1977).

[16] 624 F.2d 1312 (5th Cir.1980).

the Second Circuit's thesis, the Fifth Circuit focused its analysis not on Section 10(a), but on the violence *Manor Nursing* does to other sections of the Securities Act. False or misleading statements in a prospectus are the subject of specific antifraud provisions, and in these provisions Congress provided for defenses available in certain circumstances. By finding that a false or misleading prospectus violates Section 5(b)(2), the Second Circuit pushed aside the tailor-made antifraud provisions, rendering them, in the words of the Fifth Circuit, "essentially superfluous as remedial provisions" and obliterating the defenses they provide.

When events occur after the effectiveness of a registration statement that make the final prospectus materially false or misleading, or when prior defects are discovered after effectiveness, the prospectus must be corrected (because of the antifraud provisions of the securities laws, if for no other reason). This correction can be performed in one of two ways. First, an issuer may file a post-effective amendment to the registration statement containing the correction, which correction may be contained in either an amended final prospectus or a supplement to the final prospectus. (In industry usage, an amended prospectus is one that has been rewritten to reflect changes, while a supplemented prospectus is one to which a sticker incorporating changes has been added to the cover page.) Second, an issuer may amend or supplement the final prospectus without filing a post-effective amendment, as long as, under Rule 424(b), the new form of prospectus is filed with the Commission within a specified number of days. Traditionally, issuers handle relatively discrete corrections by the Rule 424(b) mechanism and more extensive corrections through the filing of a post-effective amendment.

IV. FINAL PROSPECTUS DELIVERY REQUIREMENTS

As described above, Section 5(b)(2) stipulates that securities cannot be delivered unless accompanied or preceded by a final prospectus. This presents interesting theoretical questions about what constitutes delivery in, *e.g.*, the case of uncertificated shares, and whether delivery to a "street name" holder constitutes delivery to the beneficial owner. These questions largely are moot owing to Rule 172(b)'s "access equals delivery" approach (providing that section 5(b)(2) generally is satisfied when the registration statement becomes effective) and the requirement in Rule 173 that issuers, underwriters and some dealers deliver either a final prospectus or a prescribed form of notice within two days of completing a sale.

Section 5(b)(2) aside, there is an additional reason why final prospectuses must be delivered to purchasers as part of the initial distribution of shares. Exchange Act Rule 15c2–8, which was discussed in connection with the waiting period, establishes much the same requirements for limited distributions of final prospectuses that it establishes for preliminary prospectuses. Basically, they are to be furnished to sales personnel, and to other persons on written request. Remember, however, that the commission has approved the delivery of prospectuses through electronic means, provided specified conditions are met.

If no written offers (or offers by radio or television) ever were made in the post-effective period other than by Section 10 prospectus, the provisions discussed thus far (Section 5(b)(2), Securities Act Rules 172 and 173, and Exchange Act Rule 15c2–8) would tell the whole story about final prospectus delivery requirements. Inevitably, however, such offers will be made, giving rise to additional obligations by way of Section 5(b)(1), discussed in connection with the waiting period. As mentioned above, Rule 172 usually takes care of the problem that otherwise would be presented by the confirmations of sale mandated by Exchange Act Rule 10b–10. Other writings and broadcasts must be separately analyzed.

Many of the purchasers in a public offering retain their securities for a substantial period, but others sell them in the trading markets shortly after their purchase. Under Section 4(a)(3) of the Securities Act, which generally exempts from the Act's registration requirements transactions by dealers not participating in the distribution of a security, such dealers are still subject to the final prospectus delivery requirements of Section 5 when (and only when) they sell securities that have been registered within the previous ninety days (forty if the issuer previously has registered securities under the Securities Act). This is true regardless of how many times the securities have changed hands in the trading markets. Rule 174, however, provides that for such dealers compliance with Rule 172 satisfies any prospectus delivery obligation imposed by Section 4(a)(3). Thus, in the case of non-participating dealers, "access equals delivery" for Section 5(b)(1) purposes, as well as for purposes of Section 5(b)(2). Underwriters and other dealers who did participate in the initial distribution must find other ways to satisfy Section 5(b)(1) if they choose to make use of written (or broadcast) information. The simplest way often will be to make sure that information is accompanied or preceded by a final prospectus.

E. SUMMARY

The following chart provides, in general terms, a summary of the communications that are specifically permitted (or, in some cases, required) by the regulatory framework discussed in this chapter.

Type of Issuer	Pre-Filing Period	Waiting Period	Post-Effective Period
Non-Reporting	**Permitted:**	**Permitted:**	**Permitted:**
	-Preliminary negotiations and agreements with underwriters (Section 2(a)(3)	-Oral offers	-Oral offers
	-Communications pursuant to Rule 135	-Preliminary negotiations and agreements with underwriters (Section 2(a)(3))	-Sales
	-Communications more than 30 days in advance that do not reference the offering (Rule 163A)	-Communications pursuant to Rule 134 or Section 2(a)(10)(b)	-Communications pursuant to Rule 134 or Section 2(a)(10)(b)
	-Regularly released factual information (Rule 169)	-Section 10 prospectuses:	-Section 10 prospectuses (no longer including the preliminary prospectus)
	If also an emerging growth company:	-Preliminary (Rule 430)	-Free writing (Section 2(a)(10(a); must be accompanied or preceded by a final prospectus)
	-Communications with certain institutional investors (Section 5(d))	-Summary (Rule 431	**If also an emerging growth company:**
	-Brokers' and dealers' research reports (Section 2(a)(3))	-Free writing (Rules 164 and 433; must be accompanied or preceded by preliminary prospectus)	-Communications with certain institutional investors (Section 5(d))
		If also an emerging growth company:	-Brokers' and dealers' research reports (Section 2(a)(3)

Type of Issuer	Pre-Filing Period	Waiting Period	Post-Effective Period
		-Communications with certain institutional investors (Section 5(d))	**Required:**
		-Brokers' and dealers' research reports (Section 2(a)(3))	-Written confirmation (Exchange Act Rule 10b–10)
		Required:	-Delivery of final prospectus or Rule 173 notice unless exempt under Section 4(a)(3) or Rule 174
		-Distribution of preliminary prospectus in accordance with Exchange Act Rule 15c2–8	-Delivery of final prospectus to accompany or precede delivery of securities (deemed under Rule 172(b) to occur at effectiveness)
			-Distribution of final prospectus in accordance with Exchange Act Rule 15c2–8
Unseasoned	Same as Non-Reporting, *plus*:	Same as Non-Reporting, *except*:	Same as Non-Reporting, *except*:
	-Regularly released forward-looking information (Rule 168)	-Exchange Act Rule 15c2–8 compliance less demanding	-Rule 174 exempts all non-participants from Securities Act prospectus delivery rules
			-Exchange Act Rule 15c2–8 compliance less demanding

Type of Issuer	Pre-Filing Period	Waiting Period	Post-Effective Period
Seasoned	Same as Unseasoned	Same as Unseasoned, *except*: -Free writing prospectuses need not be accompanied or preceded by preliminary prospectuses (Rule 433)	Same as Unseasoned, *except*: -Free writing prospectuses need not be accompanied or preceded by final prospectuses (Rule 433). (Note that a final prospectus must still accompany free writing under Section 2(a)(10))
Well-known Seasoned	Same as Unseasoned and Seasoned, *plus*: -Oral offers at any time (Rule 163) -Free writing prospectuses at any time; need not be accompanied or preceded by any other prospectus (Rule 163)	Generally not applicable	Same as Seasoned

CHAPTER 4

SECURITIES ACT REGISTRATION PROCESS

SITUATION 4

Assume Microtec is back at the pre-filing stage, with a letter of intent just having been signed, and that you are given the job of drafting the registration statement and seeing it through to effectiveness. One of your tasks will be to decide whether to obtain the comments of the Commission's staff before filing the registration statement and to assess the effect of a pre-filing submission on the obligations described in Chapter 3.

In addition to what you have learned about Microtec from earlier situations, you receive the following additional information.

Microtec currently has 2,000 no par value shares outstanding. These were purchased in equal amounts by Moore and Simpson, when the company was formed, for $100 per share. This created $200,000 of paid-in capital. Earned surplus is $2,800,000. A bank loan, payable over five years in equal installments, is outstanding in the amount of $2,000,000. In the loan agreement, Microtec covenanted to maintain earned surplus of at least $700,000. Profits in the last three years have been $400,000, $1,000,000 and $2,000,000. Microtec's financial statements for the last three years have been audited by a local certified public accountant.

As indicated in Situation 3d, the proposed offering is for 1,000,000 shares at an expected price of $10 per share. Microtec will split its currently outstanding shares so that 1,500,000 will be outstanding prior to the public sale. After the sale, the public will, then, own 40% of Microtec.

Microtec leases its business facility under a lease expiring in three years. The building is a modern office-factory combination located in an industrial park. The lease charges are competitive for the area, and relations are good with the owner of the building. No problem with renewal at reasonable terms is expected, but if problems were to develop, suitable new space could be found. There would, however, be fairly substantial costs related to moving and the attendant business disruption. All equipment and fixtures are owned by Microtec, with some of the equipment being financed under extended payment terms over an average of three years.

The directors are Moore, Simpson, and Elizabeth Hillman, a partner in your law firm. James Johnson, a partner in Nielson, is expected to become a director after the offering. The only officer besides Moore and

Simpson is William Tate, an accountant by training. Tate serves as Secretary and Treasurer and is Simpson's brother-in-law.

Sometime after the offering is completed, Microtec hopes to acquire J & H Software Corp., a small software development firm. Preliminary discussions have taken place, and the owners of J & H are clearly interested. The form of acquisition is uncertain, but a merger is most likely.

———————

In considering this situation, refer to the following, in addition to the materials in this chapter: Securities Act Sections 2(a)(8) and 6–8 and Rules 415, 424 and 430C through 430C under the Securities Act. In addition, quickly survey Registration Statement Form S–1, Regulation C under the Securities Act, and Regulations S–K and S–T under the Securities Act and the Exchange Act.

A. REGISTRATION STATEMENT PREPARATION AND PROCESSING

I. STATUTORY SCHEME AND REAL WORLD PRACTICE

a. STATUTORY SCHEME

Sections 6, 7, and 8 of the Securities Act contain the statutory scheme for the registration process. As general matters, Section 6: (1) provides that securities may be registered by filing a registration statement with the Commission, (2) specifies who must sign the registration statement, and (3) sets the formula for the registration fee, which as of December 2016 was to be $92 per $1 million of the maximum proposed offering price. (In succeeding fiscal years, the rate is to be adjusted by the Commission so that its projected fees are expected to equal a target amount set by Congress for that year. Note, however, that under Section 6 any change in the fee must be provided for in an appropriation act. If such act is not enacted before the end of a fiscal year (September 30), the pre-existing fee stays in effect until five days after a new appropriation act is enacted. Congress often does not pass an appropriation act in timely fashion.) The registration statement must be signed by the issuer, the principal executive officer, the principal financial officer, the comptroller or principal accounting officer, and a majority of the directors or persons performing similar functions. (Everyone who signs the registration statement is subject to liability under Section 11 for any material misstatement or omission in the registration statement.)

Section 6(e), added by the JOBS Act of 2012, provides that emerging growth companies (as defined in Chapter 3) contemplating their initial public offerings may submit a confidential draft registration statement to the Commission for feedback. Public filing must occur at least 21 days before the date on which the issuer conducts a road show.

Section 7 deals primarily with what a registration statement must contain and sets forth Schedule A to the Securities Act as the technical starting point for most issuers. This schedule is a thirty-two item list presenting a few pages of disclosure requirements. Congress did not intend to tie the Commission's hands with this schedule, however, and, until 2010, Section 7 itself gave the Commission full authority to add or subtract information requirements. The Commission exercised its authority to such a degree that Schedule A is now essentially irrelevant. The registration statement forms promulgated by the Commission have become the practical starting point for determining disclosure requirements. In 2010, however, the Dodd-Frank Act amended Section 7 to direct the Commission to require certain disclosures from the issuers of asset-backed securities (which were deemed to have contributed to the financial turmoil beginning in 2008). In 2012, the JOBS Act limited the financial information that could be required from an emerging growth company.

Section 8 covers the effectiveness of registration statements. This section provides that a registration statement automatically becomes effective twenty days after filing, or after the filing of any amendment. This provision is in Section 8(a), which also gives the Commission the power to accelerate the effective date. The rest of Section 8 gives the Commission the means to prevent materially defective registration statements from becoming effective or to suspend the effectiveness of such statements. These means are refusal order proceedings under Section 8(b) and stop order proceedings under Section 8(d). Section 8(e) covers examinations that the Commission may make to determine whether a stop order should be issued. As the following materials indicate, practice deviates substantially from what might be expected after reading Section 8.

As will be seen below, the Commission has done much tinkering with the statutory scheme. Two of its changes have been particularly significant. First, the Commission has devised a method to delay effectiveness in order to permit time for review and comment. Second, it has provided that the registration statements of well-known seasoned issuers (as discussed in Chapter 3, those issuers that have been Exchange Act reporting companies for at least twelve months and that meet certain size requirements) become effective immediately.

A third change, announced on the Commission's website by the Division of Corporation Finance in June 2017,[1] permits all issuers to submit IPO registration statements for pre-filing review. Multiple revisions are permitted, provided filing occurs at least 15 days before any

---

[1]   The announcement may be viewed at https://www.sec.gov/corpfin/announcement/draft-registration-statement-processing-procedures-expanded.

road show. Pre-filing review also is available for most of an issuer's registration statements filed within a year of its IPO, although in the case of these "follow on" offerings, responses to comments must take the form of actual filings.

b.   REVIEW AND COMMENT PROCEDURE

Following the 1932 election, Franklin Roosevelt and his programs were not willingly embraced by much of the business community. Capital formation was an obvious need for business recovery, and Roosevelt's detractors warned that the Securities Act would further break down the economic machine rather than help fix it. It was in this atmosphere that Congress passed the Act in May 1933, with a July 27 effective date. Many companies then offering securities to the public needed to file registration statements to continue their offerings. Under Section 8(a), registration statements filed by July 7 would become effective on the Act's effective date, unless the Federal Trade Commission, which administered the Act prior to the establishment of the Securities and Exchange Commission in 1934, issued a refusal order under Section 8(b) or a stop order under Section 8(d). The situation was thus set to give the Securities Act its first test.

Development of S.E.C. Practices in Processing Registration Statements and Proxy Statements

Byron D. Woodside.*
24 Business Lawyer 375 (1969).**

* * *

On July 7, more than 80 registration statements were filed with the Federal Trade Commission * * * . There were approximately 12 to 15 persons on the staff of the newly created Securities Division when this mass of documents arrived. No one was very sure just what a registration statement should contain or what should be done with it.

Since the few people assigned to this new work could not hope to review such a volume of material quickly, the statements were assigned to various persons in different offices of the Trade Commission, and an attempt was made to check them against the requirements of the registration form and Schedule A of the Act. A substantial number of recommendations for stop order proceedings resulted.

Almost immediately there must have been a realization, on the part of those in charge, that the procedural provisions of Section 8 of the Act

---

   *   Former Commissioner of the Securities and Exchange Commission; associated with the SEC from the time of its establishment until his retirement in April, 1967 * * * .

   **   Copyright © 1969 by the American Bar Association. All rights reserved. Reprinted with the permission of the American Bar Association and its Section of Business Law.

were too cumbrous to be useful as a means of disposing of routine business with efficiency and dispatch. * * *

These circumstances—short staff, the desire on the part of business to proceed promptly, the willingness on the part of most to comply with the requirements, the awkwardness of the statutory administrative processes, and most important I think, the desire on the part of issuers and underwriters to avoid the risk of being second-guessed by the government after beginning a public offering—inevitably led to the conference table and informal procedures. Thus, the pre-effective deficiency letter came almost spontaneously, and by common consent, to be the principal means of communication of the Administrator's views as to apparent compliance, in the conduct of routine business. * * *

The significance of "time" became apparent at once. It was clear to everyone that delay, careless or otherwise, on the part of the agency or the issuer or underwriter might be the cause of missing a market or ruining a schedule. Prolonged argumentation over less than crucial matters, or indecisiveness, could be very expensive. It was understandable, therefore, that staff recommendations, in those very early days, urging widespread use of stop order proceedings were largely rejected. Had they been followed the whole operation would have been bogged down in a morass of formal proceedings, and the worst fears of the critics would have been realized.

* * *

———————

Thus was born the Commission's review and comment procedure, which is with us still, although it now appears that for IPOs and follow-on offerings much of the process will take place out of the public eye before registration statements formally are filed. The general idea, however, is that registration statements of first time issuers are given a thorough review by the staff of the Commission's Division of Corporation Finance, and statements filed by second and later time issuers are reviewed selectively. A number of staff members work on a registration statement. An examiner takes responsibility for reviewing the bulk of the document. The financial disclosures are reviewed by an accountant. The examining team reports to an assistant director, who makes the final decision concerning comments to be made to the issuer. Staff experts in particular areas, such as engineers, are added to the team as required.

The goal of securities lawyers is compliance with staff comments, and any suggested change in the registration statement that can be made with a reasonable expenditure of time and effort is typically made with little question. Sometimes, however, the cost of compliance would be too great or the time required would be too long. Occasionally, a requested change would cause the registration statement to be materially false or misleading. In one of these instances, the issuer's counsel calls the examiner and tries to reach an agreement on changes. If they cannot come to terms, issuer's counsel sometimes then appeals informally, by telephone, to the assistant director and, if necessary, to those higher up in the Division of Corporation Finance.

Changes in an IPO registration statement not yet filed may be handled informally by resubmission to the staff; as noted above, changes to the draft of a "follow on" registration statement must take the form of the filing itself. Changes to a filed registration statement may be handled in a number of ways. When the changes are extensive, or of substantial importance to investors, an amendment is filed and a revised preliminary prospectus is recirculated. One copy of the amendment filed is marked to show all changes ("redlined"), and the staff starts its review from that point. A number of amendments may be required before the staff gives its clearance. When recirculation is not required, an amendment still may be filed for the staff's review, with the idea of including the changes in the final prospectus. Often, when the changes to be made are relatively minor, draft language is given to the examiner for informal clearance without the filing of an amendment. In this case, agreed to changes are included in the so-called price amendment, which often is filed just before effectiveness to make final corrections and changes and to add previously unknown information to the registration statement (for example, the price of the securities and the names of the underwriters). The price amendment then forms the basis for the final prospectus.

If substantial final corrections and changes are not necessary, Rule 430A often allows the issuer in a traditional registered offering to forego the filing of a price amendment and simply add to the final prospectus information about pricing and the underwriting arrangements. (For issuers utilizing "shelf" registration, discussed below, Rule 430B permits even more flexibility in omitting information from the prospectus contained in the registration statement when it becomes effective and adding the information when it becomes known.) Under Rule 424, copies of the final prospectus must be filed shortly after they are used. The information that is added is deemed to be a part of the registration statement. Under Rule 430C, this is also true of prospectuses filed to reflect substantive changes in prior information.

In terms of timing, the first staff review typically takes a month or a little more, but this varies somewhat depending on the staff's workload. After the assistant director issues comments, the staff usually responds quickly to inquiries from the issuer's counsel and to amendments. Depending on the time it takes to comply with staff comments and the number of resubmissions, it may take anywhere from another few days to a few months before the registration statement is ready to become effective. In light of this, one might wonder what has happened to the twenty day waiting period written into Section 8(a), especially in the case of registration statements that cannot be submitted for pre-filing review.

c.   EFFECTIVENESS OF REGISTRATION STATEMENTS AND SHELF REGISTRATION UNDER RULE 415

i.   *Delaying and Accelerating Effectiveness in a Traditional Registration*

The twenty-day automatic effectiveness provided by Section 8(a) was virtually a dead letter from the beginning. The review and comment process cannot consistently be completed during this period. In addition, the twenty-day automatic effectiveness scheme could not work in most offerings in any case because a registration statement rarely can be complete when filed. In the typical offering (now including those that involve pre-filing review), the registration statement needs to have added to it information that cannot be determined twenty days in advance. The resulting problem is that, under Section 8(a), if an issuer files an amendment adding this information, the twenty day waiting period begins again (unless, as provided in Section 8(a), the amendment is filed with the consent of, or pursuant to an order of, the Commission). Even when no such amendment is needed in a particular offering, the issuer and the underwriters usually do not like to be bound to an effective date chosen twenty days in advance. They wish to control the effective date so as to hit the market at an opportune time. Circumventing both the automatic twenty-day effectiveness and the twenty-day waiting period after filing an amendment has been, therefore, a practical necessity from the beginning.

The only way to avoid automatic effectiveness is to amend the registration statement before the twenty-day period has run. For many years after passage of the Securities Act, this was done on or shortly before the nineteenth day by filing a so-called delaying amendment. By means of a creative mechanism provided in Rule 473, an issuer may include a paragraph on the cover of a registration statement that effects its continuing amendment. The paragraph reads:

> The registrant hereby amends this registration statement on such date or dates as may be necessary to delay its effective date until the registrant shall file a further amendment which specifically states that this registration statement shall thereafter become effective in accordance with section 8(a) of the Securities Act of 1933 or until the registration statement shall become effective on such date as the Commission acting pursuant to said section 8(a), may determine.

The idea of this paragraph serving as a continuing amendment may seem a little strange, but it is clever and it works.

Avoiding the twenty-day wait after filing an amendment is more problematical. Under the original wording of Section 8(a), the Commission would, when satisfied with a registration statement, formally agree to the filing of the price amendment, and this would prevent the waiting period from beginning anew. In 1940, Congress rewrote Section 8(a) to give the Commission power to accelerate the twenty day period, essentially in its discretion. The mechanisms of this procedure are simple. After the Commission's staff is satisfied that a registration statement is ready to become effective, the issuer and the managing underwriter decide the timing of effectiveness and agree on final business terms. Then, as provided in Rule 461, each requests acceleration, specifying the day and time they desire the registration statement to become effective. In the usual case, acceleration is granted pro forma, with the staff working to meet any reasonable time schedule.

The Commission extracts a price for this cooperation, however, in that it uses the threat of acceleration denial to force actions not required by the statute. This power was examined in the last chapter in the discussion of distribution of preliminary prospectuses. Although the Securities Act does not require use of preliminary prospectuses, the Commission may deny acceleration unless they are distributed during the waiting period (assuming a sales effort went on during that period). Another example of the Commission's power over acceleration involves indemnification. The Commission has long disfavored the idea that officers, directors, or other persons controlling an issuer might be indemnified by the issuer for Securities Act liability, on the basis that such indemnity is against public policy and, therefore, that any agreement to provide such indemnity is unenforceable. The threat to deny acceleration is the tool the Commission uses to enforce this theory. When an issuer wishes to request acceleration, the Commission requires that the issuer include in its registration statement an undertaking to submit the public policy question concerning indemnification to a court test before paying any such indemnity.[2] Rule 461 contains a list of other factors the Commission considers in connection with acceleration requests, including whether "the Commission is currently making an investigation of the issuer, a person controlling the issuer, or one of the underwriters * * * pursuant to any of the Acts administered by the Commission."

Perhaps more important than these specific uses of the acceleration denial threat is the power the threat generally places behind staff comments on registration statements. The refusal of an issuer to accede to a particular comment clearly may not be grounds for a stop order, but the risk of refusal is usually too great because of the need for acceleration.

Technically, of course, an issuer does not have to use a delaying amendment or ask for acceleration. It has the right simply to go for twenty day effectiveness. The following case illustrates what an issuer may face in this instance.

---

[2] Regulation S–K, Item 512(h).

Las Vegas Hawaiian Development Co. v. SEC

United States District Court, District of Hawaii, 1979.
466 F.Supp. 928.

■ SAMUEL P. KING, CHIEF JUDGE.

* * *

Plaintiffs Las Vegas Hawaiian Development Company (LVH) [and others], on November 7, 1978, filed a Complaint for Declaratory Judgment against the Securities and Exchange Commission (SEC or Commission) and its commissioners. They seek a declaration that section 8(e) of the Securities Act of 1933 cannot be utilized by the Commission to delay indefinitely the sale of securities under an effective registration statement * * *.

* * *

On May 26, 1977, LVH filed a Form S–11 registration statement covering a proposed offering of limited partnerships in LVH * * *. * * * A delaying amendment was attached to this registration.

By letter dated July 21, 1977, the Commission's Division of Corporation Finance forwarded to counsel for LVH sixteen pages of comments regarding the registration statement. An amended registration statement, with attached delaying amendment, was received by the Commission from LVH on December 23, 1977. The Commission's staff forwarded a second comment letter, dated May 15, 1978, to counsel for LVH, discussing unresolved deficiencies, and stating that additional comments might be forthcoming.

On July 7, 1978, LVH filed a second amendment to its registration statement. This time no delaying amendment was attached.[3] This meant that, absent Commission action, the effective date of the registration statement (as amended as of July 7, 1978) would be "the twentieth day after the filing thereof" pursuant to section 8(a) of the Securities Act of 1933.

On July 25, 1978, the Commission issued an order authorizing its staff (1) to conduct an examination, pursuant to section 8(e), to determine whether a stop order proceeding under section 8(d) was necessary with respect to LVH's proposed public offering, and (2) to conduct a private investigation of the circumstances surrounding the proposed offer, pursuant to section 20(a) of the Act of 1933 and section 21(a) of the Act of 1934.

* * *

Since then, the Commission's staff has been conducting the ordered examinations. No recommendation has been made to the Commission. The Commission has not yet considered whether to institute a stop order

---

[3]   Presumably this amendment did not simply omit delaying amendment language, but rather included language provided for in Rule 473(b), rescinding the delaying action. [Eds.]

proceeding under section 8(d). In argument, counsel for the SEC stated that a recommendation for a section 8(d) proceeding was in process of being put together by the staff, but he could not predict when it would be completed or when the Commission might take action on the recommendation.

An effect of the Commission's July 25, 1978, order is to bring into operation the prohibition contained in section 5(c) of the Securities Act of 1933 against use of interstate communications to offer to sell or to offer to buy the registered securities "while the registration statement is the subject of * * * (prior to the effective date of the registration statement) any public proceeding or examination under section [8(e)]." Thus, although LVH's second amended registration statement became effective on the twentieth day after July 7, 1978, prior thereto, that is on July 25, 1978, it became the subject of a public examination under section 8(e) pursuant to the Commission's order of that date. As a consequence, any sales activity involving the registered securities was effectively blocked by the provisions of section 5(c).

* * *

Plaintiffs argue that the Commission is engaging in a ploy which denies LVH procedural and substantive due process. By not noticing an order delaying the effectiveness of a registration statement pursuant to section 8(b), or an order suspending the effectiveness of a registration statement pursuant to section 8(d), the Commission has prevented the registrant from having a hearing.

Defendants argue that the Commission has not done anything which is reviewable. The Commission's decision to conduct a section 8(e) examination of LVH's registration statement is not a final position. The registration statement has become effective, and until the Commission notices an intention to issue a stop order, it is only conducting an examination which may or may not result in further action.

Furthermore, say defendants, a section 8(e) examination is a matter within the Commission's discretionary powers, both as to scope and length, which may not be judicially reviewed unless there is an abuse of discretion or action which exceeds the authority of the Commission, neither of which have been supported by factual allegations in the complaint.

Finally, defendants argue that plaintiffs have not exhausted their administrative remedies.

* * *

In my opinion, a district court may, upon the petition of a registrant under the Securities Act of 1933, compel the SEC to make a determination within a reasonable time whether to notice a hearing on the issuance of a stop order under section 8(d), where the Commission has ordered an examination under section 8(e) prior to the effective date of a registration statement and the determination whether a stop order should issue has been unreasonably delayed.

* * *

In light of the foregoing discussion, has LVH alleged sufficient facts to state a claim upon which relief can be granted? The allegations of Count I of the complaint do not state that the Commission's determination of whether to institute a section 8(d) proceeding has been unreasonably delayed. The complaint merely alleges the actions taken, the time sequence involved, and the legal effect on the sale or purchase of a security of an order authorizing a section 8(e) examination *prior* to the effective date of the registration statement covering that security.

How much detail may be required under Fed.R.Civ.P. 8 and 9 need not be decided now. But certainly something must be alleged. The mere fact of delay is not in and of itself sufficient. * * *

* * *

It is Ordered that Defendants' Motion to Dismiss the complaint is granted as to [Count I], with leave to Plaintiffs to file an amended complaint in 30 days from the date of this order * * *.

———————

In the following article, the author recounts the story of an issuer that had better luck in a showdown with the Commission over effectiveness than did the issuer in *Las Vegas Hawaiian*.

"Acceleration" Under the Securities Act of 1933—A Postscript

John Mulford.
22 Business Lawyer 1087 (1967).[*]

* * *

* * * [A]n obdurate registrant was found in Phoenix Steel Corporation ("Phoenix"). Phoenix filed a registration statement * * * on September 27, 1966, to register under the Act nine-year warrants to purchase 125,000 shares of common stock and the stock underlying the warrants.[4] The warrants are exercisable initially at $23 per share, and after four years at $28 per share. The common stock had a market value at the time of filing of about $15.50 per share.

* * *

———————

[*]   Copyright © 1967 by the American Bar Association. All rights reserved. Reprinted with the permission of the American Bar Association and its Section of Business Law.

[4]   Presumably the registration statement included the delaying amendment language contemplated by Rule 473(a), since as indicated in the next paragraph, the Commission's letter of comments was not issued until after the 20-day period provided in Section 8(a) would otherwise have run, and since Mulford mentions no amendment filed before the expiration of the 20-day period (which would have started the period running anew). [Eds.]

On October 25, 1966, the Commission issued its usual letter of comments. * * *

Phoenix * * * in two amendments cleared up to the satisfaction of the Commission's staff * * * comments relating to disclosure.

Except for a statement that Phoenix would not request acceleration, the amendments and their covering letters ignored the following comments regarding undertakings:

> In the event the Company intends to request acceleration of the registration statement, there should be an undertaking [agreeing to submit the public policy questions relating to indemnification of officers and directors to a court test before paying such indemnification].

> An undertaking should be included (a) to file any prospectus required by Section 10(a)(3) of the Securities Act of 1933[5] as a post-effective amendment to the registration statement, and (b) that the effective date of each such amendment shall be deemed the effective date of the registration statement with respect to securities sold after such amendment becomes effective.

> The registration statement should also include an undertaking to remove from registration by a post-effective amendment any securities which remain unsold at the termination of the offering.

After these amendments were filed, the last on December 7, 1966,[6] it developed that a conference with the staff of the Commission was necessary to discuss an entirely distinct problem. At this conference the staff was advised that Phoenix did not intend to comply with the request for undertakings on the ground that the Commission had no authority to compel it to do so. After the conference, [the staff and counsel for Phoenix engaged in a mildly acrimonious exchange.] * * * On December 29, counsel for Phoenix [issued its last word]:

* * *

> At this point it would seem to serve no useful purpose to discuss the matter further except to state that we seem to have arrived at a fundamental disagreement as to the construction of th[e] act.

> Please be assured that my client intends to comply with the act, and that I will do my best to insure its doing so.

> I am glad to know that at least we appear to agree on one point, namely, that the Commission has no authority under the

---

[5] Section 10(a)(3) relates to prospectuses used more than nine months after the effective date of a registration statement. [Eds.]

[6] Presumably this amendment, or an earlier amendment, included language, provided for in Rule 473(b), rescinding the delaying action. [Eds.]

act to compel registrants to file undertakings whether such undertakings would be, in effect, promises to comply with the law, or whether they are promises to take some action not required by law.

On January 3, 1967, the staff replied:

> Just in order to set the record straight with respect to your letter of December 29, 1966, I do not agree that the Commission has no authority under the Securities Act of 1933 to compel registrants to file undertakings. An undertaking of the character under discussion is expressly required by the Commission's Form S–11 and is proposed to be required by Form S–7.

Meanwhile, the registration statement had become effective "through lapse of time" on December 26. No stop order or other proceeding has been instituted in the matter by the time this article went to press.

ii. Shelf Registration Under Rule 415

The last sentence of Section 6(a) provides that "[a] registration statement shall be deemed effective only as to the securities specified therein proposed to be offered." The Commission traditionally has interpreted this language to mean that securities generally can not be registered unless there is an intention to offer them in the "proximate future." Major exceptions to this approach have been embodied in Rule 415, which has taken on great significance. This rule allows the registration, in certain circumstances, of securities that are to be offered on a continuous or delayed basis. In popular terminology, it provides for "shelf registration."

The traditional offering focused on so far, which is designed to be completed promptly after effectiveness, does not satisfy the needs of all issuers. Sometimes the transaction an issuer contemplates requires that securities be offered and sold over a long period, on a continuous basis. A good example is common stock offered under an employee stock purchase plan, when the plan gives employees the right to purchase shares anytime they wish during the life of the plan. In other cases, issuers may wish to register securities and put them "on the shelf" so the securities will be immediately available for sale when needed. A traditional example of this is an issuer which is engaged in a program of acquiring other companies and wishes to have registered securities available to use as consideration for the purchase of these companies. The Commission long ago established exceptions for these (and similar) transactions; these exemptions now are included in Rule 415.

Rule 415 also is available for, among other things, offerings by issuers eligible to use Form S–3 or F–3, both described in Part II of this chapter. Another important, permitted use is for sales of mortgage-related securities by other companies. Once the registration is accomplished, issuers relying on Rule 415 can watch the advances and declines in market prices and wait for an advantageous market window through which to slip their securities. This ability to time an offering precisely can greatly minimize the qualifying issuer's cost of capital. Further savings to issuers can be made through registering the securities without naming underwriters and then shopping for the best underwriting deal, or choosing underwriters by competitive bid at the last minute. Empirical studies of issuance costs have found Rule 415 costs to have been lower than in traditional offerings.

Described in broad strokes, Rule 415 permits a registration statement to become effective even though the prospectus it contains omits information that is not yet known (such as the names of the underwriters) but which otherwise would be required. The information then is added, either through post-effective amendment or (more usually) by use of the Rule 424 process, when the information becomes available. (Rule 430B deals with the interim use of prospectuses omitting the otherwise required information.)

Of particular note, Rule 415 permits the shelf registrations of well-known seasoned issuers (as described in Chapter 3, companies meeting more stringent requirements than merely seasoned companies) to become effective automatically upon filing. The registration statement may cover unspecified amounts of specified classes of securities, and easily may be amended to add to or change the classes that are covered. Filing fees may be paid in advance or on a "pay-as-you-go" basis at the time of an actual offering. Shelf registrations of this type (as well as certain others) remain in effect for three years. Any unused pre-paid filing fees are refunded at that time.

d. REFUSAL ORDERS, STOP ORDERS, AND WITHDRAWAL OF REGISTRATION STATEMENTS

Because of the Commission's review and comment procedure, refusal and stop orders rarely are used to prevent the effectiveness of a registration statement. Refusal orders are, in fact, unlikely ever to be used, because the requirements are tougher on the Commission in refusal order proceedings under Section 8(b) than in stop order proceedings under Section 8(d), and because it has long been held that stop orders may be used in the place of refusal orders. The Section 8(e) examination also has been rarely used. Only when the Commission is faced with what it considers an egregious case, or a particularly recalcitrant issuer, is an examination or stop order at all likely. When the Commission and an issuer cannot come to terms on a registration statement, voluntary withdrawal, as provided for in Rule 477, is much more likely. Voluntary withdrawal was in fact the ultimate outcome in the *Las Vegas Hawaiian* situation. Two weeks after the district judge handed down the opinion reproduced above, the Commission initiated stop order proceedings. It also brought an enforcement action in the district court, under Securities Act Section 20(b), against affiliates of the company. This action resulted in permanent injunctions against three of the company's principals. The Commission, on the request of the company, then permitted voluntary withdrawal of the registration statement. A significant number of withdrawals do take place every year, although the new pre-filing review process almost certainly will reduce the need for them.

Not only may a stop order be issued before or after the effectiveness of a registration statement; a stop order may be issued long after all the securities covered by a registration statement have been sold. This procedure is sometimes the most effective tool available to the Commission when deficiencies are discovered after the fact. The major result of such action is publicity, and the furnishing of ammunition to private plaintiffs. Post-effective stop orders are, like pre-effective orders, rare.

II. WORKING THROUGH THE REGISTRATION PROCESS

a. REGISTRATION STATEMENT FORMS

The registration statement forms promulgated by the Commission provide the starting point for determining what must be included in a registration statement. Securities Act Rules 130 and 401 give these forms the force of law, which makes their requirements mandatory. There are a number of different forms, each for use in a specific situation. The forms are generally short because the bulk of the disclosure requirements are not usually contained in the forms themselves, but in a repository called Regulation S–K. (There is also a repository called Regulation S–X for information required in financial statements). In the main, the forms simply contain lists of Regulation S–K items with which an issuer must comply. The forms break the disclosure requirements into two parts: information required, and not required, in the prospectus. The former is information to be provided to investors, while the latter is basically for the Commission's review.

Form S–1 is the general, catch-all form that is used when no other form is authorized or prescribed. For the typical issuer and the garden variety security, it contains the Commission's most extensive disclosure requirements. A Form S–1 registration statement may be several dozen pages in length. Some issuers, however, may take advantage of a Commission initiative called integration. For most of the history of the Securities Act and the Exchange Act, the disclosure requirements of the two acts operated independently. When a company wished to register securities under the Securities Act, it filed a registration statement containing full disclosure about itself and its business. Although this requirement made sense for a first time issuer, it ignored the fact that for others essentially the same information had been disclosed, and continuously updated, in reports filed under the Exchange Act and that this information had almost certainly found its way into the marketplace through the work of securities analysts and others in the securities industry.

In recognition of these factors, and the fact that Exchange Act reports now easily may be accessed via the Internet, the Commission now permits issuers that are reporting companies under the Exchange Act to incorporate into their Form S–1 registration statements a significant amount of information by reference to their already-filed Exchange Act reports. In order to take advantage of incorporation by reference, an issuer must have filed an annual report under the Exchange Act for its most recent fiscal year and meet certain other tests. When a company meets the tests, its registration statement for most transactions may be a combination of spelled-out disclosures and the incorporation of reference of information from Exchange Act sources (which must be made accessible on the issuer's website). The prospectus used by such an issuer must state where the information incorporated by reference may be found and state that the issuer will deliver that information upon request.

Form S–3 is available for specified transactions to companies that meet certain additional tests. For instance, companies that have filed Exchange Act reports for twelve months and satisfy one of four requirements relating either to past issuance of non-convertible securities registered under the Securities Act or to specified relationships with a well-known seasoned issuer may register non-convertible debt on Form S–3. Companies that have filed Exchange Act reports for twelve months and are issuing common stock for cash may use Form S–3 if the company's outstanding voting and non-voting common equity held by non-affiliates[7] ("public float") has a market value of at least $75 million. (These two groups also comprise the class of "seasoned" issuers referred to in Chapter 3; the seasoned issuer concept, in fact, is identified by reference to these types of eligibility to use Form S–3 for primary offerings.) In addition, issuers that have a class of common equity listed and registered on a national exchange and have not been a "shell" company within the last twelve months may use Form S–3 for primary offerings of common equity not exceeding, in a twelve-month period, one-third of their public float. (These issuers, however, are not "seasoned.") In a Form S–3 registration statement, the issuer basically gives information particular to the transaction at hand and then incorporates by reference from Exchange Act documents—both those that have been filed and those that will be filed before the offering is complete. This registration statement usually runs only to several pages. Qualification

---

[7]   Under Securities Act Rule 405, an "affiliate" is someone in a control relationship with someone else either controlling, controlled by, or under common control. "Control" is a tricky concept that will be discussed in Chapter 7. Generally, directors, at least some officers, and substantial shareholders are affiliates of an issuer.

for the use of Form S–3 is, for many transactions, a condition of the use of shelf registration under Rule 415.

The Commission has long realized that the burdens of registration were greater than could be borne by many small companies and that this burden created an impediment to capital formation. It has moved to build into Regulation S–K special, less demanding requirements with which qualifying small issuers may elect to comply on an *"a la carte,"* or item-by-item, basis. These qualifying small issuers, known as "smaller reporting companies" (although the designation is not dependent on reporting status under the Exchange Act), must have either less than $75 million of public float, or, if they have no public float, less than $50 million in annual revenue. Congress also has exhibited concern for what it considers smaller companies and, as indicated above, decreed in the JOBS Act that the financial information required from emerging growth companies was to be limited.

Other registration statement forms relate to particular kinds of issuers (for example, Forms F–1 and F–3 for certain private foreign issuers, S–6 for unit investment trusts, and S–11 for certain real estate companies) and special types of transactions (for example, S–4 for mergers and other acquisitions). In some instances, one of these specialized forms must be used, but in others an issuer can use the specialized form or one of the general forms.

b. RULES, REGULATIONS, AND INDUSTRY GUIDES

Regulation S–K, entitled "Standard Instructions for Filing Forms Under the Securities Act of 1933, Securities Exchange Act of 1934 and Energy Policy and Conservation Act of 1975", serves as the Commission's general repository of disclosure requirements. It is long and highly technical, but relatively straightforward. As indicated above, it now has a number of alternative disclosure requirements that may be elected by small reporting companies. Since the adoption of the JOBS Act in 2012, the Commission has had underway a project to review and rid Regulation S–K of surplusage and redundancy and proposed changes have been exposed for comment.

Regulation C under the Securities Act contains rules in the 400 series and relates to various aspects of the registration process. Basically, it is a catch-all of rules relating to registration matters that are not specifically covered in a form or in Regulation S–K. It sometimes seems fortuitous whether an item is covered in one place rather than another, but clearly most disclosure requirements are contained in a form or in Regulation S–K, with Regulation C governing mostly formal and procedural matters. As examples, the requirements of Regulation C address such matters as dating prospectuses (Rule 423) and procedures for abandoning registration statements (Rule 479).

A detailed discussion of Regulation C would not be helpful here, but a few of the rules do merit some attention. One is Rule 405, which contains definitions. It is critical that these definitions be checked because some of them are unusual. For example:

> The term "officer" means a president, vice president, secretary, treasurer or principal financial officer, comptroller or principal accounting officer, *and any person routinely performing corresponding functions* with respect to any organization whether incorporated or unincorporated. (Emphasis added.)

Even with respect only to corporations, this may be less inclusive than state law and ordinary usage in some instances, and clearly it is more inclusive in others.

The most important rule in Regulation C, and perhaps the most significant statement of any type by the Commission on registration, is Rule 408(a):

> In addition to the information expressly required to be included in a registration statement, there shall be added such further material information, if any, as may be necessary to make the required statements, in the light of the circumstances under which they are made, not misleading.

It might be argued in litigation after-the-fact that this rule literally calls for assuring that specifically mandated disclosure not be misleading. As a planning matter, however, Rule 408(a) reduces to a requirement that anything material[8] must be disclosed. And in real-world securities practice, Rule 408(a) is the centerpiece of disclosure. Good securities lawyers make certain they cover all the specific disclosure requirements, but this is somewhat mechanical. For the securities lawyer worrying about disclosure, digging to find nonspecified information and then determining whether it is material takes the most skill and judgment.

Also worthy of attention is Rule 421(d), which states that issuers must prepare the front and back cover pages of prospectuses, as well as the summary and risk factors sections, in what the Commission refers to as "plain English." The thrust of the rule is that these parts of the prospectuses must comply with six basic plain English principles such as the use of short sentences and of the active voice. Rule 421 relates in general to the understandable presentation of information in prospectuses and, as a practical matter, the staff expects the entire prospectus to be written in what might be called plain English.

The forms and rules discussed above are promulgated by the Commission itself and have the force of law. In a different category are the Industry Guides, which are expressions of the policies and practices

---

[8]   The concept of "materiality" is significant in securities law. A good starting point for an understanding of the concept is Rule 405, which provides:

> The term "material," when used to qualify a requirement for the furnishing of information as to any subject, limits the information required to those matters to which there is a substantial likelihood that a reasonable investor would attach importance in determining whether to purchase the security registered.

of the Commission's Division of Corporation Finance. Although these guides lack the legal status of forms and rules, in practical terms they are not of much less real importance. The Industry Guides are as follows:

1.   [Reserved]

2.   Disclosure of oil and gas operations.

3.   Statistical disclosure by bank holding companies.

4.   Prospectus relating to interests in oil and gas programs.

5.   Preparation of registration statements relating to interests in real estate limited partnerships.

6.   Disclosures concerning unpaid claims and claim adjustment expenses of property-casualty insurance underwriters.

7.   Description of property by issuers engaged or to be engaged in significant mining operations.

The guides generally have the look of Regulation S–K disclosure requirements, except for Guide 5, which goes much further and is essentially a blueprint for drafting the prospectus.

c.   PREPARING AND FILING REGISTRATION STATEMENTS

i.   *Registration Statement Drafting and Filing with the Commission*

Although the registration statement form is the starting point for determining disclosure requirements, it does not provide a model for drafting. Assuming a first public offering, the issuer's counsel invariably uses prospectuses from other issuers for this purpose. The managing underwriter typically is the best source for hard copies of these prospectuses, and they are easily available online as a result of the Commission's Electronic Data Gathering, Analysis and Retrieval System ("EDGAR").[9] The registration statement drafter may be lucky and find one or more recent prospectuses that tell the same basic story the drafter has to tell. Sometimes the most closely related models are old, or the only ones available relate to companies in industries that are only analogous to that of the issuer's. The more recent the models the better, because if they are final prospectuses they may give a good idea of disclosures favored by the current Commission staff.

There are other ways to find out what currently favored disclosures are. Sometimes the Commission issues a release on particular disclosure points. Also, the Commission makes the staff's comment letters and issuer responses to staff comment letters available on EDGAR no earlier than 20 business days following the effective date of a registration statement. It intends to continue this practice with respect to comments

---

[9]   Information on how to access documents filed under EDGAR is available at the Commission's website, www.sec.gov.

generated in a pre-filing review process for any company that is not an emerging growth company (although confidential treatment for certain submitted information may be sought).

After studying other prospectuses, and keeping in mind the various other sources of information concerning disclosure, the drafter is ready to begin work. The first thing to do is to amass information about the issuer. This task is easy in the case of an Exchange Act reporting company because most of the work has already been done. For non-reporting companies, such research can be difficult, and it requires good investigative skills. Many discussions with company officers are required, along with much digging in the company's files and examining its operations. Many companies have prepared, often in connection with loan applications, a report that describes the company and its business. These reports can be helpful. If a company has sold securities in an exempt offering, an offering memorandum was probably prepared. Depending largely on the type of exemption involved, and the ability of the lawyers who drafted it, the memorandum may be good enough to use as a rough prospectus draft.

Once enough information concerning the issuer is at hand, a lawyer can begin drafting the registration statement. Drafting the prospectus portion is the challenge, since the rest of the registration statement is pretty straightforward.

Drafts of the registration statement are circulated to the managing underwriter, its counsel, officers, and perhaps directors of the issuer. Each of these persons may give comments, and typically one or two all-day meetings are held to discuss the registration statement before it is put in final form. In connection with their review of registration statement drafts, the managing underwriter and its counsel do a so-called due diligence examination designed to ensure as best they can that the registration statement is completely accurate and contains no material omission. This examination includes having discussions with the issuer's officers, examining documents in the issuer's files, and visiting the issuer's facilities.

At some point in the drafting process, a registration statement usually is sent to a financial printer to be set in type, even though much dissemination of the prospectus will be electronic. Financial printers are high-quality, quick-turnaround businesses found only in a few financial centers. When necessary, they can produce a registration statement overnight. When everyone is satisfied with the document, the printer makes the final agreed changes, often in a late-night session attended by junior members of the various teams, and the issuer files the registration statement with the Commission. (As noted above, IPO and "follow on" registration statements now may be submitted for feedback from the Commission's staff before making a public filing.) Under the EDGAR system, the registration statement (as well as any amendments) must be filed electronically. This will be handled by the financial printer.

(Regulation S–T and the Commission's EDGAR Filer Manual govern EDGAR filings.)

Many exhibits to the registration statement, including certain major contracts of the issuer, are required by the various registration statement forms, and they too must be filed on EDGAR, where they will go into the public database. Company counsel may request confidential treatment of an exhibit or, much more likely, certain provisions of the exhibit. A typical example is a provision in a contract that, if made public, would give competitors an unfair advantage.

ii. *Blue Sky Qualifications and FINRA Clearance*

Going Public
Michael J. Halloran.
Published by Sorg Printing Company Incorporated (5th ed. 1983).*

* * *

The securities of a company *Going Public* must * * * be qualified under the "Blue Sky" or securities laws of each state in which they are intended to be offered, unless [preempted by federal law or] there is an exemption from qualification available under the applicable state law. * * *

* * *

[FINRA] Clearance. [The registration statement and the underwriting agreements must be filed with the Financial Industry Regulatory Authority so that it may determine] whether the underwriting arrangements are fair and reasonable[.] [FINRA] reviews not only the underwriting discount (i.e., the difference between the purchase price to the public and the price to the underwriters), but also other compensation which the underwriters are deemed to receive in connection with the offering (such as reimbursement by the company of expenses normally payable by the underwriters, finder's fees, consulting or advisory fees, and securities, options or warrants of the company). [FINRA] gives particular scrutiny to purchases of securities of the company by underwriters or their partners, officers, directors or branch managers prior to the filing of the registration statement. [FINRA] will normally require such holders to commit not to resell or transfer such securities for a period of [180 days] following effectiveness of the registration statement, and may treat the difference between the purchase price of any such securities * * * and the value of such securities at the effective date as additional underwriters' compensation whether or not any of such securities are being sold in the offering. * * *

* * *

---

*   Copyright © 1983 by Sorg Printing Company Incorporated. Reprinted with permission.

d.　PURCHASE OF SECURITIES BY THE UNDERWRITERS

Going Public

Michael J. Halloran.
Published by Sorg Printing Company Incorporated (5th ed. 1983).[**]

* * *

[A binding legal agreement between the underwriters and the company] occurs only on the morning of the date the registration statement is to be declared effective by the SEC * * *

* * *

Even when the underwriting agreement is signed, the underwriters' obligations are subject to satisfaction of various conditions and to the nonoccurrence of certain adverse events (sometimes called "outs") specifically provided for in the underwriting agreement. Should events such as a banking moratorium, a closing of the New York * * * Stock Exchange[ ], commencement of armed hostilities or other drastic events, or a materially adverse development involving the company, occur shortly after the offering commences, the underwriters are often given the right to terminate the offering. The underwriters also condition their obligations in the underwriting agreement upon receipt of various closing documents, including certificates by company officials as to factual and financial matters, opinions of counsel as to legal matters, and representations ("cold comfort letters") from the company's independent public accountants regarding the financial condition of the company, just prior to the closing.

Purchase by the underwriters of the company's securities and payment for them in a firm commitment offering take place at a "closing" usually [two] business days after the registration statement becomes effective and the offering commences. This period gives the underwriters sufficient time to receive payment from most of their customers for the securities in response to confirmations of sales sent out when the offering commences.

* * *

B.　SEC DISCLOSURE REQUIREMENTS

As should be clear by this point, the Commission has substantial discretion over the content of the disclosure made in registration statements. It should be kept in mind, however, that Congress does not

---

[**]　Copyright © 1983 by Sorg Printing Company Incorporated. Reprinted with permission.

always give the Commission free reign in designing its requirements. As only one example, the Dodd-Frank Act of 2010 directed the Commission to draft rules calling for the disclosure of certain payments in connection with resource extraction and development. The SEC eventually complied, but its rule was struck down as an unconstitutional attempt to compel speech. In June 2016 a revised rule was adopted designed for effectiveness in 2019, but was repealed by Congressional action in 2017. On the flip-side, so to speak, a December 2015 spending bill prohibited the Commission from using any of its 2016 funding to adopt rules requiring disclosure of corporate political spending. Such micromanaging may well continue.

That said, this section focuses on the Commission's traditional concerns. Aside from truthfulness, the most notable of these probably has to do with the overall tone of disclosure. Since a prospectus is the main document that offers a security, one might expect it to be upbeat. The following materials provide a good introduction to the Commission's prospectus disclosure requirements. As will be seen, upbeat drafting does not fit well with these requirements.

In re Universal Camera Corp.

Securities and Exchange Commission, 1945.
19 S.E.C. 648.

This case comes before us on a motion to dismiss a stop order proceeding commenced with respect to a registration statement filed under the Securities Act of 1933 by Universal Camera Corporation (Universal). * * *

* * *

BACKGROUND OF THE PROPOSED OFFERING

* * * Universal's normal peace time business is the manufacture and distribution of popular priced still and motion picture cameras, projectors, film and photographic accessories.

Early in 1942 Universal virtually discontinued making these products and since then has been engaged almost exclusively in making binoculars under prime contracts for the Army and Navy. Its resumption of the manufacture of nonwar products is dependent upon the freeing of facilities from war production requirements and a relaxation of Government regulations and restrictions imposed to meet exigencies of the current national emergency.

* * *

THE TERMS OF THE OFFERING

The registration statement covers 530,500 Class A shares to be offered to the public by Universal's present common stockholders. That is all but 1,500 of the 532,000 Class A shares which the controlling stockholders [are to] receive (together with all of the new Class B stock and warrants for 308,400 shares of Class A stock) in exchange for the 300,000 shares of Universal's common stock which they now hold. The proceeds of sale of such Class A shares would go not to Universal but to the selling stockholders.

The registration statement covers also 133,000 Class A shares to be offered to the public by Universal itself. The proceeds of sale of such shares would go to Universal.

* * *

After deducting the underwriter's commission the sellers would receive $4 a share, or a total of $2,654,000 as proceeds of the offering. Of this amount, after all selling commissions and estimated expenses are deducted, the selling stockholders, who paid $30,000 for their common stock, would receive $2,100,865 and the company would receive $524,985. The selling stockholders, through their retention of * * * 500,000 shares of Class B stock, would still have exclusive voting power and a 43 percent share in the earnings after preferred dividends. They would also have * * * 1,500 shares of Class A stock remaining unsold and warrants to purchase 162,300 shares of Class A stock. * * *

* * *

SPECULATIVE CHARACTER OF THE
SHARES TO BE OFFERED

The facing page of the prospectus states: "These Shares Are Offered As a Speculation."

Where the nature of the securities requires the employment of such a legend the registrant is under a duty to describe the speculative features of the offering in the registration statement and the prospectus so clearly that they will be plainly evident to the ordinary investor. This Universal failed to do. The statement as originally filed did not plainly disclose the prospective investor's relative interest in the assets, earnings or voting power of the company. Nor did it give a clear description of Universal's proposed business activities.

A. Omissions of Material Facts in Respect of the Registrant's Proposed Financial Structure

All of Universal's outstanding common stock was acquired by the present holders * * * for $30,000. As of December 31, 1944, it had a liquidating value of $279,438 according to Universal's books. On that basis the 532,000 shares of new Class A stock to be issued in exchange for the outstanding common would have a liquidating value of about 53 cents a share according to Universal's books.

The proceeds of Universal's sale of 133,000 Class A shares at $5 per share would increase the Class A stock's liquidating value to an aggregate of $804,423 for the 665,000 shares, or $1.21 per share according to Universal's books.[10] The New Class B stock would have no asset value although it would have exclusive voting power.

Of their 532,000 shares of the new Class A stock, the selling stockholders propose to sell 530,500 shares to the public at $5 per share.[11]

Through that sale they would realize $2,100,865 for the part which they propose to sell of the stock to be received in exchange for the common they originally purchased for $30,000. At the same time they would retain exclusive voting power and a 43 percent participation in earnings after preferred dividends by retaining all of the B stock also to be received in the exchange of their common. Beyond that they would still have the earning power and liquidating value represented by 1,500 shares of Class A stock not to be offered for sale * * * .

The failure to state these facts in the registration statement or in the prospectus in such a way that they would be plainly evident was of extreme importance in view of Universal's past earning record. In 1942, when it was engaged almost exclusively in war work, Universal had the best earnings of its history. If it had then been capitalized as proposed in the registration statement the 1942 earnings would have amounted to about 23 cents a share of Class A and Class B stock after taxes. The earnings for 1944 would have amounted to only about 5 cents a share on the proposed new capitalization.[12]

The omission of facts disclosing plainly the contrast between the proposed offering price and the book value of the shares to be offered would have made it practically impossible for anyone but an astute and experienced security analyst to discover, from the information as it was set out in the statement, that on the basis of the company's past earning

---

[10] Stated another way, out of $5 paid by a public purchaser for one of the 133,000 shares to be sold by Universal, the purchaser would receive an interest having an asset value, according to Universal's books, of $1.21. Of the remaining $3.79 paid for the share, $1 would go to the underwriter as a selling commission and the balance, $2.79, would go towards raising the asset value of the present common stockholders' 532,000 new Class A shares from approximately 53 cents a share to $1.21 a share. Stated in aggregate amounts, if all the 133,000 shares to be offered by Universal should be sold at $5 a share, a total public investment of $665,000, the public purchasers would receive interests in the corporation having an asset value of $160,930; whereas $133,000 would go to the underwriter as a selling commission and $371,070 (less selling expenses of $7,015) would go to raising the asset value of the present common stockholders' new Class A shares from approximately 53 cents to $1.21 a share.

[11] Out of the $5.00 per share (or an aggregate of $2,652,500) paid by public purchasers for the 530,500 Class A shares to be sold by the selling stockholders, the purchasers would receive an interest in Universal having an asset value, according to Universal's books, of $1.21 per share (or $641,905 in the aggregate). The remaining $3.79 paid for each share (or an aggregate of $2,010,595) would represent an excess over book value that would be realized in cash by the selling stockholders, out of which they would pay $1 per share (or an aggregate of $530,500) to the underwriter as selling commission.

Of the $1.21 per share interest in book assets received by the purchasers from selling stockholders, about 53 cents (or about $281,000 in the aggregate) would represent their proportionate interest in the present net worth of Universal and about 68 cents (or about $361,000 in the aggregate) would represent the amount contributed to Universal's asset value by public purchasers who had bought stock at $5 a share from Universal.

[12] The proposed offering price was therefore more than 21 times the 1942 earnings and 100 times the 1944 earnings.

experience it would require an accumulation of many years earnings to enable an investor, buying the Class A stock and holding it, to regain through earnings, even the difference between its book value and the price at which it was offered to him.

A disclosure which makes the facts available in such form that their significance is apparent only upon searching analysis by experts does not meet the standards imposed by the Securities Act of 1933 as we understand that Act. [Disclosure] should be plainly understandable to the ordinary investor. * * *

Another aspect of the financial structure which the registration statement and prospectus did not adequately describe to the ordinary investor was the significance and effect of the proposed issuance of option warrants. * * *

* * *

[W]e believe that for a fair and complete disclosure it would be requisite for Universal to state that for the life of the warrants, until December 31, 1948, the company might be deprived of favorable opportunities to procure additional equity capital, if it should be needed for the purpose of the business, and that at any time when the holders of such warrants might be expected to exercise them, the company would, in all likelihood, be able to obtain equity capital, if it needed capital then, by public sale of a new issue on terms more favorable than those provided for by the warrants.

B. Omissions and Misstatements With Respect to Registrant's Business

The original registration statement touched but lightly upon competitive conditions in the industry before the war. On the other hand it made broad general assertions concerning Universal's postwar prospects. For example, on p. 6 of the prospectus it stated:

> The Company believes that its competitive position in the postwar market will be maintained by reason of the fact that it is currently designing and preparing improved and additional photographic products which should find a ready sale.

and again at p. 8 it said:

> While other manufacturers have also gained skill and knowledge in the field of Optical Instruments in connection with their war work, the Company, by reason of its ability to successfully compete as to quality and price in the manufacture of binoculars, feels that it will be able to maintain its competitive position in the postwar market.

With respect to the first statement quoted the prospectus contained no disclosure of the extent of its progress in the development of what it described as "improved and additional photographic products." Nor were representatives of the company able to testify to a substantial basis for their opinions relative to sales prospects.

With respect to the second statement quoted it appears that the only competition the registrant has ever met in the sale of binoculars has been in sales to the government under war contracts. Obviously that is not the kind of competition in which it is likely to be engaged primarily after the war. Furthermore, the registration statement failed to state that the market for binoculars before the war was a relatively limited market.

The original prospectus made much of Universal's ability to manufacture all of its lens requirements by mass production methods by using machines it has developed. Great emphasis was placed also upon the fact that designs for such machines were donated to the government and that the machines used by other manufacturers bear the mark "built from designs donated by Universal Camera Corporation to the U.S. Government." The prospectus did not reveal, however, that these designs are not covered by patents and that, except for some relatively recent developments, competitors are well acquainted with the machines.

Of like character was the failure of the prospectus to indicate in connection with statements made concerning the pending development for manufacture of a 16 mm. sound projector and a self-contained table model phonograph with automatic record changer, that in fact, in the case of the first and possibly in the case of the second, it would be necessary for Universal to obtain licenses under certain electronic patents before it would manufacture the new products if and when their development is completed. Furthermore, there was no indication of the time necessary to perfect such products for marketing.

* * *

EVENTS SINCE NOTICE OF PROCEEDING

* * *

On April 23 and May 5 Universal filed material amendments designed to correct some of the deficiencies in the original statement. * * * On May 24 Universal filed an additional amendment making further material changes in the statement.

* * *

It appears * * * that Universal is considering some modifications in the terms of the offering and will file amendments designed to make the statement describe the offering as modified, including appropriate amendments relative to any warrants that may be involved.

* * *

CONCLUSION
* * *

[I]n view of the corrections accomplished by the amendments already filed we see no necessity for issuing a stop order or continuing further with this proceeding. Accordingly Universal's motion to dismiss the proceeding will be granted.

* * *

In re Texas Glass Mfg. Corp.
Securities and Exchange Commission, 1958.
38 S.E.C. 630.

This is a proceeding under Section 8(d) of the Securities Act of 1933 ("Act") to determine whether a stop order should issue suspending the effectiveness of a registration statement filed on Form S–2 by Texas Glass Manufacturing Corporation ("Texas Glass") covering a proposed public offering of $1.00 par value common stock.

* * *

ALLEGED DEFICIENCIES
* * *

Organization, Development, and Description of Business

[Here the Commission detailed numerous deficiencies, reminiscent of those discussed in In re Universal Camera Corp.]

Prior Sales of Securities

The notes to the financial statements included in the prospectus state that since January 1956 the company has sold 83,708 shares of stock at $2.00 per share, and 15,425 shares of optioned stock at $1.00 per share, and that all such sales have been made pursuant to the exemption provided for under Section 3(a)(11) of the Act.[13] [Here the Commission concludes that the exemption was not in fact available.]

Under the circumstances, we find that it was materially misleading for the prospectus to state that the prior sales of securities were made pursuant to an exemption under Section 3(a)(11) of the Act. We also find that the financial statements included in the prospectus were misleading in failing to disclose that there was at that time a contingent liability under Section [12(a)(1)] of the Act arising from the sales of unregistered securities.[14] * * *

---

[13] Section 3(a)(11) of the Act provides that any security which is part of an issue offered and sold only to residents of a single state by a corporation incorporated by and doing business within such state shall be exempt from registration under the Act.

[14] Section [12(a)(1)] of the Act provides in pertinent part that a person who sells a security in violation of Section 5 shall be liable to the purchaser for recovery of the consideration or damages. * * *

Use of Proceeds

* * *

The prospectus sets forth, in a chart, costs applicable to plant construction contracts, including an item captioned "Amounts of Deferred Payments Plus Interest," without indicating at that point that such contracts have not yet been executed, that the amounts set forth do not include interest, and that the interest rates on deferred payments, which will add to the costs, have not yet been determined. The chart also allocates substantial sums for items described as "Next 90 Days Production" and "Reserve Fund" without any explanation of what these items comprise. In addition, the prospectus fails to state the order of priority in which the proceeds will be used, if the funds raised are insufficient to carry out the company's entire program.

* * *

CONCLUSIONS

In view of the numerous and serious deficiencies which we have found in the registration statement * * * , we conclude that an order should be issued suspending the effectiveness of the registration statement.

* * *

Avoiding Delays in Processing Registration Statements Under the Securities Act of 1933

Barry C. Maloney.*
24 Business Lawyer 1143 (1969).**

In the practice of Federal Securities law there appears to be a lack of empathy for the task of the regulator. The shibboleth for avoiding delays is simply to "anticipate" the examiner's comments. A great deal of an examiner's time is spent eliciting responses that could have been anticipated in the letter of transmittal * * * or in the initial filing * * * .

What does an examiner look for? The examiner's task under the securities laws is to obtain full and fair disclosure. Concerning full disclosure, oftentimes the registration is deficient because it fails to state a fact and the examiner must make a request to solicit the response, e.g. that the company is conducting negotiations concerning possible acquisitions or mergers for which the proceeds will be applied. Of course there are many areas that are difficult to anticipate but counsel should approach the registration from an examiner's point of view and

---

*   The Securities and Exchange Commission, as a matter of policy, disclaims responsibility for any private publication by any of its employees. The views expressed herein are those of the author and do not necessarily reflect the views of the Commission or of the author's colleagues upon the staff of the Commission.

**   Copyright © 1969 by the American Bar Association. All rights reserved. Reprinted with the permission of the American Bar Association and its Section of Business Law.

determine where there may be questions. In the penumbra, if disclosure appears adequate and negative assertions are not necessary then the letter of transmittal should so indicate with supporting reasons or references.

Concerning fair disclosure, the overall approach can be best expressed by viewing the prospectus as a liability document and not a selling document. The unfavorable data must be disclosed as well as the favorable. * * *

* * *

Unmentioned thus far is one additional factor which now influences greatly the drafting of prospectuses. This is the judicially-invented "bespeaks caution" doctrine discussed in Chapter 8. As also discussed in Chapter 8, Section 27A of the Securities Act provides somewhat similar statutory relief from liability for forward-looking statements accompanied by "meaningful cautionary language," but Section 27A is not available in the context of initial public offerings.

C. PERSPECTIVES ON SEC DISCLOSURE REQUIREMENTS

The Myth of the Informed Layman

Homer Kripke.
28 Business Lawyer 631 (1973).*

For the past several years, I have taught Securities Regulation * * * . Each year I distribute a prospectus to my students and say, "Let's see what we can learn about the desirability of an investment in this company." I have reluctantly come to the conclusion that the Securities Act of 1933 is not operating as it should and that the prospectus has become a routine, meaningless document which does not serve its purpose. * * *

* * *

If one searches for a clue [as to why this is so], a single thread appears. * * * That thread is simply that the Commission has misconceived its market.

It has never admitted any hypothesis other than that the prospectus is intended for the man in the street, the unsophisticated lay investor. My theme is that the theory that the prospectus can be and is used by the lay investor is a myth. It is largely responsible for the fact that the securities prospectus is fairly close to worthless.

* * *

*   Copyright © 1973 by the American Bar Association. All rights reserved. Reprinted with the permission of the American Bar Association and its Section of Business Law.

We have the fact that many of the companies coming to market are very high technology companies. No layman could really understand either the products or their technical competitive positions; nor could even an expert get a solid understanding as long as disclosure is circumscribed by the push to make the prospectus short and readable for the layman.

* * *

Yet the SEC goes on the theory that in the selection of investments from the numerous offerings of this very intricate merchandise, a simple readable prospectus on one company will enable the man in the street to make a wise choice between one company and the thousands of others about which no one may be telling him anything.

* * *

In the first place, the myth recognizes that the man in the street would not read a technical prospectus. Therefore it requires that the prospectus be made short and readable, no matter how much length might be realistically necessary in a prospectus to give a proper picture of a complex company.

Second, the myth forces the SEC into requiring emphasis on risk features of the offering with a simplicity that is sometimes less than a full picture. * * *

* * *

We find oversimplification for the layman working in many other fields of SEC law. The myth forces the Commission to forbid the disclosure in a prospectus of estimated values that might exist in excess of cost, e.g., in real estate, for fear that the lay investor could not be properly skeptical of an appraisal. * * * We read again and again in statements of Commission spokesmen that once the Commission permits something to be said in a document filed with the Commission, there is a danger that the investor will accept these assertions as gospel truth, despite all the disclaimers on the first page.

But this concern is only for the lay investor, not the professional who would be grateful for the opportunity to receive value estimates, and to consider them skeptically.

* * *

These factors have pushed the SEC into a perpetually negativistic, pessimistic approach. * * *

We could parody all prospectuses of promotional companies in one sentence: "Our competition is too much for us, and no representation is made that we will stay out of bankruptcy after the closing date." A prospectus loses its effect if every prospectus cries "wolf" all the time.

* * *

New Approaches to Disclosure in Registered Security Offerings

A Panel Discussion.
28 Business Lawyer 505 (1973).*

* * *

■ [HAROLD] MARSH: * * *

* * *

The Commission and the Securities Bar have * * * come under fire from Professor Homer Kripke of New York University, who has asserted in various published articles and speeches that "the prospectus has become a routine, meaningless document which does not serve its purpose." * * *

* * *

Are Prospectuses Too Negative?

One of Professor Kripke's major complaints about present day prospectuses is that they are too "negative." He asserts that "a prospectus loses its effect if every prospectus cries 'Wolf' all the time." Of course, this has been a common complaint about Registration Statements for many years. It may, indeed, be possible to go too far in this direction.

* * *

It is easy to criticize the drafting of a prospectus as being merely an "insurance policy" against potential civil liability, and there is little doubt investors would probably get more meaningful disclosures if this could be changed. * * * Certainly, so long as crushing civil liabilities exist for the slightest misstatement in a prospectus, any conscientious securities lawyer drafting a Registration Statement must try to protect his clients to the extent possible against that liability; and he is not going to change that approach merely because Professor Kripke would prefer to have the prospectus read some other way.

* * *

To Whom Is the Prospectus Addressed?

* * * The official position of the Commission * * * is that the prospectus must be completely informative both to the "unsophisticated investor" and to the "knowledgeable student of finance." In other words, the drafter of a prospectus is enjoined to be "all things to all men." Of course, if he attempts this, he runs an extreme danger, to paraphrase the same Apostle, of "saying those things which he should have left unsaid, and leaving unsaid those things which he should have said."

---

*   Copyright © 1973 by the American Bar Association. All rights reserved. Reprinted with the permission of the American Bar Association and its Section of Business Law.

On the other hand, Professor Kripke denounces what he calls the "myth of the informed layman," which he asserts has colored the Commission's concept of disclosure and rendered the prospectus useless. He asserts that the prospectus should be written solely for the "professional" or "expert."

With regard to Professor Kripke's obeisance to the so-called experts in securities investment, one can, I believe, with equal justification oppose his concept of the "myth of the informed layman" with the "myth of the 'expert' expert." It would be very interesting to have some graduate student in a business college conduct a research project to determine how much of the worthless junk securities sold by conglomerates in the last few years were bought by those self-appointed "expert money managers" advising mutual funds and other institutional investors, as compared to the percentage foisted off on the general public.

It seems to me that the only common sense approach to the question of the audience to whom the disclosure should be directed is that it should be directed to those persons who are capable of understanding the transactions being described. In my opinion, this will include only a small minority of the general public and only a small minority of the self-appointed experts. But to attempt to explain to a person who is incapable of understanding is a complete waste of time. If a physicist attempted to make "full disclosure" to me regarding the theory of relativity, his attempt would be doomed to failure, whatever his talents.

* * *

Where Did We Go Wrong?

Assuming that the criticisms of the usefulness of the type of disclosure presently found in most Registration Statements have some validity, and I think that few securities lawyers would assert that they are totally without foundation, the question arises as to where we went wrong. I think that this can be pinpointed with some precision. The story has often been told as to how the official in charge of the processing of 1933 Act registrations was presented with recommendations from his Staff that stop order proceedings be instituted against every single one of the more than 100 statements that were initially filed. Instead of following these recommendations, he invented the letter of comment procedure whereby the issuers were given an opportunity to rewrite their Registration Statements in the way that the SEC Staff wanted them written.

There was, however, another clear choice which he had and presumably rejected, other than instituting over 100 stop order proceedings, and that was to inform his Staff in connection with 95% to 99% of their comments that if they ever made any more asinine comments like that, they would be fired. In my opinion, the development of disclosure in registered offerings would unquestionably have been different, and very probably more useful, if the SEC Staff had stayed out of it.

It is still not too late to retrieve that error.

All that it would take is an act of will on the part of the Commission to permit the Securities Act of 1933 to operate in the manner in which it was originally written and a public announcement that the SEC Staff would never again read a Registration Statement for the purpose of issuing a "letter of comment," but would make every Registration Statement effective at any time requested by the issuer and underwriter unless a prior notice of stop order proceedings had been issued. For 39 years the Securities Bar and the SEC Staff have been attempting *jointly* to write prospectuses and, if * * * Professor Kripke [is] to be believed, all they have produced is an abortion.

Isn't it time we tried another way?

The SEC and Corporate Disclosure

A Program by the ABA Committee on Federal Regulation of Securities.
36 Business Lawyer 119 (1980).*

* * *

■ A.A. SOMMER, JR.: * * * I am not going to discuss the disclosure philosophy all the way back to [Genesis], but I am going to go back as far as 1914, or thereabouts, when Brandeis made his famous statement: "Sunshine is said to be the best of disinfectants; electric light the most efficient policeman." To some extent that statement has been the touchstone of disclosure philosophy. When you analyze that statement, it is perfectly obvious that he was not talking about disclosure for the purpose of informing investors. He was, rather, thinking of disclosure as a therapeutic or remedial means to assure honesty and decency in society.

* * *

Few fundamental questions were raised through the 1930s, 1940s and the 1950s. In the 1960s some basic questions were raised. Was the system worth the cost? Was the system really necessary?

* * *

At the same time, a number of theories were being developed with regard to the markets, the economics of information and the manner in which stock prices reacted to various kinds of events. Let me summarize them.

The first one arose about 1959 and was really a revival of a theory that had been discussed back in the early part of the century in a somewhat different context: the so-called "random walk" theory. It is

* Copyright © 1980 by the American Bar Association. All rights reserved. Reprinted with the permission of the American Bar Association and its Section of Business Law.

simple—the price of a security yesterday does not say anything about the price of the security today or tomorrow. Anyone who has followed the securities markets is readily willing to accept that and it appears to be fairly well accepted among economists today. Nonetheless, the chartists continue to make a lot of money selling charts that say if the Dow-Jones Averages are interpreted properly, "shoulders" and "heads" and various other things will appear; indeed, there are patterns, they say, in the movements of stock prices and money can be made from an awareness of them, despite all the statistical evidence to the contrary.

The random walk theory is generally regarded as the weak form of the "efficient market hypothesis." Most of the discussion about "portfolio" theory in recent years has at least started with the efficient market hypothesis. The medium-strong form of the efficient market hypothesis says simply that the market price of a security at any time has been affected by all of the publicly available information. The people who are making investments day to day, preeminently the analysts, take all available information and very quickly assimilate it in their judgment making process. That judgment eventuates in a buy, sell or hold decision. The price at any moment will reflect this myriad of judgments being made by informed investors; therefore, there is no way that the market can consistently be beaten by superior analysis of publicly available information and the exercise that analysts go through is essentially futile.

The strong form of the efficient market hypothesis says that not only is the price of a security affected by publicly available information, but also "inside" information, so that even insiders cannot make money with their inside information. I will stand corrected by * * * other people who know more about this than I, but I do not believe many people accept the strong form these days, although it is still discussed.

Out of all this there came other theories, e.g., the "capital asset pricing model" which Markowitz began to elaborate in the 1950s. The "modern portfolio" theory tried to distinguish between systematic and unsystematic risk and said that one area of risk could be eliminated simply by diversification. The information about a particular company was not as critical as the "betas" of securities. The "beta" of a security was the measure of it in relation to the market as a whole. A security with a beta over one generally moved up faster when the market was moving up than the market itself, and it also fell faster when the market was falling. If the beta was less than one, the opposite was the effect: the security moved up and down more slowly. This theory suggested that you decided the average beta (i.e., risk) you wanted in your portfolio; and then you simply selected securities that produced that average beta. It did not make any difference whether they were in the steel business, the automotive business, or the chemical business. What mattered was the beta.

These theories have become part and parcel of every analyst's equipment regardless of whether he intellectually accepts the consequences of the efficient market hypothesis.

This has led, I think, and quite rightly, as Homer [Kripke] points out in his book, [The SEC and Corporate Disclosure: Regulation in Search of a Purpose (1979),] to a reevaluation of the importance of information about individual companies. Some analysts will contend that data regarding individual companies constitutes less than 20 percent of the data that they use in making investment decisions; they are more concerned with market movements as a whole and industry trends. Homer in his book, suggests that "firm specific" information may run as high as 40 percent of the data content of a manager's judgment. In any event, I believe it is generally accepted today that industry and macroeconomic data, such as newspaper reports about the President's anti-inflation program, in the aggregate are probably more important in market decisions than firm specific information.

* * *

The main point of Homer's book, as I see it, is twofold. First, he contends that the efficient market hypothesis has rendered fundamental analysis a useless exercise, although I must say Homer fudges on this proposition every now and then in the book. The elaboration of that would suggest that the whole exercise the Commission engages in, assuming timely and accurate information for fundamental analysis, is a pretty useless exercise because you cannot make money on fundamental analysis. Homer recognizes that there is a strange anomaly lurking here that nobody knows the answer to, namely, to have an efficient market you have to have [people] *thinking* that it makes a difference and going through this exercise and spending all this money; otherwise, the efficient market will not work. Homer confesses he does not have the answer to that conundrum, and neither do I. And I suspect even the SEC does not.

Homer's second basic proposition is that there are market forces at work today that seriously undercut, if not totally eliminate, the need to *compel* corporations to make disclosures; first, the analysts (and I guess there are about 13,000 of them) who bang on the doors of corporations and in effect say, "Unless you really make full disclosure to us, we are not going to treat your stock kindly," and second, corporations which are apparently anxious to make full disclosure because they want the analysts to think well of them and reflect their good judgment in the price of the stock.

* * *

* * * I would concede that sometimes the Commission staff acts as if the information they review is totally sufficient for investor needs and that the prospectus is really all that is necessary to make an investment decision. We all know that that is nonsense, and I suspect the SEC knows it is nonsense.

The fact is that the Commission does well, with some exceptions, the limited job that they have been asked by Congress to do, namely, require prompt, accurate and full disclosure of firm specific information. Fortunately they do not get into requirements related to industry information, macroeconomic information and the like. I would suggest that criticizing the SEC for what it is presently doing is like saying to Secretariat, "You're a lousy horse because you cannot fly."

* * *

Mandatory Disclosure and the
Protection of Investors

Frank H. Easterbrook and Daniel R. Fischel.
70 Virginia Law Review 669 (1984).*

The Securities Act of 1933 and the Securities Exchange Act of 1934 have escaped the fate of many other early New Deal programs. Some of their companions, such as the National Industrial Recovery Act, were declared unconstitutional; others such as the Robinson-Patman Act, have fallen into desuetude; still others, such as Social Security, have been so changed that they would be unrecognizable to their creators. Many of the New Deal programs of regulation lost their political support and were replaced by deregulation; communications and transportation are prime examples.

The securities laws, however, have retained not only their support but also their structure. They had and still have two basic components: a prohibition against fraud, and requirements of disclosure when securities are issued and periodically thereafter. The notorious complexities of securities practice arise from defining the details of disclosure and ascertaining which transactions are covered by the disclosure requirements. There is very little substantive regulation of investments.

To be sure, the Securities and Exchange Commission (SEC) occasionally uses the rubric of disclosure to affect substance, as when it demands that insiders not trade without making "disclosures" that would make trading pointless, when it requires that a going private deal "disclose" that the price is "fair," and when it insists that the price of accelerated registration of a prospectus is "disclosure" that directors will not be indemnified for certain wrongs. * * * Although several of these refinements are important, they are not the principal components of regulation. The dominating principle of securities regulation is that anyone willing to disclose the right things can sell or buy whatever he wants at whatever price the market will sustain.

---

*   Copyright © 1984 by the Virginia Law Review Association. Reprinted with permission.

Why have the laws survived? Those who enacted these statutes asserted that they were necessary to eliminate fraud from the market and ensure that investors would receive the returns they expected; otherwise, the argument ran, people would withdraw their capital and the economy would stagnate. This explanation seemed especially pressing in 1933, for there had been frauds preceding the Depression and much disinvestment during. On this public interest story, the interests served by the laws are the same now as they were then, and so the laws have retained their beneficial structure.

No scholar should be comfortable with this simple tale. Fraud was unlawful in every state in 1933; we did not need a federal law to penalize lying and deceit. Fraud in the sale of education is more important to most people of moderate means (the supposed beneficiaries of the securities acts) than fraud in the sale of securities; these people have a much greater portion of their wealth invested in human capital than in the stock market. Yet there are no federal laws addressing these other assets. There were many securities frauds before 1933, and there have been many since. The Investors Overseas Services, National Student Marketing, Equity Funding, and OPM Leasing frauds of the last decade are every bit as spectacular as the frauds of the 1920s.

The modern recognition, backed up by evidence, that much legislation is the outcome of the interplay of pressure groups—and that only by accident will interest group laws serve the broader public interest suggests another hypothesis. The securities laws may be designed to protect special interests at the expense of investors.

The securities laws possess many of the characteristics of classic interest group legislation. Existing rules give larger issuers an edge, because many of the costs of disclosure are the same regardless of the size of the firm or the offering. Thus larger or older firms face lower flotation costs per dollar than do smaller issuers. The rules also help existing investment banks and auditing firms obtain an advantage because they acquire expertise and because rivals cannot compete by offering differentiated products. The securities laws' routinization of disclosure reduces the number of paths to the marketplace and insists that all firms give investors "the best," just as airline regulation stifled the high-density, low-fare strategies that have flourished recently.

Many lawyers are specialized in securities work, and other market professionals depend on the intricacies of the law for much revenue. Although there may be too many members of these favored groups (larger issuers, investment banks, the securities bar) for them to charge monopoly prices, the members would suffer windfall losses if existing regulations were repealed. Thus they have every incentive to support the status quo on an interest-group basis. And if the losses from existing laws are spread across a large number of people (individual investors), each of whom would benefit only slightly from abolition, the current regulation could survive even if it reduces social welfare.

Unfortunately, no one knows why some pieces of legislation are enacted and survive while others do not. The interest group explanation that might account for securities legislation also could explain airline and trucking regulation, yet these systems have been almost obliterated. Perhaps securities laws have survived because they are not predominantly interest-group legislation. But it is parlous to equate survival of legislation with public interest. Tobacco, milk, and farm price supports, for example, have survived despite the recent emphasis on deregulation. Few would seriously argue that these laws are anything other than the most naked forms of interest-group legislation.

The survival of securities regulation thus is consistent with either the interest-group or the public interest perspective. * * * We think it appropriate, therefore, to search for the "public interest" justifications of those laws.

* * *

The principal benefit usually asserted for mandatory disclosure is that investors will make more money. They will suffer fewer losses from deceit; even if the level of fraud is unaffected, they will invest more wisely when they know more. * * *

George Stigler has done the best-known study of the returns to investors before and after the creation of the disclosure requirements. Stigler looked at the market for new issues, computing for each stock the percentage difference between the purchase price and its price at some later date. He looked at purchases of new issues in 1923–1927 and asked how these investors fared if they held for one, two, three, four, or five years. They fared well by his test only if they gained relative to investors in existing firms. Then he did the same for purchasers of new issues in 1949–1955. He reached two conclusions. First, although the investors in new issues seemed to lose money relative to the market, and the investors of 1923–1928 lost a little more than the investors of 1949–1955, this difference was not statistically significant. Second, the standard deviation of investors' profits was much lower in the second period than in the first. Stigler concluded that the securities laws had been ineffectual in saving money for new investors, but that they had excluded some small firms from the market, thus reducing the variance of returns.

Gregg Jarrell did essentially the same comparison, but he used methods that had been developed after Stigler's study. * * * After holding degree of risk constant, Jarrell concluded that investors in 1926–1933 did not pay "too much" for their stock in light of later returns, and neither did the subsequent investors. Over a five-year period, those who bought new issues in 1926–1933 actually did better relative to the rest of the market than those who bought later. Like Stigler, he found a substantial reduction in volatility after the passage of the '33 Act.

Stigler and Jarrell agree that in the first year after issuance, stocks in new firms decline relative to the market, after making adjustment for risk. Any subsequent gains must be attributable to new information. Irwin Friend has concluded from this and from other work that the '33 Act produces net benefits. Stigler and Jarrell, on the other hand, find Friend's methods flawed (as he finds theirs flawed) and believe that his conclusions are unreliable. No matter which conclusion we credit, none shows substantial effects of the securities laws on investors' returns.

* * *

* * * Because securities are not homogeneous products, and direct inspection of business prospects by investors is not cost-effective, there may be gains from collective insistence on certain disclosures.

This is a far cry from saying that our existing securities rules are optimal. No satisfactory data suggest that the SEC's rules are beneficial. Perhaps problems in implementation prevent realization of whatever savings are available in principle. There is less reason to regulate securities than, say, the funeral industry, which also lacks standardized transactions and in which shopping by informed traders may not lead to efficient prices. We have not constructed a compelling case for regulation of any sort, let alone for the particular regulations the SEC uses.

There is nonetheless *a* case for mandatory disclosure, and it is a far different case from that usually advanced by those who endorse the securities laws. Our approach suggests that the telling blows that can be struck against the usual case are not fatal.

What is the appropriate response to this "conclusion," if something so uncertain may be called that? The proponent of change in the legal order bears a substantial burden. Rules of law may be beneficial in ways we do not understand, and if all we can say is that we cannot identify either benefit or detriment from a given set of rules, the injunction to leave well enough alone has great force. * * * The final difficulty * * * is that the question for decision is not regulation versus the market but one kind of regulation (disclosure rules enforced by the SEC) versus another (fraud and "material omission" rules, and perhaps disclosure rules, enforced by state courts and agencies). We cannot say that the existing securities laws are beneficial, but we also are not confident that their probable replacements would be better.

Market Failure and the Economic Case
for a Mandatory Disclosure System

John C. Coffee, Jr.
70 Virginia Law Review 717 (1984).[*]

Recent academic commentary on the securities laws has much in common with the battles fought in historiography over the origins of the First World War. The same progression of phases is evident. First, there is an orthodox school, which tends to see historical events largely as a

---

[*] Copyright © 1984 by the Virginia Law Review Association. Reprinted with permission.

moral drama of good against evil. Next come the revisionists, debunking all and explaining that the good guys were actually the bad. Eventually, a new wave of more professional, craftsmanlike scholars arrives on the scene to correct the gross overstatements of the revisionists and produce a more balanced, if problematic, assessment.

This same cycle is evident in the recent securities law literature. Not so long ago, academic treatment of the securities laws was clearly at the first or "motherhood" stage: to criticize the SEC was tantamount to favoring fraud. Then came the revisionists—most notably Professors Stigler, Benston, and Manne—who argued that the securities laws produced few benefits and considerable costs. According to Professor Benston, the passage of these statutes did not even significantly improve the quality of information provided to investors. These claims provoked a flurry of critical responses, both from academic critics and the SEC.
* * *

We therefore may be approaching a new stage, which can be called "post-revisionism." Among post-revisionism's defining characteristics are (1) a recognition of the Efficient Capital Market Hypothesis as, at the least, the best generalization by which to summarize the available empirical evidence;[15] (2) a clearer sense of the difficulties inherent in relying on aggregate statistical evidence either to prove or rebut any broad thesis about the impact and effects of disclosure; and (3) a shift in focus from continued debate over the impact the federal securities laws had fifty years ago to an examination of contemporary market structure and the needs of investors under existing conditions.

In this typology of phases, the article by Professors Easterbrook and Fischel [that appears directly above] seems at the threshold of "post-revisionism." This categorization may overstate the degree to which they

---

[15] Conventionally, the Efficient Capital Market Hypothesis (ECMH) is subdivided into three distinct versions: the "weak" form, the "semi-strong," and the "strong." As so often happens in the relationship between the law and social sciences, at the very moment that judicial and administrative decisions have begun to accept the ECMH, anomalies have begun to appear in the research data. These anomalies call into question either the extent of the ECMH's applicability or suggest the need for technical reformation. Research in three areas has identified fissures in the foundation of the ECMH. First, studies of the volatility of securities prices suggest that the response of securities prices may be excessive in relation to the significance of the underlying events. Second, studies demonstrate a "small firm" effect under which small firms (typically, the bottom 20% of publicly traded companies) earn abnormally high returns, even after risk adjustment. Other anomalies involving seasonal and weekly variations in stock returns and similar cyclical regularities are also recurrently documented. Third, the conceptual and practical utility of beta-the measure of stock market volatility-remains in serious doubt and some theorists are trying to replace it with a reformulated definition of non-diversifiable risk.

Although none of these anomalies seem likely to weaken the basic point that investors cannot "beat" the market based on diligent search efforts, they do suggest that distinctions should be drawn in terms of the degree to which the ECMH is used as a justification for deregulation—particularly since very little evidence exists with respect to any market other than the New York Stock Exchange. This article will suggest that a mandatory disclosure system should focus on disclosures that assist the investor in assessing beta and better enable him to reduce diversifiable risk; greater disclosure seems also justified in the case of small firms given their apparent immunity to the predictions of the ECMH.

have moved beyond the simple catechism of Professors Stigler and Benston, but at least their article recognizes that the statistical studies are not clearly dispositive and that a faint possibility remains open that benefits might accrue to investors from a mandatory disclosure system.
* * *

* * *

[T]he strongest arguments for a mandatory disclosure system may be efficiency-based. Empirical data strongly suggests that the adoption of a mandatory disclosure system reduced price dispersion and thereby enhanced the allocative efficiency of our capital markets. Nor need we rely only on historical evidence. Economic logic also points to the conclusion that there will be inadequate securities research and verification in the absence of a mandatory disclosure system. In the computerized securities marketplace of the future, individual investor review of corporate disclosures will be the exception, rather than the rule, and clients will increasingly rely on professional advice, both to select individual securities and to diversify their portfolios efficiently. In this world, collectivization of financial data within the SEC is best justified as a strategy for making more efficient use of securities analysts and other market professionals, both by eliminating duplication and by making it feasible for them, at the margin, to cover smaller firms.

* * *

In summary, the federal securities laws ain't necessarily broke, so let's be careful about fixing them.

Technology, Property Rights in Information, and Securities Regulation

Paul G. Mahoney
F. Hodge O'Neal Corporate and Securities Law Symposium:
Markets and Information Gathering in an Electronic Age:
Securities Regulation in the 21st Century.
75 Washington University Law Quarterly 815 (1997).*

* * *

As the combination of technology and globalization creates new choices for investors, some of which are outside the coverage of the U.S. regulatory system, regulators will increasingly receive feedback from markets indicating which elements of the regulatory system add value and which do not. Investors' decisions to risk or not risk money in particular foreign markets will convey important information about the value of the extensive protections afforded by U.S. law. Similarly, the use of technology to create new products and new markets that fall outside

---

* Copyright © 1997 by the Washington University Law Quarterly. Reprinted with permission.

particular regulatory restrictions will give insights into how much investors value those restrictions. * * *

Investors' growing tendency to opt out of the U.S. regulatory system is creating a crisis of confidence for that system. * * * One might conclude that technology and low barriers to the movement of capital will challenge the very survival of U.S. securities law. * * *

The equality-of-information paradigm treats securities law as a form of consumer protection law. * * * The underlying philosophy is that ordinary investors are at a severe informational disadvantage with respect to issuers and market professionals and are insufficiently sophisticated to recognize the magnitude of their disadvantage and to discount the value of securities offered them accordingly. * * * As such, they must both be given disclosures and barred from waiving the protections the regulatory system gives them.

This rationale implies that the SEC should strongly resist issuers' and investors' attempts to avoid regulatory costs through unregistered offerings or offerings that require reduced disclosure. The SEC has taken precisely the opposite tack through innovations like the integrated disclosure system, shelf registration, [and] the expansion * * * of exemptions * * * . The traditional registration model involving a one-shot offering and a lengthy, comprehensive prospectus is now the exception rather than the rule. A substantial portion of securities offerings takes place with voluntary rather than mandatory disclosures through unregistered private placements and offshore offerings.

These developments reflect the SEC's desire to assure that the regulatory costs associated with using the U.S. securities markets are not so substantial as to drive issuers and investors elsewhere—whether "elsewhere" means London or cyberspace. * * *

* * *

Regulatory Initiatives and the Internet: A New Era of Oversight for Securities and Exchange Commission

Roberta S. Karmel
Symposium: Regulation of Securities and Securities
Exchanges in the Age of the Internet.
5 New York University Journal of Legislation and Public Policy 33 (2001–2002).*

Though merely a communications medium, the acceptance of the Internet in the business world has led to a technological revolution in the securities market. The trading of securities over the Internet has challenged securities regulators to adjust old legal constructs to fit this new medium. However, these constructs do not neatly fit the medium of

    *   Copyright © 2001–2002 NYU Journal of Legislation and Public Policy; Roberta S. Karmel. Reprinted with permission.

the Internet. The global nature of Internet communications can lead to the conclusion that Internet activities occur everywhere, nowhere, or both simultaneously, creating jurisdictional conflicts in laws and courts.

As a result, Internet activity has given rise to the conflicting fears of overregulation and underregulation. Because geography is a meaningless construct in cyberspace, a "single actor might be subject to haphazard, uncoordinated, and even outright inconsistent regulation by states that the actor never intended to reach and possibly was unaware were being accessed." On the other hand, there is a contrary risk that significant harms will result from governments' inability or reluctance to enforce existing legal prohibitions.

Regulators are confronted with a plethora of substantive and jurisdictional issues arising out of Internet securities offerings and trading. This Article will argue that the Securities and Exchange Commission has endeavored to tailor its rules to a cyberspace environment without relaxing any of its regulations. However, since the Internet is a free and wide ranging communications medium, and SEC regulations, in essence, control speech, the Internet has forced the SEC to deregulate in certain areas. Further deregulation seems inevitable, especially where United States law is out of sync with foreign laws.

I do not see how the SEC can continue to stand with its finger in the dike while a flood of information washes over the walls. Further, the Internet and the increasing globalization of capital markets have curtailed the SEC's traditional claim to worldwide jurisdiction over antifraud claims. In response, the SEC has been working on cooperating with both domestic and foreign securities regulators and upgrading securities regulations around the world through the harmonization of standards by the International Organization of Securities Commissions (IOSCO). Internet fraud does not respect national boundaries.

* * *

Investors, IPOs, and the Internet

Donald C. Langevoort.
2 Entrepreneurial Business Law Journal 767 (2007).*

The Internet seems a natural home for the conduct of public offerings, including IPOs. By now, nearly all investors with the inclination and resources to purchase in a public offering have the technological resources to do so electronically. Email and websites offer a low-cost way to communicate information quickly and gauge interest easily with respect to large numbers of potential buyers. The SEC's 2005 Public Offering Reforms, though no doubt more cumbersome than they should be, have a carefully thought out approach to electronic

* Copyright © 2007 The Ohio State University Entrepreneurial Business Law Journal; Donald C. Langevoort. Reprinted with permission.

communications. Indeed, their most important innovation—permitting the use of "free writing prospectuses" (i.e., sales literature) prior to the effective date of the registration statement—treats electronic communication as the preferred means by treating an active hyperlink as the equivalent of delivery of the preliminary prospectus. Other forms of written communication require actual physical delivery in the IPO setting, which is more costly and burdensome.

There are more dramatic possibilities * * * . Most notably, the Internet makes it possible to change the very nature of the public offering process, shifting away from the book-building system—which is very expensive for the issuer—to an auction-style model in which investors will simply bid electronically for shares, with the price set at the level that clears the market. * * *

The basic point, with which I fully agree, is that the IPO is only partly about efficient communication. * * * The old adage is that stocks are sold, not bought—in other words, that it takes marketing and sales work to get people to want to buy securities in a company with no track record and hence little or no pre-existing credibility in the financial markets. In addition to bringing marketing expertise to the task, the underwriters act as reputational intermediaries, using their credibility to vouch for the issuer. This is naturally expensive and risky, and it is hard to imagine low-cost solutions to the problem of informational asymmetry in capital-raising transactions because of this. * * *

I suspect, then, that sales and marketing efforts by securities professionals will continue to dominate the public offering process, whether through electronic or more old-fashioned forms of communication. While book-building efforts will no doubt change in response to new technology, specialist intermediaries will best be able to exploit these opportunities, meaning that the securities industry will continue to play a dominant role in public offerings. The potential problems—* * * anti-competitive behavior, under-pricing, self-dealing and manipulation * * *—will be with us for some time to come.

If so, then regulating the IPO will continue to involve casting a wary eye on, among other things, underwriter and broker sales efforts. For instance, we encounter an interesting regulatory point, because the argument is sometimes heard that technology empowers investors (through greater access to information) in such a way that they are now better able to protect themselves. That might suggest that regulatory oversight is less important. My secondary point in this commentary is that there is an interesting and fast-growing body of empirical research on investor behavior, much of which now deals with Internet-based investing. Understanding how investors make their choices is key to setting the right policy, and so regulators should pay very close attention to this work. * * *

* * *

The bottom line of all this is that making information available to investors does not mean that they will use it at all, much less use it well. That is the concern, because as noted earlier it would be nice to think (and securities industry advocates certainly claim) that Internet-based information availability can be a good substitute for sales conduct regulation. Information lets investors protect themselves. That will sometimes be so, but the game still favors the skilled salespeople.

This is not an argument against either liberalization of public offering processes or encouragement of Internet-based offerings, but just a note of caution. The trend, to be sure, is against prior restraint in sales practices and in favor of investor choice. My point is simply that regulators and policy-makers keep a careful eye on Internet-based sales practices to see where unfair exploitation might occur, and respond accordingly. For this to be effective, however, there is a need for much more empirical work about investor behavior, online and otherwise, than we presently have. And this is a task that the SEC should attend to as well in the future.

CHAPTER 5

REACH OF SECURITIES ACT REGULATION

Earlier discussions, such as of "What is an offer?", showed the broad reach of Securities Act regulation. The Act's reach is wider in many ways than the uninitiated would suppose. But in other ways, it is also narrower. This dichotomy forms the countervailing themes of this chapter. These themes will be explored through two questions: "What is a security?" and "What is a sale?"

A. WHAT IS A SECURITY?

SITUATION 5A

Sometime after Microtec's public offering, William Tate, the treasurer, and Helen Thompson, the director of product development, approach Moore and Simpson with an intriguing idea. Thompson and her staff have done preliminary work on developing a module for microcomputers that would permit vastly improved data usage and internet connectivity. Others have developed such modules, but no economical one is very successful. Thompson believes Microtec can develop and produce a relatively inexpensive, yet sophisticated, module of this type. If so, sales potential would be high. Tate is convinced the project shows a good chance for success, but says Microtec's funds are currently committed to the expansion of production capacity.

Tate and Thompson have come up with a plan for pre-selling the modules to dealers, thus generating needed cash. The idea is to offer dealers the opportunity to order a minimum of ten modules at $500 each, paying one-half down. The dealers would be guaranteed their price and, if Microtec could not deliver within two years, the dealers would have the right to cancel their orders and receive refunds. Dealers would also be promised delivery in the sequence in which their orders are received, and they would be allowed to transfer their purchase rights to other dealers. There is a good chance many dealers would place orders. If the module is successful, the wholesale price in a year or two may be well in excess of $500, and Microtec would likely have a large backlog of orders, causing delays in deliveries to dealers who do not order in advance.

Moore and Simpson are taken with this idea and are considering going ahead with it.

I. STATUTORY SCHEME

The substantive provisions of the Securities Act begin with this definition:

> Section 2(a). When used in this title, unless the context otherwise requires—

> (1) the term "security" means any note, stock, treasury stock, security future, security-based swap, bond, debenture, evidence of indebtedness, certificate of interest or participation in any profit-sharing agreement, collateral-trust certificate, preorganization certificate or subscription, transferable share, investment contract, voting-trust certificate, certificate of deposit for a security, fractional undivided interest in oil, gas, or other mineral rights, any put, call, straddle, option, or privilege on any security, certificate of deposit, or group or index of securities (including any interest therein or based on the value thereof), or any put, call, straddle, option, or privilege entered into on a national securities exchange relating to foreign currency, or, in general, any interest or instrument commonly known as a "security," or any certificate of interest or participation in, temporary or interim certificate for, receipt for, guarantee of, or warrant or right to subscribe to or purchase, any of the foregoing.

The bulk of Section 2(a)(1) is clear, and most questions concerning whether a security exists for purposes of the Securities Act can be answered by reference to this section. Further, since the Securities Act definition is virtually identical to the definition found in Exchange Act Section 3(a)(10), most such questions under the Exchange Act may also be answered by references to this same language. One item in the Section 2(a)(1) list of securities has caused the majority of the trouble. This item is the "investment contract," and it will be focused on as a paradigm of the Securities Act's inclusiveness. At the other end of the spectrum is the phrase "unless the context otherwise requires," which is found at the beginning of each act's definitions. This language offers the greatest exclusiveness in terms of defining a security. It will be taken up later in the chapter.

The term "security-based swap" was added to Section 2(a)(1) in 2010. In general, "swaps" are contracts providing that the parties will exchange obligations to make payments on specified financial instruments, and jurisdiction over other than security-based swaps has been allocated to the Commodity Futures Trading Commission. A "security-based swap" is a swap on a single security or loan or narrow-based security index (generally one with fewer than nine component securities). A regulatory regime for security-based swaps was established by the SEC in 2012; it is distinct from the regime described in Chapters Three and Four and is beyond the scope of this book. That said, it is still necessary to address "security-based swap *agreements*," which are discussed more specifically below. Section 2A provides that these agreements (which basically are agreements individually negotiated by a limited group of eligible persons) are *not* securities.

II. INVESTMENT CONTRACT

There has long been confusion about just what constitutes an investment contract. The main reason for this confusion is that the term has no meaning in a commercial context. As will be seen, it is purely a legal construct. SEC v. W.J. Howey Co., which appears directly below, is the leading case.

SEC v. W.J. Howey Co.

Supreme Court of the United States, 1946.
328 U.S. 293.

■ MR. JUSTICE MURPHY delivered the opinion of the Court.

This case involves the application of § 2[(a)](1) of the Securities Act of 1933 to an offering of units of a citrus grove development coupled with a contract for cultivating, marketing and remitting the net proceeds to the investor.

The Securities and Exchange Commission instituted this action to restrain the respondents from using the mails and instrumentalities of interstate commerce in the offer and sale of unregistered and non-exempt securities in violation of § 5(a) of the Act. The District Court denied the injunction, and the Fifth Circuit Court of Appeals affirmed the judgment. * * *

Most of the facts are stipulated. The respondents, W.J. Howey Company and Howey-in-the-Hills Service, Inc., are Florida corporations under direct common control and management. The Howey Company owns large tracts of citrus acreage in Lake County, Florida. During the past several years it has planted about 500 acres annually, keeping half of the groves itself and offering the other half to the public "to help us finance additional development." Howey-in-the-Hills Service, Inc., is a service company engaged in cultivating and developing many of these groves, including the harvesting and marketing of the crops.

Each prospective customer is offered both a land sales contract and a service contract, after having been told that it is not feasible to invest in a grove unless service arrangements are made. While the purchaser is free to make arrangements with other service companies, the superiority of Howey-in-the-Hills Service, Inc., is stressed. Indeed, 85% of the acreage sold during the 3-year period ending May 31, 1943, was covered by service contracts with Howey-in-the-Hills Service, Inc.

* * * Upon full payment of the purchase price the land is conveyed to the purchaser by warranty deed. Purchases are usually made in

narrow strips of land arranged so that an acre consists of a row of 48 trees. * * *

The service contract, generally of a 10-year duration without option of cancellation, gives Howey-in-the-Hills Service, Inc., a leasehold interest and "full and complete" possession of the acreage. For a specified fee plus the cost of labor and materials, the company is given full discretion and authority over the cultivation of the groves and the harvest and marketing of the crops. The company is well established in the citrus business and maintains a large force of skilled personnel and a great deal of equipment, including 75 tractors, sprayer wagons, fertilizer trucks and the like. Without the consent of the company, the land owner or purchaser has no right of entry to market the crop; thus there is ordinarily no right to specific fruit. The company is accountable only for an allocation of the net profits based upon a check made at the time of picking. All the produce is pooled by the respondent companies, which do business under their own names.

The purchasers for the most part are non-residents of Florida. They are predominantly business and professional people who lack the knowledge, skill and equipment necessary for the care and cultivation of citrus trees. They are attracted by the expectation of substantial profits. It was represented, for example, that profits during the 1943–1944 season amounted to 20% and that even greater profits might be expected during the 1944–1945 season, although only a 10% annual return was to be expected over a 10-year period. * * *

* * *

* * * The legal issue in this case turns upon a determination of whether, under the circumstances, the land sales contract, the warranty deed and the service contract together constitute an "investment contract" within the meaning of § [2(a)(1)]. * * *

The term "investment contract" is undefined by the Securities Act or by relevant legislative reports. But the term was common in many state "blue sky" laws in existence prior to the adoption of the federal statute and, although the term was also undefined by the state laws, it had been broadly construed by state courts so as to afford the investing public a full measure of protection. Form was disregarded for substance and emphasis was placed upon economic reality. An investment contract thus came to mean a contract or scheme for "the placing of capital or laying out of money in a way intended to secure income or profit from its employment." State v. Gopher Tire & Rubber Co., 146 Minn. 52, 56, 177 N.W. 937, 938. This definition was uniformly applied by state courts to a variety of situations where individuals were led to invest money in a common enterprise with the expectation that they would earn a profit solely through the efforts of the promoter or of some one other than themselves.

By including an investment contract within the scope of § [2(a)(1)] of the Securities Act, Congress was using a term the meaning of which had been crystallized by this prior judicial interpretation. It is therefore reasonable to attach that meaning to the term as used by Congress, especially since such a definition is consistent with the statutory aims. In other words, an investment contract for purposes of the Securities Act means a contract, transaction or scheme whereby a person invests his money in a common enterprise and is led to expect profits solely from the efforts of the promoter or a third party, it being immaterial whether the shares in the enterprise are evidenced by formal certificates or by nominal interests in the physical assets employed in the enterprise. * * *

The transactions in this case clearly involve investment contracts as so defined. The respondent companies are offering something more than fee simple interests in land, something different from a farm or orchard coupled with management services. They are offering an opportunity to contribute money and to share in the profits of a large citrus fruit enterprise managed and partly owned by respondents. They are offering this opportunity to persons who reside in distant localities and who lack the equipment and experience requisite to the cultivation, harvesting and marketing of the citrus products. Such persons have no desire to occupy the land or to develop it themselves; they are attracted solely by the prospects of a return on their investment. Indeed, individual development of the plots of land that are offered and sold would seldom be economically feasible due to their small size. Such tracts gain utility as citrus groves only when cultivated and developed as component parts of a larger area. A common enterprise managed by respondents or third parties with adequate personnel and equipment is therefore essential if the investors are to achieve their paramount aim of a return on their investments. Their respective shares in this enterprise are evidenced by land sales contracts and warranty deeds, which serve as a convenient method of determining the investors' allocable shares of the profits. The resulting transfer of rights in land is purely incidental.

Thus all the elements of a profit-seeking business venture are present here. The investors provide the capital and share in the earnings and profits; the promoters manage, control and operate the enterprise. It follows that the arrangements whereby the investors' interests are made manifest involve investment contracts, regardless of the legal terminology in which such contracts are clothed. The investment contracts in this instance take the form of land sales contracts, warranty deeds and service contracts which respondents offer to prospective investors. * * *

This conclusion is unaffected by the fact that some purchasers choose not to accept the full offer of an investment contract by declining to enter into a service contract with the respondents. The Securities Act prohibits the offer as well as the sale of unregistered, non-exempt securities. Hence it is enough that the respondents merely offer the essential ingredients of an investment contract.

* * *

After more than a half century, *Howey* still states the test for determining the existence of an investment contract. In the intervening years, litigation has not focused on the correctness of the test, but rather on the precise meaning of one or more of its parts. For purposes of study, it is helpful to break the test down into these elements:

1. investment of money;
2. common enterprise;
3. expectation of profits; and
4. solely from the efforts of others.

Because of the way these elements are handled in the major cases, we will treat "investment of money" and "expectation of profits" together and then also combine the examinations of "common enterprise" and "solely from the efforts of others."

a. INVESTMENT OF MONEY AND EXPECTATION OF PROFITS

United Housing Foundation, Inc. v. Forman

Supreme Court of the United States, 1975.
421 U.S. 837.

■ MR. JUSTICE POWELL delivered the opinion of the Court.

The issue in these cases is whether shares of stock entitling a purchaser to lease an apartment in Co-op City, a state subsidized and supervised nonprofit housing cooperative, are "securities" within the purview of the Securities Act of 1933 and the Securities Exchange Act of 1934.

I

Co-op City is a massive housing cooperative in New York City. * * * The project was organized, financed, and constructed under the New York State Private Housing Finance Law, * * * , enacted to ameliorate a perceived crisis in the availability of decent low-income urban housing. * * *

The United Housing Foundation (UHF), a nonprofit membership corporation established for the purpose of "aiding and encouraging" the creation of "adequate, safe and sanitary housing accommodations for wage earners and other persons of low or moderate income," was responsible for initiating and sponsoring the development of Co-op City. * * * UHF organized the Riverbay Corporation (Riverbay) to own and operate the land and buildings constituting Co-op City. Riverbay, a nonprofit cooperative housing corporation, issued the stock that is the subject of this litigation. * * *

To acquire an apartment in Co-op City an eligible prospective purchaser must buy 18 shares of stock in Riverbay for each room desired. The cost per share is $25, making the total cost $450 per room, or $1,800 for a four-room apartment. The sole purpose of acquiring these shares is to enable the purchaser to occupy an apartment in Co-op City; in effect, their purchase is a recoverable deposit on an apartment. The shares are explicitly tied to the apartment: they cannot be transferred to a nontenant; nor can they be pledged or encumbered; and they descend, along with the apartment, only to a surviving spouse. No voting rights attach to the shares as such: participation in the affairs of the cooperative appertains to the apartment, with the residents of each apartment being entitled to one vote irrespective of the number of shares owned.

Any tenant who wants to terminate his occupancy, or who is forced to move out, must offer his stock to Riverbay at its initial selling price of $25 per share. In the extremely unlikely event that Riverbay declines to repurchase the stock, the tenant cannot sell it for more than the initial purchase price plus a fraction of the portion of the mortgage that he has paid off, and then only to a prospective tenant satisfying the statutory income eligibility requirements.

* * *

[I]ncreases in the [monthly rental charges for the apartments] precipitated the present lawsuit. Respondents, 57 residents of Co-op City, sued in federal court on behalf of all 15,372 apartment owners, and derivatively on behalf of Riverbay, seeking upwards of $30 million in damages, forced rental reductions, and other "appropriate" relief. * * * [R]espondents asserted * * * claims under the fraud provisions of the federal Securities Act of 1933, as amended, § 17(a); the Securities Exchange Act of 1934, as amended, § 10(b); and [Rule 10b–5]. * * *

Petitioners * * * moved to dismiss the complaint on the ground that federal jurisdiction was lacking. They maintained that shares of stock in Riverbay were not "securities" within the definitional sections of the federal Securities Act. * * *

The District Court granted the motion to dismiss. * * *

The Court of Appeals for the Second Circuit reversed. * * *

* * *

II

* * *

A

We reject at the outset any suggestion that the present transaction, evidenced by the sale of shares called "stock," must be considered a security transaction simply because the statutory definition of a security includes the words "any * * * stock." Rather we adhere to the basic principle that has guided all of the Court's decisions in this area:

> "[I]n searching for the meaning and scope of the word 'security' in the Act[s], form should be disregarded for substance and the emphasis should be on economic reality." Tcherepnin v. Knight, 389 U.S. 332, 336 (1967).

* * *

In holding that the name given to an instrument is not dispositive, we do not suggest that the name is wholly irrelevant to the decision whether it is a security. There may be occasions when the use of a traditional name such as "stocks" or "bonds" will lead a purchaser justifiably to assume that the federal securities laws apply. This would clearly be the case when the underlying transaction embodies some of the significant characteristics typically associated with the named instrument.

In the present case respondents do not contend, nor could they, that they were misled by use of the word "stock" into believing that the federal securities laws governed their purchase. Common sense suggests that people who intend to acquire only a residential apartment in a state-subsidized cooperative, for their personal use, are not likely to believe that in reality they are purchasing investment securities simply because the transaction is evidenced by something called a share of stock. * * * Despite their name, they lack what the Court in *Tcherepnin* deemed the most common feature of stock: the right to receive "dividends contingent upon an apportionment of profits." Nor do they possess the other characteristics traditionally associated with stock: they are not negotiable; they cannot be pledged or hypothecated; they confer no voting rights in proportion to the number of shares owned; and they cannot appreciate in value. In short, the inducement to purchase was solely to acquire subsidized low-cost living space; it was not to invest for profit.

B

The Court of Appeals, as an alternative ground for its decision, concluded that a share in Riverbay was also an "investment contract" as defined by the Securities Acts. * * * [T]he basic test for distinguishing the transaction [including an investment contract] from other commercial dealings is

> "whether the scheme involves an investment of money in a common enterprise with profits to come solely from the efforts of others." [SEC v. W.J. Howey Co., 328 U.S. 293, 301 (1946)].[1]

---

[1] This test speaks in terms of "profits to come *solely* from the efforts of others." (Emphasis supplied.) Although the issue is not presented in this case, we note that the Court of Appeals for the Ninth Circuit has held that "the word 'solely' should not be read as a strict or literal limitation on the definition of an investment contract, but rather must be construed realistically, so as to include within the definition those schemes which involve in substance, if not form,

This test, in shorthand form, embodies the essential attributes that run through all of the Court's decisions defining a security. The touchstone is the presence of an investment in a common venture premised on a reasonable expectation of profits to be derived from the entrepreneurial or managerial efforts of others. By profits, the Court has meant either capital appreciation resulting from the development of the initial investment * * * or a participation in earnings resulting from the use of investors' funds * * * . In such cases the investor is "attracted solely by the prospects of a return" on his investment. *Howey,* supra, at 300. By contrast, when a purchaser is motivated by a desire to use or consume the item purchased—"to occupy the land or to develop it themselves," as the *Howey* Court put it, ibid.—the securities laws do not apply.

In the present case there can be no doubt that investors were attracted solely by the prospect of acquiring a place to live, and not by financial returns on their investments. The Information Bulletin distributed to prospective residents emphasized the fundamental nature and purpose of the undertaking * * * . Nowhere does the Bulletin seek to attract investors by the prospect of profits resulting from the efforts of the promoters or third parties. On the contrary, the Bulletin repeatedly emphasizes the "nonprofit" nature of the endeavor. It explains that if rental charges exceed expenses the difference will be returned as a rebate, not invested for profit. It also informs purchasers that they will be unable to resell their apartments at a profit since the apartment must first be offered back to Riverbay "at the price * * * paid for it." In short, neither of the kinds of profits traditionally associated with securities was offered to respondents.

* * * Two * * * supposed sources of income or profits may be disposed of summarily. We turn first to the Court of Appeals' reliance on the deductibility for tax purposes of the portion of the monthly rental charge applied to interest on the mortgage. We know of no basis in law for the view that the payment of interest, with its consequent deductibility for tax purposes, constitutes income or profits. These tax benefits are nothing more than that which is available to any homeowner who pays interest on his mortgage.

The Court of Appeals also found support for its concept of profits in the fact that Co-op City offered space at a cost substantially below the going rental charges for comparable housing. Again, this is an inappropriate theory of "profits" that we cannot accept. The low rent derives from the substantial financial subsidies provided by the State of New York. This benefit cannot be liquidated into cash; nor does it result from the managerial efforts of others. In a real sense, it no more embodies the attributes of income or profits than do welfare benefits, food stamps, or other government subsidies.

---

securities." SEC v. Glenn W. Turner Enterprises, 474 F.2d 476, 482 (1973). We express no view, however, as to the holding of this case.

The final source of profit relied on by the Court of Appeals was the possibility of net income derived from the leasing by Co-op City of commercial facilities, professional offices and parking spaces, and its operation of community washing machines. The income, if any, from these conveniences, all located within the common areas of the housing project, is to be used to reduce tenant rental costs. Conceptually, one might readily agree that net income from the leasing of commercial and professional facilities is the kind of profit traditionally associated with a security investment. But in the present case this income—if indeed there is any—is far too speculative and insubstantial to bring the entire transaction within the Securities Acts.

Initially we note that the prospect of such income as a means of offsetting rental costs is never mentioned in the Information Bulletin. Thus it is clear that investors were not attracted to Co-op City by the offer of these potential rental reductions. Moreover, nothing in the record suggests that the facilities in fact return a profit in the sense that the leasing fees are greater than the actual cost to Co-op City of the space rented. The short of the matter is that the stores and services in question were established not as a means of returning profits to tenants, but for the purpose of making essential services available for the residents of this enormous complex. * * *

There is no doubt that purchasers in this housing cooperative sought to obtain a decent home at an attractive price. But that type of economic interest characterizes every form of commercial dealing. What distinguishes a security transaction—and what is absent here—is an investment where one parts with his money in the hope of receiving profits from the efforts of others, and not where he purchases a commodity for personal consumption or living quarters for personal use.

* * *

International Brotherhood of Teamsters v. Daniel

Supreme Court of the United States, 1979.
439 U.S. 551.

■ MR. JUSTICE POWELL delivered the opinion of the Court.

This case presents the question whether a noncontributory, compulsory pension plan constitutes a "security" within the meaning of the Securities Act of 1933 and the Securities Exchange Act of 1934 (Securities Acts).

I

In 1954 multiemployer collective bargaining between Local 705 of the International Brotherhood of Teamsters, Chauffeurs, Warehousemen, and Helpers of America and Chicago trucking firms produced a pension plan for employees represented by the Local. The plan was compulsory and noncontributory. Employees had no choice as to participation in the plan, and did not have the option of demanding that the employer's contribution be paid directly to them as a substitute for pension eligibility. The employees paid nothing to the plan themselves.

* * * at the time respondent brought suit, employers contributed $21.50 per employee man-week and pension payments ranged from $425 to $525 a month depending on age at retirement. In order to receive a pension an employee was required to have 20 years of continuous service, including time worked before the start of the plan.

The meaning of "continuous service" is at the center of this dispute. * * * [Respondent] retired in 1973 and applied to the plan's administrator for a pension. The administrator determined that respondent was ineligible because of a break in service between December 1960 and July 1961. After the trustees refused to waive the [continuous service] rule, respondent brought suit in federal court * * *.

Respondent's complaint alleged that the Teamsters * * * misrepresented and omitted to state material facts with respect to the value of a covered employee's interest in the pension plan. Count I of the complaint charged that these misstatements and omissions constituted a fraud in connection with the sale of a security in violation of § 10(b) of the Securities Exchange Act of 1934 and the Securities and Exchange Commission's Rule 10b–5. Count II charged that the same conduct amounted to a violation of § 17(a) of the Securities Act of 1933. * * * respondent sought to proceed on behalf of all prospective beneficiaries of Teamsters pension plans and against all Teamsters pension funds.

* * * [T]he District Court denied the motion. It held that respondent's interest in the Pension Fund constituted a security within the meaning of § [2(a)(1)] of the Securities Act, and § 3(a)(10) of the Securities Exchange Act, because the plan created an "investment contract" as that term had been interpreted in SEC v. W.J. Howey Co., 328 U.S. 293 (1946). * * *

* * * [T]he Court of Appeals for the Seventh Circuit affirmed. * * *

II

* * *

To determine whether a particular financial relationship constitutes an investment contract, "[t]he test is whether the scheme involves an investment of money in a common enterprise with profits to come solely from the efforts of others." *Howey,* 328 U.S., at 301. This test is to be applied in light of "the substance—the economic realities of the transaction—rather than the names that may have been employed by the parties." United Housing Foundation, Inc. v. Forman, 421 U.S. 837, 851–852 (1975). Looking separately at each element of the *Howey* test, it is apparent that an employee's participation in a noncontributory, compulsory pension plan such as the Teamsters' does not comport with the commonly held understanding of an investment contract.

A.   Investment of Money

An employee who participates in a noncontributory, compulsory pension plan by definition makes no payment into the pension fund. He only accepts employment, one of the conditions of which is eligibility for a possible benefit on retirement. Respondent contends, however, that he has "invested" in the Pension Fund by permitting part of his compensation from his employer to take the form of a deferred pension benefit. By allowing his employer to pay money into the Fund, and by contributing his labor to his employer in return for these payments, respondent asserts he has made the kind of investment which the Securities Acts were intended to regulate.

In order to determine whether respondent invested in the Fund by accepting and remaining in covered employment, it is necessary to look at the entire transaction through which he obtained a chance to receive pension benefits. In every decision of this Court recognizing the presence of a "security" under the Securities Acts, the person found to have been an investor chose to give up a specific consideration in return for a separable financial interest with the characteristics of a security. * * * in every case the purchaser gave up some tangible and definable consideration in return for an interest that had substantially the characteristics of a security.

In a pension plan such as this one, by contrast, the purported investment is a relatively insignificant part of an employee's total and indivisible compensation package. No portion of an employee's compensation other than the potential pension benefits has any of the characteristics of a security, yet these noninvestment interests cannot be segregated from the possible pension benefits. Only in the most abstract sense may it be said that an employee "exchanges" some portion of his labor in return for these possible benefits. He surrenders his labor as a whole, and in return receives a compensation package that is substantially devoid of aspects resembling a security. His decision to accept and retain covered employment may have only an attenuated relationship, if any, to perceived investment possibilities of a future pension. Looking at the economic realities, it seems clear that an employee is selling his labor primarily to obtain a livelihood, not making an investment.

Respondent also argues that employer contributions on his behalf constituted his investment into the Fund. But it is inaccurate to describe these payments as having been "on behalf" of any employee. The trust agreement used employee man-weeks as a convenient way to measure an employer's overall obligation to the Fund, not as a means of measuring the employer's obligation to any particular employee. Indeed, there was no fixed relationship between contributions to the Fund and an employee's potential benefits. A pension plan with "defined benefits," such as the Local's, does not tie a qualifying employee's benefits to the time he has worked. One who has engaged in covered employment for 20 years will receive the same benefits as a person who has worked for 40, even though the latter has worked twice as long and induced a substantially larger employer contribution. Again, it ignores the economic realities to equate employer contributions with an investment by the employee.

B. Expectation of Profits From a Common Enterprise

As we observed in *Forman,* the "touchstone" of the *Howey* test "is the presence of an investment in a common venture premised on a reasonable expectation of profits to be derived from the entrepreneurial or managerial efforts of others." 421 U.S., at 852. The Court of Appeals believed that Daniel's expectation of profit derived from the Fund's successful management and investment of its assets. To the extent pension benefits exceeded employer contributions and depended on earnings from the assets, it was thought they contained a profit element. The Fund's trustees provided the managerial efforts which produced this profit element.

As in other parts of its analysis, the court below found an expectation of profit in the pension plan only by focusing on one of its less important aspects to the exclusion of its more significant elements. It is true that the Fund, like other holders of large assets, depends to some extent on earnings from its assets. In the case of a pension fund, however, a far larger portion of its income comes from employer contributions, a source in no way dependent on the efforts of the Fund's managers. The Local 705 Fund, for example, earned a total of $31 million through investment of its assets between February 1955 and January 1977. During this same period employer contributions totaled $153 million. Not only does the greater share of a pension plan's income ordinarily come from new contributions, but unlike most entrepreneurs who manage other people's money, a plan usually can count on increased employer contributions, over which the plan itself has no control, to cover shortfalls in earnings.

The importance of asset earnings in relation to the other benefits received from employment is diminished further by the fact that where a plan has substantial preconditions to vesting, the principal barrier to an individual employee's realization of pension benefits is not the financial health of the fund. Rather, it is his own ability to meet the fund's eligibility requirements. Thus, even if it were proper to describe the benefits as a "profit" returned on some hypothetical investment by the employee, this profit would depend primarily on the employee's efforts to meet the vesting requirements, rather than the fund's investment success. When viewed in light of the total compensation package an employee must receive in order to be eligible for pension benefits, it becomes clear that the possibility of participating in a plan's asset earnings "is far too speculative and insubstantial to bring the entire transaction within the Securities Acts," *Forman,* 421 U.S., at 856.

* * *

V

We hold that the Securities Acts do not apply to a noncontributory, compulsory pension plan. * * *

* * *

As can be seen from reading *Forman* and *Daniel,* "investment of money" is a tricky concept. The "of money" element is easily disposed of, since it is clear that "money" in this context is simply shorthand for "something of value." (This is not to say, however, that this clarity is not sometimes overlooked by defendants' counsel. For instance, in SEC v. Shavers, the argument that bitcoins were not "money" because they were not legal tender was made, though easily rejected.[2])

"Investment" is another story. The word clearly denotes the laying out of something of value in the hope of future return. But this does not necessarily mean that, for there to be an "investment" in some sense of the word, the return must be financial. It could be any return the investor hopes for. The Supreme Court, in fact, used the term in this general sense in *Forman* when it said that the "investors were attracted solely by the prospect of acquiring a place to live, and not by financial returns on their investments."

In the course of its discussion in *Daniel* of the "investment of money" element of the *Howey* test, the Court found that the employees made no investment, saying that "it seems clear that an employee is selling his labor primarily to obtain a livelihood, not making an investment." Regrettably, the opinion does not address the question of whether, for an investment to exist, the person putting out money must look forward to receiving income or a *financial* gain in return. The Court noted, however, that in all previous cases in which it had found a security to exist, "the person found to have been an investor chose to give up a specific consideration in return for a separable financial interest with the characteristics of a security."

In the usual situation, the "investment of money" and the "expectation of profits" elements of the *Howey* test are so interrelated that they seem almost to be two focuses of essentially the same test. This is not, however, always true. Because the Teamster union members did not contribute to the pension fund established for their benefit, *Daniel* presented one of the rare instances in which the Court could have found there to have been an expectation of profits, but no investment, on the part of the purported security holders. But, of course, in *Daniel,* as in *Forman,* the Court declined to find an expectation of profits because it found the possibility of profits—if there were any—to be "far too

---

[2]   2014 WL 12622292 (E.D.Tex. Aug. 26, 2014).

speculative and insubstantial to bring the entire transaction within the Securities Acts."

The following case represents the Supreme Court's latest word on the "expectation of profit" leg of the *Howey* test.

SEC v. Edwards

Supreme Court of the United States, 2004.
540 U.S. 389.

■ JUSTICE O'CONNOR delivered the opinion of the Court.

"Opportunity doesn't always knock . . . sometimes it rings." * * * (ETS Payphones promotional brochure). And sometimes it hangs up. So it did for the 10,000 people who invested a total of $300 million in the payphone sale-and-leaseback arrangements touted by respondent under that slogan. The Securities and Exchange Commission (SEC) argues that the arrangements were investment contracts, and thus were subject to regulation under the federal securities laws. In this case, we must decide whether a moneymaking scheme is excluded from the term "investment contract" simply because the scheme offered a contractual entitlement to a fixed, rather than a variable, return.

I

Respondent Charles Edwards was the chairman, chief executive officer, and sole shareholder of ETS Payphones, Inc. (ETS). ETS, acting partly through a subsidiary also controlled by respondent, sold payphones to the public via independent distributors. The payphones were offered packaged with a site lease, a 5-year leaseback and management agreement, and a buyback agreement. All but a tiny fraction of purchasers chose this package, although other management options were offered. The purchase price for the payphone packages was approximately $7,000. Under the leaseback and management agreement, purchasers received $82 per month, a 14% annual return. Purchasers were not involved in the day-to-day operation of the payphones they owned. ETS selected the site for the phone, installed the equipment, arranged for connection and long-distance service, collected coin revenues, and maintained and repaired the phones. Under the buyback agreement, ETS promised to refund the full purchase price of the package at the end of the lease or within 180 days of a purchaser's request.

Because the Court of Appeals ordered the complaint dismissed, we treat the case as we would an appeal from a successful motion to dismiss and accept as true the allegations in the complaint. * * * .

In its marketing materials and on its website, ETS trumpeted the "incomparable pay phone" as "an exciting business opportunity," in which recent deregulation had "open[ed] the door for profits for individual pay phone owners and operators." According to ETS, "[v]ery few business opportunities can offer the potential for ongoing revenue generation that is available in today's pay telephone industry." * * * .

The payphones did not generate enough revenue for ETS to make the payments required by the leaseback agreements, so the company depended on funds from new investors to meet its obligations. In September 2000, ETS filed for bankruptcy protection. The SEC brought this civil enforcement action the same month. It alleged that respondent and ETS had violated the registration requirements of §§ 5(a) and (c) of the Securities Act of 1933, * * * the antifraud provisions of both § 17(a) of the Securities Act of 1933, * * * and § 10(b) of the Securities Exchange Act of 1934, * * * and Rule 10b–5 thereunder * * * . The District Court concluded that the payphone sale-and-leaseback arrangement was an investment contract within the meaning of, and therefore was subject to, the federal securities laws. * * * . The [Eleventh Circuit] Court of Appeals reversed. * * * . It held that respondent's scheme was not an investment contract, on two grounds. First, it read this Court's opinions to require that an investment contract offer either capital appreciation or a participation in the earnings of the enterprise, and thus to exclude schemes, such as respondent's, offering a fixed rate of return. * * * . Second, it held that our opinions' requirement that the return on the investment be "derived solely from the efforts of others" was not satisfied when the purchasers had a contractual entitlement to the return. * * * . We conclude that it erred on both grounds.

II

"Congress' purpose" in enacting the securities laws was to regulate *investments*, in whatever form they are made and by whatever name they are called." Reves v. Ernst & Young, 494 U.S. 56, 61 * * * (1990). To that end, it enacted a broad definition of "security," sufficient "to encompass virtually any instrument that might be sold as an investment." *Ibid.* Section 2(a)(1) of the 1933 Act, * * * and § 3(a)(10) of the 1934 Act, * * * in slightly different formulations which we have treated as essentially identical in meaning, * * * define "security" to include "any note, stock, treasury stock, security future, bond, debenture, * * * investment contract, * * * [or any] instrument commonly known as a 'security'." "Investment contract" is not itself defined.

The test for whether a particular scheme is an investment contract was established in our decision in SEC v. W.J. Howey Co., 328 U.S. 293 * * * (1946). We look to "whether the scheme involves an investment of money in a common enterprise with profits to come solely from the efforts of others." *Id.* * * * at 301 * * * . This definition "embodies a flexible rather than a static principle, one that is capable of adaptation to meet the countless and variable schemes devised by those who seek the use of the money of others on the promise of profits." *Id.* * * * at 299 * * * .

In reaching that result, we first observed that when Congress included "investment contract" in the definition of security, it "was using a term the meaning of which had been crystallized" by the state courts' interpretation of their "'blue sky'" laws. *Id.* * * * at 298 * * * . (Those laws were the precursors to federal securities regulation and were so named, it seems, because they were "aimed at promoters who 'would sell building lots in the blue sky in fee simple.'" 1 L. Loss & J. Seligman, Securities Regulation 36, 31–43 (3d ed. 1998) (quoting Mulvey, Blue Sky Law, 36 Can. L. Times 37 (1916)).) The state courts had defined an investment contract as "a contract or scheme for 'the placing of capital or laying out of money in a way intended to secure income or profit from its employment,'" and had "uniformly applied" that definition to "a variety of situations where individuals were led to invest money in a common enterprise with the expectation that they would earn a profit solely through the efforts of the promoter or [a third party]." *Howey, supra,* * * * at 298 * * * . Thus, when we held that "profits" must "come solely from the efforts of others," we were speaking of the profits that investors seek on their investment, not the profits of the scheme in which they invest. We used "profits" in the sense of income or return, to include, for example, dividends, other periodic payments, or the increased value of the investment.

There is no reason to distinguish between promises of fixed returns and promises of variable returns for purposes of the test, so understood. In both cases, the investing public is attracted by representations of investment income, as purchasers were in this case by ETS' invitation to "'watch the profits add up.'" * * * . Moreover, investments pitched as low-risk (such as those offering a "guaranteed" fixed return) are particularly attractive to individuals more vulnerable to investment fraud, including older and less sophisticated investors. See S. Rep. No. 102–261, Vol. 2, App., p. 326 (1992) (Staff Summary of Federal Trade Commission Activities Affecting Older Consumers). Under the reading respondent advances, unscrupulous marketers of investments could evade the securities laws by picking a rate of return to promise. We will not read into the securities laws a limitation not compelled by the language that would so undermine the laws' purposes.

Respondent protests that including investment schemes promising a fixed return among investment contracts conflicts with our precedent. We disagree. No distinction between fixed and variable returns was drawn in the blue sky law cases that the *Howey* Court used, in formulating the test, as its evidence of Congress' understanding of the term. *Howey, supra,* * * * at 298 * * * . Indeed, two of those cases involved an investment contract in which a fixed return was promised. * * *

None of our post-*Howey* decisions is to the contrary. In United Housing Foundation, Inc. v. Forman, 421 U.S. 837 * * * (1975), we considered whether "shares" in a nonprofit housing cooperative were investment contracts under the securities laws. We identified the "touchstone" of an investment contract as "the presence of an investment in a common venture premised on a reasonable expectation of profits to be derived from the entrepreneurial or managerial efforts of others," and then laid out two examples of investor interests that we had previously found to be "profits." * * * Those were "capital appreciation resulting from the development of the initial investment" and "participation in earnings resulting from the use of investors' funds." * * * We contrasted those examples, in which "the investor is 'attracted solely by the prospects of a return'" on the investment, with housing cooperative shares, regarding which the purchaser "is motivated by a desire to use or consume the item purchased." *Id.* at 852–853 * * *. Thus, *Forman* supports the commonsense understanding of "profits" in the *Howey* test as simply "financial returns on . . . investments." *Id.* at 853 * * *.

Concededly, *Forman*'s illustrative description of prior decisions on "profits" appears to have been mistaken for an exclusive list in a case considering the scope of a different term in the definition of a security, "note." See *Reves*, 494 U.S. 56 at 68 n. 4[3] * * *. But that was a misreading of *Forman*, and we will not bind ourselves unnecessarily to passing dictum that would frustrate Congress' intent to regulate all of the "countless and variable schemes devised by those who seek the use of the money of others on the promise of profits." *Howey*, 328 U.S. 293 at 299 * * *.

Given that respondent's position is supported neither by the purposes of the securities laws nor by our precedents, it is no surprise that the SEC has consistently taken the opposite position, and maintained that a promise of a fixed return does not preclude a scheme from being an investment contract. It has done so in formal adjudications * * * and in enforcement actions * * *.

The Eleventh Circuit's perfunctory alternative holding, that respondent's scheme falls outside the definition because purchasers had a contractual entitlement to a return, is incorrect and inconsistent with our precedent. We are considering investment *contracts*. The fact that investors have bargained for a return on their investment does not mean that the return is not also expected to come solely from the efforts of others. Any other conclusion would conflict with our holding that an investment contract was offered in *Howey* itself. 328 U.S. 293 at 295–296 * * * (service contract entitled investors to allocation of net profits).

We hold that an investment scheme promising a fixed rate of return can be an "investment contract" and thus a "security" subject to the federal securities laws. The judgment of the United States Court of Appeals for the Eleventh Circuit is reversed, and the case is remanded for further proceedings consistent with this opinion.

---

[3]   The *Reves* case, including the footnote the Edwards Court refers to (re-numbered as n. 16), is set out later in this chapter. [Eds.]

Given the foregoing authorities, one would have thought that the Commission Release excerpted below would not really have been necessary.

Securities Exchange Act Release No. 81207

Securities and Exchange Commission, July 25, 2017.

REPORT OF INVESTIGATION PURSUANT TO SECTION 21(a) OF THE SECURITIES EXCHANGE ACT OF 1934: THE DAO

I.   Introduction and Summary

The United States Securities and Exchange Commission's ("Commission") Division of Enforcement ("Division") has investigated whether The DAO, an unincorporated organization; Slock.it UG ("Slock.it"), a German corporation; Slock.it's co-founders; and intermediaries may have violated the federal securities laws. * * *

* * * The DAO is one example of a Decentralized Autonomous Organization, which is a term used to describe a "virtual" organization embodied in computer code and executed on a distributed ledger or blockchain. The DAO was created by Slock.it and Slock.it's co-founders, with the objective of operating as a for-profit entity that would create and hold a corpus of assets through the sale of DAO Tokens to investors, which assets would then be used to fund "projects." The holders of DAO Tokens stood to share in the anticipated earnings from these projects as a return on their investment in DAO Tokens. In addition, DAO Token holders could monetize their investments in DAO Tokens by re-selling DAO Tokens on a number of web-based platforms ("Platforms") that supported secondary trading in the DAO Tokens.

After DAO Tokens were sold, but before The DAO was able to commence funding projects, an attacker used a flaw in The DAO's code to steal approximately one-third of The DAO's assets. * * *

The investigation raised questions regarding the application of the U.S. federal securities laws to the offer and sale of DAO Tokens, including the threshold question whether DAO Tokens are securities. Based on the investigation, and under the facts presented, the Commission has determined that DAO Tokens are securities under the Securities Act of 1933 ("Securities Act") and the Securities Exchange Act of 1934 ("Exchange Act").

The Commission deems it appropriate and in the public interest to issue this report of investigation ("Report") pursuant to Section 21(a) of the Exchange Act to advise those who would use a Decentralized Autonomous Organization ("DAO Entity"), or other distributed ledger or blockchain-enabled means for capital raising, to take appropriate steps to ensure compliance with the U.S. federal securities laws. * * *

This Report reiterates these fundamental principles of the U.S. federal securities laws and describes their applicability to a new paradigm—virtual organizations or capital raising entities that use distributed ledger or blockchain technology to facilitate capital raising and/or investment and the related offer and sale of securities. The automation of certain functions through this technology, "smart contracts," or computer code, does not remove conduct from the purview of the U.S. federal securities laws. This Report also serves to stress the obligation to comply with the registration provisions of the federal securities laws with respect to products and platforms involving emerging technologies and new investor interfaces. * * *

---

b.   COMMON ENTERPRISE AND SOLELY FROM THE EFFORTS OF OTHERS

The Supreme Court has never spelled out the requirements of the common enterprise element of the *Howey* test. Two clear and disparate formulations have emerged, however. One is "vertical commonality," which focuses on the community of interest of an individual investor and the manager of the enterprise, and the other is "horizontal commonality," which concentrates on the interrelated interests of the various investors in a particular scheme. The vertical commonality formula has been succinctly stated in SEC v. Koscot Interplanetary, Inc., the case that follows.

SEC v. Koscot Interplanetary, Inc.

United States Court of Appeals, Fifth Circuit, 1974.
497 F.2d 473.

■ Before RIVES, GEWIN and RONEY, CIRCUIT JUDGES.

■ GEWIN, CIRCUIT JUDGE:

This appeal emanates from a district court order denying an injunction sought by the Securities & Exchange Commission (SEC) against Koscot Interplanetary, Inc., (Koscot) for allegedly violating the federal securities laws. Specifically, the SEC maintained that the pyramid promotion enterprise operated by Koscot was within the ambit of the term security, as employed by the Securities Act of 1933 and * * * that as such it had to be registered with the SEC pursuant to the '33 Act * * * . * * *

I

A.   *The Koscot Scheme*

The procedure followed by Koscot in the promotion of its enterprise can be synoptically chronicled. A subsidiary of Glenn W. Turner Enterprises, Koscot thrives by enticing prospective investors to participate in its enterprise, holding out as a lure the expectation of galactic profits. All too often, the beguiled investors are disappointed by paltry returns.

The vehicle for the lure is a multi-level network of independent distributors, purportedly engaged in the business of selling a line of cosmetics. At the lowest level is a "beauty advisor" whose income is derived solely from retail sales of Koscot products made available at a discount, customarily of 45%. Those desirous of ascending the ladder of the Koscot enterprise may also participate on a second level, that of supervisor or retail manager. For an investment of $1,000, a supervisor receives cosmetics at a greater discount from retail price, typically 55%, to be sold either directly to the public or to be held for wholesale distribution to the beauty advisors. In addition, a supervisor who introduces a prospect to the Koscot program with whom a sale is ultimately consummated receives $600 of the $1,000 paid to Koscot. The loftiest position in the multi-level scheme is that of distributor. An investment of $5,000 with Koscot entitles a distributor to purchase cosmetics at an even greater discount, typically 65%, for distribution to supervisors and retailers. Moreover, fruitful sponsorship of either a supervisor or distributor brings $600 or $3,000 respectively to the sponsor.

* * *

The modus operandi of Koscot and its investors is as follows. Investors solicit prospects to attend Opportunity Meetings at which the latter are introduced to the Koscot scheme. Significantly, the investor is admonished not to mention the details of the business before bringing the prospect to the meeting, a technique euphemistically denominated the "curiosity approach." * * * thus, in the initial stage, an investor's sole task is to attract individuals to the meeting.

Once a prospect's attendance at a meeting is secured, Koscot employees, frequently in conjunction with investors, undertake to apprise prospects of the "virtues" of enlisting in the Koscot plan. The meeting is conducted in conformity with scripts prepared by Koscot. Indeed, Koscot distributes a bulletin which states: " * * * this program is to be presented by the script. It is strongly recommended that you consider replacing any individual who does not present the program verbatim." The principal design of the meetings is to foster an illusion of affluence. Investors and Koscot employees are instructed to drive to meetings in expensive cars, preferably Cadillacs, to dress expensively, and to flaunt large amounts of money. It is intended that prospects will be galvanized into signing a contract by these ostentations displayed in the evangelical atmosphere of the meetings. Go-Tours, characterized by similar histrionics, are designed to achieve the same goal.

The final stage in the promotional scheme is the consummation of the sale. If a prospect capitulates at either an Opportunity Meeting or a Go-Tour, an investor will not be required to expend any additional effort. Less fortuitous investors whose prospects are not as quickly enticed to invest do have to devote additional effort to consummate a sale, the amount of which is contingent upon the degree of reluctance of the prospect.

* * *

A.   *The First Two Elements [of the Howey test]*

Since it cannot be disputed that purchasers of supervisorships and distributorships made an investment of money, our initial concern is whether the Koscot scheme functions as a common enterprise. As defined by the Ninth Circuit, "[a] common enterprise is one in which the fortunes of the investor are interwoven with and dependent upon the efforts and success of those seeking the investment or of third parties." SEC v. Glenn W. Turner Enterprises, Inc., [474 F.2d 476, 482 n. 7 (9th Cir.1973)]. The critical factor is not the similitude or coincidence of investor input, but rather the uniformity of impact of the promoter's efforts.

* * *

[T]he fact that an investor's return is independent of that of other investors in the scheme is not decisive. Rather, the requisite commonality is evidenced by the fact that the fortunes of all investors are inextricably tied to the efficacy of the Koscot meetings and guidelines on recruiting prospects and consummating a sale.

B.   *The Third Element—Solely from the Efforts of Others*

[T]he critical issue in this case is whether a literal or functional approach to the "solely from the efforts of others" test should be adopted, i.e., whether the exertion of some effort by an investor is inimical to the holding that a promotional scheme falls within the definition of an investment contract. * * *

1.   *The Legal Standard*

* * *

A literal application of the *Howey* test would frustrate the remedial purposes of the Act. As the Ninth Circuit noted in SEC v. Glenn W. Turner Enterprises, Inc., supra at 482, "[i]t would be easy to evade [the *Howey* test] by adding a requirement that the buyer contribute a modicum of effort." * * * [I]t would be anomalous to maintain that the Court in *Howey* intended to formulate the type of intractable rule which it had decried. The admitted salutary purposes of the Acts can only be safeguarded by a functional approach to the *Howey* test.

Moreover, a close reading of the language employed in *Howey* and the authority upon which the Court relied suggests that, contrary to the view of the district court, we need not feel compelled to follow the "solely from the efforts of others" test literally. Nowhere in the opinion does the Supreme Court characterize the nature of the "efforts" that would render a promotional scheme beyond the pale of the definition of an investment contract. Clearly the facts presented no issue of how to assess a scheme in which an investor performed mere perfunctory tasks. Indeed, just prior to concluding that the sales of units of citrus grove development, coupled with contracts for cultivating, marketing and remitting the net proceeds to investors constituted sales of investment contracts, the Court observed that "the promoters *manage, control* and *operate* the enterprise." 328 U.S. at 300 (emphasis added). One commentator has seized upon the italicized words in concluding that only schemes in which investors exercise managerial control are excluded from the definition of investment contracts. See Long, An Attempt to Return "Investment Contracts" to the Mainstream of Securities Regulation, 24 Okla.L.Rev. 135, 176 (1971).

* * *

* * * [W]e hold that the proper standard in determining whether a scheme constitutes an investment contract is that explicated by the Ninth Circuit in SEC v. Glenn W. Turner Enterprises, Inc., supra. In that case, the court announced that the critical inquiry is "whether the efforts made by those other than the investor are the undeniably significant ones, those essential managerial efforts which affect the failure or success of the enterprise."

* * *

2.   *Application of the Test to the Instant Facts*

Having concluded that the district court misperceived the controlling standard, it becomes incumbent upon us to determine whether Koscot's scheme falls within the standard adopted. * * *

Our task is greatly simplified by the Ninth Circuit's decision in SEC v. Glenn W. Turner Enterprises, Inc., supra. The promotional scheme confronting the Ninth Circuit is largely paralleled by that exposed before this court. Dare to be Great, (Dare) which like Koscot, is a subsidiary of Turner Enterprises, offered five plans [, called "Adventures,"] in its self-improvement program, three of which entitled an investor to earn money for coaxing additional prospects into the Dare fold. * * *

[As described by the Ninth Circuit,]

"* * * Dare's source of income is from selling the Adventures and the Plan. The purchaser is sold the idea that he will get a fixed part of the proceeds of the sales. In essence, to get that share, he invests three things: his money, his efforts to find prospects and bring them to the meetings, and whatever it costs him to create an illusion of his own affluence. He invests them in Dare's get-rich-quick scheme. What he buys is a share in the proceeds of the selling efforts of Dare. Those efforts are the *sine qua non* of the scheme; * * * those efforts are what produces the money which is to make him rich. In essence, it is the right to share in the proceeds of those efforts that he buys. In our view, the scheme is no less an investment contract merely because he contributes some effort as well as money to get into it."

We conclude that the facts in the instant case can be evaluated along similar lines.

The recruitment role played by investors in Koscot coincides with that played by investors in Dare to be Great. That investors in the latter did not participate in Adventure Meetings while they do in the Koscot scheme is insignificant. Since Koscot's Opportunity Meetings are run according to preordained script, the deviation from which would occasion disapprobation or perhaps exclusion from the meetings, the role of investors at these meetings can be characterized as little more than a perfunctory one. Nor does the fact that Koscot investors may have devoted more time than did Dare investors to closing sales transmute the essential congruity between the two schemes. The act of consummating a sale is essentially a ministerial not managerial one, one which does not alter the fact that the critical determinant of the success of the Koscot Enterprise lies with the luring effect of the opportunity meetings. * * * without the scenario created by the Opportunity Meetings and Go-Tours, an investor would invariably be powerless to realize any return on his investment.

III

We confine our holding to those schemes in which promoters retain immediate control over the essential managerial conduct of an enterprise and where the investor's realization of profits is inextricably tied to the success of the promotional scheme. Thus, we acknowledge that a conventional franchise arrangement, wherein the promoter exercises merely remote control over an enterprise and the investor operates largely unfettered by promoter mandates presents a different question than the one posed herein. * * *

* * *

Two years before *Koscot,* the Seventh Circuit had reached a different conclusion on the proper formulation of the common enterprise element of the *Howey* test. In Milnarik v. M–S Commodities, Inc.,[4] the court had to decide whether a discretionary commodity trading account with a broker involved a common enterprise. The court focused on the fact that the profitability of the plaintiffs' account was not influenced by the success or failure of other such accounts managed by the same broker. What existed, the court found, was simply an agency for hire. The broker's "various customers were represented by a common agent, but they were not joint participants in the same investment enterprise."

Five years later, the same court reexamined the question in Hirk v. Agri-Research Council, Inc.,[5] another case involving a discretionary futures trading account. By this time, *Glenn W. Turner* and *Koscot* had

---

[4]   457 F.2d 274 (7th Cir.1972).

[5]   561 F.2d 96 (7th Cir.1977).

been decided, as had SEC v. Continental Commodities Corp.,[6] a Fifth Circuit case involving discretionary commodity trading accounts. The court in *Continental Commodities* followed the vertical commonality approach of *Koscot* and expressly rejected *Milnarik's* horizontal commonality formulation. In *Hirk,* the Seventh Circuit took the opportunity both to discuss these other cases and to reject their common enterprise formulation. In doing so, it sharpened the horizontal commonality formulation of *Milnarik,* stating even more clearly than before that both multiple investors and a sharing or pooling of funds is required in the Seventh Circuit.

To complicate matters further, some courts have identified different versions of the vertical commonality formulation. One version, called strict vertical commonality, requires that the fortunes of the investor be linked to the *fortunes* of the promoter or some third party. The other version, called broad vertical commonality, requires only that the fortunes of the investor be linked to the *efforts* of the promoter or a third party. The Second Circuit, in Revak v. SEC Realty Corp.,[7] firmly rejected broad vertical commonality, but district courts within the Circuit have ruled that either horizontal commonality or strict vertical commonality will suffice.

The "solely from the efforts of others" element of the *Howey* test is perhaps the most interesting. One question, of course, has been whether or not to apply the test literally. In the usual case, the answer to this question does not matter, since any scheme that is likely to satisfy the other parts of the test typically involves entirely passive investors. *Koscot* and *Glenn W. Turner* offered interesting exceptions. One might note that the focus in these cases on managerial efforts as the "undeniably significant ones" is interesting, since the skills that seemed most important in these cases were technical rather than managerial—the ability to run an efficient meeting and, since those running the meetings followed detailed, rigid scripts, the knowledge of how to set one up.

The post-*Koscot* history of the "solely" element is confused. In *Forman,* the Supreme Court reaffirmed the *Howey* test and also said that its "touchstone is the presence of an investment in a common venture premised on a reasonable expectation of profits to be derived from the entrepreneurial or managerial efforts of others." This seemed clearly to put the Court's imprimatur on the *Glenn W. Turner-Koscot* interpretation of "solely." But in a curious footnote on the same page, the Court indicated that it "express[ed] no view" on the holding of *Glenn W. Turner* that "solely" should be read flexibly rather than literally. Perhaps all the Court meant here was that its *Forman* holding did not reach this question, but it is impossible to be sure. What is known is that three years later, in *Daniel,* the Court repeated the "touchstone" formulation from *Forman* and then proceeded briefly to discuss the managerial efforts of

---

[6]   497 F.2d 516 (5th Cir.1974).

[7]   18 F.3d 81 (2d Cir.1994).

the pension fund's trustees. But as in *Forman,* the "solely" element was not in question in *Daniel* because the purported investors were all clearly passive. Thus, the Supreme Court has never confronted the issue presented in *Glenn W. Turner* and *Koscot.* Perhaps this, more than anything else, accounts for the confusion in its opinions.

Lower courts, however, have repeatedly confronted the "solely" element. It has been an issue in many cases involving general partnerships and limited partnerships, as well as in more esoteric situations.

SEC v. Life Partners, Incorporated

United States Court of Appeals, D.C. Circuit, 1996.
102 F.3d 587.

[Life Partners, Inc. is a participant in the "viatical settlement" industry. This means that it markets, through a network of licensees, fractional interests in insurance policies on the lives of the terminally ill. It is responsible for screening the insureds and for collecting and disbursing insurance proceeds. The District of Columbia Circuit reversed and remanded a district court holding that the interests offered were securities. A petition for rehearing was denied *per curiam.*]

■ Statement of CIRCUIT JUDGE GINSBURG, joined by CIRCUIT JUDGE HENDERSON:

First, the Commission says that the Court [in its earlier ruling on this case] declared an "artificial bright-line" rule that an investment is not a security "if the efforts of promoters or others on which investors rely occur just before, rather than after, the investors commit their money." Indeed, according to the Commission, the Court holds that all pre-purchase efforts are "irrelevant." While that position may have been the one originally advanced by Life Partners, Inc., it is not the one taken by the Court.

In order to qualify as a security, an investment must have been made in an enterprise the profits of which are derived from the efforts of others. SEC v. W.J. Howey. * * * to the extent that we established any rule [in the earlier ruling on this case] in applying the "efforts of others" test, we held only "that [1] pre-purchase services cannot by themselves suffice to make the profits of an investment arise predominantly from the efforts of others, and that [2] ministerial functions should receive a good deal less weight than entrepreneurial activities." * * * we examined both "LPI's pre-purchase services as a finder-promoter and its largely ministerial post-purchase services," and we concluded that the two in combination were not enough to establish that the investors' profits flow predominantly from the efforts of others. * * * nothing in our application of the Howey test can reasonably be construed to suggest that pre-purchase efforts are "irrelevant."

Absent even one entrepreneurial post-purchase service—and the SEC could identify none—there simply is no on-going common enterprise involved in owning an interest in an insurance contract from which the profit depends entirely upon the mortality of the insured. * * * indeed, the Commission concedes in its petition that "in other cases where pre-purchase efforts were considered, those courts also found significant post-purchase efforts." See, *e.g.,* Rodriguez v. Banco Central Corp., 990 F.2d 7, 10 (1st Cir.1993) (interest in undeveloped land not security without post-purchase managerial efforts by promoter); Noa v. Key Futures, Inc., 638 F.2d 77, 79–80 (9th Cir.1980) (same with respect to silver bars); McCown v. Heidler, 527 F.2d 204, 211 (10th Cir.1975) (interest in undeveloped land would not have been security but for "substantial improvements pledged by" promoters).

The second matter worthy of comment is the totally unsubstantiated assertion in the Commission's petition for rehearing that the Court has "placed in question the applicability of the federal securities laws to * * * certain asset-backed securities," including mortgages and securitized interests in commercial real estate, which account for a vast amount of investment capital. Having leveled this astonishing charge, however, the Commission does not favor us with a single example of a formerly regulated instrument that will now escape SEC scrutiny. In fact, the Commission admits that "many asset-backed securities may be encompassed under other definitional terms in the securities laws * * * and some might have sufficient post-purchase efforts" to make LPI distinguishable.

In contrast to an LPI viatical settlement, a mortgage pool must be managed on a continuing basis. Among the post-purchase services that should easily meet the "efforts of others" test as we have interpreted it are: collecting late mortgage payments, initiating foreclosures, structuring and monitoring work-outs, negotiating concessions in order to avoid refinancing, and arranging for a secondary market. In the case of commercial real estate, the property must be kept in compliance with an array of tax, safety, and environmental laws; it must be advertised, leased, re-leased, improved, repaired, cleaned, heated, and perhaps resold. It seems fair to say, therefore, that the Commission's concern with the effect of this decision is, at the least, overblown.

* * *

———————

The Eleventh Circuit has rejected the D.C. Circuit's approach in *Life Partners*.[8]

Limited liability companies (like general partnerships) present interesting questions having to do with the amount of efforts contractually permitted or required, as opposed to the amount of efforts

———————

[8]   SEC v. Mutual Benefits Corp., 408 F.3d 737 (11th Cir. 2005).

realistically expected, of investors. The following is a recent case on the subject.

United States v. Leonard

United States Court of Appeals, Second Circuit, 2008.
529 F.3d 83.

■ KATZMANN, CIRCUIT JUDGE.

* * *

Appellants Dickau and Silverstein were two of twenty-five individuals indicted for criminal fraud for their role in marketing investment interests in film companies. Following a jury trial, they were each convicted of securities fraud and conspiracy to commit securities and mail fraud. On appeal, they challenge their convictions, claiming, *inter alia,* that insufficient evidence supported the determination that the interests at issue were securities * * * . We find [this objection] to the conviction to be without merit. * * * .

BACKGROUND

Appellants Paul C. Dickau and Nanci Silverstein each operated an independent sales office ("ISO") selling interests in companies formed to finance the production and distribution of motion pictures. Dickau's ISO sold interests in Little Giant. LLC, an entity created to produce the film *Carlo's Wake*. Both appellants' ISOs sold interests in Heritage Film Group, LLC, which was established to produce the film *The Amati Girls*. As their names suggest, Little Giant and Heritage are limited liability companies ("LLCs"), and the interests in the companies took the form of investment "units," priced at $10,000 each.

* * *

The government charged Dickau with four counts: one count of conspiracy to commit securities and mail fraud in relation to each of Little Giant and Heritage, and one count of securities fraud in relation to each of Little Giant and Heritage. The government charged Silverstein with one conspiracy count and one fraud count in relation to Heritage. All counts centered around the failure to disclose accurately the sales commission that the ISOs would be taking on the investment units. Following a trial in the Eastern District of New York, the jury returned a verdict of guilty on all counts against Dickau and Silverstein. Judge Wexler sentenced Dickau to forty-three months' imprisonment and ordered him to pay $499,989.64 in restitution. Judge Wexler sentenced Silverstein to six months' imprisonment, ordering her to pay $14,490 in restitution.

DISCUSSION

* * *

I.   Whether Sufficient Evidence Supported the Finding that the Units Were Securities

Although federal statutes enumerate many different instruments that fit the definition of security, the parties agree that the only category that potentially applies to this case is "investment contract." In the seminal case, SEC v. W.J. Howey Co., 328 U.S. 293 (1946), the Supreme Court provided the following definition of investment contract:

> an investment contract for purposes of the Securities Act means a contract, transaction or scheme whereby a person invests his money in a common enterprise and is led to expect profits solely from the efforts of the promoter or a third party, it being immaterial whether the shares in the enterprise are evidenced by formal certificates or by nominal interests in the physical assets employed in the enterprise.

Id. at 298–99. Appellants suggest that the Little Giant and Heritage units cannot constitute securities because investors never expected profits "solely from the efforts" of the promoters or others.

Following the Ninth Circuit's lead, *see* SEC v. Glenn W. Turner Enterprises, 474 F.2d 476, 482 (9th Cir. 1973), we have held that the word "solely" should not be construed as a literal limitation; rather, we "consider whether, under all the circumstances, the scheme was being promoted primarily as an investment or as a means whereby participants could pool their own activities, their money and the promoter's contribution in a meaningful way." SEC v. Aqua-Sonic Prods. Corp., 687 F.2d 577, 582 (2d Cir. 1982). Thus, in *Aqua-Sonic* we distinguished between companies that seek the "passive investor" and situations where there is a "reasonable expectation . . . of significant investor control." *Id.* at 585. It is the passive investor "for whose benefit the securities laws were enacted"; where there is a reasonable expectation of significant investor control, "the protection of the 1933 and 1934 Acts would be unnecessary." Id.

Our consideration of whether the investors in Little Giant and Heritage viewed the units primarily as a passive investment is complicated by the fact that Little Giant and Heritage were each structured as an LLC—a relatively new, hybrid vehicle that combines elements of the traditional corporation with elements of the general partnership while retaining flexibility for federal tax purposes. * * * although "common stock is the quintessence of a security," Reves v. Ernst & Young, 494 U.S. 56, 62 (1990) (citing Landreth Timber Co. v. Landreth, 471 U.S. 681, 693 (1985)), and "[n]ormally, a general partnership interest is not considered a 'security,'" Odom v. Slavik, 703 F.2d 212, 215 (6th Cir. 1983), because of the sheer diversity of LLCs, membership interests therein resist categorical classification. Thus, an interest in an LLC is the sort of instrument that requires "case-by-case analysis" into the "economic realities" of the underlying transaction, Reves, 494 U.S. at 62.

One of the original promoters of Little Giant and Heritage, Russell Finnegan, testified at trial that the LLCs were structured so as to minimize the possibility that the investment units would constitute securities—"to get into . . . the gray areas of the securities law." Indeed, were we to confine ourselves to a review of the organizational documents, we would likely conclude that the interests in Little Giant and Heritage could not constitute securities because the documents would lead us to believe that members were expected to play an active role in the management of the companies. For example, the sheet titled "Summary of Business Opportunity: Heritage Film Group, LLC" explains:

> Each Member is required to participate in the management of the Company retaining one (1) vote for each Unit acquired. Each important decision relating to the business of the Company must be submitted to a vote of the Members.

> The purchase of interests in the Company is not a passive investment. While specific knowledge and expertise in the day to day operation of a film producing and distributing company is not required, Members should have such knowledge and experience in general business, investment and/or financial affairs as to intelligently exercise their management and voting rights. . . . Further, each Member is required to participate in the management of the Company by serving on one or more committees established by the Members.

The summary further states that a manager may be chosen to perform certain "ministerial functions," such as keeping books and records, keeping the members informed, and circulating ballots to members, but the members retain the right to replace the manager and appoint his successor upon majority vote. Likewise, the operating agreement for Heritage provides that the "Company shall be managed by the Members. . . . [E]ach Member shall have the right to act for and bind the Company in the ordinary course of its business." * * *

In actuality, however, the Little Giant and Heritage members played an extremely passive role in the management and operation of the companies. At trial, members testified that they voted, at most, "a couple of times." Although the organizational documents provided for the formation of a number of committees, only two committees were formed for each of Heritage and Little Giant—a financial committee and a management committee. Of the 250–300 investors in Little Giant, five served on the management committee and seven served on the financial committee. Of the 350–400 investors in Heritage, ten served on the management committee and seven served on the financial committee. Thus, the vast majority of investors in both companies did not actively participate in the venture, exercising almost no control.

Record evidence allowed the jury to conclude that—notwithstanding the language in the organizational documents suggesting otherwise—from the start there could be no "reasonable expectation" of investor control, *Aqua-Sonic Prods. Corp.,* 687 F.2d at 585. * * *

For one, under the organizational documents, the members' managerial rights and obligations did not accrue until the LLCs were "fully organized." As promoter James Alex testified, so-called "interim managers" initially held legal control rights, and they decided almost every significant issue prior to the completion of fundraising: "The script, the director, the cast, the crew, scoring of it, editing. The entire picture was pretty well preproduced. . . . " Thus, the jury could reasonably have found the managerial rights contained in the organizational documents were hollow and illusory.

The jury was also entitled to consider the fact that the members appear not to have negotiated any terms of the LLC agreements. Rather, they were presented with the subscription agreements on a take-it-or-leave-it basis. That they played no role in shaping the organizational agreements themselves raises doubts as to whether the members were expected to have significant control over the enterprise.

Moreover, the members had no particular experience in film or entertainment and therefore would have had difficulty exercising their formal right to take over management of the companies after they were fully organized. Cf. Aqua-Sonic Prods. Corp., 687 F.2d at 583–84 (noting that investors had no experience in selling dental products and therefore would be unlikely to feel capable of undertaking distribution themselves); Bailey v. J.W.K. Props., Inc., 904 F.2d 918, 923–24 (4th Cir. 1990) (finding that investors had "little to no control over the ultimate success or failure" of their cattle breeding investments where they had the contractual authority to direct the breeding but no expertise in selecting embryos or cross-breeding). And their number and geographic dispersion left investors particularly dependent on centralized management. We echo the Fifth Circuit in finding that investors may be so lacking in requisite expertise, so numerous, or so dispersed that they become utterly dependent on centralized management, counteracting a legal right of control. See Williamson v. Tucker, 645 F.2d 404, 423–24 (5th Cir. 1981). * * *

* * *

III. EVIDENCE OF INDEBTEDNESS

"Investment contract" is not the only broad term used in Section 2(a)(1). It has, however, consumed a lion's share of attention by litigants. Other broad terms, such as "evidence of indebtedness," may be sleeping giants.

The first case below involves the question of what kind of document constitutes an "evidence of indebtedness," as that term is used in a definition of "securities." Interestingly, the definition in this case is found not in the securities laws, but in the chapter of the United States Code dealing with crimes relating to stolen property. As will be seen, this definition is quite like Securities Act Section 2(a)(1). The second case below is a decision by the Commission on the question of whether a particular series of transactions constituted the sale of securities. The Commission does not indicate what type of security is involved in the case, but "evidence of indebtedness" seems most likely. In the third case, a district court equates "evidence of indebtedness" and "note."

United States v. Jones

United States Court of Appeals, Fifth Circuit, 1971.
450 F.2d 523.

■ Before TUTTLE, INGRAHAM and RONEY, CIRCUIT JUDGES.

■ TUTTLE, CIRCUIT JUDGE:

This appeal raises the narrow question whether an airline ticket is a "security" within the meaning of 18 U.S.C. § 2311. Appellant Jones, who caused forged airline tickets to be transported in interstate commerce, was convicted of violating 18 U.S.C. § 2314 which proscribes the interstate carriage of "any falsely made, forged, altered, or counterfeited securities." We reverse.

The case was tried by the court without a jury on stipulated facts. Jones, an employee of Braniff International Airlines, obtained through an acquaintance two blank airline tickets belonging to Braniff. Jones filled out and validated these tickets for use by third parties, although he had not been authorized by Braniff to do so. Subsequently the tickets were used by the third parties for roundtrip passage between San Antonio, Texas and Acapulco, Mexico.

As a matter of general business practice Braniff permits the redemption of its tickets for cash or for another ticket of equal value, should the ticket holder choose to cancel his reservation. In addition, although the tickets state that they are not transferable, Braniff does not ordinarily check the identification of its passengers, but will simply admit on board the holder of its ticket without requiring proof of ownership.

The District Court found appellant guilty * * *. Appellant here argues that airline tickets are not securities and that therefore he cannot be convicted of this particular crime. We agree.

The term "securities", as used in § 2314, is defined by 18 U.S.C. § 2311 to include:

"* * * any note, stock certificate, bond, debenture, check, draft, warrant, traveler's check, letter of credit, warehouse receipt, negotiable bill of lading, *evidence of indebtedness,* certificate of interest or participation in any profit-sharing agreement, collateral-trust certificate, preorganization certificate or subscription, transferable share, investment contract, voting-trust certificate; certificate of interest in property, tangible or intangible; instrument or document or writing evidencing ownership of goods, wares, and merchandise, or transferring or assigning any right, title, or interest in or to goods, wares, and merchandise; or, in general, any instrument commonly known as a "security", or any certificate of interest or participation in, temporary or interim certificate for, receipt for, warrant, or right to subscribe to or purchase any of the foregoing, or any forged, counterfeited, or spurious representation of any of the foregoing; * * * ." (Emphasis added.)

The government argues that since a Braniff airline ticket is redeemable for cash, it is an "evidence of indebtedness" and, thus, a security within the meaning of the statute. However, the term "evidence of indebtedness" must be construed in the context of the entire definition. It is to be noted that "Securities" is defined with great particularity and that except for "evidence of indebtedness" each of the other documents listed in Section 2311 has a specific and commercially-cognizable referent. We therefore think it doubtful that Congress intended "evidence of indebtedness" to be viewed as a catchall rubric embracing any and all writings, not otherwise specifically listed, which represent an obligation on the part of the writer to do something for the holder.

* * *

The term "evidence of indebtedness" embraces only such documents as promissory notes which on their face establish a primary obligation to pay the holders thereof a sum of money. Since airline tickets do not establish a primary obligation to pay money, they are not evidences of indebtedness. * * *

* * *

In re Tucker Corp.

Securities and Exchange Commission, 1947.
26 S.E.C. 249.

[Tucker Corporation filed a registration statement in May 1947 covering a proposed offering of common stock. A few days later the Commission began a private examination under Section 8(e) of the Securities Act, leading in June 1947 to stop order proceedings under Section 8(d).]

* * * [W]e have considered [the amendments filed to correct deficiencies in the registration statement], and since they appear to have sufficiently corrected the matters in dispute, we have determined to dismiss the stop order proceedings. In doing so, however, we deem it imperative in the public interest and for the protection of investors to comment on certain facts developed in these proceedings.

* * *

SALE OF FRANCHISES

In August of 1946, Tucker Corporation began to sell automobile franchises to prospective distributors and dealers under the terms of which for a certain allotment of cars a $25 deposit per car was required to be paid to the corporation with a promise of repayment at a future date. The major part of these sales was made upon an assurance that the funds would be held in escrow until $15,000,000 was received at which time they would be available for general corporate purposes. A total of $372,400 was received by the corporation up to December of 1946 from the sale of these franchises. * * *

Since these franchise agreements provided for the repayment of deposits received they were "securities" within the meaning of Section [2(a)(1)] of the Securities Act and as such required registration with this Commission under the provisions of that Act. Counsel for the corporation were so advised by the staff of the Commission as early as August 6, 1946. Tucker had similar advice from the law firm of Holthusen and Pinkham as early as April 1946. The sale of these agreements without an effective registration statement constituted a violation of Section 5 of the Securities Act. * * *

* * *

Procter & Gamble Company v. Bankers Trust Company and BT Securities Corporation

United States District Court, Sourthern District of Ohio, Western Division, 1996.
925 F.Supp. 1270.

■ FEIKENS, DISTRICT JUDGE, sitting by Designation.

* * *

This case involves two interest rate swap agreements. A swap is an agreement between two parties ("counterparties") to exchange cash flows over a period of time. Generally, the purpose of an interest rate swap is to protect a party from interest rate fluctuations. The simplest form of swap, a "plain vanilla" interest-rate swap, involves one counterparty paying a fixed rate of interest, while the other counterparty assumes a floating interest rate based on the amount of the principal of the underlying debt. This is called the "notional" amount of the swap, and this amount does not change hands; only the interest payments are exchanged.

In more complex interest rate swaps, such as those involved in this case, the floating rate may derive its value from any number of different securities, rates or indexes. In each instance, however, the counterparty with the floating rate obligation enters into a transaction whose precise value is unknown and is based upon activities in the market over which the counterparty has no control. How the swap plays out depends on how market factors change.

* * *

[Plaintiff Procter & Gamble Company ("P & G")] argues that if the swaps are not notes, they are evidence of indebtedness because they contain bilateral promises to pay money and they evidence debts between the parties. It argues that the counterparties promised to pay a debt, which consists of future obligations to pay interest on the notional amounts. Indeed, [defendant] now claims that it is owed millions of dollars on the swaps. P & G points out that the phrase "evidence of indebtedness" in the statute must have a meaning other than that given to a "note" so that the words "evidence of indebtedness" are not redundant. Thus, it argues, without citation to authority, that if the swaps are not notes, then they should be construed as an evidence of indebtedness "either because they may contain terms and conditions well beyond the typical terms of a note and beyond an ordinary investor's ability to understand, or because the debt obligation simply does not possess the physical characteristics of a note."

The test whether an instrument is within the category of "evidence of indebtedness" is essentially the same as whether an instrument is a note. Holloway v. Peat, Marwick, Mitchell & Co., 879 F.2d 772, 777 (10th Cir.1989), judgment vacated on other grounds *sub nom.* Peat Marwick Main Co. v. Holloway, 494 U.S. 1014, 108 L. Ed. 2d 490, 110 S. Ct. 1314 (1990), reaff'd on remand, 900 F.2d 1485 (10th Cir.1990), *cert. den.* 498 U.S. 958 (1990) (passbook savings certificates and thrift certificates were analyzed under the "note" or "evidence of indebtedness" categories, as they represented a promise to repay the principal amount, plus accrued interest); In re Tucker Freight Lines, Inc., 789 F. Supp. 884, 885 (W.D.Mich.1991) (The Court's "method [in Reves v. Ernst and Young[9]] seems applicable to all debt instruments, including evidences of indebtedness.").

I do not accept P & G's definition of "evidence of indebtedness" in large part because that definition omits an essential element of debt instruments—the payment or repayment of principal. Swap agreements do not involve the payment of principal; the notional amount never changes hands.

* * *

———————

Section 2A of the '33 Act, added in 2000, is intended to exclude from the Act's coverage individually negotiated swap transactions involving

———————————————

[9]   The *Reves* case is discussed later in this chapter. [Eds.]

entities like the ones in the *Proctor & Gamble* case. It does so in a somewhat arcane manner—by reference to Section 3(a)(78) of the Exchange Act, which in turn refers to Section 206A of the Gramm-Leach-Bliley Act of 2000, thus incorporating a definition of "swap agreements" that includes, among other things, transactions that—

> [provide] on an executory basis for the exchange, on a fixed or contingent basis, of one or more payments based on the value or level of one or more interest or other rates, currencies, commodities, securities, instruments of indebtedness, indices, quantitative measures, or other financial or economic interests or property of any kind, or any interest therein or based on the value thereof, and that transfers, as between the parties to the transaction, in whole or in part, the financial risk associated with a future change in any such value or level without also conveying a current or future direct or indirect ownership interest in an asset (including any enterprise or investment pool) or liability that incorporates the financial risk so transferred, including any such agreement, contract, or transaction commonly known as an interest rate swap, including a rate floor, rate cap, rate collar, cross-currency rate swap, basis swap, equity index swap, equity swap, debt index swap, debt swap, credit spread, credit default swap, credit swap, weather swap, or commodity swap.

The definition excludes, however, "any note, bond, or evidence of indebtedness that is a security as defined in section 2(a)(1) of the Securities Act of 1933 * * * ." This literally means that if courts, unlike the *Proctor & Gamble* court, otherwise were inclined to find swap transactions to be "evidences of indebtedness," those transactions would not be "swap agreements" and therefore would not be entitled to the exclusion of Section 2A. Since 2010, the definition of "swap agreement" also has excluded "security-based swaps," which in that year were added to Section 2(a)(1)'s basic definition of a security.

IV. Unless the Context Otherwise Requires

The definitional sections of both the Securities Act and the Exchange Act begin with the same words: "When used in this title, unless the context otherwise requires * * * ." These clauses seem to have been forgotten for the first few decades after these acts were passed, at least as a stated basis for a court's analysis of whether something fell within or outside of a particular definition. Since the 1982 Supreme Court decision below, however, these words should be much in the minds of lawyers wrestling with the question of what constitutes a security. Either explicitly or implicitly, the phrase accounts for a large percentage of the decisions in which courts have found, after struggling with one theory or another, that a security does not exist.

Marine Bank v. Weaver

Supreme Court of the United States, 1982.
455 U.S. 551.

■ CHIEF JUSTICE BURGER delivered the opinion of the Court.

We granted certiorari to decide whether two instruments, a conventional certificate of deposit and a business agreement between two families, could be considered securities under the antifraud provisions of the federal securities laws.

I

Respondents, Sam and Alice Weaver, purchased a $50,000 certificate of deposit from petitioner Marine Bank on February 28, 1978. The certificate of deposit has a 6-year maturity, and it is insured by the Federal Deposit Insurance Corporation. The Weavers subsequently pledged the certificate of deposit to Marine Bank on March 17, 1978, to guarantee a $65,000 loan made by the bank to Columbus Packing Co. Columbus was a wholesale slaughterhouse and retail meat market which owed the bank $33,000 at that time for prior loans and was also substantially overdrawn on its checking account with the bank.

In consideration for guaranteeing the bank's new loan, Columbus' owners, Raymond and Barbara Piccirillo, entered into an agreement with the Weavers. Under the terms of the agreement, the Weavers were to receive 50% of Columbus' net profits and $100 per month as long as they guaranteed the loan. It was also agreed that the Weavers could use Columbus' barn and pasture at the discretion of the Piccirillos, and that they had the right to veto future borrowing by Columbus.

The Weavers allege that bank officers told them Columbus would use the $65,000 loan as working capital, but instead it was immediately applied to pay Columbus' overdue obligations. * * * Columbus became bankrupt four months later. * * *

* * * [T]he District Court granted summary judgment in favor of the bank. It concluded that, if a wrong occurred, it did not take place "in connection with the purchase or sale of any security," as required for liability under § 10(b). * * * [T]he Court of Appeals for the Third Circuit reversed. A divided court held that a finder of fact could reasonably conclude that either the certificate of deposit or the agreement between the Weavers and the Piccirillos was a security. * * *

We * * * reverse. * * *

II

The definition of "security" in the Securities Exchange Act of 1934 is quite broad. The Act was adopted to restore investors' confidence in the financial markets, and the term "security" was meant to include "the many types of instruments that, in our commercial world, fall within the ordinary concept of a security." H.R.Rep. No. 85, 73d Cong., 1st Sess., 11 (1933). * * * [T]he broad statutory definition is preceded, however, by the statement that the terms mentioned are not to be considered securities if "the context otherwise requires. . . ." Moreover, we are satisfied that Congress, in enacting the securities laws, did not intend to provide a broad federal remedy for all fraud.

III

The Court of Appeals concluded that * * * a certificate of deposit is similar to any other long-term debt obligation commonly found to be a security.[10] In our view, however, there is an important difference between a bank certificate of deposit and other long-term debt obligations. This certificate of deposit was issued by a federally regulated bank which is subject to the comprehensive set of regulations governing the banking industry. Deposits in federally regulated banks are protected by the reserve, reporting, and inspection requirements of the federal banking laws; advertising relating to the interest paid on deposits is also regulated. In addition, deposits are insured by the Federal Deposit Insurance Corporation. Since its formation in 1933, nearly all depositors in failing banks insured by the FDIC have received payment in full, even payment for the portions of their deposits above the amount insured.

We see, therefore, important differences between a certificate of deposit purchased from a federally regulated bank and other long-term debt obligations. The Court of Appeals failed to give appropriate weight to the important fact that the purchaser of a certificate of deposit is virtually guaranteed payment in full, whereas the holder of an ordinary long-term debt obligation assumes the risk of the borrower's insolvency. The definition of "security" in the 1934 Act provides that an instrument which seems to fall within the broad sweep of the Act is not to be considered a security if the context otherwise requires. It is unnecessary to subject issuers of bank certificates of deposit to liability under the antifraud provisions of the federal securities laws, since the holders of bank certificates of deposit are abundantly protected under the federal banking laws. We therefore hold that the certificate of deposit purchased by the Weavers is not a security.

IV

The Court of Appeals also held that a finder of fact could conclude that the separate agreement between the Weavers and the Piccirillos is a security. Examining the statutory language, the court found that the agreement might be a "certificate of interest or participation in any profit-sharing agreement" or an "investment contract." It stressed that the agreement gave the Weavers a share in the profits of the slaughterhouse which would result from the efforts of the Piccirillos.

---

[10] The Court already had concluded that a pledge of a security constitutes a sale. Rubin v. United States, 449 U.S. 424 (1981). In reaching this conclusion, the Court focused on the fact that Securities Act Section 2(a)(3) defines "sale" to include the concept of a "disposition of [an] interest in a security for value." A pledge unmistakably constitutes a sale, the Court found, because, although less than a transfer of absolute title is involved, an interest in a security is transferred nonetheless. [Eds.]

Accordingly, in that court's view, the agreement fell within the definition of "investment contract" stated in [SEC v. W.J. Howey Co., 328 U.S. 293 (1946)], because "the scheme involves an investment of money in a common enterprise with profits to come solely from the efforts of others." Id. at 298–99.

Congress intended the securities laws to cover those instruments ordinarily and commonly considered to be securities in the commercial world, but the agreement between the Weavers and the Piccirillos is not the type of instrument that comes to mind when the term "security" is used, and does not fall within "the ordinary concept of a security." The unusual instruments found to constitute securities in prior cases involved offers to a number of potential investors, not a private transaction as in this case. In Howey, for example, 42 persons purchased interests in a citrus grove during a 4-month period. 328 U.S. at 295. * * * [T]he instruments involved in * * * Howey had equivalent values to most persons, and could have been traded publicly.

Here, in contrast, the Piccirillos distributed no prospectus to the Weavers or to other potential investors, and the unique agreement they negotiated was not designed to be traded publicly. The provision that the Weavers could use the barn and pastures of the slaughterhouse at the discretion of the Piccirillos underscores the unique character of the transaction. Similarly, the provision that the Weavers could veto future loans gave them a measure of control over the operation of the slaughterhouse not characteristic of a security. Although the agreement gave the Weavers a share of the Piccirillos' profits, if any, that provision alone is not sufficient to make that agreement a security. Accordingly, we hold that this unique agreement, negotiated one-on-one by the parties, is not a security.

Lower courts have readily adopted *Marine Bank*'s reasoning in several cases involving comprehensive regulatory schemes; for instance, in Dubach v. Weitzel,[11] the Eighth Circuit found that applying the federal securities laws to the pledge of a certificate of deposit issued by a credit union regulated by federal and state law would unnecessarily "double-coat" the transaction. Occasionally, however, a court has balked at permitting a state regulatory scheme to preempt the federal securities laws.[12]

Even though *Marine Bank* is apparently the first case in which the Supreme Court explicitly used the securities statutes' contextual exception as a basis for a decision, the exception arguably had underpinned earlier opinions. For example, the much quoted statement in Tcherepnin v. Knight that "in searching for the meaning and scope of

---

[11]   135 F.3d 590 (8th Cir.1998).

[12]   Such a case is Holloway v. Peat, Marwick, Mitchell & Co., 900 F.2d 1485 (10th Cir. 1990).

the word 'security' in the Act[s], form should be disregarded for substance and the emphasis should be on economic reality,"[13] seems clearly to call for a contextual analysis. Further, this is exactly the kind of analysis the Court applied in *Forman* and *Daniel*. In *Forman* the Court said: "In holding that there is no federal jurisdiction, we do not address the merits of respondents' allegations * * *. We decide only that the *type of transaction* before us * * * is not within the scope of the federal securities laws" (emphasis added). And in *Daniel* the Court, citing *Tcherepnin* and *Forman,* found that the *Howey* test needs to be applied in the light of the "economic realities of the transaction."

The analysis of economic reality has led to two lines of cases fitting the "unless the context otherwise requires" mold. One line involves the question of whether the sale of a business, which is consummated by the sale of stock of the corporation that conducts the business, involves the sale of a security. The other line deals with the question of whether promissory notes are securities.

a. SALE OF A BUSINESS

Beginning in the 1970's, courts of appeals began to struggle with the "sale of business" doctrine. This doctrine, which arguably extended the "unless the context otherwise requires" exception to its logical conclusion, held that when a corporate business is sold by means of a sale of the corporation's stock, the stock is not a "security," as the term is used in the securities acts. Interesting logical practical problems are involved here. The idea that common stock—the archetypical security—could fall outside the statutory definitions of "security" is somewhat baffling. Perhaps more baffling, however, is the effect of the opposite conclusion. When a corporation's common stock is a security in this context, a strange anomaly results. An owner of a business who sells 100 percent of a corporation's stock to someone who wants to own and manage the corporation, in an arm's length and face-to-face transaction, is subject to all of the registration and antifraud provisions of the securities acts while another, who sells his or her business by selling all of its assets, is subject only to the common law fraud rules. The illogic of this is greater than it may at first appear, because the means by which the sale of a business is accomplished is usually a technical question, the resolution of which depends largely upon lawyers' and accountants' advice. From a business standpoint, a stock sale and an assets sale look very much the same. Perhaps choosing one form of bafflement over the other, circuit courts went both ways on the sale of business doctrine. The Supreme Court states its choice in the following case.

---

[13]   389 U.S. 332, 336 (1967).

Landreth Timber Co. v. Landreth

Supreme Court of the United States, 1985.
471 U.S. 681.

■ JUSTICE POWELL delivered the opinion of the Court.

This case presents the question whether the sale of all of the stock of a company is a securities transaction subject to the antifraud provisions of the federal securities laws (the Acts).

I

Respondents Ivan K. Landreth and his sons owned all of the outstanding stock of a lumber business they operated in Tonasket, Washington. The Landreth family offered their stock for sale through both Washington and out-of-state brokers. Before a purchaser was found, the company's sawmill was heavily damaged by fire. Despite the fire, the brokers continued to offer the stock for sale. Potential purchasers were advised of the damage, but were told that the mill would be completely rebuilt and modernized.

Samuel Dennis, a Massachusetts tax attorney, received a letter offering the stock for sale. On the basis of the letter's representations concerning the rebuilding plans, the predicted productivity of the mill, existing contracts, and expected profits, Dennis became interested in acquiring the stock. [Through a series of transactions, beginning with the purchase of the lumber company's stock, Dennis and a former client named John Bolten ended up owning 85%, and six other investors 15%, of Landreth Timber Co.] Ivan Landreth agreed to stay on as a consultant for some time to help with the daily operations of the mill. * * *

After the acquisition was completed, the mill did not live up to the purchasers' expectations. Rebuilding costs exceeded earlier estimates, and new components turned out to be incompatible with existing equipment. Eventually, petitioner sold the mill at a loss and went into receivership. Petitioner then filed this suit seeking rescission of the sale of stock and $2,500,000 in damages, alleging that respondents had widely offered and then sold their stock without registering it as required by the Securities Act of 1933 (the 1933 Act). Petitioner also alleged that respondents had negligently or intentionally made misrepresentations and had failed to state material facts as to the worth and prospects of the lumber company, all in violation of the Securities Exchange Act of 1934 (the 1934 Act).

Respondents moved for summary judgment on the ground that the transaction was not covered by the Acts because under the so-called "sale of business" doctrine, petitioner had not purchased a "security" within the meaning of those Acts. The District Court granted respondents' motion and dismissed the complaint for want of federal jurisdiction. * * *

The United States Court of Appeals for the Ninth Circuit affirmed the District Court's application of the sale of business doctrine. * * *

II

* * *

As we * * * recognized in [United Housing Foundation, Inc. v. Forman, 421 U.S. 837 (1975)], the fact that instruments bear the label "stock" is not of itself sufficient to invoke the coverage of the Acts. Rather, we concluded that we must also determine whether those instruments possess "some of the significant characteristics typically associated with" stock, recognizing that when an instrument is both called "stock" and bears stock's usual characteristics, "a purchaser justifiably [may] assume that the federal securities laws apply." We identified those characteristics usually associated with common stock as (i) the right to receive dividends contingent upon an apportionment of profits; (ii) negotiability; (iii) the ability to be pledged or hypothecated; (iv) the conferring of voting rights in proportion to the number of shares owned; and (v) the capacity to appreciate in value.

* * *

[I]t is undisputed that the stock involved here possesses all of the characteristics we identified in *Forman* as traditionally associated with common stock. * * * Moreover, unlike in *Forman,* the context of the transaction involved here—the sale of stock in a corporation—is typical of the kind of context to which the Acts normally apply. It is thus much more likely here than in *Forman* that an investor would believe he was covered by the federal securities laws. Under the circumstances of this case, the plain meaning of the statutory definition mandates that the stock be treated as "securities" subject to the coverage of the Acts.

* * *

III

Under other circumstances, we might consider the statutory analysis outlined above to be a sufficient answer compelling judgment for petitioner. Respondents urge, however, that language in our previous opinions, including *Forman,* requires that we look beyond the label "stock" and the characteristics of the instruments involved to determine whether application of the Acts is mandated by the economic substance of the transaction. Moreover, the Court of Appeals rejected the view that the plain meaning of the definition would be sufficient to hold this stock covered, because it saw "no principled way," to justify treating notes, bonds, and other of the definitional categories differently. We address these concerns in turn.

A

It is fair to say that our cases have not been entirely clear on the proper method of analysis for determining when an instrument is a "security." This Court has decided a number of cases in which it looked to the economic substance of the transaction, rather than just to its form, to determine whether the Acts applied. * * *

* * *

Respondents contend that *Forman* and the cases on which it was based require us to reject the view that the shares of stock at issue here may be considered "securities" because of their name and characteristics. Instead, they argue that our cases require us in every instance to look to the economic substance of the transaction to determine whether the *Howey* test has been met. According to respondents, it is clear that petitioner sought not to earn profits from the efforts of others, but to buy a company that it could manage and control. Petitioner was not a passive investor of the kind Congress intended the Acts to protect, but an active entrepreneur, who sought to "use or consume" the business purchased just as the purchasers in *Forman* sought to use the apartments they acquired after purchasing shares of stock. Thus, respondents urge that the Acts do not apply.

We disagree with respondents' interpretation of our cases. First, it is important to understand the contexts within which these cases were decided. All of the cases on which respondents rely involved unusual instruments not easily characterized as "securities." Thus, if the Acts were to apply in those cases at all, it would have to have been because the economic reality underlying the transactions indicated that the instruments were actually of a type that falls within the usual concept of a security. In the case at bar, in contrast, the instrument involved is traditional stock, plainly within the statutory definition. There is no need here, as there was in the prior cases, to look beyond the characteristics of the instrument to determine whether the Acts apply.

* * *

Second, we would note that the *Howey* economic reality test was designed to determine whether a particular instrument is an "investment contract," not whether it fits within *any* of the examples listed in the statutory definition of "security." * * * Moreover, applying the *Howey* test to traditional stock and all other types of instruments listed in the statutory definition would make the Acts' enumeration of many types of instruments superfluous.

Finally, we cannot agree with respondents that the Acts were intended to cover only "passive investors" and not privately negotiated transactions involving the transfer of control to "entrepreneurs." The 1934 Act contains several provisions specifically governing tender offers, disclosure of transactions by corporate officers and principal stockholders, and the recovery of short-swing profits gained by such persons. Eliminating from the definition of "security" instruments involved in transactions where control passed to the purchaser would contravene the purposes of these provisions. Furthermore, although § 4(2) of the 1933 Act, exempts transactions not involving any public offering from the Act's registration provisions, there is no comparable exemption from the antifraud provisions. Thus, the structure and language of the Acts refute respondents' position.

B

We now turn to the Court of Appeals' concern that treating stock as a specific category of "security" provable by its characteristics means that other categories listed in the statutory definition, such as notes, must be treated the same way. Although we do not decide whether coverage of notes or other instruments may be provable by their name and characteristics, we do point out several reasons why we think stock may be distinguishable from most if not all of the other categories listed in the Acts' definition.

Instruments that bear both the name and all of the usual characteristics of stock seem to us to be the clearest case for coverage by the plain language of the definition. First, traditional stock "represents to many people, both trained and untrained in business matters, the paradigm of a security." Daily v. Morgan, [701 F.2d 496, 500 (5th Cir.1983)]. Thus persons trading in traditional stock likely have a high expectation that their activities are governed by the Acts. Second, as we made clear in *Forman*, "stock" is relatively easy to identify because it lends itself to consistent definition. Unlike some instruments, therefore, traditional stock is more susceptible of a plain meaning approach.

Professor Loss has agreed that stock is different from the other categories of instruments. He observes that it "goes against the grain" to apply the *Howey* test for determining whether an instrument is an "investment contract" to traditional stock. L. Loss, Fundamentals of Securities Regulation 211–212 (1983). As Professor Loss explains,

> "It is one thing to say that the typical cooperative apartment dweller has bought a home, not a security; or that not every installment purchase 'note' is a security; or that a person who charges a restaurant meal by signing his credit card slip is not selling a security even though his signature is an 'evidence of indebtedness.' But *stock* (except for the residential wrinkle) is so quintessentially a security as to foreclose further analysis." Id., at 212 (emphasis in original).

* * * We here expressly leave until another day the question whether "notes" or "bonds" or some other category of instrument listed in the definition might be shown "by proving [only] the document itself." SEC v. C.M. Joiner Leasing Corp., [320 U.S. 344, 355 (1943)]. We hold only that "stock" may be viewed as being in a category by itself for purposes of interpreting the scope of the Acts' definition of "security."

IV

We also perceive strong policy reasons for not employing the sale of business doctrine under the circumstances of this case. By respondents' own admission, application of the doctrine depends in each case on whether control has passed to the purchaser. It may be argued that on the facts of this case, the doctrine is easily applied, since the transfer of 100% of a corporation's stock normally transfers control. We think even that assertion is open to some question, however, as Dennis and Bolten had no intention of running the sawmill themselves. Ivan Landreth apparently stayed on to manage the daily affairs of the business. Some commentators who support the sale of business doctrine believe that a purchaser who has the ability to exert control but chooses not to do so may deserve the Acts' protection if he is simply a passive investor not engaged in the daily management of the business. In this case, the District Court was required to undertake extensive fact-finding, and even requested supplemental facts and memoranda on the issue of control, before it was able to decide the case.

More importantly, however, if applied to this case, the sale of business doctrine would also have to be applied to cases in which less than 100% of a company's stock was sold. This inevitably would lead to difficult questions of line-drawing. The Acts' coverage would in every case depend not only on the percentage of stock transferred, but also on such factors as the number of purchasers and what provisions for voting and veto rights were agreed upon by the parties. As we explain more fully in Gould v. Ruefenacht, decided today as a companion to this case, coverage by the Acts would in most cases be unknown and unknowable to the parties at the time the stock was sold. These uncertainties attending the applicability of the Acts would hardly be in the best interests of either party to a transaction. Respondents argue that adopting petitioner's approach will increase the workload of the federal courts by converting state and common law fraud claims into federal claims. We find more daunting, however, the prospect that parties to a transaction may never know whether they are covered by the Acts until they engage in extended discovery and litigation over a concept as often elusive as the passage of control.

V

In sum, we conclude that the stock at issue here is a "security" within the definition of the Acts, and that the sale of business doctrine does not apply. * * *

* * *

---

b. PROMISSORY NOTES

Promissory notes are interesting devices for securities lawyers. The term "note" is the first item mentioned in the definition of "security" in both the Securities Act and the Exchange Act. Complicating the matter somewhat, each act then excludes certain notes, basically those having an original maturity not exceeding nine months, at least from certain of the act's provisions. Irrespective of the language of these provisions, however, courts have used an economic reality analysis to determine whether a particular note is a security for purposes of the Securities Act or the Exchange Act. In applying this analysis, a number of courts of appeals established a dichotomy between commercial and investment notes. An Exchange Act case relatively early in the line set up the dichotomy this way:

> [T]he mere fact that a note has a maturity of less than nine months does not take the case out of Rule 10b–5, unless the note fits the general notion of "commercial paper" * * * .

> [Nor does it] follow * * * that every transaction within the introductory clause of § 10, which involves promissory notes, whether of less or more than nine months maturity, is within Rule 10b–5. The Act is for the protection of investors, and its provisions must be read accordingly.[14]

In other words, when a note is of the investment variety it is a security, but when the note is of the commercial variety (ordinary commercial paper) it is not an Exchange Act security unless its original maturity is more than nine months.

In the case appearing directly below, the Supreme Court rejects the commercial-investment dichotomy in favor of a test it thinks "provides a more promising framework for analysis."

Reves v. Ernst & Young

Supreme Court of the United States, 1990.
494 U.S. 56.

■ JUSTICE MARSHALL delivered the opinion of the Court.

This case presents the question whether certain demand notes issued by the Farmer's Cooperative of Arkansas and Oklahoma are "securities" within the meaning of § 3(a)(10) of the Securities Exchange Act of 1934. We conclude that they are.

I

The Co-Op is an agricultural cooperative that, at the time relevant here, had approximately 23,000 members. In order to raise money to support its general business operations, the Co-Op sold promissory notes payable on demand by the holder. Although the notes were uncollateralized and uninsured, they paid a variable rate of interest that was adjusted monthly to keep it higher than the rate paid by local financial institutions. The Co-Op offered the notes to both members and nonmembers, marketing the scheme as an "Investment Program." Advertisements for the notes, which appeared in each Co-Op newsletter, read in part: "YOUR CO-OP has more than $11,000,000 in assets to stand behind your investments. The Investment is not Federal [*sic*] insured but it is * * * safe * * * secure * * * and available when you need it." Despite

---

[14] Zeller v. Bogue Electric Manufacturing Corp., 476 F.2d 795, 800 (2d Cir.1973).

these assurances, the Co-Op filed for bankruptcy in 1984. At the time of the filing, over 1,600 people held notes worth a total of $10 million.

After the Co-Op filed for bankruptcy, petitioners, a class of holders of the notes, filed suit against Arthur Young & Co., the firm that had audited the Co-Op's financial statements (and the predecessor to respondent Ernst & Young). Petitioners alleged, *inter alia,* that Arthur Young had intentionally failed to follow generally accepted accounting principles in its audit, specifically with respect to the valuation of one of the Co-Op's major assets, a gasohol plant. Petitioners claimed that Arthur Young violated these principles in an effort to inflate the assets and net worth of the Co-Op. Petitioners maintained that, had Arthur Young properly treated the plant in its audits, they would not have purchased demand notes because the Co-Op's insolvency would have been apparent. On the basis of these allegations, petitioners claimed that Arthur Young had violated the antifraud provisions of the 1934 Act as well as Arkansas' securities laws.

Petitioners prevailed at trial on both their federal and state claims, receiving a $6.1 million judgment. Arthur Young appealed, claiming that the demand notes were not "securities" under either the 1934 Act or Arkansas law, and that the statutes' antifraud provisions therefore did not apply. A panel of the Eighth Circuit, agreeing with Arthur Young on both the state and federal issues, reversed. We granted certiorari to address the federal issue, and now reverse the judgment of the Court of Appeals.

II

A

This case requires us to decide whether the note issued by the Co-Op is a "security" within the meaning of the 1934 Act. * * *

* * * Congress * * * did not attempt precisely to cabin the scope of the Securities Acts.[15] Rather, it enacted a definition of "security" sufficiently broad to encompass virtually any instrument that might be sold as an investment.

* * * In discharging our duty, we are not bound by legal formalisms, but instead take account of the economics of the transaction under investigation. Congress' purpose in enacting the securities laws was to regulate *investments,* in whatever form they are made and by whatever name they are called.

A commitment to an examination of the economic realities of a transaction does not necessarily entail a case-by-case analysis of every instrument, however. Some instruments are obviously within the class Congress intended to regulate because they are by their nature

---

[15] We have consistently held that "[t]he definition of a security in § 3(a)(10) of the 1934 Act, is virtually identical [to the 1933 Act's definition] and, for present purposes, the coverage of the two Acts may be considered the same." United Housing Foundation, Inc. v. Forman, 421 U.S. 837, 847, n. 12 (1975) (citations omitted). We reaffirm that principle here.

investments. In Landreth Timber Co. v. Landreth, 471 U.S. 681 (1985), we held that an instrument bearing the name "stock" that, among other things, is negotiable, offers the possibility of capital appreciation, and carries the right to dividends contingent on the profits of a business enterprise is plainly within the class of instruments Congress intended the securities laws to cover. *Landreth Timber* does not signify a lack of concern with economic reality; rather, it signals a recognition that stock is, as a practical matter, always an investment if it has the economic characteristics traditionally associated with stock. Even if sparse exceptions to this generalization can be found, the public perception of common stock as a paradigm of a security suggests that stock, in whatever context it is sold, should be treated as within the ambit of the Acts.

We made clear in *Landreth Timber* that stock was a special case, explicitly limiting our holding to that sort of instrument. Although we refused finally to rule out a similar *per se* rule for notes, we intimated that such a rule would be unjustified. Unlike "stock," we said, " 'note' may now be viewed as a relatively broad term that encompasses instruments with widely varying characteristics, depending on whether issued in a consumer context, as commercial paper, or in some other investment context.' " While common stock is the quintessence of a security, and investors therefore justifiably assume that a sale of stock is covered by the Securities Acts, the same simply cannot be said of notes, which are used in a variety of settings, not all of which involve investments. Thus, the phrase "any note" should not be interpreted to mean literally "any note," but must be understood against the backdrop of what Congress was attempting to accomplish in enacting the Securities Acts.

Because the *Landreth Timber* formula cannot sensibly be applied to notes, some other principle must be developed to define the term "note." A majority of the Courts of Appeals that have considered the issue have adopted, in varying forms, "investment versus commercial" approaches that distinguish, on the basis of all of the circumstances surrounding the transactions, notes issued in an investment context (which are "securities") from notes issued in a commercial or consumer context (which are not).

The Second Circuit's "family resemblance" approach begins with a presumption that *any* note with a term of more than nine months is a "security." See, e.g., Exchange Nat'l Bank of Chicago v. Touche Ross & Co., 544 F.2d 1126, 1137 (2d Cir.1976). Recognizing that not all notes are securities, however, the Second Circuit has also devised a list of notes that it has decided are obviously not securities. Accordingly, the "family resemblance" test permits an issuer to rebut the presumption that a note is a security if it can show that the note in question "bear[s] a strong family resemblance" to an item on the judicially crafted list of exceptions, id., at 1137–1138, or convinces the court to add a new instrument to the list.

* * *

The "family resemblance" and "investment versus commercial" tests * * * are really two ways of formulating the same general approach. Because we think the "family resemblance" test provides a more promising framework for analysis, however, we adopt it. The test begins with the language of the statute; because the Securities Acts define "security" to include "any note," we begin with a presumption that every note is a security. We nonetheless recognize that this presumption cannot be irrebuttable. * * * Congress was concerned with regulating the investment market, not with creating a general federal cause of action for fraud. In an attempt to give more content to that dividing line, the Second Circuit has identified a list of instruments commonly denominated "notes" that nonetheless fall without the "security" category. See *Exchange Nat'l Bank,* supra (types of notes that are not "securities" include "the note delivered in consumer financing, the note secured by a mortgage on a home, the short-term note secured by a lien on a small business or some of its assets, the note evidencing a 'character' loan to a bank customer, short-term notes secured by an assignment of accounts receivable, or a note which simply formalizes an open-account debt incurred in the ordinary course of business (particularly if, as in the case of the customer of a broker, it is collateralized)").

We agree that the items identified by the Second Circuit are not properly viewed as "securities." More guidance, though, is needed. It is impossible to make any meaningful inquiry into whether an instrument bears a "resemblance" to one of the instruments identified by the Second Circuit without specifying what it is about *those* instruments that makes *them* non-"securities." Moreover, as the Second Circuit itself has noted, its list is "not graven in stone," and is therefore capable of expansion. Thus, some standards must be developed for determining when an item should be added to the list.

An examination of the list itself makes clear what those standards should be. In creating its list, the Second Circuit was applying the same factors that this Court has held apply in deciding whether a transaction involves a "security." First, we examine the transaction to assess the motivations that would prompt a reasonable seller and buyer to enter into it. If the seller's purpose is to raise money for the general use of a business enterprise or to finance substantial investments and the buyer is interested primarily in the profit the note is expected to generate, the instrument is likely to be a "security." If the note is exchanged to facilitate the purchase and sale of a minor asset or consumer good, to correct for the seller's cash-flow difficulties, or to advance some other commercial or consumer purpose, on the other hand, the note is less sensibly described as a "security." Second, we examine the "plan of distribution" of the instrument to determine whether it is an instrument in which there is "common trading for speculation or investment." Third, we examine the reasonable expectations of the investing public: The

Court will consider instruments to be "securities" on the basis of such public expectations, even where an economic analysis of the circumstances of the particular transaction might suggest that the instruments are not "securities" as used in that transaction. Finally, we examine whether some factor such as the existence of another regulatory scheme significantly reduces the risk of the instrument, thereby rendering application of the Securities Acts unnecessary.

We conclude, then, that in determining whether an instrument denominated a "note" is a "security," courts are to apply the version of the "family resemblance" test that we have articulated here: a note is presumed to be a "security," and that presumption may be rebutted only by a showing that the note bears a strong resemblance (in terms of the four factors we have identified) to one of the enumerated categories of instrument. If an instrument is not sufficiently similar to an item on the list, the decision whether another category should be added is to be made by examining the same factors.

B

Applying the family resemblance approach to this case, we have little difficulty in concluding that the notes at issue here are "securities." Ernst & Young admits that "a demand note does not closely resemble any of the Second Circuit's family resemblance examples." Nor does an examination of the four factors we have identified as being relevant to our inquiry suggest that the demand notes here are not "securities" despite their lack of similarity to any of the enumerated categories. The Co-Op sold the notes in an effort to raise capital for its general business operations, and purchasers bought them in order to earn a profit in the form of interest.[16] Indeed, one of the primary inducements offered purchasers was an interest rate constantly revised to keep it slightly above the rate paid by local banks and savings and loans. From both sides, then, the transaction is most naturally conceived as an investment in a business enterprise rather than as a purely commercial or consumer transaction.

As to the plan of distribution, the Co-Op offered the notes over an extended period to its 23,000 members, as well as to nonmembers, and more than 1,600 people held notes when the Co-Op filed for bankruptcy. To be sure, the notes were not traded on an exchange. They were, however, offered and sold to a broad segment of the public, and that is all

---

[16] We emphasize that by "profit" in the context of notes, we mean "a valuable return on an investment," which undoubtedly includes interest. We have, of course, defined "profit" more restrictively in applying the *Howey* test to what are claimed to be "investment contracts." See, *e.g.*, United Housing Foundation, Inc. v. Forman, 421 U.S. 837, 852 (1975), ("[P]rofit" under the *Howey* test means either "capital appreciation" or "a participation in earnings"). To apply this restrictive definition to the determination whether an instrument is a "note" would be to suggest that notes paying a rate of interest not keyed to the earning of the enterprise are not "notes" within the meaning of the Securities Acts. Because the *Howey* test is irrelevant to the issue before us today, we decline to extend its definition of "profit" beyond the realm in which that definition applies.

we have held to be necessary to establish the requisite "common trading" in an instrument.

The third factor—the public's reasonable perceptions—also supports a finding that the notes in this case are "securities". We have consistently identified the fundamental essence of a "security" to be its character as an "investment." The advertisements for the notes here characterized them as "investments," and there were no countervailing factors that would have led a reasonable person to question this characterization. In these circumstances, it would be reasonable for a prospective purchaser to take the Co-Op at its word.

Finally, we find no risk-reducing factor to suggest that these instruments are not in fact securities. The notes are uncollateralized and uninsured. Moreover, * * * the notes here would escape federal regulation entirely if the Acts were held not to apply.

The court below found that "[t]he demand nature of the notes is very uncharacteristic of a security," on the theory that the virtually instant liquidity associated with demand notes is inconsistent with the risk ordinarily associated with "securities." This argument is unpersuasive. Common stock traded on a national exchange is the paradigm of a security, and it is as readily convertible into cash as is a demand note. The same is true of publicly traded corporate bonds, debentures, and any number of other instruments that are plainly within the purview of the Acts. The demand feature of a note does permit a holder to eliminate risk quickly by making a demand, but just as with publicly traded stock, the liquidity of the instrument does not eliminate risk all together. Indeed, publicly traded stock is even more readily liquid than are demand notes, in that a demand only eliminates risk when and if payment is made, whereas the sale of a share of stock through a national exchange and the receipt of the proceeds usually occur simultaneously.

We therefore hold that the notes at issue here are within the term "note" in § 3(a)(10).

* * *

B. WHAT IS A SALE?

SITUATION 5B

After the public offering, Microtec continued acquisition discussions with J & H Software Corp., but the companies could not agree on terms. Instead, Microtec has come to a tentative agreement with the officers and directors of Compuform Corp., whose operations are in the same city as Microtec's.

Compuform offers not only the software development capability Microtec desires, but it also manufactures some of the components

Microtec needs for its computer production. The company is available on favorable terms for two reasons. First, the former president and 30% shareholder recently died unexpectedly, and his stock is now in the hands of his widow. For various reasons, she wishes to see the company acquired or sold. Second, cash will have to be put into the company if it is to reach its potential. Compuform has nineteen other shareholders, and at least a majority in interest are agreeable to the acquisition on the terms being discussed.

The basic terms call for a merger of Compuform into Microtec, which is simplified because both are incorporated in the same state, the one in which each mainly operates. In the merger, Compuform shareholders would receive Microtec common stock. The arrangements are complicated somewhat, however, because of Compuform's ownership of a 51% interest in Hill-Daniels, Inc., a corporation operated, and 49% owned, by two of Compuform's shareholders. Hill-Daniels produces components for large, main-frame computers. Microtec is not interested in becoming involved in this segment of the industry, and the 49% owners would like to obtain for themselves effective control of Hill-Daniels. They would also like to see a public market established for Hill-Daniels stock. The parties have, therefore, tentatively agreed that immediately after the merger Microtec will "spin off" to its shareholders its newly acquired interest in Hill-Daniels, by means of a dividend or distribution of the Hill-Daniels stock.

In considering this situation, refer to the following, in addition to the materials in this section: Sections 2(a)(3) and 2(a)(11) of the Securities Act, Securities Act Rules 145, 153a, 165, and 172 and Registration Statement Form S–4.

I. ACQUISITIONS

There never has been any question regarding the existence of a sale in the context of an acquisition by means of a stock-for-stock tender offer. When the acquiring company asks the target company's shareholders to tender their shares, and promises its own stock in return, this is an offering of securities. And a sale inarguably occurs when the parties become bound by contract to consummate the transaction as planned, since under Securities Act Section 2(a)(3) entering into a contract of sale constitutes a "sale." In this situation, the analysis is made easy because the acquiring company deals directly with the target's shareholders, each of whom makes an individual investment decision.

When dealing with mergers and stock-for-assets acquisitions, the issues are more complex. In these transactions the target's shareholders often receive securities issued by the acquiring company, either because the plan of merger provides for this or because after the target company has sold its assets in exchange for stock of the acquiring company, it dissolves and distributes the stock to its shareholders as part of the liquidation process. Unlike the tender offer, however, the decisions behind the stock's finding its way into the hands of the target's shareholders are not, on the surface at least, the shareholders' individual decisions. Rather, these decisions can be viewed simply as decisions of the target corporation.

For a number of years, the Commission followed this reasoning and maintained that the transactions described above involve no sale of the acquiring company's securities to the target's shareholders. As a result, no registration of the securities was necessary. In 1972, the Commission reversed field, saying in Securities Act Release No. 5316 that "formalism should no longer deprive investors of the disclosure to which they are entitled." It accomplished this change of position in Rule 145, which fits the described transactions, and some similar ones, into the ordinary framework of a Securities Act offering.

Under Rule 145, an offering of securities is made to the target's shareholders when certain acquisition plans are presented to them for approval, and a sale occurs when the requisite contract is entered. The acquiring company is the issuer. It has no direct dealings with the target's shareholders, but rather those dealings are handled within the target company in the context of a shareholders' meeting. In other words, the target company acts as a middleman, and the Securities Act provides that in certain circumstances such a middleman is considered to be an underwriter. Rule 145 used to specifically provide that the target company and its affiliates were deemed to be underwriters when publicly offering or selling securities received by the target in an acquisition covered by the rule. In 2007, the rule was amended to apply the "deemed underwriter" doctrine only if one of the parties to a covered transaction is a shell company (basically, one with neither significant business operations nor significant assets other than cash or cash equivalents). For the target company deemed to be an underwriter, the primary result is that it is subject to underwriter's liability, most directly under Section 11 of the Securities Act, for disclosure problems in connection with the offering. What may be of more immediate concern to affiliates of the target is the notion that underwriter status brings restrictions on their ability to resell any securities they receive in a Rule 145 transaction. Resale limitations on affiliates are discussed in Chapter 7. For now, it is perhaps best just to note that the rule creates these limitations and that it then provides a mechanism for resales by affiliates on certain conditions

Included below are two Securities Act releases that aid in an understanding of Rule 145. The first is the release in which the Commission announced the adoption of the rule, and the second is an interpretive release issued by the Commission's Division of Corporation Finance.

Securities Act Release No. 5316

Securities and Exchange Commission, October 6, 1972.

Notice of Adoption of Rule 145

* * *

Background and Purpose

* * *

Rule 145 is * * * intended to inhibit the creation of public markets in securities of issuers about which adequate current information is not available to the public. This approach is consistent with the philosophy underlying the Act, that a disclosure law provides the best protection for investors. If a security holder who is offered a new security in a Rule 145 business combination transaction has available to him the material facts about the transaction, he will be in a position to make an informed investment judgment. In order to provide such information in connection with public offerings of these securities, Rule 145 will require the filing of a registration statement with the Commission and the delivery to security holders of a prospectus containing accurate and current information concerning the proposed business combination transaction.

Explanation and Analysis

I.   Rescission of Rule 133. Definition for Purposes of Section 5 of "Sale," "Offer to Sell," and "Offer for Sale"

Rule 133 provides that for purposes only of Section 5 of the Act, the submission to a vote of stockholders of a corporation of a proposal for certain mergers, consolidations, reclassifications of securities or transfers of assets is not deemed to involve a "sale", "offer", "offer to sell", or "offer for sale" of the securities of the new or surviving corporation to the security holders of the disappearing corporation. * * *

The "no-sale" theory embodied in Rule 133 is based on the rationale that the types of transactions specified in the rule are essentially corporate acts, and the volitional act on the part of the individual stockholder required for a "sale" was absent. The basis of this theory was that the exchange or alteration of the stockholder's security occurred not because he consented thereto, but because the corporate action, authorized by a specified majority of the interests affected, converted his security into a different security.

[T]he Commission is of the view that the "no-sale" approach embodied in Rule 133 overlooks the substance of the transactions specified therein and ignores the fundamental nature of the relationship between the stockholders and the corporation. The fact that such relationships are in part controlled by statutory provisions of the state of incorporation does not preclude as a matter of law the application of the broad concepts of "sale", "offer", "offer to sell", and "offer for sale" in Section 2(a)(3) of the Act which are broader than the commercial or common law meanings of such terms.

Transactions of the type described in Rule 133 do not, in the Commission's opinion, occur solely by operation of law without the element of individual stockholder volition. A stockholder faced with a Rule 133 proposal must decide on his own volition whether or not the proposal is one in his own best interest. The basis on which the "no-sale" theory is predicated, namely, that the exchange or alteration of the stockholder's security occurs not because he consents thereto but because the corporation by authorized corporate action converts his securities, in the Commission's opinion, is at best only correct in a formalistic sense and overlooks the reality of the transaction. The corporate action, on which such great emphasis is placed, is derived from the individual consent given by each stockholder in voting on a proposal to merge or consolidate a business or reclassify a security. In voting, each consenting stockholder is expressing his voluntary and individual acceptance of the new security, and generally the disapproving stockholder is deferring his decision as to whether to accept the new security or, if he exercises his dissenter's rights, a cash payment. The corporate action in these circumstances, therefore, is not some type of independent fiat, but is only the aggregate effect of the voluntary decisions made by the individual stockholders to accept or reject the exchange. Formalism should no longer deprive investors of the disclosure to which they are entitled.

* * *

II. Adoption of Rule 145. Reclassifications of Securities, Mergers, Consolidations and Acquisitions of Assets

* * *

B. *Rule 145(a). Transactions Within the Rule*

Paragraph (a) of Rule 145 provides that the submission to a vote of security holders of a proposal for certain reclassifications of securities, mergers, consolidations, or transfers of assets, is deemed to involve an "offer", "offer to sell", "offer for sale", or "sale" of the securities to be issued in the transaction. The effect of the Rule is to require registration of the securities to be issued in connection with such transactions, unless an exemption from registration is available. * * *

* * *

C. *Rule 145(b). Communications Not Deemed to Be a "Prospectus" or "Offer to Sell"*

Notice of a proposed action or of a meeting of security holders for voting on transactions of the character specified in Rule 145 is generally sent or furnished to security holders. Because the Rule will make the registration provisions of the Act applicable to these transactions, questions have been raised as to whether such notices will constitute statutory prospectuses or involve an offer for sale of a security. Paragraph (b) of Rule 145 is designed to resolve these questions by providing that any written communication which contains no more than the information [permitted by] paragraph (b) of the Rule shall not be deemed a prospectus for purposes of Section 2[a](10) of the Act and shall not be deemed an "offer for sale" of the security involved for the purposes of Section 5 of the Act.

* * * [T]he * * * rule [by cross reference to Rule 135] permits the identification of all parties to the transaction; a brief description of their business; a description of the basis upon which the transaction will be made; and any legend or similar statement required by federal law or state or administrative authority. * * * [Cross references to Rules 165 and 166 permit substantial additional information.]

* * *

Securities Act Release No. 5463

Securities and Exchange Commission, February 28, 1974.

DIVISION OF CORPORATION FINANCE'S
INTERPRETATIONS OF RULE 145

* * *

I.   Relationship of Rule 145 to Exemptions Set Forth in Sections 3 and 4 of the Act (See Generally Preliminary Note to Rule 145)

Illustration A

Facts: X Company proposes to issue common stock in exchange for the assets of Y Company after Y Company obtains the approval of its several stockholders, as required by state law, with respect to an agreement setting forth the terms and conditions of the exchange and providing for a distribution of the X Company common stock to the Y Company stockholders. X Company has determined that the private offering exemption afforded by Section 4(2) of the Act would be available for the transaction.

Question: In light of Rule 145, may X Company choose between relying upon the private offering exemption available under Section 4(2) and registering the securities to be issued in the transaction * * * ?

Interpretative Response: Yes, X Company may choose between relying upon the private offering exemption available under Section 4(2) and registering the securities to be issued in the transaction * * * . Rule 145 does not affect statutory exemptions which are otherwise available. * * *

* * *

II.   SPIN-OFFS AND "FREE" STOCK GIVE-AWAYS

The question of whether and under what circumstances the corporate spin-off involves a sale is both interesting and slippery in terms of analysis. In a spin-off, a corporation takes stock that it owns in another corporation and distributes this stock to its shareholders as a dividend. When the corporation engaging in the spin-off is publicly held, the spun-off corporation becomes publicly held also. Some shareholders will immediately want to sell their newly acquired shares, and a trading market will develop to facilitate this. That those purchasing these shares in the trading market will not have the benefits of disclosure that registration provides has greatly disturbed the Commission, and this has led it to apply the "sale" definition somewhat creatively, as shown in the following materials.

Securities Act Release No. 4982
Securities and Exchange Commission, July 2, 1969.

APPLICATION OF THE SECURITIES ACT OF 1933 AND THE SECURITIES EXCHANGE ACT OF 1934 TO SPIN OFFS OF SECURITIES

The Securities and Exchange Commission today made publicly known its concern with the methods being employed by a growing number of companies and persons to effect distributions to the public of unregistered securities in possible violation of the registration requirements of the Securities Act of 1933 and of the anti-fraud and anti-manipulative provisions of the Securities Act of 1933 and the Securities Exchange Act of 1934. The methods employed can take and in fact have taken a variety of patterns.

I

Frequently, the pattern involves the issuance by a company, with little, if any, business activity, of its shares to a publicly-owned company in exchange for what may or may not be nominal consideration. The publicly-owned company subsequently spins off the shares to its shareholders with the result that active trading in the shares begins with no information on the issuer being available to the investing public.[17] Despite this lack of information, moreover, the shares frequently trade in an active market at increasingly higher prices. Under such a pattern, when the shares are issued to the publicly-owned or acquiring company, a sale takes place within the meaning of the Securities Act and if the shares are then distributed to the shareholders of the acquiring company, that company may be an underwriter within the meaning of section [2(a)(11)] of the Act as a person "who purchased from an issuer with a view to * * * the distribution of any security" or as a person who "has a direct or indirect participation in any such undertaking."

While the distribution of the shares to the acquiring company's shareholders may not, in itself, constitute a distribution for the purposes

---

[17] Exchange Act Rule 15c2–11, originally adopted in 1976, now mandates that certain minimal information about the issuer of a security be in the records of any securities firm acting as a market maker. [Eds.]

of the Act, the entire process, including the redistribution in the trading market which can be anticipated and which may indeed be a principal purpose of the spin off, can have that consequence. It is accordingly the Commission's position that the shares which are distributed in certain spin offs involve the participation of a statutory underwriter and are thus, in those transactions, subject to the registration requirements of the Act and subsequent transactions in the shares by dealers, unless otherwise exempt, would be subject to the provisions of section 5 requiring the delivery of a prospectus during the 40 or 90 day period set forth in section 4(3).

The theory has been advanced that since a sale is not involved in the distribution of the shares in a spin off that registration is not required and that even if it is required, no purpose would be served by filing a registration statement and requiring the delivery of a prospectus since the persons receiving the shares are not called upon to make an investment judgment.

This reasoning fails, however, to take into account that there is a sale by the issuer and the distribution thereafter does not cease at the point of receipt by the initial distributees of the shares but continues into the trading market involving sales to the investing public at large. Moreover, it ignores what appears to be primarily the purpose of the spin off in numerous circumstances which is to create quickly, and without the disclosure required by registration, a trading market in the shares of the issuer. Devices of this kind contravene the purpose, as well as the specific provisions, of the Act which, in the words of the statutory preamble, are "to provide full and fair disclosure of the character of the securities sold in interstate and foreign commerce and through the mails, and to prevent frauds in the sale thereof." In the circumstances of a spin off, when the shares are thereafter traded in the absence of information about the issuer, the potential for fraud and deceit is manifest.

This release does not attempt to deal with any problems attributable to more conventional spin offs, which do not involve a process of purchase of securities by a publicly-owned company followed by their spin off and redistribution in the trading markets.

* * *

SEC v. Datronics Engineers, Inc.

United States Court of Appeals, Fourth Circuit, 1973.
490 F.2d 250.

■ Before BRYAN, SENIOR CIRCUIT JUDGE, and FIELD and WIDENER, CIRCUIT JUDGES.

■ ALBERT V. BRYAN, SENIOR CIRCUIT JUDGE:

The Securities and Exchange Commission in enforcement of the Securities Act of 1933, § 20(b), sought a preliminary injunction to restrain Datronics Engineers, Inc., its officers and agents, as well as related corporations, from continuing in alleged violation of the registration * * * provisions of the [Act]. * * *

Summary judgment went for the defendants, and the Commission appeals. We reverse.

Specifically, the complaint charged transgressions of the [statute] by Datronics, assisted by the individual defendants, in declaring, and effectuating through the use of the mails, "spin-offs" to and among its stockholders of the unregistered shares of stock owned by Datronics in other corporations. * * * [Datronics'] capital stock was held by 1000 shareholders and was actively traded on the market. * * *

The pattern of the spin-offs in each instance was this: Without any business purpose of its own, Datronics would enter into an agreement with the principals of a private company. The agreement provided for the organization by Datronics of a new corporation, or the utilization of one of Datronics' subsidiaries, and the merger of the private company into the new or subsidiary corporation. It stipulated that the principals of the private company would receive the majority interest in the merger-corporation. The remainder of the stock of the corporation would be delivered to, or retained by, Datronics for a nominal sum per share. Part of it would be applied to the payment of the services of Datronics in the organization and administration of the proposed spin-off, and to Datronics' counsel for legal services in the transaction. Datronics was bound by each of the nine agreements to distribute among its shareholders the rest of the stock.

Before such distribution, however, Datronics reserved for itself approximately one-third of the shares. Admittedly, none of the newly acquired stock was ever registered; its distribution [was] accomplished by use of the mails.

* * * [I]n our judgment each of these spin-offs violated § 5 of the Securities Act, in that Datronics caused to be carried through the mails an unregistered security "for the purpose of sale or for delivery after sale". * * *

* * *

As the term "sale" includes a "disposition of a security", the dissemination of the new stock among Datronics' stockholders was a sale. However, the appellees urged, and the District Court held, that this disposition was not a statutory sale because it was not "for value", as demanded by the definition. Here, again, we find error. Value accrued to Datronics in several ways. First, a market for the stock was created by its transfer to so many new assignees—at least 1000, some of whom were stockbroker-dealers, residing in various States. Sales by them followed at once—the District Judge noting that "[i]n each instance dealing promptly began in the spun-off shares". This result redounded to the benefit not only of Datronics but, as well, to its officers and agents who had received some of the spun-off stock as compensation for legal or other services to the spin-off corporations. Likewise, the stock retained by Datronics was thereby given an added increment of value. The record discloses that in fact the stock, both that disseminated and that kept by Datronics, did appreciate substantially after the distributions.

* * *

Garden variety spin-offs, as opposed to the type of spin-offs just discussed, may or may not involve sales, depending on the details of the transaction. The Commission's staff issued a large number of no-action letters involving spin-offs. Then, in 1997, the Division of Corporation Finance issued a Staff Legal Bulletin about spin-offs. In this bulletin the staff indicated its view that registration is not necessary if (1) the spin-off is pro-rata to the parent company's shareholders, (2) the recipients of the spun-off securities provide no consideration, (3) the parent provides to its shareholders and the public adequate information about the spin-off and about the company being spun-off, (4) the parent has a valid business purpose for the spin-off, and (5) if the parent spins-off "restricted securities," it has held the securities for a specified holding period. (Restricted securities are non-registered securities purchased in specified transactions. They are discussed below in Chapter 7.)[18]

On a related front, the Commission issued a 1999 press release addressing its attempt to prohibit unregistered offerings of "free" stock over the Internet. The typical "free" stock offering required the "investor" to sign up with the issuers' web site and disclose personal information in order to obtain shares. In some cases, additional shares were given for soliciting additional investors, for linking the investor's own web site to the issuer's web site, or for purchasing additional services. According to the Commission, "[t]hrough these techniques, issuers received value by spawning a fledging public market for their shares, increasing their business, creating publicity, increasing traffic to their web sites, and, in two cases, generating possible interest in projected public offerings."

---

[18] It probably is worth noting that the holding period set out in the Bulletin is two years— which is the holding period for resales of restricted securities that more generally pertained in 1997. The generally applicable holding period subsequently was changed to one year, but the Bulletin has not been updated.

CHAPTER 6

EXEMPTIONS FROM SECURITIES ACT REGISTRATION REQUIREMENTS

SITUATION 6

The Compuform merger has not yet been accomplished. The officers of Microtec wish to do the acquisition, but only if an exemption from the registration requirements can be found for the Microtec securities to be used in the acquisition.

As indicated in Situation 5b, Compuform needs an infusion of cash if it is to reach its potential. Microtec has no interest in doing another registered offering of securities to raise this cash, but would be interested in the possibility of selling securities, perhaps preferred stock or debt securities, if a registration exemption were available.

In considering this situation, refer to the following, in addition to the materials in this chapter: Securities Act Sections 2(a)(15), 3, 4(a)(2), 4(a)(5), 4(a)(6), 4(b), 4A and 28, Securities Act Rules 147, 147A, 215, 701, 801 and 802, Regulations A, CE, D and Crowdfunding under the Securities Act, and Form D under the Securities Act.

A. STATUTORY SCHEME

Statutory exemptions from the Securities Act's registration requirements are found in Sections 3 and 4, and Section 28 gives the Commission broad powers to create other exemptions. Section 4 is entitled "Exempted Transactions," which provides an accurate description of its contents. The title of Section 3, "Exempted Securities," is, however, somewhat of a misnomer. It is true that most of the securities referred to in Section 3(a) are, in all circumstances, exempted from the registration requirements of Section 5. Examples are government securities (Section 3(a)(2)), securities issued by religious, educational, charitable, and other such organizations (Section 3(a)(4)), and interests in a railroad equipment trust (Section 3(a)(6)). Regardless of whose hands these securities may fall into, and regardless of the means or frequency with which they change hands, these securities never have to be registered under the Securities Act. These truly are exempted securities.

The misnomer mainly exists in three other situations: securities exchanged with existing security holders (Section 3(a)(9)), securities issued under a plan of exchange approved by a court or other governmental authority (Section 3(a)(10)), and securities issued in an intrastate transaction (Section 3(a)(11)). These subsections do not deal with exempted securities, but rather with exempted transactions. In light of this, it may be well to reemphasize an earlier caution. Section 5 is absolute in its prohibitions: No offers are permitted without a filed registration statement, and no sales are permitted until the registration statement is effective. For each offer or sale—by any person—of a security other than an exempted security, the registration requirements must be met or an exemption for the transaction must exist. Thus, when buyers in an exempted transaction wish to resell, they must find a transaction exemption or the securities must be registered.

Section 3(b)(1) authorizes the Commission to add other securities to those exempted by Section 3 when it finds that registration is not necessary "by reason of the small amount involved or the limited character of the public offering." This subsection, however, places a dollar limit on the aggregate offering price of an issue of securities that may come within its coverage. This limit was raised in increments over the years, from $100,000 to $5,000,000. It is important to realize that, like certain exemptions provided in Section 3(a), those exemptions established by the Commission under the authority of Section 3(b)(1) are transaction exemptions only. Pursuant to Section 3(b)(1), the Commission has adopted various exempting rules. The most important of them will be discussed below.

Two developments complicate the study of Section 3(b)(1). First, in 1996, Section 28 was enacted. This new section gives the Commission authority to "exempt any person, security, or transaction, or any class or classes of persons, securities, or transactions, from any provision" of the Securities Act, so long as the "exemption is necessary or appropriate in the public interest, and is consistent with the protection of investors." (Note that under Section 2(b), added along with Section 28, the Commission must, when considering what is in the public interest, also consider whether a rulemaking action "will promote efficiency, competition, and capital formation.") One important aspect of Section 28 is the ability it gives the Commission to raise the dollar limit of exemptive rules it previously adopted under Section 3(b).

The second complicating development was the enactment in 2012 of Section 3(b)(2) (which required the provision previously numbered 3(b) to be renumbered as 3(b)(1)). Section 3(b)(2) requires the Commission to adopt an exemption for offerings not exceeding $50,000,000.

Section 4 contains only transaction exemptions. Of these, the private placement exemption provided in Section 4(a)(2), the accredited investors exemption found in Section 4(a)(5), and the new crowdfunding exemption contained in Section 4(a)(6) will be discussed in this chapter. Section

4(a)(3) was examined briefly in Chapter 3, and Sections 4(a)(1), 4(a)(4), and 4(a)(7) will be discussed in the next chapter.

It is important to understand the limits of any exemption provided by statute, rule, etc. Section 4 states that the registration requirements of Section 5 do not apply to the transactions covered in Section 4. All the other sections of the Securities Act, of which the liability provisions are the most important, do apply. Section 3 provides that the provisions of the Securities Act do not apply to the securities enumerated in Section 3 "except as * * * expressly provided." One of the major liability sections[1] of the Act, Section 12(a)(2), provides that offers or sales of all securities, except government securities and securities futures products, exempted from the registration provisions by Section 3 are nevertheless subject to Section 12(a)(2). Another liability provision, Section 17, is expressly applicable to all securities that are exempted from the registration requirements by Section 3. By its terms, Section 11, the other liability provision (except for Section 12(a)(1), which establishes liability for offering or selling securities without registration or an exemption), is applicable only to misstatements or omissions in registration statements. The terms of any exemption adopted by the Commission under Section 28 need careful examination.

In addition to the registration exemptions provided under the Securities Act, certain specialized exemptions are contained in Section 1145 of the Bankruptcy Reform Act of 1978.

B. PRIVATE PLACEMENTS: SECTION 4(a)(2)

The private placement exemption finds its statutory base in Securities Act Section 4(a)(2), which provides that the registration requirements of Section 5 do not apply to "transactions by an issuer not involving any public offering." Since the definition of "issuer" in Section 2(a)(4) is straightforward, the only thing necessary to understand the legal requirements for a private placement is knowing what constitutes a "public offering." Regrettably, this term is not defined in the statute. The basic contours of a public offering, however, are well established in case law and in pronouncements by the Commission.

The most important Commission action under Section 4(a)(2) has been the adoption of Rule 506. This rule is part of Regulation D, which is a collection of rules that govern the limited offer and sale of securities without Securities Act registration. Rule 506 is a safe harbor rule that an issuer is free to use as it pleases. When an issuer tries to comply with the rule and fails to meet all of its requirements, it may still rely on the statutory exemption. Except in the case of this auxiliary use of the statutory exemption found in Section 4(a)(2), the private placement exemption under this section and the limited offering exemption under Rule 506 tend as a practical matter to be regarded as separate

---

[1]   Liability issues will be discussed in Chapter 8.

exemptions. For this reason, the statutory exemption is discussed here and Rule 506 is examined later in the chapter when Regulation D is considered.

The private placement traditionally has been the most important registration exemption available to issuers. It retains major importance even with the safe harbor of Rule 506. There are a number of reasons for this. First, the importance of having a fallback exemption, available for use when a Rule 506 limited offering, or some other exemption, is tried but fails, should not be underestimated. The backstopping ability of the private placement exemption may prevent the scrapping of an offering in progress or the imposition of crippling liability on an issuer that has completed an offering. Second, in some types of transactions there is no doubt about the private nature of the transaction, and no safe harbor rule is needed to help secure the Section 4(a)(2) exemption. A company offering and selling securities only to insurance companies or other institutional investors illustrates this. Third, the requirements of Section 4(a)(2) can more easily be satisfied by chance than most other exemptions, some of which contain filing or other requirements that require advance planning. In cases when a lawyer is called in after the fact, the private placement exemption may be the only exemption available to save a client from civil and criminal liability.

The leading case concerning the requirements for a private placement is SEC v. Ralston Purina Co.:

SEC v. Ralston Purina Co.

Supreme Court of the United States, 1953.
346 U.S. 119.

■ MR. JUSTICE CLARK delivered the opinion of the Court.

Section [4(a)(2)][2] of the Securities Act of 1933 exempts "transactions by an issuer not involving any public offering" from the registration requirements of § 5. We must decide whether Ralston Purina's offerings of treasury stock to its "key employees" are within this exemption. On a complaint brought by the Commission under § 20(b) of the Act seeking to enjoin respondent's unregistered offerings, the District Court held the exemption applicable and dismissed the suit. The Court of Appeals affirmed. * * *

* * * At least since 1911 [Ralston Purina] has had a policy of encouraging stock ownership among its employees; more particularly, since 1942 it has made authorized but unissued common shares available to some of them. Between 1947 and 1951, the period covered by the record in this case, Ralston Purina sold nearly $2,000,000 of stock to employees without registration and in so doing made use of the mails.

---

[2] Originally Section 4(1). [Eds.]

In each of these years, a corporate resolution authorized the sale of common stock "to employees * * * who shall, without any solicitation by the Company or its officers or employees, inquire of any of them as to how to purchase common stock of Ralston Purina Company." A memorandum sent to branch and store managers after the resolution was adopted advised that "The only employees to whom this stock will be available will be those who take the initiative and are interested in buying stock at present market prices." Among those responding to these offers were employees with the duties of artist, bakeshop foreman, chow loading foreman, clerical assistant, copywriter, electrician, stock clerk, mill office clerk, order credit trainee, production trainee, stenographer, and veterinarian. * * *

The company bottoms its exemption claim on the classification of all offerees as "key employees" in its organization. Its position on trial was that "A key employee * * * is not confined to an organization chart. It would include an individual who is eligible for promotion, an individual who especially influences others or who advises others, a person whom the employees look to in some special way, an individual, of course, who carries some special responsibility, who is sympathetic to management and who is ambitious and who the management feels is likely to be promoted to a greater responsibility." That an offering to all of its employees would be public is conceded.

The Securities Act nowhere defines the scope of § [4(a)(2)]'s private offering exemption. Nor is the legislative history of much help in staking out its boundaries. The problem was first dealt with in § 4(1) of the House Bill, H.R. 5480, 73d Cong., 1st Sess., which exempted "transactions by an issuer not with or through an underwriter; * * * ." The bill, as reported by the House Committee, added "and not involving any public offering." H.R.Rep. No.85, 73d Cong., 1st Sess. 1. This was thought to be one of those transactions "where there is no practical need for [the bill's] application or where the public benefits are too remote." Id., at 5. The exemption as thus delimited became law. It assumed its present shape with the deletion of "not with or through an underwriter" by § 203(a) of the Securities Exchange Act of 1934, a change regarded as the elimination of superfluous language.

Decisions under comparable exemptions in the English Companies Acts and state "blue sky" laws, the statutory antecedents of federal securities legislation, have made one thing clear: to be public an offer need not be open to the whole world. In Securities and Exchange Comm'n v. Sunbeam Gold Mines Co., 95 F.2d 699 (C.A. 9th Cir.1938), this point was made in dealing with an offering to the stockholders of two corporations about to be merged. Judge Denman observed that:

> "In its broadest meaning the term 'public' distinguishes the populace at large from groups of individual members of the public segregated because of some common interest or characteristic. Yet such a distinction is inadequate for practical

purposes; manifestly, an offering of securities to all redheaded men, to all residents of Chicago or San Francisco, to all existing stockholders of the General Motors Corporation or the American Telephone & Telegraph Company, is no less 'public', in every realistic sense of the word, than an unrestricted offering to the world at large. Such an offering, though not open to everyone who may choose to apply, is none the less 'public' in character, for the means used to select the particular individuals to whom the offering is to be made bear no sensible relation to the purposes for which the selection is made. * * * [T]o determine the distinction between 'public' and 'public' in any particular context, it is essential to examine the circumstances under which the distinction is sought to be established and to consider the purposes sought to be achieved by such distinction."

* * *

* * * The design of the statute is to protect investors by promoting full disclosure of information thought necessary to informed investment decisions. The natural way to interpret the private offering exemption is in light of the statutory purpose. Since exempt transactions are those as to which "there is no practical need for [the bill's] application," the applicability of § [4(a)(2)] should turn on whether the particular class of persons affected needs the protection of the Act. An offering to those who are shown to be able to fend for themselves is a transaction "not involving any public offering."

The Commission would have us go one step further and hold that "an offering to a substantial number of the public" is not exempt under § [4(a)(2)]. We are advised that "whatever the special circumstances, the Commission has consistently interpreted the exemption as being inapplicable when a large number of offerees is involved." But the statute would seem to apply to a "public offering" whether to few or many. It may well be that offerings to a substantial number of persons would rarely be exempt. Indeed nothing prevents the commission, in enforcing the statute, from using some kind of numerical test in deciding when to investigate particular exemption claims. But there is no warrant for superimposing a quantity limit on private offerings as a matter of statutory interpretation.

The exemption, as we construe it, does not deprive corporate employees, as a class, of the safeguards of the Act. We agree that some employee offerings may come within § [4(a)(2)], e.g., one made to executive personnel who because of their position have access to the same kind of information that the Act would make available in the form of a registration statement. Absent such a showing of special circumstances, employees are just as much members of the investing "public" as any of their neighbors in the community. * * *

Keeping in mind the broadly remedial purposes of federal securities legislation, imposition of the burden of proof on an issuer who would plead the exemption seems to us fair and reasonable. * * * The focus of inquiry should be on the need of the offerees for the protections afforded by registration. The employees here were not shown to have access to the kind of information which registration would disclose. The obvious opportunities for pressure and imposition make it advisable that they be entitled to compliance with § 5.

* * *

Next to Rule 506, the most important Commission pronouncement on Section 4((a)(2) has been Securities Act Release No. 4552, which appears directly below.

Securities Act Release No. 4552

Securities and Exchange Commission, November 6, 1962.

NONPUBLIC OFFERING EXEMPTION

The Commission today announced the issuance of a statement regarding the availability of the exemption from the registration requirements of section 5 of the Securities Act of 1933 afforded by [Section 4(a)(2)] of the Act for "transactions by an issuer not involving any public offering," the so-called "private offering exemption." Traditionally, the [Section] has been regarded as providing an exemption from registration for bank loans, private placements of securities with institutions, and the promotion of a business venture by a few closely related persons. However, an increasing tendency to rely upon the exemption for offerings of speculative issues to unrelated and uninformed persons prompts this statement to point out the limitations on its availability.

Whether a transaction is one not involving any public offering is essentially a question of fact and necessitates a consideration of all surrounding circumstances, including such factors as the relationship between the offerees and the issuer, the nature, scope, size, type and manner of the offering.

The Supreme Court in S.E.C. v. Ralston Purina Co., 346 U.S. 119, 124, 125 (1953), noted that the exemption must be interpreted in the light of the statutory purpose to "protect investors by promoting full disclosure of information thought necessary to informed investment decisions" and held that "the applicability of Section [4(a)(2)] should turn on whether the particular class of persons affected need the protection of the Act." The court stated that the number of offerees is not conclusive as to the availability of the exemption, since the statute seems to apply to an offering "whether to few or many." * * * It should be emphasized, therefore, that the number of persons to whom the offering is extended is relevant only to the question whether they have the requisite association with and knowledge of the issuer which make the exemption available.

Consideration must be given not only to the identity of the actual purchasers but also to the offerees. Negotiations or conversations with or general solicitations of an unrestricted and unrelated group of prospective purchasers for the purpose of ascertaining who would be willing to accept an offer of securities is inconsistent with a claim that the transaction does not involve a public offering even though ultimately there may only be a few knowledgeable purchasers.

* * *

The sale of stock to promoters who take the initiative in founding or organizing the business would come within the exemption. On the other hand, the transaction tends to become public when the promoters begin to bring in a diverse group of uninformed friends, neighbors and associates.

The size of the offering may also raise questions as to the probability that the offering will be completed within the strict confines of the exemption. An offering of millions of dollars to non-institutional and non-affiliated investors or one divided, or convertible, into many units would suggest that a public offering may be involved.

When the services of an investment banker, or other facility through which public distributions are normally effected, are used to place the securities, special care must be taken to avoid a public offering. If the investment banker places the securities with discretionary accounts and other customers without regard to the ability of such customers to meet the tests implicit in the *Ralston Purina* case, the exemption may be lost. Public advertising of the offerings would, of course, be incompatible with a claim of a private offering. Similarly, the use of the facilities of a securities exchange to place the securities necessarily involves an offering to the public.

An important factor to be considered is whether the securities offered have come to rest in the hands of the initial informed group or whether the purchasers are merely conduits for a wider distribution. Persons who act in this capacity, whether or not engaged in the securities business, are deemed to be "underwriters" within the meaning of Section 2(a)(11) of the Act. If the purchasers do in fact acquire the securities with a view to public distribution, the seller assumes the risk of possible violation of the registration requirements of the Act and consequent civil liabilities. This has led to the practice whereby the issuer secures from the initial purchasers representations that they have acquired the securities for investment. Sometimes a legend to this effect is placed on the stock certificates and stop-transfer instructions issued to the transfer agent. However, a statement by the initial purchaser, at the time of his acquisition that the securities are taken for investment and not for distribution is necessarily self-serving and not conclusive as to his actual intent. Mere acceptance at face value of such assurances will not provide a basis for reliance on the exemption when inquiry would suggest to a reasonable person that these assurances are formal rather than real. The additional precautions of placing a legend on the security and issuing stop-transfer orders have proved in many cases to be an effective means of preventing illegal distributions. Nevertheless, these are only precautions and are not to be regarded as a basis for exemption from registration. The nature of the purchaser's past investment and trading practices or the character and scope of his business may be inconsistent with the purchase of large blocks of securities for investment. In particular, purchases by persons engaged in the business of buying and selling securities require careful scrutiny for the purpose of determining whether such person may be acting as an underwriter for the issuer.

* * *

Integration of Offerings[3]

A determination whether an offering is public or private would also include a consideration of the question whether it should be regarded as a part of a larger offering made or to be made. The following factors are relevant to such question of integration: whether (1) the different offerings are part of a single plan of financing, (2) the offerings involve issuance of the same class of security, (3) the offerings are made at or about the same time, (4) the same type of consideration is to be received, (5) the offerings are made for the same general purpose.

What may appear to be a separate offering to a properly limited group will not be so considered if it is one of a related series of offerings. A person may not separate parts of a series of related transactions, the sum total of which is really one offering, and claim that a particular part is a nonpublic transaction. * * *

* * *

The "integration" concept described in Release No. 4552 has received important refinements other the years. These include a number of specific "safe harbors" protecting against the integration of particular types of offerings and/or offerings that are separated by enough time. Most recently, SEC releases indicate that in many—but not all—contexts the five-factor test has been supplanted by an inquiry into whether advertising and solicitation in one offering has the effect of improperly conditioning the market for another.

Courts of appeals deciding cases following *Ralston Purina* have gone a long way in answering questions about the requirements for a valid

---

[3]   Rule 152 provides help in determining if transactions involving a private offering will be integrated with a later public offering. Rule 155 now provides a safe harbor from integration of private and registered offerings. A waiting period of 30 days and certain other conditions apply. [Eds.]

private placement. In doing so, they have devised their own lists of factors to consider, based on *Ralston Purina* and Release No. 4552. It may be helpful to recite some of the lists here. First, here is a list of relevant factors from two often cited Fifth Circuit cases: (1) the number of offerees and their relationship to each other and to the issuer, (2) the number of units offered, (3) the size of the offering, and (4) the manner of offering.[4] Second, here is a list from a First Circuit opinion: "Sales may * * * be exempted * * * if a private offering is made in which the purchasers (1) are limited in number, (2) are sophisticated, and (3) have a relationship with the issuer enabling them to command access to information that would otherwise be contained in a registration statement."[5] Third, here is a list of "flexible tests" from the Ninth Circuit: (1) the number of offerees, (2) the sophistication of the offerees, (3) the size and manner of the offering, and (4) the relationship of the offerees to the issuer.[6]

A committee of the American Bar Association attempted to combine and distill these factors in a 1975 position paper. After looking at judicial precedent and Commission pronouncements, the ABA committee decided that there are only four factors of real significance in determining the availability of the private placement exemption: (1) offeree qualification, (2) availability of information, (3) manner of offering, and (4) absence of redistribution. This position paper appears as the next reading.

Section [4(a)(2)] and Statutory Law

A Position Paper of the Federal Regulation of Securities Committee, Section of Corporation, Banking and Business Law of the American Bar Association. 31 Business Lawyer 485 (1975).*

* * *

SOURCES OF STATUTORY LAW

Legislative History

In our search for Statutory Law [, which is the law relating to private placements outside of a safe harbor rule], there are several sources upon which we can draw. First, there is the legislative history, which referred to:

[A] specific or isolated sale * * * to a particular person.

[W]here there is no practical need for the bill's application.

[W]here the public benefits are too remote.

---

[4]   Doran v. Petroleum Management Corp., 545 F.2d 893, 900 (5th Cir.1977); Hill York Corp. v. American International Franchises, Inc., 448 F.2d 680, 687–689 (5th Cir.1971).

[5]   Cook v. Avien, Inc., 573 F.2d 685, 691 (1st Cir.1978).

[6]   SEC v. Murphy, 626 F.2d 633, 644–645 (9th Cir.1980).

*   Copyright © 1975 by the American Bar Association. All rights reserved. Reprinted with the permission of the American Bar Association and its Section of Business Law.

[U]nless the stockholders are so small in number that the sale to them does not constitute a public offering.

Administrative

An early opinion of the SEC General Counsel set the interpretative stage for many years. This opinion focused on the number of offerees as a prime consideration, indicating that under ordinary circumstances an offering to approximately 25 or fewer persons would presumably not involve a public offering. It went on to enumerate the following factors as being relevant:

The number of offerees;

The relationship of the offerees to each other;

The relationship of the offerees to the issuer;

The number of units offered;

The size of the offering; and

The manner of the offering.

An administrative interpretation in 1962 [, Securities Act Release No. 4552,] stressed another aspect found in earlier interpretations, namely, that the offerees must have access to information about the issuer. * * *

* * *

Judicial Precedents

Turning to the judicial precedents, SEC v. Ralston Purina Co. focused on the offerees' lack of need for the Act's protection. * * *

The subsequent judicial precedents have not been particularly helpful. In most of the reported cases decided since *Ralston Purina,* the issuers and their control persons lost. Many of these cases involved egregious fact situations, typically tainted with a clearly public distribution and misrepresentation, in which the issuers should have lost. The courts, however, have used extremely broad dicta which, if taken literally, would leave little viability in the exemption under the statute. * * *

In those cases where the issuer prevailed on the merits, it is clear that the courts did not require full compliance with the dicta enunciated in those cases where the issuers lost.

We add a caveat. Certain of the early cases which were decided favorably to the issuers might not be decided the same way today, in the light of later circuit court precedents. * * * Nonetheless, we believe it is fair to conclude that a distinctly different attitude toward the exemption emerges from a reading of the cases in which the issuers prevailed, as contrasted with the more numerous cases where the exemption was held to be unavailable. When the facts were more favorable to the issuer, the courts seemed to interpret the requirements for exemption in a less demanding manner.

SEC Chairman Garrett * * * (when he was still a private practitioner) characterized the result of the various authorities, legislative, judicial and administrative, as:

[A] kind of mishmash. The issuer is now told that all of these factors have something to do with whether he has an exemption under Section [4(a)(2)], but he is never given a hint as to the proper proportions in the brew. The saving recipe is kept secret, a moving target which he can never be sure he has hit.

GUIDELINES

Where does this leave us? We believe that there are only four attributes of any real significance in determining whether the exemption is available under Statutory Law * * *—(1) offeree qualification; (2) availability of information; (3) manner of offering; and (4) absence of redistribution. * * *

* * *

To a large extent, our discussion focuses on the type of equity private placements which are typically sold to individuals or others who are not professional investors or venture capitalists, and which often involve a relatively high degree of risk. * * *

* * *

Offeree Qualification

* * * We believe that offerees in a private placement should be deemed qualified on any one of several bases. They may be qualified on the basis of their ability to understand the risk. This attribute is sometimes called "sophistication." They may be qualified on the basis of their ability to assume the investment risk, so called "wealth." Or, they may be qualified on the basis of a personal relationship to the issuer or a promoter. The qualifying relationships include, but are not necessarily limited to, family ties, friendship, an employment relationship or a pre-existing business relationship. In our view, *Ralston Purina* does not exclude these alternative approaches. * * * We believe that the public benefits are too remote and there is no practical need for the burdens of applying the registration provisions (as contrasted with anti-fraud provisions) when the offerees have such close relationships to the offeror. We note that when such close personal ties exist, a decision to make an investment may be motivated, wholly or in part, by non-economic factors unrelated to financial risks and benefits of the investment.

We suggested above that an offeree might qualify solely on the basis of his ability to assume the risk. We add a caveat. We might have serious reservations about including a very wealthy person as an offeree in a highly risky private placement, based solely upon his ability to assume the risk, if he had no understanding of financial matters, and no competent advisor. On the other hand, if an equally wealthy offeree was an experienced business man with some general understanding of financial matters, we would consider him qualified as an offeree based upon his ability to assume the risk, even though he lacked a high degree of sophistication.

Several other observations concerning offeree qualification are relevant.

(1) *Risk Bearing Ability:* First, with respect to the offeree's ability to assume the risk, we believe it is relevant to consider, in very broad and general terms, the extent of the risk of loss in judging whether the offeree can assume it. There have been expressions from the Commission that the appropriate inquiry is whether the offeree can afford to lose all of the money to be invested. Notwithstanding such suggestions, * * * we believe that both the total amount of money invested, and also the likelihood that all or part of it will be lost, must be considered.

* * *

(2) *The Offeree Representative Principle:* We believe that Statutory Law gives some recognition to the offeree representative principle which is formalized in Rule 146[7]—that is, a person other than an offeree may be able to advise an offeree or otherwise protect the offeree's interests so as to qualify the offeree. Two cases seem to recognize this principle in the acquisition setting. The point is also recognized tangentially in at least one non-acquisition case. In Klinkel v. Krekow, an unreported U.S. District Court memorandum decision the court accepted the parties' agreement in a rescission suit that information disclosed to the son of the plaintiff-purchaser was deemed known by plaintiff and "to the extent sophistication and investment philosophy of an offeree are relevant, those of [the son] should control."

(3) *Manner of Disclosure:* We suggest that a determination of the offeree's ability to understand the risk may well vary with the manner and scope of the disclosure made to him. The more careful, painstaking and detailed the disclosure is, the more readily one may find that a particular offeree is able to understand the risk. * * *

* * *

(4) *Degrees of Sophistication:* We consider it important to recognize that there are degrees of sophistication. The inquiry as to whether an offeree is adequately sophisticated should not be approached in a categorical or absolute fashion, since the concept entails weighing of relative factors. All those who are not sufficiently sophisticated to qualify as offerees of every type of security for every type of offering should not be lumped together. The unsophisticated range from the total

---

[7]   Rule 146 was replaced with Rule 506 of Regulation D, and the offeree representative principle was carried over into the new rule. [Eds.]

incompetent in financial matters, and possibly other matters as well, to the worldly man of business who knows a good deal about money matters but who has had limited experience in corporate finance and private placements. A good many presidents of companies going public are not "sophisticated" in matters of corporate finance, in the normal sense of the term "sophisticated."

Indeed, we suggest that the term "sophistication" is somewhat misused in this context. It is a shorthand way of expressing a rather complex thought, and quite possibly the use of the term is not entirely accurate. The relevant inquiry should be whether the investor can understand and evaluate the nature of the risk based upon the information supplied to him. The relevant inquiry should not be whether the investor is *au courant* in all of the latest nuances and techniques of corporate finance. To the extent that the term "sophistication" raises inquiries of the latter type, the use of the term may tend to becloud the inquiry.

(5) *Non-Qualified Offerees:* Is the exemption lost for the entire transaction where one or more of the offerees (or purchasers) fails to meet the appropriate tests? The question may arise in a variety of factual settings, as illustrated by the following extreme hypotheticals. Assume that the issue concerning the availability of the exemption is raised in each case in a Section [12(a)(1)] rescission suit brought by a qualified purchaser, who is seeking a return of his purchase price after the investment turns out to be unprofitable. The plaintiff charges that the offering as a whole did not qualify for the exemption.

> *Case No. 1:* The offeror makes the offers with total disregard as to the qualifications of the offerees. In fact, most of the offerees and purchasers are not qualified.

> *Case No. 2:* The offeror uses a high degree of care in pre-clearing offerees. In hindsight, it appears that only one offeree was not appropriately qualified. When the offer was made to him, the offeror had reasonable grounds to believe that the offeree was qualified, relying in part on information supplied by the offeree which was subsequently discovered to be untrue. Prior to the sale, when the true facts were discovered, the non-qualified offeree was eliminated from the private placement and the securities were sold only to qualified offerees, but no effort was made to terminate the pending offering as to the qualified offerees.

The language in the cases discussing the point indicates that the exemption is unavailable unless every offeree (even those who did not become purchasers) meets the qualification test. However, virtually all such cases more closely resemble Case No. 1 above, rather than Case No. 2. If the issue were to arise in a circumstance similar to Case No. 2, we believe that a court should, and probably would, either find the exemption available vis-à-vis the plaintiff, or find some other basis for denying the plaintiff the right to rescind his transaction.

* * *

(6) *Economic Bargaining Power:* The concept of economic bargaining power has become a widely accepted concept under Statutory Law, and is used in a somewhat imprecise way to describe an attribute of offerees who have "access" to information.

If the plain meaning of the expression "economic bargaining power" is considered, the term would seem to have no necessary connection with the sophistication of the offeree or his background in financial matters * * * . * * *

[H]owever, we think the term economic bargaining power, as used in the private placement context, should be understood as a term of art. It is, to a large extent, an attribute which an offeree may be presumed to have based upon several factors including, but not necessarily limited to, available resources, financial experience and history as an investor. It is not to be determined primarily from a factual analysis of the relative bargaining strengths of a particular issuer vis-à-vis a particular offeree in a given factual setting.

Information

A second general attribute relates to the scope and manner of disclosure of information. It is generally considered necessary that each offeree have some information about the issuer, or at least access to that information, prior to the sale. * * *

* * *

The information required to be supplied need not be nearly as extensive as the information called for by Schedule A of the 1933 Act, or by Form S–1, although the Form S–1 requirements provide a useful guideline. The statutory exemption does reflect a legislative policy decision that occasions exist where there is no need for the expense and delay of providing a registration statement, or its non-filed equivalent. It is probably adequate to give basic information concerning the issuer's financial condition, results of operations, business, property and management.

Indeed, it is doubtful whether all of the foregoing categories of information are required in every case. Many private placements by a small closely-held company are completed with little or no formal disclosure documentation. If the buyer shows no interest in information regarding executive compensation, for example, the exemption should not be lost by the failure of the issuer to supply such information, especially if the remuneration is reasonable and just about what the buyer would have expected had he considered the matter.

* * *

Manner of the Offering

The third general attribute of a proper private placement under Statutory Law relates to the manner of offering. In general, the offering should be made through direct communication with qualified offerees or their representatives, whether by the issuer itself or through an agent of the issuer. All forms of general advertising and mass media circulation should be avoided. * * *

* * *

Absence of Redistribution

A fourth general attribute of a proper private placement under Statutory Law is the absence of an immediate redistribution by the first-tier purchasers which would transform the overall transaction into a public offering. * * *

* * *

Statutory Law does not require any mechanical procedures to avoid redistribution, such as the endorsement of legends on certificates, investment (non-distribution) letters or stop transfer instructions to transfer agents, although these devices are very useful to evidence the absence of distributive purpose or intent (and they may be required under applicable state law). As long as no redistribution occurs in fact, the absence of these mechanical procedures does not render the exemption unavailable.

* * *

Significance of the Factors

If all the foregoing attributes are met—qualification of the offerees, availability of information, manner of the offering and absence of a redistribution—the exemption should apply to the transaction notwithstanding the failure of that transaction to meet some of the other tests sometimes articulated in the traditional sources.

To a large extent, this position paper reviews minimum requirements necessary to establish the Section [4(a)(2)] exemption. Assuming that the events have already occurred, we believe that the principles set forth should be of assistance in predicting how a court may decide if a transaction is challenged. We do not necessarily imply, however, that sound counseling or good business judgment dictates the planning of transactions to meet only the minimal standards. * * *

* * *

Number of Offerees

A much discussed subject regarding private placements is the significance of the number of offerees. It is the official dogma that the number of offerees (or purchasers) is not conclusive as to the availability or unavailability of the exemption. For many years, however, experienced counsel attached great significance to the number of offerees. Assuming an otherwise proper transaction, traditionally 25 qualified offerees was a widely accepted rule of thumb as an appropriate ceiling, at least when the non-institutional type of offeree was involved. However, in *Ralston Purina,* the Supreme Court pointedly rejected the SEC contention that there could be a *maximum* number which could never be *exceeded* for the exemption to remain available. * * *

* * *

As a practical matter, we believe there has always been some relationship between the number of offerees considered acceptable and the level of the offerees' sophistication. Other things being equal most counsel would feel comfortable with a larger number of offerees and purchasers, where the offerees are all sophisticated institutions rather than individuals. It is widely known that institutional private placements have occurred involving well over 100 purchasers.

We doubt that many experienced counsel would have felt comfortable with a private placement involving the same number of individual purchasers under similar circumstances.

* * *

A very important development in private offerings has been the sale of securities in a private offering where the issuer, as part of the transaction, contracts with the purchasers immediately to file a registration statement covering the resale into the public markets of the privately-purchased securities. These transactions are called PIPEs, which stands for "private investment in public equity." By use of a PIPE, an issuer can receive cash more quickly than if it had to wait until a registration statement relating to a sale by the issuer to the public was drafted and taken through the registration process. Also, since the requirements for using the short-form registration Form S–3 are easily met by most publicly held companies for resales by security holders, registration for some companies is much easier and less expensive for resales than it would be for a sale by the company to the public. Along these same lines, an issuer in a PIPE transaction avoids the expense of having underwriters involved in the registration (the buyers in the private offering will sell, as provided for in the registration statement, directly into the public market). Finally, the securities can be sold for a higher price in a PIPE than in a regular private offering, because in the latter the securities lack liquidity as they are "restricted securities" that have restrictions on their resale (as discussed in the following chapter).

C. INTRASTATE OFFERINGS: SECTION 3(a)(11), RULE 147 AND RULE 147A

Securities Act Section 3(a)(11) exempts from the registration requirements of the Act:

> Any security which is a part of an issue offered and sold only to persons resident within a single State or Territory, where the issuer of such security is a person resident and doing business within, or, if a corporation, incorporated by and doing business within, such State or Territory.

As in the case of Section 4(a)(2), the Commission has adopted a safe harbor rule, Rule 147, that issuers may use to secure a Section 3(a)(11) exemption. Exercising its broad Section 28 exemptive authority it also has adopted the related, more liberal, Rule 147A.

Before examining those rules, however, it is important to understand the statutory exemption outside the rules. It is impossible to appreciate the importance of the rules without understanding the situation without them. In addition, it is often wise to comply with the requirements of the statutory exemption and one of the rules, so that if for some reason the requirements of the rule are not satisfied, the issuer has a fallback position. Also, in some limited situations, especially when the statutory exemption is considered a remote backup for the private placement or other exemption, an issuer may not wish to comply with one of the rules. Finally, the rules are usually not satisfied by chance, and lawyers giving after-the-fact advice concerning the availability of an exemption typically find the rules of no help.

I. STATUTORY EXEMPTION

Securities Act Release No. 4434
Securities and Exchange Commission, December 6, 1961.

SECTION 3(a)(11) EXEMPTION FOR LOCAL OFFERINGS

* * *

General Nature of Exemption

* * *

The legislative history of the Securities Act clearly shows that [the Section 3(a)(11)] exemption was designed to apply only to local financing that may practicably be consummated in its entirety within the state or territory in which the issuer is both incorporated and doing business. * * *

"Issue" Concept

A basic condition of the exemption is that the entire issue of securities be offered and sold exclusively to residents of the state in question. Consequently, an offer to a nonresident which is considered a part of the intrastate issue will render the exemption unavailable to the entire offering.

Whether an offering is "a part of an issue," that is, whether it is an integrated part of an offering previously made or proposed to be made, is a question of fact and depends essentially upon whether the offerings are a related part of a plan or program. Thus, the exemption should not be relied upon in combination with another exemption for the different parts of a single issue where a part is offered or sold to nonresidents.

The determination of what constitutes an "issue" is not governed by state law. Any one or more of the following factors may be determinative of the question of integration: (1) are the offerings part of a single plan of financing; (2) do the offerings involve issuance of the same class of security; (3) are the offerings made at or about the same time; (4) is the same type of consideration to be received, and (5) are the offerings made for the same general purpose.

Moreover, since the exemption is designed to cover only those security distributions, which, as a whole, are essentially local in character, it is clear that the phrase "sold only to persons resident" as used in Section 3(a)(11) cannot refer merely to the initial sales by the issuing corporation to its underwriters, or even the subsequent resales by the underwriters to distributing dealers. To give effect to the fundamental purpose of the exemption, it is necessary that the entire issue of securities shall be offered and sold to, and come to rest only in the hands of residents within the state. If any part of the issue is offered or sold to a nonresident, the exemption is unavailable not only for the securities so sold, but for all securities forming a part of the issue, including those sold to residents. It is incumbent upon the issuer, underwriter, dealers and other persons connected with the offering to make sure that it does not become an interstate distribution through resales. It is understood to be customary for such persons to obtain assurances that purchases are not made with a view to resale to nonresidents.

Doing Business Within the State

In view of the local character of the Section 3(a)(11) exemption, the requirement that the issuer be doing business in the State can only be satisfied by the performance of substantial operational activities in the state of incorporation. The doing business requirement is not met by functions in the particular state such as bookkeeping, stock record and similar activities or by offering securities in the state. Thus, the exemptions would be unavailable to an offering by a company made in the state of its incorporation of undivided fractional oil and gas interests located in other states even though the company conducted other business in the state of its incorporation. While the person creating the fractional interests is technically the "issuer" as defined in Section [2(a)(4)] of the Act, the purchaser of such security obtains no interest in the issuer's separate business within the state. Similarly, an intrastate exemption would not be available to a "local" mortgage company offering interests in out-of-state mortgages which are sold under circumstances to constitute them investment contracts. Also, the same position has been taken of a sale of an interest, by a real estate syndicate organized in one state to the residents of that state, in property acquired under a sale and leaseback arrangement with another corporation organized and engaged in business in another state.

If the proceeds of the offering are to be used primarily for the purpose of a new business conducted outside of the state of incorporation and unrelated to some incidental business locally conducted, the exemption should not be relied upon. So also, a Section 3(a)(11) exemption should not be relied upon for each of a series of corporations organized in different states where there is in fact and purpose a single business enterprise or financial venture whether or not it is planned to merge or consolidate the various corporations at a later date.

Residence Within the State

Section 3(a)(11) requires that the entire issue be confined to a single state in which the issuer, the offerees and the purchasers are residents. Mere presence in the state is not sufficient to constitute residence as in the case of military personnel at a military post. The mere obtaining of formal representations of residence and agreements not to resell to nonresidents or agreements that sales are void if the purchaser is a nonresident should not be relied upon without more as establishing the availability of the exemption.

An offering may be so large that its success as a local offering appears doubtful from the outset. Also, reliance should not be placed on the exemption for an issue which includes warrants for the purchase of another security unless there can be assurance that the warrants will be exercised only by residents. * * *

* * *

Resales

From these general principles it follows that if during the course of distribution any underwriter, any distributing dealer (whether or not a member of the formal selling or distributing group), or any dealer or other person purchasing securities from a distributing dealer for resale were to offer or sell such securities to a nonresident, the exemption would be defeated. In other words, Section 3(a)(11) contemplates that the exemption is applicable only if the entire issue is distributed pursuant to the statutory conditions. Consequently, any offers or sales to a nonresident in connection with the distribution of the issue would destroy the exemption as to all securities which are a part of that issue, including those sold to residents regardless of whether such sales are made directly to nonresidents or indirectly through residents who as part of the distribution thereafter sell to nonresidents. * * *

This is not to suggest, however, that securities which have actually come to rest in the hands of resident investors, such as persons purchasing without a view to further distribution or resale to nonresidents, may not in due course be resold by such persons, whether directly or through dealers or brokers, to nonresidents without in any way affecting the exemption. The relevance of any such resales consists only of the evidentiary light which they might cast upon the factual question whether the securities had in fact come to rest in the hands of resident investors. If the securities are resold but a short time after their acquisition to a nonresident this fact, although not conclusive, might support an inference that the original offering had not come to rest in the state, and that the resale therefore constituted a part of the process of primary distribution; a stronger inference would arise if the purchaser involved were a security dealer. It may be noted that the nonresidence of the underwriter or dealer is not pertinent so long as the ultimate distribution is solely to residents of the state.

* * *

Securities Regulation
Louis Loss and Joel Seligman.
Pp. 1274–93 (3rd ed. 1995).*

INTRASTATE ISSUES [§ 3(a)(11)]

* * *

(i) The "Issue" Concept:

* * *

As early as 1937, the Commission's General Counsel expressed the following view: "In any consideration of the exemption it is essential to appreciate that its application is . . . expressly limited to cases in which the entire issue of securities is offered and sold exclusively to residents of the state in question." * * * An offer to a single nonresident that is considered part of the intrastate issue will destroy the exemption for the entire offering even if no sales are made to nonresidents. * * * "No reason has been suggested," as one court put it, "why the broad language of Section 3(a)(11) should exempt issues, where some allegedly sporadic and unintentional sales have been made to non-residents, provided that the remainder are sold only to residents." * * *

* * *

(ii) "Doing Business":

There is both administrative and judicial interpretation of the requirement that an issuer be a person "doing business within . . . such State or Territory." The fact that the word *only* does not modify the "doing

---

*   Copyright © 1995 by Louis Loss and Joel Seligman. Reprinted with the permission of the authors and the publisher, Little, Brown and Company.

business" clause indicates quite clearly that the issuer's business need not be *confined* to the state in which it is resident or incorporated. * * * but the language gives no precise guidance as to what degree of the issuer's business must be confined to a single state, or how one defines "business."

* * *

* * * It is clear that the "doing business" requirement is not satisfied by incidental business within a state such as bookkeeping, stock record, or similar activities. But would it ever be sufficient for a corporation's principal factory or income-producing property to be in one state and most sales to occur in a second state? Can a corporation whose headquarters are in one state and which executes sales in that state use the exemption if a substantial but minority percentage of its income-production occurs out-of-state? Suppose a corporation does all of its business entirely in one state. Could it rely on the intrastate exemption solely to finance an incidental activity in a second state? Underlying these types of questions are two discrete inquiries: (1) What activities should be defined as "doing business" under § 3(a)(11)? (2) What percentage of a firm's business must be done in a given state to qualify for the § 3(a)(11) exemption?

(iii) Residence within the State:

The statute does not define "resident," but the Commission at least at one time construed it to mean domicil in the conflict-of-laws sense. The legislative committees in 1954 referred without elaboration to "persons domiciled in one state." * * *

* * *

(iv) Use of Facilities of Interstate Commerce:

In the words of a 1937 opinion of the Commission's General Counsel (substantially reiterated in the 1961 Commission Release):

> [T]he so-called "intrastate exemption" is not in any way dependent upon absence of use of the mails or instruments of transportation or communication in interstate commerce in the distribution. * * * Securities thus exempt may without registration be offered and sold through the mails, may be made the subject of general newspaper advertisement (provided the advertisement is appropriately limited to indicate that offers to purchase are solicited only from, and sales will be made only to, residents of the particular state involved), and may even be delivered in interstate commerce to the purchasers, if such purchasers, though resident, are temporarily out of the state or should direct delivery to some non-resident agent or custodian.[8]

---

[8]   Sec. Act Rels. 1459 (1937). * * *

(v) The Statutory Exemption in General:

The several conditions of § 3(a)(11) and their strict reading by the Commission quite justify the Chairman's statement in 1958 that "as a practical matter the intrastate exemption is loaded with dynamite and must be handled with very great care." * * * Its limited usefulness is all the more apparent in the light of other exemptions. * * *

* * *

Nevertheless, the exemption is there and was presumably intended to be used. It is in fact used. This inevitably raises the question: If a single sale or offer—or, indeed a single resale or reoffer by a resident buyer before the completion of the distribution—to a nonresident destroys the exemption forevermore for the entire issue, what are the practical consequences of a mistake made in good faith, or of a properly supervised salesman's disregard of his instructions to confine his activities to residents? * * * [I]t has been the Commission's policy, once the exemption has been lost under its view, however innocently, to threaten injunctive proceedings if the offering is continued without registration, to require that the registration statement disclose a contingent liability under § 12[(a)](1) with respect to the shares already sold in violation of § 5, and to insist that the issuer offer rescission to those persons on the basis of a statutory prospectus. In one case, the Commission took this position although (1) the only offers or sales to nonresidents of Mississippi out of more than 700,000 shares sold or subscribed for at $3 per share had been a few sales made in violation of instructions by a sub-agent of the best-efforts underwriter to residents of Louisiana who had used Mississippi "dummies" to sign their subscription contracts; (2) those contracts had required every subscriber to "warrant" that he was a "bona fide resident"; and (3) the issuer, as soon as it had learned of those sales, had terminated its relationship with the underwriter and had refunded the moneys paid in by the Louisiana buyers on the ground that their purported subscription contracts had been void *ab initio*. * * *

* * *

Busch v. Carpenter

United States Court of Appeals, Tenth Circuit, 1987.
827 F.2d 653.

■ Before SEYMOUR and TACHA, CIRCUIT JUDGES, and WEINSHIENK, DISTRICT JUDGE.

■ SEYMOUR, CIRCUIT JUDGE.

Paul and Linda Busch brought this action under [Securities Act Section 12] against Craig Carpenter, George Jensen, and Ronald Burnett to recover the purchase price of shares of stock in Sonic Petroleum, Inc. Plaintiffs alleged that the * * * stock did not qualify for the intrastate offering exemption set out in [Securities Act Section 3(a)(11)]. * * * The parties filed cross motions for summary judgment, and the district court granted judgment for defendants * * * .

I.

BACKGROUND

* * * Sonic was incorporated in Utah on October 2, 1980. The three defendants were officers and directors of Sonic at its inception. * * * Sonic publicly offered and sold shares of Sonic stock to Utah residents through Olsen & Company, Inc. Although Sonic complied with Utah state registration requirements, it did not file a registration statement under federal securities law, relying on the exemption from registration provided for intrastate offerings. Sonic, which had no prior operating history at the time of this offering, was incorporated in Utah and purportedly organized to acquire, extract, and market natural resources such as oil, gas, and coal. Although the company had not undertaken this activity in Utah or anywhere else, it maintained its corporate office, books, and records in Utah at the time of the initial offering. It is not disputed that the offering of 25,000,000 shares of Sonic was sold for $500,000 entirely to Utah residents.

In late March or early April of 1981, Carpenter was contacted by William Mason, an Illinois oil and gas promoter, about a merger of Sonic with Mason's operations in Illinois. Sonic and Mason reached an agreement, effective May 25, 1981, under which Sonic issued Mason a controlling block of stock and acquired an Illinois drilling corporation privately owned by Mason. * * * Shortly after Mason Oil was formed, William Mason drew $351,126 from the remainder of the $435,000 net proceeds of the original Sonic offering and deposited it in Illinois. This money was not used in Utah.

In May 1981, Mason and Carpenter set up Norbil Investments, a brokerage account in Utah, so that Mason and his friends could buy shares of the company's stock. Plaintiffs, who are California residents, bought their stock through Norbil. Plaintiffs also presented evidence of purchases through Norbil of stock by other non-residents between May and August 1981.

II.

THE INTRASTATE OFFERING EXEMPTION

* * *

A.   Coming to Rest

The district court ruled that the resale of stock to non-residents occurred after the issued securities had come to rest in Utah and concluded that the public offering was therefore consummated in Utah within the meaning of Section 3(a)(11). * * *

* * * The SEC has consistently maintained that a distribution of securities must have "actually come to rest in the hands of resident investors—persons purchasing for investment and not with a view to

further distribution or for purposes of resale." Securities Act Release No. 1459, 11 Fed.Reg. 10,958 (May 29, 1937). We agree.

During the proceedings below, plaintiffs contended that the resale to non-residents within seven months of the initial offering in and of itself precluded the application of the intrastate offering exemption. The Amicus [the SEC] raises a new argument on appeal, contending that because defendants had the burden to show their right to the exemption, they had the burden below to present evidence that the original buyers bought with investment intent. The Amicus argues that without such a showing, summary judgment for defendants was improper. Plaintiffs have abandoned their claim that resale alone was enough to defeat the exemption. They now join in the Amicus argument, and rely on that argument to assert that they are entitled to summary judgment.

We reject the Amicus' argument. The intrastate offering exemption requires that the issue be "offered and sold only to persons resident within a single State." In our view, a seller seeking summary judgment makes a prima facie showing that the offering was consummated within a state by showing that the stock was sold only to residents of that state. We disagree with Amicus that, in order to be entitled to summary judgment, the issuer should be required to disprove all the possible circumstances that might establish the stock has not come to rest. It seems more logical to us to impose on the other party the burden of producing some contrary evidence on this issue when the seller claiming the exemption has satisfied the facial requirement of the statute. In the face of defendants' undisputed showing that all of the original buyers were Utah residents, plaintiffs were therefore required to produce evidence that the stock had not come to rest but had been sold to people who intended to resell it out of state.

The evidence fails to suggest that any of Sonic's publicly offered shares were issued under questionable circumstances. Carpenter and Mason did not know each other until their initial conversation in the spring of 1981. Mason's subsequent acquisition of control over Sonic was accomplished strictly by means of recapitalization, not via a tender of shares from the company's public offering. Moreover, the interstate purchases by Mason and others of freely trading shares several months after the completion of the intrastate offering do not, without more, impugn the investment intent of the original buyers or otherwise imply an effort to evade the federal securities laws. Norbil served as a conduit for over-the-counter purchases made by Olsen & Company on behalf of Mason and various acquaintances. Although Carpenter did collect from buyers, pay Olsen, and transfer the stock certificates to their new owners, there is simply no indication that those who sold through Norbil had not originally purchased their stock for investment purposes. * * * Accordingly, the trial court did not err in concluding that no genuine question of fact was raised on whether the issue had come to rest in the hands of Utah residents.

B.   Doing Business

Plaintiffs alternatively contend that defendants were not entitled to the intrastate offering exemption because the corporate issuer was not doing business in Utah as required by Section 3(a)(11). There is no dispute that the newly formed company, not yet operational, maintained its offices, books, and records in Salt Lake City. The decisive issue concerns whether, under the circumstances of this case, Sonic's failure to invest a portion of the proceeds from its initial public offering in Utah could defeat the intrastate exemption.

Although neither the statute nor its legislative history defines the doing business requirement, courts have uniformly held that it refers to activity that actually generates revenue within an issuer's home state. The leading case is Chapman v. Dunn, 414 F.2d 153 (6th Cir.1969), which involved a company that maintained its offices and issued stock in Michigan while operating its sole productive venture, an oil and gas business, in Ohio. The *Chapman* court reasoned that "doing business" in the context of securities regulation connotes substantially more activity than that which would warrant exercising personal jurisdiction in ordinary civil suits. Effective supervision of stock offerings, the court added, can entail on-site inspections, familiarity with local economic conditions, and sometimes reliance upon judicial process. State oversight of business operations located elsewhere could often prove cumbersome, costly, and ineffective. The *Chapman* court therefore approved the SEC's view that the intrastate exemption applies only in cases of local financing for local industries. The court held that "doing business" refers to income-producing activity, and that an issuer must conduct a "predominant amount" of that activity within its home state.

Cases involving somewhat different facts have reached the same result. SEC v. Truckee Showboat, Inc., 157 F.Supp. 824 (S.D.Cal.1957), involved a California corporation that planned to use the proceeds of an intrastate stock offering to acquire and operate a Nevada hotel. Although the company had not begun operations beyond maintaining its books and records in California, the intent to invest proceeds elsewhere sufficed to defeat a claim of exemption. In SEC v. McDonald Investment Co., 343 F.Supp. 343 (D.Minn.1972), an established Minnesota corporation that maintained its offices there while doing business elsewhere, planned to invest the proceeds from a local offering in unspecified, out-of-state real estate ventures. The court recognized that although the company operated outside of Minnesota, all land development agreements would be governed by Minnesota law, and interest income would be earned in Minnesota. Even so, because exemptions from registration are to be narrowly construed, the court reasoned that only local industries may be properly excused. Finally, in SEC v. Asset Management Corp., [1979– 1980 Transfer Binder] Fed.Sec.L.Rep. (CCH) ¶ 97,278, at 96,970 (S.D.Ind.1979), a case similar to *Truckee* but involving coal leases rather than a hotel, the court flatly limited the intrastate exemption to cases of "local financing by local industries."

These cases make clear that an issuer cannot claim the exemption simply by opening an office in a particular state. Conducting substantially all income-producing operations elsewhere defeats the exemption, as do the plans of recently organized companies to invest the net proceeds of initial public offerings only in other states. Doing business under the 1933 Act means more than maintaining an office, books, and records in one state.

Viewing the evidence and drawing reasonable inferences most favorably to plaintiffs, a fact issue exists regarding whether Sonic's plans for the use of proceeds are distinguishable from the issuers' plans in *Truckee* and *Asset Management*. Here the corporation never did more than maintain its office, books, and records in Utah. * * * The issue is not whether a newly formed company performs such minimal corporate functions within a state, but whether subsequent proceeds are to be employed in that same state. A newly formed company may not claim the exemption while planning covertly to invest the proceeds of a local offering in other states. As this court has cautioned in a related context, "a person will not be permitted to do indirectly what he cannot do directly." Stadia Oil [& Uranium Co. v. Wheelis, 251 F.2d 269, 275 (10th Cir.1957)]. Accordingly, we conclude that a genuine issue of material fact exists precluding summary judgment in favor of all defendants.

* * *

II. RULES 147 AND 147A

As a consequence of the substantial uncertainties involved in the statutory intrastate offering exemption, it is only the safe harbor of Rule 147 that makes Section 3(a)(11) generally very useful. A careful planner will follow either that rule or its close relative, Rule 147A, discussed below. Rule 147 usually is not satisfied by chance, and lawyers giving after-the-fact advice concerning the availability of the intrastate exemption typically will find themselves making arguments based on the statutory language.

Rule 147 goes through the elements of § 3(a)(11) step by step and adds a note of certainty at each point. For example, it establishes that sales efforts that are made more than six months apart typically will be treated as different issuances. In securities lingo, this means that the efforts will not be "integrated" with one another. For the purposes of the rule, the issuer's good faith belief with respect to an offeree's "principal residence" satisfies the residence requirement of individuals. In addition, the rule provides objective tests for determining the residence of corporations, partnerships, and other types of business organizations. The rule also sets objective tests for the "doing business" requirement, basically pitched at the 80 percent level for assets located in, gross revenues derived from, and proceeds to be used in the state in which the offering is made. If any **one** of the three is satisfied, the issuer will be regarded as doing business in the relevant state. In the alternative, the issuer will be regarded as doing business in any state in which a majority of its employees are located. The rule also deals with the possibility that issuers might sell securities to residents of the same state knowing they will immediately resell them by prohibiting out-of-state resales for six months after the issuer's last sale.

In late 2016, the SEC relied on a different statutory provision in adding a second intrastate offering exemption. Section 28 allows the Commission to add exemptions it deems to be in the public interest, and it was on this authority that it adopted new Rule 147A. That rule parallels Rule 147 but specifies that issuers need not be incorporated in the state in which they seek to make the relevant offering. It also permits widespread offers to be made (including over the internet) if those offers bear appropriate legends and the only purchasers are residents of the state in question. These modifications would not be permitted under § 3(a)(11).

The following is a more technical summary of the two rules drawn largely from the release adopting Rule 147A and most recently amending Rule 147:[9]

Geographic Limitations on Making Offers: Rule 147 permits an issuer to make offers and sales only to in-state persons, Under Rule 147A, an issuer can advertise, including online, to reach in-state residents not then located within the state. The issuer must, however, include a disclaimer noting that sales will be made only to residents in the same state or territory in which the issuer resides.

Issuer Residency: Under Rule 147, the issuer must be incorporated by the state in which it maintains its "principal place of business." "Principal place of business" is the "location from which the officers, partners, or managers of the issuer primarily direct, control and coordinate the activities of the issuer." Rule 147A uses "principal place of business" as the sole standard to determine a business entity's residence. If the issuer's state of residence changes, it cannot conduct a 147 or 147A offering in the new state within 6 months after the last 147 or 147A offering in the prior state.

Doing Business Requirement: Under revised Rule 147 and Rule 147A, an issuer only needs to satisfy one of the listed 80% thresholds to satisfy the doing business requirement. These thresholds relate to (1) assets located in, (2) gross revenues derived from, and (3) proceeds to be used in, the state in which the offering is made. Alternatively, an issuer can satisfy the doing business requirement under Rule 147 and Rule

---

[9]   Release No. 33–10238.

147A by showing a majority of its employees are based in the state of the issuer's residency.

Purchasers Requirement: An issuer can satisfy the in-state-purchasers-only requirement either if all purchasers are indeed in-state residents or the issuer reasonably believes they are in-state residents. The requirement of obtaining a written representation of residency from each purchaser pertains under both Rule 147 and Rule 147A. If a purchaser is a business entity, its residence is determined by the same test that applies to issuers.

Resale Limitations: For a period of six months from the date of the issuer's sale, any resale of the security shall be made only to persons whose residences are within the state or territory in which the issuer was resident at the time of the sale by the issuer. Bona fide gifts are exempt from this limitation. This requirement is satisfied as long as the subsequent purchasers are in-state residents at the time of the issuer's initial sale. Tacking starts on the day of the original investor's purchase.

Integration: Under revised Rule 147 and Rule 147A, an offering will be integrated with another offering within 6 months after completion unless the other offering is registered under the Securities Act, is exempted by Rule 147, Rule 147A, Regulation A, Rule 701, Regulation S, or Section 4(a)(6), or is made under an employee benefit plan.

Disclosure to Investors: An issuer is required to communicate the limitations on resale to all purchasers. Written disclosure is not required and there is no requirement of a legend relating to stop transaction instructions.

D. LIMITED OFFERINGS AND USE OF THE COMMISSION'S EXEMPTIVE AUTHORITY: SECTIONS 3(b)(1), 3(b)(2), 4(a)(2), 4(a)(5), 4(a)(6), AND 28; REGULATIONS A, D, CE AND CROWDFUNDING; RULES 701, 801, AND 802

Securities Act Section 3(b)(1) authorizes the Commission to exempt securities from registration when it finds that registration is not necessary because of the small dollar amount involved or the limited character of the public offering. The Commission's exempting authority is limited, however, to offerings not in excess of $5,000,000. The Commission has established various exemptions under Section 3(b), the most important of which are Rule 504 of Regulation D and Regulation CE.

Going much further than Section 3(b)(1) is Section 28, which was adopted in 1996. This section gives the Commission authority to "exempt any person, security, or transaction, or any class or classes of persons, securities, or transactions, from any provision" of the Securities Act, so long as the "exemption is necessary or appropriate in the public interest, and is consistent with the protection of investors." The Commission's first use of this power was to make changes to Rule 701 (originally a rule under Section 3(b)(1)) that raised the dollar limit above $5,000,000.

In 2012, the JOBS Act threw new Section 3(b)(2) into the mix. This Section was intended to liberalize Regulation A, discussed directly below. It required the Commission to add an exempted class of securities the aggregate offering amount of which that is "offered and sold within the prior 12-month period in reliance on the exemption" does not exceed $50 million (subject to inflation adjustment every two years).

I.   REGULATION A

Although Regulation A, which consists of Rules 251 through 263, provides an exemption from the registration requirements of the Securities Act, as a practical matter it is more closely related to registration than to any of the other exemptions. For example, Regulation A provides for the filing of an offering statement. This document, which approximates a registration statement, contains a copy of the offering circular to be used in selling the securities. As in the case of registered offerings, under Regulation A securities tend to be sold by securities firms working for issuers rather than by the issuers themselves. In the vernacular of securities lawyers, a Regulation A transaction has, in fact, traditionally been called a short-form registration.

Technically, there is no concept of effectiveness involved in Regulation A. The regulation does, however, call for the "qualification" of the offering statement under circumstances that are reminiscent of those applicable to the effectiveness of registration statements.

Regulation A also mimics registration in many other ways. For example, after an offering statement is filed, oral offers may be made freely, as is allowed under Securities Act Section 5 after the filing of a registration statement. Along these same lines, written offers may be made by a preliminary offering circular and, after the offering statement is qualified, other written offers may be made if they are accompanied or proceeded by a final offering circular.

Regulation A offerings differ significantly from registered offerings in certain respects, however. One of the more important differences is that, in Regulation A offerings, an issuer may "test the waters," before the filing of an offering statement, by oral and written communications to potential buyers that are designed to gauge interest in the offering.

Regulation A is available only to certain United States or Canadian companies. Among other requirements, the issuer cannot be an Exchange Act reporting company or an investment company, and (unless the Commission decides otherwise) it cannot have run afoul of specified laws in the past.

For many years, the maximum dollar amount of securities that could be sold under Regulation A was capped at $5,000,000 in a twelve month period (up to $1,500,000 of this amount could be sold by security holders). Because the cost and effort associated with a Regulation A offering was akin to that of a registered offering, the utility of the exemption was somewhat limited.

The Commission now has responded to its JOBS Act mandate, creating two tiers of offering rules. The Tier 1 rules permit the offering of up to $20 million in a twelve month period (no more than $6 million of which can be on behalf of security holders). The rules governing such offerings are largely the same as those governing prior Regulation A offerings. Tier 2 rules permit an issuer to raise up to $50 million in a twelve month period (no more than $15 of which can be on behalf of security holders). Individual Tier 2 purchasers who are not "accredited investors" as defined in Rule 501 (which is part of Regulation D) are limited to investing no more than 10 percent of their net worth or annual income, whichever is greater. State regulation of Tier 2 offerings is preempted (which is not the case with Tier 1); the most significant trade-offs are (1) supplying audited financial statements in the offering circular and (2) complying with ongoing semiannual reporting requirements. Under certain conditions which include maintaining a "public float" of no more than $75 million (or in the absence of public float, revenues of no more than $50 million), a Regulation A issuer can, however, avoid Exchange Act registration.

Securities issued pursuant to Regulation A are not "restricted securities" subject to the resale limitations described in Chapter 7. Still, during the first twelve months following the qualification of a Regulation A offering statement, resales attributable to issuer affiliates cannot exceed 30 percent of the value of the relevant offering.

The following is a more technical summary drawn largely from the adopting Release:[10]

The SEC has revised Regulation A pursuant to Section 401 of the JOBS Act. The new Regulation A permits two tiers of offering: Tier 1 for up to $20 million in a 12-month period and Tier 2 for up to $50 million in a 12-month period. The new Regulation A and its Forms became effective on June 19, 2015.

Eligibility: The only eligible securities for Regulation A are the securities in the specifically enumerated list of securities under Securities Act Section 3(b)(3). Asset-backed securities defined in Regulation AB are ineligible for Regulation A.

Offering Limitations and Secondary Sales:

	Tier 1	Tier 2
Amount of offering allowed within a 12-month period of time	$20 million	$50 million

---

[10]   Release No. 33–9741 (2015).

Amount of offering allowed by affiliate security holders within a 12-month period of time (note: resale both by affiliates and non-affiliates is aggregated with the issuer's offering when determining the possible maximum amount of securities allowed to offer.)	30% of the maximum offering allowed in the same tier	30% of the maximum offering allowed in the same tier

If a security underlies any rights to acquire that are convertible, exercisable or exchangeable within the first year of qualification or at the issuer's discretion, and the security's qualification is currently sought, the issuer should include the security when calculating the amount of offering. The issuer must use the highest estimated price of the security may be converted, exercised, or exchanged.

Investment Limitation: An investor cannot invest more than 10% of the greater of annual income or net worth in one Tier 2 offering, unless the investor is an accredited investor as defined in Rule 501 or unless the securities will be listed on a national securities exchange. If the investor is non-accredited and not a natural person, it cannot invest more than 10% of the greater of its annual revenue or assets. If the investor purchases securities convertible, exercisable or exchangeable for other securities within one year and the investor exercises such rights, the calculation should include both purchase price and aggregate conversion, exercise or exchange price. The issuer should notify investors such limitations exist and can rely on investors' representation when determining whether investors have met their investment limitations.

Integration Safe Harbor: A Regulation A offering will not be integrated with prior offers or sales of securities, or subsequent offers and sales of the following securities: securities registered under the Securities Act except as provided in Rule 255(c), securities sold pursuant to an employee benefit plan, securities sold pursuant to an exemption provided by Rule 701, Regulation S or Section 4(a)(6) crowdfunding, and securities offered more than six months after completion of the Regulation A offering.

Treatment Under 12(g): Securities in a Tier 2 offering are exempted from Exchange Act Section 12(g) registration if the issuer is (1) subject to, and currently satisfying, Regulation A periodic reporting requirements and (2) is engaging the services of a transfer agent registered with the SEC under Exchange Act Section 17A. Only an issuer with a public float of less than $75 million, or with revenue of less than $50 million (in the absence of a public float) is eligible for this exemption.

Qualification: The issuer must file the offering statement no later than 21 calendar days before qualification. New Regulation A requires that the SEC issue a notice of qualification before an offering may become qualified.

Solicitation of Interest (Testing the Waters): An issuer is allowed to test the waters and use solicitation materials with all potential investors, before and after filing an offering statement, subject to filing rules and disclaimers.

After the issuer publicly files an offering statement, the testing the waters materials must be accompanied by the current preliminary offering circular or URL where the current circular can be obtained. The issuer is also required to update and distribute materials in the event the original materials become materially inadequate or inaccurate.

Testing the water materials are required to include certain legends and disclaimers, including one to the effect that offers are contingent upon the qualification of the offering statement.

Ongoing Reporting Requirement: Tier 1 issuers should report completion or termination of sales but have no other reporting obligations. Tier 2 issuers must report completion or termination of sales and have ongoing reporting obligations, including annual reports (Form 1–K), semiannual reports (Form 1–SA), and current event reports (Form 1–U). A Tier 2 issuer's ongoing filing obligations immediately stop when it becomes a reporting company under Section 12(g) of the Exchange Act.

Bad Actor Disqualifications: The new regulation adopts "bad actor" disqualifications similar to those in Rule 506 of Regulation D. The disqualifications cover persons including managing members of LLCs, compensated solicitors, underwriters, executive officers and officers participating in the offering, and beneficial owners with at least 20% outstanding voting equity securities. The triggering events include both (1) final orders or bars by certain federal and state agencies, and (2) SEC cease-and-desist orders regarding scienter-based antifraud violations or violations of Securities Act Section 5.

Relationship with State Laws: All Regulation A offerees and all Tier 2 purchasers are preempted from state registration and qualifications requirements.

II. SECTION 4(a)(5)

Section 4(a)(5) provides a registration exemption for offerings to "accredited investors," in amounts up to the dollar limit of Section 3(b)(1), as long as the issuer files the required notice with the Commission. The term "accredited investor" is defined in Section 2(a)(15) to include certain institutions, such as banks and insurance companies, and "any person, who, on the basis of such factors as financial sophistication, net worth, knowledge, and experience in financial matters, or amount of assets under management qualifies as an accredited investor under rules and regulations which the Commission shall prescribe." The Commission has adopted Rule 215, which sets forth accredited investor qualification requirements. For natural persons, the basic tests are either net worth, with one's spouse, of more than $1,000,000 (calculated without regard to the value of a primary residence) or net income of more than $200,000 in each of the two most recent years (or $300,000 jointly with one's spouse.)

Section 4(a)(5) has been on the books since 1980. It has, however, been regarded as largely superfluous since the adoption of Regulation D in 1982. Regulation D, discussed below, incorporates the accredited investor concept in a somewhat more useful way. Regulation D has, in Rule 501, its own definition of an accredited investor, which the Commission attempts to keep in sync with Rule 215.

III. Regulation D

Regulation D is an interesting amalgam. Of its two exempting rules, Rule 504 is a rule under Section 3(b)(1) and Rule 506 is a rule under Section 4(a)(2). Rule 506 is a safe harbor rule that exists along with the basic private placement exemption provided in the statute. Rules 504 is not a safe harbor rule, however, since Section 3(b)(1) provides no exemption. All Section 3(b)(1) does is give the Commission the power to pass rules that provide exemptions. One of the more important things to remember about Regulation D is that when a Rule 506 transaction is attempted but fails, the requirements for the basic private placement exemption may still be met. But when a Rule 504 exemption fails, the seller has nothing in Section 3(b)(1) to fall back on.

Regulation D begins with rules that provide information and establish requirements that are applicable to the two exempting rules. Rule 501 is the definitional rule. Among other things, it establishes the requirements for classification as an accredited investor, which has substantial Regulation D consequences. As in the case of Rule 215, referred to above in connection with Section 4(a)(5), the basic accredited investor tests for natural persons are either net worth, with one's spouse, of more than $1,000,000 (not including primary residence) or net income in each of the two most recent years of more than $200,000 (or $300,000 with one's spouse). Rule 502 provides a number of conditions for establishing a Regulation D exemption, which may or may not apply to a particular exempting rule. For example, it sets forth requirements for the information to be furnished to investors. These requirements vary with the exemption used and with the nature of both issuers and investors. It also proscribes general solicitations or advertisements and sets forth a requirement designed to prevent illegal resales by purchasers. The rule also provides help with the integration question by, in most cases, removing from the possibility of integration offers and sales that occur more than six months before the start of a Regulation D offering or more than six months after its completion. The last of these rules of general applicability, Rule 503, provides the requirements for filing notices of sales, and the Commission has provided Form D for the purpose. Form D is a simple, fill-in-the-blanks form. Interestingly, as the existing rules are written, one can get the benefit of the Regulation D exemptions without filing the Form D.

Rule 507 provides, however, that if an issuer or a predecessor or affiliate has been the subject of an injunction because of a failure to file the Form D as required by Rule 503, then Regulation D is no longer available for use by that issuer, unless the Commission specifically determines otherwise. Finally, Rule 508 provides that, in certain circumstances, an insignificant deviation from the requirements of one of Regulation D's exempting rules—Rule 504 or 506—will not result in the loss of the registration exemption provided by the Rule. Main among these circumstances is a good faith and reasonable attempt by the issuer to comply with the Rule.

The following table shows the basic requirements and limitations on offerings under Rules 504 and 506. Note that although Rule 506 is a safe harbor under Section 4(a)(2), it was given something of a life of its own in 2012. Section 201 of the JOBS Act required the Commission to revise the rule so as to permit general solicitation and advertising, provided that all actual purchasers are accredited investors. Issuers are to be required to make such efforts as the Commission specifies to make sure that purchasers indeed are accredited investors. Section 4 of the Securities Act simultaneously was amended, by the addition of new sub-section (b), to provide that offerings under Rule 506 will be non-public (and thus exempt under Section 4(a)(2)) notwithstanding general solicitation or advertising.

REGULATION D EXEMPTIONS

	Rule 504	**Rule 506**
Aggregate Offering Price Limitation	$1,000,000 (12 mos.)	Unlimited
Number of Investors	Unlimited	35 plus unlimited accredited
Investor Qualification	None required	Purchaser must be sophisticated (alone or with representative)—Accredited presumed to be qualified
Sales Commissions	Permitted	Permitted
Limitations on Manner of Offering	Usually no general solicitation permitted*	General solicitation to be permitted provided all purchasers are accredited
Limitations on Resale	Usually restricted**	Restricted**
Issuer Qualifications	No Exchange Act reporting, "blank-check,"*** investment companies, or "bad actors"****	No "bad actors" ****
Notice of Sales	Five copies of Form D to be filed with Commission within 15 days after first sale (called for by Regulation D, but not required for exemption)	

Information Requirements	None	1. If purchased solely by accredited investors, no information specified
		2. If purchased by non-accredited investors,

a.   nonreporting companies under the Exchange Act must furnish the same kind of information as in registered offering, or in a Regulation A offering if eligible, but with lesser financial statement requirements

b.   reporting companies must furnish (i) specified Exchange Act documents or (ii) information contained in the most recent specified Exchange Act report or Securities Act registration statement on specified forms, plus, in any case, (iii) updating information and limited additional information about the offering

c.   issuers must make available prior to sale

i.   exhibits

ii.   written information given to accredited investors

iii.   opportunity to ask questions and receive answers

d.   issuers must advise purchasers of the limitations on resale

*   This requirement, and the "restricted" nature of the securities (see following item in table) are lifted basically when (I) the securities are registered under a state law requiring public filing and delivery of a disclosure document before sale, and such a document is delivered, or (ii) the securities are offered and sold exclusively under a state law exemption that permits general solicitations, so long as sales are made only to accredited investors.

**   "Restricted" securities are defined in Rule 144, which is discussed in the next chapter. For the purposes of this table, they can be viewed as securities that cannot be resold in a public sale until certain requirements, including in most cases a one-year holding period, are met.

***   A "Blank-check" company is a development-stage company that either has no specific business plan or purpose or has indicated that its business plan is to engage in a merger or acquisition with an unidentified company or companies or other entity or person.

****   "Bad actors" are those who have a relevant conviction, regulatory or court order, or the like.

Over the years, the Commission's staff has responded to a large number of requests for interpretation of Regulation D. Here is a small sample taken from a release containing 92 questions and answers.

Securities Act Release No. 6455

Securities and Exchange Commission, March 3, 1983.

INTERPRETIVE RELEASE ON REGULATION D

The Commission has authorized the issuance of this release setting forth the views of its Division of Corporation Finance on various interpretive questions regarding the rules contained in Regulation D under the Securities Act of 1933. These views are being published to answer frequently raised questions with respect to the regulation.

* * *

(1) *Question:* A director of a corporate issuer purchases securities offered under Rule [506]. Two weeks after the purchase, and prior to completion of the offering, the director resigns due to a sudden illness. Is the former director an accredited investor?

Answer: Yes. The preliminary language to Rule 501(a) provides that an investor is accredited if he falls into one of the enumerated categories "at the time of the sale of securities to that person." One such category includes directors of the issuer. *See* Rule 501(a)(4). The investor in this case had that status at the time of the sale to him.[11]

* * *

(24) *Question:* All but one of the shareholders of a corporation are accredited investors by virtue of net worth or income. The unaccredited shareholder is a director who bought one share of stock in order to comply with a requirement that all directors be shareholders of the corporation. Is the corporation an accredited investor under Rule 501(a)(8)?

Answer: No. Rule 501(a)(8) requires "all of the equity owners" to be accredited investors. The director is an equity owner and is not accredited. Note that the director cannot be accredited under Rule 501(a)(4). That provision extends accreditation to a director of the issuer, not of the investor.

* * *

(37) *Question:* The executive officer of the parent of the Regulation D issuer performs a policy making function for its subsidiary. May that individual be deemed an "executive officer" of the subsidiary?

Answer: Yes.

* * *

(40) *Question:* An issuer furnishes potential investors a short form offering memorandum in anticipation of actual selling activities and the delivery of an expanded disclosure document. Does Regulation D permit the delivery of disclosure in two installments?

Answer: So long as all the information is delivered prior to sale, the use of a fair and adequate summary followed by a complete disclosure document is not prohibited under Regulation D. Disclosure in such a manner, however, should not obscure material information.

* * *

---

[11] Preliminary Note 6 to Regulation D would support a different analysis if it could be shown that the director's appointment or resignation was "part of a plan or scheme to evade the registration provisions of the Act."

(54) *Question:* One purchaser in a Rule 506 offering is an accredited investor. Another is a first cousin of that investor sharing the same principal residence. Each purchaser is making his own investment decision. How must the issuer count these purchasers for purposes of meeting the 35 purchaser limitation?

Answer: The issuer is not required to count either investor. The accredited investor may be excluded under Rule 501(e)(1)(iv), and the first cousin may then be excluded under Rule 501(e)(1)(i).[12]

* * *

(57) *Question:* An investor in a Rule 506 offering is a general partnership that was not organized for the specific purpose of acquiring the securities offered. The partnership has ten partners, five of whom do not qualify as accredited investors. The partnership will make an investment of $100,000. How is the partnership counted and must the issuer make any findings as to the sophistication of the individual partners?

Answer: Rule 501(e)(2) provides that the partnership shall be counted as one purchaser. The issuer is not obligated to consider the sophistication of each individual partner.

* * *

(74) *Question:* If an issuer relies on one exemption, but later realizes that exemption may not have been made available, may it rely on another exemption after the fact?

Answer: Yes, assuming the offering met the conditions of the new exemption. No one exemption is exclusive of another.

* * *

The letter that follows provides an interesting look at offering practices as of 2015.

CITIZENVC, Inc.

(SEC NO-ACTION LETTER)

(Publicly Available Aug. 6, 2015)

DANIEL I. DEWOLF, ESQ.

MINTZ, LEVIN, COHEN, FERRIS, GLOVSKY & POPEO, P.C.

CHRYSLER CENTER, 666 THIRD AVENUE

NEW YORK, NEW YORK 10017

Re: Citizen VC, Inc.

---

[12] The Note to Rule 501(e) provides that the issuer must satisfy all other conditions of Regulation D with respect to purchasers that have been excluded from the count. Thus, for instance, the issuer would have to ensure the sophistication of the first cousin under Rule 506(b)(2)(ii).

Dear [Mr.] DeWolf:

* * *

You have requested the staff concur in your conclusion that the policies and procedures described in your letter will create a substantive, pre-existing relationship between CitizenVC and prospective investors such that the offering and sale on the Site of Interests in special purpose vehicles (SPVs) that will invest in a particular Portfolio Company will not constitute general solicitation or general advertising within the meaning of Rule 502(c) of Regulation D.

We agree that the quality of the relationship between an issuer (or its agent) and an investor is the most important factor in determining whether a "substantive" relationship exists. As the Division has stated before, a "substantive" relationship is one in which the issuer (or a person acting on its behalf) has sufficient information to evaluate, and does, in fact, evaluate, a prospective offeree's financial circumstances and sophistication, in determining his or her status as an accredited or sophisticated investor. See, e.g., *Bateman Eichler, Hill Richards, Inc.* ([publicly available] Dec. 3, 1985). We note your representation that CVC's policies and procedures are designed to evaluate the prospective investor's sophistication, financial circumstances and ability to understand the nature and risks of the securities to be offered. We also agree that there is no specific duration of time or particular short form accreditation questionnaire that can be relied upon solely to create such a relationship. Whether an issuer has sufficient information to evaluate, and does in fact evaluate, a prospective offeree's financial circumstances and sophistication will depend on the facts and circumstances.

In expressing these views, we note your representation that the relationship with new Members will pre-exist any offering, consistent with the Division's previous guidance. In this regard, we note that a prospective Member is not presented with any investment opportunity when being qualified to join the platform. Any investment opportunity would only be presented after the prospective investor becomes a Member. Further, we understand that CVC creates SPVs for investment in particular Portfolio Companies and not as blind pools for a later investment opportunity.

Because this position is based on the representations in your letter, any different facts or conditions might require the Division to reach a different conclusion.

Sincerely,

David R. Fredrickson

Chief Counsel

LETTER TO SEC

August 3, 2015

DAVID R. FREDRICKSON, ESQ.

CHIEF COUNSEL

DIVISION OF CORPORATION FINANCE

U.S. SECURITIES AND EXCHANGE COMMISSION

100 F. STREET, NE

WASHINGTON, DC 20549

Re: Citizen VC, Inc.

Dear Mr. Fredrickson:

Our client, Citizen VC, Inc. and its affiliates (collectively, "CitizenVC"), proposes to offer and sell from time to time, without registration, limited liability company interests ("Interests") of special purpose vehicles ("SPVs") established and managed by a wholly owned subsidiary of CitizenVC, Inc. (the "Manager") in order to aggregate investments made by members ("Members") of the CitizenVC online venture capital investment platform (the "Site"). The SPVs invest in seed, early-stage, emerging growth and late-stage private companies, and offer accredited investors the SPVs' Interests in reliance upon the exemption provided pursuant to Rule 506(b) of Regulation D promulgated under the Securities Act of 1933, as amended (the "Securities Act"). CitizenVC does not intend to rely on the exemption from registration provided under Rule 506(c), and will not engage in any general solicitation or general advertising. In connection with, and prior to, the offering of the Interests of SPVs, CitizenVC intends to establish pre-existing, substantive relationships with prospective members of the Site in accordance with the policies and procedures described in this letter. We note that current practices among online venture capital and angel investing sites vary substantially in the methodology for establishing a pre-existing, substantive relationship for purposes of complying with Rule 506(b). It is our opinion that the policies and procedures described in this letter will be sufficient to create the necessary relationship between CitizenVC and prospective investors such that the offering and sale of Interests on the Site will not constitute general solicitation or general advertising within the meaning of Rule 502(c) of Regulation D, On behalf of CitizenVC, we request that the staff of the Division of Corporation Finance (the "Staff") concur with our conclusion.

Background

Citizen VC, Inc. is an online venture capital firm that owns and administers a website (https://citizen.vc) that facilitates indirect investment by its pre-qualified, accredited and sophisticated Members in seed, early-stage, emerging growth and late-stage private companies ("Portfolio Companies") through SPVs organized and managed by the Manager. The SPVs are created to invest in specific Portfolio Companies and not as blind pool investment vehicles. Further, the SPVs will purchase equity interests either from the Portfolio Companies or from selling shareholders (subject to the consent of the Portfolio Companies).

CitizenVC is focused on technology, both its own and those of its portfolio companies, and desires to utilize the Internet and the Site to modernize and streamline traditionally offline venture capital investing activities, including presenting Portfolio Company offering materials to its Members and consummating ail transactions online.

The Site is hosted on the publicly accessible Internet and CitizenVC is cognizant of the fact that prospective investors may search the Internet and land on its Site. CitizenVC wants to be prepared to accept membership applications from prospective investors with whom a pre-existing relationship has not yet been formed, but with whom it will establish a relationship prior to offering Interests.

CitizenVC has developed qualification policies and procedures that it intends to use to establish substantive relationships with, and to confirm the suitability of, prospective investors that visit the Site, Upon landing on the homepage of the Site,[13] a visitor that wishes to investigate the password protected sections of the Site accessible only to Members must first register and be accepted for membership. In order to apply for membership, CitizenVC requires all prospective investors, as a first step, to complete a generic online "accredited investor" questionnaire. The satisfactory completion of the online questionnaire is, however, only the beginning of Citizen VC's relationship building process.

Once a prospective investor has completed the online questionnaire and CitizenVC has evaluated the investor's self-certification of accreditation, CitizenVC will initiate the "relationship establishment period," During this period, CitizenVC will undertake various actions to connect with the prospective investor and collect information it deems sufficient to evaluate the prospective investor's sophistication, financial circumstances, and its ability to understand the nature and risks related to an investment in the Interests. Such activities include (1) contacting the prospective investor offline by telephone to introduce representatives of CitizenVC and to discuss the prospective investor's investing experience and sophistication, investment goals and strategies, financial suitability, risk awareness, and other topics designed to assist CitizenVC in understanding the investor's sophistication, (2) sending an introductory email to the prospective investor, (3) contacting the

---

[13] The publicly accessible homepage contains only generic information about CitizenVC, There is no information accessible on the publicly accessible homepage about any of the current SPVs, Portfolio Companies, investment opportunities or offering materials. The publicly accessible homepage is designed so that no reasonable person could construe it as a solicitation for any particular offering.

prospective investor online to answer questions they may have about CitizenVC, the Site, and potential investments, (4) utilizing third party credit reporting services to confirm the prospective investor's identity, and to gather additional financial information and credit history information to support the prospective investor's suitability, (5) encouraging the prospective investor to explore the Site and ask questions about the Manager's investment strategy, philosophy, and objectives, and (6) generally fostering interactions both online and offline between the prospective investor and CitizenVC. Additionally, prospective investors will be advised that every SPV offering will have a significant minimum capital investment requirement for each investor, which will be not less than $50,000 per individual investment, and in some offerings significantly higher. All of the foregoing activities and interactions are specifically designed to create and strengthen a real, substantive relationship between CitizenVC and the prospective investor, and to verify and ensure that the offering of Interests is suitable for them.

The duration of the relationship establishment period is not limited by a specific time period. Rather, it is a process based on specific written policies and procedures created to ensure that the offering of Interests is suitable for each prospective investor.

After CitizenVC is satisfied that (i) the prospective investor has sufficient knowledge and experience in financial and business matters to enable it to evaluate the merits and risks of the investment opportunities on the Site, and (ii) it has taken all reasonable steps it believes necessary to create a substantive relationship with the prospective investor, only then will CitizenVC admit the prospective investor as a Member of the Site. Thereafter, CitizenVC will provide the new Member access to the password protected sections of the Site, where the new Member can investigate investment opportunities curated by CitizenVC and the offering materials related thereto. The relationship with a new Member will exist prior to any offering of securities to such new Member.

Once a sufficient number of qualified Members have expressed interest in the private placement investment opportunity of a particular Portfolio Company, those Members will be provided subscription materials for investment in the SPY formed by CitizenVC to aggregate such Members' investments, which materials shall include additional risk disclosure and detailed "accredited investor" certifications and representations. Thereafter, the offering and sale of Interests of such SPV will be consummated. The SPV will then invest such funds in, and become an equity holder of, the Portfolio Company, Each SPV will be managed by the Manager, which shall become a registered investment adviser as required under the Investment Advisers Act of 1940, as amended (the "IAA").

Legal Analysis

* * *

Rule 506(b) of Regulation D provides a safe harbor for issuers to engage in private placements, Private placements undertaken pursuant to Rule 506(b) are limited, however, by Rule 502(c) of Regulation D; which imposes as a condition on offers and sales under Rule 506(b) that " * * * neither the issuer nor any person acting on its behalf shall offer or sell the securities by any form of general solicitation or general advertising * * * ."

Since the adoption of Regulation D, the Staff has issued various interpretive letters ("No Action Letters") that have further clarified the contours of the regulation and established the "important and well-known principle * * * [that] a general solicitation is not present when there is a pre-existing, substantive relationship between an issuer, or its [agent], and the offerees."

Through these No Action Letters, the Staff has endorsed the position that an issuer, through its agent (generally, registered brokers-dealers), may establish a pre-existing, substantive relationship with the use of a questionnaire that, once completed by the investor, provides such agent sufficient information to evaluate the investor's sophistication or accreditation. It is less clear from the guidance, however, whether an issuer itself can rely solely on a questionnaire that relates only to "accredited investor" status (particularly in an online transaction) to establish the necessary pre-existing relationship without a waiting period or additional policies and procedures that would establish a pre-existing and substantive relationship. * * *

Conclusion

We interpret the Staffs No Action Letter guidance to mean that the *quality* of the relationship between an issuer and an investor is the most important factor to be considered in determining whether a pre-existing, substantive relationship has been established for purposes of offerings made in private placements pursuant to Rule 506(b) of Regulation D. It is our opinion that the No Action Letter guidance of the Staff points to establishing a process for issuers to develop substantive relationships with previously unknown investors, and that this process can be undertaken in a manner that will not contravene the prohibition of general solicitation and general advertising under Rule 502(c). The relationship between issuer and investor is not built through a specific duration of time or a short form accreditation questionnaire. Rather, it can be established by adhering to specific policies and procedures both online and offline (where appropriate), which enable the issuer to evaluate the prospective investor's financial sophistication, circumstances, suitability, and his or her ability to understand the nature and risks of the Interests to be offered. It is this substantive relationship that is necessary to execute an offering of securities online in a password protected area that does not violate Rule 502(c).

* * *

It is our opinion that the substantive relationship building policies and procedures developed by CitizenVC and described in this letter establish a pre-existing, substantive relationship between CitizenVC and its prospective investors such that granting access to such prospective investors in a password protected area of the CitizenVC Site to materials related to the offering of unregistered Interests in SPVs will not involve any form of general solicitation or general advertising, and will enable CitizenVC to offer Interests online without contravening Rule 502(c). We respectfully request the Staffs concurrence with our opinion.

* * *

Very truly yours,

Daniel I. DeWolf

Daniel I. DeWolf, Esq.

IV. SECTION 4(a)(6) AND REGULATION CROWDFUNDING

Section 4(a)(6) was added in 2012 by a title of the JOBS Act. The title refers to itself as the " 'Capital Raising Online While Deterring Fraud and Unethical Non-Disclosure Act of 2012' or the 'CROWDFUND Act.' " The exemption itself is stated in Section 4(a)(6), but Section 4A (added at the same time) imposes additional requirements for issuers and financial intermediaries involved in crowdfunding and also must be considered. Although the Commission was given both fairly broad discretion to tinker with the details and a list of instructions to address such matters as "bad boy" disqualifiers, the statutory exemption has the following notable requirements:[14]

(1) The issuer must be a domestic company that is not an investment company and is not required to file Exchange Act reports;

(2) The aggregate amount of securities sold to all investors by the issuer and its controlled or controlling entities within a 12-month period cannot exceed $1,000,000 (subject, as are all dollar amounts in Section 4(a)(6), to inflation adjustments at least every five years, and now set at $1,070,000);

(3) The aggregate amount sold to any investor within a 12-month period cannot exceed (a) for investors with an annual income or net worth less than $100,000 (now $107,000), the

---

[14] By reason of a simultaneous amendment to the Exchange Act, holders of securities sold in a crowdfunding transaction do not count toward the threshold that requires a company to register its securities under Exchange Act Section 12(g) if the company is current in its annual reporting obligations, retains the services of a registered transfer agent and has less than $25 million in total assets as of the end of its most recently completed fiscal year.

greater of $2,000 (now $2,200) or 5 percent of annual income or net worth; and (b) for investors with an annual income or net worth of at least $100,000 (now $107,000), 10 percent of annual income or net worth, not to exceed a maximum aggregate amount sold of $100,000 (now $107,000);

(4)   The transaction must be conducted through a broker or "funding portal" complying with a panoply of requirements, including registration under the Exchange Act, ensuring investor understanding of, and ability to bear, the risk of investment, and taking steps to ensure that no investor in a 12-month period purchases under 4(a)(6) securities that, in the aggregate from all issuers, exceed the limits described in (3) above;

(5)   The issuer must file with the Commission, and provide to investors and the relevant broker or funding portal, a variety of information including a description of the issuer's financial condition (to be updated on an annual basis) requiring levels of review ranging from officer certification to external audit, depending on the offering's target size;

(6)   The issuer must not advertise the terms of the offering, except for notices which direct investors to the relevant funding portal or broker; and

(7)   Securities acquired subject to the exemption cannot be transferred for one year other than to a list of specified parties including family members and accredited investors or as part of a registered offering.

Unfortunately, Section 4(a)(6) is not a model job of legislative drafting (the same, incidentally, is true for the rest of the JOBS Act). For instance, if an investor has (before inflation adjustments) an annual income of less than $100,000 and a net worth of $100,000 or more (or vice versa), both sets of limits on sales to specific investors literally apply. Regulation Crowdfunding, which was adopted in a release running to more than 600 pages,[15] conformed to its statutory mandate and also generated solutions to the legislative mysteries created (for instance, if, under the statute, two sets of limitations apply, the rules provide that the more restrictive set prevails).

Regulation Crowdfunding also adds to the list of companies not eligible to use the exemption, which now includes non-U.S. companies, Exchange Act reporting companies, investment companies, certain "bad actors," companies that have failed to comply with the annual reporting requirements under Regulation Crowdfunding during the two years immediately preceding the filing of the offering statement, and companies that have no specific business plan or have indicated that

---

[15]   Release No. 33–9974 (2015).

their business plan is to engage in a merger or acquisition with an unidentified company or companies.

The Regulation specifies that a funding portal is required to register with the Commission on new Form Funding Portal, and become a member of a national securities association (currently, FINRA). A company relying on the rules is required to conduct its offering exclusively through one intermediary platform at a time. The rules governing intermediaries are extensive.

V. REGULATION CE

Regulation CE is exceedingly short. It contains only one rule, Rule 1001. Basically, the rule provides a registration exemption for offers and sales of securities that satisfy the conditions of Section 25102(n) of the California Corporations Code, up to a total of $5 million per offering. (Note the implications of the fact that the amount limitation is "per offering." If, for example, $3 million of an offering were under Section 25102(n) and $3 million were under another exemption, the amount limitation would be exceeded.)

The availability of the California exemption generally is limited to California issuers and non-California issuers that have more than 50% of their property, payroll, and sales in that state, so long as more than 50% of the non-California issuer's voting securities are held of record by persons having addressees in California. Under this exemption, sales (and most offers) are limited to qualified purchasers, which include, for example, affiliates of the issuer and certain of their relatives, institutions, and persons who qualify under one or another test relating to wealth. In the case of most purchasers who are natural persons, the issuer must provide extensive written disclosure. In all cases, filings must be made with the California Corporations Commissioner. All securities sold under Regulation CE are restricted securities, a concept that will be further discussed in Chapter 7.

VI. RULE 701

Prior to the passage of Rule 701 in 1988, issuers who wished to offer securities to employees under stock purchase, stock option, or other benefit plans or contracts often found that an exemption from the Securities Act's registration requirements was not available. Perhaps recognizing the special relationship between an issuer and its employees, the Commission adopted Rule 701 to make an exemption quite freely available for such offerings, along with offerings to others having specified relationships with the issuer. Rule 701 is not available to Exchange Act reporting companies or investment companies. The maximum amount of securities that can be sold in a twelve-month period is the greater of $1,000,000, an amount equal to 15 percent of the issuer's total assets, or 15 percent of the outstanding securities of the class. If more than $5,000,000 of securities are sold, specified disclosures must be provided.

VII. RULES 801 AND 802

The Commission has long been interested in helping facilitate international securities transactions, for example by providing the specialized registration forms F–1 and F–3 for foreign issuers that correspond to Form S–1 and S–3. By the late 1990s, it became clear to the Commission that registration exemptions were necessary for international transactions involving rights offerings, exchange offers, and business combinations contemplated by foreign private issuers. Rule 801 was the Commission's response with respect to rights offerings and Rule 802 its response for exchange offers and business combinations. These Rules are further discussed in Chapter 20.

CHAPTER 7

REGULATION OF RESALES OF SECURITIES

SITUATION 7

Microtec accomplished the Compuform merger, issuing its common stock, without registration, in reliance on Securities Act Section 4(2) and Rule 506 of Regulation D. (It did not, however, sell securities to raise cash for infusion into the Compuform operations, but rather decided to rely on bank borrowings.) Within four months of the merger, five shareholders holding shares taken in connection with the Compuform merger request that Microtec allow the transfer of their shares. One is David Gordon, who was a Vice President of Compuform and is now a Vice President of Microtec. He received 1,000 shares in connection with the merger. In addition, three months ago he purchased 400 shares in the trading market. In order to raise cash to lend to his daughter, who is just starting a business, he wishes to sell in the trading market 700 of his shares, or as many as he can.

None of the other shareholders who wishes to transfer shares has any relationship with Microtec except as a shareholder. The reasons for their requests are as follows:

    1.   One shareholder wishes to make a gift of 100 shares to her recently married son.

    2.   Another shareholder is faced with paying for unexpected and expensive medical procedures. He wishes to sell 2,000 shares immediately in the trading market.

    3.   The estate of a former Compuform shareholder wishes to sell 1,000 shares in the trading market, to raise cash to pay estate taxes.

    4.   One shareholder wishes to sell 800 shares to a local executive, in a face to face transaction, to raise cash for investment in another company.

———————

In considering this situation, refer to the following, in addition to the materials in this chapter: Securities Act Sections 2(a)(11), 4(a)(1), 4(a)(4), 4(a)(7), 4(d) and 4(e), and Securities Act Rules 144 and 144A.

A. CONTROL AND RESTRICTED SECURITIES

The Securities Act registration exemption that allows most security holders to sell securities without registration is Section 4(a)(1), which covers "transactions by any person other than an issuer, underwriter, or dealer." It is easiest to determine the availability of this exemption when a preliminary question is answered first: Are the securities proposed to be sold control securities or restricted securities?

Control securities are securities owned by a person who is an affiliate of the issuer. To understand the concept of control securities, it is helpful first to look to Securities Act Rule 405, which contains definitions of terms. "Affiliate" and "control" are both defined.[1]

> *Affiliate.* An "affiliate" of, or person "affiliated" with, a specified person, is a person that directly, or indirectly through one or more intermediaries, controls or is controlled by, or is under common control with, the person specified.

> *Control.* The term "control" (including the terms "controlling," "controlled by" and "under common control with") means the possession, direct or indirect, of the power to direct or cause the direction of the management and policies of a person, whether through the ownership of voting securities, by contract, or otherwise.

To understand the concept of "control," one must understand what the Commission means by "the power to direct or cause the direction of * * * management and policies." Familiarity with two theories concerning control aids in this understanding. One is the idea that the unexercised ability to control is control. When, for example, a shareholder owns sufficient stock in a corporation that management is likely to be responsive to the shareholder's requests or demands, the Commission says the shareholder is an affiliate of the corporation. It is immaterial that the shareholder pays no attention to the management of the corporation. This leads to the question of how much stock is enough to control a corporation. There is no fixed answer, but 10 percent equity ownership is a rule of thumb. Obviously, many shareholders who own this percentage of stock, or even a much greater percentage, are not in control of a corporation. For example, a shareholder who owns a large minority interest may be excluded from power by a management that holds a majority interest. When a shareholder has a 10 percent interest, however, the Commission will probably consider the shareholder to be an affiliate, unless someone convinces it otherwise. Securities lawyers begin worrying about control when well below this percentage of stock is involved.

The other theory to understand is that of the control group. Under this theory, a person is in control if he or she is a member of a group that controls. This theory applies to shareholders who may be considered part

---

[1]   Technically, the definitions contained in Rule 405 relate to terms used in Securities Act Rules 400 through 494 or terms used in a Securities Act registration form. The definitions of "affiliate" and "control," however, are reliable definitions for general Securities Act purposes. In connection with Securities Act Rule 144, discussed below in this chapter, note that the Rule 405 definition of "affiliate" is carried over into the definition of this term contained in Rule 144(a)(1).

of a control group. A family is a classic example. This theory is also used to bring corporate officers and directors under the concept of "control."

The concept of "restricted securities" is somewhat simpler than that of "control securities." A definition is contained in Rule 144(a)(3):

The term "restricted securities" means:

(i)   Securities acquired directly or indirectly from the issuer, or from an affiliate of an issuer, in a transaction or chain of transactions not involving any public offering;

(ii)   Securities acquired from the issuer that are subject to the resale limitations of Rule 502(d) under Regulation D or Rule 701(g);

(iii)   Securities acquired in a transaction or chain of transactions meeting the requirements of Rule 144A;

(iv)   Securities acquired from the issuer in a transaction subject to the conditions of Regulation CE;

(v)   Equity securities of domestic issuers acquired in a transaction or chain of transactions subject to the conditions of Rule 901 or Rule 903 under Regulation S;

(vi)   Securities acquired in a transaction made under Rule 801 to the same extent and proportion that the securities held by the security holder of the class with respect to which the rights offering was made were as of the record date for the rights offering "restricted securities" * * * ;

(vii)   Securities acquired in a transaction made under Rule 802 to the same extent and proportion that the securities that were tendered or exchanged in the exchange offer or business combination were "restricted securities" * * * ; and

(viii)   Securities acquired from the issuer in a transaction subject to an exemption under Section [4(a)(5)] of the Act.

This definition is convoluted, but it is readily understandable with a little explanation. The best way to accomplish this explanation is to break the definition into parts, and then discuss each part in turn.

The first part of this definition relates to "Securities that are acquired directly or indirectly from the issuer, or from an affiliate of the issuer, in a transaction or chain of transactions not involving any public offering." This part of the definition covers securities (1) that at one point were sold by the issuer under a Section 4(a)(2) nonpublic offering exemption (either in a statutory private placement or in a sale under Securities Act Rule 506) or a Section 4(a)(5) limited offering exemption, or (2) that at one point were sold by an affiliate of the issuer in a private resale using the Section 4(a)(1) exemption (which is discussed below). The current holder may have purchased the restricted securities directly from the issuer or an affiliate of the issuer, or there may have been a chain of transactions that separate the current holder from one of these sellers. When there is such a chain of transactions, each intervening sale must be a private resale that uses the Section 4(a)(1) exemption. Thus, the straightforward thrust of this part of the definition is that purchasers in transactions under Section 4(a)(2) or 4(a)(5) buy restricted securities.[2]

The second part of the definition of restricted securities covers "Securities acquired from the issuer that are subject to the resale limitations of Rule 502(d) of Regulation D or Rule 701(g)." This phrase includes all securities purchased directly from an issuer in any transaction under Rule 505 or 506 of Regulation D, as well as many of the securities purchased under Rule 504.[3] There is some overlap between this part of the definition and the part discussed above, because securities purchased directly from an issuer under Rule 506 of Regulation D are included under both parts.

The third part of the definition covers "Securities that are acquired in a transaction or chain of transactions meeting the requirements of Rule 144A." Rule 144A is discussed at the end of this chapter. It relates to resales of securities by security holders to "qualified institutional buyers."

The fourth part of the definition covers "Securities acquired from the issuer in a transaction subject to the conditions of Regulation CE." Regulation CE exempts offerings and sales of securities that satisfy the conditions of Section 25102(n) of the California Corporations Code, up to a total of $5 million per offering. Regulation CE provides that all securities issued under the regulation are restricted securities.

The fifth part of the definition covers "Equity securities of domestic issuers acquired in a transaction or chain of transactions subject to the conditions of Rule 901 or Rule 903 under Regulation S." Regulation S permits certain offshore offers and sales of securities to be conducted without compliance with the Securities Act's registration requirements and is discussed in more detail in Chapter 20.

Like the fifth part of the definition of restricted securities, the sixth and seventh parts of the definition exemplify the Commission's initiative to facilitate international securities transactions. They relate, respectively, to cross-border rights offerings by foreign private issuers and to cross-border exchange offers and business combinations involving such issuers. Rules 801 and 802 are further discussed in Chapter 20.

---

[2]   Securities acquired by gift, directly or indirectly from the issuer, or an affiliate of the issuer, also meet the criteria for restricted securities.

[3]   Rule 502(d) states the resale restrictions of Regulation D as follows: "Except as provided in Rule 504(b)(1), securities acquired in a transaction under Regulation D shall have the status of securities acquired in a transaction under section 4(2)." Rule 701(g)(1) provides that "Securities issued pursuant to [Rule 701] are deemed to be 'restricted securities' as defined in [Rule 144]."

The eighth part was added in 2007 to clarify the treatment of securities acquired under section 4(a)(5) (which, as discussed above, already were covered in part one).

Before leaving the discussion of restricted securities, it will be helpful to introduce one further concept: fungibility. Under that concept, if a person owns both restricted and nonrestricted securities of the same class and from the same issuer, the nonrestricted securities would take on the taint of restricted status. This occurs because, for some purposes, securities are considered to be fungible. In the release in which it adopted Rule 144, however, the Commission indicated that the concept of fungibility will not apply for the purposes of the rule.

B. PUBLIC RESALES OUTSIDE RULE 144

Rule 144, which the Commission adopted in 1972, provides a means for selling both control and restricted securities. However, Rule 144 is not exclusive, and sellers sometimes wish to sell outside the rule. Also, the rule often is of no use when lawyers are called in after the fact, since it has requirements that may demand advance planning. In addition, the rule is mechanistic rather than analytic, and it provides little help in understanding Section 4(a)(1) and its place in the regulatory scheme. Without this understanding, some of the provisions of the rule are quite opaque. For these reasons, public resales of control and restricted securities outside Rule 144 are discussed at this point.

I. SALES OF CONTROL SECURITIES

As indicated at the beginning of this chapter, Section 4(a)(1) provides the exemption that allows most security holders to sell securities without registration. To determine when this exemption is available, it is important to determine whether the proposed transaction is "by an issuer, underwriter or dealer." Here are the Section 2 definitions of "issuer" and "dealer":

> The term "issuer" means every person who issues or proposes to issue any security * * * .

> The term "dealer" means any person who engages either for all or part of his time, directly or indirectly, as agent, broker, or principal, in the business of offering, buying, selling, or otherwise dealing or trading in securities issued by another person.

In the usual situation, the Securities Act definition of "issuer" parallels the usage of the term in corporate law generally, and means the company that originally sells the security. The term "dealer" refers to one type or other of securities professional, and not to an ordinary investor. Except in an unusual situation, then, an investor who wishes to sell securities under Section 4(a)(1) is neither an issuer nor a dealer.

The consequences of holding control securities are found in the definition of "underwriter." In its most basic provision, Section 2(a)(11) defines the term to mean "any person who has purchased from an issuer with a view to, or offers or sells for an issuer in connection with, the distribution of any security." For an affiliate who holds securities that are control securities and not also restricted securities, there would be little problem if the definition stopped here. It does not, however. The last sentence of Section 2(a)(11) adds: "As used in this [Section 2(a)(11)] the term 'issuer' shall include, in addition to an issuer, any person directly or indirectly controlling or controlled by the issuer, or any person under direct or indirect common control with the issuer." In other words, the basic definition of "underwriter" should be treated as if it read: "The term 'underwriter' means any person who has purchased from an issuer or an affiliate of the issuer with a view to, or offers or sells for an issuer or an affiliate of the issuer in connection with, the distribution of any security." "Distribution" is not defined in the statute, but it is understood essentially to be synonymous with "public offering." For example, in an early case the Commission established that a distribution comprises "the entire process by which in the course of a public offering a block of securities is dispersed and ultimately comes to rest in the hands of the investing public."[4]

Because of the way in which the term "underwriter" is defined, a securities firm that handles the sale of control securities in the public markets may be considered an underwriter. If it handles the sale as a dealer (as the term is used in the securities industry; that is, if it buys the securities itself with the idea of reselling them), it may be considered to have "purchased from an issuer with a view to * * * distribution." If it handles the transaction as a broker (that is, if it merely sells the securities for the affiliate), it may be considered to have offered or sold "for an issuer in connection with * * * the distribution." In either case, the series of transactions by which the securities pass from the affiliate to the public is considered to constitute one distribution that is partially "by" an underwriter. When this is the case, Section 4(a)(1) is not available, and the registration requirement of Section 5 is violated.

The typical sale in the trading markets by an ordinary investor is a transaction partially by a dealer (as defined in Section 2(a)(12), where brokers and real world dealers are lumped together as "dealers") in the same sense that a similar sale by an affiliate is by an underwriter. Since Section 4(a)(1) is not available when a transaction is by an issuer, underwriter, or dealer, it may seem that Section 4(a)(1) is not available when an ordinary investor sells through a dealer. This is not the case, however.

There is in the Securities Act no exemption available to underwriters in any circumstance. There are, on the other hand, exemptions provided

---

4   In re Oklahoma-Texas Trust, 2 S.E.C. 764, 769 (1937).

for dealers, both when operating as dealers in the ordinary sense of the term (Section 4(a)(3)) and as brokers (Section 4(a)(4)). It is clear that it would make little sense for the Securities Act to provide these exemptions to dealers while not at the same time providing an exemption to the investor selling to or through the dealer. And, of course, there is no question but that the 4(a)(1) exemption was designed to exempt most transactions by ordinary investors. Perhaps the way to think about such a transaction involving a dealer is that the investor is covered by Section 4(a)(1) and the dealer by Section 4(a)(3) or 4(a)(4). It may be argued that in a transaction involving an underwriter, Section 4(a)(1) is not available because neither it nor any other exemption would cover the underwriter.

It may appear that securities would always have to be registered before an affiliate can sell them publicly, because it may seem that such a sale would always constitute a distribution. Considering the costs involved in registration, this would mean that it would not be economically feasible for an affiliate to sell control securities except in a transaction involving at least some hundreds of thousands of dollars. This result is not what was contemplated by the drafters of the Securities Act, and the Commission has never taken this extreme position. Rather, the Commission has built some flexibility into the Securities Act by manipulating the concept of distribution. This is discussed in the next case, which is the seminal one on the subject.

In re Ira Haupt & Co.

Securities Exchange Commission, 1946.
23 S.E.C. 589.

This proceeding was instituted under Sections 15(b) and 15A(*l*)(2) of the Securities Exchange Act of 1934 to determine whether Ira Haupt & Co. ("Respondent") willfully violated Section 5(a) of the Securities Act of 1933 and, if so, whether the revocation of its registration as a broker-dealer and its expulsion or suspension from membership in the National Association of Securities Dealers, Inc. ("NASD"), a registered securities association, would be in the public interest.

The alleged violation of Section 5(a) is based on respondent's sale, for the accounts of David A. Schulte, a controlled corporation of Schulte's, and the David A. Schulte Trust (sometimes hereinafter referred to collectively as the "Schulte interests"), of approximately 93,000 shares of the common stock of Park & Tilford, Inc., during the period November 1, 1943, to June 1, 1944. It is conceded that the Schulte interests [, which together owned over 90 percent of Park & Tilford's common stock,] were in control of Park & Tilford during this period, that the sales were effected by use of the mails and instrumentalities of interstate commerce, and that the stock was not covered by a registration statement under the Securities Act.

* * *

THE STIPULATED FACTS

* * *

On November 30, 1943, there were 243,731 shares of Park & Tilford common stock outstanding. * * *

On or about December 14, 1943, Schulte called [Ira] Haupt to his office. George Ernst, counsel for Schulte, was also present. Haupt testified that at this meeting Schulte told him that:

> * * * The Park & Tilford Company are going to announce a plan, a liquor plan. * * * Mr. George Ernst spoke up and said that in the announcement of this liquor plan very likely the stock would become terribly active, or very active and that Mr. Schulte would like to have an orderly market and that they were contemplating putting in a hundred shares of stock to sell every quarter or half point or point, what they decide, would that create an orderly market. I said I think it would take a little more stock than that, due to the fact that if somebody came in to the crowd to buy a couple of thousand shares of stock it would put the market up 3 or 4 dollars. So George Ernst turned to Mr. Schulte and says I think Mr. Haupt might have something there, what do you think of making the order 2 or 3 hundred shares. So Mr. Schulte said, well, I will consider it, and if I am ready to do anything, Mr. Haupt, I will phone down to Mr. Scherk [Respondent's order clerk]. On the morning of December 15 he telephoned down to Mr. Herbert Scherk an order to sell 200 shares of stock at 59 and every quarter up.

* * *

On the morning of December 15, Schulte publicly announced that Park & Tilford was contemplating a distribution of whiskey at cost to its shareholders. In 2 days, the stock advanced 13¼ points, from 57⅞ to a closing price of 70⅞ on December 16; during those 2 days Schulte sold 15,700 shares through respondent.

The price declined between December 18, 1943, and January 19, 1944, and Schulte sold only 200 shares while purchasing 3,300 shares.

When the price began rising on January 20, Schulte resumed selling. By the end of January, he disposed of 5,900 shares at 60¾ to 76½. In February 14,553 shares, including the 4,853 shares held by the 1924 Corporation, were sold at 72¼ to 80¾; 11,800 shares were sold in March at prices ranging from 75 to 83; 4,400 shares were sold in April; and 1,042 were sold in May at 89½ to 95½. All sales were effected by respondent for the account of Schulte or the 1924 Corporation on orders to sell a specific number of shares at a limited price.

On February 24 Reinach[, a Haupt partner,] was called to a conference with Arthur Schulte (son of David A. Schulte and a trustee of the Trust) and George Ernst to discuss a proposed sale of 50,000 shares by Respondent for the account of the Trust. According to Reinach's testimony:

> * * * [E]ither he [Arthur Schulte] or George Ernst, I don't remember, gave me a letter to read. In this letter it stated that we should sell 50,000 shares of Park & Tilford at 80. To the best of my recollection the stock was selling in the low 70's at the time. Arthur Schulte then said we want to sell 300 shares every quarter and if the market runs away and gets wild you can tell Ira to sell a thousand or two thousand shares extra * * * .

There was some discussion about the form of the letter of authorization. In accordance with the discussion, the Trust sent respondent a revised letter dated February 25, 1944, which was received on March 7. This letter read in part as follows:

> You are hereby authorized to sell for the account of the undersigned * * * up to but not in excess of 50,000 shares of Park & Tilford, Inc. common stock at $80 per share or better. Said order is to remain good until cancelled by us in writing. We will not hold you responsible for sales at or above $80 which are not executed for our account.

By letter dated March 31, the number of shares to be sold for the Trust was increased from 50,000 shares to 73,000 shares. The increased number was to be sold subject to the same authority and conditions as the original 50,000 shares.

Pursuant to this authorization respondent sold 38,900 shares for the account of the Trust: 8,000 shares between March 23 and March 31 at $80^{1}/_{4}$ to $86^{3}/_{4}$; 4,700 shares in April; and 26,200 shares in May at prices of 84 to 98.

On May 26 Park & Tilford offered to sell to stockholders at a reduced price six cases of whiskey for each share of stock. On that day the stock reached a high of $98^{1}/_{4}$. On May 31 the Office of Price Administration limited the negotiability of the purchase rights and the maximum profits on the resale of the liquor. That day the price of the stock dropped $10^{1}/_{8}$ points. It reached a low of $30^{5}/_{8}$ in June. Neither Schulte nor the Trust sold any stock in June.

All told, respondent sold approximately 93,000 shares of stock for the account of the Schulte interests, from December 15, 1943, to May 31, 1944. * * * During the same period, the public's holdings were increased from 18,249 shares or 8 percent to 115,344 or 46 percent.

* * *

Counsel for the staff contends that the foregoing facts show a willful violation of Section 5(a) of the Securities Act. Respondent asserts that its transactions were exempt from registration and that, in any event, it lacked the requisite intent for a "willful" violation. * * *

* * *

THE ISSUES INVOLVED

It is conceded that respondent's transactions in Park & Tilford stock for the account of the Schulte interests constitute a violation of Section 5(a) unless an exemption was applicable to such transactions. Respondent contends that [the following exemption] was applicable:

* * *

Section [4(a)(4)] which exempts

Brokers' transactions, executed upon customers' orders on any exchange or in the open or counter market, but not the solicitation of such orders.

The applicability of the foregoing [exemption] involves the following subissues:

(1) Was Respondent an "underwriter" as that term is defined in Section [2(a)(11)]?

* * *

(3) Is the brokerage exemption of Section [4(a)(4)] available to an underwriter who effects a distribution of an issue for the account of a controlling stockholder through the mechanism of a stock exchange?

* * *

1.   Was Respondent an "Underwriter"?

Section [2(a)(11)] defines an "underwriter" as

any person who * * * sells for an issuer in connection with, the distribution of any security * * * as used in this paragraph the term "issuer" shall include * * * any person * * * controlling * * * the issuer * * * .

The purpose of the last sentence of this definition is to require registration in connection with secondary distributions through underwriters by controlling stockholders. * * *

It is conceded that the Schulte interests controlled Park & Tilford and the respondent was, therefore, "selling for" a person in control of the issuer. However, respondent denies that these sales were effected "in connection with the distribution of any security." It asserts that at no time did it intend, nor was it aware that Schulte intended, a distribution of a large block of stock. It emphasizes that, in connection with the sales by which Schulte disposed of approximately 52,000 shares over a period of 6 months, each order was entered by Schulte to maintain an orderly market and was limited to 200 to 300 shares at a specific price; that the authority to sell 73,000 shares for the Trust was dependent upon a market price of at least 80; that the total amount which would be sold was never fixed or ascertained, and that consequently it did not intend to sell in connection with a distribution.

"Distribution" is not defined in the Act. It has been held, however, to comprise "the entire process by which in the course of a public offering the block of securities is dispersed and ultimately comes to rest in the hands of the investing public." * * * We think [the] facts clearly fall within the above quoted definition and constitute a "distribution." We find no validity in the argument that a predetermination of the precise number of shares which are to be publicly dispersed is an essential element of a distribution. Nor do we think that a "distribution" loses its character as such merely because the extent of the offering may depend on certain conditions such as the market price. * * *

* * *

At the time of the first discussion with Schulte, respondent knew that the Schulte orders were to be placed after an announcement of a possible liquor dividend which was expected to create greatly increased market activity and a sharp rise in price and that the stated purpose of these orders was "to have an orderly market." Moreover, the fact that the public announcement of the possible liquor dividend was made much in advance of the date the dividend was actually declared, together with Schulte's statement as to the probable effect of the general announcement, was additional evidence that Schulte intended to distribute his holdings to the public at rising prices. The only reasonable conclusion that could have been reached by respondent was that it was intended that a large block would be sold. This is, of course, what actually happened. * * *

* * *

We conclude from the foregoing facts that respondent was selling for the Schulte interests, controlling stockholders of Park & Tilford, in connection with the distribution of their holdings in the stock and was, therefore, an "underwriter" within the meaning of the Act.

* * *

3. Is the Brokerage Exemption of Section [4(a)(4)] Available to an Underwriter Who Effects a Distribution of an Issue for the Account of a Controlling Stockholder Through the Mechanism of a Stock Exchange?

Respondent's final argument on this phase of the case is that, notwithstanding the inapplicability of [Section] [4(a)(1)] and even though respondent may be found to be an underwriter, its transactions fall within Section [4(a)(4)] which exempts "brokers' transactions, executed upon customers' orders on any exchange * * * but not the solicitation of such orders." Counsel for the staff takes the position * * * that Section [4(a)(4)] can never apply to exempt the transactions of an underwriter engaged in a distribution for a controlling stockholder * * * .

* * *

It is clear from Section [4(a)(1)], read in conjunction with Section [2(a)(11)], that public distributions by controlling persons, through underwriters, are intended generally to be subject to the registration and prospectus requirements of the Act. * * *

* * *

We find nothing in the language or legislative history of Section [4(a)(4)] to compel the exemption of this type of secondary distribution and the consequent overriding of the general objectives and policy of the Act. On the contrary, there are affirmative indications that Section [4(a)(4)] was meant to preserve the distinction between the "trading" and "distribution" of securities which separates the exempt and non-exempt transactions under Section [4(a)(1)]. This conclusion becomes apparent on examination of the legislative comments on Sections [4(a)(1)] and [4(a)(3)].

In referring to the exemption in Section [4(a)(1)] for transactions by a person "other than an issuer, underwriter, or dealer," the House Report states:

> Paragraph (1) broadly draws the line between *distribution* of securities and trading in securities, indicating that the act is, in the main, concerned with the problem of distribution as distinguished from trading. It, therefore, exempts all transactions except by an issuer, underwriter or dealer * * * . (Emphasis added.)

And, in discussing the limited exemption for dealers * * * ,[5] the House Report again emphasized the distinction between "trading" and "distribution":

> * * * Recognizing that a dealer is often concerned not only with the *distribution* of securities but also with *trading* in securities, the dealer is exempted as to *trading* when such *trading* occurs a year[6] after the public offering of the securities. Since before that year the dealer might easily evade the provisions of the act by a claim that the securities he was offering for sale were not acquired by him in the process of *distribution* but were acquired after such process had ended, transactions during that year are not exempted. The period of a year is arbitrarily taken because, generally speaking, the average public offering has been distributed within a year and the imposition of requirements upon the dealer so far as that year is concerned is not burdensome. (Emphasis added.)

From the foregoing, it is apparent that transactions by an issuer or underwriter and transactions by a dealer during the period of

---

[5]   Now Section 4(a)(3), the dealers' exemption. [Eds.]

[6]   Now 40 or 90 days as a matter of statutory language and, pursuant to Rule 174, in most cases even less. [Eds.]

distribution (which period for purposes of administrative practicality is arbitrarily set at one year) must be preceded by registration and the use of a prospectus. It is likewise apparent that Congress intended that, during this period, persons other than an issuer, underwriter, or dealer should be able to *trade* in the security without use of a prospectus. Since such persons would carry on their trading largely through the use of brokers (who are included in the general definition of dealers), such trading through brokers without the use of a prospectus could be permitted during the first year after the initial offering only if there were a special exemption for dealers acting as brokers. The importance of this special exemption is emphasized in the case where a stop order might be entered against a registration statement. For, although such a stop order was intended to and would operate to stop all *distribution* activities, it would also result in stopping all *trading* by individuals through dealers acting as brokers unless a special exemption were provided for brokers. It was in recognition of this fact and to permit a dealer to act as a broker for an individual's trading transactions, while the security is being distributed and during the period of a stop order, that Section [4(a)(4)] was enacted. * * *

To summarize: Section [4(a)(4)] permits individuals to sell their securities through a broker in an ordinary brokerage transaction, during the period of distribution or while a stop order is in effect, without regard to the registration and prospectus requirements of Section 5. But the process of distribution itself, however carried out, is subject to Section 5.

* * *

We conclude that Section [4(a)(4)] cannot exempt transactions by an underwriter executed over the Exchange in connection with a distribution for a controlling stockholder. Respondent has suggested that this conclusion is contrary to administrative interpretations issued by our staff and to the implications in recent orders issued in connection with applications of *The United Corporation* under the Public Utility Holding Company Act with respect to United's sale of common stock of a subsidiary through brokers on the New York Stock Exchange. The administrative interpretations referred to were to the general effect that an underwriter selling for a controlling stockholder over the exchange might conceivably be entitled to the exemption under Section [4(a)(4)] if his activities were confined strictly to the usual brokerage functions, but that, as a practical matter, his activities could not be so confined in connection with a distribution of any substantial block of securities. These interpretations arrived at the same ultimate result as that which we have reached here. But the theory and the qualification of the interpretations—which we agree are inconsistent with our conclusion herein—were developed against the background of a very different market than is now prevalent. It has been only comparatively recently that the problem has been presented in the context of a market in which large blocks can frequently be sold without solicitations or other sales activity. In that context, the invalidity of the theory on which the interpretations were based has become apparent. We have reached our present conclusion on this phase of the case after careful consideration of the entire problem and, to the extent that the administrative interpretations referred to and the principle involved in the *United* case may be inconsistent with that conclusion, they must be overruled.

* * *

PUBLIC INTEREST

Even though Respondent willfully violated the Securities Act, its registration as a broker-dealer may not be revoked, and it may not be suspended or expelled from the NASD, unless such action is found to be in the public interest.

The cumulative effect of certain considerations impels us to conclude that neither revocation nor expulsion is necessary or appropriate in the public interest. As Respondent points out, the interpretation of Section [4(a)(4)] has been the subject of considerable doubt. This is the first case in which we have held the brokerage exemption of Section [4(a)(4)] to be inapplicable to a distribution over the Exchange by an underwriter acting for a controlling person. And, to the extent we have indicated, this conclusion represents a departure from previous interpretations.

* * * Accordingly, we find it appropriate in the public interest and for the protection of investors to suspend Respondent from membership in the NASD for a period of 20 days.

* * *

The problem with *Haupt* was that its facts were too far from the garden variety sale of securities by an affiliate for securities firms to get much guidance from it. The firms knew they would be underwriters if they replicated the facts of *Haupt,* but they did not know where the Commission would draw its line separating allowable transactions from distributions. Particularly troubling was the fact that the Commission, while failing to give guidelines, overruled the prior staff interpretations that had allowed at least small scale market sales by affiliates through brokers.

It was not until 1954, when it adopted Rule 154, that the Commission took definitive action on the questions left open in *Haupt.* This rule, which was later superseded by Rule 144, used the old Commission staff interpretations as a starting point and added a numbers test to determine the existence of a distribution. Under the rule, no distribution occurred when: (1) all sales were by a broker, who performed only ordinary brokers' functions and who received only the usual commission; (2) neither the broker, nor to his knowledge the seller, solicited any orders; (3) the broker was not aware of circumstances indicating that the sales were part of a distribution; and (4) the amount of securities sold in six months did not exceed approximately one percent of the total outstanding securities of the same class. This rule alleviated a good bit of the problem generated by *Haupt*. As discussed below, its concepts were carried over into Rule 144.

It may be helpful to examine the most important case decided under Rule 154. As will be seen, in this case the Second Circuit was, because of compliance by brokers with Rule 154, backed into accepting that the brokers that sold control securities for controlling persons had the benefit of the Section 4(a)(4) brokers' exemption even though the controlling persons themselves had no exemption. This same result could obtain under Rule 144.

United States v. Wolfson

United States Court of Appeals, Second Circuit, 1968.
405 F.2d 779.

■ Before MOORE, WOODBURY and SMITH, CIRCUIT JUDGES.

■ WOODBURY, SENIOR CIRCUIT JUDGE:

It was stipulated at the trial that at all relevant times there were 2,510,000 shares of Continental Enterprises, Inc., issued and outstanding. The evidence is clear, indeed is not disputed, that of these the appellant Louis E. Wolfson himself with members of his immediate family and his right hand man and first lieutenant, the appellant Elkin B. Gerbert, owned 1,149,775 or in excess of 40%. The balance of the stock was in the hands of approximately 5,000 outside shareholders. The government's undisputed evidence at the trial was that between August 1, 1960, and January 31, 1962, Wolfson himself sold 404,150 shares of Continental through six brokerage houses, that Gerbert sold 53,000 shares through three brokerage houses and that members of the Wolfson family, including Wolfson's wife, two brothers, a sister, the Wolfson Family Foundation and four trusts for Wolfson's children sold 176,675 shares through six brokerage houses.

Gerbert was a director of Continental. Wolfson was not, nor was he an officer, but there is ample evidence that nevertheless as the largest individual shareholder he was Continental's guiding spirit in that the officers of the corporation were subject to his direction and control and that no corporate policy decisions were made without his knowledge and consent. Indeed Wolfson admitted as much on the stand. No registration statement was in effect as to Continental; its stock was traded over-the-counter.

The appellants do not dispute the foregoing basic facts. They took the position at the trial that they had no idea during the period of the alleged conspiracy, stipulated to be from January 1, 1960, to January 31, 1962, that there was any provision of law requiring registration of a security before its distribution by a controlling person to the public. On the stand in their defense they took the position that they operated at a level of corporate finance far above such "details" as the securities laws; as to whether a particular stock must be registered. They asserted and their counsel argued to the jury that they were much too busy with large affairs to concern themselves with such minor matters and attributed the fault of failure to register to subordinates in the Wolfson organization and to failure of the brokers to give notice of the need. Obviously in finding the appellants guilty the jury rejected this defense, if indeed, it is any defense at all.

* * *

The appellants argue that they come within [the Section 4(a)(1)] exemption for they are not issuers, underwriters or dealers. At first blush there would appear to be some merit in this argument. The immediate difficulty with it, however, is that Section [4(a)(1)] by its terms exempts only "transactions," not classes of persons, and ignores Section [2(a)(11)] of the Act which defines an "underwriter" to mean any person who has purchased from an issuer with a view to the distribution of any security, or participates directly or indirectly in such undertaking unless that person's participation is limited to the usual and customary seller's commission, and then goes on to provide:

> "As used in this paragraph the term 'issuer' shall include, in addition to an issuer, any person directly or indirectly *controlling* or controlled by *the issuer,* or any person under direct or indirect common control with the 'issuer.' " (Italics supplied.)

In short, the brokers provided outlets for the stock of issuers and thus were underwriters. Wherefore the stock was sold in "transactions by underwriters" which are not within the exemption of Section [4(a)(1)].

But the appellants contend that the brokers in this case cannot be classified as underwriters because their part in the sales transactions came within Section [4(a)(4)], which exempts "brokers' transactions executed upon customers' orders on any exchange or in the over-the-counter market but not the solicitation of such orders."[7] The answer to this contention is that Section [4(a)(4)] was designed only to exempt the brokers' part in security transactions. Control persons must find their own exemptions.

There is nothing inherently unreasonable for a broker to claim the exemption of Section [4(a)(4)] when he is unaware that his customer's part in the transaction is not exempt. Indeed, this is indicated by the definition of "brokers' transaction" * * * in Rule 154 which provides:

> "(a) The term "brokers' transaction' in Section [4(a)(4)] of the act shall be deemed to include transactions by a broker acting as agent for the account of any person controlling,

---

[7]   It is undisputed that the brokers involved in this case did not solicit orders from the appellants.

controlled by, or under common control with, the issuer of the securities which are the subject of the transaction where:

"(4) The broker is *not aware* of circumstances indicating * * * that the transactions are part of a distribution of securities on behalf of his principal."

And there can be no doubt that appellants' sale of over 633,000 shares (25% of the outstanding shares of Continental and more than 55% of their own holdings), was a distribution rather than an ordinary brokerage transaction. See Rule 154(6) which defines "distribution" for the purpose of paragraph (a) generally as "substantial" in relation to the number of shares outstanding and specifically as a sale of 1% of the stock within six months preceding the sale if the shares are traded on a stock exchange.

Certainly if the appellants' sales, which clearly amounted to a distribution under the above definitions had been made through a broker or brokers with knowledge of the circumstances, the brokers would not be entitled to the exemption. It will hardly do for the appellants to say that because they kept the true facts from the brokers they can take advantage of the exemption the brokers gained thereby.

* * *

II. SALES OF RESTRICTED SECURITIES

Outside of Rule 144, there never has been a corollary to Rule 154 relating to the sale of restricted securities. There are, however, administrative interpretations that allow restricted securities to be sold publicly without the sale being treated as a distribution. Before the adoption of Rule 144 in 1972, these interpretations had a great deal of vitality, and securities lawyers spent substantial amounts of time struggling with them. In Securities Act Release No. 5223 (January 10, 1972), the release in which the Commission announced Rule 144, the Commission asserted that the rule is not exclusive. Subsequently, the Commission amended the rule to provide this explicitly. It must be remembered, however, that the Commission almost certainly lacked the power to adopt an exclusive resale rule, and so its failure to do so tells little about its real desires in the matter. The language the Commission used in Release No. 5223 is the best gauge of these desires, and it clearly discourages reliance on the preexisting interpretations for sales of restricted securities, except for securities purchased before the effective date of the rule. The tone of the release accomplishes this discouragement, as do two statements in the release relating to restricted securities purchased after the effective date of the rule: (1) the change of circumstances doctrine (discussed below) would have no further effect and (2) the Commission's staff would no longer issue no-action letters in connection with resales. (The Commission later relented on the latter point and will give no-action letters on resale questions that are unusual.)

Still, Rule 144 is not exclusive for restricted securities purchased after its effective date, and there may be an occasion for a holder of such securities purposely to sell them publicly outside the rule. This rarely would be wise, however. The interpretations preexisting Rule 144 are of much greater current importance for two other reasons: (1) they foster an understanding of the workings and effect of the rule, and (2) they may have to be relied upon in cases in which a holder of restricted securities, without proper planning, sells these securities without following the requirements of the rule.

One interpretation relates to how long restricted securities are held before resale. This factor is important because it is thought that the length of the holding period is objective evidence of the holder's investment intent, or the lack thereof, at the time of original purchase. A purchaser's investment intent is important because the opposite of investment intent is "view to distribution." And, under Section 2(a)(11), purchasing with a view to distribution makes the holder an underwriter.

Alternatively, a person who sells restricted securities too soon after their purchase may be considered an underwriter under the theory that the sale is "for an issuer in connection with [a] distribution." Reasoning to this conclusion starts with the idea that a distribution is not complete until the securities have come to rest in the hands of persons who are not "merely conduits for a wider distribution." The argument may then proceed that: (1) the issuer knows or should know that some purchasers of restricted securities will want to resell fairly quickly after their purchase; (2) a purchaser is able to resell quickly only because the issuer does not take effective steps to prevent it (such as contractual provisions prohibiting the resale and legends on the certificates representing the securities); and (3) since the issuer is responsible for the resale, the resale will be considered as simply a part of a larger distribution of the securities, by the issuer, to the public through an underwriter.

Notice that from the point of view of the purchaser who has resold, the alternative theory is the more dangerous theory. Under the first theory, a purchaser may have a good chance of convincing a court that he or she did not purchase securities with a view to distribution, notwithstanding the shortness of the holding period. Under the second theory, however, the intent of the purchaser is irrelevant, as is the intent of the issuer.

The obvious question, of course, is how long a holding period is required to avoid these problems. It is clear that no holding period removes the taint of underwriter status from someone who has purchased with a distribution in mind. In the usual situation, however, a sufficiently long holding period dispels any notion that a reseller of restricted securities is an underwriter. United States v. Sherwood, which appears directly below, has been the most helpful case on this subject.

United States v. Sherwood

United States District Court, Southern District of New York, 1959.
175 F.Supp. 480.

■ SUGARMAN, DISTRICT JUDGE.

By order to show cause filed February 6, 1959, the United States of America moves * * * for an order adjudging Robert Maurice Sherwood to be in criminal contempt for not obeying a final decree of permanent injunction entered against him on consent * * * .

The application for the order to show cause alleges *inter alia* that:

* * *

"2. On November 24, 1958, United States District Judge Sidney Sugarman, sitting in the Southern District of New York, issued a permanent injunction enjoining Robert Maurice Sherwood and others from, among other things, * * * violations of the registration provisions of the Securities Act of 1933, in the offer and sale of common shares of Canadian Javelin Limited.

"3. On November 24, 1958, Robert Maurice Sherwood through his American Counsel, Simpson Thacher and Bartlett, by Albert C. Bickford, a partner, consented to the entry of this final decree of permanent injunction. * * *

* * *

"5. No registration statement covering shares of Canadian Javelin Limited has ever been filed with the Securities and Exchange Commission, and none has ever been in effect.

* * *

"7. Since November 24, 1958 * * * Robert Maurice Sherwood has offered and sold more than 8,000 shares of Canadian Javelin Limited * * * .

"8. These shares were all shares received by Robert Maurice Sherwood from John Christopher Doyle who in turn received them from the issuer. * * * "

* * *

* * * A reading of the language of the injunction, to which Sherwood gave his consent, * * * demonstrates that * * * Sherwood undertook to refrain from selling, offering to sell, or transporting Canadian Javelin Limited shares *only if a registration statement should then be required* * * * .

* * *

That the post-decree sales were made from the block of shares received by Sherwood from Doyle under [a] September 2, 1954 agreement was proven. The crucial issue therefore is, "Were the shares of Canadian

Javelin Limited sold by Sherwood required to be registered before sale thereof by him?"

* * *

* * * I am not satisfied beyond a reasonable doubt that at the time Sherwood took his shares from the issuer through Doyle, he purchased them with a view to the distribution thereof.

Defendant points to the long period between his purchase of and the first sale from his block of Canadian Javelin Limited shares. From this, he argues that:

"From such behavior, it is impossible to infer the intention to distribute, *at the time of acquisition,* that it is necessary under the Act to qualify Sherwood as an underwriter within the meaning of the Act. His retention of the shares for a minimum of two full years after he personally had obtained physical possession of them belies any inference that he had originally acquired them 'with a view to distribution,' and is inconsistent with any such intention."

On the proof before me it appears that Sherwood took the unrestricted ownership of the block of shares out of which the post-decree sales were made in September 1955 when they were delivered to his agents, Lombard & Odier. No sales or other transactions were made out of this block until September 1957. The passage of two years before the commencement of distribution of any of these shares is an insuperable obstacle to my finding that Sherwood took these shares with a view to distribution thereof, in the absence of any relevant evidence from which I could conclude he did not take the shares for investment. No such evidence was offered at the trial. In fact, the only reference to Sherwood's intention with regard to the block of stock which he received appears when government counsel was cross-examining Sherwood's Canadian counsel, Courtois. The testimony, if anything, indicates Sherwood's intention not to sell his stock. Courtois' testimony on this score is as follows:

"A. I remember asking Mr. Sherwood if he had any intention of selling any of his shares or disposing of his holdings in Canadian Javelin.

"Q. And what was his answer?

"A. His answer was no because he said for the time being he had a large block and he thought as such it had some value. * * * "

* * *

Based partly on the *Sherwood* case, two years came to be viewed by lawyers as the minimum safe holding period for restricted securities before a public sale. Before the passage of Rule 144, the Commission's staff responded to a multitude of no-action letter requests in connection with potential resales of restricted securities. The staff freely granted no-action letters when restricted securities were held for three years, but was much less likely to do so in the case of a two year holding period.

The other interpretation preexisting Rule 144 that must be discussed is the change in circumstances doctrine. Since the Commission has asserted that the doctrine should no longer be relied upon in the case of securities purchased after the effective date of Rule 144, a change in circumstances is of much less help to a post-Rule 144 purchaser than is a sufficiently long holding period. In fact, it has always been of less importance than the holding period. The thrust of the change in circumstances doctrine is that the inference of underwriter status that may accompany a too short holding period can be avoided when the holder of restricted securities proves that the desire to resell arose because of changed circumstances. The Commission made it clear in Securities Act Release No. 4552 (November 6, 1962) that factors such as an advance or decline in a stock's price or in an issuer's earnings "are normal investment risks and do not usually provide an acceptable basis for [a] claim of changed circumstances." And an examination of pre-Rule 144 no-action letter requests and responses shows little staff acceptance of change in circumstances arguments. Perhaps the usual effect of the doctrine in the pre-Rule 144 period was to give comfort to those involved in a transaction by a security holder who barely met a minimally acceptable holding period.

C. PUBLIC RESALES UNDER RULE 144

As indicated by the title of Rule 144, "Persons Deemed Not to Be Engaged in a Distribution and Therefore Not Underwriters," the rule is designed to provide a mechanism for avoiding underwriter status. It is complex because it is detailed and covers a variety of circumstances, and also because it combines provisions relating to control and restricted securities. Nonetheless, for those familiar with the rudiments of the Section 4(a)(1) exemption, which is what compliance with the rule secures, understanding the rule should present few problems.

Rule 144 begins with definitions, the most important of which are those of "affiliate" and "restricted securities." Both of these definitions are discussed above. The next most important definition is that of "person" when that term is used to refer to the seller of securities under the rule. Here the Commission has played a little drafting trick by including other people within the definition, such as certain relatives who share the same home. This has significant importance, including for the purpose of determining whether certain limitations in the rule are satisfied.

Rule 144(b) declares, by cross-referencing other parts of the rule, the basic terms with which persons hoping to take advantage of the rule's protection must comply. For purposes of further analysis, these persons should be divided into two groups and separately considered. These two groups are (1) non-affiliates who hold restricted securities, and (2) affiliates and those who act on their behalf.

I. NON-AFFILIATES

Analysis of the position of non-affiliates holding restricted securities is relatively simple. (Note, however, that to qualify as a non-affiliate one must not have been an affiliate during the three months prior to the contemplated sale.) If the securities were issued by a company that has been subject to the Exchange Act's reporting requirements for at least 90 days prior to the contemplated sale, and has filed all of its required reports for the preceding twelve months (or such shorter period as it has been subject to reporting requirements), a six-month holding period must be satisfied. Otherwise—that is, if the issuer has not been an Exchange Act reporting company for an adequate period or has not complied with its reporting requirements—the non-affiliate must satisfy a twelve-month holding period.[8]

Holding periods are calculated in accordance with Rule 144(d)(3). An important special situation dealt with is when restricted securities are resold in a private transaction. In that case, the holding period of a new owner generally begins when the securities were purchased from the issuer or an affiliate of the issuer. Also of importance is the treatment of gift shares (which are deemed to have been acquired by the donee when acquired by the donor) and shares owned by an estate (which, in the case of non-affiliates, are exempt from the holding period requirement). The rule deals with a number of other situations as well.

II. AFFILIATES AND THOSE SELLING ON THEIR BEHALF

The analysis of the position of affiliates and those selling on their behalf is, of necessity, more complicated. There are three steps to understanding why this is so. (1) An affiliate (like a non-affiliate) may have purchased restricted securities from the issuer with a view to distribution, and thus be an underwriter under Section 2(a)(11). Satisfaction of some holding period thus comes into play to establish that no such view was held. (2) An affiliate may be acting on behalf of an issuer in connection with a distribution and thus be an underwriter under Section 2(a)(11). This is trickier to handle; basically, the Commission seeks to assure that when any securities are sold by an affiliate the effect on the market is sufficiently minimal to allay any concerns that a distribution is taking place. (3) Someone selling on behalf of an affiliate in connection with a distribution may, by reason of Section

---

[8] This is a significantly shorter period than the one mandated in the original version of the Rule.

2(a)(11)'s wording, also be an underwriter. Once again, the matter is handled by assuring that no distribution is taking place.

a.   AFFILIATES AND UNRESTRICTED SHARES

The first situation to consider, then, is that of an affiliate (or a broker acting on behalf of an affiliate) who wishes to sell unrestricted securities. This can occur, under Rule 144, only if (a) there is specified information currently available to the public about the issuer, (b) the sale occurs subject to restrictions on volume, (c) the sale occurs subject to limitations on the manner of sale, and (d) appropriate notice of reliance on the rule is given.

Under Rule 144(c), it is theoretically possible for an issuer to satisfy the "publicly available information" requirement simply by making public the required information. As a practical matter, it is rarely met other than by companies who are Exchange Act reporting companies. Because of this, some companies that have not been legally required to register securities under the Exchange Act have done so to make Rule 144 available for use by their affiliates. Although it may not be strictly obvious why an informational requirement is relevant to a determination of when a distribution occurs, it can be explained in two ways. First, of course, it simply goes to the Commission's assessment of the public's need for protection in various situations. Second, it is reasonable to think that securities sold into a fully informed market will have less of an impact on market price.

The generally applicable volume limitation for affiliates' sales (including those made on their behalf) is, under Rule 144(e), the greater of one percent of the class of securities outstanding or of the average weekly trading volume of the class of securities during the preceding four weeks. Again, there are a number of provisions for special situations (including for debt securities).

In the usual case, Rule 144(f) provides that all securities sold by an affiliate or on an affiliate's behalf must be sold in a broker's transaction (as defined in Rule 144(g)) or directly to a market maker. In the case of a broker's transaction, no solicitation of buyers or extraordinary commission is allowed, and other limitations pertain. The requirements of Rule 144(f) do not, however, apply to debt securities or securities sold by an estate (provided the estate itself is not an affiliate of the issuer).

Finally, Rule 144(h) states the circumstances in which a notice of reliance on Rule 144 must be filed with the Commission. Basically, Form 144 must be filed if sales during a three-month period exceed 5,000 shares or $50,000.

b.   AFFILIATES AND RESTRICTED SHARES

The last task in understanding Rule 144 is the treatment of an affiliate's sale (or a sale on behalf of an affiliate) of restricted shares. One might think that if the volume and manner of the sale of shares has a sufficiently negligible impact on the market for a security, it would not also be necessary to assure that the seller harbored no "view" to resale at the time the shares were acquired. This has not, however, been the view adopted by the Commission. Restricted shares held by an affiliate are subject to the requirements described immediately above and are subject to mandatory holding periods. These holding periods are the same as in the case of a non-affiliate.

Selling Restricted Securities Under Rule 144—A Practical Guide

Robert S. Green.
The Practical Lawyer, May 1972, at 13.[*]

* * *

Let us assume that your client, Mr. Peter, comes in with a certificate for 10,000 shares of common stock of Lunar Realty Corp., which he purchased from Lunar [several months ago], in a private placement pursuant to an investment letter. Lunar is now selling on the American Stock Exchange at $20 per share. The certificate bears the usual restrictive legend prohibiting the sale of shares without registration or an opinion of counsel that the sale can be made without registration.

* * *

A PROCEDURE FOR COMPLIANCE

Let us assume that you have satisfied yourself that Mr. Peter is entitled to avail himself of Rule 144 in selling the Lunar shares. * * *

Mr. Peter * * * proposes to sell the shares through the brokerage firm of Planetary Securities Corporation, in the usual way, and has solicited no buy orders.

THE REQUIRED PAPERWORK

You now have an assortment of paperwork ahead of you, to confirm that the Rule is in fact available in this situation as well as to meet the requirements of Lunar (the issuer), Planetary (the broker), and the SEC. Moreover, since the Commission in a number of releases interpreting Rule 144 specifically charges the transfer agent, as well as the issuer and the broker, with an obligation to be sure securities are not transferred in violation of the Rule, transfer agents may also begin to develop their own "fail-safe" criteria to double check the requirements of the issuer and broker.

While various issuers and brokers will have their own requirements, you will probably be dealing with something like this:

---

   *   Copyright © 1972 by The American Law Institute. Reprinted with the permission of *The Practical Lawyer*. Subscription rates $55–$169/year.

The Issuer

Start by writing or calling Lunar's counsel; tell him Mr. Peter wishes to sell his 10,000 shares of Lunar pursuant to Rule 144, and ask him what conditions must be met for counsel to instruct Lunar's transfer agent to permit the sale to go through.

Lunar's counsel, Messrs. Quick & Eager, will probably require:

- A letter of representations from Peter [The form of this letter will likely be furnished by the issuer's counsel. Typically these letters contain representations on virtually all relevant factors relating to Rule 144.];

- A letter from Planetary as to the proposed method of sale [Basically, the broker will represent that its actions will comply with the requirements of Rule 144.]; and

- A completed copy of Form 144 * * * .

- He may also require an opinion from you that Rule 144 is available to Mr. Peter; this does not appear to be strictly necessary, but you may have to give one.

On your part, you will need from Lunar confirmation as to the number of shares outstanding and that it is current in its filings, as well as other details for Form 144 * * * .

* * *

The Broker

Next, call the broker and ask him what documentation he requires to effect a sale of Mr. Peter's restricted shares pursuant to Rule 144.

The broker (or his counsel) will probably require:

- A letter from Lunar confirming that Lunar is current in its SEC filings * * *;

- A copy of a form of Customer Questionnaire * * *, completed and signed by Mr. Peter [This will be provided by the broker. Typically it will be quite extensive.];

- One copy of Form 144 itself, completed by Mr. Peter * * *;

- The certificate or certificates for the shares, duly endorsed in blank for transfer; and

- Either a copy of the letter Lunar's counsel will ultimately send to Lunar's transfer agent, permitting transfer of the shares without restriction, or, perhaps, written assurance from the transfer agent itself that the shares can be so transferred. * * *

* * *

D. PRIVATE RESALES OF CONTROL AND RESTRICTED SECURITIES

When certain conditions are satisfied, the Section 4(a)(1) exemption can be available for a private offering of control or restricted securities. Here the analysis proceeds in the same way that it does for the public resale of control and restricted securities. This analysis leads to the conclusion that, as in the case of a public sale, the troublesome question is whether an underwriter will be involved in a proposed transaction. Also as with public resales, this question is answered by answering a more basic question: Will the transaction involve a distribution? When there is no distribution, there is no underwriter, since the concept of underwriter is tied in Section 2(a)(11) exclusively to a distribution. When there is no underwriter involved in a sales transaction, the Section 4(a)(1) exemption is available to any security holder other than the issuer or a dealer.

Since "distribution" essentially is synonymous with "public offering," the necessity for doing an exempt private resale of control or restricted securities is that the sale not involve a public offering. It is apparent that there is substantial learning available on the question of what constitutes a public offering and its statutory opposite, the Section 4(a)(2) private placement. What must be done, then, is an offering that, although technically under Section 4(a)(1), has some of the basic characteristics of a Section 4(a)(2) transaction. For these reasons, private resales of control or restricted securities historically were referred to as "Section 4(a)(1½)" transactions. Rule 144A was adopted as a safe harbor but was subject to the strict limitations described below.

Now, however, new Section 4(a)(7) provides an exemption for resales making reliance on either Section 4(a)(1) or Rule 144A unnecessary in the indicated circumstances.

I. SECTION 4(a)(1) AND RULE 144A

a. PRIVATE RESALES OUTSIDE RULE 144A

For private resales of restricted securities that fall outside Rule 144A, a seller relying on Section 4(a)(1) must structure the transaction so that the seller is (1) not an underwriter and (2) cannot be made an underwriter by actions of the purchaser. Analytically, this would seem to involve offering and selling only to persons who can meet the requirements for purchasing in a private placement, although no-action letters issued by the Commission's staff have shown some flexibility in this respect, as indicated in the following reading. It further involves structuring the transaction in such a way that the new purchasers cannot resell in a non-exempt transaction, since this will likely destroy the exemption or exemptions that supported sales earlier in the chain. This mainly involves having the new purchaser agree to contractual restrictions, of the type used in private placements, and insuring that the certificates representing the securities that are sold are legended against resale without an exemption.

The situation is somewhat different in the case of control securities. In that case, the seller must insure that the purchaser is not an underwriter. Theoretically, at least, it seems that the purchaser would not have to meet any requirements (such as investment sophistication), except those that go to the question of underwriter status. At a minimum, the seller would want to obtain a representation that the purchaser is not purchasing with a view to distribution and, in addition, would want to insist on the same type of contractual restrictions and legends on certificates that are needed in the case of restricted securities.

The following reading summarizes positions taken by the Commission's staff, in no-action letters, on the requirements for a private resale that complies with the requirements of Section 4(a)(1).

The Section "[4(a)(1½)]" Phenomenon: Private Resales of "Restricted" Securities

A Report to the ABA Committee on Federal Regulation of Securities from the Study Group on Section "[4(a)(1½)]" of the Subcommittee on 1933 Act–General. 34 Business Lawyer 1961 (1979).*

* * *

SEC INTERPRETATIONS

The Staff No-Action Letters

* * *

Purchaser's Intent; Number of Purchasers

[T]he staff letters seem to parallel closely the requirements of a private offering by an issuer in reliance upon the section [4(a)(2)] exemption. The staff has, for example, issued no-action letters with respect to private sales of large blocks of securities, even where there was an absence of a trading market, providing the purchaser acquired the shares for investment. On a number of occasions, the staff has conditioned its granting of no-action requests upon the sales' being made to a single purchaser or a limited number of purchasers * * *. On the other hand, the staff has only rarely expressed concern with the number of *offerees,* often taking no-action positions on transactions involving public solicitations of sales, for example where a pledgor is required to advertise a proposed sale of collateral.

Qualification of Purchasers

The staff letters are mixed with respect to the necessity that the purchaser be a sophisticated investor. Most staff letters make no

*   Copyright © 1979 by the American Bar Association. All rights reserved. Reprinted with the permission of the American Bar Association and its Section of Business Law.

reference to this requirement. A few, however, grant no-action requests upon the express condition that the purchaser be somewhat sophisticated. This latter category generally includes foreclosure sales by secured lenders designed to meet certain public sale requirements under the Uniform Commercial Code. On at least three occasions the staff has declined to take a no-action position, citing its own inability to determine whether the offerees require the protection of the Act. In two letters the staff went even further, requiring the purchaser to be able "to afford the risk of the highly speculative investment."

Access to or Furnishing of Information

The staff has grappled somewhat unsuccessfully with the question whether the Purchaser must have access to registration-type information or be supplied such information by the Holder. In one letter the staff required that "prospective purchasers * * * be limited to persons who have access to the same information about [the issuer's] stock that a registration statement would provide." In others, the staff has required that the seller advise all offerees where information regarding the issuer might be obtained, and in one letter the staff merely required the seller to disclose all information regarding the issuer that was known to the seller.

Restrictions on Purchaser's Resales

The staff letters tend uniformly to provide that Purchasers of restricted securities are deemed to have received restricted shares and may not resell them *publicly* without compliance with the registration provisions of the Act. * * *

* * *

As the foregoing indicates, there are issues about what information must be provided by a seller of restricted or control securities in a private resale. A seller needs to insure that he or she does not violate Section 17(a) of the Securities Act (discussed in Chapter 8) or Rule 10b–5 of the Exchange Act (discussed in Chapters 12 and 13) by selling while in possession of material inside information. If an affiliate sells securities of an Exchange Act reporting company, generally no information should have to be disclosed, unless there is material information that the issuer has not disclosed publicly. If the issuer has not publicly disclosed material information, an affiliate could sell privately by disclosing the inside information to the purchaser (presumably subject to a non-disclosure agreement). If an affiliate sells securities in a privately-held company, the seller needs to provide enough information so that the purchaser is in possession of all material information about the issuer, so as to avoid Section 17(a) and Rule 10b–5 questions. If the purchaser is not an affiliate, the only safe way to avoid liability is to make sure the purchaser has the kind of information that the purchaser would receive in a Section 4(a)(2) private placement (or, in the case of institutional buyers, that they have access to the information). In any case where information is provided, care dictates that it be provided in writing.

b. RULE 144A

In the case of restricted securities, the seller needs to avoid assuming the status of an underwriter. Rule 144A establishes a safe harbor for certain private resales of restricted securities, by providing that the seller in a transaction qualified under the rule will not be deemed to be an underwriter. The rule is available only if the buyer is a "qualified institutional buyer" or an institution that the seller and any person acting on its behalf reasonably believe to be a "qualified institutional buyer." The rule is not available, however, for the resale of securities (1) that, at the time of their issuance, were of the same class of securities listed on a national securities exchange or quoted in a U.S. automated inter-dealer quotation system or (2) that were issued by one of enumerated types of companies that are or are required to be registered under the Investment Company Act of 1940.

For transactions to be covered by Rule 144A, the seller and any person acting on its behalf must take reasonable steps to ensure that the purchaser is aware that the seller may rely on the exemption from the registration requirements provided by the rule. Also, in the case of securities issued by certain companies (basically those that are not subject to the reporting requirements of the Exchange Act), the rule provides that, upon request, the purchaser has a right to obtain from the seller, and the seller and the purchaser have a right to obtain from the issuer, certain basic information about the issuer. The rule also provides that the requested information must be received by the purchaser at or prior to the time of sale. Although Rule 144A originally permitted offers, as well as sales, only to those reasonably believed to be "qualified institutional buyers," the rule now permits general solicitation.

In conjunction with its adoption of Rule 144A, the Commission approved the creation of "PORTAL" (Private Offering, Resale and Trading through Automated Linkages System). PORTAL is an electronic market on which pre-approved "qualified institutional investors" may trade securities qualifying under Rule 144A. In light of the extreme popularity of private offerings designed for the Rule 144A market (the size of which is estimated to be in the hundreds of billions) other trading venues for Rule 144A securities also have been created.

II. RULE 4(a)(7)

In late 2015, Section 4(a) of the Securities Act was amended to recognize a new, non-exclusive exemption for "certain accredited investor transactions." A new sub-part (7) was added to refer to "transactions meeting the requirements of subsection (d)." The following is a brief description of the new exemption, which actually requires a careful reading of Section 4(a)(7), 4(d), and 4(e). As should quickly appear, however, the new exemption effectively codifies many of the presumed requirements of the "Section 4(a)(1½)" exemption.

A resale of securities is exempt under Section 4(a)(7) if all of the following conditions are met:

- The purchaser is an "accredited investor" within the meaning of Regulation D, as it may be amended from time to time;

- Neither the seller, nor any person acting on its behalf, uses any form of general solicitation or advertising;

- The seller is not the issuer or a subsidiary of the issuer;

- Neither the seller nor any person who has been or will be paid for its participation in the transaction is a "bad actor" as defined in Regulation D;

- The issuer is engaged in business, not in the organizational stage or in bankruptcy or receivership, and is not a blank check, blind pool, or shell company that has no specific business plan or purpose and has not indicated that its primary business plan is to engage in a merger with an unidentified person;

- The transaction does not relate to an unsold allotment to, or a subscription or participation by, a broker or dealer as an underwriter of the securities;

- The securities are of a class that has been authorized and outstanding for at least 90 days; and

- For securities of issuers not subject to periodic reporting under the Securities Exchange Act, specified information (including financial statements) has been delivered to prospective purchasers.

Securities sold pursuant to Section 4(a)(7) are "restricted securities" for purposes of Rule 144. They also are "covered securities" under Section 18 of the '33 Act, which means that blue-sky registration requirements have been preempted.

CHAPTER 8

LIABILITY FOR SECURITIES ACT VIOLATIONS

SITUATION 8

Shortly after the Compuform merger, occurring a few months following the public offering, the market price of Microtec stock begins falling from its high of $12. When it reaches $7 a few weeks later, two groups of plaintiffs, represented by the same law firm, file class action suits. The first is on behalf of all purchasers in the public offering and is against Microtec, Microtec's officers and directors, Microtec's accounting firm, and Nielson Securities Co. and each of the other underwriters. The second is on behalf of the former Compuform shareholders who received Microtec shares in the merger. This suit names the same defendants, with the exception of Nielson and the other underwriters. The first suit alleges violations of Securities Act Sections 11, 12, and 17(a), and the second violations of Sections 12 and 17(a).

Each suit makes basically the same allegations: that the prospectus delivered in the public offering, or the offering statement delivered in connection with the Compuform merger, materially overstated Microtec's income in prior years; and that management's discussion of future prospects was far too optimistic. Discovery has not begun, so the allegations are unrefined. With respect to the overstatement of prior years' income, however, they center on two points. First, that certain costs of development and refinement of Microtec's products were capitalized rather than expensed, as allegedly required under generally accepted accounting principles. Second, that Microtec's allowance for bad debts was substantially too low. The suit arising out of the public offering further alleges that illegal offers were made before the registration became effective, and the suit involving the merger alleges that the requirements of neither Section 4(a)(2) nor Rule 506 were met by Microtec.

Two shareholders who purchased in the public offering also have written letters to the Securities and Exchange Commission complaining about the alleged misstatements. The regional office of the Commission has begun an informal investigation.

Income for the current year is below that for the same period of last year, and bad debts have been greater than provided for in last year's income statement. Microtec's officers attribute these developments to the fact that the economy has entered a recession, and that the impact of the recession has been particularly great on the micro-computer industry. The accounting firm that audited Microtec's financial statements maintains that development and refinement costs were properly capitalized, but they admit that this is an area involving large measures of judgment.

In considering this situation, refer to the following, in addition to the materials in this chapter: Securities Act Sections 4(a)(c), 8A, 11–13, 15–17, 20, 24, and 27A, Rules 159A, 175 and 176 under the Securities Act and Exchange Act Section 21D(f).

A. CRIMINAL AND OTHER GOVERNMENTAL ACTIONS

The Securities Act can be viewed as a criminal statute. Its nature may be seen by examining Section 5, the centerpiece registration provision: "Unless a registration statement is in effect as to a security, it shall be unlawful * * * ." The main antifraud provision, Section 17(a), begins the same way: "It shall be unlawful for any person in the offer or sale of any securities [, by the use of jurisdictional means, to commit various 'fraudulent' acts]." Of more direct effect is Section 24, the penalties provision. It makes the willful violation of any provision of the Act, or of any of its rules, a felony punishable by up to five years imprisonment and a $10,000 fine.

Those who are not familiar with the interpretation of the term "willful" in the securities laws sometimes take undue comfort from its inclusion as a requirement for criminal prosecution. "Willful" does not mean what it may seem at first. Referring to what is required in the case of a violation of the Section 5 registration requirements, the Commission has said in an administrative action:

> [A]s is well settled, a finding of willfulness * * * does not require a finding of intention to violate the law. It is sufficient that registrants be shown to have known what they were doing. Registrants [in this case], of course, knew that no registration statement had been filed and the [press] release [violating Securities Act Section 5] was intentionally composed and publicized.[1]

"Willfulness" can take a different cast in a criminal action because of the issue of scienter. Even so, the willfulness requirement may offer scant shielding for a violator.[2] The following case nicely points this up, while at the same time providing a helpful discussion of the willfulness requirement generally.

---

[1]   In re Carl M. Loeb, Rhoades & Co., 38 S.E.C. 843, 854 n. 21 (1959).

[2]   Whether scienter is required in a criminal prosecution under the securities laws is confused. The main issue here is whether it is required in prosecutions for violations not involving fraud, for example a failure to file a registration statement in a situation where the defendant did not know that what it was offering to the public was a security. The most pointed question here is whether strict liability applies in such a situation.

United States v. Brown

United States Court of Appeals, Ninth Circuit, 1978.
578 F.2d 1280.

■ Before WRIGHT and HUG, CIRCUIT JUDGES, and INGRAM, DISTRICT JUDGE.

■ INGRAM, DISTRICT JUDGE.

Robert Edwin Brown appeals from his conviction after trial by court of 10 counts of violations of [Securities Act § 17(a) for securities fraud].

* * *

In attacking his conviction of the alleged violations of [§ 17(a)], appellant principally contends that the government's burden includes the obligation to prove beyond a reasonable doubt that appellant knew that the items sold were securities within the meaning of the act. Appellant argues that the use of the word "willful" in [§ 24], the penalty provision for violations of [§ 17(a)], imports the requirement of specific knowledge of the identity of instruments as securities. We are therefore required in determining this issue to construe the word "willfully" as it appears in the context of this statute. We are mindful that "willful" and "willfully" are words of many meanings, and that their construction is often influenced by context.

Appellant, relying upon United States v. Lizarraga-Lizarraga, 541 F.2d 826 (9th Cir.1976), and United States v. Klee, 494 F.2d 394 (9th Cir.1974), argues that the court erred as a matter of law in entering judgments of conviction upon the counts alleging violations of [§ 17(a)] in that the court did not require proof of specific intent to sell a security, or proof of specific knowledge on the part of appellant that the instruments sold were securities within the meaning of the Securities Act of 1933. Appellant contends that the word "willfully" as used in [§ 24] requires this proof in order to convict.

Lizarraga-Lizarraga finds that Congress intended the requirement of proof of specific intent by its use of the word "willful" in enacting 22 U.S.C. § 1934, which proscribes the exportation of such contraband articles as may be defined by regulation promulgated thereunder. Within the context of that statute, the court found that, absent proof of specific intent, prosecutions and convictions might ensue because of the unwitting and innocent exportation of innocuous articles that were in fact contraband because the regulations so defined them. Reference to the statute alone, without the regulations at hand, would not enlighten the unwary, and the Congressional intent was inferred from that circumstance. In *Klee,* an income tax "failure to file" case, the court approved the giving of an instruction which required proof of a knowing violation of law, as distinguished from innocent error or inadvertence, or even from reckless disregard. In sum, these cases find a requirement of the necessity of proof of specific intent in the use of the term "willful" as a necessary inference of Congressional intent to avoid the prosecution of the innocent, feckless or reckless.

In contrast, [§ 17(a)] in substance proscribes the offer or sale of a security through the use of instruments or communications in commerce or by the use of the mails where the offer or sale involves:

> (1) The employment of a device or scheme to defraud, or

> (2) The obtaining of money or property through untrue statements of material facts or the omission to state material facts, the omission of which makes statements made misleading, or

> (3) Conduct amounting to fraud and deceit.

This prohibition of conduct is not a trap for the unwary because the thrust of it is fraud. Our question is whether the government is required to prove that one otherwise transgressing this statute must specifically know that the vehicle of his perfidy is a security within the meaning of the Securities Act.

We think that the government is required to prove specific intent only as it relates to the action constituting the fraudulent, misleading or deceitful conduct, but not as to the knowledge that the instrument used is a security under the Securities Act. The government need only prove that the object sold or offered is, in fact, a security; it need not be proved that the defendant had specific knowledge that the object sold or offered was a security.

In United States v. Riedel, 126 F.2d 81 (7th Cir.1942), a prosecution for six counts of violations of [§§ 17 and 24] and three counts of mail fraud, defendant contended that the instruments in question (trust certificates) were not securities within the meaning of the Securities Act of 1933 as amended. The court held that the question of whether or not the instrument in issue was a security was determinable from the evidence, and that where the issuance of such instruments was a part of a fraud practiced upon a purchaser, a violation of the Securities Act occurred. While the question of specific knowledge of the nature of the instruments as securities was neither raised by the parties nor addressed by the court, it is implicit in the holding that where inclusion of the instrument in question in the definition of a security in the context of a fraud case is itself a jural fact, the knowledge and belief of the defendant with respect to this is not a relevant fact requiring proof.

* * *

In marked contrast to such holdings as *Lizarraga-Lizarraga* and *Klee,* it is interesting to note that when considering the securities acts, an eminent court has held that one may violate the rule of the Securities Exchange Commission without knowing of the existence of such rule. Judge Friendly, in United States v. Peltz, 433 F.2d 48 (2nd Cir.1970), reached this conclusion in construing the provisions of § 32(a) of the

Securities Exchange Act of 1934. In his consideration of the terms "willfully" and "willfully and knowingly" within the context of that section he writes:

> "The language makes one point entirely clear. A person can willfully violate an SEC rule even if he does not know of its existence. This conclusion follows from the difference between the standard for the violation of the statute or a rule or regulation, to wit, 'willfully,' and that for false and misleading statements, namely, 'willfully and knowingly' * * * ."

[Securities Act Section 24] uses the term "willfully" rather than the term "willfully and knowingly."

* * *

It is true that the use of the word "willful" in the context of § 32(a) is easier to determine than it is in [§ 24] because the former section only permits the imposition of a fine, and not imprisonment where it is shown that the actor was not aware of the statute, rule or regulation violated. However, we are satisfied that the use of the word "willful" as employed in [§ 24] does not import a requirement of specific knowledge that an instrument is a security as defined in the Act.

* * *

Before the corporate scandals that began with the Enron debacle, the Commission often found U.S. Attorneys reluctant to prosecute all but the most egregious securities violations. This has changed dramatically, with U.S. Attorneys now being eager to prosecute violators, especially for fraud.

The Securities Act, as well as the other securities statutes, is tricky in one other respect involving its criminal provisions. In Chapter 2, the difficulty of avoiding the jurisdictional means requirement of the Securities Act (use of the mails or some means or instrument of interstate commerce) was discussed. The requirement provides little comfort for someone who hopes to escape prosecution based on the absence of jurisdictional means from a transaction. Because of the way the Securities Act prohibitions are tied to uses of jurisdictional means, each separate use of these means is a separate violation. Since the average securities transaction involves multiple uses of jurisdictional means, a violator usually faces a multiple count indictment. (Additionally, when an antifraud provision is involved, the violator usually also faces a multiple count indictment for violations of the federal mail fraud and wire fraud statutes, along with multiple counts under the general conspiracy statute.)

Although the Securities Act gives the Commission substantial powers with respect to the Act's implementation and enforcement, the power to bring criminal actions is not one of them. On the subject of those actions, Section 20(b) provides: "The Commission may transmit such evidence as may be available concerning [violations] to the Attorney General who may, in his discretion, institute the necessary criminal proceedings * * * ." That section, however, does give the Commission the power to bring actions seeking injunctive relief (including disgorgement of ill-gotten profits) whenever it appears that the Act, or any rule under the Act, has been or is about to be violated. That authority has long been a powerful tool, one that created much of the case law interpreting the Securities Act. Moreover, the Sarbanes-Oxley Act of 2002 amended Exchange Act Section 21(d) by adding a new subsection (5), which provides the possibility of equitable relief in the context of *all* federal securities laws. It reads: "In any action or proceeding brought or instituted by the Commission under any provision of the securities laws, the Commission may seek, and any Federal court may grant, any equitable relief that may be appropriate or necessary for the benefit of investors."

In addition, the Commission may (under Securities Act Section 20(d)) seek judicially-imposed civil monetary penalties for violations of the Securities Act, a rule under the Securities Act, or one of the Commission's own cease-and-desist orders (discussed below).[3] The maximum civil monetary penalty a court can impose under Section 20(d) (read along with Rule of Practice 1004, which relates to the adjustment of civil monetary penalties) varies with culpability and with risk to the public presented by the violator's actions, with maximums of $75,000 for individuals and $725,000 for others.[4] If the gross amount of gain to the violator as a result of the violation is greater than the scheduled amount, however, the penalty can be as high as the amount of the gain.

Pursuant to Securities Act Section 15(b), the Commission's authority to seek the remedies available under Sections 20(b) and (d) extends not just to primary violators but also to all those who knowingly or recklessly provide substantial assistance to primary violators.

In addition to imposing a civil penalty in an action brought by the Commission under Section 20(d), a court may, under Section 20(e), prohibit a person who has violated Section 17(a)(1) (relating to fraud in the offer or sale of securities) from acting as an officer or director of a company that is an Exchange Act reporting company. Under Section 20(g), a court may, in a Commission injunctive action, bar persons from participating in an offering of penny stock if their alleged misconduct

---

[3]   Exchange Act Sections 21(d)(3), 21A and 21B cover the Commission's power in this area under that Act.

[4]   Under Rule 9 of the Commission's rules of informal and other procedures, the Commission may, on a case-by-case basis, reduce the amount of penalty it seeks against a "small entity" (which includes a "Small Business" as defined by the Commission). Under the rule, the Commission considers a number of issues in making this determination, including the willfulness and egregiousness of the conduct, the violator's history of legal or regulatory violations, and the financial ability of the entity to pay the penalty. The Commission's policies in this respect are discussed in Securities Act Release 33–7408 (effective March 29, 1997).

related to an offering of penny stock. These bars may be conditional or unconditional and temporary or permanent.

As the foregoing material suggests, the Commission also has its own power (under Securities Act Section 8A)[5] to issue cease-and-desist orders whenever it finds, after notice and an opportunity for a hearing, that someone has violated, is violating, or is about to violate the Securities Act or one of the rules thereunder. As part of this authority, the Commission can itself impose monetary penalties, pursuant to guidelines based on culpability and risk to the public, of from $7500 to $150,000 for individuals and from $75,000 to $725,000 for others. In addition, it has its own power to bar those who have violated Securities Act Section 17(a)(1), or any rule thereunder, from serving as an officer or director of an Exchange Act reporting company.

Rounding out the enforcement scheme, under Exchange Act Section 21F (which extends to all federal securities laws), the Commission has the authority to reward whistleblowers. The basic thrust of the effectuating rules is that persons who voluntarily provide the Commission information leading to imposition of more than $1 million in sanctions are to receive between 10 and 30% of the amount of any government recovery in excess of $1 million.

B. PRIVATE CIVIL LIABILITY

The Securities Act contains a number of provisions that may lead to private civil liability, either under their explicit terms or as a result of an implied civil remedy found by the courts. Under the Securities Litigation Uniform Standards Act of 1998, which among other things amended Securities Act Section 16, most class actions involving fraud or defects in disclosure relating to the securities of most publicly held companies must be brought in federal courts under federal law. (This act was passed after plaintiffs' lawyers began circumventing provisions in the private Securities Litigation Reform Act of 1995 by bringing class actions in state courts.)

I. SECTION 11

a. OVERVIEW

Securities Act Section 11 provides a civil remedy in the case of a registration statement that contains "an untrue statement of a material fact or [omits] to state a material fact required to be stated therein or necessary to make the statements therein not misleading." Joint and several liability under this section may fall on a number of persons, including the issuer; its chief executive, financial, and accounting

---

[5]   Comparable provisions are found in Exchange Act Section 21C.

officers;[6] each director; each underwriter; and each accountant or other expert who has taken responsibility for some portion of the registration statement. Until 2010, Rule 436(g) conferred an exemption from liability on credit rating agencies, which could be named (with their consent) in a registration statement as having assigned a disclosed rating. The Dodd-Frank Act removed the exemption, with the result that at least some credit rating agencies now refuse to be named. This means that disclosure of ratings takes place outside of the registration statement.

Under longstanding interpretations, a purchaser of a registered security may sue under Section 11, irrespective of whether he or she purchased the security in the registered offering or later in the trading markets.[7] The only limitation, besides being able to trace one's securities back to the registered offering, is that the purchaser must bring suit before the statute of limitations, provided in Section 13, has run. Proof of causation is not a requirement for recovery, nor is proof of reliance in the usual situation.[8]

The effect of these factors on defendants is softened somewhat by other factors. Damages cannot exceed the difference between the offering price in the registered offering and the value of the securities at the time of suit (or the price at which the plaintiff disposed of them earlier). The defendants are not, therefore, responsible for the extra damages that result when a plaintiff purchases securities in the trading market for more than the original public offering price. Further, no underwriter can be held responsible for damages in excess of the aggregate public offering price of the securities underwritten by it. Also, a number of circuit courts have held that the "pleading with particularity" requirement of Rule 9(b) of the Federal Rules of Civil Procedure applies in Section 11 cases where the allegations relate to fraud, even though Section 11 is based on strict liability and does not even require proof of negligence.

A more general softening effect comes from the defenses available under Section 11. Each defendant other than the issuer has a defense, called a due diligence defense, that provides an escape from liability.

---

[6]   Although they are not specifically identified in Section 11 as being liable, the issuer and these officers will be liable under Section 11(a)(1) because, as required by Section 6(a), they will have signed the registration statement. Under Section 11(f), the liability of outside directors is determined in accordance with Exchange Act Section 21D(f), which generally distributes liability proportionally by responsibility and requires a violation to be knowingly committed before joint and several liability attaches.

[7]   The Circuit Courts of Appeal considering whether after-market purchasers can invoke the protections of Section 11 have concluded that they can. *See, e.g.*, DeMaria v. Andersen, 318 F.3d 170 (2d Cir. 2003); Lee v. Ernst & Young, LLP, 294 F.3d 969 (8th Cir. 2002). Several District Courts had ruled to the contrary based on the analysis of Gustafson v. Alloyd, discussed below in connection with Section 12(a)(2).

[8]   Section 11(e) contains a "negative causation" defense, which allows a defendant to escape or lessen liability by proving that all or part of a plaintiff's damages resulted from something other than a disclosure defect in the registration statement. Under Section 11(a), a plaintiff must prove reliance only if he or she purchased the securities after the issuer had made generally available to its security holders an earnings statement covering a period of at least 12 months beginning after the date of the registration statement that is the subject of the complaint.

These defenses take two basic forms, depending first upon whether a particular defendant is an "expert" and, second, upon whether the portion of the registration statement that is the subject of the complaint is "expertized."[9] Of all the possible permutations, the due diligence defense requires the least when a non-expert defendant is sued for a problem in an expertized part of the registration statement. In that situation, ignorance is sufficient to escape liability. Basically, the defendant needs to show that he or she had no reasonable ground to believe, and did not believe, that the expertized part of the registration statement contained a material misstatement or omission. More is required of an expert, and also of a non-expert when a non-expertized portion of the registration statement is the subject of a complaint. In these cases, the defendant must have had, after reasonable investigation, reasonable ground to believe, and he or she must have believed, that the statements in the portion of the registration statement in question were true and that there was no material omission.

b.   ESTABLISHING "DUE DILIGENCE"

As might be imagined, one of the biggest problem involving Section 11 is determining what constitutes a reasonable investigation for purposes of establishing the due diligence defence. The Commission has here used its rulemaking power only to a minor extent. Its one rule directly on point, Rule 176, lists a few relevant circumstances (such as the office held, when the defendant is an officer, and the presence or absence of another relationship to the issuer, when the defendant is a director) to consider in making this determination. Regrettably, case law is also sparse. Escott v. BarChris Construction Corp. is the leading case:

Escott v. BarChris Construction Corp.

United States District Court, Southern District of New York, 1968.
283 F.Supp. 643.

■ MCLEAN, DISTRICT JUDGE.

This is an action by purchasers of 5$\frac{1}{2}$ per cent convertible subordinated fifteen year debentures of BarChris Construction Corporation (BarChris). * * *

The action is brought under Section 11 of the Securities Act of 1933. Plaintiffs allege that the registration statement with respect to these debentures filed with the Securities and Exchange Commission, which became effective on May 16, 1961, contained material false statements and material omissions.

---

[9]   Under Section 11(a)(4), an expert is a person whose profession gives authority to his statements. An expertized portion of a registration statement is one that has been, directly or indirectly, prepared or certified by an expert who is named as such in the registration statement. Audited financial statements are the most common example.

Defendants fall into three categories: (1) the persons who signed the registration statement; (2) the underwriters, consisting of eight investment banking firms, led by Drexel & Co. (Drexel); and (3) BarChris's auditors, Peat, Marwick, Mitchell & Co. (Peat, Marwick).

The signers, in addition to BarChris itself, were the nine directors of BarChris, plus its controller, defendant Trilling, who was not a director. Of the nine directors, five were officers of BarChris, i.e., defendants Vitolo, president; Russo, executive vice president; Pugliese, vice president; Kircher, treasurer; and Birnbaum, secretary. Of the remaining four, defendant Grant was a member of the firm of Perkins, Daniels, McCormack & Collins, BarChris's attorneys. He became a director in October 1960. Defendant Coleman, a partner in Drexel, became a director on April 17, 1961, as did the other two, Auslander and Rose, who were not otherwise connected with BarChris.

* * *

* * * At the time relevant here, BarChris was engaged primarily in the construction of bowling alleys, somewhat euphemistically referred to as "bowling centers." * * *

* * *

By early 1961, BarChris needed additional working capital. The proceeds of the sale of the debentures involved in this action were to be devoted, in part at least, to fill that need.

* * *

By [the time the debentures were sold,] BarChris was experiencing difficulties in collecting amounts due from some of its customers. * * * as time went on those difficulties increased. Although BarChris continued to build alleys in 1961 and 1962, it became increasingly apparent that the industry was overbuilt. Operators of alleys, often inadequately financed, began to fail. Precisely when the tide turned is a matter of dispute, but at any rate, it was painfully apparent in 1962.

* * * In October 1962 BarChris came to the end of the road. On October 29, 1962, it filed in this court a petition for an arrangement under Chapter XI of the Bankruptcy Act. BarChris defaulted in the payment of the interest due on November 1, 1962 on the debentures.

The Debenture Registration Statement

* * *

Plaintiffs challenge the accuracy of a number of [the financial] figures [in the prospectus]. They also charge that the text of the prospectus, apart from the figures, was false in a number of respects, and that material information was omitted. * * *

* * *

Summary

For convenience, the various falsities and omissions which I have [found] are recapitulated here. * * *

1. *1960 Earnings*

    (a) *Sales*

As per prospectus	$9,165,320
Correct figure	8,511,420
Overstatement	$ 653,900

    (b) *Net Operating Income*

As per prospectus	$1,742,801
Correct figure	1,496,196
Overstatement	$ 246,605

    (c) *Earnings per Share*

As per prospectus	$ .75
Correct figure	.65
Overstatement	$ .10

2. *1960 Balance Sheet*

    Current Assets

As per prospectus	$4,524,021
Correct figure	3,914,332
Overstatement	$ 609,689

3. *Contingent Liabilities as of December 31, 1960 on Alternative Method of Financing*

As per prospectus	$ 750,000
Correct figure	1,125,795
Understatement	$ 375,795
Capitol Lanes should have been shown as a direct liability	$ 325,000

4. *Contingent Liabilities as of April 30, 1961*

As per prospectus	$ 825,000
Correct figure	1,443,853
Understatement	$ 618,853
Capitol Lanes should have been shown as a direct liability	$ 314,166

5.   *Earnings Figures for Quarter ending March 31, 1961*

    (a) *Sales*

As per prospectus	$2,138,455
Correct figure	1,618,645
Overstatement	$ 519,810

    (b) *Gross Profit*

As per prospectus	$ 483,121
Correct figure	252,366
Overstatement	$ 230,755

6.   *Backlog as of March 31, 1961*

As per prospectus	$6,905,000
Correct figure	2,415,000
Overstatement	$4,490,000

7.   *Failure to Disclose Officers' Loans Outstanding and Unpaid on May 16, 1961* $ 386,615

8.   *Failure to Disclose Use of Proceeds in Manner not Revealed in Prospectus*

    Approximately $1,160,000

9.   *Failure to Disclose Customers' Delinquencies in May 1961 and BarChris's Potential Liability with Respect Thereto*

    Over $1,350,000

10.   *Failure to Disclose the Fact that BarChris was Already Engaged, and was about to be More Heavily Engaged, in the Operation of Bowling Alleys*

Materiality

It is a prerequisite to liability under Section 11 of the Act that the fact which is falsely stated in a registration statement, or the fact that is omitted when it should have been stated to avoid misleading, be "material." The regulations of the Securities and Exchange Commission pertaining to the registration of securities define the word as follows [Rule 405]:

> "The term 'material', when used to qualify a requirement for the furnishing of information as to any subject, limits the information required to those matters as to which an average

prudent investor ought reasonably to be informed before purchasing the security registered."[10]

* * *

The average prudent investor is not concerned with minor inaccuracies or with errors as to matters which are of no interest to him. The facts which tend to deter him from purchasing a security are facts which have an important bearing upon the nature or condition of the issuing corporation or its business.

Judged by this test, there is no doubt that many of the misstatements and omissions in this prospectus were material. This is true of all of them which relate to the state of affairs in 1961 * * * .

The misstatements and omissions pertaining to BarChris's status as of December 31, 1960, however, present a much closer question. The 1960 earnings figures, the 1960 balance sheet and the contingent liabilities as of December 31, 1960 were not nearly as erroneous as plaintiffs have claimed. But they were wrong to some extent, as we have seen. * * *

* * *

Since no one knows what moves or does not move the mythical "average prudent investor," it comes down to a question of judgment, to be exercised by the trier of the fact as best he can in the light of all the circumstances. It is my best judgment that the average prudent investor would not have cared about these errors in the 1960 sales and earnings figures, regrettable though they may be. I therefore find that they were not material within the meaning of Section 11.

The same is true of the understatement of contingent liabilities in footnote 9 by approximately $375,000. * * *

This leaves for consideration the errors in the 1960 balance sheet figures * * * . * * *

* * *

Would it have made any difference if a prospective purchaser of these debentures had been advised of [the correct 1960 balance sheet figures]? There must be some point at which errors in disclosing a company's balance sheet position become material, even to a growth-oriented investor. On all the evidence I find that these balance sheet errors were material within the meaning of Section 11.

* * *

---

[10] Note that the Rule 405 definition of "material" has been changed. It now reads:

    The term "material," when used to qualify a requirement for the furnishing of information as to any subject, limits the information required to those matters to which there is a substantial likelihood that a reasonable investor would attach importance in determining whether to purchase the security registered. [Eds.]

The "Due Diligence" Defenses

* * *

Every defendant, except BarChris itself, to whom, as the issuer, [the due diligence defenses of Section 11] are not available, and except Peat, Marwick, whose position rests on a different statutory provision, has pleaded these affirmative defenses. Each claims that (1) as to the part of the registration statement purporting to be made on the authority of an expert (which, for convenience, I shall refer to as the "expertised portion"), he had no reasonable ground to believe and did not believe that there were any untrue statements or material omissions, and (2) as to the other parts of the registration statement, he made a reasonable investigation, as a result of which he had reasonable ground to believe and did believe that the registration statement was true and that no material fact was omitted. * * *

* * *

* * * The only expert, in the statutory sense, was Peat, Marwick * * * .

* * *

* * * The registration statement contains a report of Peat, Marwick as independent public accountants dated February 23, 1961. This relates only to the consolidated balance sheet of BarChris and consolidated subsidiaries as of December 31, 1960, and the related statement of earnings and retained earnings for the five years then ended. This is all that Peat, Marwick purported to certify. * * *

I turn now to the question of whether defendants have proved their due diligence defenses. The position of each defendant will be separately considered.

Russo

Russo was, to all intents and purposes, the chief executive officer of BarChris. He was a member of the executive committee. He was familiar with all aspects of the business. * * *

* * *

* * * Russo knew all the relevant facts. He could not have believed that there were no untrue statements or material omissions in the prospectus. Russo has no due diligence defenses.

Vitolo and Pugliese

They were the founders of the business who stuck with it to the end. Vitolo was president and Pugliese was vice president. * * *

Vitolo and Pugliese are each men of limited education. It is not hard to believe that for them the prospectus was difficult reading, if indeed they read it at all.

But whether it was or not is irrelevant. The liability of a director who signs a registration statement does not depend upon whether or not he read it or, if he did, whether or not he understood what he was reading.

* * *

All in all, the position of Vitolo and Pugliese is not significantly different, for present purposes, from Russo's. They could not have believed that the registration statement was wholly true and that no material facts had been omitted. And in any case, there is nothing to show that they made any investigation of anything which they may not have known about or understood. They have not proved their due diligence defenses.

Kircher

Kircher was treasurer of BarChris and its chief financial officer. He is a certified public accountant and an intelligent man. He was thoroughly familiar with BarChris's financial affairs. * * *

Moreover, as a member of the executive committee, Kircher was kept informed as to those branches of the business of which he did not have direct charge. * * * In brief, Kircher knew all the relevant facts.

* * *

* * * Knowing the facts, Kircher had reason to believe that the expertised portion of the prospectus, i.e., the 1960 figures, was in part incorrect. He could not shut his eyes to the facts and rely on Peat, Marwick for that portion.

As to the rest of the prospectus, knowing the facts, he did not have a reasonable ground to believe it to be true. On the contrary, he must have known that in part it was untrue. * * *

Kircher has not proved his due diligence defenses.

Trilling

Trilling's position is somewhat different from Kircher's. He was BarChris's controller. He signed the registration statement in that capacity, although he was not a director.

* * *

Trilling may well have been unaware of several of the inaccuracies in the prospectus. But he must have known of some of them. As a financial officer, he was familiar with BarChris's finances and with its books of account. * * * I cannot find that Trilling believed the entire prospectus to be true.

But even if he did, he still did not establish his due diligence defenses. He did not prove that as to the parts of the prospectus expertised by Peat, Marwick he had no reasonable ground to believe that it was untrue. He also failed to prove, as to the parts of the prospectus not expertised by Peat, Marwick, that he made a reasonable investigation which afforded him a reasonable ground to believe that it was true. As far as appears he made no investigation. * * * Trilling did not sustain the burden of proving his due diligence defenses.

Birnbaum

Birnbaum was a young lawyer, * * * employed by BarChris as house counsel and assistant secretary in October 1960. Unfortunately for him, he became secretary and a director of BarChris on April 17, 1961, after the first version of the registration statement had been filed with the Securities and Exchange Commission. He signed the later amendments, thereby becoming responsible for the accuracy of the prospectus in its final form.

* * * He did not participate in the management of the company. As house counsel, he attended to legal matters of a routine nature. * * *

* * *

One of Birnbaum's more important duties, first as assistant secretary and later as full-fledged secretary, was to keep the corporate minutes of BarChris and its subsidiaries. This necessarily informed him to a considerable extent about the company's affairs. * * *

It seems probable that Birnbaum did not know of many of the inaccuracies in the prospectus. He must, however, have appreciated some of them. In any case, he made no investigation and relied on the others to get it right. Unlike Trilling, he was entitled to rely upon Peat, Marwick for the 1960 figures, for as far as appears, he had no personal knowledge of the company's books of account or financial transactions. But he was not entitled to rely upon Kircher, Grant and Ballard [, a partner in the law firm representing the underwriters,] for the other portions of the prospectus. As a lawyer, he should have known his obligations under the statute. He should have known that he was required to make a reasonable investigation of the truth of all the statements in the unexpertised portion of the document which he signed. Having failed to make such an investigation, he did not have reasonable ground to believe that all these statements were true. Birnbaum has not established his due diligence defenses except as to the audited 1960 figures.

Auslander

Auslander was an "outside" director, i.e., one who was not an officer of BarChris. He was chairman of the board of Valley Stream National Bank in Valley Stream, Long Island. * * *

* * *

Auslander was elected a director on April 17, 1961. The registration statement in its original form had already been filed, of course without his signature. On May 10, 1961, he signed a signature page for the first amendment to the registration statement which was filed on May 11, 1961. This was a separate sheet without any document attached.

Auslander did not know that it was a signature page for a registration statement. He vaguely understood that it was something "for the SEC."

Auslander attended a meeting of BarChris's directors on May 15, 1961. At that meeting, he along with the other directors, signed the signature sheet for the second amendment which constituted the registration statement in its final form. Again, this was only a separate sheet without any document attached. Auslander never saw a copy of the registration statement in its final form.

* * * A copy of the registration statement in its earlier form as amended on May 11, 1961 was passed around at the meeting. Auslander glanced at it briefly. He did not read it thoroughly.

At the May 15 meeting, Russo and Vitolo stated that everything was in order and that the prospectus was correct. Auslander believed this statement.

In considering Auslander's due diligence defenses, a distinction is to be drawn between the expertised and non-expertised portions of the prospectus. As to the former, Auslander knew that Peat, Marwick had audited the 1960 figures. He believed them to be correct because he had confidence in Peat, Marwick. He had no reasonable ground to believe otherwise.

As to the non-expertised portions, however, Auslander is in a different position. He seems to have been under the impression that Peat, Marwick was responsible for all the figures. This impression was not correct, as he would have realized if he had read the prospectus carefully. Auslander made no investigation of the accuracy of the prospectus. * * *

* * *

Section 11 imposes liability in the first instance upon a director, no matter how new he is. He is presumed to know his responsibility when he becomes a director. He can escape liability only by using that reasonable care to investigate the facts which a prudent man would employ in the management of his own property. * * *

I find and conclude that Auslander has not established his due diligence defense with respect to the misstatements and omissions in those portions of the prospectus other than the audited 1960 figures.

* * *

Grant

Grant became a director of BarChris in October 1960. His law firm was counsel to BarChris in matters pertaining to the registration of securities. Grant * * * drafted the registration statement for the debentures. In the preliminary division of work between him and Ballard, the underwriters' counsel, Grant took initial responsibility for preparing the registration statement, while Ballard devoted his efforts in the first instance to preparing the indenture.

Grant is sued as a director and as a signer of the registration statement. This is not an action against him for malpractice in his capacity as a lawyer. Nevertheless, in considering Grant's due diligence defenses, the unique position which he occupied cannot be disregarded. As the director most directly concerned with writing the registration statement and assuring its accuracy, more was required of him in the way of reasonable investigation than could fairly be expected of a director who had no connection with this work.

* * * Having seen him testify at length, I am satisfied as to his integrity. I find that Grant honestly believed that the registration statement was true and that no material facts had been omitted from it.

In this belief he was mistaken, and the fact is that for all his work, he never discovered any of the errors or omissions which have been recounted at length in this opinion, with the single exception of Capitol Lanes. He knew that BarChris had not sold this alley and intended to operate it, but he appears to have been under the erroneous impression that Peat, Marwick had knowingly sanctioned its inclusion in sales because of the allegedly temporary nature of the operation.

* * *

Much of this registration statement is a scissors and paste-pot job. Grant lifted large portions from the earlier prospectuses, modifying them in some instances to the extent that he considered necessary. But BarChris's affairs had changed for the worse by May 1961. Statements that were accurate in January were no longer accurate in May. Grant never discovered this. He accepted the assurances of Kircher and Russo that any change which might have occurred had been for the better, rather than the contrary.

It is claimed that a lawyer is entitled to rely on the statements of his client and that to require him to verify their accuracy would set an unreasonably high standard. This is too broad a generalization. It is all a matter of degree. To require an audit would obviously be unreasonable. On the other hand, to require a check of matters easily verifiable is not unreasonable. Even honest clients can make mistakes. The statute imposes liability for untrue statements regardless of whether they are intentionally untrue. The way to prevent mistakes is to test oral information by examining the original written record.

* * *

Grant was entitled to rely on Peat, Marwick for the 1960 figures. He had no reasonable ground to believe them to be inaccurate. But the [other] matters * * * were not within the expertised portion of the prospectus. As to [these], Grant, was obliged to make a reasonable investigation. I am forced to find that he did not make one. After making all due allowances for the fact that BarChris's officers misled him, there are too many instances in which Grant failed to make an inquiry which he could easily have made which, if pursued, would have put him on his guard. In my opinion, this finding on the evidence in this case does not establish an unreasonably high standard in other cases for company counsel who are also directors. Each case must rest on its own facts. I conclude that Grant has not established his due diligence defenses except as to the audited 1960 figures.

The Underwriters and Coleman

The underwriters other than Drexel made no investigation of the accuracy of the prospectus. * * * They all relied upon Drexel as the "lead" underwriter.

Drexel did make an investigation. The work was in charge of Coleman, a partner of the firm, assisted by Casperson, an associate. Drexel's attorneys acted as attorneys for the entire group of underwriters. Ballard did the work, assisted by Stanton.

On April 17, 1961 Coleman became a director of BarChris. He signed the first amendment to the registration statement filed on May 11 and the second amendment, constituting the registration statement in its final form, filed on May 16. He thereby assumed a responsibility as a director and signer in addition to his responsibility as an underwriter.

The facts as to the extent of the investigation that Coleman made may be briefly summarized. He was first introduced to BarChris on September 15, 1960. Thereafter he familiarized himself with general conditions in the industry * * * . He also acquired general information on BarChris * * * . * * *

* * *

By mid-March, Coleman was in a position to make more specific inquiries. By that time Grant had prepared a first draft of the prospectus, consisting of a marked-up copy of the January 1961 warrant prospectus. Coleman attended three meetings to discuss the prospectus with BarChris's representatives. * * *

At these discussions, which were extensive, successive proofs of the prospectus were considered and revised. At this point the 1961 figures were not available. * * *

Coleman and Ballard asked pertinent questions and received answers which satisfied them. * * *

* * *

After Coleman was elected a director on April 17, 1961, he made no further independent investigation of the accuracy of the prospectus. He assumed that Ballard was taking care of this on his behalf as well as on behalf of the underwriters.

In April 1961 Ballard instructed Stanton to examine BarChris's minutes for the past five years and also to look at "the major contracts of the company."[11] Stanton went to BarChris's office for that purpose on April 24. He asked Birnbaum for the minute books. He read the minutes of the board of directors and discovered interleaved in them a few minutes of executive committee meetings in 1960. He asked Kircher if there were any others. Kircher said that there had been other executive committee meetings but that the minutes had not been written up.

Stanton read the minutes of a few BarChris subsidiaries. His testimony was vague as to which ones. * * *

As to the "major contracts," all that Stanton could remember seeing was an insurance policy. Birnbaum told him that there was no file of major contracts. Stanton did not examine the agreements with Talcott [, a firm that purchased BarChris' accounts receivable and otherwise assisted in financing bowling lanes]. He did not examine the contracts with customers. He did not look to see what contracts comprised the backlog figure. Stanton examined no accounting records of BarChris. His visit, which lasted one day, was devoted primarily to reading the directors' minutes.

On April 25 Ballard wrote to Grant about certain matters which Stanton had noted on his visit to BarChris the day before, none of which Ballard considered "very earth shaking." * * *

On May 9, 1961, Ballard came to New York and conferred with Grant and Kircher. They discussed the Securities and Exchange Commission's deficiency letter of May 4, 1961 which required the inclusion in the prospectus of certain additional information, notably net sales, gross profits and net earnings figures for the first quarter of 1961. They also discussed the points raised in Ballard's letter to Grant of April 25. * * *

* * *

Ballard did not insist that the executive committee minutes be written up so that he could inspect them, although he testified that he knew from experience that executive committee minutes may be extremely important. If he had insisted he would have found the minutes highly informative, as has previously been pointed out. Ballard did not ask to see BarChris's schedule of delinquencies or Talcott's notices of delinquencies, or BarChris's correspondence with Talcott.

Ballard did not examine BarChris's contracts with Talcott. He did not appreciate what Talcott's rights were under those financing agreements or how serious the effect would be upon BarChris of any exercise of those rights.

Ballard did not investigate the composition of the backlog figure to be sure that it was not "puffy." He made no inquiry after March about any new officers' loans, although he knew that Kircher had insisted on a provision in the indenture which gave loans from individuals priority

---

[11] Stanton was a very junior associate. He had been admitted to the bar in January 1961, some three months before. This was the first registration statement he had ever worked on.

over the debentures. He was unaware of the seriousness of BarChris's cash position and of how BarChris's officers intended to use a large part of the proceeds. He did not know that BarChris was operating Capitol Lanes.

Like Grant, Ballard, without checking, relied on the information which he got from Kircher. He also relied on Grant who, as company counsel, presumably was familiar with its affairs.

* * *

Coleman testified that Drexel had an understanding with its attorneys that "we expect them to inspect on our behalf the corporate records of the company including, but not limited to, the minutes of the corporation, the stockholders and the committees of the board authorized to act for the board." Ballard manifested his awareness of this understanding by sending Stanton to read the minutes and the major contracts. It is difficult to square this understanding with the formal opinion of Ballard's firm which expressly disclaimed any attempt to verify information supplied by the company and its counsel.

In any event, it is clear that no effectual attempt at verification was made. The question is whether due diligence required that it be made. Stated another way, is it sufficient to ask questions, to obtain answers which, if true, would be thought satisfactory, and to let it go at that, without seeking to ascertain from the records whether the answers in fact are true and complete?

I have already held that this procedure is not sufficient in Grant's case. Are underwriters in a different position, as far as due diligence is concerned?

* * *

There is no direct authority on this question, no judicial decision defining the degree of diligence which underwriters must exercise to establish their defense under Section 11.

* * *

The purpose of Section 11 is to protect investors. To that end the underwriters are made responsible for the truth of the prospectus. * * * in order to make the underwriters' participation in this enterprise of any value to the investors, the underwriters must make some reasonable attempt to verify the data submitted to them. They may not rely solely on the company's officers or on the company's counsel. A prudent man in the management of his own property would not rely on them.

It is impossible to lay down a rigid rule suitable for every case defining the extent to which such verification must go. It is a question of degree, a matter of judgment in each case. In the present case, the underwriters' counsel made almost no attempt to verify management's representations. I hold that that was insufficient.

On the evidence in this case, I find that the underwriters' counsel did not make a reasonable investigation of the truth of those portions of the prospectus which were not made on the authority of Peat, Marwick as an expert. Drexel is bound by their failure. It is not a matter of relying upon counsel for legal advice. Here the attorneys were dealing with matters of fact. Drexel delegated to them, as its agent, the business of examining the corporate minutes and contracts. It must bear the consequences of their failure to make an adequate examination.

The other underwriters, who did nothing and relied solely on Drexel and on the lawyers, are also bound by it. It follows that although Drexel and the other underwriters believed that those portions of the prospectus were true, they had no reasonable ground for that belief, within the meaning of the statute. Hence, they have not established their due diligence defense, except as to the 1960 audited figures.[12]

The same conclusions must apply to Coleman. * * *

Peat, Marwick

* * *

The part of the registration statement purporting to be made upon the authority of Peat, Marwick as an expert was, as we have seen, the 1960 figures. [T]he question is whether * * * peat, Marwick, after reasonable investigation, had reasonable ground to believe and did believe that the 1960 figures were true and that no material fact had been omitted from the registration statement which should have been included in order to make the 1960 figures not misleading. * * *

* * *

The 1960 Audit

Peat, Marwick's work was in general charge of a member of the firm, Cummings, and more immediately in charge of Peat, Marwick's manager, Logan. Most of the actual work was performed by a senior accountant, Berardi, who had junior assistants, one of whom was Kennedy.

* * *

In substance, what Berardi did is similar to what Grant and Ballard did. He asked questions, he got answers which he considered satisfactory, and he did nothing to verify them. * * *

* * *

Accountants should not be held to a standard higher than that recognized in their profession. I do not do so here. Berardi's review did not come up to that standard. He did not take some of the steps which Peat, Marwick's written program prescribed. He did not spend an

---

[12] In view of this conclusion, it becomes unnecessary to decide whether the underwriters other than Drexel would have been protected if Drexel had established that as lead underwriter, it made a reasonable investigation.

adequate amount of time on a task of this magnitude. Most important of all, he was too easily satisfied with glib answers to his inquiries.

* * *

Here again, the burden of proof is on Peat, Marwick. I find that that burden has not been satisfied. I conclude that Peat, Marwick has not established its due diligence defense.

* * *

A few subsequent cases have sounded a somewhat more cheerful note for outside directors. For instance, in Weinberger v. Jackson, [1990–1991 Transfer Binder] Fed.Sec.L.Rep. (CCH) Par. 95,693 (N.D.Cal.1990), the court permitted an outside director to rely on the reasonable representations of management, provided his own conduct was reasonable in the circumstances:

> [Valentine] was reasonably familiar with the company's business and operations. He regularly attended board meetings at which the board discussed every aspect of the company's business. And he reviewed the company's financial statements. He was familiar with the company's development of its new product lines. He was involved with various company decisions. He reviewed six drafts of the registration statement and saw nothing suspicious or inconsistent with the knowledge that he had acquired as a decision. And he discussed certain aspects of the registration statement with management.

> * * *

> Plaintiffs argue that Valentine did not make specific inquiries of the company's management with respect to the representations contained in the prospectus. But he had no duty to do so as long as the prospectus statements were consistent with the knowledge of the company which he had reasonably acquired in his position as director. He was also given comfort by the fact that the prospectus and the information in it were reviewed by underwriters, counsel and accountants. This met the standards of due diligence and reasonable inquiry. * * *

> * * *

Despite the sparsity of case law on the subject, since *BarChris* there is no great uncertainty concerning what in general must be done by underwriters during a due diligence investigation—a lot. The starting point is the registration statement itself, and here two steps are required. The information in the registration statement must be verified, and the issuer and its affairs must be examined in an attempt to uncover what must be added to the registration statement to prevent it from containing a material omission. In a relatively small company, these jobs can be done fairly simply. With large issuers that have multiple product lines and operations in a number of locations, thorough due diligence can require a great deal of effort. Underwriters will find themselves (or will have attorneys on their behalf) reviewing all publicly available information (including the issuer's website, Commission filings, and press releases), conducting interviews with multiple members of management, touring facilities, reviewing board and committee minutes, reading contracts (both with the issuer's business partners and with its employees), analyzing the reasonableness of financial assumptions and projections, and otherwise engaging in activities that, in published lists of suggestions, go on for pages.

In re WorldCom, Inc. Securities Litigation[13] is an important decision for underwriters and others. It rejected the claim by WorldCom's underwriters that they were entitled to rely, without question, on audited financial figures. The court said that "the existence of red flags can create a duty to investigate even audited financial statements," and found that because some of WorldCom's financial ratios were significantly lower than those of its two closest competitors, a reasonable person would have inquired further. The defendant underwriters wound up settling the case for $6 billion.

c.   MATERIAL FACTS AND THE "BESPEAKS CAUTION" DOCTRINE

Section 11 imposes liability for misrepresentation or omission of material facts. The following case is an important one dealing with the issue of what constitutes a "fact."

The following is a recent case addressing the question of what constitutes a "fact" for purposes of liability under Section 11.

Omnicare Inc. v. Laborers District Council Construction Industry Pension Fund

Supreme Court of the United States, 2015.
135 S.Ct. 1318.

■ JUSTICE KAGAN delivered the opinion of the Court.

Before a company may sell securities in interstate commerce, it must file a registration statement with the Securities and Exchange Commission (SEC). If that document either "contain[s] an untrue statement of a material fact" or "omit[s] to state a material fact * * * necessary to make the statements therein not misleading," a purchaser of the stock may sue for damages. 15 U.S.C. § 77k(a). This case requires us to decide how each of those phrases applies to statements of opinion.

---

[13]   346 F.Supp. 2d 628 (S.D.N.Y. 2004).

I.

* * *

This case arises out of a registration statement that petitioner Omnicare filed in connection with a public offering of common stock. Omnicare is the nation's largest provider of pharmacy services for residents of nursing homes. Its registration statement contained (along with all mandated disclosures) analysis of the effects of various federal and state laws on its business model, including its acceptance of rebates from pharmaceutical manufacturers. Of significance here, two sentences in the registration statement expressed Omnicare's view of its compliance with legal requirements:

- "We believe our contract arrangements with other healthcare providers, our pharmaceutical suppliers and our pharmacy practices are in compliance with applicable federal and state laws."

- "We believe that our contracts with pharmaceutical manufacturers are legally and economically valid arrangements that bring value to the healthcare system and the patients that we serve."

* * *

Respondents here, pension funds that purchased Omnicare stock in the public offering (hereinafter Funds), brought suit alleging that the company's two opinion statements about legal compliance give rise to liability under § 11. Citing lawsuits that the Federal Government later pressed against Omnicare, the Funds' complaint maintained that the company's receipt of payments from drug manufacturers violated anti-kickback laws. Accordingly, the complaint asserted, Omnicare made "materially false" representations about legal compliance. And so too, the complaint continued, the company "omitted to state [material] facts necessary" to make its representations not misleading. The Funds claimed that none of Omnicare's officers and directors "possessed reasonable grounds" for thinking that the opinions offered were truthful and complete. Indeed, the complaint noted that one of Omnicare's attorneys had warned that a particular contract "carrie[d] a heightened risk" of liability under anti-kickback laws. At the same time, the Funds made clear that in light of § 11's strict liability standard, they chose to "exclude and disclaim any allegation that could be construed as alleging fraud or intentional or reckless misconduct."

The District Court granted Omnicare's motion to dismiss. In the court's view, "statements regarding a company's belief as to its legal compliance are considered 'soft' information" and are actionable only if those who made them "knew [they] were untrue at the time." The court concluded that the Funds' complaint failed to meet that standard because it nowhere claimed that "the company's officers knew they were violating the law." The Court of Appeals for the Sixth Circuit reversed. See 719

F.3d 498 (2013). It acknowledged that the two statements highlighted in the Funds' complaint expressed Omnicare's "opinion" of legal compliance, rather than "hard facts." *Id.*, at 504. But even so, the court held, the Funds had to allege only that the stated belief was "objectively false"; they did not need to contend that anyone at Omnicare "disbelieved [the opinion] at the time it was expressed." *Id.* at 506.

We granted certiorari to consider how § 11 pertains to statements of opinion. We do so in two steps, corresponding to the two parts of § 11 and the two theories in the Funds' complaint. We initially address the Funds' claim that Omnicare made "untrue statement[s] of * * * material fact" in offering its views on legal compliance. § 77k(a). We then take up the Funds' argument that Omnicare "omitted to state a material fact * * * necessary to make the statements [in its registration filing] not misleading." § 77k(a). Unlike both courts below, we see those allegations as presenting different issues. In resolving the first, we discuss when an opinion itself constitutes a factual misstatement. In analyzing the second, we address when an opinion may be rendered misleading by the omission of discrete factual representations. Because we find that the Court of Appeals applied the wrong standard, we vacate its decision.

II

The Sixth Circuit held, and the Funds now urge, that a statement of opinion that is ultimately found incorrect—even if believed at the time made—may count as an "untrue statement of a material fact." 15 U.S.C § 77k(a). As the Funds put the point, a statement of belief may make an implicit assertion about the belief's "subject matter": To say "we believe X is true" is often to indicate that "X is in fact true." In just that way, the Funds conclude, an issuer's statement that "we believe we are following the law" conveys that "we in fact are following the law"—which is "materially false," no matter what the issuer thinks, if instead it is violating an anti-kickback statute.

But that argument wrongly conflates facts and opinions. A fact is "a thing done or existing" or "[a]n actual happening." Webster's New International Dictionary 782 (1927). An opinion is "a belief[,] a view," or a "sentiment which the mind forms of persons or things." *Id.*, at 1509. Most important, a statement of fact ("the coffee is hot") expresses certainty about a thing, whereas a statement of opinion ("I think the coffee is hot") does not. See *ibid.* ("An opinion, in ordinary usage * * * does not imply * * * definiteness * * * or certainty"); 7 Oxford English Dictionary 151 (1933) (an opinion "rests[s] on grounds insufficient for complete demonstration"). Indeed, that difference between the two is so ingrained in our everyday ways of speaking and thinking as to make resort to old dictionaries seem a mite silly. And Congress effectively incorporated just that distinction in § 11's first part by exposing issuers to liability not for "untrue statement[s]" full stop (which would have included ones of opinion), but only for "untrue statement[s] of * * * *fact*." § 77k(a) (emphasis added).

Consider that statutory phrase's application to two hypothetical statements, couched in ways the Funds claim are equivalent. A company's CEO states: "The TVs we manufacture have the highest resolution available on the market." Or, alternatively, the CEO transforms that factual statement into one of opinion: "I *believe*" (or "I think") "the TVs we manufacture have the highest resolution available on the market." The first version would be an untrue statement of fact if a competitor had introduced a higher resolution TV a month before—even assuming the CEO had not yet learned of the new product. The CEO's assertion, after all, is not mere puffery, but a determinate, verifiable statement about her company's TVs; and the CEO, however innocently, got the facts wrong. But in the same set of circumstances, the second version would remain true. Just as she said, the CEO really did believe, when she made the statement, that her company's TVs had the sharpest picture around. And although a plaintiff could later prove that opinion erroneous, the words "I believe" themselves admitted that possibility, thus precluding liability for an untrue statement of fact. That remains the case if the CEO's opinion, as here, concerned legal compliance. If, for example, she said, "I believe our marketing practices are lawful," and actually did think that, she could not be liable for a false statement of fact—even if she afterward discovered a longtime violation of law. Once again, the statement would have been true, because all she expressed was a view, not a certainty, about legal compliance.

That still leaves some room for § 11's false-statement provision to apply to expressions of opinion. As even Omnicare acknowledges, every such statement explicitly affirms one fact: that the speaker actually holds the stated belief. * * * For that reason, the CEO's statement about product quality ("I believe our TVs have the highest resolution available on the market") would be an untrue statement of fact—namely, the fact of her own belief—if she knew that her company's TVs only placed second. And so too the statement about legal compliance ("I believe our marketing practices are lawful") would falsely describe her own state of mind if she thought her company was breaking the law. In such cases, § 11's first part would subject the issuer to liability (assuming the misrepresentation were material).[14]

---

[14] Our decision in Virginia Bankshares, Inc. v. Sandberg, 501 U.S. 1083 (1991), qualifies this statement in one respect. There, the Court considered when corporate directors' statements of opinion in a proxy solicitation give rise to liability under § 14(a) of the Securities Exchange Act, 15 U.S.C. § 78n(a), which bars conduct similar to that described in § 11. In discussing that issue, the Court raised the hypothetical possibility that a director could think he was lying while actually (*i.e.*, accidentally) telling the truth about the matter addressed in his opinion. See *Virginia Bankshares,* 501 U.S., at 1095–1096. That rare set of facts, the Court decided, would not lead to liability under § 14(a). See *ibid.* The Court reasoned that such an inadvertently correct assessment is unlikely to cause anyone harm and that imposing liability merely for the "impurities" of a director's "unclean heart" might provoke vexatious litigation. We think the same is true (to the extent this scenario ever occurs in real life) under § 11. So if our CEO did not believe that her company's TVs had the highest resolution on the market, but (surprise!) they really did, § 11 would not impose liability for her statement.

In addition, some sentences that begin with opinion words like "I believe" contain embedded statements of fact—as, once again, Omnicare recognizes. Suppose the CEO in our running hypothetical said: "I believe our TVs have the highest resolution available because we use a patented technology to which our competitors do not have access." That statement may be read to affirm not only the speaker's state of mind, as described above, but also an underlying fact: that the company uses a patented technology. See Virginia Bankshares, Inc. v. Sandberg, 501 U.S. 1083, 1109 (1991) (SCALIA, J., concurring in part and concurring in judgment) (showing that a statement can sometimes be "most fairly read as affirming separately both the fact of the [speaker's] opinion and the accuracy of the facts" given to support or explain it). Accordingly, liability under § 11's false-statement provision would follow (once again, assuming materiality) not only if the speaker did not hold the belief she professed but also if the supporting fact she supplied were untrue.

But the Funds cannot avail themselves of either of those ways of demonstrating liability. The two sentences to which the Funds object are pure statements of opinion: To simplify their content only a bit, Omnicare said in each that "we believe we are obeying the law." And the Funds do not contest that Omnicare's opinion was honestly held. Recall that their complaint explicitly "exclude[s] and disclaim[s]" any allegation sounding in fraud or deception. What the Funds instead claim is that Omnicare's belief turned out to be wrong—that whatever the company thought, it was in fact violating anti-kickback laws. But that allegation alone will not give rise to liability under § 11's first clause because, as we have shown, a sincere statement of pure opinion is not an "untrue statement of material fact," regardless whether an investor can ultimately prove the belief wrong. That clause, limited as it is to factual statements, does not allow investors to second-guess inherently subjective and uncertain assessments. In other words, the provision is not, as the Court of Appeals and the Funds would have it, an invitation to Monday morning quarterback an issuer's opinions.

III

A

That conclusion, however, does not end this case because the Funds also rely on § 11's omissions provision, alleging that Omnicare "omitted to state facts necessary" to make its opinion on legal compliance "not misleading." [S]ee § 77k(a). As all parties accept, whether a statement is "misleading" depends on the perspective of a reasonable investor: The inquiry (like the one into materiality) is objective. Cf. TSC Industries, Inc. v. Northway, Inc., 426 U.S. 438, 445 (1976) (noting that the securities laws care only about the "significance of an omitted or misrepresented fact to a reasonable investor"). We therefore must consider when, if ever, the omission of a fact can make a statement of opinion like Omnicare's, even if literally accurate, misleading to an ordinary investor.

Omnicare claims that is just not possible. On its view, no reasonable person, in any context, can understand a pure statement of opinion to convey anything more than the speaker's own mindset. As long as an opinion is sincerely held, Omnicare argues, it cannot mislead as to any matter, regardless what related facts the speaker has omitted. Such statements of belief (concludes Omnicare) are thus immune from liability under § 11's second part, just as they are under its first.

That claim has more than a kernel of truth. A reasonable person understands, and takes into account, the difference we have discussed above between a statement of fact and one of opinion. She recognizes the import of words like "I think" or "I believe," and grasps that they convey some lack of certainty as to the statement's content. See, *e.g.,* Restatement (Second) of Contracts § 168, Comment *a,* p. 456 (1979) (noting that a statement of opinion "implies that [the speaker] * * * is not certain enough of what he says" to do without the qualifying language). And that may be especially so when the phrases appear in a registration statement, which the reasonable investor expects has been carefully wordsmithed to comply with the law. When reading such a document, the investor thus distinguishes between the sentences "we believe X is true" and "X is true." And because she does so, the omission of a fact that merely rebuts the latter statement fails to render the former misleading. In other words, a statement of opinion is not misleading just because external facts show the opinion to be incorrect. Reasonable investors do not understand such statements as guarantees, and § 11's omissions clause therefore does not treat them that way.

But Omnicare takes its point too far, because a reasonable investor may, depending on the circumstances, understand an opinion statement to convey facts about how the speaker has formed the opinion—or, otherwise put, about the speaker's basis for holding that view. And if the real facts are otherwise, but not provided, the opinion statement will mislead its audience. Consider an unadorned statement of opinion about legal compliance: "We believe our conduct is lawful." If the issuer makes that statement without having consulted a lawyer, it could be misleadingly incomplete. In the context of the securities market, an investor, though recognizing that legal opinions can prove wrong in the end, still likely expects such an assertion to rest on some meaningful legal inquiry—rather than, say, on mere intuition, however sincere. Similarly, if the issuer made the statement in the face of its lawyers' contrary advice, or with knowledge that the Federal Government was taking the opposite view, the investor again has cause to complain: He expects not just that the issuer believes the opinion (however irrationally), but that it fairly aligns with the information in the issuer's possession at the time. Thus, if a registration statement omits material facts about the issuer's inquiry into or knowledge concerning a statement of opinion, and if those facts conflict with what a reasonable investor would take from the statement itself, then § 11's omissions clause creates liability.

An opinion statement, however, is not necessarily misleading when an issuer knows, but fails to disclose, some fact cutting the other way. Reasonable investors understand that opinions sometimes rest on a weighing of competing facts; indeed, the presence of such facts is one reason why an issuer may frame a statement as an opinion, thus conveying uncertainty. Suppose, for example, that in stating an opinion about legal compliance, the issuer did not disclose that a single junior attorney expressed doubts about a practice's legality, when six of his more senior colleagues gave a stamp of approval. That omission would not make the statement of opinion misleading, even if the minority position ultimately proved correct: A reasonable investor does not expect that *every* fact known to an issuer supports its opinion statement.[15]

Moreover, whether an omission makes an expression of opinion misleading always depends on context. Registration statements as a class are formal documents, filed with the SEC as a legal prerequisite for selling securities to the public. Investors do not, and are right not to, expect opinions contained in those statements to reflect baseless, off-the-cuff judgments, of the kind that an individual might communicate in daily life. At the same time, an investor reads each statement within such a document, whether of fact or of opinion, in light of all its surrounding text, including hedges, disclaimers, and apparently conflicting information. And the investor takes into account the customs and practices of the relevant industry. So an omission that renders misleading a statement of opinion when viewed in a vacuum may not do so once that statement is considered, as is appropriate, in a broader frame. The reasonable investor understands a statement of opinion in its full context, and § 11 creates liability only for the omission of material facts that cannot be squared with such a fair reading.

* * *

Finally, [responding to Omnicare's argument to the contrary,] we see no reason to think that liability for misleading opinions will chill disclosures useful to investors. Nothing indicates that § 11's application to misleading factual assertions in registration statements has caused such a problem. And likewise, common-law doctrines of opinion liability have not, so far as anyone knows, deterred merchants in ordinary commercial transactions from asserting helpful opinions about their products. That absence of fallout is unsurprising. Sellers (whether of stock or other items) have strong economic incentives to * * * well, *sell*

---

[15] We note, too, that a reasonable investor generally considers the specificity of an opinion statement in making inferences about its basis. Compare two new statements from our ever-voluble CEO. In the first, she says: "I believe we have 1.3 million TVs in our warehouse." In the second, she says: "I believe we have enough supply on hand to meet demand." All else equal, a reasonable person would think that a more detailed investigation lay behind the former statement.

(*i.e.,* hawk or peddle). Those market-based forces push back against any inclination to underdisclose. And to avoid exposure for omissions under § 11, an issuer need only divulge an opinion's basis, or else make clear the real tentativeness of its belief. Such ways of conveying opinions so that they do not mislead will keep valuable information flowing. And that is the only kind of information investors need. To the extent our decision today chills *misleading* opinions, that is all to the good: In enacting § 11, Congress worked to ensure better, not just more, information.

B

* * *

[F]or the reasons stated, we vacate the judgment below and remand the case for further proceedings.

The Second Circuit has made the point that audit reports are statements of opinion and subject to the *Omnicare* standard.[16]

Omnicare was not decided until 2015 and well may have changed the analysis—but not the outcome—of the case set out below. *Trump*, however, is presented not for what it says about facts but for what it says about materiality.

In re Donald J. Trump Casino Securities Litigation—Taj Mahal Litigation

United States Court of Appeals, Third Circuit, 1993.
7 F.3d 357.

■ Before BECKER, ALITO, CIRCUIT JUDGES and ATKINS, DISTRICT JUDGE.

■ BECKER, CIRCUIT JUDGE.

This is an appeal from orders of the district court for the District of New Jersey dismissing a number of complaints brought under [Sections 11, 12(a)(2) and 15] of the Securities Act of 1933 and [Sections 10(b) and 20(a)] of the Securities Exchange Act of 1934 by a class of investors who purchased bonds to provide financing for the acquisition and completion of the Taj Mahal, a lavish casino/hotel on the boardwalk in Atlantic City, New Jersey. The defendants are Donald J. Trump ("Trump"), Robert S. Trump, Harvey S. Freeman, the Trump Organization Inc., Trump Taj Mahal Inc., Taj Mahal Funding Inc. and Trump Taj Mahal Associates Limited Partnership (the "Partnership") (collectively the "Trump defendants") and Merrill Lynch, Pierce, Fenner and Smith Inc. ("Merrill Lynch"). The complaints allege that the prospectus accompanying the issuance of the bonds contained affirmatively misleading statements and materially misleading omissions in contravention of the federal securities laws.

----

[16]   Querub v. Moore Stephens Hong Kong, 649 Fed.Appx. 55 (2d Cir.2016).

The district court dismissed the securities law claims under Fed.R.Civ.P. 12(b)(6) for failure to state a claim upon which relief can be granted. The linchpin of the district court's decision was what has been described as the "bespeaks caution" doctrine, according to which a court may determine that the inclusion of sufficient cautionary statements in a prospectus renders misrepresentations and omissions contained therein nonactionable. While the viability of the bespeaks caution doctrine is an issue of first impression for this court, we believe that it primarily represents new nomenclature rather than substantive change in the law. As we see it, "bespeaks caution" is essentially shorthand for the well-established principle that a statement or omission must be considered in context, so that accompanying statements may render it immaterial as a matter of law.

* * *

I.   Facts and Procedural History

In November, 1988 the Trump defendants offered to the public $675 million in first mortgage investment bonds (the "bonds") with Merrill Lynch acting as the sole underwriter. The interest rate on the bonds was 14%, a high rate in comparison to the 9% yield offered on quality corporate bonds at the time. The Trump defendants issued the bonds to raise capital to: (1) purchase the Taj Mahal, a partially-completed casino/hotel located on the boardwalk, from Resorts International, Inc. (which had already invested substantial amounts in its construction); (2) complete construction of the Taj Mahal; and (3) open the Taj Mahal for business.

* * *

Plaintiffs ground their lawsuits in the text of the prospectus. Their strongest attack focuses on the "Management Discussion and Analysis" ("MD & A") section of the prospectus, which stated: "The Partnership believes that funds generated from the operation of the Taj Mahal will be sufficient to cover all of its debt service (interest and principal)." The plaintiffs' primary contention is that this statement was materially misleading because the defendants possessed neither a genuine nor a reasonable belief in its truth. * * *

After learning that the Trump defendants planned to file Chapter 11 bankruptcy proceedings and establish a reorganization plan, various bondholders filed separate complaints in the United States District Courts for the Southern District of New York, the Eastern District of New York and the District of New Jersey. * * *

* * *

IV. The Alleged Affirmative Material Misrepresentations in the Prospectus

* * *

B.   The Text of the Prospectus

The prospectus at issue contained an abundance of warnings and cautionary language which bore directly on the prospective financial success of the Taj Mahal and on the Partnership's ability to repay the bonds. We believe that given this extensive yet specific cautionary language, a reasonable factfinder could not conclude that the inclusion of the statement "[t]he Partnership believes that funds generated from the operation of the Taj Mahal will be sufficient to cover all of its debt service (interest and principal)" would influence a reasonable investor's investment decision. More specifically, we believe that due to the disclaimers and warnings the prospectus contains, no reasonable investor could believe anything but that the Taj Mahal bonds represented a rather risky, speculative investment which might yield a high rate of return, but which alternatively might result in no return or even a loss. We hold that under this set of facts, the bondholders cannot prove that the alleged misrepresentation was material.

The statement the plaintiffs assail as misleading is contained in the MD & A section of the prospectus, which follows the sizable "Special Considerations" section, a section notable for its extensive and detailed disclaimers and cautionary statements. More precisely, the prospectus explained that, because of its status as a new venture of unprecedented size and scale, a variety of risks inhered in the Taj Mahal which could affect the Partnership's ability to repay the bondholders. For example, it stated:

The casino business in Atlantic City, New Jersey has a seasonal nature of which summer is the peak season. * * * Since the third interest payment date on the Bonds [(which constitutes the first interest payment not paid out of the initial financing)] occurs before the summer season, the Partnership will not have the benefit of receiving peak season cash flow prior to the third interest payment date, which could adversely affect its ability to pay interest on the Bonds.

* * * The Taj Mahal has not been completed and, accordingly, has no operating history. The Partnership, therefore, has no history of earnings and its operations will be subject to all of the risks inherent in the establishment of a new business enterprise. Accordingly, the ability of the Partnership to service its debt to [Taj Mahal Funding Inc., which issued the bonds,] is completely dependent upon the success of that operation and such success will depend upon financial, business, competitive, regulatory and other factors affecting the Taj Mahal and the casino industry in general as well as prevailing economic conditions. * * *

The Taj Mahal will be the largest casino/hotel complex in Atlantic City, with approximately twice the room capacity and casino space of many of the existing casino/hotels in Atlantic City. [No] other casino/hotel operator has had experience operating a complex the size of the Taj Mahal in Atlantic City. Consequently, no assurance can be given that, once opened, the Taj Mahal will be profitable or that it will generate cash flow sufficient to provide for the payment of the debt service * * * .

The prospectus went on to relate, as part of its "Security for the Bonds" subsection, the potential effect of the Partnership's default on its mortgage payments. For example, this subsection unreservedly explained that if a default occurred prior to completion of the Taj Mahal, "there would not be sufficient proceeds [from a foreclosure sale of the Taj Mahal] to pay the principal of, and accrued interest on, the Bonds."

The "Special Considerations" section also detailed the high level of competition for customers the completed Taj Mahal would face once opened to the public:

Competition in the Atlantic City casino/hotel market is intense. At present, there are twelve casino/hotels in Atlantic City. * * * Some Atlantic City casino/hotels recently have completed renovations or are in the process of expanding and improving their facilities * * * . The Partnership believes that, based upon historical trends, casino win per square foot of casino space will decline in 1990 as a result of a projected increase in casino floor space, including the opening of the Taj Mahal.

In a section following the MD & A section, the prospectus reiterated its reference to the intense competition in the Atlantic City casino industry * * * . The prospectus additionally reported that there were risks of delay in the construction of the Taj Mahal and a risk that the casino might not receive the numerous essential licenses and permits from the state regulatory authorities.

In this case the Partnership did not bury the warnings about risks amidst the bulk of the prospectus. Indeed, it was the allegedly misleading statement which was buried amidst the cautionary language. * * * Moreover, an investor would have read the sentence immediately following the challenged statement, which cautioned: "no assurance can be given, however, that actual operating results will meet the Partnership's expectations."

As we explained above, we must consider an alleged misrepresentation within the context in which the speaker communicated it. Here the context clearly and precisely relayed to the bondholders the substantial uncertainties inherent in the completion and operation of the Taj Mahal. The prospectus contained both general warnings that the Partnership could not assure the repayment of the bonds as well as specific discussions detailing a variety of risk factors that rendered the completion and profitable operation of the Taj Mahal highly uncertain. Within this broad context the statement at issue was, at worst, harmless.

C.   The Bespeaks Caution Doctrine

The district court applied what has come to be known as the "bespeaks caution" doctrine. In so doing it followed the lead of a number of courts of appeals which have dismissed securities fraud claims under Rule 12(b)(6) because cautionary language in the offering document negated the materiality of an alleged misrepresentation or omission. We are persuaded by the *ratio decidendi* of these cases and will apply bespeaks caution to the facts before us.

The application of bespeaks caution depends on the specific text of the offering document or other communication at issue, i.e., courts must assess the communication on a case-by-case basis. Nevertheless, we can state as a general matter that, when an offering document's forecasts, opinions or projections are accompanied by meaningful cautionary statements, the forward-looking statements will not form the basis for a securities fraud claim if those statements did not affect the "total mix" of information the document provided investors. In other words, cautionary language, if sufficient, renders the alleged omissions or misrepresentations immaterial as a matter of law.

The bespeaks caution doctrine is, as an analytical matter, equally applicable to allegations of both affirmative misrepresentations and omissions concerning soft information. * * * Of course, a vague or blanket (boilerplate) disclaimer which merely warns the reader that the investment has risks will ordinarily be inadequate to prevent misinformation. To suffice, the cautionary statements must be substantive and tailored to the specific future projections, estimates or opinions in the prospectus which the plaintiffs challenge.

Because of the abundant and meaningful cautionary language contained in the prospectus, we hold that the plaintiffs have failed to state an actionable claim regarding the statement that the Partnership believed it could repay the bonds. We can say that the prospectus here truly bespeaks caution because, not only does the prospectus generally convey the riskiness of the investment, but its warnings and cautionary language directly address the substance of the statement the plaintiffs challenge. That is to say, the cautionary statements were tailored precisely to address the uncertainty concerning the Partnership's prospective inability to repay the bondholders.

* * *

Most courts limit the "bespeaks caution" doctrine to situations that involve forward-looking statements, but this is not universal. Picking up on the judicial "bespeaks caution" doctrine, Congress added Section 27A to the Securities Act. This section, unlike the "bespeaks caution" doctrine, does not apply in the context of an issuer's IPO. It provides, to Exchange Act reporting companies and some other persons, a safe harbor for certain forward-looking statements that are accompanied by cautionary statements meeting the section's requirements. This section should be read along with Rule 175, which also relates to liability for certain forward-looking statements. Note that the "bespeaks caution" doctrine, the safe harbor provided by Section 27A, and Rule 175 apply not only to Section 11, but to applicable situations arising under any section of the Securities Act.

The following case provides further insight into the meaning of "materiality," both in the context of Section 11 and for other purposes under the Securities and Exchange Acts.

Kapps v. Torch Offshore, Inc.

United States Court of Appeals, Fifth Circuit, 2004.
379 F.3d 207.

■ Before Garwood, Jones, and Stewart, Circuit Judges.

■ Garwood, Circuit Judge:

* * *

FACTS AND PROCEEDINGS BELOW

Torch Offshore, Inc. (Torch) is a service provider that installs and maintains underwater oil and natural gas pipelines and related infrastructure on the Gulf of Mexico's Continental Shelf. Torch's customers include major energy companies and independent oil and natural gas producers.

Commencing on June 7, 2001, Torch conducted an Initial Public Offering (IPO) during which it sold 5,000,000 shares of its common stock at $16 per share, raising $80 million. The IPO was conducted pursuant to a registration statement and prospectus dated June 7, 2001 which Torch filed with the Securities and Exchange Commission (SEC).

In the prospectus, Torch disclosed the volatile nature of oil and natural gas prices, the dependence of Torch's business upon oil and natural gas prices, and the time lags between the prices and the demand for Torch's services.

The prospectus asserted, truthfully, that natural gas prices had increased by approximately 133% from February 1999 through June 6, 2001. However, during the some five and one-third months immediately preceding the June 7, 2001 IPO, natural gas prices had in fact declined approximately 60%. That information was not included anywhere in the prospectus. Though it did discuss the volatile nature of oil and natural gas prices, the prospectus made no mention of any particular decline in the price of natural gas.

During the two month period after the issuance of the IPO, Torch's share prices declined to below $8 per share. On August 2, 2001, Torch issued a press release stating that during the period after the IPO, domestic natural gas and crude oil prices declined. The press release also noted that Torch had begun to note delays in the completion of shallow water drilling projects.

On March 1, 2002, Kapps filed a putative class action suit on behalf of all persons and entities who purchased Torch common stock between June 7, 2001 and August 1, 2001. * * *

The district court granted the [defendants'] motions to dismiss on December 18, 2002, holding that federal securities laws do not impose a duty on issuers to disclose industry-wide trends or publicly available information. The plaintiffs timely appealed.

DISCUSSION

* * *

It appears that the district court granted the motions to dismiss on the ground that the price of natural gas is publicly available information, and therefore, the defendants could not have been in violation of Section 11. If this is the interpretation intended by the district court, it is incorrect. Specifically, we hold that the definition of "material" under Section 11 is not strictly limited to information that is firm-specific and non-public. While all material information need not be included in the registration statement, an issuer is not free to make material misrepresentations, or to omit material information that is either required to be disclosed by law or that is necessary to disclose in order to prevent statements made in the registration statement from being misleading.

A *fact* is material "if there is a substantial likelihood that a reasonable shareholder would consider it important" in making an investment decision. Basic Inc. v. Levinson, 485 U.S. 224 (1988), *quoting* TSC Industries, Inc. v. Northway, 426 U.S. 438 (1976). For an *omission* to be material, "there must be a *substantial* likelihood that the disclosure of the omitted fact would have been viewed by the *reasonable investor* as having *significantly* altered the 'total mix' of information made available." *Id.* (emphasis added). This Court must determine whether "the information allegedly omitted or misrepresented in the prospectus was material, in the sense that it would have altered the way a reasonable investor would have perceived the total mix of information available in the prospectus as a whole." Krim v. BancTexas Group, Inc., 989 F.2d 1435, 1445 (5th Cir. 1993) (holding that certain omitted information was not material, but based on the ground that the substance of the information was adequately set forth in the prospectus, not simply because the information was not firm-specific or was publicly available). *But see* Ward v. Succession of Freeman, 854 F.2d 780, 792–93 (5th Cir. 1988). * * * .

* * *

In Wielgos v. Commonwealth Edison, Co., 892 F.2d 509 (7th Cir. 1989), the court stated, "Issuers of securities must reveal firm-specific information. Investors combine this with public information to derive estimates about the securities' value. It is pointless and costly to compel firms to reprint information already in the public domain." *Id.* At 517. Contrary to the way the district court may have understood that passage, we conclude that the *Wielgos* court likely did not mean for it to be taken as a strict rule that securities laws *never* require disclosure of any information that is not firm-specific or that is publicly available. For example, * * * the SEC requires an issuer to disclose certain "trends" that could affect its business, and in appropriate circumstances this requirement may extend to certain trends that are not firm-specific or are publicly available. Moreover, the court in *Wielgos* stated that it was not addressing the question of whether omitted facts were material, but was rather ruling on whether the disclosures complied with SEC rules.

* * *

Though in a Section 10 case, the Fifth Circuit has defined materiality as a " '*substantial* likelihood' that a *reasonable* investor would consider . . . [the challenged] statements . . . to have '*significantly* altered the "*total mix*" of information.' " * * * Nathenson v. Zonagen Inc., 267 F.3d 400, 422 (5th Cir. 2001) (emphasis added). The "total mix" of information normally includes information that is and has been in the readily available general public domain and facts known or reasonably available to the shareholders. United Paperworkers Intern. Union v. International Paper Co., 985 F.2d 1190, 1199 (2d Cir. 1993).

Natural gas prices are listed in daily papers. The Wall Street Journal, for example, compares the day's price with the price one year ago (and historic daily prices are also available through other sources, such as the New York Mercantile Exchange, or NYMEX). While not of itself necessarily dispositive, such common public ready availability must be considered in determining whether the "total mix" of information was altered because the price decline was not included in the prospectus. When viewed in context, and taking into consideration the cautionary language used in relation to the volatility of natural gas prices and the ready public availability of natural gas prices, neither of the statements at issue were materially misleading. It was not materially misleading for the prospectus to state that over the specified period the price had increased by 133%, or, in the particular context where the language appears, that there had been "recent increases in the price of natural gas," not simply because the omitted information was not firm-specific or was publicly available, but because there is no substantial likelihood that including the fact that the price of natural gas had declined since December 27, 2000 would have significantly altered a reasonable investor's perception of the "total mix of information available in the prospectus as a whole." *Krim*, 989 F.2d at 1445.

* * *

CONCLUSION

The district court properly granted defendants' motions to dismiss because the statements in the prospectus concerning natural gas prices were neither false nor materially misleading. * * *

* * *

II. SECTION 12(a)(1)

Section 12(a)(1) provides for civil liability when a person "offers or sells a security in violation of Section 5." That is, liability flows under this section when unregistered securities are offered or sold without an available exemption. Under Section 12(a)(1), a purchaser may not recover from an issuer, or any other seller (e.g., an intermediate seller if there has been a chain of purchases and sales), unless there is a direct link between the purchaser and seller. That limitation flows from the provision in the section that provides that a seller is "liable, subject to subsection (b), to the person purchasing * * * from him." But an intermediate seller (for example, one between the issuer who originally sells securities illegally and the plaintiff who first brings suit) can, of course, sue his seller, who can in turn sue his seller, and so on up the line. Other than the requirement that the suit be commenced before the statute of limitations has run, there is generally nothing else standing in the way of a plaintiff's obtaining rescission of his purchase, with recovery of interest, or damages when he has sold his securities at a loss. An obstacle that does stand in the way of a plaintiff's recovery under Section 12(a)(1) arose in the next case:

Fuller v. Dilbert

United States District Court, Southern District of New York, 1965.
244 F.Supp. 196.

■ WEINFELD, DISTRICT JUDGE.

This litigation revolves about a contract for the sale of a block of unregistered stock of Dilbert's Quality Supermarkets, Inc., a corporation which had been engaged in the supermarket and food store business in the Metropolitan New York area. The litigants are (1) Arthur and Samuel Dilbert, the sellers of the stock; (2) Abraham Dilbert, their cousin, the purchaser of the stock; and (3) the partners of an investment and underwriting concern, S.D. Fuller & Co., who jointly and severally guaranteed the performance by Abraham Dilbert of the purchase contract [the "Fullers"].

Under the terms of the contract entered into on March 10, 1961, Abraham Dilbert agreed to purchase from his cousins, Arthur and Samuel, 164,540 shares of common stock, including the common stock to be obtained on conversion of preferred shares, at a price of $6 per share, for a total of $987,240. Upon execution of the contract $210,000 was paid for 35,000 shares, which were delivered on May 9, 1961. The balance of the shares as they came into the sellers' possession were to be deposited in escrow, and the purchaser was obligated to draw these down in five equal annual installments beginning on March 10, 1962, delivery to be made upon payment at the agreed price per share.

No registration statement was in effect as to the 164,540 shares, which represented approximately twenty-seven per cent of the then outstanding stock. However, "Abraham Dilbert and his designees" agreed that the purchased shares were being acquired for investment so that the transaction would come within the exemption provision of Section [4(a)(2)] of the Securities Act of 1933.

The Fullers, upon execution of the contract and as required by its terms, signed the following guaranty: "Performance of the foregoing agreement by Abraham Dilbert is hereby guaranteed." Simultaneously, the Fullers entered into a separate agreement (referred to as the designation agreement) with the purchaser under which (as permitted by the stock purchase agreement) they, the Fullers, purchased 8,500 shares of Abraham Dilbert's initial acquisition of 35,000 shares, for which they paid $51,000; in addition, they agreed to purchase fifty-five per cent of the balance of the shares that Abraham was to take down in installments.

In March 1962 the sellers, upon the failure of the purchaser or the guarantors to take down and pay for the first installment, declared a default; in April 1962, by reason thereof, they claimed the entire purchase price and gave notice they intended to sue. But before the sellers instituted any action, the guarantors commenced this suit for a declaratory judgment that the contract for the sale of the stock was void and unenforceable on the grounds that the sale was not for investment, but was a public distribution in violation of Section 5 of the Securities Act of 1933 * * * . * * *

* * *

The Fullers contend that the stock purchase agreement of March 10, 1961 and their guaranty of its provisions involved a transaction that was a public offering or distribution of unregistered stock in violation of Section 5 of the Securities Act of 1933, and consequently they are entitled under Section [12(a)(1)] of the Act to have them declared void and unenforceable.

All parties were aware that the purchaser, the primary obligor under the stock purchase agreement, could not himself finance the transaction. Thus, although obligated for the entire purchase price, it was contemplated that he could designate other investors, described as designees, to take and hold portions of the stock. The Fullers were "designees" and, as already noted, purchased 8,500 shares of the initial 35,000 acquired by Abraham Dilbert. Contemporaneously, they also committed themselves under their separate designation agreement with

Abraham to purchase fifty-five per cent of the installment shares as they were taken down by Abraham. Another designee was the North River Securities Company, an investment concern which, simultaneously with the contract closing, purchased from Abraham 8,000 shares of the initial 35,000.

Paragraph 8 of the stock purchase agreement provides that:

"Abraham Dilbert and his designees agree that the shares purchased hereunder are being acquired for investment and that appropriate letters of investment, as required by the attorneys for the seller, will be given by Abraham Dilbert and/or his designees, so that the sale herein made shall be deemed to be exempt from the Securities Act of 1933 * * * in accordance with the provisions of Section [4(a)(2)]."

On its face, the agreement was within Section [4(a)(2)], which exempts from registration transactions not involving a public distribution. Also, it is clear from paragraph 8 that, while the purchaser could designate others to take a portion of the stock, compliance therewith required this be done consistently with its purpose that no public offering or distribution be effected, and that he and his designees would take the stock only for investment so that the exemption under the Act would be preserved.

Notwithstanding, the Fullers, and Abraham too, contend that the distribution to Abraham and to his designees, and a sale of shares to one Sol Davis, hereafter considered, constituted a public offering. Their contention must be rejected. Certainly the purchaser, who was the executive vice president and a director of Dilbert's, the Fullers and the North River Securities Company, the only offerees known to the sellers and the Court so finds satisfied the statutory requirements as interpreted by the courts. * * *

* * *

They also seek to vitiate the agreement by reason of a sale of 3,500 shares on March 10, 1961 by Abraham Dilbert to one Sol Davis, then in Miami, Florida, who immediately cut in two friends for forty per cent of the stock and thereafter sold the balance at a profit through the facilities of the American Stock Exchange. The offer appears to have preceded the actual signing of the contract. The Court finds that the Davis transaction was unknown to and concealed from the sellers by the purchaser. It was not only a breach of his express commitment that he and his designees would hold the stock for investment, but also a violation of Section 5. Thus, the question is posed whether in consequence the contract is unenforceable. The legislative purpose of the securities acts was the protection of innocent purchasers of securities, and public policy does not command that every violation of the acts renders contracts void and unenforceable.

The Court accepts the view urged by the Securities and Exchange Commission in its amicus curiae brief submitted in this matter on the motion for summary judgment before Judge Dawson that no public interest is served or protected by depriving the sellers of their rights under the contract-in short, that Abraham Dilbert, who undertook that he and his designees would not violate the statute, and the Fullers, who guaranteed performance of his undertaking, are not among those entitled to take advantage of an alleged Section 5 violation resulting from Abraham's distribution of stock in breach of his covenant.

Section 12 of the Securities Act which creates civil liability on the part of one who sells stock in violation of Section 5 does not require that a purchaser and his guarantor be permitted to escape their contractual obligations where the violation is brought about by the purchaser's wrongdoing in which the seller did not participate and of which he was without knowledge. No public interest requires this result. * * * On the other hand, as the Commission pointed out, permitting the sellers to enforce the contract "would establish the salutary precedent of enabling those who sell securities to enforce undertakings to hold for investment." This is not to say that members of the investing public in whose hands the stock eventually comes to rest may not resort to Section 12. * * *

* * *

Another Section 12(a)(1) question is whether a claim for rescission or damages is allowed when an illegal offer is followed by registration of the offered securities, and delivery of a proper prospectus, prior to sale. The Second Circuit examined this question in Diskin v. Lomasney & Co.:

Diskin v. Lomasney & Co.

United States Court of Appeals, Second Circuit, 1971.
452 F.2d 871.

■ Before FRIENDLY, CHIEF JUDGE, FEINBERG, CIRCUIT JUDGE, and DAVIS, ASSOCIATE JUDGE.

■ FRIENDLY, CHIEF JUDGE:

During the summer of 1968 plaintiff Diskin had conversations with defendant Lomasney, general partner of defendant Lomasney & Co., a broker-dealer, with respect to securities of two companies, Ski Park City West, S.I. and Continental Travel, Ltd. Lomasney & Co. had agreed to sell up to 60,000 common shares of the former on a "best efforts" basis and was the principal underwriter for the sale of 350,000 common shares of the latter. A preliminary registration statement with respect to the shares of Continental Travel had been filed with the Securities and Exchange Commission on August 28, 1968, but did not become effective until February 11, 1969. On September 17, 1968, Lomasney sent Diskin a final prospectus for the Ski Park City West, S.I., stock, along with a letter, the body of which read as follows:

> I am enclosing herewith, a copy of the Prospectus on SKI PARK CITY WEST. This letter will also assure you that if you take 1,000 shares of SKI PARK CITY WEST at the issue price, we will commit to you the sale at the public offering price when, as and if issued, 5,000 shares of CONTINENTAL TRAVEL, LTD.

On the same day Diskin placed an order for the 1,000 shares of Ski Park City West and received a written confirmation. He later paid for these, and the validity of their offer and sale is unquestioned.

On February 12, 1969, Lomasney sent Diskin a confirmation of the sale of 5,000 shares of Continental Travel at $12 per share, apparently without any further communication. Diskin received from Lomasney a final prospectus and registration statement for these shares prior to February 28, 1969, when he paid the bill of $60,000, and received delivery. On November 19, 1969, Diskin demanded rescission. Having received no answer, he brought this action in the District Court for the Southern District of New York on January 6, 1970, claiming that the letter of September 17, 1968, insofar as it related to shares of Continental Travel, was a violation of § 5(b)(1) of the Securities Act of 1933. * * *

* * *

The parties submitted agreed findings of fact and stipulated that the case should be decided thereon. The district judge dismissed the complaint * * * . * * *

* * *

We pass [to the argument] * * * that the violation [of § 5(b)(1)] was cured by Diskin's receipt of a prospectus prior to the actual purchase * * * .

* * *

[Prior to 1954 amendments to the Securities Act, offers were included within the definition of "sale," making them illegal during the waiting period. We] agree with Professor Loss that "[w]hatever doubt there may once have been as to the applicability of § [12(a)(1)] to illegal offers [followed by legal sales after registration] was resolved when the original definition of sale was split into separate definitions of 'sale' and 'offer' in 1954, with the incidental amendment of § [12(a)(1)] to refer to any person 'who offers or sells a security in violation of section 5' so as 'to preserve the effect of the present law' by not excluding the newly permissible pre-effective offers from liabilities under § 12." III Loss, [Securities Regulation (2d ed. 1961)], at 1695–96. * * *

The result here reached may appear to be harsh, since Diskin had an opportunity to read the final prospectus before he paid for the shares. But the 1954 Congress quite obviously meant to allow rescission or damages in the case of illegal offers as well as of illegal sales. Very likely Congress thought that, when it had done so much to broaden the methods for making legal offers during the "waiting period" between the filing and the taking effect of a registration statement, it should make sure that still other methods were not attempted. Here all Lomasny needed to have done was to accompany the September 17, 1968 letter with [a] prospectus for the Continental shares * * * . Very likely Congress thought a better time for meaningful prospectus reading was at the time of the offer rather than in the context of confirmation and demand for payment. In any event, it made altogether clear that an offeror of a security who had failed to follow one of the allowed paths could not achieve absolution simply by returning to the road of virtue before receiving payment.

* * *

Diskin points up the fact that Section 12(a)(1) is a strict liability section in which Congress used a Draconian remedy to discourage violation of the registration provisions. Clients often wonder what happens if they commit an inadvertent, minor violation of these provisions. The answer under Section 12(a)(1) is simple: they guarantee one or more purchasers against loss. If the securities purchase turns out well for purchasers, there will never be a Section 12(a)(1) suit. But if it turns out badly, purchasers who can prove the few necessary elements of a Section 12(a)(1) claim can get back their money.

As is apparent from the above discussion, primary liability under Section 12(a)(1) flows only to a seller or, in the language of the section, only to a "person who * * * sells a security." But courts have interpreted that language more broadly than one might at first expect. The leading case is Pinter v. Dahl.

Pinter v. Dahl

Supreme Court of the United States, 1988.
486 U.S. 622.

■ JUSTICE BLACKMUN delivered the opinion of the Court.

[A question] presented by this case [is] whether one must intend to confer a benefit on himself or on a third party in order to qualify as a "seller" within the meaning of § [12(a)(1)].

I

The controversy arises out of the sale prior to 1982 of unregistered securities (fractional undivided interests in oil and gas leases) by petitioner Billy J. "B.J." Pinter to respondents Maurice Dahl and Dahl's friends, family, and business associates. Pinter is an oil and gas producer in Texas and Oklahoma, and a registered securities dealer in Texas. Dahl is a California real estate broker and investor, who, at the time of his dealings with Pinter, was a veteran of two unsuccessful oil and gas ventures. In pursuit of further investment opportunities, Dahl employed an oilfield expert to locate and acquire oil and gas leases. This expert introduced Dahl to Pinter. Dahl advanced $20,000 to Pinter to acquire leases, with the understanding that they would be held in the name of Pinter's Black Gold Oil Company and that Dahl would have a right of first refusal to drill certain wells on the leasehold properties. Pinter located leases in Oklahoma, and Dahl toured the properties, often without Pinter, in order to talk to others and "get a feel for the properties." Upon examining the geology, drilling logs, and production history assembled by Pinter, Dahl concluded, in the words of the District Court, that "there was no way to lose."

After investing approximately $310,000 in the properties, Dahl told the other respondents about the venture. Except for Dahl and respondent Grantham, none of the respondents spoke to or met Pinter or toured the properties. Because of Dahl's involvement in the venture, each of the other respondents decided to invest about $7,500.

Dahl assisted his fellow investors in completing the subscription-agreement form prepared by Pinter. Each letter-contract signed by the purchaser stated that the participating interests were being sold without the benefit of registration under the Securities Act, in reliance on Securities and Exchange Commission (SEC or Commission) Rule 146.[17] In fact, the oil and gas interests involved in this suit were never registered with the Commission. Respondents' investment checks were made payable to Black Gold Oil Company. Dahl received no commission from Pinter in connection with the other respondents' purchases.

When the venture failed and their interests proved to be worthless, respondents brought suit against Pinter in the United States District Court for the Northern District of Texas, seeking rescission under § [12(a)(1)] of the Securities Act for the unlawful sale of unregistered securities.

In a counterclaim, Pinter alleged that Dahl, by means of fraudulent misrepresentations and concealment of facts, induced Pinter to sell and deliver the securities. Pinter averred that Dahl falsely assured Pinter that he would provide other qualified, sophisticated, and knowledgeable investors with all the information necessary for evaluation of the investment. Dahl allegedly agreed to raise the funds for the venture from those investors, with the understanding that Pinter would simply be the "operator" of the wells. * * *

The District Court, after a bench trial, granted judgment for respondent-investors. * * *

A divided panel of the Court of Appeals for the Fifth Circuit affirmed. * * *

* * *

---

[17]   Rule 146 was the forerunner of the current Rule 506. [Eds.]

In determining whether Dahl may be deemed a "seller" for purposes of § [12(a)(1)], such that he may be held liable for the sale of unregistered securities to the other investor-respondents, we look first at the language of § [12(a)(1)]. That statute provides, in pertinent part: "Any person who * * * offers or sells a security" in violation of the registration requirement of the Securities Act "shall be liable to the person purchasing such security from him." This provision defines the class of defendants who may be subject to liability as those who offer or sell unregistered securities. But the Securities Act nowhere delineates who may be regarded as a statutory seller, and the sparce legislative history sheds no light on the issue. The courts, on their part, have not defined the term uniformly.

At the very least, however, the language of § [12(a)(1)] contemplates a buyer-seller relationship not unlike traditional contractual privity. Thus, it is settled that § [12(a)(1)] imposes liability on the owner who passed title, or other interest in the security, to the buyer for value. Dahl, of course, was not a seller in this conventional sense, and therefore may be held liable only if § [12(a)(1)] liability extends to persons other than the person who passes title.[18]

A

In common parlance, a person may offer or sell property without necessarily being the person who transfers title to, or other interest in, that property. We need not rely entirely on ordinary understanding of the statutory language, however, for the Securities Act defines the operative terms of § [12(a)(1)]. Section [2(a)(3)] defines "sale" or "sell" to include "every contract of sale or disposition of a security or interest in a security, for value," and the terms "offer to sell," "offer for sale," or "offer" to include "every attempt or offer to dispose of, or solicitation of an offer to buy, a security or interest in a security, for value." Under these definitions, the range of persons potentially liable under § [12(a)(1)] is not limited to persons who pass title. The inclusion of the phrase "solicitation of an offer to buy" within the definition of "offer" brings an individual who engages in solicitation, an activity not inherently confined to the actual owner, within the scope of § 12. Indeed, the Court has made clear, in the context of interpreting § 17(a) of the Securities Act, that transactions other than traditional sales of securities are within the

---

[18] The "offers or sells" and the "purchasing such security from him" language that governs § [12(a)(1)] also governs § [12(a)(2)], which provides a securities purchaser with a similar rescissionary cause of action for misrepresentation. Most courts and commentators have not defined the defendant class differently for purposes of the two provisions. See [e.g.] *Schillner v. H. Vaughan Clarke & Co.,* 134 F.2d 875, 878 (CA2 1943) ("Clearly the word [sell] has the same meaning in subdivision (2) as in subdivision (1) of Section 12").

The question whether anyone beyond the transferor of title, or immediate vendor, may be deemed a seller for purposes of § 12 has been litigated in actions under both § [12(a)(1)] and § [12(a)(2)]. Decisions under § [12(a)(2)] addressing the "seller" question are thus relevant to the issue presented to us in this case, and, to that extent, we discuss them here. Nevertheless, this case does not present, nor do we take a position on, the scope of a statutory seller for purposes of § [12(a)(2)].

scope of § [2(a)(3)] and passage of title is not important. See United States v. Naftalin, 441 U.S. 768, 773 (1979). We there explained: "The statutory terms ['offer' and 'sell'], which Congress expressly intended to define broadly, * * * are expansive enough to encompass the entire selling process, including the seller/agent transaction." See also Rubin v. United States, 449 U.S. 424, 430 (1981) ("It is not essential under the terms of the Act that full title pass to a transferee for the transaction to be an 'offer' or a 'sale' ").

Determining that the activity in question falls within the definition of "offer" or "sell" in § [2(a)(3)], however, is only half of the analysis. The second clause of § [12(a)(1)], which provides that only a defendant "from" whom the plaintiff "purchased" securities may be liable, narrows the field of potential sellers. Several courts and commentators have stated that the purchase requirement necessarily restricts § 12 primary liability to the owner of the security. In effect, these authorities interpret the term "purchase" as complementary to only the term "sell" defined in § [2(a)(3)]. Thus, an offeror, as defined by § [2(a)(3)], may incur § 12 liability only if the offeror also "sells" the security to the plaintiff, in the sense of transferring title for value.

We do not read § [12(a)(1)] so restrictively. The purchase requirement clearly confines § 12 liability to those situations in which a sale has taken place. Thus, a prospective buyer has no recourse against a person who touts unregistered securities to him if he does not purchase the securities. The requirement, however, does not exclude solicitation from the category of activities that may render a person liable when a sale has taken place. A natural reading of the statutory language would include in the statutory seller status at least some persons who urged the buyer to purchase. For example, a securities vendor's agent who solicited the purchase would commonly be said, and would be thought by the buyer, to be among those "from" whom the buyer "purchased," even though the agent himself did not pass title.

The Securities Act does not define the term "purchase." The soundest interpretation of the term, however, is as a correlative to both "sell" and "offer," at least to the extent that the latter entails active solicitation of an offer to buy. This interpretation is supported by the history of the phrase "offers or sells," as it is used in § [12(a)(1)]. As enacted in 1933, § [12(a)(1)] imposed liability on "[a]ny person who sells a security." The statutory definition of "sell" included "offer" and the activities now encompassed by that term, including solicitation. The words "offer or" were added to § [12(a)(1)] by the 1954 amendments to the Securities Act, when the original definition of "sell" in § [2(a)(3)] was split into separate definitions of "sell" and "offer" in order to accommodate changes in § 5. Since "sells" and "purchases" have obvious correlative meanings, Congress' express definition of "sells" in the original Securities Act to include solicitation suggests that the class of those from whom the buyer "purchases" extended to persons who solicit him. The 1954 amendment to § [12(a)(1)] was intended to preserve existing law, including the liability provisions of the Act. Hence, there is no reason to think Congress intended to narrow the meaning of "purchased from" when it amended the statute to include "solicitation" in the statutory definition of "offer" alone.

The applicability of § 12 liability to brokers and others who solicit securities purchases has been recognized frequently since the passage of the Securities Act. It long has been "quite clear," that when a broker acting as agent of one of the principals to the transaction successfully solicits a purchase, he is a person from whom the buyer purchases within the meaning of § 12 and is therefore liable as a statutory seller. Indeed, courts had found liability on this basis prior to the 1954 amendment of the statute. Had Congress intended liability to be restricted to those who pass title, it could have effectuated its intent by not adding the phrase "offers or" when it split the definition of "sell" in § [2(a)(3)].

An interpretation of statutory seller that includes brokers and others who solicit offers to purchase securities furthers the purposes of the Securities Act-to promote full and fair disclosure of information to the public in the sales of securities. In order to effectuate Congress' intent that § [12(a)(1)] civil liability be *in terrorem,* the risk of its invocation should be felt by solicitors of purchases. The solicitation of a buyer is perhaps the most critical stage of the selling transaction. It is the first stage of a traditional securities sale to involve the buyer, and it is directed at producing the sale. In addition, brokers and other solicitors are well positioned to control the flow of information to a potential purchaser, and, in fact, such persons are the participants in the selling transaction who most often disseminate material information to investors. Thus, solicitation is the stage at which an investor is most likely to be injured, that is, by being persuaded to purchase securities without full and fair information. Given Congress' overriding goal of preventing this injury, we may infer that Congress intended solicitation to fall under the mantle of § [12(a)(1)].

Although we conclude that Congress intended § [12(a)(1)] liability to extend to those who solicit securities purchases, we share the Court of Appeals' conclusion that Congress did not intend to impose rescission based on strict liability on a person who urges the purchase but whose motivation is solely to benefit the buyer. When a person who urges another to make a securities purchase acts merely to assist the buyer, not only is it uncommon to say that the buyer "purchased" from him, but it is also strained to describe the giving of gratuitous advice, even strongly or enthusiastically, as "soliciting." Section [2(a)(3)] defines an offer as a "solicitation of an offer to buy * * * for value." The person who gratuitously urges another to make a particular investment decision is not, in any meaningful sense, requesting value in exchange for his suggestion or seeking the value the titleholder will obtain in exchange for the ultimate sale. The language and purpose of § [12(a)(1)] suggest that liability extends only to the person who successfully solicits the purchase, motivated at least in part by a desire to serve his own financial interests or those of the securities owner. If he had such a motivation, it is fair to say that the buyer "purchased" the security from him and to align him with the owner in a rescission action.

B

Petitioner is not satisfied with extending § [12(a)(1)] primary liability to one who solicits securities sales for financial gain. Pinter assumes, without explication, that liability is not limited to the person who actually parts title with the securities, and urges us to validate, as the standard by which additional defendant-sellers are identified, that version of the "substantial factor" test utilized by the Fifth Circuit before the refinement espoused in this case.[19] Under that approach, grounded in tort doctrine, a nontransferor § [12(a)(1)] seller is defined as one "whose participation in the buy-sell transaction is a substantial factor in causing the transaction to take place." Pharo v. Smith, 621 F.2d 656, 667 (CA5 1980).[20] * * *

* * *

We do not agree that Congress contemplated imposing § [12(a)(1)] liability under the broad terms petitioner advocates. There is no support in the statutory language or legislative history for expansion of § [12(a)(1)] primary liability beyond persons who pass title and persons who "offer," including those who "solicit" offers. Indeed, § 12's failure to impose express liability for mere participation in unlawful sales transactions suggests that Congress did not intend that the section impose liability on participants collateral to the offer or sale. When Congress wished to create such liability, it had little trouble doing so.

The deficiency of the substantial-factor test is that it divorces the analysis of seller status from any reference to the applicable statutory language and from any examination of § 12 in the context of the total statutory scheme. Those courts that have adopted the approach have not attempted to ground their analysis in the statutory language. Instead, they substitute the concept of substantial participation in the sales transaction, or proximate causation of the plaintiff's purchase, for the words "offers or sells" in § 12. The "purchase from" requirement of § 12 focuses on the defendant's relationship with the plaintiff-purchaser. The

---

[19] The Fifth Circuit's test is only one of several approaches that have emerged in expanding § 12 liability beyond the security titleholder. All but one of these theories reflect the courts' views of who constitutes a § 12 seller. The remaining approach the aiding and abetting theory is actually a method by which courts create secondary liability in persons other than the statutory seller. Because this case deals exclusively with primary liability under § [12(a)(1)], we need not consider whether civil liability for aiding and abetting is appropriate under that section.

[20] The substantial factor test reflects a conviction that § 12 liability "must lie somewhere between the narrow view, which holds only the parties to the sale, and the too-liberal view which would hold all who remotely participated in the events leading up to the transaction." Lennerth v. Mendenhall, 234 F.Supp. 59, 65 (ND Ohio 1964). That court elected to "borrow a phrase from the law of negligence" and to premise liability on proximate cause. * * *

substantial-factor test, on the other hand, focuses on the defendant's degree of involvement in the securities transaction and its surrounding circumstances. Thus, although the substantial-factor test undoubtedly embraces persons who pass title and who solicit the purchase of unregistered securities as statutory sellers, the test also would extend § [12(a)(1)] liability to participants only remotely related to the relevant aspects of the sales transaction. Indeed, it might expose securities professionals, such as accountants and lawyers, whose involvement is only the performance of their professional services, to § [12(a)(1)] strict liability for rescission. The buyer does not, in any meaningful sense, "purchas[e] the security from" such a person.[21]

Further, no congressional intent to incorporate tort law doctrines of reliance and causation into § [12(a)(1)] emerges from the language or the legislative history of the statute. Indeed, the strict liability nature of the statutory cause of action suggests the opposite. By injecting these concepts into § [12(a)(1)] litigation, the substantial-factor test introduces an element of uncertainty into an area that demands certainty and predictability. As the Fifth Circuit has conceded, the test affords no guidelines for distinguishing between the defendant whose conduct rises to a level of significance sufficient to trigger seller status, and the defendant whose conduct is not sufficiently integral to the sale. None of the courts employing the approach has articulated what measure of participation qualifies a person for seller status, and logically sound limitations would be difficult to develop. As a result, decisions are made on an ad hoc basis, offering little predictive value to participants in securities transactions. We find it particularly unlikely that Congress would have ordained *sub silentio* the imposition of strict liability on such an unpredictably defined class of defendants.

* * *

C

We are unable to determine whether Dahl may be held liable as a statutory seller under § [12(a)(1)]. The District Court explicitly found that "Dahl solicited each of the other plaintiffs (save perhaps Grantham) in connection with the offer, purchase, and receipt of their oil and gas interests." We cannot conclude that this finding was clearly erroneous. It is not clear, however, that Dahl had the kind of interest in the sales that make him liable as a statutory seller. We do know that he received no

---

[21] For similar reasons, we reject the Commission's suggestion that persons who "participate in soliciting the purchase" may be liable as statutory sellers. The Commission relies on Katz v. Amos Treat & Co., 411 F.2d 1046 (CA2 1969), where the court held that an attorney who had been "a party to the solicitation" of the plaintiff-purchaser was liable under § [12(a)(1)] because he had placed the brokerage firm for which he worked in a position "to tackle [the purchaser] for the money" owed on an investment he had made. Although in *Katz* the attorney spoke directly to the plaintiff prior to the delivery of money in plaintiff's investment, the "party to a solicitation" concept could easily embrace those who merely assist in another's solicitation efforts. It is difficult to see more than a slight difference between this approach and the participation theory, which we have concluded does not comport with Congress' intent.

commission from Pinter in connection with the other sales, but this is not conclusive. Typically, a person who solicits the purchase will have sought or received a personal financial benefit from the sale, such as where he "anticipat[es] a share of the profits," Lawler v. Gilliam, 569 F.2d [1283 (CA4 1978)], or receives a brokerage commission. But a person who solicits the buyer's purchase in order to serve the financial interests of the owner may properly be liable under § [12(a)(1)] without showing that he expects to participate in the benefits the owner enjoys.

The Court of Appeals apparently concluded that Dahl was motivated entirely by a gratuitous desire to share an attractive investment opportunity with his friends and associates. This conclusion, in our view, was premature. The District Court made no findings that focused on whether Dahl urged the other purchases in order to further some financial interest of his own or of Pinter. Accordingly, further findings are necessary to assess Dahl's liability.

* * *

The judgment of the Court of Appeals is vacated and the case is remanded for further proceedings consistent with this opinion.

* * *

III. SECTIONS 12(a)(2) AND 4A(c)

a. SECTION 12(a)(2)

Section 12(a)(2) is a very different kind of provision from Section 12(a)(1). It provides that any person who offers or sells a security by means of a material misstatement or omission is liable to his purchaser for rescission or damages (subject to the loss causation provisions found in Section 12(b)).

Although Congress would be hard pressed to provide a justification, it chose to exempt government securities from the coverage of Section 12(a)(2). Political realities were the obvious reason. Jurisdictional means must be used for the section to apply, but of course this requirement is likely to cause a plaintiff little problem. Section 12(a)(2) provides that a plaintiff cannot win if he or she knew about the misstatement or omission complained of, which is as close as 12(a)(2) itself comes to requiring reliance or causation. Section 12(b), however, states that if a defendant proves that any or all of the amount otherwise recoverable under Section 12(a)(2) arose from something other than the defective disclosure complained of, then that amount is not recoverable. As provided in Section 13, an action under Section 12(a)(2) must be brought within one year after discovery of the misstatement or omission, or after its discovery should have been made by the exercise of reasonable diligence.

In any event, the action must be brought within three years after the sale.

Many decades after the Securities Act was passed, some courts began finding for the first time that section 12(a)(2) applies only to initial sales of securities by issuers (or affiliates) and not to secondary trading transactions. This reached its zenith in Gustafson v. Alloyd Co., Inc.

Gustafson v. Alloyd Co., Inc.

Supreme Court of the United States, 1995.
513 U.S. 561.

■ JUSTICE KENNEDY delivered the opinion of the Court.

Under § [12(a)(2)] of the Securities Act of 1933 buyers have an express cause of action for rescission against sellers who make material misstatements or omissions "by means of a prospectus." The question presented is whether this right of rescission extends to a private, secondary transaction, on the theory that recitations in the purchase agreement are part of a "prospectus."

I

Petitioners Gustafson, McLean, and Butler (collectively Gustafson) were in 1989 the sole shareholders of Alloyd, Inc., a manufacturer of plastic packaging and automatic heat sealing equipment. Alloyd was formed, and its stock was issued, in 1961. In 1989, Gustafson decided to sell Alloyd and engaged KPMG Peat Marwick to find a buyer. In response to information distributed by KPMG, Wind Point Partners II, L.P., agreed to buy substantially all of the issued and outstanding stock through Alloyd Holdings, Inc., a new corporation formed to effect the sale of Alloyd's stock. The shareholders of Alloyd Holdings were Wind Point and a number of individual investors.

* * *

On December 20, 1989 Gustafson and Alloyd Holdings executed a contract of sale. Alloyd Holdings agreed to pay Gustafson and his coshareholders $18,709,000 for the sale of the stock plus a payment of $2,122,219, which reflected the estimated increase in Alloyd's net worth from the end of the previous year, the last period for which hard financial data were available. Article IV of the purchase agreement, entitled "Representations and Warranties of the Sellers," included assurances that the company's financial statements "present fairly * * * the Company's financial condition "and that between the date of the latest balance sheet and the date the agreement was executed "there ha[d] been no material adverse change in * * * [Alloyd's] financial condition." The contract also provided that if the year-end audit and financial statements revealed a variance between estimated and actual increased value, the disappointed party would receive an adjustment.

The year-end audit of Alloyd revealed that Alloyd's actual earnings for 1989 were lower than the estimates relied upon by the parties in negotiating the adjustment amount of $2,122,219. Under the contract, the buyers had a right to recover an adjustment amount of $815,000, from the sellers. Nevertheless, on February 11, 1991, the newly formed company (now called Alloyd, Co., the same as the original company) and Wind Point brought suit in the United States District Court for the Northern District of Illinois, seeking outright rescission of the contract under § [12(a)(2)] of the Securities Act of 1933. Alloyd (the new company) claimed that statements made by Gustafson and his coshareholders regarding the financial data of their company were inaccurate, rendering untrue the representations and warranties contained in the contract. The buyers further alleged that the contract of sale was a "prospectus," so that any misstatements contained in the agreement gave rise to liability under § [12(a)(2)] of the 1933 Act. Pursuant to the adjustment clause, the defendants remitted to the purchasers $815,000 plus interest, but the adjustment did not cause the purchasers to drop the lawsuit.

Relying on the decision of the Court of Appeals for the Third Circuit in Ballay v. Legg Mason Wood Walker, Inc., 925 F.2d 682 (1991), the District Court granted Gustafson's motion for summary judgment, holding "that Section [12(a)(2)] claims can only arise out of the initial stock offerings." Although the sellers were the controlling shareholders of the original company, the District Court concluded that the private sale agreement "cannot be compared to an initial offering" because "the purchasers in this case had direct access to financial and other company documents, and had the opportunity to inspect the seller's property."

On review, the Court of Appeals for the Seventh Circuit vacated the District Court's judgment and remanded for further consideration in light of that court's intervening decision in Pacific Dunlop Holdings Inc. v. Allen & Co. Inc., 993 F.2d 578 (1993). In *Pacific Dunlop* the court reasoned that the inclusion of the term "communication" in the Act's definition of prospectus meant that the term prospectus was defined "very broadly" to include all written communications that offered the sale of a security. Rejecting the view of the Court of Appeals for the Third Circuit in *Ballay*, the Court of Appeals decided that § [12(a)(2)]'s right of action for rescission "applies to any communication which offers any security for sale[,] * * * including the stock purchase agreement in the present case." We granted certiorari to resolve this Circuit conflict, and we now reverse.

II

The rescission claim against Gustafson is based upon § [12(a)(2)] of the 1933 Act. * * * [A]s this case reaches us, we must assume that the stock purchase agreement contained material misstatements of fact made by the sellers and that Gustafson would not sustain its burden of proving due care. On these assumptions, Alloyd would have a right to obtain rescission if those misstatements were made "by means of a prospectus or oral communication." The parties (and the courts of appeals) agree that the phrase "oral communication" is restricted to oral communications that relate to a prospectus. The determinative question, then, is whether the contract between Alloyd and Gustafson is a "prospectus" as the term is used in the 1933 Act.

Alloyd argues that "prospectus" is defined in a broad manner, broad enough to encompass the contract between the parties. This argument is echoed by the dissents. Gustafson, by contrast, maintains that prospectus in the 1933 Act means a communication soliciting the public to purchase securities from the issuer.

Three sections of the 1933 Act are critical in resolving the definitional question on which the case turns: § [2(a)(10)], which defines a prospectus; § 10, which sets forth the information that must be contained in a prospectus; and § 12, which imposes liability based on misstatements in a prospectus. In seeking to interpret the term "prospectus," we adopt the premise that the term should be construed, if possible, to give it a consistent meaning throughout the Act. That principle follows from our duty to construe statutes, not isolated provisions.

A

We begin with § 10. * * * Section 10 does not provide that some prospectuses must contain the information contained in the registration statement. Save for the explicit and well-defined exemptions for securities listed under § 3, its mandate is unqualified: "a prospectus * * * shall contain the information contained in the registration statement."

Although § 10 does not define what a prospectus is, it does instruct us what a prospectus cannot be if the Act is to be interpreted as a symmetrical and coherent regulatory scheme, one in which the operative words have a consistent meaning throughout. There is no dispute that the contract in this case was not required to contain the information contained in a registration statement and that no statutory exemption was required to take the document out of § 10's coverage. It follows that the contract is not a prospectus under § 10. That does not mean that a document ceases to be a prospectus whenever it omits a required piece of information. It does mean that a document is not a prospectus within the meaning of that section if, absent an exemption, it need not comply with § 10's requirements in the first place.

An examination of § 10 reveals that, whatever else "prospectus" may mean, the term is confined to a document that, absent an overriding exemption, must include the "information contained in the registration statement." By and large, only public offerings by an issuer of a security, or by controlling shareholders of an issuer, require the preparation and filing of registration statements. It follows, we conclude, that a prospectus under § 10 is confined to documents related to public offerings by an issuer or its controlling shareholders.

This much (the meaning of prospectus in § 10) seems not to be in dispute. Where the courts are in disagreement is with the implications of this proposition for the entirety of the Act, and for § 12 in particular. We conclude that the term "prospectus" must have the same meaning under §§ 10 and 12. In so holding, we do not, as the dissent by Justice GINSBURG suggests, make the mistake of treating § 10 as a definitional section. Instead, we find in § 10 guidance and instruction for giving the term a consistent meaning throughout the Act.

The Securities Act of 1933, like every Act of Congress, should not be read as a series of unrelated and isolated provisions. Only last term we adhered to the normal rule of statutory construction that "identical words used in different parts of the same act are intended to have the same meaning." Department of Revenue of Oregon v. ACF Industries, Inc., 114 S.Ct. 843, 845 (1994). That principle applies here. If the contract before us is not a prospectus for purposes of § 10—as all must and do concede—it is not a prospectus for purposes of § 12 either.

The conclusion that prospectus has the same meaning, and refers to the same types of communications (public offers by an issuer or its controlling shareholders), in both §§ 10 and 12 is reinforced by an examination of the structure of the 1933 Act. Sections 4 and 5 of the Act together require a seller to file a registration statement and to issue a prospectus for certain defined types of sales (public offerings by an issuer, through an underwriter). Sections 7 and 10 of the Act set forth the information required in the registration statement and the prospectus. Section 11 provides for liability on account of false registration statements; § [12(a)(2)] for liability based on misstatements in prospectuses. Following the most natural and symmetrical reading, just as the liability imposed by § 11 flows from the requirements imposed by §§ 5 and 7 providing for the filing and content of registration statements, the liability imposed by § [12(a)(2)], cannot attach unless there is an obligation to distribute the prospectus in the first place (or unless there is an exemption).

* * *

The primary innovation of the 1933 Act was the creation of federal duties—for the most part, registration and disclosure obligations—in connection with public offerings. We are reluctant to conclude that § [12(a)(2)] creates vast additional liabilities that are quite independent of the new substantive obligations the Act imposes. It is more reasonable to interpret the liability provisions of the 1933 Act as designed for the primary purpose of providing remedies for violations of the obligations it had created. Indeed, §§ 11 and [12(a)(1)]—the statutory neighbors of § [12(a)(2)]—afford remedies for violations of those obligations. Under our interpretation of "prospectus," § [12(a)(2)] in similar manner is linked to the new duties created by the Act.

On the other hand, accepting Alloyd's argument that any written offer is a prospectus under § 12 would require us to hold that the word "prospectus" in § 12 refers to a broader set of communications than the same term in § 10. The Court of Appeals was candid in embracing that conclusion: "[T]he 1933 Act contemplates many definitions of a prospectus. Section [2(a)(10)] gives a single, broad definition; Section 10(a) involves an isolated, distinct document—a prospectus within a prospectus; section 10(d) gives the Commission authority to classify many." Pacific Dunlop Holdings Inc. v. Allen & Co., 993 F.2d, at 584. The dissents take a similar tack. In the name of a plain meaning approach to statutory interpretation, the dissents discover in the Act two different species of prospectuses: formal (also called § 10) prospectuses, subject to both §§ 10 and 12, and informal prospectuses, subject only to § 12 but not to § 10. Nowhere in the statute, however, do the terms "formal prospectus" or "informal prospectus" appear. Instead, the Act uses one term—"prospectus"—throughout. In disagreement with the Court of Appeals and the dissenting opinions, we cannot accept the conclusion that this single operative word means one thing in one section of the Act and something quite different in another. The dissenting opinions' resort to terms not found in the Act belies the claim of fidelity to the text of the statute.

Alloyd, as well as Justice THOMAS in his dissent, respond that if Congress had intended § [12(a)(2)] to govern only initial public offerings, it would have been simple for Congress to have referred to the § 4 exemptions in § [12(a)(2)]. The argument gets the presumption backwards. Had Congress meant the term "prospectus" in § [12(a)(2)] to have a different meaning than the same term in § 10, that is when one would have expected Congress to have been explicit. Congressional silence cuts against, not in favor of, Alloyd's argument. The burden should be on the proponents of the view that the term "prospectus" means one thing in § 12 and another in § 10 to adduce strong textual support for that conclusion. And Alloyd adduces none.

B

Alloyd's contrary argument rests to a significant extent on § [2(a)(10)], or, to be more precise, on one word of that section. Section [2(a)(10)] provides that "[t]he term 'prospectus' means any prospectus, notice, circular, advertisement, letter, or communication, written or by radio or television, which offers any security for sale or confirms the sale of any security." Concentrating on the word "communication," Alloyd argues that any written communication that offers a security for sale is a "prospectus." Inserting its definition into § [12(a)(2)], Alloyd insists that a material misstatement in any communication offering a security for sale gives rise to an action for rescission, without proof of fraud by the seller or reliance by the purchaser. In Alloyd's view, § [2(a)(10)] gives the term "prospectus" a capacious definition that, although incompatible with § 10, nevertheless governs in § 12.

The flaw in Alloyd's argument, echoed in the dissenting opinions, is its reliance on one word of the definitional section in isolation. To be sure, § [2(a)(10)] defines a prospectus as, *inter alia*, a "communication, written or by radio or television, which offers any security for sale or confirms the sale of any security." The word "communication," however, on which Alloyd's entire argument rests, is but one word in a list, a word Alloyd reads altogether out of context.

* * *

There is a better reading. From the terms "prospectus, notice, circular, advertisement, or letter," it is apparent that the list refers to documents of wide dissemination. In a similar manner, the list includes communications "by radio or television," but not face-to-face or telephonic conversations. Inclusion of the term "communication" in that list suggests that it too refers to a public communication.

When the 1933 Act was drawn and adopted, the term "prospectus" was well understood to refer to a document soliciting the public to acquire securities from the issuer. See Black's Law Dictionary 959 (2d ed. 1910) (defining "prospectus" as a "document published by a company * * * or by persons acting as its agents or assignees, setting forth the nature and objects of an issue of shares * * * and inviting the public to subscribe to the issue"). In this respect, the word prospectus is a term of art, which accounts for Congressional confidence in employing what might otherwise be regarded as a partial circularity in the formal, statutory definition. See § [2(a)(10)] ("The term 'prospectus' means any prospectus * * * ."). The use of the term prospectus to refer to public solicitations explains as well Congress' decision in § [12(a)(2)] to grant buyers a right to rescind without proof of reliance. See H.R.Rep. No. 85, 73d Cong., 1st Sess., 10 (1933) ("The statements for which [liable persons] are responsible, although they may never actually have been seen by the prospective purchaser, because of their wide dissemination, determine the market price of the security * * * .").

The list of terms in § [2(a)(10)] prevents a seller of stock from avoiding liability by calling a soliciting document something other than a prospectus, but it does not compel the conclusion that Alloyd urges us to reach and that the dissenting opinions adopt. Instead, the term "written communication" must be read in context to refer to writings that, from a functional standpoint, are similar to the terms "notice, circular, [and] advertisement." The term includes communications held out to the public at large but that might have been thought to be outside the other words in the definitional section.

C

Our holding that the term "prospectus" relates to public offerings by issuers and their controlling shareholders draws support from our earlier decision interpreting the one provision of the Act that extends coverage beyond the regulation of public offerings, § 17(a) of the 1933 Act. See

United States v. Naftalin, 441 U.S. 768 (1979). In *Naftalin*, though noting that "the 1933 Act was primarily concerned with the regulation of new offerings," the Court held that § 17(a) was "intended to cover any fraudulent scheme in an offer or sale of securities, whether in the course of an initial distribution or in the course of ordinary market trading." The Court justified this holding—which it termed "a major departure from th[e] limitation [of the 1933 Act to new offerings]"—by reference to both the statutory language and the unambiguous legislative history. The same considerations counsel in favor of our interpretation of § [12(a)(2)].

The Court noted in *Naftalin* that § 17(a) contained no language suggesting a limitation on the scope of liability under § 17(a). ("the statutory language * * * makes no distinctions between the two kinds of transactions"). Most important for present purposes, § 17(a) does not contain the word "prospectus." In contrast, as we have noted, § [12(a)(2)] contains language, *i.e.*, "by means of a prospectus or oral communication," that limits § [12(a)(2)] to public offerings. Just as the absence of limiting language in § 17(a) resulted in broad coverage, the presence of limiting language in § [12(a)(2)] requires a narrow construction.

Of equal importance, the legislative history relied upon in *Naftalin* showed that Congress decided upon a deliberate departure from the general scheme of the Act in this one instance, and "made abundantly clear" its intent that § 17(a) have broad coverage. See *Naftalin*, 441 U.S., at 778 (quoting legislative history stating that " 'fraud or deception in the sale of securities may be prosecuted regardless of whether * * * or not it is of the class of securities exempted under sections 11 or 12.' " S.Rep. No. 47, 73d Cong., 1st Sess., 4 (1933)). No comparable legislative history even hints that § [12(a)(2)] was intended to be a free-standing provision effecting expansion of the coverage of the entire statute. The intent of Congress and the design of the statute require that § [12(a)(2)] liability be limited to public offerings.

D

It is understandable that Congress would provide buyers with a right to rescind, without proof of fraud or reliance, as to misstatements contained in a document prepared with care, following well established procedures relating to investigations with due diligence and in the context of a public offering by an issuer or its controlling shareholders. It is not plausible to infer that Congress created this extensive liability for every casual communication between buyer and seller in the secondary market. It is often difficult, if not altogether impractical, for those engaged in casual communications not to omit some fact that would, if included, qualify the accuracy of a statement. Under Alloyd's view any casual communication between buyer and seller in the aftermarket could give rise to an action for rescission, with no evidence of fraud on the part of the seller or reliance on the part of the buyer. In many instances buyers in practical effect would have an option to rescind, impairing the stability of past transactions where neither fraud nor detrimental reliance on misstatements or omissions occurred. We find no basis for interpreting the statute to reach so far.

III

The SEC, as *amicus*, and Justice GINSBURG in dissent, rely on what they call the legislative background of the Act to support Alloyd's construction. With a few minor exceptions, however, their reliance is upon statements by commentators and judges written after the Act was passed, not while it was under consideration. Material not available to the lawmakers is not considered, in the normal course, to be legislative history. After-the-fact statements by proponents of a broad interpretation are not a reliable indicator of what Congress intended when it passed the law, assuming extratextual sources are to any extent reliable for this purpose.

* * *

If legislative history is to be considered, it is preferable to consult the documents prepared by Congress when deliberating. The legislative history of the Act concerning the precise question presented supports our interpretation with much clarity and force. Congress contemplated that § [12(a)(2)] would apply only to public offerings by an issuer (or a controlling shareholder). The House Report stated: "[t]he bill affects only new offerings of securities * * *. It does not affect the ordinary redistribution of securities unless such redistribution takes on the characteristics of a new offering." The observation extended to § [12(a)(2)] as well. Part II, § 6 of the House Report is entitled "Civil Liabilities." It begins: "Sections 11 and 12 create and define the civil liabilities imposed by the act * * *. Fundamentally, these sections entitle the buyer of securities sold upon a registration statement * * * to sue for recovery of his purchase price." It will be recalled that as to private transactions, such as the Alloyd purchase, there will never have been a registration statement. If § [12(a)(2)] liability were imposed here, it would cover transactions not within the contemplated reach of the statute.

* * *

Nothing in the legislative history, moreover, suggests Congress intended to create two types of prospectuses, a formal prospectus required to comply with both §§ 10 and 12, and a second, less formal prospectus, to which only § 12 would be applicable. The Act proceeds by definitions more stable and precise. * * *

* * *

In sum, the word "prospectus" is a term of art referring to a document that describes a public offering of securities by an issuer or controlling shareholder. The contract of sale, and its recitations, were not held out to the public and were not a prospectus as the term is used in the 1933 Act.

The judgment of the Court of Appeals is reversed, and the case is remanded for further proceedings consistent with this opinion.

It is so ordered.

■ JUSTICE THOMAS, with whom JUSTICE SCALIA, JUSTICE GINSBURG, and JUSTICE BREYER join, dissenting.

From the majority's opinion, one would not realize that § [12(a)(2)] was involved in this case until one had read more than half-way through. In contrast to the majority's approach of interpreting the statute, I believe the proper method is to begin with the provision actually involved in this case, § [12(a)(2)], and then turn to the 1933 Act's definitional section, § [2(a)(10)], before consulting the structure of the Act as a whole. Because the result of this textual analysis shows that § [12(a)(2)] applies to secondary or private sales of a security as well as to initial public offerings, I dissent.

* * *

As we have emphasized in our recent decisions, " '[t]he starting point in every case involving construction of a statute is the language itself.' " * * * Unfortunately, the majority has decided to interpret the word "prospectus" in § [12(a)(2)] by turning to sources outside the four corners of the statute, rather than by adopting the definition provided by Congress.

* * * I agree with the majority that the only way to interpret § [12(a)(2)] as limited to initial offerings is to read "by means of a prospectus or oral communication" narrowly. I also agree that in the absence of any other statutory command, one could understand "prospectus" as "a term of art which describes the transmittal of information concerning the sale of a security in an initial distribution." But the canon that "we construe a statutory term in accordance with its ordinary or natural meaning," applies only "[i]n the absence of [a statutory] definition." FDIC v. Meyer, 114 S.Ct. 996, 1001 (1994).

There is no reason to seek the meaning of "prospectus" outside of the 1933 Act, because Congress has supplied just such a definition in § [2(a)(10)]. That definition is extraordinarily broad * * *. For me, the breadth of these terms forecloses the majority's position that "prospectus" applies only in the context of initial distributions of securities. Indeed, § [2(a)(10)]'s inclusion of a prospectus as only one of the many different documents that qualify as a "prospectus" for statutory purposes indicates that Congress intended "prospectus" to be more than a mere "term of art." Likewise, Congress' extension of prospectus to include documents that merely *confirm* the sale of a security underscores Congress' intent to depart from the term's ordinary meaning. Section [2(a)(10)]'s definition obviously concerns different types of communications rather than different types of transactions. Congress left the job of exempting certain classes of transactions to §§ 3 and 4, not to § [2(a)(10)]. We should use

§ [2(a)(10)] to define "prospectus" for the 1933 Act, rather than, as the majority does, use the 1933 Act to define "prospectus" for § [2(a)(10)].

* * *

■ JUSTICE GINSBURG, with whom JUSTICE BREYER joins, dissenting.

* * *

I

To construe a legislatively defined term, courts usually start with the defining section. Section [2(a)(10)] defines prospectus capaciously as "any prospectus, notice, circular, advertisement, letter, or communication, written or by radio or television, which offers any security for sale or confirms the sale of any security." The items listed in the defining provision, notably "letters" and "communications," are common in private and secondary sales, as well as in public offerings. The § [2(a)(10)] definition thus does not confine the § [12(a)(2)] term "prospectus" to public offerings.

The Court bypasses § [2(a)(10)], and the solid support it gives the Court of Appeals' disposition. Instead of beginning at the beginning, by first attending to the definition section, the Court starts with § 10, a substantive provision. The Court correctly observes that the term "prospectus" has a circumscribed meaning in that context. A prospectus within the contemplation of § 10 is a formal document, typically a document composing part of a registration statement; a § 10 prospectus, all agree, appears only in public offerings. The Court then proceeds backward; it reads into the literally and logically prior definition section, § [2(a)(10)], the meaning "prospectus" has in § 10.

To justify its backward reading—proceeding from § 10 to § [2(a)(10)] and not the other way round—the Court states that it "cannot accept the conclusion that [the operative word prospectus] means one thing in one section of the Act and something quite different in another." Our decisions, however, constantly recognize that "a characterization fitting in certain contexts may be unsuitable in others." NationsBank of N.C., N.A. v. Variable Annuity Life Ins. Co., 115 S.Ct. 810, 816 (1995) * * *. * * *

According "prospectus" discrete meanings in § 10 and § [12(a)(2)] is consistent with Congress' specific instruction in § [2(a)] that definitions apply "unless the context otherwise requires." * * *

* * *

II

Most provisions of the Securities Act govern only public offerings, and the legislative history pertaining to the Act as a whole shares this orientation. Section § 17(a) of the Act, however, is not limited to public offerings; that enforcement provision, this Court has recognized, also covers secondary trading. See United States v. Naftalin, 441 U.S. 768

(1979). The drafting history is at least consistent with the conclusion that § [12(a)(2)], like § 17(a), is not limited to public offerings.

The drafters of the Securities Act modeled this federal legislation on the British Companies Act. The Companies Act defined "prospectus" as "any prospectus, notice, circular, advertisement, or other invitation, *offering to the public* for subscription or purchase any shares or debentures of a company" (emphasis added). Though the drafters of the Securities Act borrowed the first four terms of this definition, they did not import from the British legislation the language limiting prospectuses to communications "offering [securities] to the public." This conspicuous omission suggests that the drafters intended the defined term "prospectus" to reach beyond communications used in public offerings.[22]

* * *

Commentators writing shortly after passage of the Act understood § [12(a)(2)] to cover resales and private sales, as well as public offerings. Felix Frankfurter, organizer of the team that drafted the statute, firmly stated this view. * * * William O. Douglas expressed the same understanding. * * *

Most subsequent commentators have agreed that § [12(a)(2)], like § 17(a), is not confined to public offerings. * * *

While Courts of Appeals have divided on § [12(a)(2)]'s application to secondary transactions, every Court of Appeals to consider the issue has ruled that private placements are subject to § [12(a)(2)]. * * * "[L]ongstanding acceptance by the courts [of a judicial interpretation], coupled with Congress's failure to reject" that interpretation, "argues significantly in favor of accept[ing]" it. Blue Chip Stamps v. Manor Drug Stores, 421 U.S. 723 (1975).

* * *

In light of the text, drafting history, and longstanding scholarly and judicial understanding of § [12(a)(2)], I conclude that § [12(a)(2)] applies to a private resale of securities. If adjustment is in order, as the Court's opinion powerfully suggests it is, * * * congress is equipped to undertake the alteration. Accordingly, I dissent from the Court's opinion and judgment.

_____

There is a great deal in *Gustafson* that requires consideration. Among these matters is the fact that much of the logic of the opinion

---

[22]   Though the Court cites legislative history to show Congress' intent to follow, rather than depart from, the British statute, these sources suggest an intention to afford *at least as much* protection from fraud as the British statute provides. ("What is deemed necessary for sound financing in conservative England ought not to be unnecessary for the more feverish pace which American finance has developed.") Congress' provision for liability beyond "offering[s] to the public," however, suggests a legislative conclusion that the "feverish pace" of American finance called for greater protection from fraud than the British Act supplied.

hinges on the Court's understanding of the structure of the Securities Act. In this connection, it should be noted that the Court explains that part of the structure made up of Sections 11 and 12(a)(2) by the following statement: "Section 11 provides for liability on account of false registration statements; § [12(a)(2)] for liability based on misstatements in prospectuses." From this statement it seems clear that the Court did not know that the bulk of a registration statement consists of a prospectus and that virtually all cases involving false or misleading statements will involve the prospectus part of a registration statement. Because of this evident failure of understanding, the Court has these two sections covering the same thing. That could not have been intended by the drafters or by Congress.

It is noteworthy that when the Commission, in 2005, adopted provisions allowing the use of "free writing prospectuses," it took care to specify that these writings would constitute "prospectuses" under Section 2(a)(10) and would be deemed to relate to public offerings. Moreover, when in 2012 Congress adopted Securities Act Section 3(b)(2), effectively directing the Commission to liberalize Regulation A, it provided that any person offering or selling a security exempt by reason of the liberalization is subject to Section 12(a)(2).

As in the case of Section 12(a)(1), a plaintiff-purchaser can collect, as a matter of primary liability, only from a person who has "sold" to him. But, also as with Section 12(a)(1), courts have stretched the requirements to allow plaintiffs the targets provided by Pinter v. Dahl, which appears in the preceding section of this chapter. (Note, however, that Pinter v. Dahl did not purport to resolve the question under Section 12(a)(2)). Rule 159A, adopted in 2005, specifies that the issuer of securities is a seller of those securities for purposes of Section 12(a)(2), notwithstanding the type of underwriting method used in a particular transaction. This was an issue about which there previously had been some doubt, which still lingers given the rejection of the rule by some courts as being contrary to *Pinter*.[23]

Although a plaintiff can prevail under Section 12(a)(2) without proving knowledge or awareness of improper activity on the part of a defendant, the section provides that a defendant can defeat a claim by showing that he did not know, and in the exercise of reasonable care could not have known, of the material misstatement or omission that gives rise to the claim. This defense is reminiscent of the due diligence defense provided under Section 11. The question is, how similar are they? This question was considered by the Seventh Circuit in the next case.

---

[23] In re Kosmos Energy Ltd. Securities Litigation, 955 F.Supp.2d 658 (N.D.Tex.2013); Capital Ventures International v. UBS Securities LLC, 2012 WL 4469101 (D. Mass. Sept. 28, 2012).

Sanders v. John Nuveen & Co., Inc.

United States Court of Appeals, Seventh Circuit, 1980.
619 F.2d 1222.

■ Before TONE and WOOD, CIRCUIT JUDGES, and DUMBAULD, SENIOR DISTRICT JUDGE.

■ TONE, CIRCUIT JUDGE.

The issue we decide on this appeal is whether plaintiff class members have established their claims under § [12(a)(2)] of the Securities Act of 1933. Holding that they have, we affirm the district court's judgment in their favor.

* * *

Plaintiff class consists of forty-two purchasers of unsecured short term promissory notes aggregating $1,612,500 issued by Winter & Hirsch, Inc. (WH), a consumer finance company. The purchases were made from John Nuveen & Co., Inc. during a seven-month period immediately preceding WH's default on the notes in February 1970. * * *

Nuveen was the exclusive underwriter of the WH notes, which were sold, like other commercial paper, through its branch offices throughout the United States. As the underwriter, it bought the notes from WH and resold them to customers at a profit. * * *

* * *

WH's default was the product of a fraud it perpetrated with the connivance of the certified public accountants who audited its financial statements and rendered opinions thereon. In summary, over a period of ten years WH continually issued financial statements in which accounts receivable were overstated and some of its indebtedness was omitted. * * *

Nuveen was not aware of the fraud and held "the mistaken but honest belief that financial statements [of WH] prepared by certified public accountants correctly represented the condition of" WH. It accordingly proceeded to sell the WH notes and also to issue commercial paper reports thereon that reflected the false WH financial statements.

* * *

Defendants * * * argue that they have established a defense under § [12(a)(2)] by sustaining their burden of proving that they "in the exercise of reasonable care could not have known" of the claimed untruth or omission. * * *

* * *

* * * Defendants attempt to distinguish *Sanders II* [an earlier decision of the court in connection with the same litigation] on the ground that while this court relied heavily in that case on decisions construing § 11, which explicitly requires a "reasonable investigation," § [12(a)(2)] requires only that defendants show exercise of "reasonable care." We find no significance in this difference in language in the case at bar.

It is not at all clear that Congress intended to impose a higher standard of care under § 11 than under § [12(a)(2)]. The difference in language appeared in the House bill and was retained in the Act as agreed to by the Joint Conference Committee and as passed by both Houses. The Conference Committee report, in its discussion of the standard of liability imposed for a misleading registration statement, describes the standard adopted not as one of "reasonable investigation," but one of "reasonable care." H.R.Rep. No. 152, 73d Cong., 1st Sess. 26 (1933). More specifically, Congress does not appear to have intended that a different standard apply to underwriters. Thus, the House Report draws no distinction between an underwriter's burden in the case of misleading statements in a prospectus, for which it can be liable only under § [12(a)(2)], and its § 11 duty to conduct a "reasonable investigation." H.R.Rep. No. 85, 73d Cong., 1st Sess. 9 (1933). The difference in language can be explained not as an attempt to impose different duties of care under §§ 11 and 12, but by the fact that § [12(a)(2)] imposes the duty on all sellers of securities, while § 11 imposes liability only on specified groups of persons having such a close relationship with the registration statement that the 1933 Act, before it was amended the following year, treated them as fiduciaries. Thus the general duty of reasonable care, the specific requirements of which are determined by the circumstances of the case, was to be applied in § 11 only to persons who had a stronger connection with a registration statement than a seller necessarily has to a prospectus, so a more stringent articulation of the standard was appropriate.

* * * Since what constitutes reasonable care under § [12(a)(2)] depends upon the circumstances, we, of course, do not intimate that the duty of a seller under § [12(a)(2)] is always the same as that of an underwriter in a registration offering under § 11.

* * *

The Seventh Circuit's equivalent reading of the Section 11 and Section [12(a)(2)] standards in *Sanders* was criticized by Justice Powell in a dissent from a denial of certiorari in the case. In his dissent, Justice Powell stressed that "in the securities acts Congress has used its words with precision" and that " '[i]nvestigation' commands a greater undertaking than 'care'." He also pointed out that, in its amicus brief filed with the court of appeals, the Commission argued that the standard of care under Section [12(a)(2)] was less demanding than under Section 11. What the circuit courts generally will hold on this question remains to be seen, although a panel of the Seventh Circuit itself has criticized *Sanders.*[24]

b. SECTION 4A(c)

As noted above, when Congress adopted new Section 3(b)(2) under the Securities Act, it simply stated that those offering or selling securities exempted by reason of the new section would be subject to Section 12(a)(2). It took a somewhat different approach with respect to the new crowdfunding exemption. Section 4A(c) provides for recovery from an issuer by way of rescission (or rescissory damages) by purchasers in an exempt crowdfunding transaction if the issuer, through means of interstate commerce and by means of any written or oral communication, makes an untrue statement of material fact or omits to state a material fact required to be stated or necessary in order to make the statements made not misleading. This is obviously quite similar to the liability imposed under Section 12(a)(2). The similarity is enhanced by (1) the requirement that the purchaser must not have known of the untruth or omission, (2) the availability of a reasonable care defense, (3) incorporation by reference of the lack of loss causation defense available under Section 12(b), and (4) invocation of the statute of limitations contained in Section 13. Critical differences are the fact that the new provision makes no reference to a "prospectus" and that the term "issuer" includes directors, partners and specified officers of issuers, as well as anyone who offers or sells a security in the transaction.

IV. SECTION 15

Section 15 is an important part of the liability scheme of the Securities Act. It provides that anyone who controls a person liable under Section 11 or 12 is jointly and severally liable to the same extent as the controlled person, with one exception: the controlling person can escape liability provided he or she "had no knowledge of or reasonable grounds to believe in the existence of the facts by reason of which the liability of the controlled person is alleged to exist." As will be remembered from the discussion at the beginning of the preceding chapter, "control" is in general a broad concept, and the language used in Section 15 to describe the means by which control can exist parallel the general meaning of the term:

> Every person who, by or through stock ownership, agency, or otherwise, or who, pursuant to or in connection with an agreement or understanding with one or more other persons by or through stock ownership, agency, or otherwise, controls any person liable under section 11 or 12 * * * .

---

[24] Associated Bank v. Griffin, Kubik, Stephens & Thompson, Inc., 3 F.3d 208 (7th Cir. 1993).

The exact limits of the concept of "control" in this context are uncertain and vary by circuit. There is no doubt, however, that the concept easily can include major shareholders, directors, and officers. The following case is instructive in this regard.

Stadia Oil & Uranium Co. v. Wheelis

United States Court of Appeals, Tenth Circuit, 1957.
251 F.2d 269.

■ Before HUXMAN, MURRAH and BREITENSTEIN, CIRCUIT JUDGES.

■ BREITENSTEIN, CIRCUIT JUDGE.

Appellees, plaintiffs below, recovered judgment upon their claims that the appellants sold them stock in the Stadia Oil & Uranium Company without the registration of that stock with, or the exemption of the stock by, the Securities and Exchange Commission, and that such stock sales were made by use of interstate means of transportation and of the United States mail.

* * *

Defendant Rankin contends that he is not liable to the plaintiffs because he did not participate in the stock sales to them. Plaintiffs concede that Rankin's liability arises only by reason of [Section 15] of the [Securities] Act. The statute does not define the terms "controls," "controlled," or "controlling." These terms should be given a broad definition to permit the applicable provisions of the Act to become effective wherever the fact of control actually exists. This fact is one for determination by the jury and was submitted to the jury under careful instructions which were not objected to by the defendants so far as this issue is concerned. The jury in returning a verdict against Rankin necessarily found that he was liable under the control section of the Act. On appeal we are required only to ascertain whether there is substantial evidence to support the verdict and judgment of the court. A verdict based on such evidence and approved by the trial court is conclusive and will not be disturbed on appeal. On the issue here presented the evidence was sharply conflicting. Rankin was one of the organizers of the company, its vice-president, and one of its three directors. His connection with the stock sales is shown by evidence that he presided over, and participated in, board meetings where the sale and disposition of the company stock was discussed and authorized. As vice-president he signed two of the [stock] certificates [issued to the securities firm that assisted in the stock sales]. * * * While he flatly denied any knowledge of, or participation in, the stock sales here under consideration, the evidence is such that the jury could reasonably infer that he "controlled the corporation" and had knowledge of the stock sales in question. The jury resolved this factual issue against Rankin. Under the circumstances, the verdict of the jury must stand.

* * *

———

Culpability for the actions complained of typically plays an important role in litigation under section 15. Some courts require a showing of culpability by the plaintiff, while others require a lack of culpability to be raised by the defendant as an affirmative defense.

V.　Section 17(a)

Section 17(a) provides:

It shall be unlawful for any person in the offer or sale of any securities by the use of any means or instruments of transportation or communication in interstate commerce or by the use of the mails, directly or indirectly—

(1)　to employ any device, scheme, or artifice to defraud, or

(2)　to obtain money or property by means of any untrue statement of a material fact or any omission to state a material fact necessary in order to make the statements made, in the light of the circumstances under which they were made, not misleading, or

(3)　to engage in any transaction, practice, or course of business which operates or would operate as a fraud or deceit upon the purchaser.

As indicated at the beginning of the chapter, Section 17(a) is a criminal provision. It is discussed here because a few courts have over the years found that an implied private right of action exists under it.

Those familiar with Exchange Act Rule 10b–5 (discussed in Chapters 12 and 13) will notice a close resemblance between it and Section 17(a). The reason is that when the Commission drafted Rule 10b–5, it copied the numbered subdivisions of Section 17(a) almost word for word. There is, in fact, only one substantive difference in the language of the two provisions: Section 17(a) covers fraud in the sale of securities, while Rule 10b–5 covers fraud in the purchase *or* sale of securities. Fairly early, courts implied a private right of action under the rule, and the growth of case law involving the rule has been unparalleled in securities law. As a result, cases that might otherwise have been handled under Section 17(a) were instead decided under Rule 10b–5, and Section 17(a) therefore saw little use.

This mattered little until the Supreme Court handed down Aaron v. SEC in 1980.[25] In that case, the Court held that scienter (defined as a state of mind that is more culpable than negligence) must be proven under Rule 10b–5 in an action by the Commission seeking an injunction. The Court also determined that the Commission must only show scienter

———

[25]　446 U.S. 680 (1980).

when it brings an action under Section 17(a)(1), not when it does so under Section 17(a)(2) or (3). Under these latter subsections, a showing of negligence is sufficient.

In view of the fact that Section 17(a) and Rule 10b–5 are virtually identical in their numerical subdivisions, *Aaron* may seem inexplicable. The holding proves logical when it is remembered that the two provisions are on different levels in the hierarchy of regulation. Section 17(a) was passed by Congress, and it must be interpreted in a way that effectuates the will of Congress. Rule 10b–5, on the other hand, is merely a rule of the Commission under Exchange Act Section 10(b). Thus, the interpretation of the rule must fall within the area Congress has circumscribed in Section 10(b). In *Aaron,* then, the Supreme Court looked at Securities Act Section 17(a) and Exchange Act Section 10(b), and discerned two different congressional intents. With respect to Section 10(b), the Court interpreted congressional intent as requiring scienter in the case of all actions brought for the violations of rules adopted under the section, but for Section 17(a), the Court found differing congressional intents with respect to the various subsections.

With *Aaron*, the issue of whether an implied right of action exists under Section 17(a) took on major importance, since for the first time plaintiffs would often prefer that section to Rule 10b–5. The Supreme Court has never spoken on the issue, but at the time of or shortly after *Aaron*, four courts of appeals had found that a private right of action existed under Section 17(a). Now, each of those circuits has reversed course, and most courts that have decided the issue have found that the right does not exist. The Sixth Circuit has, however, confirmed a private right of action under Section 17(a).[26]

In considering whether a private right of action exists under Section 17(a), it should be remembered that the liability scheme of the Securities Act was drastically altered in 1995 by the *Gustafson* case, which appears above in connection with Section 12(a)(2). *Gustafson*, of course, eliminated the usefulness of Section 12(a)(2) in non-public and most secondary offerings. By contrast, in a 1979 criminal case, the Supreme Court had held Section 17(a) applicable to fraud "in every facet" of the securities business, and *not* limited to dishonesty in the initial distribution process.[27] It therefore has seemed worthwhile to private plaintiffs to continue to attempt actions under Section 17(a).

To appreciate the issues involved in deciding whether such an action in fact exists, it is necessary to look at the rules, developed by the Supreme Court since the mid-1960s, for determining the existence of an implied private right of action under federal statutes. It is especially worthwhile to spend some time on those rules, since the question of implied rights of action arises in many securities law contexts.

---

[26] Craighead v. E.F. Hutton & Co., 899 F.2d 485 (6th Cir.1990).

[27] United States v. Naftalin, 441 U.S. 768 (1979).

In the most influential early case, J.I. Case Co. v. Borak,[28] the Supreme Court used an expansive analysis to decide that a private right of action exists under Exchange Act Section 14(a):

> The purpose of § 14(a) is to prevent management or others from obtaining authorization for corporate action by means of deceptive or inadequate disclosure in proxy solicitation. * * * While [the language of the section] makes no specific reference to a private right of action, among its chief purposes is "the protection of investors," which certainly implies the availability of judicial relief where necessary to achieve that result.

As might be expected under a test whose touchstone is the protection of investors, courts were quick to imply private rights of action in the years following *Borak.*

This expansive era of implying rights of action continued for about a decade, until Cort v. Ash.[29] In *Cort,* the Supreme Court established four factors as relevant in determining the existence of an implied remedy: (1) Is the plaintiff of the class for whose especial benefit the statute was enacted? (2) Is there any indication of legislative intent, explicit or implicit, either to create such a remedy or to deny one? (3) Is it consistent with the underlying purposes of the legislative scheme to imply such a remedy for the plaintiff? (4) Is the cause of action one traditionally relegated to state law, in an area basically the concern of the states? Compared to *Borak,* which basically focused only on the third of these factors, *Cort* was obviously more restrictive.

Four years later, the Supreme Court refined its analysis in Touche Ross & Co. v. Redington.[30] There the Court had to decide whether an implied private right of action exists under Exchange Act Section 17(a), which requires that securities firms file certain financial reports with the Commission. The Court used the *Cort* analysis, but made it clear that each of the four factors stated there do not carry equal weight. The central inquiry, it determined, is legislative intent. *Borak* was not overruled, but the Court said of it: "To the extent our analysis in today's decision differs from that of the Court in *Borak,* it suffices to say that in a series of cases since *Borak* we have adhered to a stricter standard for the implication of private causes of action, and we follow that stricter standard today."

In 1982, the focus on legislative intent took an interesting turn, one that again showed a more expansive approach to implied remedies. In Merrill Lynch, Pierce, Fenner & Smith, Inc. v. Curran,[31] the question was whether to find an implied right of action under the Commodity Exchange Act. Rather than look at the intent of Congress at the time of

---

[28]   377 U.S. 426 (1964).

[29]   422 U.S. 66 (1975).

[30]   442 U.S. 560 (1979).

[31]   456 U.S. 353 (1982).

the Act's passage, the Court chose to focus on its intent at the point it passed comprehensive amendments in 1974. Noting that prior to these amendments "the federal courts routinely and consistently had recognized an implied private cause of action," the Court reasoned that leaving "intact the statutory provisions under which the federal courts had implied a cause of action is itself evidence that Congress affirmatively intended to preserve that remedy." Based largely on this reasoning, the Court found the implied right to exist.

The next year the Court dealt with a different kind of implied right of action question and again used an expansive approach. In Herman & MacLean v. Huddleston,[32] the issue was whether the implied right of action under Rule 10b–5, which previously had been held to exist, could be pursued in a situation clearly covered by Securities Act Section 11. With seeming ease the Court determined that it could. According to the Court, the resolution of the issue turned "on the fact that the two provisions involve distinct causes of action and were intended to address different types of wrongdoing." Thus, the Court found it to be "hardly a novel proposition" that the Securities Act and the Exchange Act prohibit some of the same conduct. Picking up on *Curran,* the Court also found support for its conclusion in the fact that "when Congress comprehensively revised the securities laws in 1975, a consistent line of judicial decisions had permitted plaintiffs to sue under § 10(b) regardless of the availability of express remedies." Therefore, "Congress' decision to leave § 10(b) intact suggests that Congress ratified the cumulative nature of the § 10(b) action." It is interesting to note that the general tenor of the opinion seemed a throwback to the earlier expansive era of implying rights of action, symbolized by its inclusion of language from SEC v. Capital Gains Research Bureau, Inc.,[33] that the securities laws should be construed "not technically and restrictively, but flexibly to effectuate [their] remedial purposes."

The result of these decisions, with respect to implied private rights of action in general, is not always certain. The Fifth Circuit examined the question of the proper post-*Aaron* result under Section 17(a) in Landry v. All American Assurance Co.[34] Of the four factors set out in *Cort,* the court determined that only the last (is the cause of action one traditionally relegated to state law, in an area basically the concern of the states?) pointed toward the existence of an implied private right. It viewed the third *Cort* factor (is it consistent with the underlying purposes of the legislative scheme to imply such a remedy for the plaintiff?) as most compellingly pointed away from the existence of such a right, saying "Section 17(a)(2) prohibits the same type of conduct as §§ 11 and 12, but has none of the limitations imposed by Congress. The creation of an implied cause of action under § 17(a) under these circumstances would

---

[32]   459 U.S. 375 (1983).

[33]   375 U.S. 180 (1963).

[34]   688 F.2d 381 (5th Cir.1982).

effectively frustrate the carefully laid framework of the Act." This calculus could be affected by *Gustafson*'s alteration of the Securities Act's liability scheme, but post-*Gustafson* cases by and large do not address this possibility.[35]

Although the pendulum clearly has swung against the viability of a private right of action under Section 17(a), the section remains of vital importance to the Commission, especially given judicial developments (discussed in Chapter 12) narrowing liability under Section 10(b) and Rule 10b–5 under the Exchange Act. Three developments in use of the section by the Commission are worthy of note. First, the Commission appears to have stepped up its reliance on Section 17(a)(2) and (3), and has taken the position that they may be strict liability provisions. Second, some lower courts have extended the holding of Janus Capital Group, Inc. v. First Derivative Traders[36] to Commission actions under Section 17(a).[37] Other lower courts, however, have found the extension of Janus either to Commission actions or to Section 17(a) to be inappropriate.[38] *Janus* (discussed below in Chapter 12) held that, in the context of a private lawsuit, Rule10b–5 liability for a misleading statement will attach only to those with "ultimate control" over the statement. The Court indicated that, in the ordinary case, attribution will be critical in determining ultimate control.

C. INDEMNIFICATION AND CONTRIBUTION

Section 11(f) of the Securities Act specifically grants the right of contribution to any person liable under the section, except when the person seeking contribution is, and the person from whom contribution is sought is not, guilty of fraudulent misrepresentation. (When dealing with the liability of outside directors under Section 11, note that Section 11(f), as amended in 1995, brings the proportionate liability provisions of Exchange Act Section 21D(f) into play. One issue covered is contribution.) Contribution has also been found to be available in a private suit under Section 17(a).[39] The reasoning underlying this result in the case of Section 17(a), including "the general drift of the law today * * * toward allowance of contribution among joint tortfeasors," applies with equal force to Section 12. Also instructive is the fact that the Supreme Court has found contribution to be available in suits brought under Exchange Act Rule 10b–5. There should, therefore, be little question that contribution is generally available in Securities Act suits.

---

[35]   *See, e.g.*, Maldonado v. Dominguez, 137 F.3d 1 (1st Cir.1998)

[36]   131 S.Ct. 2296 (2011).

[37]   *See, e.g.*, SEC v. Kelly, No. 08–CV–4612 (SDNY, Sept. 22, 2011).

[38]   *See, e.g.*, SEC v. Big Apple Consulting USA, 783 F.3d 786 (11th Cir.2015); SEC v. Pentagon Capital Management PLC, No. 08 Civ. 3324 (SDNY, Feb. 14, 2012), overruled on other grounds, SEC v Pentagon Capital Management PLC, 725 F.3d 279 (2d Cir.2013).

[39]   Globus, Inc. v. Law Research Service, Inc., 318 F.Supp. 955 (S.D.N.Y.1970), aff'd 442 F.2d 1346 (2d Cir.1971).

Indemnification is a more difficult problem. The Commission has long been dissatisfied with the idea that officers, directors, and other persons controlling an issuer might be indemnified by the issuer for Securities Act liability. The Commission's position is that such indemnity is against public policy and, therefore, it believes that any provision granting it is unenforceable. The Commission's stance on the public policy issue makes it more likely, of course, that a court will take such a position itself. And, in fact, some courts have brought into question indemnification against Securities Act liability. The leading case, Globus v. Law Research Service, Inc., appears directly below.

Globus v. Law Research Service, Inc.

United States Court of Appeals, Second Circuit, 1969.
418 F.2d 1276.

■ Before WATERMAN, SMITH and KAUFMAN, CIRCUIT JUDGES.

■ IRVING R. KAUFMAN, CIRCUIT JUDGE:

This tortuous litigation raises [the issue of whether an underwriter may] be indemnified by an issuer for liabilities arising out of misstatements in an offering circular of which the underwriter had actual knowledge? We hold * * * that an underwriter may not be indemnified in a case such as this.

The plaintiffs-appellees, purchasers of the stock of Law Research Services, Inc. (LRS), initiated this action against LRS, its president Ellias C. Hoppenfeld, and the underwriter of LRS's public stock offer, Blair & Co., Granbery Marache, Inc. (Blair). They contended that the appellants violated § 17(a) of the Securities Act of 1933 * * * . The essence of their charge is that the offering circular prepared in connection with LRS's offer to sell 100,000 shares of its stock to the public under Regulation A of the Securities and Exchange Commission was misleading * * * .

Judge Mansfield presided over a ten-day trial of these claims, to a jury in the Southern District of New York. The jury * * * decided that [Blair, LRS, and Hoppenfeld] had violated * * * the Securities Act of 1933 * * * . Accordingly, the jury awarded compensatory damages to all plaintiffs * * *

The jury was also called upon to deal with a cross-claim asserted by Blair against LRS, which rested on an indemnity clause included in the underwriting agreement * * * . * * * [T]he jury found for Blair.

* * *

Judge Mansfield * * * granted the motion of LRS * * * to set aside the jury's verdict on the cross-claims granting indemnification to Blair. He thus struck down the indemnity agreement between the issuer and the underwriter, at least as it applied to the facts before us. Blair's cross-claim against LRS was based on a provision which compelled LRS to indemnify the underwriter for any loss arising out of an untrue statement of a material fact in the offering circular, except that Blair was not to obtain indemnification by reason of any willful misfeasance, bad faith or gross negligence in the performance of its duties or by reason of its reckless disregard of its obligations under the agreement. * * *

The jury, by awarding compensatory and punitive damages to the plaintiffs under [Section] 17(a) * * * , necessarily found in light of the judge's charge, that Blair had actual knowledge of the material misstatements. Accordingly the court had ample basis to find Blair not deserving of recovery under the indemnity agreement itself. But it chose instead the broader ground that where there is actual knowledge of the misstatement by the underwriter and wanton indifference by Blair to its obligations, "it would be against the public policy embodied in the federal securities legislation to permit Blair and Co. * * * to enforce its indemnification agreement." Thus it is important to emphasize at the outset that at this time we consider only the case where the underwriter has committed a sin graver than ordinary negligence.

Given this state of the record, we concur in Judge Mansfield's ruling that to tolerate indemnity under these circumstances would encourage flouting the policy of the common law and the Securities Act. It is well established that one cannot insure himself against his own reckless, willful or criminal misconduct.

Although the 1933 Act does not deal expressly with the question before us, provisions in that Act confirm our conclusion that Blair should not be entitled to indemnity from LRS. For example, § 11 of the Act makes underwriters jointly liable with directors, experts and signers of the registration statement. And, the SEC has announced its view that indemnification of directors, officers and controlling persons for liabilities arising under the 1933 Act is against the public policy of the Act. If we follow the syllogism through to its conclusion, underwriters should be treated equally with controlling persons and hence prohibited from obtaining indemnity from the issuer.

Civil liability under Section 11 and similar provisions was designed not so much to compensate the defrauded purchaser as to promote enforcement of the Act and to deter negligence by providing a penalty for those who fail in their duties. And Congress intended to impose a "high standard of trusteeship" on underwriters. Thus, what Professor Loss terms the "*in terrorem* effect" of civil liability, 3 Loss, [Securities Regulation (1969)], at 1831, might well be thwarted if underwriters were free to pass their liability on to the issuer. Underwriters who knew they could be indemnified simply by showing that the issuer was "more liable" than they (a process not too difficult when the issuer is inevitably closer to the facts) would have a tendency to be lax in their independent investigations. Cases upholding indemnity for negligence in other fields are not necessarily apposite. The goal in such cases is to compensate the injured party. But the Securities Act is more concerned with prevention than cure.

Finally, it has been suggested that indemnification of the underwriter by the issuer is particularly suspect. Although in form the underwriter is reimbursed by the issuer, the recovery ultimately comes out of the pockets of the issuer's stockholders. Many of these stockholders may be the very purchasers to whom the underwriter should have been initially liable. The 1933 Act prohibits agreements with purchasers which purport to exempt individuals from liability arising under the Act. The situation before us is at least reminiscent of the evil this section was designed to avoid.

* * *

In its discussion of indemnity in *Globus,* the Second Circuit emphasized that it was considering "only the case where the underwriter has committed a sin graver than ordinary negligence." This caveat notwithstanding, ever since *Globus* securities lawyers have viewed the enforceability of all indemnification provisions with substantial uncertainty. Underwriting agreements typically provide for cross indemnity between the issuer and the underwriters. That is, each side agrees to indemnify the other for liability flowing from problems in the registration statement that are attributable to the indemnifying party. Underwriting agreements also typically require that the underwriters receive opinions from counsel covering a number of legal matters, including the enforceability of the underwriting agreement. Since *Globus,* careful securities lawyers insist that they include in such opinions an exception stating that they express no opinion on the enforceability of the indemnification provisions contained in the underwriting agreement.

Some courts have now held that there is no implied right of action for indemnification under the Securities Act or the Exchange Act, and some have refused to enforce the indemnification provisions in an underwriting agreement irrespective of the culpability of those seeking indemnification.[40] Indemnification of a party who has successfully defended a lawsuit, however, appears to be permissible.[41]

---

[40] *See, e.g.,* Eichenholtz v. Brennan, 52 F.3d 478 (3d Cir.1995).

[41] *See, e.g.,* Credit Swisse First Boston v. Intershop Communications, 407 F. Supp. 2d 541 (S.D.N.Y. 2006).

PART 3

SECURITIES EXCHANGE ACT OF 1934

CHAPTER 9

COMMISSION'S GENERAL EXEMPTIVE AUTHORITY AND REGISTRATION OF SECURITIES AND PERIODIC REPORTING UNDER THE EXCHANGE ACT

SITUATION 9

After Microtec completed its public offering, you were given the task of helping Microtec comply with the registration and reporting requirements of the Securities Exchange Act of 1934. Assume that you are back in the period of time between the completion of that offering and the time the law suits referred to in Situation 8 are filed, and that you are working on this task.

Then assume that shortly after the law suits are filed, plaintiffs' counsel files another suit, this one on behalf of persons who purchased Microtec common stock in the trading markets. In this suit plaintiffs allege violations of Exchange Act Sections 12(g)(1), 13(a), (b)(2), and (l), and 15(d) and seek recovery both under implied rights of action under these sections and under the liability provisions of Exchange Act Section 18(a). The factual allegations are basically the same as in the earlier suits, but in this suit the alleged deficiencies in disclosure of income were in the registration statement filed under Exchange Act Section 12(g)(1) and reports filed under Sections 13(a) and 15(d). The plaintiffs maintain that Section 13(b)(2) was violated in that Microtec did not keep its books and accounts in accordance with the requirements of this section, and that section 13(l) was violated when Microtec failed to disclose changes in its financial condition in timely fashion.

In considering this situation, refer to the following, in addition to the materials in this chapter: Exchange Act Sections 3(f), 12, 13(a), (b), (c), (l), and (p), 15(d), 18, 20 and 36, and Rule 12g–1, Rule 12g5–1(a), Regulations 13A and 15D under the Exchange Act. In addition, quickly survey Exchange Act Forms 10, 10–K, 10–Q, and 8–K under the Exchange Act.

The next several chapters cover the Securities Exchange Act of 1934. Since much of what is discussed in these chapters applies only to companies that have securities registered under that Act, Exchange Act registration is the natural starting point for the discussion. One of the major consequences of registration, periodic reporting to the Commission, is intertwined with registration, since it involves the updating of information provided to the Commission at the time of registration. For that reason, it is also examined in this chapter. First, however, it is important to say something about the Commission's general exemptive authority.

A. COMMISSION'S GENERAL EXEMPTIVE AUTHORITY

In connection not only with this chapter, but with all chapters dealing with the Exchange Act, it should be noted that, under Section 36 of the Exchange Act, "the Commission, by rule, regulation, or order, may conditionally or unconditionally exempt any person, security, or transaction, or any class or classes of persons, securities, or transactions, from any provision or provisions of this title or of any rule or regulation thereunder." Section 36 contains only two caveats. First, any exemption must be "necessary or appropriate in the public interest, and consistent with the protection of investors." Second, the authority of the Commission does not extend to Exchange Act Section 15C, which relates to government securities brokers and dealers. An important element of the Commission's authority under Section 36 is that the Commission can exercise this authority by order or ad hoc.

Also to be considered in connection with Section 36 is Section 3(f), which was added to the Exchange Act at the same time as Section 36. When engaged in rulemaking, or the review of a rule by a self-regulatory organization such as a securities exchange, Section 3(f) requires the Commission to consider "whether the action will promote efficiency, competition, and capital formation," at any time it is "required to consider or determine whether an action is necessary or appropriate in the public interest."

B. REGISTRATION OF SECURITIES UNDER THE EXCHANGE ACT AND PERIODIC REPORTING

I. REGISTRATION

The Exchange Act requires the registration of securities under two distinct circumstances. First, an issuer must register securities when the securities are to be traded on a stock exchange. Second, an issuer must register securities when it meets certain tests with respect to number of shareholders and amount of assets. As a practical matter, virtually all companies initially registering do so because they meet these tests, and only a small percentage of these companies ever see their securities traded on an exchange.

Exchange Act Section 12(g)(1) now requires registration within 120 days of the last day of the first fiscal year in which an issuer (a) has total assets exceeding $10,000,000 and (b) a class of equity security "held of record" by either 2,000 or more persons or 500 or more unaccredited investors (accredited investors are discussed in Chapter 6).[1] Thus, a company could have 1999 accredited investors, or 499 unaccredited investors and 1500 accredited investors (or various other permutations, such as 1800 accredited investors and 199 unaccredited investors), without coming within the mandate of Section 12(g). Section 12(g)(5) and (6) add two additional complications. First, securities owned by persons receiving them through employee compensation plan transactions exempt from registration under the Securities Act will not be counted toward Section 12(g)'s "held of record" tests. Second, the Commission was required to adopt, and has adopted, rules excluding from Section 12(g) calculations the holders of securities acquired pursuant to the new "crowdfunding" exemption from Securities Act registration. In a final wrinkle, under Rule 12g5–1(a)(7), many issuers of securities under the Regulation A exemption from Securities Act registration will not be required to register under Section 12(g) of the Exchange Act, notwithstanding passing the thresholds indicated above, provided that they maintain less than \$75 million in "public float" or, in the absence of public float, less than \$50 million in revenue.

Companies that are not required to register securities under Section 12(g)(1) may register them nevertheless, if they wish. Over the years, a number of companies have registered securities voluntarily to meet the current public information requirement of Securities Act Rule 144(c), and thus make this rule available to shareholders who wish to sell securities under it.[2] Some companies have also registered voluntarily, in response to a proxy fight, in order to subject proxy solicitations to Exchange Act regulation.

Companies that wish to have their securities trade on an exchange must register the securities under Section 12(b). The statutory framework for requiring this registration is somewhat roundabout. It starts with Section 12(a), which makes it unlawful for any securities professional to effect a transaction in any security (except an exempted security) on a national securities exchange,[3] "unless a registration is effective as to such security for such exchange." Section 12(b) then provides the mechanism for registration, which involves filing an application with the exchange and with the Commission.

Section 12(b) serves as the starting point for establishing what disclosures must be included in the registration application. This section also grants the Commission authority to prescribe the details of this disclosure. Section 12(g)(1) gives the Commission this same power with

---

[1]   A slightly different rule pertains to banks and bank holding companies, to which the "500 unaccredited investor" test does not apply.

[2]   With the changes in the rule discussed in Chapter 7, allowing most non-affiliates who have held restricted securities for one year to sell freely, fewer companies now register under the Exchange Act voluntarily because of Rule 144.

[3]   Any exchange registered with the Commission under Section 6(a) of the Exchange Act is a "national" exchange. There now are over twenty such exchanges.

respect to registrations under that section, and the Commission has adopted the same forms for registering securities under either Section 12(b) or 12(g)(1). Form 10 is the form used by most domestic issuers. (If, as discussed in the next section of the chapter, an issuer is already subject to the Exchange Act's reporting requirements, it can register on the very simple Form 8–A.)

Exchange Act registration forms have much in common with Securities Act registration forms, because there is a great sameness in the general disclosures required for registration under each Act. Commonality also arises because the registration statement forms under each Act use Regulation S–K as the repository of detailed disclosure requirements, with each form consisting mainly of references to the items in the regulation with which a registering company must comply.

It is confusing that both the Securities Act and the Exchange Act provide for the registration of securities. The consequences of registration under the two Acts are entirely different. Registration under the Securities Act allows the securities that are registered to be sold in a particular transaction. In this case, it is only technically incorrect to say that the transaction itself is what is registered. The consequences of Exchange Act registration are that the issuer of the registered securities is subject to that Act's periodic reporting requirements and to certain other requirements, for example with respect to proxy solicitations, that will be discussed in later chapters. In the case of the Exchange Act, it is only technically incorrect to say that the issuer is what is registered.

II. PERIODIC REPORTING UNDER THE EXCHANGE ACT

By registering securities under Exchange Act Section 12, an issuer becomes a "reporting company." That is, it becomes subject to the periodic reporting requirements of Section 13(a). Under this section, reporting companies must make two kinds of filings with the Commission: (1) filings of such information and documents as the Commission requires to keep current the information provided at the time of registration and (2) filings of such annual and quarterly reports as the Commission requires irrespective of the updating requirement. The grant of power to the Commission in Section 13(a) is broad, and under it the Commission generally has power to require the filing of virtually any document or report it wishes.

An exception to the Commission's broad grant of power was added by the JOBS Act and limits the financial information that must be presented by emerging growth companies (which are, as described below and in Chapters 3 and 4 entitled to additional types of special treatment under both the Securities and the Exchange Acts). As detailed in Chapter 3, these are issuers whose initial public offering was or will be completed after Dec. 8, 2011, and had total annual gross revenues of less than $1 billion during their most recent fiscal years. Emerging growth company status terminates on the earliest of:

1.   The last day of the first fiscal year of the issuer during which it had total annual gross revenues of $1 billion or more;

2.   The last day of the fiscal year of the issuer following the fifth anniversary of the date of the issuer's initial public offering;

3.   The date on which such issuer has issued more than $1 billion in non-convertible debt during the prior three-year period; or

4.   The date on which the issuer is deemed to be a "large accelerated filer" under the Exchange Act (requiring, among other things, that it have a public float in excess of $700 million). (Since the mid-2000s, issuers have been subject to different Exchange Act reporting deadlines based on their public float.)

Moreover, Congress in some instances has directed how the Commission's power to require disclosure is to be used. For instance, the Sarbanes-Oxley Act of 2002 added Section 13(j), mandating that the Commission adopt rules with respect to the disclosure of material off-balance sheet transactions. It also ordered the Commission to impose certain officer certification requirements relating both to the integrity of reports and the efficacy of management's internal controls. More recently, the Dodd-Frank Act of 2010 required the adoption of rules calling for disclosures with respect to use of "conflict minerals" (tantalum, tin, gold, or tungsten mined in the Democratic Republic of Congo and surrounding countries) and with respect to payments made to governments to further commercial development of oil, natural gas, or minerals. The resulting rules were, however, deemed unconstitutional by the D.C. Circuit Court of Appeals[4] and their enforcement was suspended in 2017.

Regulation 13A outlines the filings required by the Commission under Section 13(a). For the typical issuer, these filings are on Form 10–K for annual reports, Form 10–Q for quarterly reports, and Form 8–K for reports upon the occurrence of certain materially important events.

A Form 10–K report is much like the Form 10 registration statement that is used to register securities under the Exchange Act. A Form 10–Q report usually consists mainly of quarterly financial statements. In each case, the forms consist primarily of references to the detailed disclosure requirements collected in Regulation S–K.

Although a report on Form 8–K typically is quite short, and can be limited to providing the specific information called for with respect to the triggering event, the matters required to be disclosed on Form 8–K are quite substantial. The form now covers a number of categories (sub-divided into specific reportable events), including the registrants' business and operations, financial information, securities and trading

---

4   Nat'l Ass'n of Mfrs., et al. v. SEC, 800 F.3d 518, 530 (D.C. Cir. 2015).

markets, matters related to accountants, corporate governance and management, Regulation FD (which requires fair, broad-based disclosure as opposed to selective disclosure and is discussed in Chapter 12), and certain other matters. A Form 8–K must be filed within four business days of a reportable event. Form 8–K also can be used to make voluntary disclosures, and may be the most practical way for a small company to publicly disseminate information.

In connection with Form 8–K it is worth noting the existence of Section 13(*l*) of the Exchange Act, added by Sarbanes-Oxley. It is headed "Real Time Issuer Disclosures" and provides that each reporting company "shall disclose to the public on a rapid and current basis such additional information (in addition to that specifically called for elsewhere) concerning material changes in the financial condition or operations of the issuer, in plain English, * * * as the Commission determines." The Commission's response was to increase the items required to be reported on Form 8–K and to shorten the time within which that form must be filed. Although issuers technically have no general duty to disclose material information, such a duty does arise in connection with a required Commission filing and (as discussed in Chapters 12 and 13) if the company is trading in its own securities, or if the disclosure is required to correct (and possibly to update) previously disclosed information that is still material. Given the number of disclosures now required on Form 8–K, combined with a duty to correct (and possibly to update) such disclosures, saying that there is no general duty to disclose may strike some as a distinction without a difference.

One of the most important, as well as most difficult to prepare, pieces of disclosure required in any report (as well as in registration statements under the Securities Act and the Exchange Act) that contains financial statements is the management's discussion and analysis of financial condition and results of operations. This disclosure is referred to by securities lawyers as "MD & A." Also required for filers of Form 10–K is plain-English disclosure of significant risk factors that might affect the value of the issuer's securities.

There is one other way in which companies become subject to the reporting requirements of the Exchange Act. Under Section 15(d), read along with Regulation 15D, a company that has registered securities under the Securities Act is subject to the same Section 13 filing requirements as are companies that have securities registered under Exchange Act Section 12. As a practical matter, the usual impact of Section 15(d) is simply earlier compliance with the periodic reporting requirements of the Exchange Act. Companies that register equity securities under the Securities Act typically meet the requirements of Section 12(g)(1) upon completion of the offering. A company does not, however, have to register securities under these provisions until 120 days after the end of the first fiscal year on the last day of which it meets the requirements. As a result of Section 15(d) and Regulation 15D, periodic reporting must begin immediately upon effectiveness of a Securities Act registration statement.

Some of the more interesting questions concerning periodic reporting relate to the liabilities that may flow from material misstatements or omissions in Exchange Act filings. Since the Exchange Act is a criminal statute, the first concern may be criminal liability. With this in mind, here is the Act's penalty provision:

> Section 32. (a). Any person who willfully violates any provision of this title (other than section 30A), or any rule or regulation thereunder the violation of which is made unlawful or the observance of which is required under the terms of this title, or any person who willfully and knowingly makes, or causes to be made, any statement in any application, report, or document required to be filed under this title or any rule or regulation thereunder * * *, which statement was false or misleading with respect to any material fact, shall upon conviction be fined not more than $5,000,000, or imprisoned not more than 20 years, or both, except that when such person is a person other than a natural person, a fine not exceeding $25,000,000 may be imposed; but no person shall be subject to imprisonment under this section for the violation of any rule or regulation if he proves that he had no knowledge of such rule or regulation.

It is important to note that since Section 32 deals with violations of the Exchange Act and its rules generally, much of what is discussed below is applicable to problems in addition to those arising in the context of periodic reporting.

A comparison of Section 32 with Securities Act Section 24 shows that the Exchange Act's penalty provision is somewhat easier on violators. There are at least two important differences. First, in a criminal prosecution under the Securities Act, willfulness must be shown. As discussed in the preceding chapter, in the context of a Securities Act prosecution for false or misleading statements, to show willfulness the government need not prove that the defendant knew of the existence of the statutory section or rule he is on trial for violating. All that is necessary is proof that the defendant knew he was committing a wrongful act. On the other hand, in a similar case brought under Exchange Act Section 32, the government must prove that the defendant acted "willfully and knowingly." To satisfy this requirement, the government must establish that the defendant knew of the existence of the section or rule he allegedly violated. Second, under Exchange Act Section 32, but not Securities Act Section 24, a defendant can avoid imprisonment (although not a fine) if he can prove that he had no knowledge of the rule or regulation he is charged with violating.

Section 18 provides an express civil remedy for false or misleading statements in Exchange Act filings. This section is not plaintiffs' first choice for relief, however, because of a number of requirements and limitations. First, under Section 18, plaintiffs must show that they purchased or sold securities in reliance on a defective filing. Second, to show damages, plaintiffs must prove that the price at which they purchased or sold was affected by the defective filing. Third, defendants can defeat a claim when they can establish that they acted in good faith and without knowledge that the filing was defective. Fourth, courts can require an undertaking for costs and can assess costs, including attorneys' fees, against any party.

As a result of their dissatisfaction with Section 18, plaintiffs who sue on the basis of a false or misleading statement hope to have a court find an implied right of action under another section of the Exchange Act. Two possibilities are Section 12(b)(1), which sets informational requirements for Exchange Act registration, and Section 13(a), which establishes the requirement of periodic reporting for Exchange Act companies. Appearing directly below are leading cases on the questions of whether a private right of action exists under these sections.

Cramer v. General Telephone & Electronics

United States District Court, Eastern District of Pennsylvania, 1977.
443 F.Supp. 516, affirmed 582 F.2d 259 (3d Cir.1978).

■ HIGGINBOTHAM, DISTRICT JUDGE

This shareholder derivative action, alleging violations of [Section] 12(b)(1) * * * of the 1934 Securities and Exchange Acts as well as breach of fiduciary duties, was commenced by Harold Cramer on behalf of the shareholders of General Telephone & Electronics Corp. (GTE) against Leslie H. Warner, Theodore F. Brophy, John G. Douglas and William Bennett, corporate officers, and Arthur Andersen & Co., GTE's auditors. * * *

* * *

Cramer, plaintiff herein, has alleged that * * * material facts were incompletely and/or inaccurately disclosed to GTE's shareholders. * * *

* * *

Plaintiff has * * * alleged a violation of Section 12(b)(1), which specifies the information an issuer must provide in an application to register a security. In order to successfully maintain an action under § 12(b)(1), plaintiff must meet the standing requirement of § 18 which limits the ability to maintain a 12(b)(1) claim to only those plaintiffs who purchased or sold a security in reliance upon information filed as required by § 12 or § 13, whose purchase or sales price was affected by said information, and who had no knowledge of omissions from or misrepresentations in the report. As Chief Judge Lord stated in In re Penn Central Securities Litigation, 347 F.Supp. 1327, 1340 (E.D.Pa.1972):

Where Congress has specifically authorized a remedy for violation of an act, the courts should not nullify the congressional scheme by implying a right of action on behalf of those not otherwise entitled to recover.

The complaint herein contains none of the allegations required to establish standing under § 18. There is no allegation that the corporation relied on any false or misleading filings in making any sale; there is no allegation that any filing affected the price of GTE securities. Finally, there is no causal nexus made, or even attempted, between any filing and any alleged loss which GTE suffered.

It is suggested by plaintiff that Kerber v. Kakos, 383 F.Supp. 625, 631 (N.D.Ill.1974), supports the position that a private cause of action will lie even when the § 18 requirements have not been completely satisfied. However, such reliance is misplaced; in Kerber v. Kakos, the court implied a cause of action under § 12(b) *only* in a case where the issuer had completely ignored the registration requirements. That situation is distinguishable from the case where the issuer is alleged to have made a false and misleading statement. * * *

In sum, as plaintiff has failed to meet the standing requirements of § 18(a), plaintiff's claims under 12(b)(1) must be dismissed.

* * *

In re Penn Central Securities Litigation

United States Court of Appeals, Third Circuit, 1974.
494 F.2d 528.

■ Before KALODNER, ADAMS and ROSENN, CIRCUIT JUDGES.

■ ROSENN, CIRCUIT JUDGE.

This appeal is another instance of the widespread litigation spawned by the reorganization in bankruptcy of the Penn Central Transportation Company. Appellants, plaintiffs in the district court, have appealed from an order granting partial summary judgment to defendants in the consolidated multidistrict proceedings known as the Penn Central Securities Litigation, which has been assigned to Chief Judge Lord of the Eastern District of Pennsylvania. * * * defendants are alleged to have violated numerous provisions of the securities acts[, including Exchange Act Section 13(a)].

The actions are predicated upon allegedly false and misleading financial information concerning the Penn Central complex which the defendants prepared, filed with the SEC, or released to the shareholders and the public in an allegedly successful attempt to inflate the market price of Penn Central Company capital stock. * * *

* * *

Section 13(a) of the Securities Exchange Act of 1934 requires the filing of information, reports and documents with the SEC as required by the rules and regulations of the SEC. Section 18(a) provides that a person making or causing to be made a false statement in a document filed under any other section of the Act shall be liable for false or misleading material facts to any person who in reliance on such misstatement *purchased or sold a security* at a price affected by such misstatement. The district court granted summary judgment to defendants as to all Section 13(a) claims by all plaintiffs. * * *

We have not been cited, nor have we found, any appellate decisions concerning the possible existence of a private right of action under 13(a). We believe the district court correctly held that § 18(a) is the exclusive remedy for alleged violations of § 13(a). Acceptance of plaintiffs' argument would result in the elimination of the purchaser-seller requirement for violations of § 13(a), a requirement which this court has recently held essential for standing under the general anti-fraud provision of § 10(b). Landy v. Federal Deposit Insurance Corporation, 486 F.2d 139, 158 (3d Cir.1973). We have not been cited to any language or to any history in the 1934 Act which indicates that Congress intended to extend the protection offered by § 13(a) beyond the class of purchasers or sellers. We also see no practical basis for creating a cause of action in a shareholder who alleges he relied on an unduly optimistic report in not selling his stock. Were we to do so, we logically should create a right of action in any non-shareholder who alleges he relied upon an unduly pessimistic report in deciding *not to buy* stock of the corporation. As we noted in *Landy,* supra, 486 F.2d at 158, as to Section 10(b),

> Were we to extend the provisions of Section 10(b) beyond the buyer or seller relationship, we would be judicially extending the terms of the statute and creating new rights. The consequences of the view urged by plaintiffs would establish a new and amorphous body of rights and obligations heretofore unrecognized in federal jurisdiction.

We believe the same considerations also apply to the contention advanced in the instant case that we should imply a private right of action in Section 13(a) to avoid the purchaser-seller requirement of Section 18. We therefore decline to do so, at least in the absence of exceptional circumstances which are not present in this case.

* * *

Rule 10b–5, which is the subject of a later chapter, is the other provision that a private plaintiff may wish to use as an alternative to Section 18. In Herman & MacLean v. Huddleston,[5] the Supreme Court held that a Rule 10b–5 action could be pursued in a situation that

---

[5]   459 U.S. 375 (1983).

Securities Act Section 11 was specifically designed to cover. The decision turned largely on the fact that the two provisions "involve distinct causes of action and were intended to address different types of wrongdoing." This distinction between provisions is also the case when comparing Section 18 and Rule 10b–5, particularly since an action under Rule 10b–5 requires scienter while one under Section 18 does not. The court in Huddleston was also persuaded that Congress intended that Section 10(b) and Rule 10b–5 be used even in cases in which an explicit remedy has been provided by statute. This argues in favor of a finding that Rule 10b–5 can be used in situations covered by Section 18.

Note that in an action under Section 18 or Rule 10b–5, or indeed in any private right of action case under the Exchange Act, the protections afforded defendants by Exchange Act Sections 21D and 21E apply. These sections relate in part to (i) the requirement of loss causation, (ii) limitations on damages, (iii) proportionate liability, and (iv) a safe harbor for certain forward-looking statements that are accompanied by appropriate cautionary statements. One would also want to consider the effect of the "bespeaks caution" doctrine and the situation with controlling person and aiding and abetting liability for Exchange Act violations. (Each of these issues, and some other important liability issues also relevant here, are discussed below in Chapter 12, which relates to securities fraud and related issues under Rule 10b–5 and under Sarbanes-Oxley.)

III. EDGAR

Filings of both Exchange Act registration statements and periodic reports must be made under the Commission's Electronic Data Gathering, Analysis and Retrieval System (EDGAR). These statements and reports, as well as accompanying exhibits, become publicly available, although in some circumstances confidential treatment can be obtained for at least portions of the documents sent.

C. FOREIGN CORRUPT PRACTICES ACT

Exchange Act Section 13(b) contains recordkeeping requirements that are intimately related to periodic reporting. The most controversial of these requirements have been Sections 13(b)(2) and (3), which were added by the Foreign Corrupt Practices Act of 1977. Under Section 13(b)(2), every Exchange Act reporting company is required to:

> (A) make and keep books, records, and accounts, which, in reasonable detail, accurately and fairly reflect the transactions and dispositions of the assets of the issuer; and

> (B) devise and maintain a system of internal accounting controls sufficient to provide reasonable assurances that—

>> (i) transactions are executed in accordance with management's general or specific authorization;

(ii) transactions are recorded as necessary (I) to permit preparation of financial statements in conformity with generally accepted accounting principles or any other criteria applicable to such statements, and (II) to maintain accountability for assets;

(iii) access to assets is permitted only in accordance with management's general or specific authorization; and

(iv) the recorded accountability for assets is compared with the existing assets at reasonable intervals and appropriate action is taken with respect to any differences.

Section 13(b)(3) exempts issuers from these requirements when they act in cooperation with certain federal officials in connection with "matters concerning the national security of the United States"—that is, when they provide cover for clandestine operations.

The Foreign Corrupt Practices Act was passed in response to what has been called "corporate Watergate." During the mid-1970s scores of United States corporations were found to have engaged in what were euphemistically called "questionable payments." Some of these payments were bribes to foreign governmental officials, some were "grease" payments to foreign governmental functionaries designed to encourage them to do their jobs efficiently, and some were foreign political contributions. To hide these payments from auditors and others, many companies doctored their books and maintained large off the books slush funds.

Section 13(b)(2) quickly came under strong and widespread criticism from the corporate community, as explained in the following address by the then Chairman of the Commission.

The Accounting Provisions of the Foreign Corrupt Practices Act: An Analysis

Harold M. Williams.[*]

Address to the SEC Developments Conference of the American Institute of Certified Public Accountants (January 13, 1981).

* * *

The anxieties created by the Foreign Corrupt Practices Act—among men and women of utmost good faith—have been, in my experience, without equal. This consternation can be attributed, in significant part, to the spectre which some commentators have raised of exposure to Commission enforcement action, and perhaps criminal liability, as a result of technical and insignificant errors in corporate records or weaknesses in corporate internal accounting controls. In fact, some

---

[*]   Chairman of the Securities and Exchange Commission. This address was published as Commission policy in Exchange Act Release No. 17500 (January 29, 1981). [Eds.]

commentators claim that, because of the broad strokes with which the accounting provisions are fashioned, no corporate executive can ever feel fully confident that his corporation is in compliance with the law. And, other commentators have expressed fear that this lack of concrete statutory parameters evidences a meaning to the Act which is far beyond its Congressional intent.

Such uncertainty can have a debilitating effect on the activities of those who seek to comply with the law. My sense is that, as a consequence, many businesses have been very cautious—sometimes overly so—in assuring at least technical compliance with the Act. And, therefore, business resources may have been diverted from more productive uses to overly-burdensome compliance systems which extend beyond the requirements of sound management or the policies embodied in the Act. The public, of course, is not well served by such reactions.

The Commission is sensitive to these concerns and considerations. The goal is to allow a business, acting in good faith, to comply with the Act's accounting provisions in an innovative and cost-effective way and with a better sense of its legal responsibilities. I have conferred, accordingly, with my colleagues before presenting these remarks, and they have authorized me to advise you that these remarks constitute a statement of the Commission's policy.

* * *

— Recordkeeping. The Act's recordkeeping provision requires that a company maintain records which reasonably and fairly reflect the transactions and dispositions of the company's assets. This provision is intimately related to the requirement for a system of internal accounting controls, and we believe that records which are not relevant to accomplishing the objectives specified in the statute for the system of internal controls are not within the purview of the recordkeeping provision. Moreover, inadvertent recordkeeping mistakes will not give rise to Commission enforcement proceedings; nor could a company be enjoined for a falsification of which its management, broadly defined, was not aware and reasonably should not have known.

— Internal accounting controls system. The Act does not mandate any particular kind of internal controls system. The test is whether a system, taken as a whole, reasonably meets the statute's specified objectives. "Reasonableness," a familiar legal concept, depends on an evaluation of all the facts and circumstances.

— Deference. Private sector decisions implementing these statutory objectives are business decisions. And, reasonable business decisions should be afforded deference. This means that the issuer need not always select the best or the most effective control measure. However, the one selected must be reasonable under all the circumstances.

— State of mind. The accounting provisions principal objective is to reach knowing or reckless conduct. Moreover, we would expect that the courts will issue injunctions only when there is a reasonable likelihood that the misconduct would be repeated. In the context of the accounting provisions, that showing is not likely to be possible when the conduct in question is inadvertent.

— Status of subsidiaries. The issuer's responsibility for the compliance of its subsidiaries varies according to the issuer's control of the subsidiary. The Commission has established percentage of ownership tests to afford guidance in this area.

— Enforcement policy. These views reflect Commission policy and practice in implementing and enforcing the accounting provisions and are consistent with the cases brought by the Commission over the last three years. During this period, the Commission has addressed these areas prudently and with common sense. Similarly, the Commission has not sought out violations of the accounting provisions for their own sake; indeed, we have not chosen to bring a single case under these provisions that did not also involve other violations of law. The Commission, instead, places its greatest emphasis on encouraging an environment in which the private sector can meet its responsibilities in complying with the Act meaningfully and creatively. In that connection, the Commission has adopted enforcement policies in furtherance of this policy * * * .

* * *

[T]he Commission is meeting its difficult mandate of administering the accounting provisions of the Foreign Corrupt Practices Act in which we believe is a constructive and pragmatic manner. We have been receptive to—and responsive to—the comments and criticisms of the public, the business community, and the legal and accounting professions. * * * as a consequence, I believe progress has been made—and will continue—in assuring that public companies meet the statutory mandate for accurate records and meaningful internal accounting controls, without inflicting unreasonable costs on the business community and with only minimal federal intrusion upon internal corporate decisionmaking.

Chairman Williams' speech, coupled with congruent Commission action, calmed management fears to a large degree. Those fears were further calmed by amendments to Section 13(b) that covered some points of concern. Main among these amendments was the addition of a new paragraph (7) that says this: "For the purposes of paragraph (2) of this subsection, the terms 'reasonable assurances' and 'reasonable detail' mean such level of detail and degree of assurance as would satisfy prudent officials in the conduct of their own affairs." It is worth noting, however, that FCPA enforcement has, for several years, been a priority for both the SEC and the Department of Justice. Although the absolute number of actions varies (with 2016 seeing a record number), sanctions have continually run quite high. In addition, both the Department of Justice and the Commission have employed new tactics, such as examining employment practices and offering reduced penalties for self-reported violations. It also is worth noting that the agencies pursue individual as well as corporate defendants for FCPA violations.

D. IMPACT OF TWENTY-FIRST CENTURY LEGISLATION

The first years of the 21st century were marked by significant financial turmoil. The Enron, WorldCom and other scandals (in large part relating to accounting irregularities) spawned the Sarbanes-Oxley Act of 2002. The financial panic beginning in 2008 gave rise to the Dodd-Frank Act of 2010. The recession lingering after the panic prompted the JOBS Act of 2012 (and public sentiment at the same time led to the adoption of the Stop Trading on Congressional Knowledge Act, discussed in Chapter 13). Each of these Acts was, at the time of its adoption, billed as "the most sweeping change in financial regulation since the Great Depression." In the case of the Dodd-Frank and JOBS Acts, most of the changes made to securities regulation—as opposed to other types of financial regulation—were amendments to portions of the Securities and/or Exchange Acts that could be, and are, described in other portions of this book. This is also true of many of the changes made by Sarbanes-Oxley. Some of Sarbanes-Oxley's innovations, however, require additional explanation, as does Dodd-Frank's expansion and, in the case of emerging growth companies, the JOBS Act's relaxation of certain of those innovations.

As noted earlier in this chapter, Sarbanes-Oxley mandated passage of rules relating to officer certifications of periodic reports and internal controls. The rules passed by the Commission are not the complete story on officer certification, however. Sarbanes-Oxley amended the general criminal provisions in title 18 of the United States Code by adding a new Section 1350. This section requires chief executive and chief financial officers of Exchange Act reporting companies to certify, with each periodic report containing financial statements, that the report "fully complies with the requirements of [the Exchange Act] and that information contained in the periodic report fairly presents, in all material respects, the financial condition and results of operations of the issuer." The new criminal provision also sets heavy penalties for false certifications. The penalty for certifying compliance of the report with Section 1350, knowing the report is not in compliance, is up to $1 million or 10 years imprisonment, or both. If the false certification is also "willful," the penalties increase to us to $5 million or 20 years imprisonment, or both. As a result, many chief executive and chief financial officers are, among other things, requiring lower-level officers and others within the issuers to make certifications to them covering the matters that have to be certified to the Commission.

Sarbanes-Oxley also contained provisions designed to improve the audit process. One of these requires auditor certification of management's internal controls; another mandates auditor rotation. The JOBS Act excuses emerging growth companies from both of these requirements. Even emerging growth companies, however, must comply with other audit-related innovations (as well as other Sarbanes-Oxley requirements). These include Exchange Act Section 10A(m) and Sarbanes-Oxley Section 303. Exchange Act Section 10A(m) relates in various ways to audit committees of publicly held companies and states a requirement that each audit committee member be an independent member of the board of directors. Sarbanes-Oxley Section 303 makes it unlawful, in contravention of the Commission's rules, fraudulently to influence the conduct of audits for the purpose of making financial statements materially misleading. (Section 303 is particularly notable insofar as it specifically indicates that there is no private right of action for violation of this provision.)

Additional Sarbanes-Oxley provisions called for the Commission to pass rules relating to codes of ethics for financial officers, and disclosures of financial experts on audit committees. Pursuant to the resulting rules, although companies are not required to adopt ethics codes or to have financial experts on their audit committees, they are required to describe any circumstances under which they have chosen not to do so.

Sarbanes-Oxley made other changes that relate more tangentially to Exchange Act reporting but are discussed here because they have become of much interest to securities lawyers. First, Section 13(k) was added to the Exchange Act. This section basically makes it unlawful for any issuer, directly or indirectly, to extend or maintain credit, or to arrange to extend credit, in the form of a personal loan, for any director or executive officer, with specified exceptions. These include loans on market terms and certain home loans. The problem for lawyers is determining just what may or may not be considered maintaining or extending credit, or making arrangements for extending credit. Minor examples are allowing an officer to bill overnight delivery or telephone charges to his or her company, for convenience and to take advantage of the company's discount, with the charges to be repaid when the company receives the vendor's invoice. A much more troubling example is the so-called cashless exercise of stock options.

Moreover, Sarbanes-Oxley gave the Commission the authority to recoup for an issuer certain executive compensation. Basically, it calls for the return of bonuses or other incentive or equity-based compensation in the event of an accounting restatement due to material noncompliance with any financial reporting requirement as a result of misconduct. This "clawback" approach was augmented by a Dodd-Frank provision requiring public companies to adopt policies compelling the return of certain overpayments made to executives on the basis of financial results that require restating (whether or not misconduct was involved).

Consider the following, which nicely contrasts the opposing views on Sarbanes-Oxley and also has something to say about subsequent rounds of legislation.

A Social Defense of Sarbanes-Oxley

James Fanto.
52 New York Law School Law Review 517 (2007–2008).*

If one were to ask today in business and financial circles what has been, five years after its passage, the impact of the Sarbanes-Oxley Act of 2002 ("Sarbanes-Oxley") on the regulation of public corporations, one would be greeted by a litany of complaints and doomsday predictions. The legislation is now perceived as a media-driven congressional overreaction to a few salient corporate scandals (as opposed to a rational legal reform governed by hard-edged empirical analysis), which ended up imposing costs on U.S. corporations that exceeded the benefits that the regulations attempted to create. According to this view, Sarbanes-Oxley has had unintended, but predictable, consequences. To avoid its heavy regulatory burdens, foreign companies have been reluctant to list their securities in the United States, and domestic public companies have been forced into the private market. According to the prevailing view, the legislation designed to protect the U.S. public capital markets ironically ended up contributing to their demise. The message from this perspective is that it is necessary to repeal or weaken the legislation before it is too late—that is, before the public capital markets atrophy and before the United States loses its dominant position as the world's center of finance.

There is, however, another perspective on Sarbanes-Oxley. The history of modern U.S. business can be seen as one of occasional overreaching by the managerial and financial elite in public companies and the financial markets. Members of this elite are checked in their misconduct by competitors and held back by social norms that, if necessary, are enforced by market regulators and prosecutors as representatives of society. The creation of a new wealth available for distribution often leads to overreaching by members of the elite, a phenomenon that generally occurs in what financial scholars call a "bubble." In a bubble, members of the elite violate social and legal restraints, often resulting in criminal prosecution and regulatory action in the short term and legislation or regulation that addresses the specific abuses in the long term.

*   Copyright © 2007–2008 New York Law School Law Review; James Fanto. Reprinted with permission.

This perspective makes sense of Sarbanes-Oxley. The pre-Sarbanes-Oxley period was one in which, because of the Internet, new technology companies emerged with promises of tremendous growth and huge amounts of wealth to be made. Funds flowed freely to these companies, although only a few ever delivered on their promises. It was a classic bubble period. Company founders, corporate executives, venture capital investors, and investment bankers who helped take these companies public, in addition to accountants, lawyers, and even lay people, were affected by the "gold rush" environment. The Securities and Exchange Commission even went so far as to issue warnings meant for the many novice day traders.

The promises of great wealth overwhelmed social checks, informal codes of conduct, and even legal restraints, in the single-minded pursuit of self-interest. Investment and commercial bankers alike began to engage in such questionable practices as abandoning longstanding client relationships, switching allegiances to other companies to obtain higher fees, and acquiring future business by allocating shares of "hot" initial public offerings to executives of prospective clients. Some large public companies that had become successful during this period, like Enron, perverted the rules of capitalism altogether when they raised funds based upon a fraudulent view of their financial condition, and some companies simply fabricated their financial results. This excessive pursuit of self-interest was widespread. When the bubble burst with the NASDAQ crash of 2000 and the corporate scandals of Enron, WorldCom, and Tyco, among others, were revealed, public disapproval of the pursuit of self-interest by the elite could finally be expressed. Since the overreaching by the elite was widespread, government authorities reacted vigorously. There were criminal prosecutions, regulatory investigations and enforcement actions, changes to SEC and self-regulatory organization regulation, and eventually, Sarbanes-Oxley, which imposed new regulations on public companies.

At its core, therefore, Sarbanes-Oxley was an expression of social outrage at misconduct by some members of the elite during the late 1990s. It is commonly understood that a healthy, vibrant society cannot endure if its dominant members, who are necessary for value creation because of their managerial, technical, and financial expertise, take most of the value for themselves and pursue their self-interest unchecked. Social norms exist to impose limits on this socially destructive behavior.

Sarbanes-Oxley was passed during a crisis after a significant fall in the U.S. public capital markets, and its passage involved all kinds of political horse-trading. The resulting legislation was imperfect—some parts were valuable and followed longstanding regulatory proposals, while others emerged in reaction to certain scandals. Sarbanes-Oxley sent a symbolic message that the excessive pursuit of self-interest was socially destructive. It did this by reaffirming the need for professionalism in the capital markets, which is itself a social value.

* * *

CHAPTER 10

PROXY REGULATION

SITUATION 10

Assume you are back at the time immediately prior to the Compuform merger and are given the task of helping Microtec obtain the approval of its shareholders, which is required under state corporation law.

In considering this situation, refer to the following, in addition to the materials in this chapter: Exchange Act Sections 10C, 10D, 14(a), (b), (c), 14A, 21D, and 21E and Regulation 14A under the Exchange Act.

A. REGULATORY SCHEME

I. GENERAL OVERVIEW

At the heart of the Exchange Act's scheme for the regulation of proxy solicitations is Section 14(a):

> It shall be unlawful for any person, by the use of the mails or by any means or instrumentality of interstate commerce or of any facility of a national securities exchange or otherwise, in contravention of such rules and regulations as the Commission may prescribe as necessary or appropriate in the public interest or for the protection of investors, to solicit or to permit the use of his name to solicit any proxy or consent or authorization in respect of any security (other than an exempted security) registered pursuant to section 12 of this title.

Although the drafters used essentially the standard formula for invoking the jurisdictional means requirement, there is in fact no such requirement in Section 14(a). The addition of the words "or otherwise" in the jurisdictional means clause makes the entire clause surplusage. Section 14(a) is a classic administrative law provision. It embodies no substantive regulation, but simply gives the Commission the power to pass rules. The section then provides that the rules have the force of law.

Section 14(b) makes it unlawful for securities firms, and banks and others exercising fiduciary powers, to violate the Commission's proxy rules in respect of registered and certain other securities that are "carried for the account of a customer"—that is, securities that are beneficially owned by a customer but that are owned of record by the securities firm, bank, or someone else. Pursuant to Rules 14a–13, 14b–1, and 14b–2, the Commission has established a system under which proxy and related materials are sent to beneficial owners so that they can decide what action should be taken.[1]

Section 14(c) is a gap closing measure. The proxy statement required by the Commission under authority of Section 14(a) fills a niche in the Commission's overall scheme of disclosure. Not all companies under the Commission's jurisdiction need to solicit proxies, however. In some cases, one or a few insiders own sufficient securities to constitute a quorum. To prevent the void in disclosure that would exist if such companies could avoid sending security holders the information mandated by Section 14(a) and its rules, Section 14(c) requires that substantially equivalent information be filed with the Commission and sent to security holders any time management does not solicit proxies, consents, or authorizations in connection with a meeting.

To give effect to Section 14(a), the Commission adopted Regulation 14A. The rules that constitute this regulation provide detailed instructions for the preparation, filing,[2] and provision to security holders of proxy materials. Under Rule 14a–16, issuers and others soliciting proxies must post their materials on an Internet website and notify shareholders that the materials are available. Shareholders must also be provided with paper copies if they so request.

The formal disclosure document that must be filed and made available or given to security holders is called a proxy statement. Rule 14a–101, which is usually simply referred to as Schedule 14A, details the information that must be included in this statement. This information varies depending on the purpose of the meeting. The rule is voluminous and has much in common with Securities Act and Exchange Act registration statement forms.

Under Rule 14a–6, preliminary copies of the proxy statement and form of proxy may or may not have to be filed with the Commission at least ten days before they are used, depending on what matters are to be acted upon at the meeting. No such filings are required, for example, in the case of proxy materials for the most mundane annual meetings. In any case, however, definitive copies of each of those documents must be filed with the Commission (and any securities exchange upon which the issuer's securities are listed) not later than the date they are first used. Besides also providing details of filing requirements in specified situations, Rule 14a–6 deals with filing fees.

Proxy statements (and information statements required by Section 14(c)) are not the only communications governed by the proxy rules. The proxy form itself is covered, as is, with some exceptions, any "other

---

[1] Under modern business practice, a large percentage of publicly traded securities are owned of record by securities firms or others acting on their behalf, with their "real" owners having beneficial ownership.

[2] Proxy filings are subject to the requirements of the Commission's Electronic Data Gathering, Analysis and Retrieval System, Known as EDGAR, which mandates the electronic filings of proxy statements and most other material filed with the Commission.

communication to security holders under circumstances reasonably calculated to result in the procurement, withholding or revocation of a proxy."[3] The scope of this last provision is broad. It is easy to imagine all manner of communications that the provision would cover, including product advertising designed to bolster the image of management and planted news stories that may affect the outcome of the contest.

II. DISCLOSURES BY MANAGEMENT

Although everyone who seeks proxy authority is subject to the proxy rules, the rules are different for solicitations conducted by management than for other solicitations. The greatest difference is that proxy statements sent by management in connection with a typical annual meeting must be accompanied or preceded by an annual report that meets detailed requirements (or specified financial statements in the case of certain small business issuers). The annual report, together with the proxy statement, provides the security holders with basic information concerning the issuer and its recent financial history, along with specific information on matters to be voted on at the annual meeting. One of the most important matters at the annual meeting is the election of directors, and a substantial portion of the proxy statement consists of information concerning management's candidates for election to the board. The proxy statement also contains extensive disclosures regarding executive and director compensation, related person transactions, security ownership by officers and directors, director independence, and other corporate governance matters. Moreover, a "Compensation Discussion & Analysis" long has been required. The motivation for requiring this disclosure presumably is to discourage executives from paying themselves too handsomely.

The Dodd-Frank Act of 2010 had a somewhat significant impact on the regulation of proxy solicitation and, more broadly, executive compensation. New Sections 10C, 10D[4] and 14A, added to the Exchange Act, deal with matters relating to executive compensation. (As detailed below, however, the JOBS Act of 2012 limited the applicability of these provisions to emerging growth companies (which are more described in Chapters 3 and 9).

Pursuant to Section 14A, the proxy statements of companies registered under the Exchange Act must include a resolution providing for an advisory vote by shareholders on the executive compensation of certain named executive officers. This vote generally is referred to as "say on pay." A separate resolution must address the frequency with which

---

³ Exchange Act Rule 14a–1(*l*). As in the case of proxies, these other communications are subject to the filing requirements of Rule 14a–6 and the antifraud prohibitions of Rule 14a–9.

⁴ Although not related to disclosure or proxy regulation, Section 10D requires the Commission to adopt rules directing stock exchanges to prohibit listing a company unless it has a policy requiring recoupment of compensation in the event a restatement of financial statements occurs.

say on pay must occur, with the permissible variation between one and three years (this is known as "say on frequency"). A separate advisory resolution (known as "say on parachutes") is called for in the event special compensation—so-called "golden parachute" compensation—is to be granted in connection with a merger or similar transaction and has not already been included in a say on pay vote. Rule 14a–21 effectuates each of these changes; the JOBS Act of 2012, however, provides that emerging growth companies need not comply with these requirements.

Under Section 10C, enhanced disclosure of executive compensation and compensation practices (such as the use of advisors) is required. Moreover, stock exchanges must mandate that listed companies have compensation committees the members of which meet certain independence standards. The JOBS Act of 2012, however, liberated emerging growth companies from the enhanced disclosure requirements.

Dodd-Frank made two other notable changes in proxy regulation. First, an issuer's proxy statement must disclose the reasons that the company has selected one person to serve as both Chairman of the Board and Chief Executive Officer (or, if it has chosen to have different individuals serve in those positions, to justify that choice). Second, and very importantly, the Act prohibits brokers from using discretionary authority to vote proxies with respect to executive compensation, the election of directors, or other matters designated by the Commission. The Commission has designated say-on-pay, say-on-frequency, and say-on-parachutes as three of those matters.

III. SHAREHOLDER SOLICITATIONS AND PROPOSALS

Because of the far reach of the proxy rules, substantial concern has been expressed over the years about how far shareholders can go in discussing corporate matters among themselves, or in making public statements about those matters, without becoming subject to the proxy rules. These issues have been particularly important in the case of large institutional shareholders, who sometimes wish to take an active role in supporting or opposing specific corporate decisions. In response to these concerns, the Commission excluded from the definition of "solicitation," in most circumstances, public communications by shareholders as to how they intend to vote and their reasons for their decision.[5] The Commission also exempted from the proxy rules (except the rule prohibiting false or misleading statements) activities that would constitute solicitations, so long as the shareholders or other people involved (1) are not affiliated with management, (2) do not have an individual interest in the proposal to which the solicitation relates, and (3) do not seek proxy authority or provide to anyone proxy or other forms, such as consents, relating to

---

[5]   Exchange Act Rule 14a–1(*l*).

voting.[6] Another useful exemption permits non-management solicitation of up to ten persons.[7]

Rule 14a–2(b)(6) further expands the ability of shareholders to communicate without being characterized as engaging in proxy solicitation. They may participate in electronic shareholder forums, provided that such participation occurs more than 60 days prior to the date announced for an annual or special meeting of the shareholders of the relevant company. (Where an announcement is made less than 60 days before a meeting, the exemption will pertain for only two days after the announcement.) A communicating party must not solicit proxy authority while relying on the exemption, but may later engage in a solicitation complying with Regulation 14A. Importantly, although the focus of the expansion was the facilitation of intra-shareholder communication, management also may participate.

In some circumstances, a security holder may wish to solicit proxies from fellow security holders. If a security holder does so, compliance with the general regulatory scheme is required. The cost of compliance, however, could be prohibitive. In light of this, the Commission adopted Rule 14a–8, which now is cast in a user-friendly question and answer format. Rule 14a–8 requires management to include in its proxy statement proposals made by security holders, along with supporting statements (up to 500 words, including the proposal itself), when certain conditions are met. These conditions cover such things as timeliness, amount of securities held, and most importantly, the subject of the proposal. An issuer may refuse to include a proposal on a number of grounds, including that the proposal: (1) under the laws of the issuer's state of incorporation is not a proper subject for action by security holders, (2) deals with a matter relating to the conduct of the ordinary business operations of the issuer, or (3) relates to an election to office. When a proxy statement includes a proposal of a security holder, the proxy form must provide security holders with a mechanism for telling the proxy holder how to vote on the proposal. If management wishes to exclude a security holder's proposal, it must make a filing with the Commission in which, among other things, it states its reasons. These filings take the form of no-action letter requests. As a result, much "law" on Rule 14a–8 can be found in the responses of the Commission's staff to those requests and in staff legal bulletins 14 through 14H, which relate to proposals of security holders. Excerpts from the most recent such bulletin appear below, addressing the possibility of excluding proposals that conflict with management's own proposals or that relate to the company's ordinary business.

---

[6]   Exchange Act Rule 14a–2(b)(1).
[7]   Exchange Act Rule 14a–2(b)(2).

Securities and Exchange Commission
Staff Legal Bulletin No. 14H (CF)

Division of Corporation Finance (Oct. 22, 2015).

* * *

A.   The purpose of this bulletin

This bulletin is part of a continuing effort by the Division to provide guidance on important issues arising under Exchange Act Rule 14a–8. Specifically, this bulletin contains information about the Division's views on:

- the scope and application of Rule 14a–8(i)(9); and

- the scope and application of Rule 14a–8(i)(7) in light of *Trinity Wall Street* v. *WalMart Stores, Inc.*[, 792 F.3d 323 (3d Cir. 2015)].

* * *

B.   Rule 14a–8(i)(9)

* * *

Based on our review of the history of the exclusion, we believe that it was intended to prevent shareholders from using Rule 14a–8 to circumvent the proxy rules governing solicitations. When a shareholder solicits in opposition to a management proposal, the Commission's proxy rules contain additional procedural and disclosure requirements that are not required by Rule 14a–8. We do not believe the shareholder proposal process should be used as a means to conduct a solicitation in opposition without complying with these requirements. * * *

Many of the Division's response letters granting no-action relief under the exclusion have expressed the view that a shareholder proposal was excludable if including it, along with a management proposal, could present "alternative and conflicting decisions for the shareholders" and create the potential for "inconsistent and ambiguous results." The response letters have used variations of this language for decades to articulate when a shareholder proposal may be excluded. This language focused on the potential for shareholder confusion and inconsistent mandates, instead of more specifically on the nature of the conflict between a management and shareholder proposal.

After reviewing the history of Rule 14a–8(i)(9) and based on our understanding of the rule's intended purpose, we believe that any assessment of whether a proposal is excludable under this basis should focus on whether there is a direct conflict between the management and shareholder proposals. For this purpose, we believe that a direct conflict would exist if a reasonable shareholder could not logically vote in favor of both proposals, *i.e.*, a vote for one proposal is tantamount to a vote against the other proposal. While this articulation may be a higher burden for some companies seeking to exclude a proposal to meet than had been the case under our previous formulation, we believe it is most consistent with the history of the rule and more appropriately focuses on whether a reasonable shareholder could vote favorably on both proposals or whether they are, in essence, mutually exclusive proposals.

In considering no-action requests under Rule 14a–8(i)(9) going forward, we will focus on whether a reasonable shareholder could logically vote for both proposals. For example, where a company seeks shareholder approval of a merger, and a shareholder proposal asks shareholders to vote against the merger, we would agree that the proposals directly conflict. Similarly, a shareholder proposal that asks for the separation of the company's chairman and CEO would directly conflict with a management proposal seeking approval of a bylaw provision requiring the CEO to be the chair at all times.

We will not, however, view a shareholder proposal as directly conflicting with a management proposal if a reasonable shareholder, although possibly preferring one proposal over the other, could logically vote for both. For example, if a company does not allow shareholder nominees to be included in the company's proxy statement, a shareholder proposal that would permit a shareholder or group of shareholders holding at least 3% of the company's outstanding stock for at least 3 years to nominate up to 20% of the directors would not be excludable if a management proposal would allow shareholders holding at least 5% of the company's stock for at least 5 years to nominate for inclusion in the company's proxy statement 10% of the directors. This is because both proposals generally seek a similar objective, to give shareholders the ability to include their nominees for director alongside management's nominees in the proxy statement, and the proposals do not present shareholders with conflicting decisions such that a reasonable shareholder could not logically vote in favor of both proposals.

Similarly, a shareholder proposal asking the compensation committee to implement a policy that equity awards would have no less than four-year annual vesting would not directly conflict with a management proposal to approve an incentive plan that gives the compensation committee discretion to set the vesting provisions for equity awards. This is because a reasonable shareholder could logically vote for a compensation plan that gives the compensation committee the discretion to determine the vesting of awards, as well as a proposal seeking implementation of a specific vesting policy that would apply to future awards granted under the plan.

In the preceding examples, the board of directors may have to consider the effects of both proposals if both the company and shareholder proposals are approved by shareholders. We do not believe, however, that such a decision represents the kind of "direct conflict" the rule was designed to address.[8]

* * *

C. Rule 14a–8(i)(7)

In *Trinity Wall Street v. Wal-Mart Stores, Inc.,* the U.S. Court of Appeals for the Third Circuit addressed the application of Rules 14a–8(i)(3) and 14a–8(i)(7).[9] Reversing a decision by the U.S. District Court for the District of Delaware which ruled that a shareholder proposal could not be excluded, a three-judge panel held that a shareholder proposal submitted to Wal-Mart Stores, Inc. ("Wal-Mart") was excludable under Rules 14a–8(i)(3) and 14a–8(i)(7). The staff had previously agreed that Wal-Mart could exclude the proposal under Rule 14a–8(i)(7).

In analyzing whether the proposal was excludable under Rule 14a–8(i)(7), the Third Circuit concluded that the proposal's subject matter related to Wal-Mart's ordinary business operations—specifically, "a potential change in the way Wal-Mart decides which products to sell." This conclusion was the same as our conclusion when responding to Wal-Mart's no-action request. We believe our analysis in this matter is consistent with the views the Commission has expressed on how to analyze proposals under the ordinary business exclusion, *i.e.,* the analysis should focus on the underlying subject matter of a proposal's request for board or committee review regardless of how the proposal is framed.

The panel also considered whether the significant policy exception to the ordinary business exclusion applied. The majority opinion employed a new two-part test, concluding that "a shareholder must do more than focus its proposal on a significant policy issue; the subject matter of its proposal must 'transcend' the company's ordinary business." [792 F.3d at 346–347.] The majority opinion found that to transcend a company's ordinary business, the significant policy issue must be "divorced from how a company approaches the nittygritty of its core business." [*Id.* at 347.] This two-part approach differs from the

---

[8]   We recognize, however, that there may be instances in which a binding shareholder and management proposal would directly conflict. We do not believe that a reasonable shareholder would logically vote for two proposals, each of which has binding effect, that contain two mutually exclusive mandates. However, consistent with the Division's practice under Rule 14a–8(i)(1), our no-action response may allow proponents to revise a proposal's form from binding to nonbinding. If revised within a specified time, and a reasonable shareholder could otherwise logically vote for both proposals, the shareholder proposal would not be excludable under Rule 14a–8(i)(9). In addition, a binding shareholder proposal on the same subject as a binding management proposal may be excludable under Rules 14a–8(i)(1) or 14a–8(i)(2) to the extent a company demonstrates that it is excludable under one of those bases.

[9]   Rule 14a–8(i)(3) permits a company to exclude a shareholder proposal "[i]f the proposal or supporting statement is contrary to * * * [Rule] 14a–9, which prohibits materially false or misleading statements in proxy soliciting materials" and Rule 14a–8(i)(7) permits a company to exclude a shareholder proposal "[i]f the proposal deals with a matter relating to the company's ordinary business operations."

Commission's statements on the ordinary business exclusion and Division practice.

In contrast, the concurring judge analyzed Rule 14a–8(i)(7) in a manner consistent with the approach articulated by the Commission and applied by the Division, including in WalMart's no-action request. Summarizing the Commission's history on this exclusion, the judge noted that "whether a proposal focuses on an issue of social policy that is sufficiently significant is not separate and distinct from whether the proposal transcends a company's ordinary business. Rather, a proposal is sufficiently significant 'because' it transcends day-to-day business matters." [Id. at 353 (Schwartz, J., concurring).] The judge also explained that the Commission "treats the significance and transcendence concepts as interrelated, rather than independent." [Id.]

Although we had previously concluded that the significant policy exception does not apply to the proposal that was submitted to Wal-Mart, we are concerned that the new analytical approach introduced by the Third Circuit goes beyond the Commission's prior statements and may lead to the unwarranted exclusion of shareholder proposals. Whereas the majority opinion viewed a proposal's focus as separate and distinct from whether a proposal transcends a company's ordinary business, the Commission has not made a similar distinction. Instead, as the concurring judge explained, the Commission has stated that proposals focusing on a significant policy issue are not excludable under the ordinary business exception "*because* the proposals would transcend the day-to-day business matters and raise policy issues so significant that it would be appropriate for a shareholder vote."[10] Thus, a proposal may transcend a company's ordinary business operations even if the significant policy issue relates to the "nitty-gritty of its core business." Therefore, proposals that focus on a significant policy issue transcend a company's ordinary business operations and are not excludable under Rule 14a–8(i)(7). The Division intends to continue to apply Rule 14a–8(i)(7) as articulated by the Commission and consistent with the Division's prior application of the exclusion, as endorsed by the concurring judge, when considering no-action requests that raise Rule 14a–8(i)(7) as a basis for exclusion.

Transcend not excluded

––––––––––––

It is fair to say that the Commission has not been entirely consistent in its interpretation of some of the grounds for excluding shareholder proposals. These notably include the meaning of "matter relating to the conduct of ordinary business operations," discussed above in Staff Legal Bulletin No. 14H, and "relates to an election to office." With respect to the latter, the Dodd-Frank Act empowered the Commission to adopt rules allowing certain shareholders (basically, groups that have held three percent of voting power for at least three years) to include director

––––––––––––

[10]   Release No. 34–40018 (May 21, 1998) (emphasis added).

nominees in the company's proxy materials. In response to this grant, the Commission finalized a rule that subsequently was declared by the District of Columbia Circuit Court of Appeals invalid as an arbitrary and capricious exercise of the Commission's discretion. The Commission then declared effective an amendment to Rule 14a–8 that is intended to require management to include in its proxy materials shareholder proposals to create proxy access procedures on a company-by-company basis. It accomplishes this by limiting the previous broad exclusion for proposals relating to elections to office. As amended, the exclusion (in Rule 14a–8(i)(8) now provides that a proposal can be excluded if it:

(1) Would disqualify a nominee who is standing for election;

(2) Would remove a director from office before his or her term expired;

(3) Questions the competence, business judgment, or character of one or more nominees or directors;

(4) Seeks to include a specific individual in the company's proxy materials for election to the board of directs; or

(5) Otherwise could affect the outcome of the upcoming election of directors.

Very importantly, however, Rule 14a–8(i)(10) also permits the exclusion of proposals that already have substantially been implemented. The vast majority of recent shareholder attempts to submit proxy access proposals have been defeated on this basis. This is because a large number of companies proactively adopted proxy access measures.

B. FALSE OR MISLEADING STATEMENTS

Most litigation in the proxy area has involved Rule 14a–9(a), which states Regulation 14A's antifraud prohibitions:

No solicitation subject to this regulation shall be made by means of any proxy statement, form of proxy, notice of meeting or other communication, written or oral, containing any statement which, at the time and in the light of the circumstances under which it is made, is false or misleading with respect to any material fact, or which omits to state any material fact necessary in order to make the statements therein not false or misleading or necessary to correct any statement in any earlier communication with respect to the solicitation of a proxy for the same meeting or subject matter which has become false or misleading.

In J.I. Case Co. v. Borak, 377 U.S. 426 (1964), the Supreme Court (utilizing a free-wheeling approach from which it has retreated) held that an implied private right of action exists for violations of Rule 14a–9. Notice, however, that this does not answer the question of who has standing to bring the action. *Borak* involved a suit by a shareholder. In Royal Business Group, Inc. v. Realist, Inc., 933 F.2d 1056 (1st Cir. 1991), for example, the court held that when a plaintiff's claim arises from its role as a proxy contestant, it does not have standing to bring a Rule 14a–9 claim.

I. MATERIALITY AND CAUSATION

Under Rule 14a–9, as well as all other antifraud rules, a misstatement or omission must be material before it gives rise to a cause of action. The current standard of materiality, which with modification is now used in all securities law contexts, was set forth by the Supreme Court in the following Rule 14a–9 case.

TSC Industries, Inc. v. Northway, Inc.

Supreme Court of the United States, 1976.
426 U.S. 438.

■ MR. JUSTICE MARSHALL delivered the opinion of the Court.

* * *

I

The dispute in this case centers on the acquisition of petitioner TSC Industries, Inc., by petitioner National Industries, Inc. * * *

This is an action brought by respondent Northway, a TSC shareholder, against TSC and National, claiming that their joint proxy statement [relating to the acquisition] was incomplete and materially misleading in violation of § 14(a) of the Securities Exchange Act of 1934 and [Rule] 14a–9 promulgated thereunder. The Rule 14a–9 claim, insofar as it concerns us, is that TSC and National omitted from the proxy statement material facts relating to the degree of National's control over TSC and the favorability of the terms of the proposal to TSC shareholders.

[The District Court denied Northway's motion for summary judgment, but the Court of Appeals reversed,] holding that certain omissions of fact were material as a matter of law.

* * *

II

* * *

C

In formulating a standard of materiality under Rule 14a–9, we are guided, of course, by the recognition in [J.I. Case Co. v. Borak, 377 U.S. 426 (1964),] and [Mills v. Electric Auto-Lite Co., 396 U.S. 375 (1970),] of the rule's broad remedial purpose. That purpose is not merely to ensure by judicial means that the transaction, when judged by its real terms, is fair and otherwise adequate, but to ensure disclosures by corporate management in order to enable the shareholders to make an informed choice. As an abstract proposition, the most desirable role for a court in a suit of this sort, coming after the consummation of the proposed transaction, would perhaps be to determine whether in fact the proposal would have been favored by the shareholders and consummated in the absence of any misstatement or omission. But as we recognized in *Mills,* such matters are not subject to determination with certainty. Doubts as to the critical nature of information misstated or omitted will be commonplace. And particularly in view of the prophylactic purpose of the Rule and the fact that the content of the proxy statement is within management's control, it is appropriate that these doubts be resolved in favor of those the statute is designed to protect.

We are aware, however, that the disclosure policy embodied in the proxy regulations is not without limit. Some information is of such dubious significance that insistence on its disclosure may accomplish more harm than good. The potential liability for a Rule 14a–9 violation can be great indeed, and if the standard of materiality is unnecessarily low, not only may the corporation and its management be subjected to liability for insignificant omissions or misstatements, but also management's fear of exposing itself to substantial liability may cause it simply to bury the shareholders in an avalanche of trivial information-a result that is hardly conducive to informed decisionmaking. Precisely these dangers are presented, we think, by the definition of a material fact adopted by the Court of Appeals in this case-a fact which a reasonable shareholder *might* consider important. We agree with Judge Friendly, speaking for the Court of Appeals in [Gerstle v. Gamble-Skogmo, Inc., 478 F.2d 1281 (2d Cir.1973)], that the "might" formulation is "too suggestive of mere possibility, however unlikely."

The general standard of materiality that we think best comports with the policies of Rule 14a–9 is as follows: An omitted fact is material if there is a substantial likelihood that a reasonable shareholder would consider it important in deciding how to vote. This standard is fully consistent with *Mills'* general description of materiality as a requirement that "the defect have a significant *propensity* to affect the voting process." It does not require proof of a substantial likelihood that disclosure of the omitted fact would have caused the reasonable investor to change his vote. What the standard does contemplate is a showing of a substantial likelihood that, under all the circumstances, the omitted fact would have assumed actual significance in the deliberations of the reasonable shareholder. Put another way, there must be a substantial likelihood that the disclosure of the omitted fact would have been viewed by the reasonable investor as having significantly altered the "total mix" of information made available.

D

The issue of materiality may be characterized as a mixed question of law and fact, involving as it does the application of a legal standard to a particular set of facts. In considering whether summary judgment on the issue is appropriate, we must bear in mind that the underlying objective facts, which will often be free from dispute, are merely the starting point for the ultimate determination of materiality. The determination requires delicate assessments of the inferences a "reasonable shareholder" would draw from a given set of facts and the significance of those inferences to him, and these assessments are peculiarly ones for the trier of fact. Only if the established omissions are "so obviously important to an investor, that reasonable minds cannot differ on the question of materiality" is the ultimate issue of materiality appropriately resolved "as a matter of law" by summary judgment.

[After analysis, the court concluded that "none of the omissions claimed to have been in violation of Rule 14a–9 were, so far as the record reveals, materially misleading as a matter of law, and Northway was not entitled to partial summary judgment."]

———————

The "bespeaks caution" doctrine needs to be considered when deciding whether a particular misstatement or omission is material. Under that doctrine, a misstatement or omission can be rendered immaterial if it appears in the context of a document that contains sufficient cautionary language that the document "bespeaks caution." Courts almost always limit the "bespeaks caution" doctrine to situations that involve forward-looking statements.

Also, forward-looking statements in proxy materials are covered by the general safe harbor provisions contained in Exchange Act Section 21E, so long as the requirements of that section are met, and subject to specified exclusions.

The Supreme Court has declared that causation is a required element in private right of action cases under Rule 14a–9. The interesting question is how to prove causation. The seminal case in this area is Mills v. Electric Auto-Lite Co.:

Mills v. Electric Auto-Lite Co.

Supreme Court of the United States, 1970.
396 U.S. 375.

■ Mr. Justice Harlan delivered the opinion of the Court.

* * *

I

Petitioners were shareholders of the Electric Auto-Lite Company until 1963, when it was merged into Mergenthaler Linotype Company. * * *

* * * They alleged that the proxy statement sent out by the Auto-Lite management to solicit shareholders' votes in favor of the merger was misleading, in violation of § 14(a) of the Act and SEC Rule 14a–9 thereunder. Petitioners recited that before the merger Mergenthaler owned over 50% of the outstanding shares of Auto-Lite common stock, and had been in control of Auto-Lite for two years. * * * Petitioners charged that in light of these circumstances the proxy statement was misleading in that it told Auto-Lite shareholders that their board of directors recommended approval of the merger without also informing them that all 11 of Auto-Lite's directors were nominees of Mergenthaler and were under the "control and domination of Mergenthaler". * * *

[T]he District Court for the Northern District of Illinois ruled as a matter of law that the claimed defect in the proxy statement was, in light of the circumstances in which the statement was made, a material omission. * * *

[T]he court found that under the terms of the merger agreement, an affirmative vote of two-thirds of the Auto-Lite shares was required for approval of the merger, and that the respondent companies owned and controlled about 54% of the outstanding shares. Therefore, to obtain authorization of the merger, respondents had to secure the approval of a substantial number of the minority shareholders. At the stockholders' meeting, approximately 950,000 shares, out of 1,160,000 shares outstanding, were voted in favor of the merger. This included 317,000 votes obtained by proxy from the minority shareholders, votes that were "necessary and indispensable to the approval of the merger." The District Court concluded that a causal relationship had thus been shown, and it granted an interlocutory judgment in favor of petitioners on the issue of liability, referring the case to a master for consideration of appropriate relief.

[T]he Court of Appeals for the Seventh Circuit * * * affirmed the District Court's conclusion that the proxy statement was materially deficient, but reversed on the question of causation. * * *

* * * [R]ightly concluding that "[r]eliance by thousands of individuals, as here, can scarcely be inquired into", the court [of appeals] ruled that the [causation] issue was to be determined by proof of the fairness of the terms of the merger. If respondents could show that the merger had merit and was fair to the minority shareholders, the trial court would be justified in concluding that a sufficient number of shareholders would have approved the merger had there been no deficiency in the proxy statement. In that case respondents would be entitled to a judgment in their favor.

* * *

II

* * * The decision below, by permitting all liability to be foreclosed on the basis of a finding that the merger was fair, would allow the stockholders to be bypassed, at least where the only legal challenge to the merger is a suit for retrospective relief after the meeting has been held. A judicial appraisal of the merger's merits could be substituted for the actual and informed vote of the stockholders.

The result would be to insulate from private redress an entire category of proxy violations-those relating to matters other than the terms of the merger. Even outrageous misrepresentations in a proxy solicitation, if they did not relate to the terms of the transaction, would give rise to no cause of action under § 14(a). Particularly if carried over to enforcement actions by the Securities and Exchange Commission itself, such a result would subvert the congressional purpose of ensuring full and fair disclosure to shareholders.

* * *

Where the misstatement or omission in a proxy statement has been shown to be "material," as it was found to be here, that determination itself indubitably embodies a conclusion that the defect was of such a character that it might have been considered important by a reasonable shareholder who was in the process of deciding how to vote. * * *

There is no need to supplement this requirement, as did the Court of Appeals, with a requirement of proof of whether the defect actually had a decisive effect on the voting. Where there has been a finding of materiality, a shareholder has made a sufficient showing of causal relationship between the violation and the injury for which he seeks redress if, as here, he proves that the proxy solicitation itself, rather than the particular defect in the solicitation materials, was an essential link in the accomplishment of the transaction. This objective test will avoid the impracticalities of determining how many votes were affected, and, by resolving doubts in favor of those the statute is designed to protect, will effectuate the congressional policy of ensuring that the shareholders are able to make an informed choice when they are consulted on corporate transactions.[11]

---

[11] We need not decide in this case whether causation could be shown where the management controls a sufficient number of shares to approve the transaction without any votes from the minority. Even in that situation, if the management finds it necessary for legal or practical reasons to solicit proxies from minority shareholders, at least one court has held that

* * *

As the Supreme Court indicates in the footnote appearing at the end of *Mills,* it left open the question of "whether causation could be shown where the management controls a sufficient number of shares to approve the transaction without any votes from the minority." The opinion in the next case addresses this issue. It also deals with an interesting issue relating to what is a material fact.

Virginia Bankshares, Inc. v. Sandberg

Supreme Court of the United States, 1991.
501 U.S. 1083.

■ JUSTICE SOUTER delivered the opinion of the Court.[12]

* * *

The questions before us are whether a statement couched in conclusory or qualitative terms purporting to explain directors' reasons for recommending certain corporate action can be materially misleading within the meaning of Rule 14a–9, and whether causation of damages compensable under § 14(a) can be shown by a member of a class of minority shareholders whose votes are not required by law or corporate bylaw to authorize the corporate action subject to the proxy solicitation. We hold that knowingly false statements of reasons may be actionable even though conclusory in form, but that respondents have failed to demonstrate the equitable basis required to extend the § 14(a) private action to such shareholders when any indication of congressional intent to do so is lacking.

I

In December 1986, First American Bankshares, Inc., (FABI), a bank holding company, began a "freeze-out" merger, in which the First American Bank of Virginia (Bank) eventually merged into the Virginia Bankshares, Inc., (VBI), a wholly owned subsidiary of FABI. VBI owned 85% of the Bank's shares, the remaining 15% being in the hands of some 2,000 minority shareholders. FABI hired the investment banking firm of Keefe, Bruyette & Woods (KBW) to give an opinion on the appropriate price for shares of the minority holders, who would lose their interests in

---

the proxy solicitation might be sufficiently related to the merger to satisfy the causation requirement.

   [12] SOUTER, J., delivered the opinion of the Court, in Part I of which REHNQUIST, C.J., and WHITE, MARSHALL, BLACKMUN, O'CONNOR, SCALIA, and KENNEDY, JJ., joined, in Part II of which REHNQUIST, C.J., and WHITE, MARSHALL, BLACKMUN, O'CONNOR, and KENNEDY, JJ., joined, and in Parts III and IV of which REHNQUIST, C.J., and WHITE, O'CONNOR, and SCALIA, JJ., joined. SCALIA, J., filed an opinion concurring in part and concurring in the judgment. STEVENS, J., filed an opinion concurring in part and dissenting in part, in which MARSHALL, J., joined. KENNEDY, J., filed an opinion concurring in part and dissenting in part, in which MARSHALL, BLACKMUN, and STEVENS, JJ., joined. [Note adopted from syllabus of Reporter of Decisions.]

the Bank as a result of the merger. Based on market quotations and unverified information from FABI, KBW gave the Bank's executive committee an opinion that $42 a share would be a fair price for the minority stock. The executive committee approved the merger proposal at that price, and the full board followed suit.

Although Virginia law required only that such a merger proposal be submitted to a vote at a shareholders' meeting, and that the meeting be preceded by circulation of a statement of information to the shareholders, the directors nevertheless solicited proxies for voting on the proposal at the annual meeting set for April 21, 1987. In their solicitation, the directors urged the proposal's adoption and stated they had approved the plan because of its opportunity for the minority shareholders to achieve a "high" value, which they elsewhere described as a "fair" price, for their stock.

* * *

The jury's verdicts were for [the plaintiff] * * * finding violations of Rule 14a–9 by all defendants and a breach of fiduciary duties by the Bank's directors. The jury awarded Sandberg $18 a share, having found that she would have received $60 if her stock had been valued adequately.

* * *

On appeal, the United States Court of Appeals for the Fourth Circuit affirmed the judgments * * * . * * *

II

The Court of Appeals affirmed petitioners' liability for two statements found to have been materially misleading in violation of § 14(a) of the Act, one of which was that "The Plan of Merger has been approved by the Board of Directors because it provides an opportunity for the Bank's public shareholders to achieve a high value for their shares." Petitioners argue that statements of opinion or belief incorporating indefinite and unverifiable expressions cannot be actionable as misstatements of material fact within the meaning of Rule 14a–9, and that such a declaration of opinion or belief should never be actionable when placed in a proxy solicitation incorporating statements of fact sufficient to enable readers to draw their own, independent conclusions.

A

We consider first the actionability *per se* of statements of reasons, opinion or belief. Because such a statement by definition purports to express what is consciously on the speaker's mind, we interpret the jury verdict as finding that the directors' statements of belief and opinion were made with knowledge that the directors did not hold the beliefs or opinions expressed, and we confine our discussion to statements so made. That such statements may be materially significant raises no serious question. The meaning of the materiality requirement for liability under

§ 14(a) was discussed at some length in TSC Industries, Inc. v. Northway, Inc., 426 U.S. 438 (1976), where we held a fact to be material "if there is a substantial likelihood that a reasonable shareholder would consider it important in deciding how to vote." We think there is no room to deny that a statement of belief by corporate directors about a recommended course of action, or an explanation of their reasons for recommending it, can take on just that importance. Shareholders know that directors usually have knowledge and expertness far exceeding the normal investor's resources, and the directors' perceived superiority is magnified even further by the common knowledge that state law customarily obliges them to exercise their judgment in the shareholders' interest. Naturally, then, the share owner faced with a proxy request will think it important to know the directors' beliefs about the course they recommend, and their specific reasons for urging the stockholders to embrace it.

B

1

But, assuming materiality, the question remains whether statements of reasons, opinions, or beliefs are statements "with respect to * * * material fact[s]" so as to fall within the strictures of the Rule. Petitioners argue that we would invite wasteful litigation of amorphous issues outside the readily provable realm of fact if we were to recognize liability here on proof that the directors did not recommend the merger for the stated reason * * * .

* * *

Attacks on the truth of directors' statements of reasons or belief, however, need carry no such threats. Such statements are factual in two senses: as statements that the directors do act for the reasons given or hold the belief stated and as statements about the subject matter of the reason or belief expressed. * * * Reasons for directors' recommendations or statements of belief are * * * characteristically matters of corporate record subject to documentation, to be supported or attacked by evidence of historical fact outside a plaintiff's control. Such evidence would include not only corporate minutes and other statements of the directors themselves, but circumstantial evidence bearing on the facts that would reasonably underlie the reasons claimed and the honesty of any statement that those reasons are the basis for a recommendation or other action, a point that becomes especially clear when the reasons or beliefs go to valuations in dollars and cents.

It is no answer to argue, as petitioners do, that the quoted statement on which liability was predicated did not express a reason in dollars and cents, but focused instead on the "indefinite and unverifiable" term, "high" value, much like the similar claim that the merger's terms were "fair" to shareholders. The objection ignores the fact that such conclusory terms in a commercial context are reasonably understood to rest on a factual basis that justifies them as accurate, the absence of which renders them misleading. Provable facts either furnish good reasons to make a conclusory commercial judgment, or they count against it, and expressions of such judgments can be uttered with knowledge of truth or falsity just like more definite statements, and defended or attacked through the orthodox evidentiary process that either substantiates their underlying justifications or tends to disprove their existence. * * * In this case, whether $42 was "high," and the proposal "fair" to the minority shareholders depended on whether provable facts about the Bank's assets, and about actual and potential levels of operation, substantiated a value that was above, below, or more or less at the $42 figure, when assessed in accordance with recognized methods of valuation.

Respondents adduced evidence for just such facts in proving that the statement was misleading about its subject matter and a false expression of the directors' reasons. Whereas the proxy statement described the $42 price as offering a premium above both book value and market price, the evidence indicated that a calculation of the book figure based on the appreciated value of the Bank's real estate holdings eliminated any such premium. The evidence on the significance of market price showed that KBW had conceded that the market was closed, thin and dominated by FABI, facts omitted from the statement. There was, indeed, evidence of a "going concern" value for the Bank in excess of $60 per share of common stock, another fact never disclosed. However conclusory the directors' statement may have been, then, it was open to attack by garden-variety evidence, subject neither to a plaintiff's control nor ready manufacture, and there was no undue risk of open-ended liability or uncontrollable litigation in allowing respondents the opportunity for recovery on the allegation that it was misleading to call $42 "high."

* * *

2

Under § 14(a), then, a plaintiff is permitted to prove a specific statement of reason knowingly false or misleadingly incomplete, even when stated in conclusory terms. In reaching this conclusion we have considered statements of reasons of the sort exemplified here, which misstate the speaker's reasons and also mislead about the stated subject matter (e.g., the value of the shares). A statement of belief may be open to objection only in the former respect, however, solely as a misstatement of the psychological fact of the speaker's belief in what he says. In this case, for example, the Court of Appeals alluded to just such limited falsity in observing that "the jury was certainly justified in believing that the directors did not believe a merger at $42 per share was in the minority stockholders' interest but, rather, that they voted as they did for other reasons, e.g., retaining their seats on the board."

The question arises, then, whether disbelief, or undisclosed belief or motivation, standing alone, should be a sufficient basis to sustain an action under § 14(a), absent proof by the sort of objective evidence described above that the statement also expressly or impliedly asserted something false or misleading about its subject matter. We think that proof of mere disbelief or belief undisclosed should not suffice for liability under § 14(a), and if nothing more had been required or proven in this case we would reverse for that reason.

On the one hand, it would be rare to find a case with evidence solely of disbelief or undisclosed motivation without further proof that the statement was defective as to its subject matter. While we certainly would not hold a director's naked admission of disbelief incompetent evidence of a proxy statement's false or misleading character, such an unusual admission will not very often stand alone, and we do not substantially narrow the cause of action by requiring a plaintiff to demonstrate something false or misleading in what the statement expressly or impliedly declared about its subject.

On the other hand, to recognize liability on mere disbelief or undisclosed motive without any demonstration that the proxy statement was false or misleading about its subject would authorize § 14(a) litigation confined solely to what one skeptical court spoke of as the "impurities" of a director's "unclean heart." Stedman v. Storer, 308 F.Supp. 881, 887 (SDNY 1969) (dealing with § 10(b)). * * * While it is true that the liability, if recognized, would rest on an actual, not hypothetical, psychological fact, the temptation to rest an otherwise nonexistent § 14(a) action on psychological enquiry alone would threaten * * * strike suits and attrition by discovery * * *. We therefore hold disbelief or undisclosed motivation, standing alone, insufficient to satisfy the element of fact that must be established under § 14(a).

* * *

III

The second issue before us, left open in Mills v. Electric Auto-Lite Co., is whether causation of damages compensable through the implied private right of action under § 14(a) can be demonstrated by a member of a class of minority shareholders whose votes are not required by law or corporate bylaw to authorize the transaction giving rise to the claim. * * *

Although a majority stockholder in *Mills* controlled just over half the corporation's shares, a two-thirds vote was needed to approve the merger proposal. * * * The question arose whether the plaintiffs' burden to demonstrate causation of their damages traceable to the § 14(a) violation required proof that the defect in the proxy solicitation had had "a decisive effect on the voting." The *Mills* Court avoided the evidentiary morass that would have followed from requiring individualized proof that enough minority shareholders had relied upon the misstatements to swing the vote. Instead, it held that causation of damages by a material proxy misstatement could be established by showing that minority proxies necessary and sufficient to authorize the corporate acts had been given in accordance with the tenor of the solicitation, and the Court described such a causal relationship by calling the proxy solicitation an "essential link in the accomplishment of the transaction." In the case before it, the Court found the solicitation essential, as contrasted with one addressed to a class of minority shareholders without votes required by law or by-law to authorize the action proposed, and left it for another day to decide whether such a minority shareholder could demonstrate causation.

In this case, respondents address *Mills'* open question by proffering two theories that the proxy solicitation addressed to them was an "essential link" under the *Mills* causation test. They argue, first, that a link existed and was essential simply because VBI and FABI would have been unwilling to proceed with the merger without the approval manifested by the minority shareholder's proxies, which would not have been obtained without the solicitation's express misstatements and misleading omissions. On this reasoning, the causal connection would depend on a desire to avoid bad shareholder or public relations, and the essential character of the causal link would stem not from the enforceable terms of the parties' corporate relationship, but from one party's apprehension of the ill will of the other.

In the alternative, respondents argue that the proxy statement was an essential link between the directors' proposal and the merger because it was the means to satisfy a state statutory requirement of minority shareholder approval, as a condition for saving the merger from voidability resulting from a conflict of interest on the part of one of the Bank's directors, Jack Beddow, who voted in favor of the merger while also serving as a director of FABI. Under the terms of Va. Code § 13.1–691(A)(1989), minority approval after disclosure of the material facts about the transaction and the director's interest was one of three avenues to insulate the merger from later attack for conflict, the two others being ratification by the Bank's directors after like disclosure, and proof that the merger was fair to the corporation. On this theory, causation would depend on the use of the proxy statement for the purpose of obtaining votes sufficient to bar a minority shareholder from commencing proceedings to declare the merger void.

Although respondents have proffered each of these theories as establishing a chain of causal connection in which the proxy statement is claimed to have been an "essential link," neither theory presents the proxy solicitation as essential in the sense of *Mills'* causal sequence, in which the solicitation links a directors' proposal with the votes legally required to authorize the action proposed. As a consequence, each theory would, if adopted, extend the scope of [J.I. Case Co. v. Borak, 377 U.S. 426 (1964),] actions beyond the ambit of *Mills*, and expand the class of plaintiffs entitled to bring *Borak* actions to include shareholders whose initial authorization of the transaction prompting the proxy solicitation is unnecessary.

Assessing the legitimacy of any such extension or expansion calls for the application of some fundamental principles governing recognition of a right of action implied by a federal statute, the first of which was not, in fact, the considered focus of the *Borak* opinion. The rule that has emerged in the years since *Borak* and *Mills* came down is that recognition of any private right of action for violating a federal statute must ultimately rest on congressional intent to provide a private remedy, Touche Ross & Co. v. Redington, 442 U.S. 560, 575 (1979). From this the corollary follows that the breadth of the right once recognized should not, as a general matter, grow beyond the scope congressionally intended.

This rule and corollary present respondents with a serious obstacle, for we can find no manifestation of intent to recognize a cause of action (or class of plaintiffs) as broad as respondents' theory of causation would entail. At first blush, it might seem otherwise, for the *Borak* Court certainly did not ignore the matter of intent. Its opinion adverted to the statutory object of "protection of investors" as animating Congress' intent to provide judicial relief where "necessary," and it quoted evidence for that intent from House and Senate Committee Reports. *Borak*'s probe of the congressional mind, however, never focused squarely on private rights of action, as distinct from the substantive objects of the legislation, and one member of the *Borak* Court later characterized the "implication" of the private right of action as resting modestly on the Act's "exclusively procedural provision affording access to a federal forum." Bivens v. Six Unknown Fed. Narcotics Agents, 403 U.S. 388, 403, n. 4 (1971) (Harlan, J., concurring in judgment). In fact, the importance of enquiring specifically into intent to authorize a private cause of action became clear only later, see Cort v. Ash, 422 U.S. [66, 78 (1975)], and only later still, in *Touche Ross*, was this intent accorded primacy among the considerations that might be thought to bear on any decision to recognize a private remedy. There, in dealing with a claimed private right under § 17(a) of the Act, we explained that the "central inquiry remains whether Congress intended to create, either expressly or by implication, a private cause of action."

Looking to the Act's text and legislative history mindful of this heightened concern reveals little that would help toward understanding the intended scope of any private right. According to the House report, Congress meant to promote the "free exercise" of stockholders' voting rights, H.R. Rep. No. 1383, 73d Cong., 2d Sess., 14 (1934), and protect "[f]air corporate suffrage," id., at 13, from abuses exemplified by proxy solicitations that concealed what the Senate report called the "real nature" of the issues to be settled by the subsequent votes, S. Rep. No. 792, 73d Cong., 2d Sess., 12 (1934). While it is true that these reports, like the language of the Act itself, carry the clear message that Congress meant to protect investors from misinformation that rendered them unwitting agents of self-inflicted damage, [it] is just as true that Congress was reticent with indications of how far this protection might depend on self-help by private action. The response to this reticence may be, of course, to claim that § 14(a) cannot be enforced effectively for the sake of its intended beneficiaries without their participation as private litigants. But the force of this argument for inferred congressional intent depends on the degree of need perceived by Congress, and we would have trouble inferring any congressional urgency to depend on implied private actions to deter violations of § 14(a), when Congress expressly provided private rights of action in §§ 9(e), 16(b) and 18(a) of the same Act.

The congressional silence that is thus a serious obstacle to the expansion of cognizable *Borak* causation is not, however, a necessarily insurmountable barrier. This is not the first effort in recent years to expand the scope of an action originally inferred from the Act without "conclusive guidance" from Congress, see Blue Chip Stamps v. Manor Drug Stores, 421 U.S. [723], 737 (1975), and we may look to that earlier case for the proper response to such a plea for expansion. There, we accepted the proposition that where a legal structure of private statutory rights has developed without clear indications of congressional intent, the contours of that structure need not be frozen absolutely when the result would be demonstrably inequitable to a class of would-be plaintiffs with claims comparable to those previously recognized. Faced in that case with such a claim for equality in rounding out the scope of an implied private statutory right of action, we looked to policy reasons for deciding where the outer limits of the right should lie. We may do no less here, in the face of respondents' pleas for a private remedy to place them on the same footing as shareholders with votes necessary for initial corporate action.

A

Blue Chip Stamps set an example worth recalling as a preface to specific policy analysis of the consequences of recognizing respondents' first theory, that a desire to avoid minority shareholders' ill will should suffice to justify recognizing the requisite causality of a proxy statement needed to garner that minority support. It will be recalled that in *Blue Chip Stamps* we raised concerns about the practical consequences of allowing recovery, under § 10(b) of the Act and Rule 10b–5, on evidence of what a merely hypothetical buyer or seller might have done on a set of facts that never occurred, and foresaw that any such expanded liability would turn on "hazy" issues inviting self-serving testimony, strike suits, and protracted discovery, with little chance of reasonable resolution by pretrial process. These were good reasons to deny recognition to such claims in the absence of any apparent contrary congressional intent.

The same threats of speculative claims and procedural interactability are inherent in respondents' theory of causation linked through the directors' desire for a cosmetic vote. Causation would turn on inferences about what the corporate directors would have thought and done without the minority shareholder approval unneeded to authorize action. A subsequently dissatisfied minority shareholder would have virtual license to allege that managerial timidity would have doomed corporate action but for the ostensible approval induced by a misleading statement, and opposing claims of hypothetical diffidence and hypothetical boldness on the part of directors would probably provide enough depositions in the usual case to preclude any judicial resolution short of the credibility judgments that can only come after trial. Reliable evidence would seldom exist. Directors would understand the prudence of making a few statements about plans to proceed even without minority endorsement, and discovery would be a quest for recollections of oral conversations at odds with the official pronouncements, in hopes of finding support for ex post facto guesses about how much heat the directors would have stood in the absence of minority approval. The issues would be hazy, their litigation protracted, and their resolution unreliable. Given a choice, we would reject any theory of causation that raised such prospects, and we reject this one.

B

The theory of causal necessity derived from the requirements of Virginia law dealing with postmerger ratification seeks to identify the essential character of the proxy solicitation from its function in obtaining the minority approval that would preclude a minority suit attacking the merger. Since the link is said to be a step in the process of barring a class of shareholders from resort to a state remedy otherwise available, this theory of causation rests upon the proposition of policy that § 14(a) should provide a federal remedy whenever a false or misleading proxy statement results in the loss under state law of a shareholder plaintiff's state remedy for the enforcement of a state right. Respondents agree with the suggestions of counsel for the SEC and FDIC that causation be recognized, for example, when a minority shareholder has been induced by a misleading proxy statement to forfeit a state-law right to an appraisal remedy by voting to approve a transaction, or when such a shareholder has been deterred from obtaining an order enjoining a damaging transaction by a proxy solicitation that misrepresents the facts on which an injunction could properly have been issued. Respondents claim that in this case a predicate for recognizing just such a causal link exists in Va. Code § 13.1–691(A)(2) (1989), which sets the conditions under which the merger may be insulated from suit by a minority shareholder seeking to void it on account of Beddow's conflict.

This case does not, however, require us to decide whether § 14(a) provides a cause of action for lost state remedies, since there is no indication in the law or facts before us that the proxy solicitation resulted in any such loss. The contrary appears to be the case. Assuming the soundness of respondents' characterization of the proxy statement as materially misleading, the very terms of the Virginia statute indicate that a favorable minority vote induced by the solicitation would not suffice to render the merger invulnerable to later attack on the ground of the conflict. The statute bars a shareholder from seeking to avoid a transaction tainted by a directors conflict if, *inter alia*, the minority shareholders ratified the transaction following disclosure of the material facts of the transaction and the conflict. Va. Code § 13.1–691(A)(2) (1989). Assuming that the material facts about the merger and Beddow's interests are not accurately disclosed, the minority votes were inadequate to ratify the merger under state law, and there was no loss of state remedy to connect the proxy solicitation with harm to minority shareholders irredressable under state law. Nor is there a claim here that the statement misled respondents into entertaining a false belief that they had no chance to upset the merger, until the time for bringing suit had run out.

IV

The judgment of the Court of Appeals is reversed.

In addition to the general form of causation referred to above, which is called transaction causation, courts began requiring loss causation in cases under Rule 14a–9. Loss causation forms the link between the wrong complained of and the fact that the plaintiff has been damaged by the wrong, and to prove loss causation in a Rule 14a–9 case the plaintiff must show that he or she suffered a loss because of a proxy violation. Originally of judicial origin, the loss causation requirement now is codified in Exchange Act Section 21D(b)(4), which provides: "In any private action arising under [the Exchange Act], the plaintiff shall have the burden of proving that the act or omission of the defendant alleged to violate [the Act] caused the loss for which the plaintiff seeks to recover damages."

Further limiting plaintiffs' recoveries is Subsection 21D(e), which relates to a limitation on damages. The limitation applies in private actions where the plaintiff seeks to establish damages by reference to the market price of a security. Basically, Subsection 21D(e) provides that such damages cannot exceed the difference between the plaintiff's purchase or sale price and the mean trading price (as defined) "during the 90-day period beginning on the date on which the information correcting the misstatement or omission that is the basis for the action is disseminated to the market."

II. DEGREE OF FAULT REQUIRED

The Supreme Court has never determined the degree of fault required to support a finding of liability under Rule 14a–9. Courts of appeal have gone both ways on the question, with the choice being between negligence and scienter. Here are two of the most influential cases on this issue.

Gerstle v. Gamble-Skogmo, Inc.

United States Court of Appeals, Second Circuit, 1973.
478 F.2d 1281.

■ Before FRIENDLY, CHIEF JUDGE, OAKES, CIRCUIT JUDGE, and DAVIS, JUDGE.

■ FRIENDLY, CHIEF JUDGE:

This appeal and cross-appeal in a class action by minority stockholders of General Outdoor Advertising Co. (GOA), attacking its merger into defendant Gamble-Skogmo, Inc. (Skogmo), raise a variety of new and difficult questions with respect to the SEC's Proxy Rules, adopted under § 14(a) of the Securities Exchange Act, and the remedy for their violation. * * *

I.   The Facts

* * * [T]he gravamen of plaintiffs' complaint concerning the Proxy Statement sent to GOA's stockholders was that its disclosure that Skogmo expected to realize large profits from the disposition of such of GOA's advertising plants as had not been sold at the date of the merger was inadequate.

* * *

The fateful paragraph is this:

> If the merger becomes effective, it is the intention of Gamble-Skogmo, as the surviving corporation, to continue the business of General Outdoor, including the policy of considering offers for the sale to acceptable prospective purchasers of outdoor advertising branches or subsidiaries of General Outdoor with the proceeds of any such sales, to the extent immediately available, being used to further expand and diversify operations now being conducted or which might be acquired and conducted by Gamble-Skogmo or its new, wholly-owned subsidiary, GOA, Inc. There have been expressions of interest in acquiring many of the remaining branches of General Outdoor and discussions have taken place in connection therewith, but at the present time there are no agreements, arrangements or understandings with respect to the sale of any branch and no negotiations are presently being conducted with respect to the sale of any branch.

* * *

The merger was approved at the October 11 stockholders' meeting and became effective on October 17. The next day, Kluge made a package offer for the New York and Chicago plants and by October 28 Skogmo had agreed to sell the Chicago and New York plants to Metromedia for $13,551,121 representing a pre-tax profit of $7,504,802. * * * By July 13, 1964, GOA had contracted to sell all the United States plants which had remained at the date of the merger. [T]he sales prices amounted to

$25,081,121 as against a book value of $10,576,418, representing a pre-tax profit of $14,504,703 and an after-tax profit of some $11,740,875—more than a 25% addition to GOA's net worth as of May 31, 1963, as shown in the balance sheet attached to the Proxy Statement.

* * *

III. Liability

* * *

A.   Was the Proxy Statement Misleading?

* * *

* * * We rest our decision on the point that * * * the Proxy Statement must be faulted * * * as failing adequately to disclose that, upon completion of the merger, Skogmo intended to pursue aggressively the policy of selling GOA's plants, which had already yielded such a substantial excess of receipts over book value.

B.   What Is the Standard of Culpability in Suits for Damages for Violation of Rule 14a–9?

In contrast to the large quantity of ink that has been spilled on the issue whether a plaintiff seeking damages under Rule 10b–5 must make some showing of "scienter" and, if so, what, there has been little discussion of what a plaintiff alleging damage because of a violation of Rule 14a–9(a) must show in the way of culpability on the part of a defendant.[13] * * *

* * *

* * * Although the language of Rule 14a–9(a) closely parallels that of Rule 10b–5, and neither says in so many words that scienter should be a requirement, one of the primary reasons that this court has held that this is required in a private action under Rule 10b–5 is a concern that without some such requirement the Rule might be invalid as exceeding the Commission's authority under Section 10(b) to regulate "manipulative or deceptive devices." In contrast, the scope of the rulemaking authority granted under Section 14(a) is broad, extending to all proxy regulation "necessary or appropriate in the public interest or for the protection of investors" and not limited by any words connoting fraud or deception. This language suggests that rather than emphasizing the prohibition of fraudulent conduct on the part of insiders to a securities transaction, as we think Section 10(b) does, in Section 14(a) Congress was somewhat more concerned with protection of the outsider whose proxy is being

---

[13] Our discussion of this point is limited to the rights of persons who were invited by a proxy statement to participate in the taking of corporate action involving a change in the character of their securities, as in a sale of assets or a consolidation or merger. It does not include persons who have traded because of information in such a proxy statement, for whom the statement would seem to stand no differently from, say, an annual report to stockholders. We likewise do not pass on the principles that should govern liability of directors and other individuals having some responsibility for such a statement, as distinguished from a controlling corporation which has been the beneficiary of the action that was induced.

solicited. Indeed, it was this aspect of the statute that the Supreme Court emphasized in recognizing a private right of action for violation of Section 14(a) in [J.I. Case Co. v. Borak]. We note also that while an open-ended reading of Rule 10b–5 would render the express civil liability provisions of the securities acts largely superfluous, and be inconsistent with the limitations Congress built into these sections, a reading of Rule 14a–9 as imposing liability without scienter in a case like the present is completely compatible with the statutory scheme.

Although this does not mean that scienter should never be required in an action under Rule 14a–9, a number of considerations persuade us that it would be inappropriate to require plaintiffs to prove it in the circumstances of this case. First, many 10b–5 cases relate to statements issued by corporations, without legal obligation to do so, as a result of what the SEC has properly called "a commendable and growing recognition on the part of industry and the investment community of the importance of informing security holders and the public generally with respect to important business and financial developments." Securities Act Release No. 3844 (Oct. 8, 1957). Imposition of too liberal a standard with respect to culpability would deter this, particularly in light of the almost unlimited liability that may result. Such considerations do not apply to a proxy statement required by the Proxy Rules, especially to one, like that in the present case, which serves many of the same functions as a registration statement. Rather, a broad standard of culpability here will serve to reinforce the high duty of care owed by a controlling corporation to minority shareholders in the preparation of a proxy statement seeking their acquiescence in this sort of transaction, a consideration which is particularly relevant since liability in this case is limited to the stockholders whose proxies were solicited. While "privity" is not required for most actions under the securities laws, its existence may bear heavily on the appropriate standard of culpability.

Furthermore, the common law itself finds negligence sufficient for tort liability where a person supplies false information to another with the intent to influence a transaction in which he has a pecuniary interest. This is particularly so when the transaction redounded directly to the benefit of the defendant, in which case the common law would provide the remedies of rescission and restitution without proof of scienter. It is unlikely that Section 14(a) and Rule 14a–9 contemplated less.

We thus hold that in a case like this, where the plaintiffs represent the very class who were asked to approve a merger on the basis of a misleading proxy statement and are seeking compensation from the beneficiary who is responsible for the preparation of the statement, they are not required to establish any evil motive or even reckless disregard of the facts. Whether in situations other than that here presented "the liability of the corporation issuing a materially false or misleading proxy statement is virtually absolute, as under Section 11 of the 1933 Act with respect to a registration statement," Jennings & Marsh, Securities

Regulation: Cases and Materials 1358 (3d ed. 1972), we leave to another day.

* * *

Adams v. Standard Knitting Mills, Inc.

United States Court of Appeals, Sixth Circuit, 1980.
623 F.2d 422.

■ Before WEICK, ENGEL and MERRITT, CIRCUIT JUDGES.

■ MERRITT, CIRCUIT JUDGE.

In this securities fraud case, Peat, Marwick, Mitchell & Co., herein referred to as "Peat," a firm of certified public accountants, appeals from a judgment of the District Court in the amount of $3.4 million, plus pre-judgment interest, plus attorneys' fees of $1.2 million. The suit is a class action based upon causes of action implied under § * * *14(a) of the Securities Exchange Act of 1934 and SEC [Rule] 14a–9. It is based on an allegedly false proxy solicitation issued in order to gain shareholder approval of a merger between two corporations, Chadbourn, Inc. and Standard Knitting Mills, Inc., herein referred to as "Chadbourn" and "Standard." The primary issue is whether Peat is liable for a negligent error-the failure to point out in the proxy statement sent to stockholders of the acquired corporation that certain restrictions on the payment of dividends by the acquiring corporation applied to preferred as well as common stock. * * *

* * *

II.   LIABILITY FOR NEGLIGENT MISREPRESENTATION UNDER SEC [RULE] 14a–9

* * *

We turn to the question of the standard of liability under Rule 14a–9 pertaining to statements made in proxy solicitations. * * * Two circuits have examined the issue. Both have prescribed a negligence standard for the corporation issuing the proxy statement. One held that the negligence standard also applies to outside, nonmanagement directors, Gould v. American-Hawaiian Steamship Co., 535 F.2d 761, 777–78 (3d Cir.1976); and the other intimated in dicta, without deciding the issue, that a *scienter* standard probably should apply to outside directors and accountants, Gerstle v. Gamble-Skogmo, Inc., 478 F.2d 1281, 1300–1301 (2d Cir. 1973).

In view of the overall structure and collective legislative histories of the securities laws, as well as important policy considerations, we conclude that scienter should be an element of liability in private suits under the proxy provisions as they apply to outside accountants.

It is not simply a question of statutory interpretation. Federal courts created the private right of action under Section 14, and they have a special responsibility to consider the consequences of their rulings and to mold liability fairly to reflect the circumstances of the parties. Although we are not called on in this case to decide the standard of liability of the corporate issuer of proxy material, we are influenced by the fact that the accountant here, unlike the corporate issuer, does not directly benefit from the proxy vote and is not in privity with the stockholder. Unlike the corporate issuer, the preparation of financial statements to be appended to proxies and other reports is the daily fare of accountants, and the accountant's potential liability for relatively minor mistakes would be enormous under a negligence standard. In contrast to Section [12(a)(2)] of the 1933 Act which imposes liability for negligent misrepresentation in a prospectus, Rule 14a–9 does not require privity. In contrast to Section 11 of the 1933 Act which imposes liability for negligent misrepresentation in registration statements, Rule 14a–9 does not require proof of actual investor reliance on the misrepresentation. Rule 14a–9, like 10b–5, substitutes the less exacting standard of materiality for reliance, and in the instant case there was no proof of investor reliance on the notes to the financial statements which erroneously described the restriction on payments of dividends. We can see no reason for a different standard of liability for accountants under the proxy provisions than under 10(b).

We may not end our consideration there, however. We must turn to the legislative history of the proxy provisions. Section 14(a) and Rule 14a–9 are silent regarding the proper standard of liability. The Senate Report to the 1934 Act, commonly known as the Fletcher Report, discussed the sort of proxy abuse that Congress was trying to stop, that of corporate officers using the proxy mechanism to ratify their own frauds upon the shareholders, or outsiders soliciting shareholders' approval to plunder a ripe company. * * * The nature of each wrong deed depicted by the Report evidenced scienter.

An even more informative section of the Report is one describing the scope of 14(a):

> It is contemplated that the rules and regulations promulgated by the Commission will protect investors from *promiscuous* solicitation of their proxies, on the one hand, by irresponsible outsiders seeking to wrest control of a corporation away from honest and conscientious corporation officials; and, on the other hand, by *unscrupulous* corporate officials seeking to retain control of the management by *concealing* and *distorting* facts. (emphasis added) Senate Committee on Banking & Currency, S.Rep. No. 1455, 73d Cong., 2d Sess. 77 (1934).

The words "unscrupulous," "concealing," and "distorting" all imply knowledge or scienter; and we interpret "promiscuous" to mean reckless. In addition the characterization of irresponsible outsiders trying to "wrest control * * * from *honest* * * * corporate officials," implies dishonesty and hence scienter on the part of the outsiders. Consequently, the Report leads us to believe that its authors contemplated that 14(a) would be applied only against the knowing or reckless wrongdoing of outsiders.

The few times the proxy section was discussed in debate paint a similar picture of the type of misconduct against which 14(a) was directed. * * *

Another important consideration is Congressional intent regarding subsequent amendments that are indirectly linked to 14(a). In passing the Williams Act of 1968 governing tender offers, Congress expressed the desire that proxy statements and tender offers be governed by the *same* rules and regulations. This would logically extend to standards of liability. Because 14(e) pertaining to tender offers requires scienter, we believe there is a strong policy reason for imposing a similar standard on 14(a).

* * *

We conclude that 14(a) and 14(e) should be governed by the same standard of liability insofar as accountants' liability is concerned, and that an action under 14(a) requires proof of scienter. Finding no evidence of scienter, we reverse the imposition of liability under 14(a) and Rule 14a–9.

* * *

_____

Of some relevance to the "degree of fault" issue is Subsection 21D(f), added to the Exchange Act in 1995. The provision is complex. Some of its basic aspects are that in private actions under the Exchange Act, (i) a defendant generally is liable solely for the portion of a judgment that corresponds to the percentage of responsibility of that defendant, as determined as provided in Section 21D; (ii) a defendant is liable for damages jointly and severally only when the trier of fact specifically determines that the defendant knowingly committed a violation of the securities laws; and (iii) a defendant has a right of contribution, based on proportionate liability.

Note that Section 21D(b)(2) of the Exchange Act provides that in any private action under the Exchange Act in which the plaintiff may recover money damages only on proof that the defendant acted with a particular state of mind, the plaintiff must plead with particularity facts giving rise to a strong inference of that state of mind. This provision is further discussed in Chapter 12.

CHAPTER 11

TENDER OFFER REGULATION

SITUATION 11

Assume the same basic facts as in Situation 5b, relating to the Compuform acquisition, except assume that Compuform is a publicly held company with its common stock trading in the over-the-counter market at $5 per share. Assume further that Microtec wishes first to buy as much Compuform stock as it can afford in the trading markets and then, after acquiring several percent ownership, make an offer to all remaining Compuform shareholders for the exchange of Compuform stock for Microtec stock, currently trading at $12 per share, on the basis of two Compuform shares for each Microtec share. Finally, assume that Compuform's management is not in favor of the acquisition of Compuform by Microtec, but that management controls relatively few Compuform shares itself.

In considering this situation, refer to the following, in addition to the materials in this chapter: Exchange Act Sections 13(d) and (g), and 14(d), (e), and (f), and Regulations 13D–G and 14D and Rules 14e–1, 14e–3, and 14e–5 under the Exchange Act.

A. REGULATION OF TENDER OFFERS: THE WILLIAMS ACT

Tender offers in which the acquiring company offers its securities in exchange for shares in the target (often called "stock tender offers") have always been subject to the registration requirements of the Securities Act. Prior to 1968, however, tender offers in which the target's shareholders were offered cash in exchange for their shares (generally called "cash tender offers") were unregulated. During this period, a standard tactic of acquiring companies was to announce a tender offer in *The Wall Street Journal* that specified little more than the percentage of the target's stock the acquiring company would purchase and the price it would pay. Acquiring companies typically gave themselves broad power to hold tendered shares in limbo pending receipt of a specified minimum percentage of shares.

In the mid-1960s, Congress began working on a legislative response. Those who viewed tender offers negatively had the upper hand at first, and they caused the proposed legislation to be anti-tender offer in its effect. By the time the legislation was passed in 1968, however, it was widely regarded as neutral. This legislation, known as the Williams Act, added to the Exchange Act Sections 13(d) and (e) and 14(d), (e), and (f).

Section 13(d) is aimed at tender offers only indirectly. It requires a person who owns beneficially more than five percent of a class of equity security registered under the Exchange Act[1] to provide certain information to the issuer, to the Commission, and to each exchange on which the security is traded, within ten days after the acquisition of securities that triggers the reporting requirement. The section contains a list of such information, but it also gives the Commission the power to add or subtract from the list. Exchange Act Regulation 13D–G is the Commission's response, and it details the disclosure requirements. The resulting disclosure document, Schedule 13D, is designed to give management of the issuer basic information concerning potential tender offerors. This information includes the number of shares beneficially owned by the reporting person, the source of funds used to purchase the shares, and, if the purpose of the purchase of shares is to acquire control of the issuer, any plans of the reporting person to liquidate the issuer, to sell its assets, to engage it in a merger, or to effect any other major change in its structure. Under Section 13(d), amendments to this schedule must be filed upon the occurrence of material changes in the disclosed information. (In specified circumstances, shareholders are allowed to file a Schedule 13G, the requirements of which are less than those of Schedule 13D.) The other Williams Act provision in Section 13 is Section 13(e). It gives the Commission the power to regulate repurchases by issuers of their own equity securities. The Commission has done this by extensive rulemaking, including the requirement to file, in specified circumstances, Schedule 13E–3 and Schedule TO, which require substantially more disclosure than Schedule 13D.

The heart of the Williams Act is Section 14(d). Under this provision, it is unlawful to make a tender offer for an Exchange Act registered equity security[2] if success in the offer would result in ownership of more than five percent of the class, unless certain filings are made. The document used here is Schedule TO.

Section 14(d) also contains substantive regulation on three points. First, the section provides that securities deposited in response to a tender offer may be withdrawn within seven days after the date of the original tender offer, and after sixty days have elapsed following this date. By Rule 14d–7, the Commission has extended the withdrawal right to cover the entire period of the tender offer (although a bidder may open a subsequent offering period, after the original offer, that does not have withdrawal rights). That withdrawal right provides easy rescission for security holders who change their minds, along with protection against

---

[1]   Acquisitions of three other types of securities are covered also: an insurance company's equity securities that would be required to be registered under the Exchange Act save for a registration exemption, equity securities issued by a closed-end investment company registered under the Investment Company Act of 1940, and equity securities issued by a Native Corporation pursuant to Section 37(d)(6) of the Alaska Native Claims Settlement Act.

[2]   Also covered are tender offers for the types of equity securities mentioned in note 1, supra. Certain exceptions to all the requirements of Section 14(d) are specified in Section 14(d)(8).

having their securities tied up indefinitely while a tender offeror waits to receive its desired number of tenders. Second, Section 14(d) says that when a tender offer is for less than all the securities of a class, a tender offeror must purchase tendered securities pro rata, according to the number of securities tendered by each security holder during the first ten days the offer is open. By Rule 14d–8, the Commission has extended the pro rata purchase requirement to cover securities tendered at any time during the period of the tender offer. That requirement helps avoid the pressure security holders might otherwise feel to tender quickly and without adequate thought. It also protects small holders from being ignored in favor of larger holders. Third, when a tender offeror increases the tender offer price after some holders have tendered, Section 14(d) provides that all tendering security holders must be paid the higher price. Rule 14d–10 provides that all securities holders must receive the same price; specifically excluded, however, are payments for employment compensation, severance, or other similar benefits.

The Williams Act's anti-fraud provision is Section 14(e). It provides:

> It shall be unlawful for any person to make any untrue statement of a material fact or omit to state any material fact necessary in order to make the statements made, in the light of the circumstances under which they are made, not misleading, or to engage in any fraudulent, deceptive, or manipulative acts or practices, in connection with any tender offer or request or invitation for tenders, or any solicitation of security holders in opposition to or in favor of any such offer, request, or invitation.

Unlike the other Williams Act provisions, Section 14(e) relates not only to tender offers for specified types of securities, but to tender offers for any kind of security.

Section 14(f) is a specialized provision that calls for certain disclosures to the Commission and to security holders when a majority of a corporation's directorships are to be filled, otherwise than at a meeting of security holders, following an acquisition of securities that is subject to the requirements of Section 13(d) or 14(d). The usual trigger of this provision is the filling of vacant directorships by sitting directors, which is generally allowed under state corporation law.

Only a few of the rules under the Williams Act have been mentioned. The rules are voluminous and cover a wide variety of situations. These rules underwent a comprehensive reworking in 2000, the drive of which was to allow greater communication with security holders and additional disclosures to the securities markets. The Commission adopted provisions relating to business combinations, including Regulation M–A (which is a sub-part of Regulation S–K), relating to mergers and acquisitions. At the same time the Commission amended and adopted Securities Act rules for the purpose of better integrating its disclosure philosophy in this area under the Exchange Act with the disclosures the Commission requires under the Securities Act.

In 2000, the Commission focused on the so-called "mini-tender," which is unregulated under Section 14(d) but captured by Section 14(e).

Securities Exchange Act Release No. 43069

Securities Exchange Commission, July 24, 2000.

COMMISSION GUIDANCE ON MINI-TENDER OFFERS AND LIMITED PARTNERSHIP TENDER OFFERS

* * *

I.   Tender Offer Regulatory Scheme

* * *

Federal tender offer regulation is based on three statutory sections of the Exchange Act and our Regulations adopted under those sections. The applicability of each section and its underlying regulations depend on: (i) the party conducting the offers, (ii) the nature of the subject security, (iii) whether the security is registered under Section 12 of the Exchange Act, and (iv) whether or not the bidder would own more than five percent of the securities after the tender offer.

A.   Section 14(d) and Regulation 14D

Section 14(d) of the Exchange Act and Regulation 14D apply to all tender offers for Exchange Act registered equity securities made by parties other than the target (or affiliates of the target), so long as upon consummation of the tender offer the bidder would beneficially own more than five percent of the class of securities subject to the offer. * * * A bidder must include any shares it owns before the commencement of the tender offer in calculating the five percent amount. For example, if a bidder owns four percent of the target's securities before it commences the tender offer, it could not make an offer for more than one percent of the target's securities without triggering Section 14(d) and Regulation 14D requirements. * * *

Regulation 14D requires the bidder to make specific disclosures to security holders and mandates certain procedural protections. The disclosure focuses on the terms of the offer and information about the bidder. * * * The procedural protections include the right to withdraw tendered securities while the offer remains open, * * * the right to have the tendered securities accepted on a pro rata basis * * * throughout the term of the offer if the offer is for less than all of the securities, and the requirement that all security holders of the subject class of securities be treated equally. * * * Also, Regulation 14D requires the bidder to file its offering documents and other information with the Commission * * * and hand deliver a copy to the target and any competing bidders. * * *

* * *

C.   Section 14(e) and Regulation 14E

Section 14(e) of the Exchange Act is the antifraud provision for all tender offers, including mini-tender offers * * * . * * * Section 14(e) prohibits fraudulent, deceptive, and manipulative acts in connection with a tender offer. Regulation 14E provides the basic procedural protections for all tender offers * * * .

Section 14(e) and Regulation 14E apply to all tender offers, even where the offer is for less than five percent of the outstanding securities and offers where the bidder would not own more than five percent after the consummation of the offer. Section 14(e) and Regulation 14E apply to tender offers for any type of security (including debt). These provisions apply both to registered and unregistered securities (including securities issued by a private company), except exempt securities under the Exchange Act, such as municipal bonds.

Regulation 14E requires that a tender offer be open for at least 20 business days, * * * that the offer remain open for 10 business days following a change in the offering price or the percentage of securities being sought, * * * and that the bidder promptly pay for or return securities when the tender offer expires. * * * Regulation 14E also requires the target company to state its position about the offer within 10 business days after the offer begins. * * * The target must state either that it recommends that its security holders accept or reject the offer; that it expresses no opinion and remains neutral toward the offer; or that it is unable to take a position on the offer. * * * With a tender offer not subject to Regulation 14D, however, the bidder is not required to send its offer to the target. Therefore, the target may not know about the tender offer. The target should take all steps to comply with its obligations under Regulation 14E within 10 business days or as soon as possible upon becoming aware of the offer.

II.   Mini-Tender Offers

A.   Background

We have observed an increase in tender offers that would result in the bidder holding not more than five percent of a company's securities. These so-called "mini-tender offers" are generally structured to avoid the filing, disclosure and procedural requirements of Section 14(d) and Regulation 14D. These offers are subject only to the provisions of Section 14(e) and Regulation 14E. * * *

We are concerned that the substance of the disclosure in many of these offers is not adequate under Section 14(e) and Regulation 14E. We also are concerned that bidders are not adequately disseminating the disclosure to security holders. Further, we are concerned that many bidders are not paying for securities promptly at the expiration of the tender offer, as required by Regulation 14E. Recently, we have brought enforcement actions that address some concerns we have with mini-tender offers. * * *

The offering documents in mini-tender offers frequently are very brief and contain very little information. Often these mini-tender offers are made at a price below the current market price. However, frequently there is no disclosure of this fact in the offering documents or in any disclosure that the security holders ultimately receive. This lack of disclosure can mislead security holders because most tender offers, especially third-party offers, historically have been made at prices that are at a premium to the current market price. Many investors could reasonably assume that a mini-tender offer also involves a premium to market price. However, because of the lack of disclosure given to shareholders, it is often difficult for shareholders to determine the actual price that will be paid in the offer and whether it is below the market price.

Some bidders have devised schemes to confuse security holders about the actual offer price. For example, we have seen situations where a bidder makes an offer at a price above market price but never intends to purchase the shares in the offer at a premium. In these cases, the bidder holds the shares tendered and continuously extends the offer until the market price rises above the offer price. During this time, security holders generally are not permitted to withdraw their securities from the offer. Then the bidder purchases the shares at the offer price. In these situations, the bidder does not disclose this plan to security holders. * * * we believe these practices are "fraudulent, deceptive or manipulative practices" within the meaning of Section 14(e) * * * .

* * *

B. WHAT IS A TENDER OFFER?

Congress used the term "tender offer" in the Williams Act without definition. The Commission has the power to provide a definition by rule, but has chosen not to do so, presumably because it does not want to lose the flexibility provided by the statute. In the years since the passage of the Williams Act, the Commission and the courts have, however, worked toward a definition. This effort has reached its most refined form in the case of Wellman v. Dickinson,[3] in which the court accepted eight factors, which had been suggested by the Commission, as characteristic of a tender offer:

> (1) active and widespread solicitation of public shareholders for the shares of an issuer; (2) solicitation made for a substantial percentage of the issuer's stock; (3) offer to purchase made at a premium over the prevailing market price; (4) terms of the offer are firm rather than negotiable; (5) offer contingent on the tender of a fixed number of shares, often subject to a fixed

---

[3]   475 F.Supp. 783 (S.D.N.Y.1979).

maximum number to be purchased; (6) offer open only a limited period of time; (7) offeree subjected to pressure to sell his stock; and (8) public announcements of a purchasing program concerning the target company precede or accompany rapid accumulation of large amounts of the target company's securities.

The *Wellman* articulation of these factors has been accepted by other courts, including the Ninth Circuit in SEC v. Carter Hawley Hale Stores, Inc.[4] In that case, the court made it clear that all eight of the *Wellman* factors do not have to be present in a particular situation before it is recognized as a tender offer: "[R]ather, they provide some guidance as to the traditional indicia of a tender offer."

Some courts have used another well known test that grew out of a district court opinion in S–G Securities, Inc. v. Fuqua Investment Co.[5] That test is much simpler than the test in *Wellman,* but it is limited in that it only relates to specialized situations that do not fit the mold of classic tender offers. This test holds that a tender offer exists, for the purposes of Section 14(d), when there is:

　　(1) a publicly announced intention by the purchaser to acquire a substantial block of the stock of the target company for purposes of acquiring control thereof, and

　　(2) a subsequent rapid acquisition by the purchaser of large blocks of stock through open market and privately negotiated purchases.

In *Carter Hawley Hale,* the Ninth Circuit rejected this test on a number of bases. The court indicated that the test is "vague and difficult to apply" and that it "offers little guidance to the issuer as to when his conduct will come within the ambit of [one Commission rule rather than another]."

Finally, as indicated in the following case, the Second Circuit has chosen to pursue a course that is, at least formally, quite different from that followed in either *Wellman* or *Fuqua.*

<h2 style="text-align:center">Hanson Trust PLC v. SCM Corp.</h2>

United States Court of Appeals, Second Circuit, 1985.
774 F.2d 47.

■ Before MANSFIELD, PIERCE and PRATT, CIRCUIT JUDGES.

■ MANSFIELD, CIRCUIT JUDGE:

Hanson Trust PLC, HSCM Industries, Inc., and Hanson Holdings Netherlands B.V. (hereinafter sometimes referred to collectively as "Hanson") appeal from an order of the Southern District of New York * * * granting SCM Corporation's motion for a preliminary injunction

---

[4]　760 F.2d 945 (9th Cir.1985).

[5]　466 F.Supp. 1114 (D.Mass.1978).

restraining them, their officers, agents, employees and any persons acting in concert with them, from acquiring any shares of SCM and from exercising any voting rights with respect to 3.1 million SCM shares acquired by them on September 11, 1985. The injunction was granted on the ground that Hanson's September 11 acquisition of the SCM stock through five private and one open market purchases amounted to a "tender offer" for more than 5% of SCM's outstanding shares, which violated §§ 14(d)(1) and (6) of the Williams Act, and rules promulgated by the Securities and Exchange Commission (SEC) thereunder. We reverse.

The setting is the familiar one of a fast-moving bidding contest for control of a large public corporation: first, a cash tender offer of $60 per share by Hanson, an outsider, addressed to SCM stockholders; next, a counter proposal by an "insider" group consisting of certain SCM managers and their "White Knight," Merrill Lynch Capital Markets (Merrill), for a "leveraged buyout" at a higher price ($70 per share); then an increase by Hanson of its cash offer to $72 per share, followed by a revised SCM-Merrill leveraged buyout offer of $74 per share with a "crown jewel" irrevocable lock-up option to Merrill designed to discourage Hanson from seeking control by providing that if any other party (in this case Hanson) should acquire more than one-third of SCM's outstanding shares (66⅔% being needed under N.Y.Bus.L. § 903(a)(2) to effectuate a merger) Merrill would have the right to buy SCM's two most profitable businesses (consumer foods and pigments) at prices characterized by some as "bargain basement." The final act in this scenario was the decision of Hanson, having been deterred by the SCM-Merrill option (colloquially described in the market as a "poison pill"), to terminate its cash tender offer and then to make private purchases, amounting to 25% of SCM's outstanding shares, leading SCM to seek and obtain the preliminary injunction from which this appeal is taken. * * *

* * *

The typical tender offer, as described in the Congressional debates, hearings and reports on the Williams Act, consisted of a general, publicized bid by an individual or group to buy shares of a publicly-owned company, the shares of which were traded on a national securities exchange, at a price substantially above the current market price. The offer was usually accompanied by newspaper and other publicity, a time limit for tender of shares in response to it, and a provision fixing a quantity limit on the total number of shares of the target company that would be purchased.

* * *

* * * The borderline between public solicitations and privately negotiated stock purchases is not bright and it is frequently difficult to determine whether transactions falling close to the line or in a type of "no man's land" are "tender offers" or private deals. This has led some to

advocate [that we] adopt the eight-factor "test" of what is a tender offer, which was recommended by the SEC and applied by the district court in Wellman v. Dickinson, 475 F.Supp. 783, 823–24 (S.D.N.Y.1979), and by the Ninth Circuit in SEC v. Carter Hawley Hale Stores, Inc., [760 F.2d 945 (9th Cir.1985)]. * * * Although many of the [eight] factors are relevant for purposes of determining whether a given solicitation amounts to a tender offer, the elevation of such a list to a mandatory "litmus test" appears to be both unwise and unnecessary. As even the advocates of the proposed test recognize, in any given case a solicitation may constitute a tender offer even though some of the eight factors are absent or, when many factors are present, the solicitation may nevertheless not amount to a tender offer because the missing factors outweigh those present.

We prefer to be guided by the principle followed by the Supreme Court in deciding what transactions fall within the private offering exemption provided by § [4(2)] of the Securities Act of 1933 * * *. That principle is simply to look to the statutory purpose. In SEC v. Ralston Purina Co., 346 U.S. 119 (1953), the Court stated, "the applicability of § [4(2)] should turn on whether the particular class of persons affected need the protection of the Act. An offering to those who are shown to be able to fend for themselves is a transaction 'not involving any public offering.'" Similarly, since the purpose of § 14(d) is to protect the ill-informed solicitee, the question of whether a solicitation constitutes a "tender offer" within the meaning of § 14(d) turns on whether, viewing the transaction in the light of the totality of circumstances, there appears to be a likelihood that unless the pre-acquisition filing strictures of that statute are followed there will be a substantial risk that solicitees will lack information needed to make a carefully considered appraisal of the proposal put before them.

Applying this standard, we are persuaded on the undisputed facts that Hanson's September 11 negotiation of five private purchases and one open market purchase of SCM shares, totalling 25% of SCM's outstanding stock, did not under the circumstances constitute a "tender offer" within the meaning of the Williams Act. Putting aside for the moment the events preceding the purchases, there can be little doubt that the privately negotiated purchases would not, standing alone, qualify as a tender offer, for the following reasons:

(1) In a market of 22,800 SCM shareholders the number of SCM sellers here involved, six in all, was minuscule compared with the numbers involved in public solicitations of the type against which the Act was directed.

(2) At least five of the sellers were highly sophisticated professionals, knowledgeable in the market place and well aware of the essential facts needed to exercise their professional skills and to appraise Hanson's offer * * *.

(3) The sellers were not "pressured" to sell their shares by any conduct that the Williams Act was designed to alleviate, but by the forces of the market place. * * *

(4) There was no active or widespread advance publicity or public solicitation, which is one of the earmarks of a conventional tender offer. * * *

(5) The price received by the six sellers, $73.50 per share, unlike that appearing in most tender offers, can scarcely be dignified with the label "premium." The stock market price on September 11 ranged from $72.50 to $73.50 per share. * * *

(6) Unlike most tender offers, the purchases were not made contingent upon Hanson's acquiring a fixed minimum number or percentage of SCM's outstanding shares. * * *

(7) Unlike most tender offers, there was no general time limit within which Hanson would make purchases of SCM stock. * * *

* * *

C. ISSUES IN WILLIAMS ACT LITIGATION

Although a wide range of issues can be raised in litigation under the Williams Act, two have been of most interest. One involves the question of who may bring suit under the various statutory provisions, particularly Sections 13(d) and 14(e). The other relates to what type of conduct is proscribed by Section 14(e). These two issues are discussed below.

I. WHO MAY BRING SUIT?

In the event of a Williams Act violation, the Commission can, under Section 21 of the Exchange Act, bring an enforcement action in a district court seeking an injunction or it can, under Section 21C, issue a cease-and-desist order on its own. The Justice Department can seek a criminal indictment when it believes willfulness was involved in a breach. As in many other areas of the securities laws, the interesting issue involves whether private individuals may bring suit and, if so, which persons have standing.

a. SECTION 13(d)

Under Section 13(d), the major issue, now settled into a clear majority-minority situation, is whether an implied private right of action exists under which an issuer can sue shareholders who have violated the disclosure requirements of the section. In the classic action, a shareholder has acquired a substantial block of the issuer's stock, but has either failed to file the required Schedule 13D or has filed one that allegedly is defective. In these cases, the issuer typically seeks an injunction against further violations, in addition to an injunction that either requires the sale of the securities or prohibits the shareholder from voting them.

The best known Section 13(d) case fits this mold. It is Rondeau v. Mosinee Paper Corp.,[6] which the Supreme Court decided in 1975. In that case, the Court had to decide whether a district court had correctly refused to issue the requested injunction. Because of the facts in the case (involving a late filing of a Schedule 13D due to a lack of familiarity with the securities laws), the Supreme Court upheld the denial. It is important to note, however, that the defendant did not challenge the plaintiff's right to bring the action, and the Court did not question the existence of the right.

In the years following *Rondeau,* a number of circuit courts decided that issuers have a private right of action under Section 13(d) when they seek injunctive relief, or they have proceeded on that assumption. Indiana National Corp. v. Rich is one of the most persuasive, since it contains a reasoned analysis of the issue based on the Supreme Court cases on implied rights of action. This case appears directly below.

Indiana National Corp. v. Rich

United States Court of Appeals, Seventh Circuit, 1983.
712 F.2d 1180.

■ Before CUDAHY and ESCHBACH, CIRCUIT JUDGES, and GRAY, SENIOR DISTRICT JUDGE.

■ CUDAHY, CIRCUIT JUDGE.

This case requires us to decide whether there is an implied private right of action for an issuer corporation to seek injunctive relief under Section 13(d) of the Securities Exchange Act (the "Act"). * * *

I

Plaintiff, Indiana National Corporation ("Indiana National"), is a bank holding company which engages principally in the banking business through its wholly owned subsidiary, Indiana National Bank. Indiana National's stock is registered pursuant to Section 12 of the Securities Exchange Act and is traded in the over-the-counter market. The defendants are a group of investors who acquired more than 5% of Indiana National's stock during 1981 and 1982. As required by Section 13(d) of the Act, they filed a Schedule 13D on September 4, 1981, and subsequently amended it six times between then and August 10, 1982.

On July 21, 1982, Indiana National filed a complaint in which it was alleged that the defendants' Schedule 13D contained materially false and

---

[6]   422 U.S. 49 (1975). *Rondeau* appears in the next subsection of this chapter.

misleading information, in that it failed to disclose the defendants' intention to acquire control of Indiana National, the Federal Reserve Bank's prior denial of an application by certain of the defendants for control of another bank, certain information concerning the members of the group and the true source of the funds used to acquire the shares. The plaintiffs sought a court order compelling defendants to file an amended Schedule 13D with full disclosure in the respects noted, as well as enjoining defendants from acquiring more shares of Indiana National, and compelling them to divest themselves of the shares they already held, which were alleged to have been unlawfully acquired.

In response, the defendants filed a motion to dismiss the complaint on the grounds, in relevant part, that Indiana National, as the issuer of the stock, had no standing to assert a claim under Section 13(d) of the Act. On December 30, 1982, the district court granted the defendants' motion to dismiss on the ground that an issuer corporation does not have an implied right of action under Section 13(d) of the Act. * * *

II

In the course of the last decade, the Supreme Court has given us substantial guidance about when to imply a private right of action in the face of statutory silence. In 1975, the Court outlined a four-part test to determine the appropriateness of such a remedy: (1) whether the plaintiff is a member of a class for whose especial benefit the statute was enacted; (2) whether there is any explicit or implicit indication of congressional intent to create or deny a private remedy; (3) whether a private remedy would be consistent with the underlying purposes of the legislative scheme; and (4) whether the cause of action is one traditionally relegated to state law. Cort v. Ash, 422 U.S. 66, 78 (1975). Several years later, however, the Court indicated that these factors were not of equal weight but that the central inquiry, at which the first three factors were all directed, was one of congressional intent. Touche Ross & Co. v. Redington, 442 U.S. 560, 575 (1979); Transamerica Mortgage Advisors, Inc. (TAMA) v. Lewis, 444 U.S. 11, 15–16 (1979).

The reduction of these questions to one of congressional intent imposes on us the challenging task of divining, as of a moment in the past, the collective state of mind of a body of legislators. But on this question as well, recent Supreme Court cases have shed additional light. In perusing the legislative history for signs of congressional intent, we are directed to pay particular attention to the contemporary legal context in which the statute was enacted. See Cannon v. University of Chicago, 441 U.S. 677, 694–703 (1979); Merrill Lynch, Pierce, Fenner & Smith, Inc. v. Curran, 456 U.S. 353, 378–82 (1982). * * * In *Merrill Lynch,* the Court described this approach in more detail:

> In determining whether a private cause of action is implicit in a federal statutory scheme when the statute by its terms is silent on that issue, the initial focus must be on the state of the law at the time the legislation was enacted. * * * When Congress acts

in a statutory context in which an implied private remedy has already been recognized by the courts, the inquiry logically is different. Congress need not have intended to create a new remedy, since one already existed; the question is whether Congress intended to preserve the pre-existing remedy.

Thus the Court was led to conclude that, when Congress undertook reexamination and significant amendment of a statute while leaving intact the provisions under which the federal courts had implied a cause of action, the evidence was that Congress had affirmatively intended to preserve that remedy. This approach, construing a statute in light of the contemporary legal context in order to determine whether Congress intended that a private right of action be implied, has recently been reaffirmed by the Supreme Court in Herman & MacLean v. Huddleston, 103 S.Ct. 683, 689 (1983); and we shall make use of it in analyzing the case at hand.

III

* * *

At the time it was enacted * * * the Williams Act was consciously patterned upon the protections already available in the proxy rules, Section 14(a) of the Act. * * * [I]n 1968 it was already established that an issuer corporation had an implied private right of action under Section 14(a). Thus, although the Williams Act did not itself contain an explicit private right of action, the statute upon which it was modeled had already been held to contain such a right by implication. We are justified in assuming, as did the Supreme Court in an analogous situation in *Cannon,* that Congress was aware of this precedent when the Williams Act was enacted upon the model of a prior statute.

More important, the Williams Act has itself been twice amended; and on neither occasion did Congress avail itself of the opportunity to overturn the accumulating precedents for a private right of action for issuer corporations under Section 13(d). * * * Moreover, the Supreme Court had assumed, without directly confronting the issue, that such a private right was available to issuer corporations, at least with respect to injunctive relief. See Rondeau v. Mosinee Paper Corp., 422 U.S. 49, 59 n. 9 (1975). * * * Since Congress amended the Act while leaving this remedy intact, we conclude that the legislature affirmatively intended to preserve the remedy of a private right of action for issuer corporations under Section 13(d).

* * *

Our conclusion is further bolstered by the fact that such an interpretation of the statutory provision at issue is the only construction which can make the Section 13(d) disclosure requirements effective at all. The filing required by Section 13(d) is sent to the S.E.C. and to the issuer corporation; it is not disseminated to the shareholders, for whose protection the information is required. The S.E.C., as friend of the court, has told us that it is unreasonable to expect the Commission to police possible Section 13(d) filing violations. The only party with both the capability and incentive to pursue these violations is the issuer corporation. Our conclusion that Congress intended that a private right of action for an issuer corporation be implied under Section 13(d) is thus inescapable if the objectives of the statute are to be realized.

* * *

Some district courts and at least one circuit court have refused to find a private right of action for injunctive relief under Section 13(d), at least in certain circumstances. The Eleventh Circuit's opinion in one of these cases, Liberty National Insurance Holding Co. v. Charter Co.,[7] involved a suit in which the plaintiff had sought divestiture of its shares that were owned by the defendant. The court examined the history of amendments to the Williams Act. It found that the first set of amendments, in 1970, came too soon after adoption of the Act for there to have developed sufficient precedent on the question of private rights of action. After examining the legislative history of the second amendments, passed in 1977, the court determined that the history did not "permit an unambiguous inference of legislative intent to preserve a judicially recognized issuer right of action." The court then concluded on other grounds that Congress did not in fact intend such a private right of action to exist. Further to muddy the waters, a year after one panel of the Eleventh Circuit decided *Liberty National,* another panel distinguished this case and held that a target company does have standing to sue under Section 13(d) when seeking corrective disclosures rather than divestiture.[8] Barring a clarifying Supreme Court decision, some uncertainties will continue about the existence of an issuer's private right of action under Section 13(d). The situation is different in the case of issuers seeking damages rather than an injunction, where courts uniformly have been unsympathetic.[9]

b.   SECTION 14(e)

There is some small question, as a technical matter, as to whether a private right of action really exists under Section 14(e). There are also the questions of who may bring the action and what remedy may be sought, damages or only an injunction. As will be seen, the leading case, Piper v. Chris-Craft Industries, Inc., touches on each of these questions, but answers only one: May an unsuccessful tender offeror sue the target or a competing offeror for damages?

---

[7]   734 F.2d 545 (11th Cir.1984).

[8]   Florida Commercial Banks v. Culverhouse, 772 F.2d 1513 (11th Cir.1985).

[9]   *See, e.g.,* Hallwood Realty Partners, L.P. v. Gotham Partners, L.P., 286 F.3d 613 (2d Cir.2002).

Piper v. Chris-Craft Industries, Inc.

Supreme Court of the United States, 1977.
430 U.S. 1.

■ MR. CHIEF JUSTICE BURGER delivered the opinion of the Court.

We granted certiorari in these cases to consider, among other issues, whether an unsuccessful tender offeror in a contest for control of a corporation has an implied cause of action for damages under § 14(e) of the Securities Exchange Act of 1934 * * *, based on alleged anti-fraud violations by the successful competitor, its investment adviser, and individuals constituting the management of the target corporation.

I

Background

The factual background of this complex contest for control, including the protracted litigation culminating in the cases now before us, is essential to a full understanding of the contending parties' claims.

The three petitions present questions of first impression, arising out of a "sophisticated and hard fought contest" for control of Piper Aircraft Corp., a Pennsylvania-based manufacturer of light aircraft. Piper's management consisted principally of members of the Piper family, who owned 31% of Piper's outstanding stock. Chris-Craft Industries, Inc., a diversified manufacturer of recreational products, attempted to secure voting control of Piper through cash and exchange tender offers for Piper common stock. Chris-Craft's takeover attempt failed, and Bangor Punta Corp. (Bangor or Bangor Punta), with the support of the Piper family, obtained control of Piper in September 1969. Chris-Craft brought suit under § 14(e) of the Securities Exchange Act of 1934 * * * alleging that Bangor Punta achieved control of the target corporation as a result of violations of the federal securities laws by the Piper family, Bangor Punta, and Bangor Punta's underwriter, First Boston Corp., who together had successfully repelled Chris-Craft's takeover attempt.

* * *

III

The Williams Act

* * *

The threshold issue in these cases is whether tender offerors such as Chris-Craft, whose activities are regulated by the Williams Act, have a cause of action for damages against other regulated parties under the statute on a claim that anti-fraud violations by other parties have frustrated the bidder's efforts to obtain control of the target corporation. Without reading such a cause of action into the Act, none of the other issues need be reached.

IV

* * *

* * * To resolve that question we turn to the legislative history to discern the congressional purpose underlying the specific statutory prohibition in § 14(e). Once we identify the legislative purpose, we must then determine whether the creation by judicial interpretation of the implied cause of action asserted by Chris-Craft is necessary to effectuate Congress' goals.

A

* * *

The legislative history * * * shows that the sole purpose of the Williams Act was the protection of investors who are confronted with a tender offer. As we stated in Rondeau v. Mosinee Paper Corp., 422 U.S. [49, 58 (1975)]: "The purpose of the Williams Act is to insure that public shareholders who are confronted by a cash tender offer for their stock will not be required to respond without adequate information * * * ." We find no hint in the legislative history, on which respondent so heavily relies, that Congress contemplated a private cause of action for damages by one of several contending offerors against a successful bidder or by a losing contender against the target corporation.

* * *

B

Our conclusion as to the legislative history is confirmed by the analysis in Cort v. Ash, 422 U.S. 66 (1975). There, the Court identified four factors as "relevant" in determining whether a private remedy is implicit in a statute not expressly providing one. The first is whether the plaintiff is " 'one of the class for whose *especial* benefit the statute was enacted * * * .' " (Emphasis in original.) As previously indicated, examination of the statute and its genesis shows that Chris-Craft is not an intended beneficiary of the Williams Act, and surely is not one "for whose *especial* benefit the statute was enacted." * * *

Second, in Cort v. Ash we inquired whether there was "any indication of legislative intent, explicit or implicit, either to create such a remedy or to deny one." Although the historical materials are barren of any express intent to deny a damages remedy to tender offerors as a class, there is, as we have noted, no indication that Congress intended to create a damages remedy in favor of the loser in a contest for control. * * *

* * *

Third, Cort v. Ash tells us that we must ascertain whether it is "consistent with the underlying purposes of the legislative scheme to imply such a remedy for the plaintiff." We conclude that it is not. As a disclosure mechanism aimed especially at protecting shareholders of target corporations, the Williams Act cannot consistently be interpreted as conferring a monetary remedy upon regulated parties, particularly where the award would not redound to the direct benefit of the protected class. * * * The class sought to be protected by the Williams Act are the shareholders of the *target* corporation; hence it can hardly be said that their interests as a class are served by a judgment in favor of Chris-Craft and against Bangor Punta. * * *

* * *

Fourth, under the Cort v. Ash analysis, we must decide whether "the cause of action [is] one traditionally relegated to state law * * * ." Despite the pervasiveness of federal securities regulation, the Court of Appeals concluded in these cases that Chris-Craft's complaint would give rise to a cause of action under common-law principles of interference with a prospective commercial advantage. Although Congress is, of course, free to create a remedial scheme in favor of contestants in tender offers, we conclude, as we did in Cort v. Ash, that "it is entirely appropriate in this instance to relegate [the offeror-bidder] and others in [that] situation to whatever remedy is created by state law," at least to the extent that the offeror seeks damages for having been wrongfully denied a "fair opportunity" to compete for control of another corporation.

C

What we have said thus far suggests that, unlike J.I. Case Co. v. Borak, judicially creating a damages action in favor of Chris-Craft is unnecessary to ensure the fulfillment of Congress' purposes in adopting the Williams Act. Even though the SEC operates in this context under the same practical restraints recognized by the Court in *Borak,* institutional limitations alone do not lead to the conclusion that any party interested in a tender offer should have a cause of action for damages against a competing bidder. First, as Judge Friendly observed in Electronic Specialty Co. v. International Controls Corp., 409 F.2d 937, 947 (CA2 1969), in corporate control contests the stage of preliminary injunctive relief, rather than post-contest lawsuits, "is the time when relief can best be given." Furthermore, awarding damages to parties other than the protected class of shareholders has only a remote, if any, bearing upon implementing the congressional policy of protecting shareholders who must decide whether to tender or retain their stock.[10] * * *

We therefore conclude that Chris-Craft, as a defeated tender offeror, has no implied cause of action for damages under § 14(e).

* * *

---

[10] Our holding is a limited one. Whether shareholder-offerees, the class protected by § 14(e), have an implied cause of action under § 14(e) is not before us, and we intimate no view on the matter. Nor is the target corporation's standing to sue in issue in this case. We hold only that a tender offeror, suing in its capacity as a takeover bidder, does not have standing to sue for damages under § 14(e).

Several district courts and at least one circuit court have examined the question of whether a tender offeror may bring a Section 14(e) action for injunctive relief. Each court has decided that the action may be brought. Interestingly, although the court of appeals opinion referred to, in Mobil Corp. v. Marathon Oil Co.,[11] grew out of one of the hardest fought tender offer battles of the early 1980s, neither party raised the issue of whether the tender offeror had standing to sue for injunctive relief. Out of what it called an "abundance of caution," the Sixth Circuit decided to resolve the issue anyway, which it did rather easily by going through the Cort v. Ash analysis.

There seems to have been little doubt over the years that target corporations can sue tender offerors when they seek an injunction, and in fact the Second Circuit so held the year after the Williams Act was passed. The case in which it did so was Electronic Specialty Co. v. International Controls Corp.,[12] and it was Judge Friendly's opinion in this case that the Supreme Court quoted approvingly in *Piper* to the effect that the best time to resolve Williams Act questions is the preliminary injunction stage. After the passage of the Williams Act, the standard response of unwilling targets to tender offers quickly became suit against the offeror under Section 14(e), and courts often relied directly or indirectly on *Electronic Specialty* to uphold the right of targets to do so.

In 1984, however, the Eleventh Circuit analyzed the question of a target's right to bring an injunction action under Section 14(e) against a tender offeror and determined that the right does not exist. The case was Liberty National Insurance Holding Co. v. Charter Co.,[13] discussed above for its holding that no private suit may be brought under Section 13(d) in a case involving a request for divestiture of stock in the plaintiff owned by the defendant. The case contains an analysis based on the factors outlined in Cort v. Ash, but the court slips lightly over the question of legislative intent as evidenced by the failure of Congress to overturn prior court interpretations when it amended the statute in other respects. The court also ignored what other courts had done with the issue of target corporation standing since the passage of the Williams Act in 1968. Further limiting the precedential value of *Liberty National* is the fact that in Florida Commercial Banks v. Culverhouse,[14] a different panel of the Eleventh Circuit distinguished *Liberty National* and determined that a target company has standing to sue under Section 14(e) when seeking corrective disclosures rather than divestiture of stock in the plaintiff owned by the defendant.

---

[11]   669 F.2d 366 (6th Cir.1981).

[12]   409 F.2d 937 (2d Cir.1969).

[13]   734 F.2d 545 (11th Cir.1984).

[14]   772 F.2d 1513 (11th Cir.1985).

In addition to holding that target corporations have a right to sue under Section 14(e), the Second Circuit determined in *Electronic Specialty* that shareholders of the target also have this right. This result came as no surprise. As indicated in *Piper,* the purpose of the Williams Act was the protection of shareholders confronted with a tender offer. So, if private plaintiffs were to line up by the strength of their right to bring a Section 14(e) action, target shareholders would be at the front of the line.

In 1985, the Supreme Court decided Schreiber v. Burlington Northern, Inc.,[15] a Section 14(e) case brought by a target shareholder. The Court took the case to resolve a split in the circuits over whether misrepresentation or nondisclosure is a necessary element in an action under Section 14(e). The existence of a private right of action under this section was not an issue in the case, and the Court did not discuss it. Considering its then-recent interest in questions relating to implied rights of action, however, it is unlikely the Court would have accepted the case for review if it had substantial doubts regarding the right of target shareholders to sue under Section 14(e).

The following case deals with a different permutation of the issue of who may bring suit for a violation of Section 14(e), with the specific question being whether shareholders of the target can sue for damages when a planned tender offer is never made because of defensive actions by the target's management.

Lewis v. McGraw

United States Court of Appeals, Second Circuit, 1980.
619 F.2d 192.

■ Before KAUFMAN, CHIEF JUDGE, MESKILL, CIRCUIT JUDGE, and BRIEANT, DISTRICT JUDGE.

■ PER CURIAM:

The instant action is a consolidation of five similar lawsuits brought on behalf of McGraw-Hill, Inc. stockholders, alleging that McGraw-Hill and its directors made false statements of material facts in response to two proposals of the American Express Company for the acquisition of substantial amounts of McGraw-Hill stock. The issue before us is whether shareholders may maintain a cause of action for damages under the Williams Act where they concede that no tender offer has been made to them. We conclude that they may not.

I

On January 8, 1979, American Express proposed to McGraw-Hill what plaintiff describes as a "friendly business combination" of the two companies through payment by American Express of $34 in cash for each McGraw-Hill share. Alternatively, American Express indicated its

---

[15]   472 U.S. 1 (1985).

willingness to acquire 49% of McGraw-Hill's shares for cash or a combination of cash and securities. McGraw-Hill common stock was trading at $26 per share immediately prior to the announcement. On January 15, 1979, McGraw-Hill announced that its Board of Directors had rejected the proposal and made public a letter to American Express characterizing the offer as "reckless," "illegal," and "improper." The following day, American Express filed Schedule 14D–1 with the Securities and Exchange Commission concerning its intention to make a cash tender offer for any and all of McGraw-Hill's stock.

The proposed offer was never made, however, for on January 29, American Express retracted its earlier announcement, and in its place submitted a new proposal to the McGraw-Hill board. This offer, at a price of $40 per share, would not become effective unless McGraw-Hill's incumbent management agreed not to oppose it by "propaganda, lobbying, or litigation." The offer was rejected by the McGraw-Hill board two days later, and expired, by its own terms, on March 1.

Plaintiffs' consolidated, amended complaint charges that:

> Defendants announced publicly that the tender offer price of $40 per share was inadequate, although they knew that the price * * * was fair.

> * * *

> Defendants, in resisting the AMEXCO [American Express Company] tender offer [*sic*], challenged the integrity and honesty of AMEXCO (by indicating that AMEXCO had illegally complied with the Arab boycott), publicly challenged the legality of the tender offer (by indicating that the federal Bank Holding Company [Act] may preclude the tender offer), and publicly stated that the tender offer somehow threatened freedom of expression under the First Amendment of the Constitution (by stating that since the McGraw-Hill [*sic*] was engaged in publishing, its independence would be smothered by a large financial institution such as AMEXCO).

These statements, as well as McGraw-Hill's characterization of the initial proposal as "reckless," "illegal," and "improper," are alleged to be false, as evidenced by the fact that, some months earlier, McGraw-Hill had advised American Express that it considered it to be a proper and desirable merger partner.

Plaintiffs concede that no tender offer ever took place—that no McGraw-Hill shareholder was ever in a position to offer his shares to American Express at a stated price. The $34 proposal was withdrawn before it became effective, and was replaced with a $40 proposal that could have ripened into an offer only upon the acquiescence of the McGraw-Hill board. Nonetheless, plaintiffs claim, "had defendants provided * * * shareholders and the public with complete and truthful information about AMEXCO and its proposed tender offer (i.e. that $40 per share was a fair price, and that AMEXCO was a company with which defendants themselves had wanted to merge), the AMEXCO tender offer would have been consummated." Accordingly, they each seek damages from the company and its directors for the difference between the $40 proposed tender price, and the $25 price to which the stock returned after the expiration of the American Express proposal.

Judge Motley dismissed the consolidated amended complaint * * * , noting that "plaintiffs fail to allege that McGraw-Hill stockholders, or anyone else for that matter, in fact relied upon the alleged misrepresentations or omissions. While plaintiffs do allege deception on the part of defendants, plaintiffs do not allege that anyone was deceived or that anyone acted in reliance upon the alleged deception to their detriment." Having found plaintiffs' federal claim critically insufficient, the district court dismissed plaintiffs' pendent state claims for want of jurisdiction.

II

The complaint was properly dismissed. Section 14(e) of the Williams Act has as its "sole purpose" the "protection of investors who are confronted with a tender offer." Piper v. Chris-Craft Industries, Inc., 430 U.S. 1, 35 (1977). It is designed "to ensure that [investors] will not be required to respond [to a tender offer] without adequate information." Rondeau v. Mosinee Paper Corp., 422 U.S. 49, 58 (1975). Accordingly, one element of a cause of action under § 14(e) is a showing "that there was misrepresentation upon which the target corporation shareholders *relied.*" Chris-Craft Industries, Inc. v. Piper Aircraft Corp., 480 F.2d 341 (2d Cir.), cert. denied, 414 U.S. 910 (1973) (emphasis supplied).[16] In the instant case, the target's shareholders simply could not have relied upon McGraw-Hill's statements, whether true or false, since they were never given an opportunity to tender their shares.

Plaintiffs do not contest this indisputable fact, but rather rest upon cases holding that reliance may sometimes be presumed from a showing of materiality. Mills v. Electric Auto-Lite Co., 396 U.S. 375 (1970); Affiliated Ute Citizens v. United States, 406 U.S. 128 (1972). These cases, however, in presuming reliance, did not abolish it as an element of the cause of action. Rather, they held that in cases in which reliance is possible, and even likely, but is unduly burdensome to prove, the resulting doubt would be resolved in favor of the class the statute was designed to protect. We therefore presume reliance only "where it is

---

[16] We note that the element of reliance has been held "irrelevant" to a cause of action under Rule 10b–5, where material misstatements can be shown to have caused the issuance of securities which, in turn, resulted in losses to plaintiff purchasers. Shores v. Sklar, 610 F.2d 235 (5th Cir.1980). In *Shores,* plaintiffs could plausibly claim that if defendants had disclosed the truth concerning the financial condition of the issuer, the bond issue in question would never have been marketed. In the case at bar, by contrast, plaintiffs must contend that but for the alleged misstatements and omissions on the part of defendants, American Express would have proceeded with a hostile tender offer, over the opposition of McGraw-Hill. Such a scenario stretches the principle of causation into the realm of mere speculation, for it depends upon proof of an offer that, for all that appears here, American Express never even contemplated.

logical" to do so. Chris-Craft Industries, Inc. v. Piper Aircraft Corp., supra, 480 F.2d at 375. Here, where no reliance was possible under any imaginable set of facts, such a presumption would be illogical in the extreme.

We note in closing that our holding today does not place statements made on the eve of a tender offer by target or tendering companies wholly outside the scope of the Williams Act. On the contrary, where the offer ultimately becomes effective, and reliance can be demonstrated or presumed, such statements may well be made "in connection with a tender offer" as required by § 14(e). Otherwise, either party would be free to disseminate misinformation up to the effective date of the tender offer, thus defeating in substantial part the very purpose of the Act—informed decision making by shareholders. Injunctive relief, moreover, may be available to restrain or correct misleading statements made during the period preceding a tender offer where it appears that such an offer is likely, and that reliance upon the statements at issue is probable under the circumstances. Finally, we must bear in mind that many of the wrongs alleged in this complaint may be recast as state law claims for breach of the fiduciary duties owed to shareholders by directors. Indeed, we note that several plaintiffs have commenced state court actions arising out of the abortive transactions at issue here. In this case, however, since American Express never made its proposed offer to the shareholders of McGraw-Hill, plaintiffs cannot state a cause of action for alleged misstatements under the Williams Act.

II. SUBSTANTIVE SECTION 13(d) ISSUES

The preceding section of this chapter dealt with the question of whether a private right of action exists under Section 13(d). The following two cases introduce some of the more important substantive Section 13(d) issues that have been raised in litigation.

GAF Corp. v. Milstein

United States Court of Appeals, Second Circuit, 1971.
453 F.2d 709.

■ Before KAUFMAN and MANSFIELD, CIRCUIT JUDGES, and LEVET, DISTRICT JUDGE.

■ KAUFMAN, CIRCUIT JUDGE:

This appeal involves the interpretation of Section 13(d) of the Securities Exchange Act * * *. Essentially, Section 13(d) requires any person, after acquiring more than 10% (now 5%) of a class of registered equity security, to send to the issuer and the exchanges on which the security is traded and file with the Commission the statement required by the Act. * * *

GAF Corporation filed its complaint in the United States District Court for the Southern District of New York alleging that Morris Milstein, his two sons, Seymour and Paul, and his daughter, Gloria Milstein Flanzer, violated Section 13(d) of the Securities Exchange Act first by failing to file the required statements and then by filing false ones. * * * Judge Pollack aptly framed the [issue] involved:

> The ultimate issue presented by the defendants' motion to dismiss * * * is whether, organizing a group of stockholders owning more than 10% of a class of equity securities with a view to seeking control is, without more, a reportable event under Section 13(d) of the Exchange Act * * *. Judge Pollack granted the Milsteins' motion to dismiss * * *, and GAF has appealed. We disagree with Judge Pollack's determination that GAF failed to state a claim under Section 13(d) and Rule 13d–1 promulgated thereunder, and thus reverse his order in this respect * * *.

Before considering the merits of the issues involved on appeal, a statement of the facts as presented in the complaint and the briefs is in order. We note also that in this posture of the proceeding we must accept as true all well pleaded allegations in the complaint.

The four Milsteins received 324,166 shares of GAF convertible preferred stock, approximately 10.25% of the preferred shares outstanding, when The Ruberoid Company, in which they had substantial holdings, was merged into GAF in May, 1967. They have not acquired any additional preferred shares since the merger.

The complaint informs us that at some time after July 29, 1968, the effective date of the Williams Act, the Milsteins "formed a conspiracy among themselves and other persons to act as a syndicate or group for the purpose of acquiring, holding, or disposing of securities of GAF with the ultimate aim of seizing control of GAF for their own personal and private purposes." It is necessary for our purposes to examine only a few of the nine overt acts GAF alleged were taken in furtherance of this conspiracy.

The complaint alleged that initially the Milsteins sought senior management and board positions for Seymour Milstein with GAF. When this sinecure was not forthcoming, the Milsteins allegedly caused Circle Floor Co., Inc., a company in their control, to reduce its otherwise substantial purchases from GAF. It also charged that the Milsteins thereafter undertook a concerted effort to disparage its management and depress the price of GAF common and preferred stock in order to facilitate the acquisition of additional shares. On May 27, 1970, the Milsteins filed a derivative action in the district court, charging the directors, *inter alia,* with waste and spoliation of corporation assets. A companion action was filed in the New York courts. GAF further alleged that these actions were filed only to disparage management, to depress the price of GAF stock and to use discovery devices to gain valuable information for their takeover conspiracy.

In the meantime, the complaint tells us, Paul and Seymour Milstein purchased respectively 62,000 and 64,000 shares of GAF common stock. When GAF contended that the Milsteins were in violation of Section 13(d) because they had not filed a Schedule 13D as required by Rule 13d–1, the Milsteins, although disclaiming any legal obligation under section 13(d), filed such a schedule on September 24, 1970. In their 13D statement (appended to the complaint), the Milsteins disclosed their preferred and common holdings and stated they "at some future time [might] determine to attempt to acquire control of GAF. * * * " They also stated that they had "no present intention as to whether or not any additional securities of GAF [might] be acquired by them in the future. * * * " Indeed, within the next two months, commencing with October 2, Paul and Seymour each purchased an additional 41,650 shares of common. The Milsteins thereafter filed a Restated and Amended Schedule 13D on November 10 to reflect these new purchases.

Then, on January 27, 1971, the Milsteins filed a third Schedule 13D, disclosing their intention to wage a proxy contest at the 1971 annual meeting. Although the statement again disclaimed any present intention to acquire additional shares, Paul purchased 28,300 shares of common stock during February, 1971. These last purchases, which brought the Milsteins' total common holdings to 237,600 shares having a value in excess of $2 million and constituting 1.7% of the common shares outstanding, were reflected in a February 23 amendment to the January 27 Schedule 13D.

The last essential datum for our purposes is the proxy contest. On May 10, 1971, it was announced that GAF management had prevailed at the April 16 meeting by a margin of some 2 to 1.

GAF's complaint in this action filed on December 16, 1970, requested that the Milsteins be preliminarily and permanently enjoined from (1) acquiring or attempting to acquire additional GAF stock; (2) soliciting any proxy from a GAF shareholder to vote GAF stock; (3) voting any shares of GAF stock held or acquired during the conspiracy; and (4) otherwise acting in furtherance of the conspiracy. It asks for this relief "until the effects of the conspiracy have been fully dissipated and the unlawful acts committed pursuant to the conspiracy fully corrected. * * * "

I.

At the time the conspiracy allegedly was formed, Section 13(d)(1) in relevant part provided:

> Any person who, after acquiring directly or indirectly the beneficial ownership of any equity security of a class which is registered pursuant to Section 12 of this title * * * , is directly or indirectly the beneficial owner of more than 10 per centum of

such class shall, within ten days after such acquisition, send to the issuer of the security at its principal executive office, by registered or certified mail, send to each exchange where the security is traded, and file with the Commission, a statement.
* * *

This section, however, exempts from its filing requirements any acquisition which, "together with all other acquisitions by the same person of securities of the same class during the preceding twelve months, does not exceed 2 per centum of that class." Section 13(d)(3), which is crucial to GAF's claim, further provides that "[w]hen two or more persons act as a partnership, limited partnership, syndicate, or other group for the purpose of acquiring, holding, or disposing of securities of an issuer, such syndicate or group shall be deemed a 'person' for the purposes of [Section 13(d)]." On the assumption that the facts alleged in the complaint are true, we cannot conclude other than that the four Milsteins constituted a "group" and thus, as a "person," were subject to the provisions of Section 13(d). We also are aware of the charge that the Milsteins agreed after July 29, 1968, to hold their GAF preferred shares for the common purpose of acquiring control of GAF. Furthermore, the individuals collectively or as a "group" held more than 10% of the outstanding preferred shares—a registered class of securities. Since the section requires a "person" to file only if he acquires more than 2% of the class of stock in a 12-month period after July 29, 1968, the principal question presented to us is whether the complaint alleges as a matter of law that the Milstein *group* "acquired" the 324,166 shares of preferred stock owned by its members after that date. We conclude that it does and thus that it states a claim under Section 13(d).

The statute refers to "acquiring directly or indirectly the beneficial ownership of securities." Thus, at the outset, we are not confronted with the relatively simple concept of legal title, but rather with the amorphous and occasionally obfuscated concepts of indirect and beneficial ownership which pervade the securities acts.

The Act nowhere explicitly defines the concept of "acquisition" as used in Section 13(d). Although we are aware of Learned Hand's warning "not to make a fortress out of the dictionary," Cabell v. Markham, 148 F.2d 737, 739 (2d Cir.), aff'd, 326 U.S. 404 (1945), some light, although dim, is shed by Webster's Third International Dictionary. It tells us that "to acquire" means "to come into possession [or] control." If the allegations in the complaint are true, then the group, which must be treated as an entity separate and distinct from its members, could have gained "beneficial control" of the voting rights of the preferred stock only after its formation, which we must assume occurred after the effective date of the Williams Act. Manifestly, according to the complaint, the group when formed acquired a beneficial interest in the individual holdings of its members. We find ourselves in agreement with the statement of the Court of Appeals for the Seventh Circuit in Bath

Industries, Inc. v. Blot, 427 F.2d 97, 112 (7th Cir.1970), that in the context of the Williams Act, where the principal concern is focused on the battle for corporate control, "voting control of stock is the only relevant element of beneficial ownership." Thus, we hardly can agree with Judge Pollack that the language of the statute compels the conclusion that individual members must acquire shares before the group can be required to file.

We are well aware of the first catechism of statutory construction which teaches that we should begin the process of interpretation with "the language of the statute itself"; that, however, is *toto caelo* from saying that the process must end there or that we are required to blind ourselves to other relevant aids to construction, particularly when dealing with a statute as complex as the one before us. * * *

The legislative history, as well as the purpose behind Section 13(d), bear out our interpretation. Any residual doubt over its soundness is obviated by the following clear statement appearing in both the House and Senate reports accompanying the Williams Act:

> "[Section 13(d)(3)] would prevent a group of persons who seek to pool their voting or other interests in the securities of any issuer from evading the provisions of the statute because no one individual owns more than 10 percent of the securities. *The group would be deemed to have become the beneficial owner, directly or indirectly, of more than 10 percent of a class of securities at the time they agreed to act in concert. Consequently, the group would be required to file the information called for in Section 13(d)(1) within 10 days after they agree to act together, whether or not any member of the group had acquired any securities at that time.*" S.Rep. No. 550, 90th Cong., 1st Sess. 8 (1967); H.R.Rep. No. 1711, 90th Cong., 2d Sess. 8–9 (1968). (Emphasis added.)

Indeed, Professor Loss, one of the foremost scholars of securities law, reached the same interpretation in his treatise, citing this passage.

The Senate and House reports and the Act as finally enacted, contrary to appellees' contention, are entirely consistent in our view. This conclusion is buttressed by a consideration of the purpose of the Act. The 1960's on Wall Street may best be remembered for the pyrotechnics of corporate takeovers and the phenomenon of conglomeration. Although individuals seeking control through a proxy contest were required to comply with Section 14(a) of the Securities Exchange Act and the proxy rules promulgated by the SEC, and those making stock tender offers were required to comply with the applicable provisions of the Securities Act, before the enactment of the Williams Act there were no provisions regulating cash tender offers or other techniques of securing corporate control. According to the committee reports:

"The [Williams Act] would correct the current gap in our securities laws by amending the Securities Exchange Act of 1934 to provide for full disclosure in connection with cash tender offers and other techniques for accumulating large blocks of equity securities of publicly held companies." S.Rep. No. 550 at 4; H.R.Rep. No. 1711 at 4.

Specifically, we were told, "the purpose of Section 13(d) is to require disclosure of information by persons who have acquired a substantial interest, or increased their interest in the equity securities of a company by a substantial amount, within a relatively short period of time." S.Rep. No. 550 at 7; H.R.Rep. No. 1711 at 8. Otherwise, investors cannot assess the potential for changes in corporate control and adequately evaluate the company's worth.

That the purpose of Section 13(d) is to alert the marketplace to every large, rapid aggregation or accumulation of securities, regardless of technique employed, which might represent a potential shift in corporate control is amply reflected in the enacted provisions. Section 13(d)(1)(C) requires the person filing to disclose any intention to acquire control. If he has such an intention, he must disclose any plans for liquidating the issuer, selling its assets, merging it with another company or changing substantially its business or corporate structure. * * *

The alleged conspiracy on the part of the Milsteins is one clearly intended to be encompassed within the reach of Section 13(d). * * *

––––––––––––

Although each of the Milsteins involved in the litigation individually was a beneficial owner of GAF Corp. stock, the Second Circuit's reasoning does not appear to demand that this be the case. In Hemispherx Biopharma Inc. v. Johannesburg Consolidated Investments,[17] the Eleventh Circuit held beneficial ownership by each member of a purported group is a requisite of liability under Section 13(d), reasoning that to do otherwise would expand that liability beyond reason. This is in agreement with an earlier Third Circuit case, Rosenberg v. XM Ventures.[18]

Rondeau v. Mosinee Paper Corp.

Supreme Court of the United States, 1975.
422 U.S. 49.

■ MR. CHIEF JUSTICE BURGER delivered the opinion of the Court.

We granted certiorari in this case to determine whether a showing of irreparable harm is necessary for a private litigant to obtain injunctive

––––––––––––

[17] Hemispherx Biopharma, Inc. v. Johannesburg Consol. Investments, 553 F.3d 1351 (11th Cir. 2009).

[18] 274 F.3d 137 (3d Cir.2001).

relief in a suit under § 13(d) of the Securities Exchange Act of 1934. The Court of Appeals held that it was not. We reverse.

I

Respondent Mosinee Paper Corp. is a Wisconsin company engaged in the manufacture and sale of paper, paper products, and plastics. Its principal place of business is located in Mosinee, Wis., and its only class of equity security is common stock which is registered under § 12 of the Securities Exchange Act of 1934. At all times relevant to this litigation there were slightly more than 800,000 shares of such stock outstanding.

In April 1971 petitioner Francis A. Rondeau, a Mosinee businessman, began making large purchases of respondent's common stock in the over-the-counter market. Some of the purchases were in his own name; others were in the name of businesses and a foundation known to be controlled by him. By May 17, 1971, petitioner had acquired 40,413 shares of respondent's stock, which constituted more than 5% of those outstanding. He was therefore required to comply with the disclosure provisions of the Williams Act, by filing a Schedule 13D with respondent and the Securities and Exchange Commission within 10 days. That form would have disclosed, among other things, the number of shares beneficially owned by petitioner, the source of the funds used to purchase them, and petitioner's purpose in making the purchases.

Petitioner did not file a Schedule 13D but continued to purchase substantial blocks of respondent's stock. By July 30, 1971, he had acquired more than 60,000 shares. On that date the chairman of respondent's board of directors informed him by letter that his activity had "given rise to numerous rumors" and "seems to have created some problems under the Federal Securities Laws * * * ." Upon receiving the letter petitioner immediately stopped placing orders for respondent's stock and consulted his attorney. On August 25, 1971, he filed a Schedule 13D which, in addition to the other required disclosures, described the "Purpose of Transaction" as follows:

> "Francis A. Rondeau determined during early part of 1971 that the common stock of the Issuer [respondent] was undervalued in the over-the-counter market and represented a good investment vehicle for future income and appreciation. Francis A. Rondeau and his associates presently propose to seek to acquire additional common stock of the Issuer in order to obtain effective control of the Issuer, but such investments as originally determined were and are not necessarily made with this objective in mind. Consideration is currently being given to making a public cash tender offer to the shareholders of the Issuer at a price which will reflect current quoted prices for such stock with some premium added."

Petitioner also stated that, in the event that he did obtain control of respondent, he would consider making changes in management "in an effort to provide a Board of Directors which is more representative of all of the shareholders, particularly those outside of present management * * * ." One month later petitioner amended the form to reflect more accurately the allocation of shares between himself and his companies.

On August 27 respondent sent a letter to its shareholders informing them of the disclosures in petitioner's Schedule 13D. The letter stated that by his "tardy filing" petitioner had "withheld the information to which you [the shareholders] were entitled for more than two months, in violation of federal law." In addition, while agreeing that "recent market prices have not reflected the real value of your Mosinee stock," respondent's management could "see little in Mr. Rondeau's background that would qualify him to offer any meaningful guidance to a Company in the highly technical and competitive paper industry."

Six days later respondent initiated this suit in the United States District Court for the Western District of Wisconsin. Its complaint named petitioner, his companies, and two banks which had financed some of petitioner's purchases as defendants and alleged that they were engaged in a scheme to defraud respondent and its shareholders in violation of the securities laws. It alleged further that shareholders who had "sold shares without the information which defendants were required to disclose lacked information material to their decision whether to sell or hold," and that respondent "was unable to communicate such information to its stockholders, and to take such actions as their interest required." Respondent prayed for an injunction prohibiting petitioner and his codefendants from voting or pledging their stock and from acquiring additional shares, requiring them to divest themselves of stock which they already owned, and for damages. A motion for a preliminary injunction was filed with the complaint but later withdrawn.

After three months of pretrial proceedings petitioner moved for summary judgment. He readily conceded that he had violated the Williams Act, but contended that the violation was due to a lack of familiarity with the securities laws and that neither respondent nor its shareholders had been harmed. The District Court agreed. It found no material issues of fact to exist regarding petitioner's lack of willfulness in failing to timely file a Schedule 13D, concluding that he discovered his obligation to do so on July 30, 1971, and that there was no basis in the record for disputing his claim that he first considered the possibility of obtaining control of respondent some time after that date. The District Court therefore held that petitioner and his codefendants "did not engage in intentional covert, and conspiratorial conduct in failing to timely file the 13D Schedule."

Similarly, although accepting respondent's contention that its management and shareholders suffered anxiety as a result of petitioner's activities and that this anxiety was exacerbated by his failure to disclose his intentions until August 1971, the District Court concluded that similar anxiety "could be expected to accompany any change in management," and was "a predictable consequence of shareholder democracy." It fell far short of the irreparable harm necessary to support an injunction and no other harm was revealed by the record; as amended, petitioner's Schedule 13D disclosed all of the information to which respondent was entitled, and he had not proceeded with a tender offer. Moreover, in the view of the District Court even if a showing of irreparable harm were not required in all cases under the securities laws, petitioner's lack of bad faith and the absence of damage to respondent made this "a particularly inappropriate occasion to fashion equitable relief * * *." Thus, although petitioner had committed a technical violation of the Williams Act, the District Court held that respondent was entitled to no relief and entered summary judgment against it.

The Court of Appeals reversed, with one judge dissenting. The majority stated that it was "giving effect" to the District Court's findings regarding the circumstances of petitioner's violation of the Williams Act, but concluded that those findings showed harm to respondent because it "was delayed in its efforts to make any necessary response to" petitioner's potential to take control of the company. In any event, the majority was of the view that respondent "need not show irreparable harm as a prerequisite to obtaining permanent injunctive relief in view of the fact that as issuer of the securities it is in the best position to assure that the filing requirements of the Williams Act are being timely and fully complied with and to obtain speedy and forceful remedial action when necessary." The Court of Appeals remanded the case to the District Court with instructions that it enjoin petitioner and his codefendants from further violations of the Williams Act and from voting the shares purchased between the due date of the Schedule 13D and the date of its filing for a period of five years. It considered "such an injunctive decree appropriate to neutralize [petitioner's] violation of the Act and to deny him the benefit of his wrongdoing."

We granted certiorari to resolve an apparent conflict among the Courts of Appeals and because of the importance of the question presented to private actions under the federal securities laws. We disagree with the Court of Appeals' conclusion that the traditional standards for extraordinary equitable relief do not apply in these circumstances, and reverse.

II

As in the District Court and the Court of Appeals, it is conceded here that petitioner's delay in filing the Schedule 13D constituted a violation of the Williams Act. The narrow issue before us is whether this record supports the grant of injunctive relief, a remedy whose basis "in the federal courts has always been irreparable harm and inadequacy of legal remedies." Beacon Theatres, Inc. v. Westover, 359 U.S. 500, 506–507 (1959).

The Court of Appeals' conclusion that respondent suffered "harm" sufficient to require sterilization of petitioner's stock need not long detain us. The purpose of the Williams Act is to insure that public shareholders who are confronted by a cash tender offer for their stock will not be required to respond without adequate information regarding the qualifications and intentions of the offering party. By requiring disclosure of information to the target corporation as well as the Securities and Exchange Commission, Congress intended to do no more than give incumbent management an opportunity to express and explain its position. The Congress expressly disclaimed an intention to provide a weapon for management to discourage takeover bids or prevent large accumulations of stock which would create the potential for such attempts. Indeed, the Act's draftsmen commented upon the "extreme care" which was taken "to avoid tipping the balance of regulation either in favor of management or in favor of the person making the takeover bid." S.Rep. No. 550, 90th Cong., 1st Sess., 3 (1967); H.R.Rep. No. 1711, 90th Cong., 2d Sess., 4 (1968).

The short of the matter is that none of the evils to which the Williams Act was directed has occurred or is threatened in this case. Petitioner has not attempted to obtain control of respondent, either by a cash tender offer or any other device. Moreover, he has now filed a proper Schedule 13D, and there has been no suggestion that he will fail to comply with the Act's requirement of reporting any material changes in the information contained therein. On this record there is no likelihood that respondent's shareholders will be disadvantaged should petitioner make a tender offer, or that respondent will be unable to adequately place its case before them should a contest for control develop. Thus, the usual basis for injunctive relief, "that there exists some cognizable danger of recurrent violation," is not present here. United States v. W.T. Grant Co., 345 U.S. 629, 633 (1953).

Nor are we impressed by respondent's argument that an injunction is necessary to protect the interests of its shareholders who either sold their stock to petitioner at predisclosure prices or would not have invested had they known that a takeover bid was imminent. As observed, the principal object of the Williams Act is to solve the dilemma of shareholders desiring to respond to a cash tender offer, and it is not at all clear that the type of "harm" identified by respondent is redressable under its provisions. In any event, those persons who allegedly sold at an unfairly depressed price have an adequate remedy by way of an action for damages, thus negating the basis for equitable relief. Similarly, the fact that the second group of shareholders for whom respondent expresses concern have retained the benefits of their stock and the lack of an imminent contest for control make the possibility of damage to them remote at best.

We turn, therefore, to the Court of Appeals' conclusion that respondent's claim was not to be judged according to traditional equitable principles, and that the bare fact that petitioner violated the Williams Act justified entry of an injunction against him. This position would seem to be foreclosed by Hecht Co. v. Bowles, 321 U.S. 321 (1944). There, the administrator of the Emergency Price Control Act of 1942 brought suit to redress violations of that statute. The fact of the violations was admitted, but the District Court declined to enter an injunction because they were inadvertent and the defendant had taken immediate steps to rectify them. This Court held that such an exercise of equitable discretion was proper despite § 205(a) of the Act, which provided that an injunction or other order "shall be granted" upon a showing of violation, observing:

> "We are dealing here with the requirements of equity practice with a background of several hundred years of history. * * * *The historic injunctive process was designed to deter, not to punish.* * * * We do not believe that such a major departure from that long tradition as is here proposed should be lightly implied." 321 U.S., at 329–330. (Emphasis added.)

This reasoning applies *a fortiori* to actions involving only "competing private claims," and suggests that the District Court here was entirely correct in insisting that respondent satisfy the traditional prerequisites of extraordinary equitable relief by establishing irreparable harm. * * *

Respondent urges, however, that the "public interest" must be taken into account in considering its claim for relief and relies upon the Court of Appeals' conclusion that it is entitled to an injunction because it "is in the best position" to insure that the Williams Act is complied with by purchasers of its stock. This argument misconceives, we think, the nature of the litigation. Although neither the availability of a private suit under the Williams Act nor respondent's standing to bring it has been questioned here, this cause of action is not expressly authorized by the statute or its legislative history. Rather, respondent is asserting a so-called implied private right of action established by cases such as J.I. Case Co. v. Borak, 377 U.S. 426 (1964). Of course, we have not hesitated to recognize the power of federal courts to fashion private remedies for securities laws violations when to do so is consistent with the legislative scheme and necessary for the protection of investors as a supplement to enforcement by the Securities and Exchange Commission. However, it by no means follows that the plaintiff in such an action is relieved of the burden of establishing the traditional prerequisites of relief. * * *

* * *

Any remaining uncertainty regarding the nature of relief available to a person asserting an implied private right of action under the securities laws was resolved in Mills v. Electric Auto-Lite Co., 396 U.S. 375 (1970). * * *

Mills could not be plainer in holding that the questions of liability and relief are separate in private actions under the securities laws, and that the latter is to be determined according to traditional principles. Thus, the fact that respondent is pursuing a cause of action which has been generally recognized to serve the public interest provides no basis for concluding that it is relieved of showing irreparable harm and other usual prerequisites for injunctive relief. Accordingly, the judgment of the Court of Appeals is reversed and the case is remanded to it with directions to reinstate the judgment of the District Court.

———————

III. CONDUCT PROSCRIBED BY SECTION 14(e)

The last Williams Act topic discussed here is the type of conduct proscribed by Section 14(e). This section of the Williams Act is phrased in the disjunctive, speaking first about making "any untrue statement of a material fact or [the omission] to state any material fact * * *" and then—separated by the word "or"—about engaging "in any fraudulent, deceptive, or manipulative acts or practices." Prior to Schreiber v. Burlington Northern, Inc., the case which appears directly below, the Sixth Circuit had found that a defendant could be held liable for conduct that was manipulative even when the conduct did not contain an element of misstatement or nondisclosure. The Second, Third, and Eighth Circuits, on the other hand, had issued opinions with the opposite conclusion. The Supreme Court took the *Schreiber* case to resolve this conflict.

Schreiber v. Burlington Northern, Inc.

Supreme Court of the United States, 1985.
472 U.S. 1.

■ CHIEF JUSTICE BURGER delivered the opinion of the Court.

* * *

I

On December 21, 1982, Burlington Northern, Inc., made a hostile tender offer for El Paso Gas Co. Through a wholly owned subsidiary, Burlington proposed to purchase 25.1 million El Paso shares at $24 per share. Burlington reserved the right to terminate the offer if any of several specified events occurred. El Paso management initially opposed the takeover, but its shareholders responded favorably, fully subscribing the offer by the December 30, 1982 deadline.

Burlington did not accept those tendered shares; instead, after negotiations with El Paso management, Burlington announced on January 10, 1983, the terms of a new and friendly takeover agreement. Pursuant to the new agreement, Burlington undertook, *inter alia*, to (1) rescind the December tender offer, (2) purchase 4,166,667 shares from El Paso at $24 per share, (3) substitute a new tender offer for only 21 million shares at $24 per share, (4) provide procedural protections against a squeeze-out merger[19] of the remaining El Paso shareholders, and (5) recognize "golden parachute"[20] contracts between El Paso and four of its senior officers. By February 8, more than 40 million shares were tendered in response to Burlington's January offer, and the takeover was completed.

The rescission of the first tender offer caused a diminished payment to those shareholders who had tendered during the first offer. The January offer was greatly oversubscribed and consequently those shareholders who retendered were subject to substantial proration. Petitioner Barbara Schreiber filed suit on behalf of herself and similarly situated shareholders, alleging that Burlington, El Paso, and members of El Paso's board violated § 14(e)'s prohibition of "fraudulent, deceptive or manipulative acts or practices * * * in connection with any tender offer." She claimed that Burlington's withdrawal of the December tender offer coupled with the substitution of the January tender offer was a "manipulative" distortion of the market for El Paso stock. Schreiber also alleged that Burlington violated § 14(e) by failing * * * to disclose the "golden parachutes" offered to four of El Paso's managers. She claims that this January nondisclosure was a deceptive act forbidden by § 14(e).

The District Court dismissed the suit for failure to state a claim. * * *

The Court of Appeals for the Third Circuit affirmed. * * *

* * *

II

A

We are asked in this case to interpret § 14(e) of the Securities Exchange Act. The starting point is the language of the statute. * * *

Petitioner relies on a construction of the phrase, "fraudulent, deceptive or manipulative acts or practices." Petitioner reads the phrase

---

[19] A "squeeze-out" merger occurs when Corporation A, which holds a controlling interest in Corporation B, uses its control to merge B into itself or into a wholly owned subsidiary. The minority shareholders in Corporation B are, in effect, forced to sell their stock. The procedural protection provided in the agreement between El Paso and Burlington required the approval of non-Burlington members of El Paso's board of directors before a squeeze-out merger could proceed. Burlington eventually purchased all the remaining shares of El Paso for $12 cash and one quarter share of Burlington preferred stock per share. The parties dispute whether this consideration was equal to that paid to those tendering during the January tender offer.

[20] Petitioner alleged in her complaint that respondent Burlington failed to disclose that four officers of El Paso had entered into "golden parachute" agreements with El Paso for "extended employment benefits in the event El Paso should be taken over, which benefits would give them millions of dollars of extra compensation." The term "golden parachute" refers generally to agreements between a corporation and its top officers which guarantee those officers continued employment, payment of a lump sum, or other benefits in the event of a change of corporate ownership. As described in the Schedule 14D–9 filed by El Paso with the Commission on January 12, 1983, El Paso entered into "employment agreements" with two of its officers for a period of not less than five years, and with two other officers for a period of three years. The Schedule 14D–9 also disclosed that El Paso's Deferred Compensation Plan had been amended "to provide that for the purposes of such Plan a participant shall be deemed to have retired at the instance of the Company if his duties as a director, officer or employee of the Company have been diminished or curtailed by the Company in any material respect."

"fraudulent, deceptive or manipulative acts or practices" to include acts which, although fully disclosed, "artificially" affect the price of the takeover target's stock. Petitioner's interpretation relies on the belief that § 14(e) is directed at purposes broader than providing full and true information to investors.

Petitioner's reading of the term "manipulative" conflicts with the normal meaning of the term. We have held in the context of an alleged violation of § 10(b) of the Securities Exchange Act:

> "Use of the word 'manipulative' is especially significant. It is and was virtually a term of art when used in connection with the securities markets. It connotes intentional or willful conduct *designed to deceive or defraud* investors by controlling or artificially affecting the price of securities." Ernst & Ernst v. Hochfelder, 425 U.S. 185, 199 (1976) (emphasis added).

Other cases interpreting the term reflect its use as a general term comprising a range of misleading practices. * * * The meaning the Court has given the term "manipulative" is consistent with the use of the term at common law, and with its traditional dictionary definition.

* * *

B

Our conclusion that "manipulative" acts under § 14(e) require misrepresentation or nondisclosure is buttressed by the purpose and legislative history of the provision * * * .

It is clear that Congress relied primarily on disclosure to implement the purpose of the Williams Act. * * *

* * *

While legislative history specifically concerning § 14(e) is sparse, the House and Senate Reports discuss the role of § 14(e). Describing § 14(e) as regulating "fraudulent transactions," and stating the thrust of the section:

> "This provision would affirm the fact that persons engaged in making or opposing tender offers or otherwise seeking to influence the decision of investors or the outcome of the tender offer are under an obligation to make *full disclosure* of material information to those with whom they deal." H.R.Rep. No. 1711, 90th Cong., 2d Sess., 11 (1968) (emphasis added); S.R.Rep. No. 550, 90th Cong., 1st Sess., 11 (1967) (emphasis added).

Nowhere in the legislative history is there the slightest suggestion that § 14(e) serves any purpose other than disclosure, or that the term "manipulative" should be read as an invitation to the courts to oversee the substantive fairness of tender offers; the quality of any offer is a matter for the marketplace.

To adopt the reading of the term "manipulative" urged by petitioner would not only be unwarranted in light of the legislative purpose but would be at odds with it. Inviting judges to read the term "manipulative" with their own sense of what constitutes "unfair" or "artificial" conduct would inject uncertainty into the tender offer process. An essential piece of information—whether the court would deem the fully disclosed actions of one side or the other to be "manipulative"—would not be available until after the tender offer had closed. This uncertainty would directly contradict the expressed Congressional desire to give investors full information.

Congress' consistent emphasis on disclosure persuades us that it intended takeover contests to be addressed to shareholders. In pursuit of this goal, Congress, consistent with the core mechanism of the Securities Exchange Act, created sweeping disclosure requirements and narrow substantive safeguards. The same Congress that placed such emphasis on shareholder choice would not at the same time have required judges to oversee tender offers for substantive fairness. It is even less likely that a Congress implementing that intention would express it only through the use of a single word placed in the middle of a provision otherwise devoted to disclosure.

C

We hold that the term "manipulative" as used in § 14(e) requires misrepresentation or nondisclosure. It connotes "conduct designed to deceive or defraud investors by controlling or artificially affecting the price of securities." Ernst & Ernst v. Hochfelder, 425 U.S., at 199. Without misrepresentation or nondisclosure, § 14(e) has not been violated.

Applying that definition to this case, we hold that the actions of respondents were not manipulative. The amended complaint fails to allege that the cancellation of the first tender offer was accompanied by any misrepresentation, nondisclosure or deception. The District Court correctly found, "All activity of the defendants that could have conceivably affected the price of El Paso shares was done openly."

Petitioner also alleges that El Paso management and Burlington entered into certain undisclosed and deceptive agreements during the making of the second tender offer. The substance of the allegations is that, in return for certain undisclosed benefits, El Paso managers agreed to support the second tender offer. But both courts noted that petitioner's complaint seeks redress only for injuries related to the cancellation of the first tender offer. Since the deceptive and misleading acts alleged by the petitioner all occurred with reference to the making of the second tender offer—when the injuries suffered by petitioner had already been sustained—these acts bear no possible causal relationship to petitioner's alleged injuries. * * *

* * *

One of the more interesting Section 14(e) developments was the adoption by the Commission of Rule 14e–3. This rule generally makes it illegal to purchase or sell, or cause to be purchased or sold, securities that are or are to be the subject of a tender offer (or certain related securities) when a person "is in possession of material information relating to such tender offer which information he knows or has reason to know is nonpublic and which he knows or has reason to know has been acquired" from the tender offeror or the target, or from someone connected with either. The rule also makes it illegal for insiders to tip others with material information about tender offers. Rule 14e–3 serves as an adjunct to Rule 10b–5, which is the main Exchange Act weapon against the purchase or sale of securities on the basis of material, nonpublic information. Rule 14e–3 is especially important in this respect because, at least as it is currently interpreted, it may be violated without the existence of a related violation of a fiduciary or other such duty, as is required in a Rule 10b–5 case. (Rule 10b–5 is the main subject of the next chapter.)

Defendants in cases brought under Rule 14e–3 used to argue that the Rule exceeded the Commission's rulemaking authority. In United States v. O'Hagan, 521 U.S. 642, decided by the Supreme Court in 1997, the Court said the following:

> We need not resolve in this case whether the Commission's authority under § 14(e) to "define * * * such acts and practices as are fraudulent" is broader than the Commission's fraud-defining authority under § 10(b), for we agree with the United States that Rule 14e–3(a), as applied to cases of this genre [a straightforward misappropriation of information case involving a lawyer who worked for a law firm that represented a bidder], qualifies under § 14(e) as a "means reasonably designed to prevent" fraudulent trading on material, nonpublic information in the tender offer context [quoting § 14(e)]. A prophylactic measure, because its mission is to prevent, typically encompasses more than the core activity prohibited. As we noted in Schreiber [v. Burlington Northern, 472 U.S. 1 (1985)], § 14(e)'s rulemaking authorization gives the Commission "latitude," even in the context of a term of art like "manipulative," "to regulate nondeceptive activities as a 'reasonably designed' means of preventing manipulative acts, without suggesting any change in the meaning of the term 'manipulative' itself." We hold, accordingly, that under § 14(e), the Commission may prohibit acts, not themselves fraudulent under the common law or § 10(b), if the prohibition is "reasonably designed to prevent * * * acts and practices [that] are fraudulent." [Quoting § 14(e).]

D. THE TENDER OFFER BATTLE

It is hard to appreciate the law relating to tender offers without an understanding of their real-world context. The following article provides an overview of the current landscape.

Takeover Law and Practice
Wachtell, Lipton, Rosen & Katz.
1712 PLI/Corp 697.[*]

* * *

Merger and acquisition activity historically has been cyclical, and recent years prove no exception. Following the merger wave of the latter half of the 1990s, the new millennium has been marked by dramatic ebbs and flows of merger activity. At the beginning of the last decade, merger activity was frenetic, marked by headline-grabbing deals such as Time Warner's $165 billion business combination with AOL in 2000. The pace of mergers then slowed dramatically from 2001 to 2003 and, for a time, subsided. Despite lingering concerns regarding deficits, terrorism and corporate governance, improving market conditions and increased optimism regarding the U.S. economy created a conducive macroeconomic environment for mergers during the 2004–2007 period, with the volume of announced transactions worldwide peaking in 2007. * * * [C]ritical to the increase in deals were the growing pools of investment capital being deployed in takeover transactions by private equity funds and hedge funds, enhanced by readily available debt financing, the "club" approach to private equity deals and the availability of equity syndication and receptivity to buyouts among companies deriving from, among other things, desire for relief from the expenses and difficulties of being public. Despite setting a new record in 2007, U.S. and global M&A volume declined steeply beginning in August 2007. The collapse of the housing bubble and the drying up of liquidity severely constrained M&A activity, particularly private equity deals, which in 2007 accounted for approximately 25% of total M&A volume. * * *

Global M&A volume continued to drop in 2008 and again in 2009, to the lowest level since 2004. Deal volumes began to increase in late 2009, however, as economic conditions improved, with momentum continuing to build in 2010. * * *

Although overall deal activity in 2011 was relatively flat compared to 2010, one type of transaction in particular—the spin-off—became increasingly popular. A spin-off can create shareholder value when a company's businesses may command higher valuations if owned and managed separately, rather than as part of the same enterprise. * * * Spin-off volume reached an aggregate of $230 billion in 2011, which was six times the level for such transactions in 2010. * * * Distressed M&A

---

    *   Copyright © 2012, Wachtell, Lipton, Rosen & Katz. Reprinted with permission.

activity, which was a prominent feature of the landscape in the aftermath of the financial crisis as companies sought to pair up with stronger rivals and companies and investors sought to acquire businesses and assets out of bankruptcy, slowed considerably in 2010 and 2011 as the economy improved and distressed acquisition opportunities diminished.

* * *

V.   Advance Takeover Preparedness and Responding to Unsolicited Offers

Although strategies implemented once an unsolicited offer has emerged can provide a board valuable time during which to evaluate a bid and determine the correct response, advance takeover preparedness is important. A corporation that carefully employs advance takeover measures can improve its ability to deter coercive or inadequate bids or secure a high premium in the event of a sale of control of the corporation. If gaps in a company's takeover defenses are found, the board must carefully consider whether to address them in the short term in the absence of any particular threat (and thus risk raising the company's profile with shareholder and governance activists), or whether to be prepared as part of a contingency plan to understand any potential vulnerabilities and move to mitigate them in the face of a specific threat. * * *

* * *

A.   Rights Plans

Rights plans are the most effective device yet developed in response to abusive takeover tactics and inadequate bids, and remain a central feature of most major corporations' takeover preparedness. Rights plans do not interfere with negotiated transactions, nor do they preclude unsolicited takeovers. The evidence is clear, however, that rights plans do have the desired effect of forcing an acquiror to deal with a target's board and ultimately may enable the board to extract from an acquiror a higher acquisition premium than may otherwise have been the case or deter offers that the board determines to be inadequate. * * *

* * *

Rights plans have long been the subject of active discussion and debate, and they continue to contribute significantly to the structure and outcome of most major contests for corporate control. This debate has only increased of late, as a number of companies have allowed their rights plans to expire, have affirmatively terminated their rights plans, have modified their rights plans with watered-down protections, and have agreed not to implement rights plans going forward absent shareholder approval or ratification within some period of time, generally one year. * * *

* * *

[O]ver 3,000 companies at one point had adopted rights plans, including almost two-thirds of the S&P 500 companies. However, recent trends in shareholder activism, as well as the ability of a board to adopt a rights plan on short notice in response to a specific threat, have led to a marked decrease in the prevalence of these plans. Today, approximately 734 U.S.-incorporated companies, including 10% of the S&P 500, have shareholder rights plans in effect. * * *

* * *

The key features of a rights plan are the "flip-in" and "flip-over" provisions of the rights, the effect of which, in specified circumstances, is to impose unacceptable levels of dilution on an acquiror. The risk of dilution, combined with the authority of a target's board to redeem the rights prior to a triggering event (generally an acquisition of 15% or 20% of the target's stock), gives a potential acquiror a powerful incentive to negotiate with the target's board rather than proceeding unilaterally.

* * *

B.   Defensive Charter and By-Law Provisions

Defensive charter and by-law provisions typically do not purport to, and will not, prevent a hostile acquisition. Rather, they provide some measure of protection against certain takeover tactics and allow a board some additional negotiating leverage, as well as the opportunity to respond appropriately to proxy and consent solicitations. Defensive charter provisions can include: (1) staggered board provisions; (2) provisions that eliminate shareholder action by written consent; (3) provisions limiting the ability of shareholders to remove directors without cause and to alter the size of a board; (4) "fair price" provisions (which require that shareholders receive equivalent consideration at both ends of a two-step bid, thus deterring coercive two-tier, front-end-loaded offers); and (5) "business combination" provisions (which commonly provide for supermajority voting in wide range of business combinations not approved by the company's continuing directors, absent the ability of the transaction to meet certain substantive requirements).

* * *

D.   Passive Responses to Unsolicited Offers—Just Say No

The developments in strategic mergers and related case law do not undercut the just say no defense to an acquisition proposal. * * *

E.   Active Responses to Unsolicited Offers

1.   White Knights and White Squires

A white knight transaction, namely a merger or acquisition transaction with a friendly acquiror, can be a successful strategy where the white knight transaction provides greater economic value to target company stockholders than the initial hostile offer. In some contexts, however, white knight transactions, because of required regulatory approvals and related procedures, are more difficult to accomplish. For example, in a banking or telecommunications acquisition, a white knight will require the same regulatory approvals as are required by the hostile acquiror and, to the extent that the white knight commences the approval process after the hostile acquiror does, the white knight will suffer a timing disadvantage. Certain target companies may also be constrained by a scarcity of available acquirors, depending upon applicable regulatory restrictions and antitrust considerations.

A white squire defense, which involves placing a block of voting stock in friendly hands, may be more quickly realized. * * *

2. Restructuring Defenses

Restructurings have been driven in part by the threat of hostile takeovers. The failure of a company's stock price to reflect fully the value of its various businesses has provided opportunities for acquirors to profit by acquiring a company, breaking it up and selling the separate pieces for substantially more than was paid for the entire company. A primary goal of any restructuring is to cause the value of a company's various businesses to be better understood and, ultimately, to be better reflected in its stock price.

* * *

In addition to asset sales, a stock repurchase plan * * * may be an effective response to a takeover threat. Buybacks at or slightly above the current market price allow stockholders to lock in current market values and reduce a company's available cash, which may be critical to any leveraged acquisition bid. * * *

* * *

3. Corporate Spin-Offs and Split-Ups

Companies have used spin-offs, split-offs and similar transactions to enhance shareholder values and, in some cases, to frustrate hostile acquisition attempts. One means of focusing stock market attention on a company's underlying assets is to place desirable assets in a corporation and exchange shares of the new company for shares of the parent company (known as a "split-off"), which usually is done after selling off some of the shares of the new company in an initial public offering; another is to distribute all of the shares of the new company to the parent company's shareholders as a dividend (known as a "spin-off"). Another means of boosting the share price of a company is to "split-up" (i.e., deconglomerate—sell off businesses that no longer fit the company's strategic plans or split the company into logically separate units). In all of these cases, a company tries to focus the market's attention on its individual businesses which, viewed separately, may enjoy a higher market valuation than when viewed together.

* * *

4.   Regulatory Action

In addition to antitrust regulation, which may itself provide an important ground for disputing the feasibility of a hostile offer, many companies are subject to other regulatory authorities that must approve a change of control. In industries such as telecommunications and banking, federal (and sometimes state) regulators may be receptive to arguments made on behalf of a target (or by a target itself) maintaining that a merger is not consistent with the policies and practices of the relevant agency. A company subject to such regulation may take full advantage of any rights it may have to file protests and comments with such agencies. * * *

* * *

CHAPTER 12

FRAUD AND RELATED ISSUES UNDER RULE 10b–5 AND THE SARBANES-OXLEY ACT

SITUATION 12

In addition to the causes of action enumerated in Situations 8 and 9, each of the shareholder suits that have been brought against Microtec also allege violations of Exchange Act Section 10(b) and Rule 10b–5 and 18 U.S.C. § 1348.

In the course of discovery in connection with these suits, both you and the plaintiffs' counsel have learned that Microtec delayed for two weeks in making its first public announcement about its decreased profits and its unfavorable bad debt experience, hoping that other microcomputer companies facing similar problems would disclose their problems first.

In considering this situation refer to the following, in addition to the materials in this chapter: Exchange Act Sections 20, 21, 21C, 21D(b), (e) and (f) and 21E and Regulation FD.

A. OVERVIEW OF RULE 10b–5

The Commission adopted Rule 10b–5 in 1942 to close a gap in the anti-fraud provisions of the securities laws. The Commission's regional administrator in Boston discovered that a company president was inducing the company's shareholders to sell their shares to him at a low price by telling the shareholders the company was doing badly, while in fact the company was doing very well. The regional administrator reported this to the Commission's staff. The general anti-fraud provision then available, Securities Act Section 17(a), was of no help because it covers fraud only in the sale of securities, not in their purchase. To solve this problem, the staff drafted Rule 10b–5 by putting the numbered subdivisions of Securities Act Section 17(a) (which describe various kinds of prohibited conduct) together with language from Exchange Act Section 10(b) (which makes it unlawful by jurisdictional means to use, "in connection with the purchase or sale of any security * * *, any manipulative or deceptive device or contrivance" in violation of any rule of the Commission). That day the staff presented the proposal to the

Commissioners, who passed it without comment, except for Sumner Pike, who said, "Well, we are against fraud, aren't we?"[1]

Here is the resulting rule:

Rule 10b–5. Employment of Manipulative and Deceptive Devices

It shall be unlawful for any person, directly or indirectly, by the use of any means or instrumentality of interstate commerce, or of the mails or of any facility of any national securities exchange,

(a) To employ any device, scheme, or artifice to defraud,

(b) To make any untrue statement of a material fact or to omit to state a material fact necessary in order to make the statements made, in the light of the circumstances under which they were made, not misleading, or

(c) To engage in any act, practice, or course of business which operates or would operate as a fraud or deceit upon any person, in connection with the purchase or sale of any security.

The first big event in the history of Rule 10b–5 was the 1946 decision in Kardon v. National Gypsum Co.[2] In this case, with which all subsequent courts have agreed, a district court found that an implied private right of action exists under the rule. From that time until the 1960s, the use of the rule grew slowly. Its use then began to soar, partially as a result of In re Cady, Roberts & Co.,[3] decided by the Commission in 1961, and SEC v. Texas Gulf Sulphur Co.,[4] handed down by the Second Circuit in 1968. Both of these cases involved what is known as "insider trading" *Cady, Roberts* appears in Chapter 13, which is devoted to that subject. *Texas Gulf Sulphur* has an additional aspect, however, and is set out immediately below as an introduction to many of the themes appearing in Rule 10b–5 jurisprudence.

SEC v. Texas Gulf Sulphur Co.

United States Court of Appeals, Second Circuit, 1968.
401 F.2d 833.

■ Before LUMBARD, CHIEF JUDGE, and WATERMAN, MOORE, FRIENDLY, SMITH, KAUFMAN, HAYS, ANDERSON and FEINBERG, CIRCUIT JUDGES.

■ WATERMAN, CIRCUIT JUDGE:

This action was commenced in the United States District Court for the Southern District of New York by the Securities and Exchange

---

[1] *Proceedings, Conference on Codification of the Federal Securities Laws* (Comments of Milton Freeman), 22 Bus.Law. 793, 922 (1967).

[2] 69 F.Supp. 512 (E.D.Pa.1946).

[3] 40 S.E.C. 907 (1961).

[4] 401 F.2d 833 (2d Cir.1968).

Commission (the SEC) pursuant to Sec. 21(e) of the Securities Exchange Act of 1934 (the Act), against Texas Gulf Sulphur Company (TGS) and several of its officers, directors and employees, to enjoin certain conduct by TGS and the individual defendants said to violate Section 10(b) of the Act and Rule 10b–5 (the Rule), promulgated thereunder, and to compel the rescission by the individual defendants of securities transactions assertedly conducted contrary to law. The complaint alleged (1) that defendants Fogarty, Mollison, Darke, Murray, Huntington, O'Neill, Clayton, Crawford, and Coates had either personally or through agents purchased TGS stock or calls thereon from November 12, 1963 through April 16, 1964 on the basis of material inside information concerning the results of TGS drilling in Timmins, Ontario, while such information remained undisclosed to the investing public generally or to the particular sellers; (2) that defendants Darke and Coates had divulged such information to others for use in purchasing TGS stock or calls[5] or recommended its purchase while the information was undisclosed to the public or to the sellers; that defendants Stephens, Fogarty, Mollison, Holyk, and Kline had accepted options to purchase TGS stock on Feb. 20, 1964 without disclosing the material information as to the drilling progress to either the Stock Option Committee or the TGS Board of Directors; and [(3)] that TGS issued a deceptive press release on April 12, 1964. The case was tried at length before Judge Bonsal of the Southern District of New York, sitting without a jury. Judge Bonsal in a detailed opinion decided, *inter alia,* that the insider activity prior to April 9, 1964 was not illegal because the drilling results were not "material" until then; that Clayton and Crawford had traded in violation of law because they traded after that date; that Coates had committed no violation as he did not trade before disclosure was made; and that the issuance of the press release was not unlawful because it was not issued for the purpose of benefiting the corporation, there was no evidence that any insider used the release to his personal advantage and it was not "misleading, or deceptive on the basis of the facts then known." Defendants Clayton and Crawford appeal from that part of the decision below which held that they had violated Sec. 10(b) and Rule 10b–5 and the SEC appeals from the remainder of the decision which dismissed the complaint against defendants TGS, Fogarty, Mollison, Holyk, Darke, Stephens, Kline, Murray, and Coates.

* * *

THE FACTUAL SETTING

This action derives from the exploratory activities of TGS begun in 1957 on the Canadian Shield in eastern Canada. In March of 1959, aerial geophysical surveys were conducted over more than 15,000 square miles of this area by a group led by defendant Mollison, a mining engineer and

---

[5]   A "call" is a negotiable option contract by which the bearer has the right to buy from the writer of the contract a certain number of shares of a particular stock at a fixed price on or before a certain agreed-upon date.

a Vice President of TGS. The group included defendant Holyk, TGS's chief geologist, defendant Clayton, an electrical engineer and geophysicists, and defendant Darke, a geologist. These operations resulted in the detection of numerous anomalies, i.e., extraordinary variations in the conductivity of rocks, one of which was on the Kidd 55 segment of land located near Timmins, Ontario. * * * These results were so remarkable that neither Clayton, an experienced geophysicists, nor four other TGS expert witnesses, had ever seen or heard of a comparable initial exploratory drill hole in a base metal deposit. So, the trial court concluded, "There is no doubt that the drill core of K–55–1 was unusually good and that it excited the interest and speculation of those who knew about it." By March 27, 1964, TGS decided that the land acquisition program had advanced to such a point that the company might well resume drilling, and drilling was resumed on March 31.

During this period, from November 12, 1963 when K–55–1 was completed, to March 31, 1964 when drilling was resumed, certain of the individual defendants * * * , and persons * * * said to have received "tips" from them, purchased TGS stock or calls thereon. Prior to these transactions these persons had owned 1135 shares of TGS stock and possessed no calls; thereafter they owned a total of 8235 shares and possessed 12,300 calls.

On February 20, 1964, also during this period, TGS issued stock options to 26 of its officers and employees whose salaries exceeded a specified amount, five of whom were the individual defendants Stephens, Fogarty, Mollison, Holyk, and Kline. Of these, only Kline was unaware of the detailed results of K–55–1, but he, too, knew that a hole containing favorable bodies of copper and zinc ore had been drilled in Timmins. At this time, neither the TGS Stock Option Committee nor its Board of Directors had been informed of the results of K–55–1, presumably because of the pending land acquisition program which required confidentiality. All of the foregoing defendants accepted the options granted them.

* * *

[The results of drilling resumed on March 31 prompted the trial court to conclude] "There was real evidence that a body of commercially minable ore might exist."

* * *

Meanwhile, rumors that a major ore strike was in the making had been circulating throughout Canada. On the morning of Saturday, April 11, Stephens at his home in Greenwich, Conn. read in the New York Herald Tribune and in the New York Times unauthorized reports of the TGS drilling which seemed to infer a rich strike from the fact that the drill cores had been flown to the United States for chemical assay. Stephens immediately contacted Fogarty at his home in Rye, N.Y., who in turn telephoned and later that day visited Mollison at Mollison's home in Greenwich to obtain a current report and evaluation of the drilling progress. The following morning, Sunday, Fogarty again telephoned Mollison, inquiring whether Mollison had any further information and told him to return to Timmins with Holyk, the TGS Chief Geologist, as soon as possible "to move things along." With the aid of one Carroll, a public relations consultant, Fogarty drafted a press release designed to quell the rumors, which release, after having been channeled through Stephens and Huntington, a TGS attorney, was issued at 3:00 P.M. on Sunday, April 12, and which appeared in the morning newspapers of general circulation on Monday, April 13. It read in pertinent part as follows:

> NEW YORK, April 12—The following statement was made today by Dr. Charles F. Fogarty, executive vice president of Texas Gulf Sulphur Company, in regard to the company's drilling operations near Timmins, Ontario, Canada. Dr. Fogarty said:
>
> "During the past few days, the exploration activities of Texas Gulf Sulphur in the area of Timmins, Ontario, have been widely reported in the press, coupled with rumors of a substantial copper discovery there. These reports exaggerate the scale of operations, and mention plans and statistics of size and grade of ore that are without factual basis and have evidently originated by speculation of people not connected with TGS.
>
> * * *
>
> "Most of the areas drilled in Eastern Canada have revealed either barren pyrite or graphite without value; a few have resulted in discoveries of small or marginal sulphide ore bodies.
>
> "Recent drilling on one property near Timmins has led to preliminary indications that more drilling would be required for proper evaluation of this prospect. The drilling done to date has not been conclusive, but the statements made by many outside quarters are unreliable and include information and figures that are not available to TGS.
>
> "The work done to date has not been sufficient to reach definite conclusions and any statement as to size and grade of ore would be premature and possibly misleading. When we have progressed to the point where reasonable and logical conclusions can be made, TGS will issue a definite statement to its stockholders and to the public in order to clarify the Timmins project."
>
> * * *

The release purported to give the Timmins drilling results as of the release date, April 12. From Mollison Fogarty had been told of the developments through 7:00 P.M. on April 10, and of the remarkable discoveries made up to that time, detailed supra, which discoveries, according to the calculations of the experts who testified for the SEC at the hearing, demonstrated that TGS had already discovered 6.2 to 8.3 million tons of proven ore having gross assay values from $26 to $29 per ton. TGS experts, on the other hand, denied at the hearing that proven or probable ore could have been calculated on April 11 or 12 because there was then no assurance of continuity in the mineralized zone.

The evidence as to the effect of this release on the investing public was equivocal and less than abundant. On April 13 the New York Herald Tribune in an article head-noted "Copper Rumor Deflated" quoted from the TGS release of April 12 and backtracked from its original April 11 report of a major strike but nevertheless inferred from the TGS release that "recent mineral exploratory activity near Timmins, Ontario, has provided preliminary favorable results, sufficient at least to require a step-up in drilling operations." Some witnesses who testified at the hearing stated that they found the release encouraging. On the other hand, a Canadian mining security specialist, Roche, stated that "earlier in the week [before April 16] we had a Dow Jones saying that they [TGS] didn't have anything basically" and a TGS stock specialist for the Midwest Stock Exchange became concerned about his long position in the stock after reading the release. The trial court stated only that "While, in retrospect, the press release may appear gloomy or incomplete, this does not make it misleading or deceptive on the basis of the facts then known."

* * *

While drilling activity ensued to completion, TGS officials were taking steps toward ultimate disclosure of the discovery. On April 13, a previously-invited reporter for The Northern Miner, a Canadian mining industry journal, visited the drillsite, interviewed Mollison, Holyk and Darke, and prepared an article which confirmed a 10 million ton ore strike. This report, after having been submitted to Mollison and returned to the reporter unamended on April 15, was published in the April 16 issue. A statement relative to the extent of the discovery, in substantial part drafted by Mollison, was given to the Ontario Minister of Mines for release to the Canadian media. Mollison and Holyk expected it to be released over the airways at 11 P.M. on April 15th, but, for undisclosed reasons, it was not released until 9:40 A.M. on the 16th. An official detailed statement, announcing a strike of at least 25 million tons of ore, based on the drilling data set forth above, was read to representatives of American financial media from 10:00 A.M. to 10:10 or 10:15 A.M. on April 16, and appeared over Merrill Lynch's private wire at 10:29 A.M. and, somewhat later than expected, over the Dow Jones ticker tape at 10:54 A.M.

Between the time the first press release was issued on April 12 and the dissemination of the TGS official announcement on the morning of April 16, the only defendants before us on appeal who engaged in market activity were Clayton and Crawford and TGS director Coates. Clayton ordered 200 shares of TGS stock through his Canadian broker on April 15 and the order was executed that day over the Midwest Stock Exchange. Crawford ordered 300 shares at midnight on the 15th and another 300 shares at 8:30 A.M. the next day, and these orders were executed over the Midwest Exchange in Chicago at its opening on April 16. Coates left the TGS press conference and called his broker son-in-law Haemisegger shortly before 10:20 A.M. on the 16th and ordered 2,000 shares of TGS for family trust accounts of which Coates was a trustee but not a beneficiary; Haemisegger executed this order over the New York and Midwest Exchanges, and he and his customers purchased 1500 additional shares.

During the period of drilling in Timmins, the market price of TGS stock fluctuated but steadily gained overall. On Friday, November 8, when the drilling began, the stock closed at 17 $3/8$; on Friday, November 15, after K–55–1 had been completed, it closed at 18. After a slight decline to 16 $3/8$ by Friday, November 22, the price rose to 20 $7/8$ by December 13, when the chemical assay results of K–55–1 were received, and closed at a high of 24 $1/8$ on February 21, the day after the stock options had been issued. It had reached a price of 26 by March 31, after the land acquisition program had been completed and drilling had been resumed, and continued to ascend to 30 $1/8$ by the close of trading on April 10, at which time the drilling progress up to then was evaluated for the April 12th press release. On April 13, the day on which the April 12 release was disseminated, TGS opened at 30 $1/8$, rose immediately to a high of 32 and gradually tapered off to close at 30 $7/8$. It closed at 30 $1/4$ the next day, and at 29 $3/8$ on April 15. On April 16, the day of the official announcement of the Timmins discovery, the price climbed to a high of 37 and closed at 36 $3/8$. By May 15, TGS stock was selling at 58 $1/4$.

I.   THE INDIVIDUAL DEFENDANTS

A.   *Introductory*

* * *

* * * Rule [10b–5] is based in policy on the justifiable expectation of the securities marketplace that all investors trading on impersonal exchanges have relatively equal access to material information. The essence of the Rule is that anyone who, trading for his own account in the securities of a corporation has "access, directly or indirectly, to information intended to be available only for a corporate purpose and not for the personal benefit of anyone" may not take "advantage of such information knowing it is unavailable to those with whom he is dealing," i.e., the investing public. Matter of Cady, Roberts & Co., 40 SEC 907, 912 (1961). Insiders, as directors or management officers are, of course, by this Rule, precluded from so unfairly dealing, but the Rule is also applicable to one possessing the information who may not be strictly termed an "insider" within the meaning of Sec. 16(b) of the Act. Cady, Roberts, supra. Thus, anyone in possession of material inside information must either disclose it to the investing public, or, if he is disabled from disclosing it in order to protect a corporate confidence, or he chooses not to do so, must abstain from trading in or recommending the securities concerned while such inside information remains undisclosed. So, it is here no justification for insider activity that disclosure was forbidden by the legitimate corporate objective of acquiring options to purchase the land surrounding the exploration site; if the information was, as the SEC contends, material, its possessors should have kept out of the market until disclosure was accomplished. Cady, Roberts, supra at 911.

B.   Material Inside Information

An insider is not, of course, always foreclosed from investing in his own company merely because he may be more familiar with company operations than are outside investors. An insider's duty to disclose information or his duty to abstain from dealing in his company's securities arises only in "those situations which are essentially extraordinary in nature and which are reasonably certain to have a substantial effect on the market price of the security if [the extraordinary situation is] disclosed." Fleischer, Securities Trading and Corporate Information Practices: The Implications of the Texas Gulf Sulphur Proceeding, 51 Va.L.Rev. 1271, 1289.

Nor is an insider obligated to confer upon outside investors the benefit of his superior financial or other expert analysis by disclosing his educated guesses or predictions. The only regulatory objective is that access to material information be enjoyed equally, but this objective requires nothing more than the disclosure of basic facts so that outsiders may draw upon their own evaluative expertise in reaching their own investment decisions with knowledge equal to that of the insiders.

[A] material fact * * * must be effectively disclosed to the investing public prior to the commencement of insider trading in the corporation's securities. * * *

In each case, then, whether facts are material within Rule 10b–5 when the facts relate to a particular event and are undisclosed by those persons who are knowledgeable thereof will depend at any given time upon a balancing of both the indicated probability that the event will occur and the anticipated magnitude of the event in light of the totality of the company activity. Here, notwithstanding the trial court's conclusion that the results of the first drill core, K–55–1, were "too 'remote' * * * to have had any significant impact on the market, i.e., to be deemed material," knowledge of the possibility, which surely was more than marginal, of the existence of a mine of the vast magnitude indicated by the remarkably rich drill core located rather close to the surface (suggesting mineability by the less expensive open-pit method) within the confines of a large anomaly (suggesting an extensive region of mineralization) might well have affected the price of TGS stock and would certainly have been an important fact to a reasonable, if speculative, investor in deciding whether he should buy, sell, or hold. * * *

* * * Our survey of the facts found below conclusively establishes that knowledge of the results of the discovery hole, K–55–1, would have been important to a reasonable investor and might have affected the price of the stock.[6] On April 16, The Northern Miner, a trade publication in wide circulation among mining stock specialists, called K–55–1, the discovery hole, "one of the most impressive drill holes completed in modern times." Roche, a Canadian broker whose firm specialized in mining securities, characterized the importance to investors of the results of K–55–1. He stated that the completion of "the first drill hole" with "a 600 foot drill core is very significant[,] * * * anything over 200 feet is considered very significant and 600 feet is just beyond your wildest imagination." * * *

Finally, a major factor in determining whether the K–55–1 discovery was a material fact is the importance attached to the drilling results by those who knew about it. In view of other unrelated recent developments favorably affecting TGS, participation by an informed person in a regular stock-purchase program, or even sporadic trading by an informed person, might lend only nominal support to the inference of the materiality of the K–55–1 discovery; nevertheless, the timing by those who knew of it of their stock purchases and their purchases of *short-term* calls—purchases in some cases by individuals who had never before purchased calls or even TGS stock—virtually compels the inference that the insiders were influenced by the drilling results. * * *

* * *

The core of Rule 10b–5 is the implementation of the Congressional purpose that all investors should have equal access to the rewards of participation in securities transactions. It was the intent of Congress that all members of the investing public should be subject to identical market risks—which market risks include, of course the risk that one's evaluative capacity or one's capital available to put at risk may exceed another's capacity or capital. The insiders here were not trading on an equal footing with the outside investors. * * *

We hold, therefore, that all transactions in TGS stock or calls by individuals apprised of the drilling results of K–55–1 were made in violation of Rule 10b–5. * * *

---

[6] We do not suggest that material facts must be disclosed immediately; the timing of disclosure is a matter for the business judgment of the corporate officers entrusted with the management of the corporation within the affirmative disclosure requirements promulgated by the exchanges and by the SEC. Here, a valuable corporate purpose was served by delaying the publication of the K–55–1 discovery. We do intend to convey, however, that where a corporate purpose is thus served by withholding the news of a material fact, those persons who are thus quite properly true to their corporate trust must not during the period of non-disclosure deal personally in the corporation's securities or give to outsiders confidential information not generally available to all the corporations' stockholders and to the public at large.

* * *

C.   *When May Insiders Act?*

Appellant Crawford, who ordered the purchase of TGS stock shortly before the TGS April 16 official announcement, and defendant Coates, who placed orders with and communicated the news to his broker immediately after the official announcement was read at the TGS-called press conference, concede that they were in possession of material information. They contend, however, that their purchases were not proscribed purchases for the news had already been effectively disclosed. We disagree.

Crawford telephoned his orders to his Chicago broker about midnight on April 15 and again at 8:30 in the morning of the 16th, with instructions to buy at the opening of the Midwest Stock Exchange that morning. The trial court's finding that "he sought to, and did, 'beat the news,'" is well documented by the record. The rumors of a major ore strike which had been circulated in Canada and, to a lesser extent, in New York, had been disclaimed by the TGS press release of April 12, which significantly promised the public an official detailed announcement when possibilities had ripened into actualities. The abbreviated announcement to the Canadian press at 9:40 A.M. on the 16th by the Ontario Minister of Mines and the report carried by The Northern Miner, parts of which had sporadically reached New York on the morning of the 16th through reports from Canadian affiliates to a few New York investment firms, are assuredly not the equivalent of the official 10–15 minute announcement which was not released to the American financial press until after 10:00 A.M. Crawford's orders had been placed before that. Before insiders may act upon material information, such information must have been effectively disclosed in a manner sufficient to insure its availability to the investing public. Particularly here, where a formal announcement to the entire financial news media had been promised in a prior official release known to the media, all insider activity must await dissemination of the promised official announcement.

Coates was absolved by the court below because his telephone order was placed shortly before 10:20 A.M. on April 16, which was after the announcement had been made even though the news could not be considered already a matter of public information. This result seems to have been predicated upon a misinterpretation of dicta in *Cady, Roberts,* where the SEC instructed insiders to "keep out of the market until the established procedures for public release of the information are *carried out* instead of hastening to execute transactions in advance of, and in frustration of, the objectives of the release" (emphasis supplied). The reading of a news release, which prompted Coates into action, is merely the first step in the process of dissemination required for compliance with the regulatory objective of providing all investors with an equal opportunity to make informed investment judgments. Assuming that the contents of the official release could instantaneously be acted upon, at the minimum Coates should have waited until the news could reasonably have been expected to appear over the media of widest circulation, the Dow Jones broad tape, rather than hastening to insure an advantage to himself and his broker son-in-law.

* * *

E. *May Insiders Accept Stock Options Without Disclosing Material Information to the Issuer?*

On February 20, 1964, defendants Stephens, Fogarty, Mollison, Holyk and Kline accepted stock options issued to them and a number of other top officers of TGS, although not one of them had informed the Stock Option Committee of the Board of Directors or the Board of the results of K–55–1, which information we have held was then material. The SEC sought rescission of these options. The trial court, in addition to finding the knowledge of the results of the K–55 discovery to be immaterial, held that Kline had no detailed knowledge of the drilling progress and that Holyk and Mollison could reasonably assume that their superiors, Stephens and Fogarty, who were directors of the corporation, would report the results if that was advisable; indeed all employees had been instructed not to divulge this information pending completion of the land acquisition program. Therefore, the court below concluded that only directors Stephens and Fogarty, of the top management, would have violated the Rule by accepting stock options without disclosure, but it also found that they had not acted improperly as the information in their possession was not material. In view of our conclusion as to materiality we hold that Stephens and Fogarty violated the Rule by accepting them. * * *

Contrary to the belief of the trial court that Kline had no duty to disclose his knowledge of the Kidd project before accepting the stock option offered him, we believe that he, a vice president, who had become the general counsel of TGS in January 1964, but who had been secretary of the corporation since January 1961, and was present in that capacity when the options were granted, and who was in charge of the mechanics of issuance and acceptance of the options, was a member of top management and under a duty before accepting his option to disclose any material information he may have possessed, and, as he did not disclose such information to the Option Committee we direct rescission of the option he received. As to Holyk and Mollison, the SEC has not appealed the holding below that they, not being then members of top management (although Mollison was a vice president) had no duty to disclose their knowledge of the drilling before accepting their options. Therefore, the issue of whether, by accepting, they violated the Act, is not before us, and the holding below is undisturbed.

II.   THE CORPORATE DEFENDANT

A.   *Introductory*

At 3:00 P.M. on April 12, 1964, evidently believing it desirable to comment upon the rumors concerning the Timmins project, TGS issued the press release quoted in pertinent part [above]. The SEC argued below and maintains on this appeal that this release painted a misleading and deceptive picture of the drilling progress at the time of its issuance, and hence violated Rule 10b–5(2). TGS relies on the holding of the court below that "The issuance of the release produced no unusual market action" and "In the absence of a showing that the purpose of the April 12 press release was to affect the market price of TGS stock to the advantage of TGS or its insiders, the issuance of the press release did not constitute a violation of Section 10(b) or Rule 10b–5 since it was not issued 'in connection with the purchase or sale of any security' " and, alternatively, "even if it had been established that the April 12 release was issued in connection with the purchase or sale of any security, the Commission has failed to demonstrate that it was false, misleading or deceptive."

Before further discussing this matter it seems desirable to state exactly what the SEC claimed in its complaint and what it seeks. The specific SEC allegation in its complaint is that this April 12 press release " * * * was materially false and misleading and was known by certain of defendant Texas Gulf's officers and employees, including defendants Fogarty, Mollison, Holyk, Darke and Clayton, to be materially false and misleading."

The specific relief the SEC seeks is * * * a permanent injunction restraining the issuance of any further materially false and misleading publicly distributed informative items.

B.   *The "In Connection With * * * " Requirement*

In adjudicating upon the relationship of this phrase to the case before us it would appear that the court below used a standard that does not reflect the congressional purpose that prompted the passage of the Securities Exchange Act of 1934.

* * *

[I]t seems clear from the legislative purpose Congress expressed in the Act, and the legislative history of Section 10(b) that Congress when it used the phrase "in connection with the purchase or sale of any security" intended only that the device employed, whatever it might be, be of a sort that would cause reasonable investors to rely thereon, and, in connection therewith, so relying, cause them to purchase or sell a corporation's securities. There is no indication that Congress intended that the corporations or persons responsible for the issuance of a misleading statement would not violate the section unless they engaged in related securities transactions * * * . * * *

* * *

C. Did the Issuance of the April 12
Release Violate Rule 10b–5?

Turning first to the question of whether the release was misleading, i.e., whether it conveyed to the public a false impression of the drilling situation at the time of its issuance, we note initially that the trial court did not actually decide this question. * * * while we certainly agree with the trial court that "in retrospect, the press release may appear gloomy or incomplete," we cannot, from the present record, by applying the standard Congress intended, definitively conclude that it was deceptive or misleading to the reasonable investor, or that he would have been misled by it. * * *

* * *

We conclude, then, that, having established that the release was issued in a manner reasonably calculated to affect the market price of TGS stock and to influence the investing public, we must remand to the district court to decide whether the release was misleading to the reasonable investor and if found to be misleading, whether the court in its discretion should issue the injunction the SEC seeks.

* * *

The most notorious use of Rule 10b–5 probably has been in insider trading cases, typically those in which an officer, director or other person who has a fiduciary relationship with a corporation buys or sells the company's securities while in the possession of material, non-public information (or selectively discloses such information to another party who then trades). As indicated above, Chapter 13 is devoted to an in-depth consideration of insider trading. *Texas Gulf Sulphur* reveals, though, that the rule is also used in other situations, notably including when a corporation issues misleading information to the public or keeps silent when it has a duty to disclose. It also has been used when a person mismanages a corporation in ways that are connected with the purchase or sale of securities. Discussion of two more specialized uses is reserved for Chapter 16, which deals with the regulation of the securities business. These are (1) when a securities firm or another person manipulates the market for a security traded in the over-the-counter market; and (2) when a securities firm or securities professional engages in certain other forms of conduct connected with the purchase or sale of securities.

In reading a case interpreting Rule 10b–5 it usually is helpful to remind oneself to ask whether the case was brought by the government or by private plaintiffs. This distinction is significant because private plaintiffs must make showings not required of the Commission or the Department of Justice. Coverage in this chapter therefore separates discussion of those showings generally required from discussion of those showings required only of private plaintiffs. Sections 12B and 12C address the most important of these respective matters. Section 12D examines the specific question of when issuers have a duty to disclose; Section 12E discusses the various penalties and damages that may be associated with violations of Rule 10b–5 that do not involve insider trading. Section 12F deals with secondary liability for violations of Rule 10b–5.

Before plunging into the story of Rule 10b–5, it should be noted that the tale of its development has not been a consistent one. The boom that started in the 1960s was more-or-less busted by two Supreme Court decisions issued in the mid-1970s. These were Blue Chip Stamps v. Manor Drug Stores[7] and Ernst & Ernst v. Hochfelder,[8] each of which appears in a later section of this chapter. The rule's history since these cases is somewhat checkered, but it nonetheless continues to occupy the preeminent position among the anti-fraud provisions in the securities laws. With the passage of the Sarbanes-Oxley Act of 2002, however, it gained interesting company. Sarbanes-Oxley amended title 18 of the United States Code to add a new Section 1348, which addresses fraud in connection with securities of Exchange Act reporting companies. This provision, along with other fraud-related provisions in Sarbanes-Oxley, is discussed below in Section 12G.

B. GENERAL REQUIREMENTS

I. THE "MANIPULATIVE OR DECEPTIVE" REQUIREMENT

The following case reminds us that Rule 10b–5 always must be understood in light of its enabling statutory provision, Exchange Act Section 10(b).

Santa Fe Industries, Inc. v. Green
Supreme Court of the United States, 1977.
430 U.S. 462.

■ MR. JUSTICE WHITE delivered the opinion of the Court.

The issue in this case involves the reach and coverage of § 10(b) of the Securities Exchange Act of 1934 and Rule 10b–5 thereunder in the context of a Delaware short-form merger transaction used by the majority stockholder of a corporation to eliminate the minority interest.

I

In 1936, petitioner Santa Fe Industries, Inc. (Santa Fe), acquired control of 60% of the stock of Kirby Lumber Corp. (Kirby), a Delaware corporation. Through a series of purchases over the succeeding years, Santa Fe increased its control of Kirby's stock to 95%; the purchase prices during the period 1968–1973 ranged from $65 to $92.50 per share. In

---

[7]   421 U.S. 723 (1975).

[8]   425 U.S. 185 (1976).

1974, wishing to acquire 100% ownership of Kirby, Santa Fe availed itself of § 253 of the Delaware Corporation Law, known as the "short-form merger" statute. Section 253 permits a parent corporation owning at least 90% of the stock of a subsidiary to merge with that subsidiary, upon approval by the parent's board of directors, and to make payment in cash for the shares of the minority stockholders. The statute does not require the consent of, or advance notice to, the minority stockholders. However, notice of the merger must be given within 10 days after its effective date, and any stockholder who is dissatisfied with the terms of the merger may petition the Delaware Court of Chancery for a decree ordering the surviving corporation to pay him the fair value of the shares, as determined by a court-appointed appraiser subject to review by the court.

Santa Fe obtained independent appraisals of the physical assets of Kirby—land, timber, buildings, and machinery—and of Kirby's oil, gas, and mineral interests. These appraisals, together with other financial information, were submitted to Morgan Stanley & Co. (Morgan Stanley), an investment banking firm retained to appraise the fair market value of Kirby stock. Kirby's physical assets were appraised at $320 million (amounting to $640 for each of the 500,000 shares); Kirby's stock was valued by Morgan Stanley at $125 per share. Under the terms of the merger, minority stockholders were offered $150 per share.

* * *

Respondents, minority stockholders of Kirby, objected to the terms of the merger, but did not pursue their appraisal remedy in the Delaware Court of Chancery. Instead, they brought this action in federal court on behalf of the corporation and other minority stockholders, seeking to set aside the merger or to recover what they claimed to be the fair value of their shares. The amended complaint asserted that, based on the fair market value of Kirby's physical assets as revealed by the appraisal included in the information statement sent to minority shareholders, Kirby's stock was worth at least $772 per share. The complaint alleged further that the merger took place without prior notice to minority stockholders; that the purpose of the merger was to appropriate the difference between the "conceded pro rata value of the physical assets" and the offer of $150 per share—to "freez[e] out the minority stockholders at a wholly inadequate price"; and that Santa Fe, knowing the appraised value of the physical assets, obtained a "fraudulent appraisal" of the stock from Morgan Stanley and offered $25 above that appraisal "in order to lull the minority stockholders into erroneously believing that [Santa Fe was] generous." This course of conduct was alleged to be "a violation of Rule 10b–5 because defendants employed a 'device, scheme, or artifice to defraud' and engaged in an 'act, practice or course of business which operates or would operate as a fraud or deceit upon any person, in connection with the purchase or sale of any security.'" * * *

The District Court dismissed the complaint for failure to state a claim upon which relief could be granted. * * *

* * *

A divided Court of Appeals for the Second Circuit reversed. * * *

* * *

II

* * * The Court of Appeals' approach to the interpretation of Rule 10b–5 is inconsistent with that taken by the Court last Term in Ernst & Ernst v. Hochfelder, 425 U.S. 185 (1976).

Ernst & Ernst makes clear that in deciding whether a complaint states a cause of action for "fraud" under Rule 10b–5, "we turn first to the language of § 10(b), for '[t]he starting point in every case involving construction of a statute is the language itself.' " * * *

* * * [A]s the Court [held in *Ernst & Ernst*], the language of the statute must control the interpretation of the Rule:

> Rule 10b–5 was adopted pursuant to authority granted the [Securities and Exchange] Commission under § 10(b). The rulemaking power granted to an administrative agency charged with the administration of a federal statute is not the power to make law. Rather, it is " 'the power to adopt regulations to carry into effect the will of Congress as expressed by the statute.' "
> * * * [The scope of the Rule] cannot exceed the power granted the Commission by Congress under § 10(b).

The language of § 10(b) gives no indication that Congress meant to prohibit any conduct not involving manipulation or deception. Nor have we been cited to any evidence in the legislative history that would support a departure from the language of the statute. * * * Thus the claim of fraud and fiduciary breach in this complaint states a cause of action under any part of Rule 10b–5 only if the conduct alleged can be fairly viewed as "manipulative or deceptive" within the meaning of the statute.

III

It is our judgment that the transaction, if carried out as alleged in the complaint, was neither deceptive nor manipulative and therefore did not violate either § 10(b) of the Act or Rule 10b–5.

As we have indicated, the case comes to us on the premise that the complaint failed to allege a material misrepresentation or material failure to disclose. The finding of the District Court, undisturbed by the Court of Appeals, was that there was no "omission" or "misstatement" in the information statement accompanying the notice of merger. On the basis of the information provided, minority shareholders could either accept the price offered or reject it and seek an appraisal in the Delaware Court of Chancery. Their choice was fairly presented, and they were furnished with all relevant information on which to base their decision.

We therefore find inapposite the cases relied upon by respondents and the court below, in which the breaches of fiduciary duty held violative of Rule 10b–5 included some element of deception. Those cases forcefully reflect the principle that "[§] 10(b) must be read flexibly, not technically and restrictively" and that the statute provides a cause of action for any plaintiff who "suffer[s] an injury as a result of deceptive practices touching its sale [or purchase] of securities * * * ." Superintendent of Insurance v. Bankers Life & Cas. Co., 404 U.S. 6, 12–13 (1971). But the cases do not support the proposition * * * that a breach of fiduciary duty by majority stockholders, without any deception, misrepresentation, or nondisclosure, violates the statute and the Rule.

It is also readily apparent that the conduct alleged in the complaint was not "manipulative" within the meaning of the statute. "Manipulation" is "virtually a term of art when used in connection with securities markets." *Ernst & Ernst,* 425 U.S., at 199. The term refers generally to practices, such as wash sales, matched orders, or rigged prices, that are intended to mislead investors by artificially affecting market activity.

* * *

IV

* * *

We thus adhere to the position that "Congress by § 10(b) did not seek to regulate transactions which constitute no more than internal corporate mismanagement." Superintendent of Insurance v. Bankers Life & Cas. Co., 404 U.S., at 12. There may well be a need for uniform federal fiduciary standards to govern mergers such as that challenged in this complaint. But those standards should not be supplied by judicial extension of § 10(b) and Rule 10b–5 to "cover the corporate universe."

* * *

A number of cases have featured Section 10(b) and Rule 10b–5 claims based on executives' failure to follow corporate ethics codes. The result in Retail Wholesale & Dept. Store Union Local 338 Ret. Fund v. Hewlett-Packard Co.[9] is not atypical. There, the CEO and Chairman of the Board had engaged in a "very close personal relationship" with an independent contractor and had falsified expense records to cover it up, all while he and the company touted Hewlett-Packard's high ethical standards. Following disclosure of his violation of those standards he resigned, and the stock of the company allegedly lost $10 billion in value. According to the Ninth Circuit, statements about ethics codes were not misrepresentations of facts. Rather, they were aspirational and not capable of objective verification. "A contrary interpretation * * * is simply

---

[9] 845 F.3d 1268 (9th Cir. 2017).

untenable, as it could turn all corporate wrongdoing into securities fraud." In the alternative, the Ninth Circuit also held that any misrepresentation or omission was not material.

II. THE "MATERIALITY" REQUIREMENT

Only the second clause of Rule 10b–5 specifically uses the word "material" but there never has been any doubt that only manipulation or deception with respect to material matters would constitute a violation under any part of the rule. Materiality is regarded as having the same definition throughout the federal securities laws, so the discussions of the concept in earlier chapters also are relevant with respect to Rule 10b–5. In addition, discussions of materiality set out in the Rule 10b–5 context, including the comments of the *Texas Gulf Sulphur* court set out earlier in this chapter, have informed understanding of the concept under other provisions of the Securities and Exchange Acts. Appearing immediately below is an important Supreme Court opinion decided under Rule 10b–5.

Basic Inc. v. Levinson

Supreme Court of the United States, 1988.
485 U.S. 224.

■ JUSTICE BLACKMUN delivered the opinion of the Court.

This case requires us to apply the materiality requirement of section 10(b) of the Securities Exchange Act of 1934 (1934 Act) and the Securities and Exchange Commission's Rule 10b–5, promulgated thereunder, in the context of preliminary corporate merger discussions. We must also determine whether a person who traded a corporation's shares on a securities exchange after the issuance of a materially misleading statement by the corporation may invoke a rebuttable presumption that, in trading, he relied on the integrity of the price set by the market. [Portions of the case relating to the latter issue appear in Section CIIb below.]

I

Prior to December 20, 1978, Basic Incorporated was a publicly traded company primarily engaged in the business of manufacturing chemical refractors for the steel industry. As early as 1965 or 1966, Combustion Engineering, Inc., a company producing mostly alumina-based refractors, expressed some interest in acquiring Basic, but was deterred from pursuing this inclination seriously because of antitrust concerns it then entertained. In 1976, however, regulatory action opened the way to a renewal of Combustion's interest. The "Strategic Plan," dated October 25, 1976, for Combustion's Industrial Products Group included the objective: "Acquire Basic Inc. $30 million."

Beginning in September 1976, Combustion representatives had meetings and telephone conversations with Basic officers and directors, including petitioners here, concerning the possibility of a merger. During 1977 and 1978, Basic made three public statements denying that it was engaged in merger negotiations.[10] On December 18, 1978, Basic asked the New York Stock Exchange to suspend trading in its shares and issued a release stating that it had been "approached" by another company concerning a merger. On December 19, Basic's board endorsed Combustion's offer of $46 per share for its common stock, and on the following day publicly announced its approval of Combustion's tender offer for all outstanding shares.

Respondents are former Basic shareholders who sold their stock after Basic's first public statement of October 21, 1977, and before the suspension of trading in December 1978. Respondents brought a class action against Basic and its directors, asserting that the defendants issued three false or misleading public statements and thereby were in violation of section 10(b) of the 1934 Act and of Rule 10b–5. Respondents alleged that they were injured by selling Basic shares at artificially depressed prices in a market affected by petitioners' misleading statements and in reliance thereon.

* * * [T]he District Court granted summary judgment for the defendants. It held that, as a matter of law, any misstatements were immaterial: there were no negotiations ongoing at the time of the first statement, and although negotiations were taking place when the second and third statements were issued, those negotiations were not "destined, with reasonable certainty, to become a merger agreement in principle."

The United States Court of Appeals for the Sixth Circuit * * * reversed the District Court's summary judgment, and remanded the case. The court reasoned that while petitioners were under no general duty to disclose their discussions with Combustion, any statement the company voluntarily released could not be "so incomplete as to mislead." Id., at 746, quoting SEC v. Texas Gulf Sulphur Co., 401 F.2d 833, 862 (C.A.2 1968) (en banc). In the Court of Appeals' view, Basic's statements that no negotiations were taking place, and that it knew of no corporate

---

[10] On October 21, 1977, after heavy trading and a new high in Basic stock, the following news item appeared in the Cleveland Plain Dealer: "Basic President Max Muller said the company knew no reason for the stock's activity and that no negotiations were under way with any company for a merger. He said Flintkote recently denied Wall Street rumors that it would make a tender offer of $25 a share for control of the Cleveland-based maker of refractors for the steel industry."

On September 25, 1978, in reply to an inquiry from the New York Stock Exchange, Basic issued a release concerning increased activity in its stock and stated that "management is unaware of any present or pending company development that would result in the abnormally heavy trading activity and price fluctuation in company shares that have been experienced in the past few days."

On November 6, 1978, Basic issued to its shareholders a "Nine Months Report 1978." This Report stated: "With regard to the stock market activity in the Company's shares we remain unaware of any present or pending developments which would account for the high volume of trading and price fluctuations in recent months."

developments to account for the heavy trading activity, were misleading. With respect to materiality, the court rejected the argument that preliminary merger discussions are immaterial as a matter of law, and held that "once a statement is made denying the existence of any discussions, even discussions that might not have been material in absence of the denial are material because they make the statement made untrue."

* * *

II

The 1934 Act was designed to protect investors against manipulation of stock prices. Underlying the adoption of extensive disclosure requirements was a legislative philosophy: "There cannot be honest markets without honest publicity. Manipulation and dishonest practices of the market place thrive upon mystery and secrecy." H. R. Rep. No. 1383, 73d Cong., 2d Sess., 11 (1934). This Court "repeatedly has described the 'fundamental purpose' of the Act as implementing a 'philosophy of full disclosure.'" Santa Fe Industries, Inc. v. Green, 430 U.S. 462, 477–478 (1977), quoting SEC v. Capital Gains Research Bureau, Inc., 375 U.S. 180, 186 (1963).

* * *

* * * The Court * * * explicitly has defined a standard of materiality under the securities laws, see TSC Industries, Inc. v. Northway, Inc., 426 U.S. 438 (1976), concluding in the proxy-solicitation context that "an omitted fact is material if there is a substantial likelihood that a reasonable shareholder would consider it important in deciding how to vote." Id., at 449. Acknowledging that certain information concerning corporate developments could well be of "dubious significance," the Court was careful not to set too low a standard of materiality; it was concerned that a minimal standard might bring an overabundance of information within its reach, and lead management "simply to bury the shareholders in an avalanche of trivial information—a result that is hardly conducive to informed decisionmaking." It further explained that to fulfill the materiality requirement "there must be a substantial likelihood that the disclosure of the omitted fact would have been viewed by the reasonable investor as having significantly altered the 'total mix' of information made available." We now expressly adopt the TSC Industries standard of materiality for the section 10(b) and Rule 10b–5 context.

III

The application of this materiality standard to preliminary merger discussions is not self-evident. Where the impact of the corporate development on the target's fortune is certain and clear, the TSC Industries materiality definition admits straightforward application. Where, on the other hand, the event is contingent or speculative in nature, it is difficult to ascertain whether the "reasonable investor" would have considered the omitted information significant at the time.

Merger negotiations, because of the ever-present possibility that the contemplated transaction will not be effectuated, fall into the latter category.

A

Petitioners urge upon us a Third Circuit test for resolving this difficulty. Under this approach, preliminary merger discussions do not become material until "agreement-in-principle" as to the price and structure of the transaction has been reached between the would-be merger partners. By definition, then, information concerning any negotiations not yet at the agreement-in-principle stage could be withheld or even misrepresented without a violation of Rule 10b–5.

Three rationales have been offered in support of the "agreement-in-principle" test. The first derives from the concern expressed in TSC Industries that an investor not be overwhelmed by excessively detailed and trivial information, and focuses on the substantial risk that preliminary merger discussions may collapse because such discussions are inherently tentative, disclosure of their existence itself could mislead investors and foster false optimism. The other two justifications for the agreement-in-principle standard are based on management concerns: because the requirement of "agreement-in-principle" limits the scope of disclosure obligations, it helps preserve the confidentiality of merger discussions where earlier disclosure might prejudice the negotiations; and the test also provides a usable, bright-line rule for determining when disclosure must be made.

None of these policy-based rationales, however, purports to explain why drawing the line at agreement-in-principle reflects the significance of the information upon the investor's decision. The first rationale, and the only one connected to the concerns expressed in TSC Industries, stands soundly rejected, even by a Court of Appeals that otherwise has accepted the wisdom of the agreement-in-principle test. "It assumes that investors are nitwits, unable to appreciate—even when told—that mergers are risky propositions up until the closing." Flamm v. Eberstadt, 814 F.2d [1169, 1175 (7th Cir.1987)]. Disclosure, and not paternalistic withholding of accurate information, is the policy chosen and expressed by Congress. We have recognized time and again, a "fundamental purpose" of the various securities acts, "was to substitute a philosophy of full disclosure for the philosophy of caveat emptor and thus to achieve a high standard of business ethics in the securities industry." SEC v. Capital Gains Research Bureau, Inc., 375 U.S. 180, 186 (1963). The role of the materiality requirement is not to "attribute to investors a child-like simplicity, an inability to grasp the probabilistic significance of negotiations," Flamm v. Eberstadt, 814 F.2d, at 1175, but to filter out essentially useless information that a reasonable investor would not consider significant, even as part of a larger "mix" of factors to consider in making his investment decision.

The second rationale, the importance of secrecy during the early stages of merger discussions, also seems irrelevant to an assessment whether their existence is significant to the trading decision of a reasonable investor. To avoid a "bidding war" over its target, an acquiring firm often will insist that negotiations remain confidential, and at least one Court of Appeals has stated that "silence pending settlement of the price and structure of a deal is beneficial to most investors, most of the time." Flamm v. Eberstadt, 814 F.2d at 1177.

We need not ascertain, however, whether secrecy necessarily maximizes shareholder wealth—although we note that the proposition is at least disputed as a matter of theory and empirical research—for this case does not concern the TIMING of a disclosure; it concerns only its accuracy and completeness. We face here the narrow question whether information concerning the existence and status of preliminary merger discussions is significant to the reasonable investor's trading decision. Arguments based on the premise that some disclosure would be "premature" in a sense are more properly considered under the rubric of an issuer's duty to disclose. The "secrecy" rationale is simply inapposite to the definition of materiality.

The final justification offered in support of the agreement-in-principle test seems to be directed solely at the comfort of corporate managers. A bright-line rule indeed is easier to follow than a standard that requires the exercise of judgment in the light of all the circumstances. But ease of application alone is not an excuse for ignoring the purposes of the securities acts and Congress' policy decisions. Any approach that designates a single fact or occurrence as always determinative of an inherently fact-specific finding such as materiality, must necessarily be over-or under-inclusive. In TSC Industries this Court explained: "The determination of materiality requires delicate assessments of the inferences a 'reasonable shareholder' would draw from a given set of facts and the significance of those inferences to him * * *." After much study, the Advisory Committee on Corporate Disclosure cautioned the SEC against administratively confining materiality to a rigid formula. Courts also would do well to heed this advice.

We therefore find no valid justification for artificially excluding from the definition of materiality information concerning merger discussions, which would otherwise be considered significant to the trading decision of a reasonable investor, merely because agreement-in-principle as to price and structure has not yet been reached by the parties or their representatives.

B

The Sixth Circuit explicitly rejected the agreement-in-principle test, as we do today, but in its place adopted a rule that, if taken literally, would be equally insensitive, in our view, to the distinction between materiality and the other elements of an action under Rule 10b–5:

When a company whose stock is publicly traded makes a statement, as Basic did, that "no negotiations" are underway, and that the corporation knows of "no reason for the stock's activity," and that "management is unaware of any present or pending corporate development that would result in the abnormally heavy trading activity," information concerning ongoing acquisition discussions becomes material *by virtue of the statement denying their existence.*

* * *

In analyzing whether information regarding merger discussions is material such that it must be affirmatively disclosed to avoid a violation of Rule 10b–5, the discussions and their progress are the primary considerations. However, once a statement is made denying the existence of any discussions, even discussions that might not have been material in absence of the denial are material because they make the statement made untrue. (emphasis in original)

This approach, however, fails to recognize that, in order to prevail on a Rule 10b–5 claim, a plaintiff must show that the statements were *misleading* as to a *material* fact. It is not enough that a statement is false or incomplete, if the misrepresented fact is otherwise insignificant.

C

Even before this Court's decision in TSC Industries, the Second Circuit had explained the role of the materiality requirement of Rule 10b–5, with respect to contingent or speculative information or events, in a manner that gave that term meaning that is independent of the other provisions of the Rule. Under such circumstances, materiality "will depend at any given time upon a balancing of both the indicated probability that the event will occur and the anticipated magnitude of the event in light of the totality of the company activity." SEC v. Texas Gulf Sulphur Co., 401 F.2d, at 849. Interestingly, neither the Third Circuit decision adopting the agreement-in-principle test nor petitioners here take issue with this general standard. Rather, they suggest that with respect to preliminary merger discussions, there are good reasons to draw a line at agreement on price and structure.

In a subsequent decision, the late Judge Friendly, writing for a Second Circuit panel, applied the Texas Gulf Sulphur probability/magnitude approach in the specific context of preliminary merger negotiations. After acknowledging that materiality is something to be determined on the basis of the particular facts of each case, he stated:

> Since a merger in which it is bought out is the most important event that can occur in a small corporation's life, to wit, its death, we think that inside information, as regards a merger of this sort, can become material at an earlier stage than would be

the case as regards lesser transactions—and this even though the mortality rate of mergers in such formative stages is doubtless high.

SEC v. Geon Industries, Inc., 531 F.2d 39, 47–48 (C.A.2 1976). We agree with that analysis. Whether merger discussions in any particular case are material therefore depends on the facts. Generally, in order to assess the probability that the event will occur, a factfinder will need to look to indicia of interest in the transaction at the highest corporate levels. Without attempting to catalog all such possible factors, we note by way of example that board resolutions, instructions to investment bankers, and actual negotiations between principals or their intermediaries may serve as indicia of interest. To assess the magnitude of the transaction to the issuer of the securities allegedly manipulated, a factfinder will need to consider such facts as the size of the two corporate entities and of the potential premiums over market value. No particular event or factor short of closing the transaction need be either necessary or sufficient by itself to render merger discussions material.[11]

As we clarify today, materiality depends on the significance the reasonable investor would place on the withheld or misrepresented information.[12] The fact-specific inquiry we endorse here is consistent

---

[11] To be actionable, of course, a statement must also be misleading. Silence, absent a duty to disclose, is not misleading under Rule 10b–5. "No comment" statements are generally the functional equivalent of silence. See In re Carnation Co., [Exchange Act Release No. 22214, 33 SEC Docket 1025 (1985)]. See also New York Stock Exchange Listed Company Manual section 202.01, reprinted in 3 CCH Fed.Sec.L.Rep. paragraph 23,515 (premature public announcement may properly be delayed for valid business purpose and where adequate security can be maintained); American Stock Exchange Company Guide sections 401–405, reprinted in 3 CCH Fed.Sec.L.Rep. paragraphs 23,124A–23,124E (similar provisions).

It has been suggested that given current market practices, a "no comment" statement is tantamount to an admission that merger discussions are underway. See Flamm v. Eberstadt, 814 F.2d, at 1178. That may well hold true to the extent that issuers adopt a policy of truthfully denying merger rumors when no discussions are underway, and of issuing "no comment" statements when they are in the midst of negotiations. There are, of course, other statement policies firms could adopt; we need not now advise issuers as to what kind of practice to follow, within the range permitted by law. Perhaps more importantly, we think that creating an exception to a regulatory scheme founded on a prodisclosure legislative philosophy, because complying with the regulation might be "bad for business," is a role for Congress, not this Court. See also id., at 1182 (opinion concurring in the judgment and concurring in part).

[12] We find no authority in the statute, the legislative history, or our previous decisions, for varying the standard of materiality depending on who brings the action or whether insiders are alleged to have profited. See, e.g., Pavlidis v. New England Patriots Football Club, Inc., 737 F.2d 1227, 1231 (C.A.1 1984) ("A fact does not become more material to the shareholder's decision because it is withheld by an insider, or because the insider might profit by withholding it"); cf. Aaron v. SEC, 446 U.S. 680, 691 (1980) ("scienter is an element of a violation of section 10(b) and Rule 10b–5, regardless of the identity of the plaintiff or the nature of the relief sought").

We recognize that trading (and profit making) by insiders can serve as *an* indication of materiality. We are not prepared to agree, however, that "in cases of the disclosure of inside information to a favored few, determination of materiality has a different aspect than when the issue is, for example, an inaccuracy in a publicly disseminated press release." SEC v. Geon Industries, Inc., 531 F.2d 39, 48 (C.A.2 1976). Devising two different standards of materiality, one for situations where insiders have traded in abrogation of their duty to disclose or abstain (or for that matter when any disclosure duty has been breached), and another covering affirmative misrepresentations by those under no duty to disclose (but under the ever-present duty not to mislead), would effectively collapse the materiality requirement into the analysis of defendant's disclosure duties.

with the approach a number of courts have taken in assessing the materiality of merger negotiations. Because the standard of materiality we have adopted differs from that used by both courts below, we remand the case for reconsideration of the question whether a grant of summary judgment is appropriate on this record.

The Supreme Court also addressed materiality under Rule 10b–5 in Matrixx Initiatives, Inc. v. Siracusano.[13] It invoked *Basic* in refusing the defendant's invitation to adopt a bright-line rule that reports of adverse events associated with a pharmaceutical company's products cannot be material absent a sufficient number of such reports to establish a statistically significant risk that the product is in fact causing the events.

Retail Wholesale & Dept. Store Union Local 338 Ret. Fund v. Hewlett-Packard, described above in Section 12BI, found representations related to Hewlett-Packard's high standards for ethics and compliance to be immaterial under *Basic* and *Matrixx*. According to the Ninth Circuit, "It cannot be said that there is 'a substantial likelihood' that [Hewlett-Packards' ethics code] and related representations altered the 'total mix' of information made available for use in stockholder decisionmaking." This was held to be the case notwithstanding the $10 billion drop in stock price following the resignation of the CEO who had engaged in violations of the code. On the other hand, in Nathanson v. Polycom, Inc.,[14] a different court held that information about an executive's misreporting of expenses could be material because "[i]nvestors have a right to know—and would consider it important—when the head of a publicly-owned company is stealing any quantity of money from their company."

III. THE "IN CONNECTION WITH" REQUIREMENT

To be subject to Rule 10b–5, the conduct prohibited by the rule must be "in connection with the purchase or sale of [a] security." In cases involving public dissemination of false or misleading information "in a medium upon which an investor would presumably rely," courts have tended to find that the "in connection with requirement" may be satisfied by a showing of materiality.[15] Under the "means of dissemination plus materiality" standard, " * * * It is irrelevant that the misrepresentations were not made for the purpose or the object of influencing the investment decision of market participants."

In cases not involving public dissemination, the "in connection with" requirement has presented some real challenges. The first Supreme Court case in this area is Superintendent of Insurance of New York v. Bankers Life & Casualty Co.:

---

[13] 563 U.S. 27 (2011).

[14] 87 F.Supp.3d 966 (D.C.N.D.CA 2015).

[15] *See, e.g.,* Semerenko v. Cendant Corp., 223 F.3d 165 (3d Cir.2000).

Superintendent of Insurance of New York
v. Bankers Life & Casualty Co.

Supreme Court of the United States, 1971.

404 U.S. 6.

■ MR. JUSTICE DOUGLAS delivered the opinion of the Court.

Manhattan Casualty Co., now represented by petitioner, New York's Superintendent of Insurance, was, it is alleged, defrauded in the sale of certain securities in violation of * * * § 10(b) of the Securities Exchange Act of 1934. The District Court dismissed the complaint, and the Court of Appeals affirmed, by a divided bench. The case is here on a petition for a writ of certiorari which we granted.

It seems that Bankers Life & Casualty Co., one of the respondents, agreed to sell all of Manhattan's stock to one Begole for $5,000,000. It is alleged that Begole conspired with one Bourne and others to pay for this stock, not out of their own funds, but with Manhattan's assets. They were alleged to have arranged, through Garvin, Bantel & Co.—a note brokerage firm—to obtain a $5,000,000 check from respondent Irving Trust Co., although they had no funds on deposit there at the time. On the same day they purchased all the stock of Manhattan from Bankers Life for $5,000,000 and as stockholders and directors, installed one Sweeny as president of Manhattan.

Manhattan then sold its United States Treasury bonds for $4,854,552.67.[16] That amount, plus enough cash to bring the total to $5,000,000, was credited to an account of Manhattan at Irving Trust and the $5,000,000 Irving Trust check was charged against it. As a result, Begole owned all the stock of Manhattan, having used $5,000,000 of Manhattan's assets to purchase it.

To complete the fraudulent scheme, Irving Trust issued a second $5,000,000 check to Manhattan which Sweeny, Manhattan's new president, tendered to Belgian-American Bank & Trust Co. which issued a $5,000,000 certificate of deposit in the name of Manhattan. Sweeny endorsed the certificate of deposit over to New England Note Corp., a company alleged to be controlled by Bourne. Bourne endorsed the certificate over to Belgian-American Banking Corp. as collateral for a $5,000,000 loan from Belgian-American Banking to New England. Its proceeds were paid to Irving Trust to cover the latter's second $5,000,000 check.

Though Manhattan's assets had been depleted, its books reflected only the sale of its Government bonds and the purchase of the certificate of deposit and did not show that its assets had been used by Begole to pay for his purchase of Manhattan's shares or that the certificate of

---

[16] Manhattan's Board of Directors was allegedly deceived into authorizing this sale by misrepresentation that the proceeds would be exchanged for a certificate of deposit of equal value.

deposit had been assigned to New England and then pledged to Belgian-American Banking.

Manhattan was the seller of Treasury bonds and, it seems to us, clearly protected by § 10(b) of the Securities Exchange Act, which makes it unlawful to use "in connection with the purchase or sale" of any security "any manipulative or deceptive device or contrivance" in contravention of the rules and regulations of the Securities and Exchange Commission.

There certainly was an "act" or "practice" within the meaning of Rule 10b–5 which operated as "a fraud or deceit" on Manhattan, the seller of the Government bonds. To be sure, the full market price was paid for those bonds; but the seller was duped into believing that it, the seller, would receive the proceeds. * * *

Section 10(b) outlaws the use "in connection with the purchase or sale" of any security of "any manipulative or deceptive device or contrivance." The Act protects corporations as well as individuals who are sellers of a security. Manhattan was injured as an investor through a deceptive device which deprived it of any compensation for the sale of its valuable block of securities.

* * *

* * * Section 10(b) must be read flexibly, not technically and restrictively. Since there was a "sale" of a security and since fraud was used "in connection with" it, there is redress under § 10(b) * * * .

We agree that Congress by § 10(b) did not seek to regulate transactions which constitute no more than internal corporate mismanagement. But we read § 10(b) to mean that Congress meant to bar deceptive devices and contrivances in the purchase or sale of securities whether conducted in the organized markets or face to face. * * *

The crux of the present case is that Manhattan suffered an injury as a result of deceptive practices touching its sale of securities as an investor. * * *

* * *

The case must be remanded for trial. We intimate no opinion on the merits, as we have dealt only with allegations and with the question of law whether a cause of action as respects the sale by Manhattan of its Treasury bonds has been charged under § 10(b). * * *

* * *

The looseness of the "touching" formulation in *Bankers Life,* and the almost summary way in which the Supreme Court disposed of the case, seemed to send a clear signal to lower courts that they were to continue to interpret Rule 10b–5 expansively. The lower courts responded affirmatively, at least until the Supreme Court sent contrary signals in two cases discussed in subsequent sections, *Blue Chip Stamps* in 1975 and *Hochfelder* in 1976. In 2002, however, in SEC v. Zandford,[17] the Court confirmed the breadth of the *Bankers Life* test in a case dealing with a broker's misappropriation of client funds.

IV. THE "SCIENTER" REQUIREMENT

Ernst & Ernst v. Hochfelder

Supreme Court of the United States, 1976.
425 U.S. 185.

■ MR. JUSTICE POWELL delivered the opinion of the Court.

The issue in this case is whether an action for civil damages may lie under § 10(b) of the Securities Exchange Act of 1934 (1934 Act), and Securities and Exchange Commission Rule 10b–5, in the absence of an allegation of intent to deceive, manipulate, or defraud on the part of the defendant.

I

Petitioner, Ernst & Ernst, is an accounting firm. From 1946 through 1967 it was retained by First Securities Company of Chicago (First Securities), a small brokerage firm and member of the Midwest Stock Exchange and of the National Association of Securities Dealers, to perform periodic audits of the firm's books and records. In connection with these audits Ernst & Ernst prepared for filing with the Securities and Exchange Commission (Commission) the annual reports required of First Securities under § 17(a) of the 1934 Act. * * *

Respondents were customers of First Securities who invested in a fraudulent securities scheme perpetrated by Leston B. Nay, president of the firm and owner of 92% of its stock. Nay induced the respondents to invest funds in "escrow" accounts that he represented would yield a high rate of return. Respondents did so from 1942 through 1966, with the majority of the transactions occurring in the 1950's. In fact, there were no escrow accounts as Nay converted respondents' funds to his own use immediately upon receipt. * * *

This fraud came to light in 1968 when Nay committed suicide, leaving a note that described First Securities as bankrupt and the escrow accounts as "spurious." Respondents subsequently filed this action for damages against Ernst & Ernst in the United States District Court for the Northern District of Illinois under § 10(b) of the 1934 Act. The complaint charged that Nay's escrow scheme violated § 10(b) and Commission Rule 10b–5, and that Ernst & Ernst had "aided and abetted" Nay's violations by its "failure" to conduct proper audits of First Securities. As revealed through discovery, respondents' cause of action

---

[17]   535 U.S. 813 (2002).

rested on a theory of negligent nonfeasance. The premise was that Ernst & Ernst had failed to utilize "appropriate auditing procedures" in its audits of First Securities, thereby failing to discover internal practices of the firm said to prevent an effective audit. The practice principally relied on was Nay's rule that only he could open mail addressed to him at First Securities or addressed to First Securities to his attention, even if it arrived in his absence. Respondents contended that if Ernst & Ernst had conducted a proper audit, it would have discovered this "mail rule." The existence of the rule then would have been disclosed in reports to the Exchange and to the Commission by Ernst & Ernst as an irregular procedure that prevented an effective audit. This would have led to an investigation of Nay that would have revealed the fraudulent scheme. Respondents specifically disclaimed the existence of fraud or intentional misconduct on the part of Ernst & Ernst.

After extensive discovery the District Court granted Ernst & Ernst's motion for summary judgment and dismissed the action. * * *

The Court of Appeals for the Seventh Circuit reversed * * * . * * *

We granted certiorari to resolve the question whether a private cause of action for damages will lie under § 10(b) and Rule 10b–5 in the absence of any allegation of "scienter"—intent to deceive, manipulate, or defraud.[18] We conclude that it will not and therefore we reverse.

II

* * *

* * * During the 30-year period since a private cause of action was first implied under § 10(b) and Rule 10b–5, a substantial body of case law and commentary has developed as to its elements. Courts and commentators long have differed with regard to whether scienter is a necessary element of such a cause of action, or whether negligent conduct alone is sufficient. * * *

A

Section 10(b) makes unlawful the use or employment of "any manipulative or deceptive device or contrivance" in contravention of

---

[18] Although the verbal formulations of the standard to be applied have varied, several Courts of Appeals have held in substance that negligence alone is sufficient for civil liability under § 10(b) and Rule 10b–5. Other Courts of Appeals have held that some type of scienter— i.e., intent to defraud, reckless disregard for the truth, or knowing use of some practice to defraud—is necessary in such an action. But few of the decisions announcing that some form of negligence suffices for civil liability under § 10(b) and Rule 10b–5 actually have involved only negligent conduct.

In this opinion the term "scienter" refers to a mental state embracing intent to deceive, manipulate, or defraud. In certain areas of the law recklessness is considered to be a form of intentional conduct for purposes of imposing liability for some act. We need not address here the question whether, in some circumstances, reckless behavior is sufficient for civil liability under § 10(b) and Rule 10b–5.

Since this case concerns an action for damages we also need not consider the question whether scienter is a necessary element in an action for injunctive relief under § 10(b) and Rule 10b–5.

Commission rules. The words "manipulative or deceptive" used in conjunction with "device or contrivance" strongly suggest that § 10(b) was intended to proscribe knowing or intentional misconduct.

In its *amicus curiae* brief, however, the Commission contends that nothing in the language "manipulative or deceptive device or contrivance" limits its operation to knowing or intentional practices. In support of its view, the Commission cites the overall congressional purpose in the 1933 and 1934 Acts to protect investors against false and deceptive practices that might injure them. The Commission then reasons that since the "effect" upon investors of given conduct is the same regardless of whether the conduct is negligent or intentional, Congress must have intended to bar all such practices and not just those done knowingly or intentionally. The logic of this effect-oriented approach would impose liability for wholly faultless conduct where such conduct results in harm to investors, a result the Commission would be unlikely to support. But apart from where its logic might lead, the Commission would add a gloss to the operative language of the statute quite different from its commonly accepted meaning. The argument simply ignores the use of the words "manipulative," "device," and "contrivance"—terms that make unmistakable a congressional intent to proscribe a type of conduct quite different from negligence. Use of the word "manipulative" is especially significant. It is and was virtually a term of art when used in connection with securities markets. It connotes intentional or willful conduct designed to deceive or defraud investors by controlling or artificially affecting the price of securities.

In addition to relying upon the Commission's argument with respect to the operative language of the statute, respondents contend that since we are dealing with "remedial legislation," it must be construed " 'not technically and restrictively, but flexibly to effectuate its remedial purposes.' " Affiliated Ute Citizens v. United States, 406 U.S. [128, 151 (1972)]. They argue that the "remedial purposes" of the Acts demand a construction of § 10(b) that embraces negligence as a standard of liability. But in seeking to accomplish its broad remedial goals, Congress did not adopt uniformly a negligence standard even as to express civil remedies. In some circumstances and with respect to certain classes of defendants, Congress did create express liability predicated upon a failure to exercise reasonable care. E.g., 1933 Act § 11(b)(3)(B) (liability of "experts," such as accountants, for misleading statements in portions of registration statements for which they are responsible). But in other situations good faith is an absolute defense. 1934 Act § 18 (misleading statements in any document filed pursuant to the 1934 Act). And in still other circumstances Congress created express liability regardless of the defendant's fault, 1933 Act § 11(a) (issuer liability for misleading statements in the registration statement).

It is thus evident that Congress fashioned standards of fault in the express civil remedies in the 1933 and 1934 Acts on a particularized basis. Ascertainment of congressional intent with respect to the standard of liability created by a particular section of the Acts must therefore rest primarily on the language of that section. Where, as here, we deal with a judicially implied liability, the statutory language certainly is no less important. In view of the language of § 10(b), which so clearly connotes intentional misconduct, and mindful that the language of a statute controls when sufficiently clear in its context, further inquiry may be unnecessary. We turn now, nevertheless, to the legislative history of the 1934 Act to ascertain whether there is support for the meaning attributed to § 10(b) by the Commission and respondents.

B

* * *

Neither the intended scope of § 10(b) nor the reasons for the changes in its operative language are revealed explicitly in the legislative history of the 1934 Act, which deals primarily with other aspects of the legislation. There is no indication, however, that § 10(b) was intended to proscribe conduct not involving scienter. The extensive hearings that preceded passage of the 1934 Act touched only briefly on § 10, and most of the discussion was devoted to the enumerated devices that the Commission is empowered to proscribe under § 10(a). The most relevant exposition of the provision that was to become § 10(b) was by Thomas G. Corcoran, a spokesman for the drafters. Corcoran indicated:

"Subsection (c) [§ 10(b)] says, 'Thou shalt not devise any other cunning devices.'

* * *

"Of course subsection (c) is a catch-all clause to prevent manipulative devices. I do not think there is any objection to that kind of clause. The Commission should have the authority to deal with new manipulative devices."

This brief explanation of § 10(b) by a spokesman for its drafters is significant. The section was described rightly as a "catchall" clause to enable the Commission "to deal with new manipulative [or cunning] devices." It is difficult to believe that any lawyer, legislative draftsman, or legislator would use these words if the intent was to create liability for merely negligent acts or omissions. Neither the legislative history nor the briefs supporting respondents identify any usage or authority for construing "manipulative [or cunning] devices" to include negligence.

* * *

C

* * *

We also consider it significant that each of the express civil remedies in the 1933 Act allowing recovery for negligent conduct, see §§ 11, 12(2), 15, is subject to significant procedural restrictions not applicable under

§ 10(b). Section 11(e) of the 1933 Act, for example, authorizes the court to require a plaintiff bringing a suit under § 11, § 12(2), or § 15 thereof to post a bond for costs, including attorneys' fees, and in specified circumstances to assess costs at the conclusion of the litigation. Section 13 specifies a statute of limitations of one year from the time the violation was or should have been discovered, in no event to exceed three years from the time of offer or sale, applicable to actions brought under § 11, § 12(2), or § 15. * * * We think these procedural limitations indicate that the judicially created private damages remedy under § 10(b)—which has no comparable restrictions—cannot be extended, consistently with the intent of Congress, to actions premised on negligent wrongdoing. Such extension would allow causes of action covered by §§ 11, 12(2), and 15 to be brought instead under § 10(b) and thereby nullify the effectiveness of the carefully drawn procedural restrictions on these express actions. We would be unwilling to bring about this result absent substantial support in the legislative history, and there is none.

* * *

Prior to *Hochfelder,* the various circuits had been split on the issue of the degree of fault required, with the generally Rule 10b–5 activist Second Circuit leading the group of those requiring scienter. If all the Supreme Court had done was agree with this position, the case would have been important for its technical holding, but it would not have created much of a stir. Seeming to take its cue from *Blue Chip Stamps*, however, the Court did more: Its discussion of the rule left no doubt that the old, expansive days of Rule 10b–5 were over.

The Supreme Court in Hochfelder specifically left open two questions: (1) Is scienter required to be proved in an enforcement action by the Commission? and (2) is recklessness sufficient by itself to constitute scienter? The first of these questions was answered affirmatively by the Supreme Court in the 1980 case of Aaron v. SEC.[19] Virtually all courts that have addressed the second question have found that recklessness in some form constitutes scienter.

C. ADDITIONAL REQUIREMENTS FOR PRIVATE PLAINTIFFS

I. THE "PURCHASER-SELLER" REQUIREMENT

Early in the life of Rule 10b–5, the Second Circuit established the requirement that a private plaintiff had to be a purchaser or seller of securities to have standing to sue under the rule. This standing

---

[19]   446 U.S. 680 (1980).

requirement, generally called the *Birnbaum* rule after the case from which it came,[20] has been universally accepted by the other circuit courts.

Over two decades after the initiation of the *Birnbaum* rule, the Supreme Court decided its first "purchaser-seller" requirement case, Blue Chip Stamps v. Manor Drug Stores:

Blue Chip Stamps v. Manor Drug Stores

Supreme Court of the United States, 1975.
421 U.S. 723.

■ MR. JUSTICE REHNQUIST delivered the opinion of the Court.

This case requires us to consider whether the offerees of a stock offering, made pursuant to an antitrust consent decree and registered under the Securities Act of 1933 (1933 Act), may maintain a private cause of action for money damages where they allege that the offeror has violated the provisions of Rule 10b–5 of the Securities and Exchange Commission, but where they have neither purchased nor sold any of the offered shares. See Birnbaum v. Newport Steel Corp., 193 F.2d 461 (CA2), cert. denied, 343 U.S. 956 (1952).

I

In 1963 the United States filed a civil antitrust action against Blue Chip Stamp Co. (Old Blue Chip), a company in the business of providing trading stamps to retailers, and nine retailers who owned 90% of its shares. In 1967 the action was terminated by the entry of a consent decree. The decree contemplated a plan of reorganization whereby Old Blue Chip was to be merged into a newly formed corporation, Blue Chip Stamps (New Blue Chip). The holdings of the majority shareholders of Old Blue Chip were to be reduced, and New Blue Chip, one of the petitioners here, was required under the plan to offer a substantial number of its shares of common stock to retailers who had used the stamp service in the past but who were not shareholders in the old company. Under the terms of the plan, the offering to nonshareholder users was to be proportional to past stamp usage and the shares were to be offered in units consisting of common stock and debentures.

The reorganization plan was carried out, the offering was registered with the SEC as required by the 1933 Act, and a prospectus was distributed to all offerees as required by § 5 of that Act. Somewhat more than 50% of the offered units were actually purchased. In 1970, two years after the offering, respondent, a former user of the stamp service and therefore an offeree of the 1968 offering, filed this suit in the United States District Court for the Central District of California. Defendants below and petitioners here are Old and New Blue Chip, eight of the nine majority shareholders of Old Blue Chip and the directors of New Blue Chip (collectively called Blue Chip).

---

[20] Birnbaum v. Newport Steel Corp., 193 F.2d 461 (2d Cir.1952).

Respondent's complaint alleged, *inter alia,* that the prospectus prepared and distributed by Blue Chip in connection with the offering was materially misleading in its overly pessimistic appraisal of Blue Chip's status and future prospects. It alleged that Blue Chip intentionally made the prospectus overly pessimistic in order to discourage respondent and other members of the allegedly large class whom it represents from accepting what was intended to be a bargain offer, so that the rejected shares might later be offered to the public at a higher price. The complaint alleged that class members because of and in reliance on the false and misleading prospectus failed to purchase the offered units. Respondent therefore sought on behalf of the alleged class some $21,400,000 in damages representing the lost opportunity to purchase the units; the right to purchase the previously rejected units at the 1968 price; and in addition, it sought some $25,000,000 in exemplary damages.

* * *

II

* * *

[In 1952] the Court of Appeals for the Second Circuit concluded that the plaintiff class for purposes of a private damage action under § 10(b) and Rule 10b–5 was limited to actual purchasers and sellers of securities. Birnbaum v. Newport Steel Corp., supra.

The Court of Appeals in this case did not repudiate *Birnbaum* * * * . But in this case a majority of the Court of Appeals found that the facts warranted an exception to the *Birnbaum* rule. For the reasons hereinafter stated, we are of the opinion that *Birnbaum* was rightly decided, and that it bars respondent from maintaining this suit under Rule 10b–5.

III

The panel which decided *Birnbaum* consisted of Chief Judge Swan and Judges Learned Hand and Augustus Hand: the opinion was written by the last named. Since both § 10(b) and Rule 10b–5 proscribed only fraud "in connection with the purchase or sale" of securities, and since the history of § 10(b) revealed no congressional intention to extend a private civil remedy for money damages to other than defrauded purchasers or sellers of securities, in contrast to the express civil remedy provided by § 16(b) of the 1934 Act, the court concluded that the plaintiff class in a Rule 10b–5 action was limited to actual purchasers and sellers.

* * *

Three principal classes of potential plaintiffs are presently barred by the *Birnbaum* rule. First are potential purchasers of shares, either in a new offering or on the Nation's post-distribution trading markets, who allege that they decided not to purchase because of an unduly gloomy representation or the omission of favorable material which made the issuer appear to be a less favorable investment vehicle than it actually was. Second are actual shareholders in the issuer who allege that they decided not to sell their shares because of an unduly rosy representation or a failure to disclose unfavorable material. Third are shareholders, creditors, and perhaps others related to an issuer who suffered loss in the value of their investment due to corporate or insider activities in connection with the purchase or sale of securities which violate Rule 10b–5. It has been held that shareholder members of the second and third of these classes may frequently be able to circumvent the *Birnbaum* limitation through bringing a derivative action on behalf of the corporate issuer if the latter is itself a purchaser or seller of securities. But the first of these classes, of which respondent is a member, cannot claim the benefit of such a rule.

A great majority of the many commentators on the issue before us have taken the view that the *Birnbaum* limitation on the plaintiff class in a Rule 10b–5 action for damages is an arbitrary restriction which unreasonably prevents some deserving plaintiffs from recovering damages which have in fact been caused by violations of Rule 10b–5. The Securities and Exchange Commission has filed an *amicus* brief in this case espousing that same view. We have no doubt that this is indeed a disadvantage of the *Birnbaum* rule, and if it had no countervailing advantages it would be undesirable as a matter of policy, however much it might be supported by precedent and legislative history. But we are of the opinion that there are countervailing advantages to the *Birnbaum* rule, purely as a matter of policy, although those advantages are more difficult to articulate than is the disadvantage.

There has been widespread recognition that litigation under Rule 10b–5 presents a danger of vexatiousness different in degree and in kind from that which accompanies litigation in general. * * *

Judge Friendly in commenting on another aspect of Rule 10b–5 litigation has referred to the possibility that unduly expansive imposition of civil liability "will lead to large judgments, payable in the last analysis by innocent investors, for the benefit of speculators and their lawyers * * * ." SEC v. Texas Gulf Sulphur Co., 401 F.2d 833, 867 (C.A.2 1968) (concurring opinion).

We believe that the concern expressed for the danger of vexatious litigation which could result from a widely expanded class of plaintiffs under Rule 10b–5 is founded in something more substantial than the common complaint of the many defendants who would prefer avoiding lawsuits entirely to either settling them or trying them. These concerns have two largely separate grounds.

The first of these concerns is that in the field of federal securities laws governing disclosure of information even a complaint which by objective standards may have very little chance of success at trial has a settlement value to the plaintiff out of any proportion to its prospect of success at trial so long as he may prevent the suit from being resolved against him by dismissal or summary judgment. The very pendency of the lawsuit may frustrate or delay normal business activity of the defendant which is totally unrelated to the lawsuit.

* * *

The potential for possible abuse of the liberal discovery provisions of the Federal Rules of Civil Procedure may likewise exist in this type of case to a greater extent than they do in other litigation. The prospect of extensive deposition of the defendant's officers and associates and the concomitant opportunity for extensive discovery of business documents, is a common occurrence in this and similar types of litigation. To the extent that this process eventually produces relevant evidence which is useful in determining the merits of the claims asserted by the parties, it bears the imprimatur of those Rules and of the many cases liberally interpreting them. But to the extent that it permits a plaintiff with a largely groundless claim to simply take up the time of a number of other people, with the right to do so representing an *in terrorem* increment of the settlement value, rather than a reasonably founded hope that the process will reveal relevant evidence, it is a social cost rather than a benefit. Yet to broadly expand the class of plaintiffs who may sue under Rule 10b–5 would appear to encourage the least appealing aspect of the use of the discovery rules.

Without the *Birnbaum* rule, an action under Rule 10b–5 will turn largely on which oral version of a series of occurrences the jury may decide to credit, and therefore no matter how improbable the allegations of the plaintiff, the case will be virtually impossible to dispose of prior to trial other than by settlement. * * *

The *Birnbaum* rule, on the other hand, permits exclusion prior to trial of those plaintiffs who were not themselves purchasers or sellers of the stock in question. The fact of purchase of stock and the fact of sale of stock are generally matters which are verifiable by documentation, and do not depend upon oral recollection, so that failure to qualify under the *Birnbaum* rule is a matter that can normally be established by the defendant either on a motion to dismiss or on a motion for summary judgment.

* * *

The second ground for fear of vexatious litigation is based on the concern that, given the generalized contours of liability, the abolition of the *Birnbaum* rule would throw open to the trier of fact many rather hazy issues of historical fact the proof of which depended almost entirely on oral testimony. We in no way disparage the worth and frequent high value of oral testimony when we say that dangers of its abuse appear to exist in this type of action to a peculiarly high degree. * * *

* * *

The manner in which the defendant's violation caused the plaintiff to fail to act could be as a result of the reading of a prospectus, as respondent claims here, but it could just as easily come as a result of a claimed reading of information contained in the financial pages of a local newspaper. * * * in the absence of the *Birnbaum* doctrine, bystanders to the securities marketing process could await developments on the sidelines without risk, claiming that inaccuracies in disclosure caused nonselling in a falling market and that unduly pessimistic predictions by the issuer followed by a rising market caused them to allow retrospectively golden opportunities to pass.

* * *

IV

The majority of the Court of Appeals in this case expressed no disagreement with the general proposition that one asserting a claim for damages based on the violation of Rule 10b–5 must be either a purchaser or seller of securities. However, it noted that prior cases have held that persons owning contractual rights to buy or sell securities are not excluded by the *Birnbaum* rule. Relying on these cases, it concluded that respondent's status as an offeree pursuant to the terms of the consent decree served the same function, for purposes of delimiting the class of plaintiffs, as is normally performed by the requirement of a contractual relationship.

* * *

A contract to purchase or sell securities is expressly defined by § 3(a) of the 1934 Act, as a purchase or sale of securities for the purposes of that Act. Unlike respondent, which had no contractual right or duty to purchase Blue Chip's securities, the holders of puts, calls, options, and other contractual rights or duties to purchase or sell securities have been recognized as "purchasers" or "sellers" of securities for purposes of Rule 10b–5, not because of a judicial conclusion that they were similarly situated to "purchasers" or "sellers," but because the definitional provisions of the 1934 Act themselves grant them such a status.

Even if we were to accept the notion that the *Birnbaum* rule could be circumvented on a case-by-case basis through particularized judicial inquiry into the facts surrounding a complaint, this respondent and the members of its alleged class would be unlikely candidates for such a judicially created exception. While the *Birnbaum* rule has been flexibly interpreted by lower federal courts, we have been unable to locate a single decided case from any court in the 20-odd years of litigation since the *Birnbaum* decision which would support the right of persons who were in the position of respondent here to bring a private suit under Rule 10b–5. * * *

* * *

* * * As a purely practical matter, it is doubtless true that respondent and the members of its class, as offerees and recipients of the prospectus of New Blue Chip, are a smaller class of potential plaintiffs than would be all those who might conceivably assert that they obtained information violative of Rule 10b–5 and attributable to the issuer in the financial pages of their local newspaper. And since respondent likewise had a prior connection with some of petitioners as a result of using the trading stamps marketed by Old Blue Chip, and was intended to benefit from the provisions of the consent decree, there is doubtless more likelihood that its managers read and were damaged by the allegedly misleading statements in the prospectus than there would be in a case filed by a complete stranger to the corporation.

But respondent and the members of its class are neither "purchasers" nor "sellers," as those terms are defined in the 1934 Act, and therefore to the extent that their claim of standing to sue were recognized, it would mean that the lesser practical difficulties of corroborating at least some elements of their proof would be regarded as sufficient to avoid the *Birnbaum* rule. While we have noted that these practical difficulties, particularly in the case of a complete stranger to the corporation, support the retention of that rule, they are by no means the only factor which does so. The general adoption of the rule by other federal courts in the 25 years since it was announced, and the consistency of the rule with the statutes involved and their legislative history, are likewise bases for retaining the rule. Were we to agree with the Court of Appeals in this case, we would leave the *Birnbaum* rule open to endless case-by-case erosion depending on whether a particular group of plaintiffs was thought by the court in which the issue was being litigated to be sufficiently more discrete than the world of potential purchasers at large to justify an exception. We do not believe that such a shifting and highly fact-oriented disposition of the issue of who may bring a damages claim for violation of Rule 10b–5 is a satisfactory basis for a rule of liability imposed on the conduct of business transactions. Nor is it as consistent as a straightforward application of the *Birnbaum* rule with the other factors which support the retention of that rule. We therefore hold that respondent was not entitled to sue for violation of Rule 10b–5, and the judgment of the Court of Appeals is

Reversed.

* * *

––––––––––

Blue Chip Stamps was a blockbuster to securities lawyers, and the reason was simple: It seemed clearly to usher in a new era in the Court's view of Rule 10b–5. Gone was the broad, loose, and expansive outlook so evident in a case like Superintendent of Insurance of New York v. Bankers Life & Casualty Co., which the Court had decided only four years before.

The issue in *Blue Chip Stamps,* of course, was whether to allow an exception to the *Birnbaum* rule for a particular type of transaction. The *Birnbaum* rule has not been without other exceptions, either before or after *Blue Chip Stamps.* One of these is for "forced sellers"—those compelled to sell or convert shares as a result of fraud. This exception, in appropriate circumstances, has permitted minority shareholders of merged or liquidated companies to seek relief under Rule 10b–5 even though they might not be sellers in the common law sense.[21] The "forced sale" doctrine does have limits. Thus, the Seventh Circuit held, in Isquith v. Caremark International, Inc.,[22] that plaintiff shareholders had no standing to sue their company for alleged misstatements made in connection with a dividend of securities in another company (a so-called spin-off) because there was no sale involved in the transaction.

The following case is the Supreme Court's reaction to a defendant's attempt to invoke *Blue Chip Stamp* in the context of an oral contract that the defendant refused to honor.

Wharf (Holdings) Limited v. United International Holdings, Inc.

Supreme Court of the United States, 2001.
532 U.S. 588.

■ JUSTICE BREYER delivered the opinion of the Court.

* * *

I.

Respondent United International Holdings, Inc., a Colorado-based company, sued petitioner The Wharf (Holdings) Limited, a Hong Kong firm, in Colorado's Federal District Court. United said that in October 1992 Wharf had [,in exchange for United's services, orally granted] it an option to buy 10% of the stock of a new Hong Kong cable system. But, United alleged, at the time of the sale Wharf secretly intended not to permit United to exercise the option. United claimed that Wharf's conduct amounted to a fraud "in connection with the * * * sale of [a] security," prohibited by Section 10(b), and violated numerous state laws as well. A jury found in United's favor. The Court of Appeals for the Tenth Circuit upheld that verdict. 210 F.3d 1207 (2000). And we granted certiorari to consider whether the dispute fell within the scope of Section 10(b).

* * *

---

[21] *See, e.g.,* Alley v. Miramon, 614 F.2d 1372 (5th Cir.1980).

[22] 136 F.3d 531 (7th Cir.1998).

II.

* * *

In deciding whether the Rule covers the circumstances present here, we must assume that the "security" at issue is not the cable system stock, but the option to purchase that stock. That is because the Court of Appeals found that Wharf conceded this point. 210 F.3d at 1221 ("Wharf does not contest on appeal the classification of the option as a security"). That concession is consistent with the language of the Securities Exchange Act, which defines "security" to include both "any * * * option * * * on any security" and "any * * * right to * * * purchase" stock. * * * Consequently, we must decide whether Wharf's secret intent not to honor the option it sold United amounted to a misrepresentation (or other conduct forbidden by the Rule) in connection with the sale of the option.

Wharf argues that its conduct falls outside the Rule's scope for two basic reasons. First, Wharf points out that its agreement to grant United an option to purchase shares in the cable system was an oral agreement. And it says that Section 10(b) does not cover oral contracts of sale. Wharf points to [Blue Chip Stamps v. Manor Drug Stores, 421 U.S. 723 (1975)], in which this Court construed the Act's "purchase or sale" language to mean that only "actual purchasers and sellers of securities" have standing to bring a private action for damages. See 421 U.S. at 730–731. Wharf notes that the Court's interpretation of the Act flowed in part from the need to protect defendants against lawsuits that "turn largely on which oral version of a series of occurrences the jury may decide to credit." Blue Chip Stamps, supra, at 742. And it claims that an oral purchase or sale would pose a similar problem of proof and thus should not satisfy the Rule's "purchase or sale" requirement.

Blue Chip Stamps, however, involved the very different question whether the Act protects a person who did not actually buy securities, but who might have done so had the seller told the truth. The Court held that the Act does not cover such a potential buyer, in part for the reason that Wharf states. But United is not a potential buyer; by providing Wharf with its services, it actually bought the option that Wharf sold. And Blue Chip Stamps said nothing to suggest that oral purchases or sales fall outside the scope of the Act. Rather, the Court's concern was about "the abuse potential and proof problems inherent in suits by investors who neither bought nor sold, but asserted they would have traded absent fraudulent conduct by others." United States v. O'Hagan, 521 U.S. 642, 664 (1997). Such a "potential purchase" claim would rest on facts, including the plaintiff's state of mind, that might be "totally unknown and unknowable to the defendant," depriving the jury of "the benefit of weighing the plaintiff's version against the defendant's version." Blue Chip Stamps, supra, at 746. An actual sale, even if oral, would not create this problem, because both parties would be able to testify as to whether the relevant events had occurred.

Neither is there any other convincing reason to interpret the Act to exclude oral contracts as a class. The Act itself says that it applies to "any contract" for the purchase or sale of a security. * * * Oral contracts for the sale of securities are sufficiently common that the Uniform Commercial Code and statutes of frauds in every State now consider them enforceable. * * * Any exception for oral sales of securities would significantly limit the Act's coverage, thereby undermining its basic purposes.

* * *

Finally, Wharf supports its claim for an exemption from the statute by characterizing this case as a "dispute over the ownership of securities." * * * Wharf expresses concern that interpreting the Act to allow recovery in a case like this one will permit numerous plaintiffs to bring federal securities claims that are in reality no more than ordinary state breach-of-contract claims—actions that lie outside the Act's basic objectives. United's claim, however, is not simply that Wharf failed to carry out a promise to sell it securities. It is a claim that Wharf sold it a security (the option) while secretly intending from the very beginning not to honor the option. And United proved that secret intent with documentary evidence that went well beyond evidence of a simple failure to perform. Moreover, Wharf has not shown us that its concern has proven serious as a practical matter in the past. * * * Nor does Wharf persuade us that it is likely to prove serious in the future. Cf. Private Securities Litigation Reform Act of 1995 * * * (imposing, beginning in 1995, stricter pleading requirements in private securities fraud actions that, among other things, require that a complaint "state with particularity facts giving rise to a strong inference that the defendant acted with the required state of mind").[23]

For these reasons, the judgment of the Court of Appeals is

Affirmed.

―――――――

The following case provides the Second Circuit's take on an important issue relating to standing.

―――――――

[23] The Supreme Court's guidance on the meaning of "strong inference" is set out in Chapter 17. [Eds.]

Ontario Public Service Employees Union Pension Trust Fund v. Nortel Networks Corp.

United States Court of Appeals, Second Circuit, 2004.
369 F.3d 27.

■ Before: OAKES, POOLER, and WESLEY, CIRCUIT JUDGES.

■ POOLER, CIRCUIT JUDGE.

This case requires us to decide whether an individual has standing to sue a company pursuant to Section 10(b) of the Securities Exchange Act of 1934 and Rule 10b–5, for making a material misstatement when the individual purchased the security of a company other than the one that made the misstatement. * * * We hold that plaintiffs lack standing under these circumstances and affirm.

BACKGROUND

* * * Nortel Networks Corporation ("Nortel") is a global supplier of telecommunications services while JDS Uniphase Corporation ("JDS") manufactures and supplies fiber optic components. Nortel and JDS had been involved in a number of business relationships, and in January, 2001, Nortel was JDS's largest customer, accounting for 10–15% of JDS's revenues. Both companies are publicly traded and, while they appear to have maintained a healthy business relationship, nothing in the record indicates that the companies shared any management structures.

On January 16, 2001, market analysts and news agencies began reporting that Nortel and JDS were on the verge of consummating a transaction that would transfer JDS's laser business to Nortel, in exchange for Nortel stock. On February 6, 2001, Nortel and JDS confirmed that JDS was selling their laser business to Nortel in exchange for $2.5 billion in Nortel stock and a promise of increased fiber optic component purchases. This announcement, plaintiffs contend, caused the price of JDS shares to increase, as market analysts determined that this transaction would make it more likely that JDS would meet its 2001 financial projections. On February 12, 2001, the transaction closed, and Nortel filed a Form 8–K with the SEC, informing the public that it had completed the deal for $2.5 billion in stock.

Meanwhile, from January 18, 2001, to February 15, 2001, Nortel publically indicated that it saw strong demand for its fiber optics products and expected 30% growth in revenue and earnings for 2001. Plaintiffs claim that these assertions not only improved the value of Nortel's stock, but that because JDS made optimistic projections for its own business based on Nortel's claims, JDS's stock price reacted positively a well. However, on February 15, 2001, Nortel announced that it was cutting revenue estimates for the quarter by $1.7 billion and that revenue growth would be closer to 15% than 30%. Following this announcement, the value of both Nortel and JDS shares tumbled in heavy trading.

Plaintiffs allege that Nortel had known since at least the third quarter of 2000 that the demand for its products was falling and that it had booked revenue from 2001 during the third and fourth quarters of 2000 in order to meet analyst expectations for 2000. The need to resort to these radical tactics in 2000 did not prevent Nortel from setting lofty goals for 2001 and making representations that the demand for its products was growing. Thus, plaintiffs contend that all of the financial filings and press releases regarding earnings made by Nortel from January 18, 2001, to February 15, 2001, were materially misleading because they incorporated inaccurate accounting results and unfounded projections.

* * *

On April 1, 2002, Nortel moved to dismiss the JDS Complaint for lack of standing pursuant to Fed. R. Civ. P. 12(b)(6). After briefing, on January 3, 2003, the district court granted Nortel's motion. Citing Blue Chip Stamps v. Manor Drug Stores, 421 U.S. 723 (1975) and Birnbaum v. Newport Steel Corp., 193 F.2d 461 (2d Cir. 1952), the court held that the JDS shareholders did not have standing because they did not purchase or sell any Nortel stock. In addition, the district court concluded that plaintiffs did not satisfy the "in connection with" requirement of Section 10(b) and Rule 10b–5 as Nortel's statements concerned only its own financial state, not that of JDS

* * *

DISCUSSION

* * *

The language of Section 10(b) and Rule 10b–5 does not explicitly create a private right of action. In fact, the legislative history fails to indicate whether Congress even contemplated creating such a right. * * * Nevertheless, courts long have held that a private right of action was indeed created. * * *

However, the private right of action is not unlimited. * * * In *Blue Chip Stamps* * * * the Supreme Court held that individuals who failed to purchase a stock due to a company's misrepresentation of the value of its stock did not have standing to sue under Rule 10b–5 because they were not purchasers or sellers of the security. 421 U.S. at 754–55.

* * *

The Court noted that "there has been widespread recognition that litigation under Rule 10b–5 presents a danger of vexatiousness different in degree and in kind from that which accompanies litigation in general." *Id.* at 739. Thus, allowing a cause of action for non-purchasers would lead to an unacceptable level of abusive litigation. This problem of abusive litigation was particularly salient in the securities litigation field because actions by non-purchasers brought under Rule 10b–5 rely heavily on oral testimony, making them extremely unpredictable until they reach a jury.

Thus, the Court was concerned companies could be forced to settle cases that were not meritorious in order to manage their risk-levels.

In this case, plaintiffs are quick to point out that they did purchase securities after the alleged misrepresentations took place. However, instead of purchasing securities of the entity that made the alleged misrepresentations, they purchased securities of a company that had a business relationship with the misrepresenter. They claim that they have met the *Blue Chip Stamps* standing requirements because they purchased the security at issue in their lawsuit. They base this argument on the references in Section 10(b) and Rule 10b–5 to fraudulent conduct "in connection with the purchase or sale of *any* security." * * * In plaintiffs' view, the word "any" indicates that the intent of Congress and the SEC was to create universal standing for purchasers of securities, allowing anyone who made use of the markets to sue under Rule 10b–5. They further argue that this interpretation is consistent with the Supreme Court's understanding that Congress intended Section 10(b) to be interpreted flexibly to protect against the ever-evolving nature of securities fraud. Affiliated Ute Citizens v. United States, 406 U.S. 128, 151 (1972).

Plaintiffs assume that the phrase "any security" includes securities of any company affected in some way by the misrepresentation and not just securities of the company that makes the material misstatements. However, in our view, the phrase indicates that the regulations reach *all types* of securities, and not *any affected company's* securities. *See* Thomas Lee Hazen, The Law of Securities Regulation § 12.4 (4th ed. 2002) (explaining that Rule 10b–5's "any security" language means that it applies to all types of securities, even those that are exempt from registration). Furthermore, plaintiffs' interpretation of this passage is entirely at odds with the purchaser-seller requirement in *Blue Chip Stamps* that "limits the class of plaintiffs to those who have at least dealt in the security to which the prospectus, representation, or omission relates. "*Blue Chip Stamps*, 421 U.S. at 747.

Plaintiffs attempt to salvage their case by arguing that *Blue Chip Stamps* merely holds that an individual who does not purchase securities cannot sue under Section 10(b) and Rule 10b–5. They contend that *Blue Chip Stamps* has no bearing on the facts of this case, as plaintiffs did purchase securities. While plaintiffs correctly identify the factual context of *Blue Chip Stamps,* the Court's reasoning is nonetheless valuable in analyzing plaintiffs' claim. First, in *Blue Chip Stamps* the Court embraced * * * standing limitations as compatible with the legislative intent of the Exchange Act. *Blue Chip Stamps*, 421 U.S. at 733–34. * * *

Furthermore, in this case, as in *Blue Chip Stamps*, to allow plaintiffs standing would encourage individuals to engage in potentially abusive litigation. This concern was based in part on the fact that an individual's claim that he did not purchase a security would rest almost exclusively on oral testimony. *Blue Chip Stamps,* 421 U.S. at 743. Because oral testimony cannot be adequately evaluated until presented to a jury, the Court wanted to protect companies from having to defend and settle cases that relied heavily on that form of evidence. * * * Here, oral testimony would play a crucial role in proving that plaintiffs relied on Nortel's financial projections when they purchased JDS's securities. In a case where the plaintiff is bringing an action against the company whose securities he purchased, this testimony is corroborated by his ownership of the company's securities. However, where a plaintiff is bringing an action based on the statements of a company whose securities he did not purchase, "plaintiffs entire testimony could be dependent upon uncorroborated oral evidence of many of the crucial elements of his claims and still be sufficient to go to the jury." *Id.* At 746.

* * *

CONCLUSION

Stockholders do not have standing to sue under Section 10(b) and Rule 10b–5 when the company whose stock they purchased is negatively impacted by the material misstatement of another company, whose stock they do not purchase. Therefore, we affirm the district court's dismissal of plaintiffs' complaint pursuant to Fed. R. Civ. P. 12(b)(6).

———————

II. RELIANCE AND CAUSATION

In thinking about reliance and causation, cases involving non-disclosure must be distinguished from those involving misstatements; non-disclosure is considered below in the context of insider trading. The cases appearing in this section deal with the requirement that a private plaintiff show that the defendant's affirmative material misrepresentations caused the plaintiff's injury. This generally requires the plaintiff to establish reliance on the misrepresentation in question. This requirement is not always what it may seem, however. Courts have adopted what is known as the "fraud-on-the-market" theory. The case appearing directly below gives the Supreme Court's exposition of the theory.

Basic Inc. v. Levinson

Supreme Court of the United States, 1988.
485 U.S. 224.

■ JUSTICE BLACKMUN delivered the opinion of the Court.

* * *

I

Prior to December 20, 1978, Basic Incorporated was a publicly traded company primarily engaged in the business of manufacturing chemical refractors for the steel industry. * * *

Beginning in September 1976, Combustion [Engineering, Inc.] representatives had meetings and telephone conversations with Basic officers and directors, including petitioners here, concerning the possibility of a merger. During 1977 and 1978, Basic made three public statements denying that it was engaged in merger negotiations. On December 18, 1978, Basic asked the New York Stock Exchange to suspend trading in its shares and issued a release stating that it had been "approached" by another company concerning a merger. On December 19, Basic's board endorsed Combustion's offer of $46 per share for its common stock, and on the following day publicly announced its approval of Combustion's tender offer for all outstanding shares.

Respondents are former Basic shareholders who sold their stock after Basic's first public statement of October 21, 1977, and before the suspension of trading in December 1978. Respondents brought a class action against Basic and its directors, asserting that the defendants issued three false or misleading public statements and thereby were in violation of section 10(b) of the 1934 Act and of Rule 10b–5. Respondents alleged that they were injured by selling Basic shares at artificially depressed prices in a market affected by petitioners' misleading statements and in reliance thereon.

The District Court adopted a presumption of reliance by members of the plaintiff class upon petitioners' public statements that enabled the court to conclude that common questions of fact or law predominated over particular questions pertaining to individual plaintiffs. The District Court therefore certified respondents' class. On the merits, however, the District Court granted summary judgment for the defendants. * * *

The United States Court of Appeals for the Sixth Circuit affirmed the class certification, but reversed the District Court's summary judgment, and remanded the case. * * *

The Court of Appeals joined a number of other circuits in accepting the "fraud-on-the-market theory" to create a rebuttable presumption that respondents relied on petitioners' material misrepresentations, noting that without the presumption it would be impractical to certify a class under Fed. Rule Civ. Proc. 23(b)(3).

* * *

IV

A

* * * Succinctly put:

The fraud on the market theory is based on the hypothesis that, in an open and developed securities market, the price of a company's stock is determined by the available material information regarding the company and its business. * * * Misleading statements will therefore defraud purchasers of stock even if the purchasers do not directly rely on the misstatements. * * * The causal connection between the defendants' fraud and the plaintiffs' purchase of stock in such a case is no less significant than in a case of direct reliance on misrepresentations.

Peil v. Speiser, 806 F.2d 1154, 1160–1161 (C.A.3 1986).

Our task, of course, is not to assess the general validity of the theory, but to consider whether it was proper for the courts below to apply a rebuttable presumption of reliance, supported in part by the fraud-on-the-market theory.

* * * In their amended complaint, the named plaintiffs alleged that in reliance on Basic's statements they sold their shares of Basic stock in the depressed market created by petitioners. Requiring proof of individualized reliance from each member of the proposed plaintiff class effectively would have prevented respondents from proceeding with a class action, since individual issues then would have overwhelmed the common ones. The District Court found that the presumption of reliance created by the fraud-on-the-market theory provided "a practical resolution to the problem of balancing the substantive requirement, of proof of reliance in securities cases against the procedural requisites of Fed. Rule Civ. Proc. 23." The District Court thus concluded that with reference to each public statement and its impact upon the open market for Basic shares, common questions predominated over individual questions, as required by Fed. Rule Civ. Proc. 23(a)(2) and (b)(3).

Petitioners and their amici complain that the fraud-on-the-market theory effectively eliminates the requirement that a plaintiff asserting a claim under Rule 10b–5 prove reliance. They note that reliance is, and long has been, an element of common-law fraud and argue that because the analogous express right of action includes a reliance requirement, see, e.g., section 18(a) of the 1934 Act, as amended, so too must an action implied under section 10(b).

We agree that reliance is an element of a Rule 10b–5 cause of action. Reliance provides the requisite causal connection between a defendant's misrepresentation and a plaintiff's injury. There is, however, more than one way to demonstrate the causal connection. Indeed, we previously have dispensed with a requirement of positive proof of reliance, where a duty to disclose material information had been breached, concluding that the necessary nexus between the plaintiff's injury and the defendant's wrongful conduct had been established. See Affiliated Ute Citizens v. United States, 406 U.S. [128, 153–154 (1972)]. Similarly, we did not require proof that material omissions or misstatements in a proxy statement decisively affected voting, because the proxy solicitation itself, rather than the defect in the solicitation materials, served as an essential link in the transaction. See Mills v. Electric Auto-Lite Co., 396 U.S. 375, 384–385 (1970).

The modern securities markets, literally millions of shares changing hands daily, differ from the face-to-face transactions contemplated by early fraud cases, and our understanding of Rule 10b–5's reliance requirement must encompass these differences.

> In face-to-face transactions, the inquiry into an investor's reliance upon information is into the subjective pricing of that information by that investor. With the presence of a market, the market is interposed between seller and buyer and, ideally, transmits information to the investor in the processed form of a market price. Thus the market is performing a substantial part of the valuation process performed by the investor in a face-to-face transaction. The market is acting as the unpaid agent of the investor, informing him that given all the information available to it, the value of the stock is worth the market price.

In re LTV Securities Litigation, 88 F.R.D. 134, 143 (N.D.Tex.1980).

B

Presumptions typically serve to assist courts in managing circumstances in which direct proof, for one reason or another, is rendered difficult. The courts below accepted a presumption, created by the fraud-on-the-market theory and subject to rebuttal by petitioners, that persons who had traded Basic shares had done so in reliance on the integrity of the price set by the market, but because of petitioners' material misrepresentations that price had been fraudulently depressed. Requiring a plaintiff to show a speculative state of facts, i.e., how he would have acted if omitted material information had been disclosed, or if the misrepresentation had not been made, would place an unnecessarily unrealistic evidentiary burden on the Rule 10b–5 plaintiff who has traded on an impersonal market.

Arising out of considerations of fairness, public policy, and probability, as well as judicial economy, presumptions are also useful devices for allocating the burdens of proof between parties. The presumption of reliance employed in this case is consistent with, and, by facilitating Rule 10b–5 litigation, supports, the congressional policy embodied in the 1934 Act. In drafting that Act, Congress expressly relied on the premise that securities markets are affected by information, and enacted legislation to facilitate an investor's reliance on the integrity of those markets:

> No investor, no speculator, can safely buy and sell securities upon the exchanges without having an intelligent basis for forming his judgment as to the value of the securities he buys or sells. The idea of a free and open public market is built upon the theory that competing judgments of buyers and sellers as to the fair price of a security brings about a situation where the market price reflects as nearly as possible a just price. Just as artificial manipulation tends to upset the true function of an open

market, so the hiding and secreting of important information obstructs the operation of the markets as indices of real value.

H.R.Rep.No. 1383, supra, at 11.

The presumption is also supported by common sense and probability. Recent empirical studies have tended to confirm Congress' premise that the market price of shares traded on well-developed markets reflects all publicly available information, and, hence, any material misrepresentations.[24] It has been noted that "it is hard to imagine that there ever is a buyer or seller who does not rely on market integrity. Who would knowingly roll the dice in a crooked crap game?" Schlanger v. Four-Phase Systems Inc., 555 F.Supp. 535, 538 (S.D.N.Y.1982). Indeed, nearly every court that has considered the proposition has concluded that where materially misleading statements have been disseminated into an impersonal, well-developed market for securities, the reliance of individual plaintiffs on the integrity of the market price may be presumed. Commentators generally have applauded the adoption of one variation or another of the fraud-on-the-market theory. An investor who buys or sells stock at the price set by the market does so in reliance on the integrity of that price. Because most publicly available information is reflected in market price, an investor's reliance on any public material misrepresentations, therefore, may be presumed for purposes of a Rule 10b–5 action.

C

The Court of Appeals found that petitioners "made public, material misrepresentations and respondents sold Basic stock in an impersonal, efficient market. Thus the class, as defined by the district court, has established the threshold facts for proving their loss." The court acknowledged that petitioners may rebut proof of the elements giving rise to the presumption, or show that the misrepresentation in fact did not lead to a distortion of price or that an individual plaintiff traded or would have traded despite his knowing the statement was false.

Any showing that severs the link between the alleged misrepresentation and either the price received (or paid) by the plaintiff, or his decision to trade at a fair market price, will be sufficient to rebut the presumption of reliance. For example, if petitioners could show that the "market makers" were privy to the truth about the merger discussions here with Combustion, and thus that the market price would

---

[24] See In re LTV Securities Litigation, 88 F.R.D. 134, 144 (N.D.Tex.1980) (citing studies); Fischel, Use of Modern Finance Theory in Securities Fraud Cases Involving Actively Traded Securities, 38 Bus.Law. 1, 4, n. 9 (1982) (citing literature on efficient-capital-market theory); Dennis, Materiality and the Efficient Capital Market Model: A Recipe for the Total Mix, 25 Wm. & Mary L.Rev. 373, 374–381, and n. 1 (1984). We need not determine by adjudication what economists and social scientists have debated through the use of sophisticated statistical analysis and the application of economic theory. For purposes of accepting the presumption of reliance in this case, we need only believe that market professionals generally consider most publicly announced material statements about companies, thereby affecting stock market prices.

not have been affected by their misrepresentations, the causal connection could be broken: the basis for finding that the fraud had been transmitted through market price would be gone. Similarly, if, despite petitioners' allegedly fraudulent attempt to manipulate market price, news of the merger discussions credibly entered the market and dissipated the effects of the misstatements, those who traded Basic shares after the corrective statements would have no direct or indirect connection with the fraud. Petitioners also could rebut the presumption of reliance as to plaintiffs who would have divested themselves of their Basic shares without relying on the integrity of the market. For example, a plaintiff who believed that Basic's statements were false and that Basic was indeed engaged in merger discussions, and who consequently believed that Basic stock was artificially underpriced, but sold his shares nevertheless because of other unrelated concerns, e.g., potential antitrust problems, or political pressures to divest from shares of certain businesses, could not be said to have relied on the integrity of a price he knew had been manipulated.

* * *

In Amgen v. Connecticut Retirement Plans and Trust Funds,[25] the Supreme Court rejected the idea that the materiality of the misrepresentation complained of must be shown before invocation of the fraud-on-the-market theory for class certification purposes. Two dissenting opinions (joined by three Justices),however, were critical of the theory, while a concurring opinion cautioned that the author joined the majority only "with the understanding that the petitioners did not ask us to revisit *Basic*'s fraud-on-the-market presumption." Although the defendant had conceded the efficiency of the market in that case, the majority opinion acknowledged that modern economic research indicates that differences in efficiency can exist in a single market and that some types of information could be more easily disseminated and digested than others. In any event, plaintiffs seeking to demonstrate market efficiency generally address five factors identified in the lower court case of Cammer v. Boom.[26] These are trading volume, number of market makers, number of research analysts, eligibility to use Securities Act Form S–3, and a demonstration of "empirical facts showing a cause and effect relationship between unexpected corporate events or financial releases and an immediate response in the stock price."

The type of causation discussed so far is called "transaction causation." Another case, Stoneridge Investment Partners, LLC v. Scientific-Atlanta, Inc., in which the Supreme Court discusses the requirement of transaction causation in connection with a different issue is set out in Section 12FIII of this chapter. In addition to transaction

---

[25] 568 U.S. 455 (2013).

[26] 711 F.Supp. 1264 (D.N.J. 1989).

causation, courts began requiring loss causation; this requirement now is codified in Section 21D(b)(4), which provides: "In any private action arising under [the Exchange Act], the plaintiff shall have the burden of proving that the act or omission of the defendant alleged to violate [the Act] caused the loss for which the plaintiff seeks to recover damages." A Supreme Court decision explaining what must be pleaded and proved to establish loss causation follows.

Dura Pharmaceuticals, Inc. v. Broudo

Supreme Court of the United States, 2005.
544 U.S. 336.

■ JUSTICE BREYER delivered the opinion of the Court.

A private plaintiff who claims securities fraud must prove that the defendant's fraud caused an economic loss. 109 Stat. 747, 15 U.S.C. § 78u–4(b)(4) ["Exchange Act Section 21D(b)(4)"]. We consider a Ninth circuit holding that a plaintiff can satisfy this requirement—a requirement that courts call "loss causation"—simply by alleging in the complaint and subsequently establishing that "the price" of the security "*on the date of purchase* was inflated because of the misrepresentation." 339 F.3d 933, 938 (2003). In our view, the Ninth Circuit is wrong, both in respect to what a plaintiff must prove and in respect to what the plaintiffs' complaint here must allege.

I

Respondents are individuals who bought stock in Dura Pharmaceuticals, Inc., on the public securities market between April 15, 1997, and February 24, 1998. They have brought this securities fraud class action against Dura and some of its managers and directors (hereinafter "Dura") in federal court. In respect to the question before us, their complaint makes substantially the following allegations:

(1) Before and during the purchase period, Dura (or its officials) made false statements concerning both Dura's drug profits and future Food and Drug Administration (FDA) approval of a new asthmatic spray device.

(2) In respect to drug profits, Dura falsely claimed that it expected that its drug sales would prove profitable.

(3) In respect to the asthmatic spray device, Dura falsely claimed that it expected the FDA would soon grant its approval.

(4) On the last day of the purchase period, February 24, 1998, Dura announced that its earnings would be lower than expected, principally due to slow drug sales.

(5) The next day Dura's shares lost almost half their value (falling from about $39 per share to about $21).

(6) About eight months later (in November 1998), Dura announced that the FDA would not approve Dura's new asthmatic spray device.

(7) The next day Dura's share price temporarily fell but almost fully recovered within one week.

Most importantly, the complaint says the following (and nothing significantly more than the following) about economic losses attributable to the spray device misstatement: *"In reliance on the integrity of the market, [the plaintiffs * * * paid artificially inflated prices for Dura securities"* and the Plaintiffs suffered *"damages"* thereby. * * * (emphasis added).

* * *

II

* * *

The courts have implied from [Exchange Act section 10(b) and Rule 10b–5] a private damages action, which resembles, but is not identical to, common-law tort actions for deceit and misrepresentation. *See, e.g.,* Blue Chip Stamps v. Manor Drug Stores, 421 U.S. 723, 730, 744 (1975); Ernst & Ernst v. Hochfelder, 425 U.S. 185 (1976). And Congress has imposed statutory requirements on that private action. *E.g.,* Exchange Act Section 21D(b)(4).

In cases involving publicly traded securities and purchases or sales in public securities markets, the action's basic elements include:

(1) a material misrepresentation (or omission), * * * *see* Basic Inc. v. Levinson, 485 U.S. 224, 231–232 (1988);

(2) scienter, *i.e.,* a wrongful state of mind, *see Ernst & Ernst, supra,* at 197, 199;

(3) a connection with the purchase or sale of a security, *see Blue Chip Stamps, supra,* at 730–731;

(4) reliance, often referred to in cases involving public securities markets (fraud-on-the-market cases) as "transaction causation," *see Basic, supra,* at 248–249;

(5) economic loss, Exchange Act Section 21D(b)(4); and

(6) "loss causation," *i.e.,* a causal connection between the material misrepresentation and the loss, ibid.

Dura argues that the complaint's allegations are inadequate in respect to these last two elements.

A

We begin with the Ninth Circuit's basic reason for finding the complaint adequate, namely, that at the end of the day plaintiffs need only "establish," *i.e.,* prove, that "the price *on the date of purchase* was inflated because of the misrepresentation." 339 F.3d at 938 * * * In our view, this statement of the law is wrong. Normally, in cases such as this one (*i.e.*, fraud-on-the market cases), an inflated purchase price will not itself constitute or proximately cause the relevant economic loss.

For one thing, as a matter of pure logic, at the moment the transaction takes place, the plaintiff has suffered no loss; the inflated purchase payment is offset by ownership of a share that *at that instant* possesses equivalent value. Moreover, the logical link between the inflated share purchase price and any later economic loss is not invariably strong. Shares are normally purchased with an eye toward a later sale. But if, say, the purchaser sells the shares quickly before the relevant truth begins to leak out, the misrepresentation will not have led to any loss. If the purchaser sells later after the truth makes its way into the market place, an initially inflated purchase price *might* mean a later loss. But that is far from inevitably so. When the purchaser subsequently resells such shares, even at a lower price, that lower price may reflect, not the earlier misrepresentation, but changed economic circumstances, changed investor expectations, new industry-specific or firm-specific facts, conditions, or other events, which taken separately or together account for some or all of that lower price. (The same is true in respect to a claim that a share's higher price is lower than it would otherwise have been—a claim we do not consider here.) Other things being equal, the longer the time between purchase and sale, the more likely that this is so, i.e., the more likely that other factors caused the loss.

Given the tangle of factors affecting price, the most logic alone permits us to say is that the higher purchase price will *sometimes* play a role in bringing about a future loss. It may prove to be a necessary condition of any such loss, and in that sense one might say that the inflated purchase price suggests that the misrepresentation (using language the Ninth Circuit used) "touches upon" a loss is not to *cause* a loss, and it is the latter that the law requires. Exchange Act Section 21D(b)(4).

For another thing, the Ninth Circuit's holding lacks support in precedent. Judicially implied private securities-fraud actions resemble in many (but not all) respects common-law deceit and misrepresentation actions. See *Blue Chip Stamps, supra,* at 744 * * * The common law of deceit subjects a person who "fraudulently" makes a "misrepresentation" to liability "for pecuniary loss caused" to one who justifiably relies upon that misrepresentation. Restatement (Second) of Torts § 525, p. 55 (1977) * * * . And the common law has long insisted that a plaintiff in such a case show not only that had he known the truth he would not have acted but also that he suffered actual economic loss. * * *

* * *

Finally, the Ninth Circuit's approach overlooks an important securities law objective. The securities statutes seek to maintain public confidence in the marketplace. *See* United States v. O'Hagan, 521 U.S.

642, 658 (1997). They do so by deterring fraud, in part, through the availability of private securities fraud actions. Randall v. Loftsgaarden, 478 U.S. 647, 664 (1986). But the statutes make these latter actions available, not to provide investors with broad insurance against market losses, but to protect them against those economic losses that misrepresentations actually cause.

The statutory provision at issue here and the paragraphs that precede it emphasize this last mentioned objective. * * * The statute insists that securities fraud complaints "specify" each misleading statement; that they set forth the facts "on which [a] belief" that a statement is misleading was "formed"; and that they "state with particularity facts giving rise to a strong inference that the defendant acted with the required state of mind." Exchange Act Sections 21D(b)(1), (2). And the statute expressly imposes on plaintiffs "the burden of proving" that the defendant's misrepresentations "caused the loss for which the plaintiff seeks to recover." Exchange Act Section 21D(b)(4).

The statute thereby makes clear Congress' intent to permit private securities fraud actions for recovery where, but only where, plaintiffs adequately allege and prove the traditional elements of causation and loss. By way of contrast, the Ninth Circuit's approach would allow recovery where a misrepresentation leads to an inflated purchase price but nonetheless does not proximately cause any economic loss. That is to say, it would permit recovery where these two traditional elements in fact are missing.

In sum, we find the Ninth Circuit's approach inconsistent with the law's requirement that a plaintiff prove that the defendant's misrepresentation (or other fraudulent conduct) proximately caused the plaintiffs economic loss. We need not, and do not, consider other proximate cause or loss-related questions.

B

Our holding about plaintiffs' need to *prove* proximate causation and economic loss leads us also to conclude that the plaintiffs' complaint here failed adequately to *allege* these requirements. We concede that the Federal Rules of Civil Procedure require only "a short and plain statement" of the claim showing that the pleader is entitled to relief: Fed. Rule Civ. Proc. 8(a)(2). And we assume, at least for argument's sake, that neither the Rules nor the securities statutes impose any special further requirement in respect to the pleading of proximate causation or economic loss. But, even so, the "short and plain statement" must provide the defendant with "fair notice of what the plaintiff's claim is and the grounds upon which it rests." Conley v. Gibson, 355 U.S. 41, 47 (1957). The complaint before us fails this simple test.

As we have pointed out, the Plaintiffs' lengthy complaint contains only one statement that we can fairly read as describing the loss caused by the defendants' "spray device" misrepresentations. That statement says that the plaintiffs "paid artificially inflated prices for Dura's securities" and suffered "damages." * * * The statement implies that the plaintiffs' loss consisted of the "artificially inflated" purchase "prices." The complaint's failure to claim that Dura's share price fell significantly after the truth became known suggests that the plaintiffs considered the allegation of purchase price inflation alone sufficient. The complaint contains nothing that suggests otherwise.

* * *

We concede that ordinary pleading rules are not meant to impose a great burden upon a plaintiff. Swierkiewicz v. Sorema N.A., 534 U.S. 506, 513–515 (2002). But it should not prove burdensome for a plaintiff who has suffered an economic loss to provide a defendant with some indication of the loss and the causal connection that the plaintiff has in mind. At the same time, allowing a plaintiff to forgo giving any indication of the economic loss and proximate cause that the plaintiff has in mind would bring about harm of the very sort the statutes seek to avoid. * * *

For these reasons, we find the plaintiffs' complaint legally insufficient. We reverse the judgment of the Ninth Circuit, and we remand the case for further proceedings consistent with this opinion.

————————

More recently, the Court held that although loss causation is an element that must be proven to prevail on the merits of a private action for securities fraud, demonstrating it is not a precondition to class certification.[27]

D. ISSUERS' DUTY TO DISCLOSE

So long as a publicly-held company is not trading in its own securities, it is said that there is no general duty, under Rule 10b–5 or otherwise, that requires it to disclose material inside information. In the absence of an explicit mandate in a given situation, or some special circumstance, a company may disclose material information or not, as suits its purposes.

It is necessary, however, to consider the explicit disclosure mandates, which now are very broad. These include, of course, the periodic and other reports discussed in Chapter 9, which incorporate by reference the various items of Regulation S–K and S–X. The Second Circuit, in Stratte-McClure v. Morgan Stanley,[28] specifically has ruled that failure to disclose known trends and uncertainties as called for by Item 303 of Regulation S–K is actionable if material. In *Stratte-McClure*, however, the court noted its conclusion was "at odds with the Ninth Circuit's recent opinion in In re NVDIA Corp. Securities Litigation."[29]

---

[27] Erica P. John Fund, Inc. v. Halliburton Co., 563 U.S. 804 (2011).

[28] 776 F.3d 94 (2d Cir.2015).

[29] 768 F.3d 1046 (9th Cir.2014).

That court held that "Item 303 does not create a duty to disclose for purposes of Section 10(b) and Rule 10b–5. Such a duty to disclose must be separately shown according to the principles set forth by the Supreme Court in *Basic* and *Matrixx Initiatives*." The *NVDIA Corp.* court regarded those principles as being embodied in the following language from *Basic*: "Disclosure is required under these provisions only when necessary 'to make . . . statements made, in the [sic] light of the circumstances under which they were made, not misleading.' " Both courts claimed consistency with the Third Circuit's opinion in Oran v. Stafford,[30] which found that an omission of information required by Item 303 is not" inevitably" a violation of Section 10(b) and Rule 10b–5. In 2017, the Supreme Court accepted certiorari over Leidos, Inc. v. Indiana Pub. Ret. Sys., another Second Circuit case following *Stratte-McClure*.[31]

Another explicit disclosure mandate is found in Regulation FD. Regulation FD imposes a duty upon issuers to intentionally reveal material information only through public disclosure. Selective (nonpublic) disclosures thus generally are prohibited, although communications with groups not reasonably expected to trade on the information, such as the press, customers, suppliers, and rating agencies, are exempt. If any issuer learns it unintentionally has made a material selective disclosure, it is required to make public disclosure of the same information within 24 hours. "Public" disclosure includes the filing of an Exchange Act Report on Form 8K or other means designed to reach the public "on a broad, nonexclusionary basis" (such as a press release). In principles-based guidance adopted in 2008,[32] the Commission made it clear that disclosure on Web sites can constitute the requisite public disclosure for purposes of Regulation FD; more recently it has indicated that disclosure through social media such as Twitter and Facebook may be sufficient. In its 2008 release, the Commission also sought to make it clear that issuers are not required to correct erroneous information posted by third-parties. Information posted by or on behalf of issuers is subject to antifraud and proxy requirements, but is only subject to the disclosure controls and certifications required by Sarbanes-Oxley if the posting is intended to comply with Exchange Act requirements. Regulation FD is not intended to give rise to liability to private plaintiffs.

What other circumstances trigger an issuer's duty to disclose? Consider the following case, decided under Rule 10b–5.

---

[30]   226 F.3d 275 (3d Cir.2000).

[31]   818 F.3d 85 (2d Cir.2016), *cert. granted* 137 S.Ct. 1395 (2017).

[32]   Exchange Act Release No. 58,288 (Aug. 1, 2008).

Stransky v. Cummins Engine Co., Inc.

United States Court of Appeals, Seventh Circuit, 1995.
51 F.3d 1329.

■ Before BAUER, KANNE, and ROVNER,[33] CIRCUIT JUDGES.

■ KANNE, CIRCUIT JUDGE:

The predicate for this case is a familiar one: a company makes optimistic predictions about future performance, the predictions turn out to be less than prophetic, and shareholders cry foul, or more specifically, fraud. Alan Stransky and Raphael Warkel filed a class action suit against Cummins Engine Company, Inc. (Cummins), alleging securities fraud. The district court dismissed * * * . * * *

Cummins is a leading designer and manufacturer of in-line and v-type diesel engines. Because of new emissions standards promulgated by the U.S. Environmental Protection Agency, in 1988 Cummins began producing redesigned engines. Stransky claims that "in internal technical memoranda, Cummins admitted that it had 'rushed' its design and production to comply with the new standards, that there was insufficient time for evaluation of the engines, and that the technical division had relied too much on the testing of prototype hardware rather than on the testing of the final production product." Cummins typically warranted its engines for two years or 100,000 miles, whichever came first.

Stransky alleges that beginning in the fall of 1988 and extending through the spring of 1989, Cummins' board of directors was informed that the newly designed engines were experiencing problems due to faulty design and that costs associated with fixing the engines (warranty costs) were rising. * * *

Of course, to state a securities fraud claim, Stransky must allege fraud. To this end, Stransky alleges that during the fall of 1988, the directors of Cummins became concerned that the Hanson Group (USA) Ltd. (Hanson), a known corporate takeover company, was preparing a hostile takeover. * * * Stransky alleges that in order to entrench themselves against the takeover, the directors plotted to increase the value of Cummins' stock by suppressing the news of the redesigned engines' problems.

Mere silence about even material information is not fraudulent absent a duty to speak. Stransky alleges that Cummins' silence about the rising warranty costs violated SEC Rule 10b–5 because a duty to disclose the warranty problems arose when Cummins made public statements that related to warranty costs and were misleading because of the withheld information about the problems. If one speaks, he must speak the whole truth.

---

[33] Due to a conflict discovered on the day the case was decided, Judge Rovner was recused from the appeal. [Eds.]

* * * The avenues of proving a false or misleading statement or omission are still uncertain. The most common and obvious method is by demonstrating that the defendant fraudulently made a statement of material fact or omitted a fact necessary to prevent a statement from being misleading. Two other avenues have been kicked around by courts, litigants and academics alike: a "duty to correct" and a "duty to update." Litigants often fail to distinguish between these theories (as did Stransky in this case) and to delineate their exact parameters. The former applies when a company makes a historical statement that, at the time made, the company believed to be true, but as revealed by subsequently discovered information actually was not. The company then must correct the prior statement within a reasonable time.

Some have argued that a duty to update arises when a company makes a forward-looking statement—a projection—that because of subsequent events becomes untrue. This court has never embraced such a theory, and we decline to do so now.

* * * [Rule 10b–5] implicitly precludes basing liability on circumstances that arise after the speaker makes the statement. In addition, the securities laws typically do not act as a Monday Morning Quarterback. * * *

Courts differ on how they examine forward-looking statements. One method, adopted by the Fourth Circuit, has focused on the requirement that the misleading statement be material. * * * In Howard v. Haddad, 962 F.2d 328 (4th Cir.1992), Howard claimed that Haddad induced him, through misrepresentations, to buy stock in a bank that subsequently went under. The alleged misrepresentations were statements by Haddad "that it was a growing bank, and that it was [a] good investment." The Fourth Circuit held that such "puffery" could not lead to liability because it "lacks the materiality essential to a securities fraud allegation." In Raab v. General Physics Corp., 4 F.3d 286 (4th Cir.1993), the Fourth Circuit expanded on this rationale by stating, "Soft, 'puffing' statements * * * generally lack materiality because the market price of a share is not inflated by vague statements predicting growth. * * * No reasonable investor would rely on those statements, and they are certainly not specific enough to perpetrate a fraud on the market."

While it often may be the case that predictions of growth are not material, we hesitate to impose a per se rule to this effect. The Supreme Court has cautioned that materiality is typically an issue to be resolved by the finder of fact. TSC Indus., Inc. [v. Northway, Inc., 426 U.S. 438, 450 (1976)]. A blanket rule that forward-looking statements are not material does not allow for the contextual, fact-specific nature of the inquiry and would potentially allow companies to engage in conjecture with impunity.

* * *

Another avenue of analysis is available. In Virginia Bankshares, Inc. v. Sandberg, 501 U.S. 1083 (1991), the Supreme Court held that statements by a board of directors of reasons for taking action and statements of present opinion or belief are statements "with respect to * * * material fact[s]" within the meaning of SEC Rule 14(a)–9. The Court reasoned that, "[s]uch statements are factual in two senses: as statements that the directors do act for the reasons given or hold the belief stated and as statements about the subject matter of the reason or belief expressed."

Applying this framework to forward-looking statements, in Kowal v. MCI Communications Corp., 16 F.3d 1271 (D.C.Cir.1994), the D.C. Circuit stated that the "only truly factual elements involved in a projection are the implicit representations that the statements are made in good faith and with a reasonable basis." (internal quotations and citations omitted). We believe this is correct. This analysis remains true to the wording of the rule, as well as limiting liability to the small number of statements that are most harmful in the marketplace. Thus, a projection can lead to liability under Rule 10b–5 only if it was not made in good faith or was made without a reasonable basis. With this discussion in mind, we turn to the facts of the case before us.

* * *

We first look to the complaint to determine whether Stransky has alleged facts that, if true, could lead to Rule 10b–5 liability under any theory. The complaint, as it relates to Stransky, alleges that four press releases lead to liability. * * * Nothing in [two of the] press releases related directly to warranty costs, and therefore Stransky cannot rely on them for alleging that Cummins violated Rule 10b–5.

Stransky also alleges that two April press releases can support liability. The complaint alleges the following about an April 4, 1989 press release.

> 43. [The press release] indicated that Cummins expected its First Quarter earnings to exceed $1.50 per share and that Second Quarter results were expected to be stronger than the First Quarter. The press release further stated that the shift by the Company to sales of their new engines had a dramatic influence on profitability since each of these products were coming down on their cost curves and were making progress toward their targets. As set forth above, however, the new engines were, in fact, beginning to show design defects and increased product and warranty costs from January to April of 1989.

* * * [T]he press release * * * made two historical statements that may relate to warranty costs: that the engines "were coming down on their cost curves," and that the engines "were making progress toward their targets." These statements, at least as represented in the complaint, are

ambiguous. We can think of at least four ways in which "cost curves" can be interpreted. It could refer to only production costs, as the district court seems to have concluded, in which case warranty costs would indeed be unrelated. On the other hand, it could refer to overall costs of a product, which conceivably, although not necessarily, include warranty costs. If warranty costs were rising so precipitously as to outweigh the decrease in other costs, thereby causing overall costs to rise, the statement could be false. Additionally, "cost curves" was stated in the plural; this could lead to two additional interpretations. One can imagine a company breaking up its overall cost curve into its derivative costs (i.e., raw materials, labor, marketing, warranty, among others) and charting and following these more particularized costs. Thus, "cost curves" could have referred to each of these derivative costs. However, the plural could have stemmed from the press releases' discussion of multiple products. The statement is unclear. What is clear is that on a motion to dismiss we should make all reasonable inferences in favor of Stransky and should not resolve the interpretation of the press release against Stransky. Similarly, if Cummins had "targets" for its warranty costs, as suggested in the complaint, then the fact that warranty costs were rising could make incorrect the statement that the engines were making progress toward their targets.

The complaint also recounts an April 20, 1989 press release that "indicated that B & C engines were now profitable and that profit margins on these engines should improve as the costs of these engines continued to decline." This statement appears to contain one historical statement, that the costs of the engines are now declining, and two predictions, 1) that profit margins should improve, and 2) that the costs of the engines should decline from current levels. The analysis of the historical statement alleged here follows that set out above and will not be repeated. The forward-looking statements can lead to liability only if they were unreasonable in light of the facts known at the time (and such unreasonableness was due to rising warranty costs as Stransky has alleged no other reason) or they were not made in good faith. We must remand to the district court for further resolution of these issues.

———————

In opposition to *Stransky* is Weiner v. Quaker Oats Co.,[34] in which the Third Circuit found that the plaintiff's case survived summary judgment on a failure to update issue, saying: "The complaint alleges facts on the basis of which a reasonable factfinder could determine that Quaker's statements regarding its total debt-to-total capitalization ratio guideline would have been material to a reasonable investor, and hence that Quaker had a duty to update such statements when they became unreliable." The Third Circuit subsequently made it clear, though, that it does regard the duty to update and the duty to correct as conceptually

———————

[34]   129 F.3d 310 (3d Cir.1997).

distinct, and believes that if the duty to update does exist it is quite narrow in scope.[35] The Seventh Circuit has hardened its distinction between the duty to correct (which it recognizes) and the duty to update (which it does not, absent a specific statutory or Commission mandate).[36]

E. DAMAGES AND PENALTIES

Considering the abundance of Rule 10b–5 cases, it might be expected that damage issues would be completely resolved. They are not. The measure of damages generally applied is the out-of-pocket measure, which is the difference between the price paid or received for securities and their actual value at the time of the purchase or sale.[37] Where this measure is sought, Section 21D(e) comes into play. This provision applies in any private action brought under the Exchange Act where the plaintiff seeks to establish damages by reference to the market price of a security. Basically, Section 21D(e) provides that such damages cannot exceed the difference between the plaintiff's purchase or sale price and the mean trading price (as defined) "during the 90-day period beginning on the date on which the information correcting the misstatement or omission that is the basis for the action is disseminated to the market."

Other measures of damages are sometimes used, however, including rescissionary damages, under which a "plaintiff is entitled to a return of the consideration paid, reduced by the amount realized when he sold the security and by any 'income received' on the security."[38] Another possibility in measuring damages is the disgorgement approach, which is discussed in Chapter 13 in the context of insider trading. Exchange Act provisions dealing with penalties specifically tailored for insider trading also are covered in that chapter.

The general penalties that may be invoked in connection with an action under Rule 10b–5 are, to put it politely, complex. First, of course, are the criminal penalties discussed in Chapter 9 (up to $5 million in fines and 20 years in prison for natural persons and up to $25 million in fines for other than natural persons). The following discussion deals with the penalties that the Commission may seek in litigation brought in federal court and the penalties the Commission may impose in its own administrative proceedings.

Section 21(d)(1) provides the Commission with the authority to seek injunctive relief (historically including orders of disgorgement) against violations of the Exchange Act and its rules. Section 21(d)(3) grants the Commission authority to seek court-ordered civil penalties under all provisions of the Exchange Act and its rules (other than for acts already subject to the civil penalty provision in Section 21A relating to insider

---

[35]   United States v. Schiff, 602 F.3d 152 (2010).

[36]   Gallagher v. Abbott Laboratories, 269 F.3d 806 (7th Cir.2001).

[37]   See, e.g., Randall v. Loftsgaarden, 478 U.S. 647, 661 (1986).

[38]   Id. at 656.

trading). The amount of possible penalty escalates in tiers, depending on the nature of the conduct involved. Under Section 308 of Sarbanes-Oxley, these amounts can be added to a disgorgement fund for the benefit of victims if the Commission also has obtained an order requiring disgorgement. Section 21(d)(5) permits the Commission to seek any equitable relief under any provision of the federal securities laws. Under Section 21(d)(2), the courts specifically are given the power to prohibit persons who violate Exchange Act Section 10(b) from serving as an officer or director of a company that has securities registered under Section 12 of the Exchange Act or that is required under Exchange Act Section 15(d) to file Exchange Act reports. Section 21(d)(6) authorizes court-ordered bars against participation in offerings of penny stock if the defendant's alleged misconduct related to an offering of penny stock.

The Commission has received progressively more significant ability to impose penalties in its own administrative proceedings. Section 21B gives the Commission the basic power to impose (tiered) civil penalties escalating in the same tiers as court-ordered penalties. Section 21C provides the Commission authority to issue cease-and-desist orders when it finds, after notice and an opportunity for a hearing, that someone is violating, has violated, or is about to violate any provision of the Exchange Act or any of its rules. This section also gives the Commission the power to order an accounting and disgorgement in cease-and-desist proceedings, and the power in cease-and-desist proceedings to issue officer and director bars, with respect to service with Exchange Act reporting companies, against those who have violated Exchange Act Section 10(b) or any of its rules. The Commission may, under Section 21(d)(3), seek court-ordered civil penalties for violations of its own cease-and-desist orders.

Under Rule 9 of the Commission's rules of informal and other procedures, the Commission may, on a case-by-case basis, reduce the amount of penalty it either seeks or assesses against a "small entity" (which includes a "Small Business" as defined by the Commission). Under the rule, the Commission considers a number of issues in making this determination, including the willfulness and egregiousness of the conduct, the violator's history of legal or regulatory violations, and the financial ability of the entity to pay the penalty.

F. SECONDARY LIABILITY AND CONTRIBUTION

I. CONTROLLING PERSON LIABILITY

Exchange Act Section 20 provides that controlling persons are jointly and severally liable for any violation of the Exchange Act or its rules committed by the company or other person they control, "unless the controlling person acted in good faith and did not directly or indirectly induce the act or acts constituting the violation or cause of action." This section also prohibits various other actions, including hindering, delaying, or obstructing an Exchange Act filing, without just cause, by a director, officer, or security owner of the filer.

II. AIDING AND ABETTING AND CONSPIRACY

Until the 1993–94 Supreme Court term, there seemed to be no question that one could be charged with aiding and abetting a Rule 10b–5 violation, both in private actions and in those brought by the government.

Central Bank of Denver, N.A. v. First Interstate Bank of Denver, N.A.

Supreme Court of the United States, 1994.
511 U.S. 164.

■ JUSTICE KENNEDY delivered the opinion of the Court.

* * *

I

[Central Bank of Denver, N.A. ("Central Bank"), served as indenture trustee for bonds secured by land that, as a matter of covenant, was to be worth at least 160% of the bonds' outstanding principal and interest. Despite reason to suspect that the land had declined in value, Central Bank delayed arranging for an independent appraisal. Before the appraisal was completed, the issuer of the bonds had gone into default. Central Bank and others then were sued as aiders and abettors. Eds.]

* * *

II

* * *

Our consideration of statutory duties, especially in cases interpreting § 10(b), establishes that the statutory text controls the definition of conduct covered by § 10(b). That bodes ill for respondents, for the language of Section 10(b) does not in terms mention aiding and abetting. Brief for SEC as *Amicus Curiae* 8 (hereinafter Brief for SEC). To overcome this problem, respondents and the SEC suggest (or hint at) the novel argument that the use of the phrase "directly or indirectly" in the text of § 10(b) covers aiding and abetting.

The federal courts have not relied on the "directly or indirectly" language when imposing aiding and abetting liability under § 10(b), and with good reason. There is a basic flaw with this interpretation. According to respondents and the SEC, the directly or indirectly language shows that Congress * * * intended to reach all persons who engage, even if only indirectly, in proscribed activities connected with securities transactions. The problem, of course, is that aiding and abetting liability extends beyond persons who engage, even indirectly, in a proscribed activity; aiding and abetting liability reaches persons who do not engage in the proscribed activities at all, but who give a degree of aid to those who do. A further problem with respondents' interpretation of the directly or indirectly language is posed by the numerous provisions of the 1934 Act that use the term in a way that does not impose aiding and abetting liability. In short, respondents' interpretation of the directly or indirectly language fails to support their suggestion that the text of § 10(b) itself prohibits aiding and abetting.

Congress knew how to impose aiding and abetting liability when it chose to do so. * * *

* * *

III

Because this case concerns the conduct prohibited by § 10(b), the statute itself resolves the case, but even if it did not, we would reach the same result. When the text of § 10(b) does not resolve a particular issue, we attempt to infer "how the 1934 Congress would have addressed the issue had the 10b–5 action been included as an express provision in the 1934 Act." Musick, Peeler [& Garrett v. Employers Ins. of Wausau, 113 S.Ct. 2085], at 2090. For that inquiry, we use the express causes of action in the securities Acts as the primary model for the § 10(b) action. The reason is evident: Had the 73d Congress enacted a private § 10(b) right of action, it likely would have designed it in a manner similar to the other private rights of action in the securities Acts.

* * *

Following that analysis here, we look to the express private causes of action in the 1933 and 1934 Acts. In the 1933 Act, § 11 prohibits false statements or omissions of material fact in registration statements; it identifies the various categories of defendants subject to liability for a violation, but that list does not include aiders and abettors. Section 12 prohibits the sale of unregistered, nonexempt securities as well as the sale of securities by means of a material misstatement or omission; and it limits liability to those who offer or sell the security. In the 1934 Act, § 9 prohibits any person from engaging in manipulative practices such as wash sales, matched orders, and the like. Section 16 prohibits short-swing trading by owners, directors, and officers. Section 18 prohibits any person from making misleading statements in reports filed with the SEC. And § 20A, added in 1988, prohibits any person from engaging in insider trading.

This survey of the express causes of action in the securities Acts reveals that each (like § 10(b)) specifies the conduct for which defendants may be held liable. Some of the express causes of action specify categories of defendants who may be liable; others (like § 10(b)) state only that "any person" who commits one of the prohibited acts may be held liable. The important point for present purposes, however, is that none of the express causes of action in the 1934 Act further imposes liability on one who aids or abets a violation.

From the fact that Congress did not attach private aiding and abetting liability to any of the express causes of action in the securities Acts, we can infer that Congress likely would not have attached aiding and abetting liability to § 10(b) had it provided a private § 10(b) cause of action. There is no reason to think that Congress would have attached aiding and abetting liability only to § 10(b) and not to any of the express private rights of action in the Act. In Blue Chip Stamps [v. Manor Drug Stores, 421 U.S. 723 (1975)], we noted that it would be "anomalous to impute to Congress an intention to expand the plaintiff class for a judicially implied cause of action beyond the bounds it delineated for comparable express causes of action." * * *

Our reasoning is confirmed by the fact that respondents' argument would impose 10b–5 aiding and abetting liability when at least one element critical for recovery under 10b–5 is absent: reliance. A plaintiff must show reliance on the defendant's misstatement or omission to recover under 10b–5. Were we to allow the aiding and abetting action proposed in this case, the defendant could be liable without any showing that the plaintiff relied upon the aider and abettor's statements or actions. Allowing plaintiffs to circumvent the reliance requirement would disregard the careful limits on 10b–5 recovery mandated by our earlier cases.

IV

* * *

The text does not support their point, but respondents and some *amici* invoke a broad-based notion of congressional intent. They say that Congress legislated with an understanding of general principles of tort law and that aiding and abetting liability was "well established in both civil and criminal actions by 1934." Brief for SEC 10. Thus, "Congress intended to include" aiding and abetting liability in the 1934 Act. *Id.*, at 11. A brief history of aiding and abetting liability serves to dispose of this argument.

* * *

More to the point, Congress has not enacted a general civil aiding and abetting statute either for suits by the Government (when the Government sues for civil penalties or injunctive relief) or for suits by private parties. Thus, when Congress enacts a statute under which a person may sue and recover damages from a private defendant for the defendant's violation of some statutory norm, there is no general presumption that the plaintiff may also sue aiders and abettors.

* * *

* * * In addition, Congress did not overlook secondary liability when it created the private rights of action in the 1934 Act. Section 20 of the 1934 Act imposes liability on "controlling persons"—persons who "contro[l] any person liable under any provision of this chapter or of any

rule or regulation thereunder." This suggests that "[w]hen Congress wished to create such [secondary] liability, it had little trouble doing so." Pinter v. Dahl, 486 U.S. [622, 650 (1988)]. Aiding and abetting is "a method by which courts create secondary liability" in persons other than the violator of the statute. Pinter v. Dahl, *supra,* 486 U.S. at 648, n. 24. The fact that Congress chose to impose some forms of secondary liability, but not others, indicates a deliberate congressional choice with which the courts should not interfere.

* * *

V

Because the text of § 10(b) does not prohibit aiding and abetting, we hold that a private plaintiff may not maintain an aiding and abetting suit under § 10(b). The absence of § 10(b) aiding and abetting liability does not mean that secondary actors in the securities markets are always free from liability under the securities Acts. Any person or entity, including a lawyer, accountant, or bank, who employs a manipulative device or makes a material misstatement (or omission) on which a purchaser or seller of securities relies may be liable as a primary violator under 10b–5, assuming *all* of the requirements for primary liability under Rule 10b–5 are met. In any complex securities fraud, moreover, there are likely to be multiple violators; in this case, for example, respondents named four defendants as primary violators.

* * *

Under the Court's reasoning, which was based primarily on its interpretation of congressional intent, it was problematic whether the Commission had authority to bring actions for aiding and abetting violations of Section 10(b). The uncertainty was cleared up when Congress in 1995 amended Exchange Act Section 20 to provide that the Commission has authority to bring actions for aiding and abetting the violation of any section of the Exchange Act or of any of its rules or regulations.[39] In 2010, the Dodd-Frank Act provided the Commission may base aiding and abetting enforcement actions on reckless conduct; a showing that conduct was knowing previously was required. Dodd-Frank also called for a study by the Government Accounting Office of the impact of creating a private right of action for aiding and abetting claims under the federal securities laws.

In Dinsmore v. Squadron, Ellenoff, Plesent, Sheinfeld & Sorkin,[40] the Second Circuit, reasoning from *Central Bank of Denver*, found that there is no conspiracy cause of action in private suits under Rule 10b–5.

---

[39] The Ninth Circuit has ruled that the section applies retroactively. SEC v. Fehn, 97 F.3d 1276 (9th Cir.1996), cert. denied 522 U.S. 813 (1997).

[40] 135 F.3d 837 (2d Cir.1998).

The court pointed out, however, that alleged conspirators can be held liable if the requirements for primary liability are met.

III. DISTINGUISHING PRIMARY AND SECONDARY LIABILITY

In the years following *Central Bank of Denver*, attempts were made to characterize those participating in a deceptive scheme but not communicating with the public as primary violators of Rule 10b–5. The theory pursuant to which liability was sought to be imposed was known as "scheme liability." The following case reveals the theory's fate.

Stoneridge Investment Partners, LLC v. Scientific-Atlanta, Inc.

Supreme Court of the United States, 2008.
552 U.S. 148.

■ JUSTICE KENNEDY delivered the opinion of the Court.

* * *

I

* * *

Charter Communications, Inc., issued the financial statements and the securities in question. It was a named defendant along with some of its executives and Arthur Andersen LLP, Charter's independent auditor during the period in question. We are concerned, though, with two other defendants, respondents here. Respondents are Scientific-Atlanta, Inc., and Motorola, Inc. They were suppliers, and later customers, of Charter.

For purposes of this proceeding, we take these facts, alleged by petitioner, to be true. Charter, a cable operator, engaged in a variety of fraudulent practices so its quarterly reports would meet Wall Street expectations for cable subscriber growth and operating cash flow. The fraud included misclassification of its customer base; delayed reporting of terminated customers; improper capitalization of costs that should have been shown as expenses; and manipulation of the company's billing cutoff dates to inflate reported revenues. In late 2000, Charter executives realized that, despite these efforts, the company would miss projected operating cash flow numbers by $15 to $20 million. To help meet the shortfall, Charter decided to alter its existing arrangements with respondents, Scientific-Atlanta and Motorola. Petitioner's theory as to whether Arthur Andersen was altogether misled or, on the other hand, knew the structure of the contract arrangements and was complicit to some degree, is not clear at this stage of the case. The point, however, is neither controlling nor significant for our present disposition, and in our decision we assume it was misled.

Respondents supplied Charter with the digital cable converter (set top) boxes that Charter furnished to its customers. Charter arranged to overpay respondents $20 for each set top box it purchased until the end of the year, with the understanding that respondents would return the overpayment by purchasing advertising from Charter. The transactions, it is alleged, had no economic substance; but, because Charter would then record the advertising purchases as revenue and capitalize its purchase of the set top boxes, in violation of generally accepted accounting principles, the transactions would enable Charter to fool its auditor into approving a financial statement showing it met projected revenue and operating cash flow numbers. Respondents agreed to the arrangement.

So that Arthur Andersen would not discover the link between Charter's increased payments for the boxes and the advertising purchases, the companies drafted documents to make it appear the transactions were unrelated and conducted in the ordinary course of business. Following a request from Charter, Scientific-Atlanta sent documents to Charter stating—falsely—that it had increased production costs. It raised the price for set top boxes for the rest of 2000 by $20 per box. As for Motorola, in a written contract Charter agreed to purchase from Motorola a specific number of set top boxes and pay liquidated damages of $20 for each unit it did not take. The contract was made with the expectation Charter would fail to purchase all the units and pay Motorola the liquidated damages.

To return the additional money from the set top box sales, Scientific-Atlanta and Motorola signed contracts with Charter to purchase advertising time for a price higher than fair value. The new set top box agreements were backdated to make it appear that they were negotiated a month before the advertising agreements. The backdating was important to convey the impression that the negotiations were unconnected, a point Arthur Andersen considered necessary for separate treatment of the transactions. Charter recorded the advertising payments to inflate revenue and operating cash flow by approximately $17 million. The inflated number was shown on financial statements filed with the Securities and Exchange Commission (SEC) and reported to the public.

Respondents had no role in preparing or disseminating Charter's financial statements. And their own financial statements booked the transactions as a wash, under generally accepted accounting principles. It is alleged respondents knew or were in reckless disregard of Charter's intention to use the transactions to inflate its revenues and knew the resulting financial statements issued by Charter would be relied upon by research analysts and investors.

Petitioner filed a securities fraud class action on behalf of purchasers of Charter stock alleging that, by participating in the transactions, respondents violated § 10(b) of the Securities Exchange Act of 1934 and SEC Rule 10b–5.

* * *

II

* * *

* * * In a typical § 10(b) private action a plaintiff must prove (1) a material misrepresentation or omission by the defendant; (2) scienter; (3) a connection between the misrepresentation or omission and the purchase or sale of a security; (4) reliance upon the misrepresentation or omission; (5) economic loss; and (6) loss causation. See Dura Pharms., Inc. v. Broudo, 544 U.S. 336, 341–342 (2005).

In Central Bank of Denver N.A. v. First Interstate Bank of Denver, N.A., 511 U.S. 164 (1994), the Court determined that § 10(b) liability did not extend to aiders and abettors. * * * The decision in *Central Bank* led to calls for Congress to create an express cause of action for aiding and abetting within the Securities Exchange Act. Then-SEC Chairman Arthur Levitt, testifying before the Senate Securities Subcommittee, cited *Central Bank* and recommended that aiding and abetting liability in private claims be established. * * * Congress did not follow this course. Instead, in § 104 of the Private Securities Litigation Reform Act of 1995 (PSLRA) it directed prosecution of aiders and abettors by the SEC.

The § 10(b) implied private right of action does not extend to aiders and abettors. The conduct of a secondary actor must satisfy each of the elements or preconditions for liability; and we consider whether the allegations here are sufficient to do so.

III

The Court of Appeals concluded petitioner had not alleged that respondents engaged in a deceptive act within the reach of the § 10(b) private right of action, noting that only misstatements, omissions by one who has a duty to disclose, and manipulative trading practices (where "manipulative" is a term of art, see, *e.g.,* Santa Fe Industries, Inc. v. Green, 430 U.S. 462, 476–477 (1977)) are deceptive within the meaning of the rule. If this conclusion were read to suggest there must be a specific oral or written statement before there could be liability under § 10(b) or Rule 10b–5, it would be erroneous. Conduct itself can be deceptive, as respondents concede. In this case, moreover, respondents' course of conduct included both oral and written statements, such as the backdated contracts agreed to by Charter and respondents.

A different interpretation of the holding from the Court of Appeals opinion is that the court was stating only that any deceptive statement or act respondents made was not actionable because it did not have the requisite proximate relation to the investors' harm. That conclusion is consistent with our own determination that respondents' acts or statements were not relied upon by the investors and that, as a result, liability cannot be imposed upon respondents.

A

Reliance by the plaintiff upon the defendant's deceptive acts is an essential element of the § 10(b) private cause of action. It ensures that, for liability to arise, the "requisite causal connection between a defendant's misrepresentation and a plaintiff's injury" exists as a predicate for liability. Basic Inc. v. Levinson, 485 U.S. 224, 243 (1988); see also Affiliated Ute Citizens of Utah v. United States, 406 U.S. 128 (1972) (requiring "causation in fact"). We have found a rebuttable presumption of reliance in two different circumstances. First, if there is an omission of a material fact by one with a duty to disclose, the investor to whom the duty was owed need not provide specific proof of reliance. *Id.,* at 153–154. Second, under the fraud-on-the-market doctrine, reliance is presumed when the statements at issue become public. The public information is reflected in the market price of the security. Then it can be assumed that an investor who buys or sells stock at the market price relies upon the statement. *Basic, supra,* at 247.

Neither presumption applies here. Respondents had no duty to disclose; and their deceptive acts were not communicated to the public. No member of the investing public had knowledge, either actual or presumed, of respondents' deceptive acts during the relevant times. Petitioner, as a result, cannot show reliance upon any of respondents' actions except in an indirect chain that we find too remote for liability.

B

Invoking what some courts call "scheme liability," see, *e.g.,* In re Enron Corp. Secs. v. Enron Corp., 439 F. Supp. 2d 692, 723 (SD Tex. 2006), petitioner nonetheless seeks to impose liability on respondents even absent a public statement. In our view this approach does not answer the objection that petitioner did not in fact rely upon respondents' own deceptive conduct.

Liability is appropriate, petitioner contends, because respondents engaged in conduct with the purpose and effect of creating a false appearance of material fact to further a scheme to misrepresent Charter's revenue. The argument is that the financial statement Charter released to the public was a natural and expected consequence of respondents' deceptive acts; had respondents not assisted Charter, Charter's auditor would not have been fooled, and the financial statement would have been a more accurate reflection of Charter's financial condition. That causal link is sufficient, petitioner argues, to apply *Basic*'s presumption of reliance to respondents' acts.

In effect petitioner contends that in an efficient market investors rely not only upon the public statements relating to a security but also upon the transactions those statements reflect. Were this concept of reliance to be adopted, the implied cause of action would reach the whole marketplace in which the issuing company does business; and there is no authority for this rule.

* * * In all events we conclude respondents' deceptive acts, which were not disclosed to the investing public, are too remote to satisfy the requirement of reliance. It was Charter, not respondents, that misled its auditor and filed fraudulent financial statements; nothing respondents did made it necessary or inevitable for Charter to record the transactions as it did.

The petitioner invokes the private cause of action under § 10(b) and seeks to apply it beyond the securities markets—the realm of financing business—to purchase and supply contracts—the realm of ordinary business operations. The latter realm is governed, for the most part, by state law. It is true that if business operations are used, as alleged here, to affect securities markets, the SEC enforcement power may reach the culpable actors. It is true as well that a dynamic, free economy presupposes a high degree of integrity in all of its parts, an integrity that must be underwritten by rules enforceable in fair, independent, accessible courts. Were the implied cause of action to be extended to the practices described here, however, there would be a risk that the federal power would be used to invite litigation beyond the immediate sphere of securities litigation and in areas already governed by functioning and effective state-law guarantees. Our precedents counsel against this extension. * * *

* * *

Petitioner's theory, moreover, would put an unsupportable interpretation on Congress' specific response to *Central Bank* * * *. Congress amended the securities laws to provide for limited coverage of aiders and abettors. Aiding and abetting liability is authorized in actions brought by the SEC but not by private parties. Petitioner's view of primary liability makes any aider and abettor liable under § 10(b) if he or she committed a deceptive act in the process of providing assistance. Were we to adopt this construction of § 10(b), it would revive in substance the implied cause of action against all aiders and abettors except those who committed no deceptive act in the process of facilitating the fraud; and we would undermine Congress' determination that this class of defendants should be pursued by the SEC and not by private litigants. * * *

* * *

The practical consequences of an expansion, which the Court has considered appropriate to examine in circumstances like these, * * * provide a further reason to reject petitioner's approach. In *Blue Chip*, the Court noted that extensive discovery and the potential for uncertainty and disruption in a lawsuit allow plaintiffs with weak claims to extort settlements from innocent companies. *Id.,* at 740–741. Adoption of petitioner's approach would expose a new class of defendants to these risks. As noted in *Central Bank*, contracting parties might find it necessary to protect against these threats, raising the costs of doing business. See 511 U.S., at 189. Overseas firms with no other exposure to our securities laws could be deterred from doing business here. This, in turn, may raise the cost of being a publicly traded company under our law and shift securities offerings away from domestic capital markets.

C

* * *

* * * In the absence of congressional intent the Judiciary's recognition of an implied private right of action "necessarily extends its authority to embrace a dispute Congress has not assigned it to resolve. This runs contrary to the established principle that 'the jurisdiction of the federal courts is carefully guarded against expansion by judicial interpretation . . . ,' American Fire & Casualty Co. v. Finn, 341 U.S. 6, 17 (1951) * * * ." * * *

Concerns with the judicial creation of a private cause of action caution against its expansion. The decision to extend the cause of action is for Congress, not for us. Though it remains the law, the § 10(b) private right should not be extended beyond its present boundaries. * * *

This restraint is appropriate in light of the PSLRA, which imposed heightened pleading requirements and a loss causation requirement upon "any private action" arising from the Securities Exchange Act. See 15 U.S.C. It is clear these requirements touch upon the implied right of action, which is now a prominent feature of federal securities regulation. * * * Congress thus ratified the implied right of action after the Court moved away from a broad willingness to imply private rights of action. * * * It is appropriate for us to assume that * * * Congress accepted the § 10(b) private cause of action as then defined but chose to extend it no further.

IV

Secondary actors are subject to criminal penalties and civil enforcement by the SEC. The enforcement power is not toothless. Since September 30, 2002, SEC enforcement actions have collected over $10 billion in disgorgement and penalties, much of it for distribution to injured investors. * * * [I]n this case both parties agree that criminal penalties are a strong deterrent. In addition some state securities laws permit state authorities to seek fines and restitution from aiders and abettors. All secondary actors, furthermore, are not necessarily immune from private suit. The securities statutes provide an express private right of action against accountants and underwriters in certain circumstances, and the implied right of action in § 10(b) continues to cover secondary actors who commit primary violations. *Central Bank, supra*, at 191.

Here respondents were acting in concert with Charter in the ordinary course as suppliers and, as matters then evolved in the not so ordinary course, as customers. Unconventional as the arrangement was, it took place in the marketplace for goods and services, not in the investment sphere. Charter was free to do as it chose in preparing its books, conferring with its auditor, and preparing and then issuing its financial statements. In these circumstances the investors cannot be said to have relied upon any of respondents' deceptive acts in the decision to purchase or sell securities; and as the requisite reliance cannot be shown, respondents have no liability to petitioner under the implied right of action. This conclusion is consistent with the narrow dimensions we must give to a right of action Congress did not authorize when it first enacted the statute and did not expand when it revisited the law.

* * *

■ JUSTICE STEVENS, with whom JUSTICE SOUTER and JUSTICE GINSBURG join, dissenting.

* * *

I

* * *

What the Court fails to recognize is that this case is critically different from *Central Bank* because the bank in that case did not engage in any deceptive act and, therefore, did not *itself* violate § 10(b). The Court sweeps aside any distinction, remarking that holding respondents liable would "revive the implied cause of action against all aiders and abettors except those who committed no deceptive act in the process of facilitating the fraud." But the fact that Central Bank engaged in no deceptive conduct whatsoever—in other words, that it was at most an aider and abettor—sharply distinguishes *Central Bank* from cases that do involve allegations of such conduct. * * *

* * * The facts of this case would parallel those of *Central Bank* if respondents had, for example, merely delayed sending invoices for set-top boxes to Charter. Conversely, the facts in *Central Bank* would mirror those in the case before us today if the bank had knowingly purchased real estate in wash transactions at above-market prices in order to facilitate the appraiser's overvaluation of the security. *Central Bank*, thus, poses no obstacle to petitioner's argument that it has alleged a cause of action under § 10(b).

II

The Court's next faulty premise is that petitioner is required to allege that Scientific-Atlanta and Motorola made it "necessary or inevitable for Charter to record the transactions in the way it did," in order to demonstrate reliance. * * *

* * *

In *Basic Inc.*, we held that the "fraud-on-the-market" theory provides adequate support for a presumption in private securities actions that shareholders (or former shareholders) in publicly traded companies rely on public material misstatements that affect the price of the company's stock. *Id.*, at 248. The holding in *Basic* is surely a sufficient response to the argument that a complaint alleging that deceptive acts which had a material effect on the price of a listed stock should be dismissed because the plaintiffs were not subjectively aware of the deception at the time of the securities' purchase or sale. * * *

The Court is right that a fraud-on-the-market presumption coupled with its view on causation would not support petitioner's view of reliance. The fraud-on-the-market presumption helps investors who cannot demonstrate that they, *themselves*, relied on fraud that reached the market. But that presumption says nothing about causation from the other side: what an individual or corporation must do in order to have "caused" the misleading information that reached the market. The Court thus has it backwards when it first addresses the fraud-on-the-market presumption, rather than the causation required. The argument is not that the fraud-on-the-market presumption is enough standing alone, but that a correct view of causation coupled with the presumption would allow petitioner to plead reliance.

* * *

* * * [R]espondents' acts had the foreseeable effect of causing petitioner to engage in the relevant securities transactions. The Restatement (Second) of Torts § 533 (1977) provides that "the maker of a fraudulent misrepresentation is subject to liability . . . if the misrepresentation, although not made directly to the other, is made to a third person and the maker intends or has reason to expect that its terms will be repeated or its substance communicated to the other." The sham transactions described in the complaint in this case had the same effect on Charter's profit and loss statement as a false entry directly on its books that included $17 million of gross revenues that had not been received. And respondents are alleged to have known that the outcome of their fraudulent transactions would be communicated to investors.

* * *

* * * In fact, our prior cases explained that to the extent that "the antifraud provisions of the securities laws are not coextensive with common-law doctrines of fraud," it is because common-law fraud doctrines might be too restrictive. Herman & MacLean v. Huddleston, 459 U.S. 375, 388–389 (1983). "Indeed, an important purpose of the federal securities statutes was to rectify perceived deficiencies in the available common-law protections by establishing higher standards of conduct in the securities industry." *Id.,* at 389. I, thus, see no reason to abandon common-law approaches to causation in § 10(b) cases.

Finally, the Court relies on the course of action Congress adopted after our decision in *Central Bank* to argue that siding with petitioner on reliance would run contrary to congressional intent. * * * That Congress chose not to restore the aiding and abetting liability removed by *Central*

Bank does not mean that Congress wanted to exempt from liability the broader range of conduct that today's opinion excludes.

* * *

III

While I would reverse for the reasons stated above, I must also comment on the importance of the private cause of action that Congress implicitly authorized when it enacted the Securities Exchange Act of 1934. A theme that underlies the Court's analysis is its mistaken hostility towards the § 10(b) private cause of action. The Court's current view of implied causes of action is that they are merely a "relic" of our prior "heady days." Correctional Services Corp. v. Malesko, 534 U.S. 61, 75 (2001) (SCALIA, J., concurring). Those "heady days" persisted for two hundred years.

During the first two centuries of this Nation's history much of our law was developed by judges in the common-law tradition. A basic principle animating our jurisprudence was enshrined in state constitution provisions guaranteeing, in substance, that "every wrong shall have a remedy." Fashioning appropriate remedies for the violation of rules of law designed to protect a class of citizens was the routine business of judges. See Marbury v. Madison, 5 U.S. 137 (1803). While it is true that in the early days state law was the source of most of those rules, throughout our history—until 1975—the same practice prevailed in federal courts with regard to federal statutes that left questions of remedy open for judges to answer. * * *

In a law-changing opinion written by Justice Brennan in 1975, the Court decided to modify its approach to private causes of action. Cort v. Ash, 422 U.S. 66 (constraining courts to use a strict four-factor test to determine whether Congress intended a private cause of action). A few years later, in Cannon v. University of Chicago, 441 U.S. 677 (1979), we adhered to the strict approach mandated by Cort v. Ash in 1975, but made it clear that "our evaluation of congressional action in 1972 must take into account its contemporary legal context." 441 U.S., at 698–699. That context persuaded the majority that Congress had intended the courts to authorize a private remedy for members of the protected class.

Until *Central Bank,* the federal courts continued to enforce a broad implied cause of action for the violation of statutes enacted in 1933 and 1934 for the protection of investors. * * *

In light of the history of court-created remedies and specifically the history of implied causes of action under § 10(b), the Court is simply wrong when it states that Congress did not impliedly authorize this private cause of action "when it first enacted the statute." * * * Congress enacted § 10(b) with the understanding that federal courts respected the principle that every wrong would have a remedy. Today's decision simply cuts back further on Congress' intended remedy. I respectfully dissent.

In 2011, the Supreme Court released yet another decision sharply limiting the ability of private plaintiffs to recover from those participating in securities fraud. Janus Capital Group, Inc. v. First Derivative Traders[41] heavily cited both *Central Bank* and *Stoneridge* in holding that, in the context of a private lawsuit, Rule 10b–5 liability for a misleading statement will attach only to those with "ultimate control" over the statement. The Court indicated that, in the ordinary case, attribution will be critical in determining ultimate control. Thus, participation in drafting and dissemination of misleading statements attributed to others generally will not suffice to sustain a private right of action under Rule 10b–5(b). The lower courts have since tended to construe *Janus* somewhat closely, holding that it does not extend to the parallel provision of Section 17 of the Securities Act,[42] and does not apply to Rule 10b–5(a) and (c).[43]

IV. CONTRIBUTION

An interesting question, unsolved until 1993, had been whether defendants in an implied private right of action suit under rule 10b–5 have a right to contribution from other defendants who have paid no damages or have paid less than their fair share. In Musick, Peeler & Garrett v. Employers Insurance of Wausau,[44] the Supreme Court put the issue to rest: there is a right of contribution in Rule 10b–5 suits. Section 21D(f) of the Exchange Act now codifies that holding and provides that contribution is to be on the basis of proportionate liability, as detailed in that section. Some of its basic aspects are that in private actions under the Exchange Act, (i) a defendant generally is liable solely for the portion of a judgment that corresponds to the percentage of responsibility of that defendant, as determined as provided in Section 21D; (ii) a defendant is liable for damages jointly and severally only when the trier of fact specifically determines that the defendant knowingly committed a violation of the securities laws; and (iii) a defendant has a right of contribution, based on proportionate liability.

---

[41]   564 U.S. 135 (2011).

[42]   *See, e.g.*, SEC v. Big Apple Consulting USA, Inc., 783 F.3d 786 (11th Cir.2015); SEC v. Strebinger 114 F.Supp.3d 1321 (N.D. Ga.2015); SEC v. Farmer, 2015 WL 5838867 (S.D.Tex. Oct. 7, 2015).

[43]   *See, e.g.*, West Virginia Pipe Trades Health & Welfare Fund v. Medtronics, Inc., 645 F.3d 384 (8th Cir.2016); Koch v. SEC, 793 F.3d 147 (D.D.C. 2015); SEC v. Strebinger 114 F.Supp.3d 1321 (N.D. Ga.2015).

[44]   508 U.S. 286 (1993).

G. FRAUD AND RELATED ISSUES UNDER THE SARBANES-OXLEY ACT

Sarbanes-Oxley Section 807 created an entirely new securities fraud provision, which appears not in the securities laws but as 18 U.S.C. § 1348. It provides:

> Whoever knowingly executes, or attempts to execute, a scheme or artifice—
>
> (1) to defraud any person in connection with any security of [an Exchange Act reporting company]; or
>
> (2) to obtain, by means of false or fraudulent pretenses, representations, or promises, any money or property in connection with the purchase or sale of any security of [an Exchange Act reporting company]shall be fined under this title, or imprisoned not more than 25 years, or both.

Here and in closely related provisions, Sarbanes-Oxley made a number of important changes in the law. For example, this provision put an attempt to commit a fraudulent act on the same plane as completion of the act, with the same 25-year penalty.

Whether a private right of action exists under new Section 1348 is an interesting question. Here it is important to consider Sarbanes-Oxley Section 303, which makes it unlawful, in contravention of Commission rules, for certain persons fraudulently to influence the conduct of audits for the purpose of making financial statements materially misleading. Section 303 specifically indicates that there is no private right of action for violation of this provision. Plaintiffs' lawyers certainly could argue that if Congress had intended there to be no private right of action under Section 1348, they would have done likewise with respect to this section. The argument has added strength when Section 1348 is analogized to Exchange Act Rule 10b–5, under which there has long been found to exist a private right of action, as discussed earlier in this chapter.

It still is unclear how the word "knowingly" should be interpreted in Section 1348, although allowing recklessness to suffice is not unlikely, since recklessness is enough to constitute scienter under Rule 10b–5, as discussed above in Chapter 12B. It also is unclear how broad the reach of Section 1348(1) will be, since it refers simply to "a scheme or artifice— to defraud any person *in connection with* any security of [an Exchange Act reporting company]." [Emphasis added.] The big difference here from Rule 10b–5 is that the rule covers only fraud in connection with *the purchase or sale* of a security. This issue harkens back to the time when the scope of Rule 10b–5 was much in issue, as discussed above in Chapter 12CI. Many courts expressed a broad view of this issue until the Supreme Court decided otherwise. Especially in light of this history, Congress may now be argued to have given the go-ahead to an exceedingly broad interpretation of Section 1348(1), since almost any fraud relating to an issuer can be said to be in connection with its securities in some way. Many more issues could be raised, but a final one deserves mentions here: whether and to what extent Section 1348(2), which contains Rule 10b–5's "purchase or sale" requirement, covers broader conduct than Rule 10b–5. The phrasing of the two provisions is very different, and this leads to the argument that Congress intended Section 1348(2) to expand upon Rule 10b–5.

CHAPTER 13

INSIDER TRADING

SITUATION 13

In addition to the causes of action enumerated in Situations 8 and 9, each of the shareholder suits that have been brought against Microtec also allege violations of Exchange Act Section 10(b) and Rule 10b–5 and 18 U.S.C. § 1348.

In the course of discovery in connection with the suits described in Situations 8, 9 and 12, both you and the plaintiffs' counsel have learned that, shortly before the first public announcement was made by Microtec about its decreased profits and its unfavorable bad debt experience, Tate, the Secretary and Treasurer, and two non-officer employees sold most of their Microtec shares in the trading markets. One of these employees is an administrative assistant to Simpson and the other is an engineer. You and plaintiffs' counsel also have learned that, before this first public announcement, Moore discussed Microtec's unfavorable information with his brother-in-law, who is an investment counselor. The brother-in-law then sold Microtec shares publicly while this information remained unannounced. Finally, you and plaintiffs' counsel have learned that one of the Commission employees investigating Microtec after the private lawsuits were filed has been buying "puts" on Microtec stock. (A "put" gives the holder the right to sell a share at a specified price, notwithstanding a lower market price prevailing at the time the put is exercised.)

In considering this situation refer to the following, in addition to the materials in this chapter: Exchange Act Sections 14(e), 20A, and 21A, and Rules 10b5–1, 10b5–2 and 14e–3.

A. USE OF RULE 10b–5 IN THE CONTEXT OF INSIDER TRADING

I. PERSONS SUBJECT TO TRADING CONSTRAINTS

The question of who is subject to the trading constraints of Rule 10b–5 has become one of the most interesting aspects of the rule. The seminal case on the subject is In re Cady, Roberts & Co.

In re Cady, Roberts & Co.

Securities and Exchange Commission, 1961.
40 S.E.C. 907.

■ By Cary, Chairman:

This is a case of first impression and one of signal importance in our administration of the Federal securities acts. It involves a selling broker who executes a solicited order and sells for discretionary accounts (including that of his wife) upon an exchange. The crucial question is what are the duties of such a broker after receiving non-public information as to a company's dividend action from a director who is employed by the same brokerage firm.

These proceedings were instituted to determine whether Cady, Roberts & Co. ("registrant") and Robert M. Gintel ("Gintel"), the selling broker and a partner of the registrant, willfully violated the "anti-fraud" provisions of Section 10(b) of the Securities Exchange Act of 1934 ("Exchange Act"), Rule 10b–5 issued under that Act and Section 17(a) of the Securities Act of 1933 ("Securities Act") and, if so, whether any disciplinary action is necessary or appropriate in the public interest. The respondents have submitted an offer of settlement which essentially provides that the facts stipulated by respondents shall constitute the record in these proceedings for the purposes of determining the occurrence of a willful violation of the designated anti-fraud provisions and the entering of an appropriate order, on the condition that no sanction may be entered in excess of a suspension of Gintel for 20 days from the New York Stock Exchange.

The facts are as follows:

Early in November 1959, Roy T. Hurley, then President and Chairman of the Board of Curtiss-Wright Corporation, invited 2,000 representatives of the press, the military and the financial and business communities to a public unveiling on November 23, of a new type of internal combustion engine being developed by the company. On November 24, 1959, press announcements concerning the new engine appeared in certain newspapers. On that day Curtiss-Wright stock was one of the most active issues on the New York Stock Exchange, closing at $35\frac{1}{4}$, up $3\frac{1}{4}$ on a volume of 88,700 shares. From November 6, through November 23, Gintel had purchased approximately 11,000 shares of Curtiss-Wright stock for about 30 discretionary accounts of customers of registrant. With the rise in the price on November 24, he began selling Curtiss-Wright shares for these accounts and sold on that day a total of 2,200 shares on the Exchange.

The activity in Curtiss-Wright stock on the Exchange continued the next morning, November 25, and the price rose to $40\frac{3}{4}$, a new high for the year. Gintel continued sales for the discretionary accounts and, between the opening of the market and about 11:00 a.m., he sold 4,300 shares.

On the morning of November 25, the Curtiss-Wright directors, including J. Cheever Cowdin ("Cowdin"), then a registered representative of registrant, met to consider, among other things, the declaration of a quarterly dividend. The company had paid a dividend, although not earned, of $.625 per share for each of the first three quarters of 1959. The Curtiss-Wright board, over the objections of Hurley, who favored declaration of a dividend at the same rate as in the prior quarters, approved a dividend for the fourth quarter at the reduced rate of $.375 per share. At approximately 11:00 a.m., the board authorized transmission of information of this action by telegram to the New York Stock Exchange. The Secretary of Curtiss-Wright immediately left the meeting room to arrange for this communication. There was a short delay in the transmission of the telegram because of a typing problem and the telegram, although transmitted to Western Union at 11:12 a.m., was not delivered to the Exchange until 12:29 p.m. It had been customary for the company also to advise the Dow Jones News Ticker Service of any dividend action. However, apparently through some mistake or inadvertence, the Wall Street Journal was not given the news until approximately 11:45 a.m. and the announcement did not appear on the Dow Jones ticker tape until 11:48 a.m.

Sometime after the dividend decision, there was a recess of the Curtiss-Wright directors' meeting, during which Cowdin telephoned registrant's office and left a message for Gintel that the dividend had been cut. Upon receiving this information, Gintel entered two sell orders for execution on the Exchange, one to sell 2,000 shares of Curtiss-Wright stock for 10 accounts, and the other to sell short 5,000 shares for 11 accounts. Four hundred of the 5,000 shares were sold for three of Cowdin's customers. According to Cowdin, pursuant to directions from his clients, he had given instructions to Gintel to take profits on these 400 shares if the stock took a "run-up." These orders were executed at 11:15 and 11:18 a.m. at $40\frac{1}{4}$ and $40\,\frac{3}{8}$, respectively.

When the dividend announcement appeared on the Dow Jones tape at 11:48 a.m., the Exchange was compelled to suspend trading in Curtiss-Wright because of the large number of sell orders. Trading in Curtiss-Wright stock was resumed at 1:59 p.m. at $36\frac{1}{2}$[,] ranged during the balance of the day between $34\,\frac{1}{8}$ and 37, and closed at $34\,\frac{7}{8}$.

Violation of Anti-Fraud Provisions

So many times that citation is unnecessary, we have indicated that the purchase and sale of securities is a field in special need of regulation for the protection of investors. To this end one of the major purposes of the securities acts is the prevention of fraud, manipulation or deception in connection with securities transactions. Consistent with this objective, Section 17(a) of the Securities Act, Section 10(b) of the Exchange Act and Rule 10b–5, issued under that Section, are broad remedial provisions aimed at reaching misleading or deceptive activities, whether or not they are precisely and technically sufficient to sustain a common law action for fraud and deceit. Indeed, despite the decline in importance of a "Federal rule" in the light of Erie R. Co. v. Tompkins, the securities acts may be said to have generated a wholly new and far-reaching body of Federal corporation law.

* * *

Section 17 and Rule 10b–5 apply to securities transactions by "any person." Misrepresentations will lie within their ambit, no matter who the speaker may be. An affirmative duty to disclose material information has been traditionally imposed on corporate "insiders," particularly officers, directors, or controlling stockholders. We, and the courts have consistently held that insiders must disclose material facts which are known to them by virtue of their position but which are not known to persons with whom they deal and which, if known, would affect their investment judgment. Failure to make disclosure in these circumstances constitutes a violation of the anti-fraud provisions. If, on the other hand, disclosure prior to effecting a purchase or sale would be improper or unrealistic under the circumstances, we believe the alternative is to forego the transaction.

The ingredients are here and we accordingly find that Gintel willfully violated Sections 17(a) and 10(b) and Rule 10b–5. We also find a similar violation by the registrant, since the actions of Gintel, a member of registrant, in the course of his employment are to be regarded as actions of registrant itself. It was obvious that a reduction in the quarterly dividend by the Board of Directors was a material fact which could be expected to have an adverse impact on the market price of the company's stock. The rapidity with which Gintel acted upon receipt of the information confirms his own recognition of that conclusion.

We have already noted that the anti-fraud provisions are phrased in terms of "any person" and that a special obligation has been traditionally required of corporate insiders, e.g., officers, directors and controlling stockholders. These three groups, however, do not exhaust the classes of persons upon whom there is such an obligation. Analytically, the obligation rests on two principal elements; first, the existence of a relationship giving access, directly or indirectly, to information intended to be available only for a corporate purpose and not for the personal benefit of anyone, and second, the inherent unfairness involved where a party takes advantage of such information knowing it is unavailable to those with whom he is dealing. In considering these elements under the broad language of the anti-fraud provisions we are not to be circumscribed by fine distinctions and rigid classifications. Thus our task here is to identify those persons who are in a special relationship with a company and privy to its internal affairs, and thereby suffer correlative duties in trading in its securities. Intimacy demands restraint lest the uninformed be exploited.

The facts here impose on Gintel the responsibilities of those commonly referred to as "insiders." He received the information prior to its public release from a director of Curtiss-Wright, Cowdin, who was associated with the registrant. Cowdin's relationship to the company clearly prohibited him from selling the securities affected by the information without disclosure. By logical sequence, it should prohibit Gintel, a partner of registrant. This prohibition extends not only over his own account, but to selling for discretionary accounts and soliciting and executing other orders. In somewhat analogous circumstances, we have charged a broker-dealer who effects securities transactions for an insider and who knows that the insider possesses non-public material information with the affirmative duty to make appropriate disclosures or disassociate himself from the transaction.

* * *

We cannot accept respondents' contention that an insider's responsibility is limited to existing stockholders and that he has no special duties when sales of securities are made to non-stockholders. This approach is too narrow. It ignores the plight of the buying public-wholly unprotected from the misuse of special information.

* * *

The Public Interest

All the surrounding circumstances and the state of mind of the participants may be taken into consideration in determining what sanctions should appropriately be imposed here.

It is clear that Gintel's conduct was willful in that he knew what he was doing. However, there is no evidence of a preconceived plan whereby Cowdin was to "leak" advance information of the dividend reduction so that Gintel could use it to advantage before the public announcement; on the contrary, the evidence points to the conclusion that Cowdin probably assumed, without thinking about it, that the dividend action was already a matter of public information and further that he called registrant's office to find out the effect of the dividend news upon the market. The record, moreover, indicates that Gintel's conduct was a spontaneous reaction to the dividend news, that he intended primarily to benefit existing clients of Cady, Roberts & Co. and that he acted on the spur of the moment and so quickly as to preclude the possibility of review by registrant or of his own more deliberate consideration of his responsibilities under the securities acts.

Gintel has been fined $3,000 by the New York Stock Exchange in connection with the instant transactions. The publication of this opinion, moreover, will in itself serve as a further sanction upon Gintel and registrant and will also induce a more careful observance of the requirements of the anti-fraud provisions in the area in question. Furthermore, registrant had no opportunity to prevent Gintel's spontaneous transactions and no contention has been made that its procedures for handling accounts did not meet proper standards. Under all the circumstances we conclude that the public interest and the protection of investors will be adequately and appropriately served if Gintel is suspended from the New York Stock Exchange for 20 days and if no sanction is imposed against the registrant. Accordingly, we accept respondents' offer of settlement.

* * *

The Commission began its analysis in *Cady, Roberts* with a focus on the fact that the prohibitions of the rule were phrased in terms of their applicability to "any person." Although the Commission then laid an analytical base for determining who has obligations under the rule, this base was virtually lost in the period of the rule's growth. In the most influential case, SEC v. Texas Gulf Sulphur Co.[1] (set out in Chapter 12), the Second Circuit largely ignored this analytical base and baldly stated the proposition of who is subject to the rule's constraints on trading: "*[A]nyone* in possession of material inside information must either disclose it to the investing public, or [refrain from trading]."[2]

In the years following *Texas Gulf Sulphur,* securities lawyers and courts tended to view the trading constraints of Rule 10b–5 as broadly as the Second Circuit did in that case. Then, however, the Supreme Court decided Chiarella v. United States:

Chiarella v. United States

Supreme Court of the United States, 1980.
445 U.S. 222.

■ MR. JUSTICE POWELL delivered the opinion of the Court.

The question in this case is whether a person who learns from the confidential documents of one corporation that it is planning an attempt to secure control of a second corporation violates § 10(b) of the Securities Exchange Act of 1934 if he fails to disclose the impending takeover before trading in the target company's securities.

I

Petitioner is a printer by trade. In 1975 and 1976, he worked as a "markup man" in the New York composing room of Pandick Press, a financial printer. Among documents that petitioner handled were five announcements of corporate takeover bids. When these documents were delivered to the printer, the identities of the acquiring and target corporations were concealed by blank spaces or false names. The true names were sent to the printer on the night of the final printing.

---

[1] 401 F.2d 833 (2d Cir.1968).

[2] Emphasis added.

The petitioner, however, was able to deduce the names of the target companies before the final printing from other information contained in the documents. Without disclosing his knowledge, petitioner purchased stock in the target companies and sold the shares immediately after the takeover attempts were made public. By this method, petitioner realized a gain of slightly more than $30,000 in the course of 14 months. Subsequently, the Securities and Exchange Commission (Commission or SEC) began an investigation of his trading activities. In May 1977, petitioner entered into a consent decree with the Commission in which he agreed to return his profits to the sellers of the shares. On the same day, he was discharged by Pandick Press.

In January 1978, petitioner was indicted on 17 counts of violating § 10(b) of the Securities Exchange Act of 1934 (1934 Act) and SEC Rule 10b–5. After petitioner unsuccessfully moved to dismiss the indictment, he was brought to trial and convicted on all counts.

The Court of Appeals for the Second Circuit affirmed petitioner's conviction. We granted certiorari, and we now reverse.

II

* * *

This case concerns the legal effect of the petitioner's silence. The District Court's charge permitted the jury to convict the petitioner if it found that he willfully failed to inform sellers of target company securities that he knew of a forthcoming takeover bid that would make their shares more valuable. * * *

* * *

* * * But one who fails to disclose material information prior to the consummation of a transaction commits fraud only when he is under a duty to do so. And the duty to disclose arises when one party has information "that the other [party] is entitled to know because of a fiduciary or similar relation of trust and confidence between them."[3] * * *

* * *

III

In this case, the petitioner was convicted of violating § 10(b) although he was not a corporate insider and he received no confidential information from the target company. Moreover, the "market information" upon which he relied did not concern the earning power or operations of the target company, but only the plans of the acquiring company. Petitioner's use of that information was not a fraud under § 10(b) unless he was subject to an affirmative duty to disclose it before trading. In this case, the jury instructions failed to specify any such duty. In effect, the trial court instructed the jury that petitioner owed a duty to everyone; to all sellers, indeed, to the market as a whole. The jury

---

[3]   Restatement of the Law 2d, Torts § 551(2)(a) (1976).

simply was told to decide whether petitioner used material, non-public information at a time when "he knew other people trading in the securities market did not have access to the same information."

* * *

We cannot affirm petitioner's conviction without recognizing a general duty between all participants in market transactions to forgo actions based on material, non-public information. Formulation of such a broad duty, which departs radically from the established doctrine that duty arises from a specific relationship between two parties, should not be undertaken absent some explicit evidence of congressional intent.

[N]o such evidence emerges from the language or legislative history of § 10(b). * * *

* * *

* * * We hold that a duty to disclose under § 10(b) does not arise from the mere possession of non-public market information.

* * *

IV

In its brief to this Court, the United States offers an alternative theory to support petitioner's conviction. It argues that petitioner breached a duty to the acquiring corporation when he acted upon information that he obtained by virtue of his position as an employee of a printer employed by the corporation. The breach of this duty is said to support a conviction under § 10(b) for fraud perpetrated upon both the acquiring corporation and the sellers.

We need not decide whether this theory has merit for it was not submitted to the jury. * * *

* * *

———————

As might be expected, lawyers trying Rule 10b–5 cases after *Chiarella* tended to plead their case using the alternative, so-called "misappropriation," theory that had been argued to the Supreme Court but that had not been submitted to the *Chiarella* jury. In one such case, Moss v. Morgan Stanley Inc.,[4] a target company shareholder, who sold shares during the period when the prohibited trading was going on, brought a class action suit against the traders and others. The district court dismissed the complaint, and the Second Circuit affirmed, basically on the idea that in a private right of action Rule 10b–5 suit, the plaintiff must show that the defendant violated a duty owed *to the plaintiff.*

It bothered many people that *Moss,* if followed generally, would allow inside traders to escape civil liability in most situations. As a result

———————

[4]   719 F.2d 5 (2d Cir.1983).

of that case, Congress in 1988 added Section 20A to the Exchange Act. That section was billed as undoing the *Moss* result: it stated explicitly that those who violate the Act's insider-trading rules are liable to anyone who "contemporaneously" trades any securities of the same class (with the key word "contemporaneously" being undefined).

Moss did not get to the Supreme Court, but a later Second Circuit Rule 10b–5 case involving the misappropriation theory did. This was Carpenter v. United States.[5] The Court split evenly on the applicability of the theory to the tippees of a reporter who traded on the basis of stock recommendations to be published by his employer, The Wall Street Journal. It did, however, find that the conduct in that case constituted a violation of federal mail and wire fraud statutes (18 U.S.C. Sections 1341 and 1343).

Finally, in 1997, the Court put its imprimatur on the misappropriation theory in United States v. O'Hagan, which appears below.

United States v. O'Hagan

Supreme Court of the United States, 1997.
521 U.S. 642.

■ JUSTICE GINSBURG delivered the opinion of the Court.

This case concerns the interpretation and enforcement of § 10(b) * * * of the Securities Exchange Act of 1934, and [Rule 10b–5] made by the Securities and Exchange Commission * * * . * * * In particular, we address and resolve this [issue:] Is a person who trades in securities for personal profit, using confidential information misappropriated in breach of a fiduciary duty to the source of the information, guilty of violating § 10(b) and Rule 10b–5? * * *

I

Respondent James Herman O'Hagan was a partner in the law firm of Dorsey & Whitney in Minneapolis, Minnesota. In July 1988, Grand Metropolitan PLC (Grand Met), a company based in London, England, retained Dorsey & Whitney as local counsel to represent Grand Met regarding a potential tender offer for the common stock of the Pillsbury Company, headquartered in Minneapolis. Both Grand Met and Dorsey & Whitney took precautions to protect the confidentiality of Grand Met's tender offer plans. O'Hagan did no work on the Grand Met representation. [O]n October 4, 1988, Grand Met publicly announced its tender offer for Pillsbury stock.

On August 18, 1988, * * * O'Hagan began purchasing call options for Pillsbury stock. Each option gave him the right to purchase 100 shares of Pillsbury stock by a specified date in September 1988. Later in August and in September, O'Hagan made additional purchases of Pillsbury call

---

[5]   484 U.S. 19 (1987).

options. By the end of September, he owned 2,500 unexpired Pillsbury options, apparently more than any other individual investor. O'Hagan also purchased, in September 1988, some 5,000 shares of Pillsbury common stock, at a price just under $39 per share. When Grand Met announced its tender offer in October, the price of Pillsbury stock rose to nearly $60 per share. O'Hagan then sold his Pillsbury call options and common stock, making a profit of more than $4.3 million.

The Securities and Exchange Commission (SEC or Commission) initiated an investigation into O'Hagan's transactions, culminating in [an] indictment. The indictment alleged that O'Hagan defrauded his law firm and its client, Grand Met, by using for his own trading purposes material, nonpublic information regarding Grand Met's planned tender offer. According to the indictment, O'Hagan used the profits he gained through this trading to conceal his previous embezzlement and conversion of unrelated client trust funds. A jury convicted O'Hagan on all * * * counts, and he was sentenced to a 41-month term of imprisonment.

A divided panel of the Court of Appeals for the Eighth Circuit reversed all of O'Hagan's convictions. Liability under § 10(b) and Rule 10b–5, the Eighth Circuit held, may not be grounded on the "misappropriation theory" of securities fraud on which the prosecution relied. * * *

Decisions of the Courts of Appeals are in conflict on the propriety of the misappropriation theory under § 10(b) and Rule 10b–5 * * * . We granted certiorari, and now reverse the Eighth Circuit's judgment.

II

* * *

A

* * *

Under the "traditional" or "classical theory" of insider trading liability, § 10(b) and Rule 10b–5 are violated when a corporate insider trades in the securities of his corporation on the basis of material, nonpublic information. Trading on such information qualifies as a "deceptive device" under § 10(b), we have affirmed, because "a relationship of trust and confidence [exists] between the shareholders of a corporation and those insiders who have obtained confidential information by reason of their position with that corporation." Chiarella v. United States, 445 U.S. 222, 228 (1980). That relationship, we recognized, "gives rise to a duty to disclose [or to abstain from trading] because of the 'necessity of preventing a corporate insider from * * * taking unfair advantage of * * * uninformed * * * stockholders.'" The classical theory applies not only to officers, directors, and other permanent insiders of a corporation, but also to attorneys, accountants, consultants, and others who temporarily become fiduciaries of a corporation.

The "misappropriation theory" holds that a person commits fraud "in connection with" a securities transaction, and thereby violates § 10(b) and Rule 10b–5, when he misappropriates confidential information for securities trading purposes, in breach of a duty owed to the source of the information. Under this theory, a fiduciary's undisclosed, self-serving use of a principal's information to purchase or sell securities, in breach of a duty of loyalty and confidentiality, defrauds the principal of the exclusive use of that information. In lieu of premising liability on a fiduciary relationship between company insider and purchaser or seller of the company's stock, the misappropriation theory premises liability on a fiduciary-turned-trader's deception of those who entrusted him with access to confidential information.

The two theories are complementary, each addressing efforts to capitalize on nonpublic information through the purchase or sale of securities. The classical theory targets a corporate insider's breach of duty to shareholders with whom the insider transacts; the misappropriation theory outlaws trading on the basis of nonpublic information by a corporate "outsider" in breach of a duty owed not to a trading party, but to the source of the information. The misappropriation theory is thus designed to "protect the integrity of the securities markets against abuses by 'outsiders' to a corporation who have access to confidential information that will affect the corporation's security price when revealed, but who owe no fiduciary or other duty to that corporation's shareholders." [Brief for United States.]

In this case, the indictment alleged that O'Hagan, in breach of a duty of trust and confidence he owed to his law firm, Dorsey & Whitney, and to its client, Grand Met, traded on the basis of nonpublic information regarding Grand Met's planned tender offer for Pillsbury common stock. This conduct, the Government charged, constituted a fraudulent device in connection with the purchase and sale of securities.

B

We agree with the Government that misappropriation, as just defined, satisfies § 10(b)'s requirement that chargeable conduct involve a "deceptive device or contrivance" used "in connection with" the purchase or sale of securities. We observe, first, that misappropriators, as the Government describes them, deal in deception. A fiduciary who "[pretends] loyalty to the principal while secretly converting the principal's information for personal gain," Brief for United States 17, "dupes" or defrauds the principal.

* * *

The misappropriation theory advanced by the Government is consistent with Santa Fe Industries, Inc. v. Green, 430 U.S. 462 (1977), a decision underscoring that § 10(b) is not an all-purpose breach of fiduciary duty ban; rather, it trains on conduct involving manipulation or deception. In contrast to the Government's allegations in this case, in Santa Fe Industries, all pertinent facts were disclosed by the persons charged with violating § 10(b) and Rule 10b–5, therefore, there was no deception through nondisclosure to which liability under those provisions could attach. Similarly, full disclosure forecloses liability under the misappropriation theory: Because the deception essential to the misappropriation theory involves feigning fidelity to the source of information, if the fiduciary discloses to the source that he plans to trade on the nonpublic information, there is no "deceptive device" and thus no § 10(b) violation—although the fiduciary-turned-trader may remain liable under state law for breach of a duty of loyalty.

We turn next to the § 10(b) requirement that the misappropriator's deceptive use of information be "in connection with the purchase or sale of [a] security." This element is satisfied because the fiduciary's fraud is consummated, not when the fiduciary gains the confidential information, but when, without disclosure to his principal, he uses the information to purchase or sell securities. The securities transaction and the breach of duty thus coincide. This is so even though the person or entity defrauded is not the other party to the trade, but is, instead, the source of the nonpublic information. A misappropriator who trades on the basis of material, nonpublic information, in short, gains his advantageous market position through deception; he deceives the source of the information and simultaneously harms members of the investing public.

The misappropriation theory targets information of a sort that misappropriators ordinarily capitalize upon to gain no-risk profits through the purchase or sale of securities. Should a misappropriator put such information to other use, the statute's prohibition would not be implicated. The theory does not catch all conceivable forms of fraud involving confidential information; rather, it catches fraudulent means of capitalizing on such information through securities transactions.

The Government notes another limitation on the forms of fraud § 10(b) reaches: "The misappropriation theory would not * * * apply to a case in which a person defrauded a bank into giving him a loan or embezzled cash from another, and then used the proceeds of the misdeed to purchase securities." In such a case, the Government states, "the proceeds would have value to the malefactor apart from their use in a securities transaction, and the fraud would be complete as soon as the money was obtained." In other words, money can buy, if not anything, then at least many things; its misappropriation may thus be viewed as sufficiently detached from a subsequent securities transaction that § 10(b)'s "in connection with" requirement would not be met.

The dissent's charge that the misappropriation theory is incoherent because information, like funds, can be put to multiple uses, misses the point. The Exchange Act was enacted in part "to insure the maintenance of fair and honest markets," 15 U.S.C. § 78(b), and there is no question that fraudulent uses of confidential information fall within § 10(b)'s prohibition if the fraud is "in connection with" a securities transaction. It is hardly remarkable that a rule suitably applied to the fraudulent uses of certain kinds of information would be stretched beyond reason were it applied to the fraudulent use of money.

* * *

The misappropriation theory comports with § 10(b)'s language, which requires deception "in connection with the purchase or sale of any security," not deception of an identifiable purchaser or seller. The theory is also well-tuned to an animating purpose of the Exchange Act: to insure honest securities markets and thereby promote investor confidence. Although informational disparity is inevitable in the securities markets, investors likely would hesitate to venture their capital in a market where trading based on misappropriated nonpublic information is unchecked by law. An investor's informational disadvantage vis-a-vis a misappropriator with material, nonpublic information stems from contrivance, not luck; it is a disadvantage that cannot be overcome with research or skill.

In sum, considering the inhibiting impact on market participation of trading on misappropriated information, and the congressional purposes underlying § 10(b), it makes scant sense to hold a lawyer like O'Hagan a § 10(b) violator if he works for a law firm representing the target of a tender offer, but not if he works for a law firm representing the bidder. The text of the statute requires no such result. The misappropriation at issue here was properly made the subject of a § 10(b) charge because it meets the statutory requirement that there be "deceptive" conduct "in connection with" securities transactions.

* * *

Rule 10b5–2 addresses the circumstances in which there is a duty based on a "relationship of trust and confidence" sufficient to find liability under the "misappropriation" theory approved by *O'Hagan*. According to the Rule, such a duty exists if (1) "a person agrees to maintain information in confidence;" (2) the person communicating the material nonpublic information and the recipient "have a history, pattern, or practice of sharing confidences" resulting in a reasonable expectation of confidentiality; or (3) the person communicating the material nonpublic information and the recipient are spouses, parents, or siblings. Family members may, however, prove that because of the particular facts and circumstances of their relationship, no duty of trust and confidence existed.

SEC v. Rocklage[6] was an interesting First Circuit case dealing with *O'Hagan*'s deception requirement in a family context. There, the court

---

[6]   470 F.3d 1 (1st Cir.2006).

held that the Commission had stated a claim against a wife who told her husband that she was going to pass his confidential information to her brother. The rationale was that the requisite deception had occurred when she initially permitted him to reveal the information while intending to leak it.

The SEC and the Department of Justice have pursued a series of securities fraud charges against computer hackers and their tippees, all of whom were strangers to the issuers of the stock involved but who acquired and traded on nonpublic information in alleged violation of Section 10(b) and Rule 10b–5. The Second Circuit has held that liability in such circumstances was not possible under the misappropriation theory, but did invite prosecution of hackers under an affirmative deception theory.[7] The court reasoned that "misrepresenting one's identity in order to gain access to information that otherwise is off limits, and then stealing that information is plainly 'deceptive.'"

Speculation that government employees trading on non-public information received in their official capacity properly are subject to liability under the misappropriation theory culminated in Congressional action. The special circumstances of federal employees are discussed separately in Section 13C.

The Supreme Court has decided two additional cases that further the discussion of who is subject to the trading constraints of Rule 10b–5. Both concern the circumstances under which tippee liability pertains.

Dirks v. SEC

Supreme Court of the United States, 1983.
463 U.S. 646.

■ JUSTICE POWELL delivered the opinion of the Court.

Petitioner Raymond Dirks received material non-public information from "insiders" of a corporation with which he had no connection. He disclosed this information to investors who relied on it in trading in the shares of the corporation. The question is whether Dirks violated the anti-fraud provisions of the federal securities laws by this disclosure.

I

In 1973, Dirks was an officer of a New York broker-dealer firm who specialized in providing investment analysis of insurance company securities to institutional investors. On March 6, Dirks received information from Ronald Secrist, a former officer of Equity Funding of America. Secrist alleged that the assets of Equity Funding, a diversified corporation primarily engaged in selling life insurance and mutual funds, were vastly overstated as the result of fraudulent corporate practices. Secrist also stated that various regulatory agencies had failed to act on

---

[7]   SEC v. Dorozhko, 574 F.3d 42 (2d Cir. 2009).

similar charges made by Equity Funding employees. He urged Dirks to verify the fraud and disclose it publicly.

Dirks decided to investigate the allegations. He visited Equity Funding's headquarters in Los Angeles and interviewed several officers and employees of the corporation. The senior management denied any wrongdoing, but certain corporation employees corroborated the charges of fraud. Neither Dirks nor his firm owned or traded any Equity Funding stock, but throughout his investigation he openly discussed the information he had obtained with a number of clients and investors. Some of these persons sold their holdings of Equity Funding securities, including five investment advisers who liquidated holdings of more than $16 million.

While Dirks was in Los Angeles, he was in touch regularly with William Blundell, the *Wall Street Journal's* Los Angeles bureau chief. Dirks urged Blundell to write a story on the fraud allegations. Blundell did not believe, however, that such a massive fraud could go undetected and declined to write the story. He feared that publishing such damaging hearsay might be libelous.

During the two-week period in which Dirks pursued his investigation and spread word of Secrist's charges, the price of Equity Funding stock fell from $26 per share to less than $15 per share. This led the New York Stock Exchange to halt trading on March 27. Shortly thereafter California insurance authorities impounded Equity Funding's records and uncovered evidence of the fraud. Only then did the Securities and Exchange Commission (SEC) file a complaint against Equity Funding and only then, on April 2, did the *Wall Street Journal* publish a front-page story based largely on information assembled by Dirks. Equity Funding immediately went into receivership.

The SEC began an investigation into Dirks' role in the exposure of the fraud. After a hearing by an administrative law judge, the SEC found that Dirks had aided and abetted violations of * * * § 10(b) of the Securities Exchange Act of 1934, and SEC Rule 10b–5, by repeating the allegations of fraud to members of the investment community who later sold their Equity Funding stock. The SEC concluded: "Where 'tippees'— regardless of their motivation or occupation—come into possession of material 'information that they know is confidential and know or should know came from a corporate insider,' they must either publicly disclose that information or refrain from trading." 21 S.E.C. Docket 1401, 1407 (1981) (footnote omitted) (quoting Chiarella v. United States, 445 U.S. 222, 230 n. 12 (1980)). Recognizing, however, that Dirks "played an important role in bringing [Equity Funding's] massive fraud to light," the SEC only censured him.

Dirks sought review in the Court of Appeals for the District of Columbia Circuit. The court entered judgment against Dirks * * * . * * *

* * *

III

We were explicit in *Chiarella* in saying that there can be no duty to disclose where the person who has traded on inside information "was not [the corporation's] agent, * * * was not a fiduciary, [or] was not a person in whom the sellers [of the securities] had placed their trust and confidence." Not to require such a fiduciary relationship, we recognized, would "depar[t] radically from the established doctrine that duty arises from a specific relationship between two parties" and would amount to "recognizing a general duty between all participants in market transactions to forgo actions based on material, non-public information." This requirement of a specific relationship between the shareholders and the individual trading on inside information has created analytical difficulties for the SEC and courts in policing tippees who trade on inside information. Unlike insiders who have independent fiduciary duties to both the corporation and its shareholders, the typical tippee has no such relationships.[8] In view of this absence, it has been unclear how a tippee acquires the * * * duty to refrain from trading on inside information.

* * *

In determining whether a tippee is under an obligation to disclose or abstain, it * * * is necessary to determine whether the insider's "tip" constituted a breach of the insider's fiduciary duty. All disclosures of confidential corporate information are not inconsistent with the duty insiders owe to shareholders. In contrast to the extraordinary facts of this case, the more typical situation in which there will be a question whether disclosure violates the insider's * * * duty is when insiders disclose information to analysts. In some situations, the insider will act consistently with his fiduciary duty to shareholders, and yet release of the information may affect the market. For example, it may not be clear—either to the corporate insider or to the recipient analyst— whether the information will be viewed as material non-public information. Corporate officials may mistakenly think the information already has been disclosed or that it is not material enough to affect the market. Whether disclosure is a breach of duty therefore depends in large part on the purpose of the disclosure. This standard was identified by the SEC itself in [In re Cady, Roberts & Co., 40 S.E.C. 907 (1961)]: a purpose of the securities laws was to eliminate "use of inside information for personal advantage." Thus, the test is whether the insider personally will benefit, directly or indirectly, from his disclosure. Absent some personal

---

[8] Under certain circumstances, such as where corporate information is revealed legitimately to an underwriter, accountant, lawyer, or consultant working for the corporation, these outsiders may become fiduciaries of the shareholders. The basis for recognizing this fiduciary duty is not simply that such persons acquired non-public corporate information, but rather that they have entered into a special confidential relationship in the conduct of the business of the enterprise and are given access to information solely for corporate purposes. When such a person breaches his fiduciary relationship, he may be treated more properly as a tipper than a tippee. For such a duty to be imposed, however, the corporation must expect the outsider to keep the disclosed non-public information confidential, and the relationship at least must imply such a duty.

gain, there has been no breach of duty to stockholders. And absent a breach by the insider, there is no derivative breach. * * *

* * * This requires courts to focus on objective criteria, *i.e.,* whether the insider receives a direct or indirect personal benefit from the disclosure, such as a pecuniary gain or a reputational benefit that will translate into future earnings. There are objective facts and circumstances that often justify such an inference. For example, there may be a relationship between the insider and the recipient that suggests a *quid pro quo* from the latter, or an intention to benefit the particular recipient. The elements of fiduciary duty and exploitation of non-public information also exist when an insider makes a gift of confidential information to a trading relative or friend. The tip and trade resemble trading by the insider himself followed by a gift of the profits to the recipient.

* * *

IV

Under the inside-trading and tipping rules set forth above, we find that there was no actionable violation by Dirks. It is undisputed that Dirks himself was a stranger to Equity Funding, with no pre-existing fiduciary duty to its shareholders. He took no action, directly or indirectly, that induced the shareholders or officers of Equity Funding to repose trust or confidence in him. There was no expectation by Dirks' sources that he would keep their information in confidence. Nor did Dirks misappropriate or illegally obtain the information about Equity Funding. Unless the insiders breached their *Cady, Roberts* duty to shareholders in disclosing the non-public information to Dirks, he breached no duty when he passed it on to investors as well as to the *Wall Street Journal.*

It is clear that neither Secrist nor the other Equity Funding employees violated their *Cady, Roberts* duty to the corporation's shareholders by providing information to Dirks. The tippers received no monetary or personal benefit for revealing Equity Funding's secrets, nor was their purpose to make a gift of valuable information to Dirks. As the facts of this case clearly indicate, the tippers were motivated by a desire to expose the fraud. In the absence of a breach of duty to shareholders by the insiders, there was no derivative breach by Dirks. Dirks therefore could not have been "a participant after the fact in [an] insider's breach of a fiduciary duty." *Chiarella,* 445 U.S., at 230, n. 12.

* * *

_____

Although it may seem obvious that *Dirks* would dictate the outcome in the following case, a number of lower courts and commentators thought otherwise.

Salman v. United States

Supreme Court of the United States, 2016.
137 S.Ct. 420.

■ JUSTICE ALITO delivered the opinion of the Court.

* * *

I

Maher Kara was an investment banker in Citigroup's healthcare investment banking group. He dealt with highly confidential information about mergers and acquisitions involving Citigroup's clients. Maher enjoyed a close relationship with his older brother, Mounir Kara (known as Michael). After Maher started at Citigroup, he began discussing aspects of his job with Michael. At first he relied on Michael's chemistry background to help him grasp scientific concepts relevant to his new job. Then, while their father was battling cancer, the brothers discussed companies that dealt with innovative cancer treatment and pain management techniques. Michael began to trade on the information Maher shared with him. At first, Maher was unaware of his brother's trading activity, but eventually he began to suspect that it was taking place.

Ultimately, Maher began to assist Michael's trading by sharing inside information with his brother about pending mergers and acquisitions. Maher sometimes used code words to communicate corporate information to his brother. Other times, he shared inside information about deals he was not working on in order to avoid detection. * * * Without his younger brother's knowledge, Michael fed the information to others—including Salman, Michael's friend and Maher's brother-in-law. By the time the authorities caught on, Salman had made over $1.5 million in profits that he split with another relative who executed trades via a brokerage account on Salman's behalf.

Salman was indicted on one count of conspiracy to commit securities fraud, * * *, and four counts of securities fraud * * *. Facing charges of their own, both Maher and Michael pleaded guilty and testified at Salman's trial.

* * *

After a jury trial in the Northern District of California, Salman was convicted on all counts. He was sentenced to 36 months of imprisonment, three years of supervised release, and over $730,000 in restitution. After his motion for a new trial was denied, Salman appealed to the Ninth Circuit. While his appeal was pending, the Second Circuit issued its opinion in *United States v. Newman,* 773 F.3d 438 (2014), cert. denied, 136 S.Ct. 242 (2015). There, the Second Circuit reversed the convictions of two portfolio managers who traded on inside information. The *Newman* defendants were "several steps removed from the corporate insiders" and the court found that "there was no evidence that either was aware of the source of the inside information." 773 F.3d, at 443. The court acknowledged that *Dirks* and Second Circuit case law allow a factfinder to infer a personal benefit to the tipper from a gift of confidential information to a trading relative or friend. 773 F.3d, at 452. But the court concluded that, "[t]o the extent" *Dirks* permits "such an inference," the inference "is impermissible in the absence of proof of a meaningfully close personal relationship that generates an exchange that is objective, consequential, and represents at least a potential gain of a pecuniary or similarly valuable nature." 773 F.3d, at 452.[9]

Pointing to *Newman,* Salman argued that his conviction should be reversed. While the evidence established that Maher made a gift of trading information to Michael and that Salman knew it, there was no evidence that Maher received anything of "a pecuniary or similarly valuable nature" in exchange—or that Salman knew of any such benefit. The Ninth Circuit disagreed and affirmed Salman's conviction. 792 F.3d 1087. The court reasoned that the case was governed by *Dirks*'s holding that a tipper benefits personally by making a gift of confidential information to a trading relative or friend. Indeed, Maher's disclosures to Michael were "precisely the gift of confidential information to a trading relative that *Dirks* envisioned." 792 F.3d, at 1092 (internal quotation marks omitted). To the extent *Newman* went further and required additional gain to the tipper in cases involving gifts of confidential information to family and friends, the Ninth Circuit "decline [d] to follow it." 792 F.3d, at 1093.

We granted certiorari to resolve the tension between the Second Circuit's *Newman* decision and the Ninth Circuit's decision in this case.

II

A

In this case, Salman contends that an insider's "gift of confidential information to a trading relative or friend," *Dirks,* 463 U.S., at 664, is not enough to establish securities fraud. Instead, Salman argues, a tipper does not personally benefit unless the tipper's goal in disclosing inside information is to obtain money, property, or something of tangible value. He claims that our insider-trading precedents, and the cases those precedents cite, involve situations in which the insider exploited confidential information for the insider's own "tangible monetary profit." He suggests that his position is reinforced by our criminal-fraud precedents outside of the insider-trading context, because those cases confirm that a fraudster must personally obtain money or property. More broadly, Salman urges that defining a gift as a personal benefit renders the insider-trading offense indeterminate and overbroad: indeterminate, because liability may turn on facts such as the closeness of the

---

[9] The Second Circuit also reversed the *Newman* defendants' convictions because the Government introduced no evidence that the defendants knew the information they traded on came from insiders or that the insiders received a personal benefit in exchange for the tips. 773 F.3d, at 453–454. This case does not implicate those issues.

relationship between tipper and tippee and the tipper's purpose for disclosure; and overbroad, because the Government may avoid having to prove a concrete personal benefit by simply arguing that the tipper meant to give a gift to the tippee. He also argues that we should interpret *Dirks's* standard narrowly so as to avoid constitutional concerns. Brief for Petitioner 36–37. Finally, Salman contends that gift situations create especially troubling problems for remote tippees—that is, tippees who receive inside information from another tippee, rather than the tipper—who may have no knowledge of the relationship between the original tipper and tippee and thus may not know why the tipper made the disclosure.

The Government disagrees and argues that a gift of confidential information to anyone, not just a "trading relative or friend," is enough to prove securities fraud. ("*Dirks's* personal-benefit test encompasses a gift to *any* person with the expectation that the information will be used for trading, not just to 'a trading relative or friend' " (quoting 463 U.S. at 664, emphasis in original)). Under the Government's view, a tipper personally benefits whenever the tipper discloses confidential trading information for a noncorporate purpose. Accordingly, a gift to a friend, a family member, or anyone else would support the inference that the tipper exploited the trading value of inside information for personal purposes and thus personally benefited from the disclosure. * * *

The Government also argues that Salman's concerns about unlimited and indeterminate liability for remote tippees are significantly alleviated by other statutory elements that prosecutors must satisfy to convict a tippee for insider trading. The Government observes that, in order to establish a defendant's criminal liability as a tippee, it must prove beyond a reasonable doubt that the tipper expected that the information being disclosed would be used in securities trading. The Government also notes that, to establish a defendant's criminal liability as a tippee, it must prove that the tippee knew that the tipper breached a duty—in other words, that the tippee knew that the tipper disclosed the information for a personal benefit and that the tipper expected trading to ensue.

B

We adhere to *Dirks,* which easily resolves the narrow issue presented here.

In *Dirks,* we explained that a tippee is exposed to liability for trading on inside information only if the tippee participates in a breach of the tipper's fiduciary duty. Whether the tipper breached that duty depends "in large part on the purpose of the disclosure" to the tippee. 463 U.S. at 662. "[T]he test," we explained, "is whether the insider personally will benefit, directly or indirectly, from his disclosure." *Ibid.* Thus, the disclosure of confidential information without personal benefit is not enough. In determining whether a tipper derived a personal benefit, we instructed courts to "focus on objective criteria, *i.e.,* whether the insider receives a direct or indirect personal benefit from the disclosure, such as a pecuniary gain or a reputational benefit that will translate into future earnings." *Id.*, at 663. This personal benefit can "often" be inferred "from objective facts and circumstances," we explained, such as "a relationship between the insider and the recipient that suggests a *quid pro quo* from the latter, or an intention to benefit the particular recipient." *Id.*, at 664. In particular, we held that "[t]he elements of fiduciary duty and exploitation of nonpublic information also exist *when an insider makes a gift of confidential information to a trading relative or friend.*" *Ibid.* (emphasis added). In such cases, "[t]he tip and trade resemble trading by the insider followed by a gift of the profits to the recipient." *Ibid.* We then applied this gift-giving principle to resolve *Dirks* itself, finding it dispositive that the tippers "received no monetary or personal benefit" from their tips to Dirks, "*nor was their purpose to make a gift of valuable information to Dirks.*" *Id.*, at 667 (emphasis added).

Our discussion of gift giving resolves this case. Maher, the tipper, provided inside information to a close relative, his brother Michael. *Dirks* makes clear that a tipper breaches a fiduciary duty by making a gift of confidential information to "a trading relative," and that rule is sufficient to resolve the case at hand. As Salman's counsel acknowledged at oral argument, Maher would have breached his duty had he personally traded on the information here himself then given the proceeds as a gift to his brother. It is obvious that Maher would personally benefit in that situation. But Maher effectively achieved the same result by disclosing the information to Michael, and allowing him to trade on it. *Dirks* appropriately prohibits that approach, as well. *Cf.* 463 U.S. at 659 (holding that "insiders [are] forbidden" both "from personally using undisclosed corporate information to their advantage" and from "giv[ing] such information to an outsider for the same improper purpose of exploiting the information for their personal gain"). *Dirks* specifies that when a tipper gives inside information to "a trading relative or friend," the jury can infer that the tipper meant to provide the equivalent of a cash gift. In such situations, the tipper benefits personally because giving a gift of trading information is the same thing as trading by the tipper followed by a gift of the proceeds. Here, by disclosing confidential information as a gift to his brother with the expectation that he would trade on it, Maher breached his duty of trust and confidence to Citigroup and its clients—a duty Salman acquired, and breached himself, by trading on the information with full knowledge that it had been improperly disclosed.

To the extent the Second Circuit held that the tipper must also receive something of a "pecuniary or similarly valuable nature" in exchange for a gift to family or friends, *Newman,* 773 F.3d, at 452, we agree with the Ninth Circuit that this requirement is inconsistent with *Dirks.*

* * *

III

* * * Accordingly, the Ninth Circuit's judgment is affirmed.

———————

In part, *Salman* is worth reading in order to see some of the things the government conceded were required for a successful prosecution. These include proof that the tipper expected that the information being disclosed would be used in securities trading and that the tippee knew that the tipper breached a duty—in other words, that the tippee knew that the tipper disclosed the information for a personal benefit and that the tipper expected trading to ensue. In United States v. Newman, discussed in *Salman*, the Second Circuit cited as additional grounds for its ruling the government's failure to introduce evidence that the defendants knew the information they traded on came from insiders or that the insiders received a personal benefit in exchange for the tips. In *Salman*, the Court specifically noted those issues were not raised.

Naturally, there are still any number of questions to be resolved. For instance, for tippee liability to exist, is it necessary that the tipper know that disclosure was improper. In United States v. Evans,[10] the answer given by the Seventh Circuit was "no."

An additional issue for courts dealing with liability for insider trading is the question of whether an insider (or the insider's illicit tippee) is entirely precluded from trading without disclosing the non-public information in question once he or she possesses it. In SEC v. Adler,[11] the Eleventh Circuit rejected this interpretation, and adopted the "use test." Under this test, it had to be shown that the defendant used inside information in trading, not merely that he or she traded while in possession of that information. In response to the "use test," the Commission adopted Rule 10b5–1. Under this rule it is enough to show that a defendant was aware of material inside information when trading. The rule does provide, however, some exceptions that are designed to allow persons to trade, while aware of inside information, in limited circumstances. The most interesting is when a trade is made pursuant to a written plan of trading that meets specified requirements. The Commission has indicated its suspicion that such plans may be the subject of abuse.

At the same time it adopted Rule 10b5–1, the Commission adopted Regulation FD. The discussion in the Dirks case suggested that communications between insiders and financial analysts could present issues somewhat different than those usually manifest in insider "tipping" cases. Regulation FD, discussed in Chapter 12D, deals with these issues in terms of the issuer's duty to disclose, rather than in terms of inside trading.

———————

[10]   486 F.3d 315 (7th Cir.2007).

[11]   137 F.3d 1325 (11th Cir.1998).

II. RELIANCE AND CAUSATION IN THE CONTEXT OF INSIDER TRADING

Reliance and causation involving non-disclosure (which of course is the hallmark of insider trading) are complex subjects under Rule 10b–5. The best starting point is Affiliated Ute Citizens v. United States,[12] decided by the Supreme Court in 1972. In that case, the Court had to struggle with reliance and causation in the context of face-to-face dealings between officers of a bank who engaged in stock transactions with members of the Ute tribe. The major allegations were the failure of the bank officers to disclose material information. The Court found that "[u]nder the circumstances of this case, involving primarily a failure to disclose, positive proof of reliance is not a prerequisite to recovery. All that is necessary is that the facts withheld be material * * * . This obligation to disclose and this withholding of a material fact establish the requisite element of causation in fact." (It would have been better if the Court had spoken in terms of the establishment of a rebuttable presumption of reliance, which is how courts have quite properly read the case.)

Complaints based on open market trading in violation of the duty to disclose or refrain from trading have presented particularly interesting issues:

Fridrich v. Bradford

United States Court of Appeals, Sixth Circuit, 1976.
542 F.2d 307.

■ Before CELEBREZZE, PECK and ENGEL, CIRCUIT JUDGES.

■ ENGEL, CIRCUIT JUDGE.

On April 27, 1972 J.C. Bradford, Jr. purchased 1,225 shares of common stock of Old Line Life Insurance Company (Old Line). The shares were purchased on inside information Bradford, Jr. had received on a tip from his father. The shares were purchased on the over-the-counter market from J.C. Bradford and Co., a Nashville brokerage firm of which Bradford, Jr. and his father are managing partners. Subsequent to the purchase, Old Line stock increased in value and on July 27, 1972, Bradford, Jr. sold the 1,225 shares, reaping a profit of $13,000 on the transaction.

* * *

Thereafter plaintiffs filed this civil action, alleging that Bradford, Jr.'s trading activities violated Rule 10b–5. By the judgment of the district court appealed from here, Bradford, Jr. has been rendered jointly and severally liable to [the three] plaintiffs for the sum of $361,186.75. He has been held liable, although plaintiffs never sold their stock to him

---

[12]   406 U.S. 128 (1972).

or his associates, nor did they sell on the same day or even in the same month in which he bought. There was no proof that Bradford, Jr.'s trading activities had any impact upon the market price of Old Line stock or upon plaintiffs' decision to trade in it. * * *

* * *

IV.

* * *

In [Shapiro v. Merrill Lynch, Pierce, Fenner & Smith, Inc., 353 F.Supp. 264 (S.D.N.Y.1972), aff'd, 495 F.2d 228 (2d Cir.1974)], plaintiffs did not allege that they had actually traded with the defendants. Neither does it appear from the opinion that defendants' act of trading had any influence upon their own decision to purchase. In their motion to dismiss, defendants contended that their violation of Rule 10b–5, even if proved, did not cause any damage to plaintiffs and that since plaintiffs would have bought the stock in any event, no injury to plaintiffs was occasioned. Judge Tenney rejected this analysis:

> But therein lies the fallacy of defendants' reasoning: it is not the act of trading which causes plaintiffs' injury, *it is the act of trading without disclosing material inside information which causes plaintiffs' injury.* * * *

The Second Circuit, in affirming the district court judgment, agreed with Judge Tenney's analysis and further concluded that any argument defendants might make that their conduct did not cause plaintiffs' damage was precluded by the [causation in fact] holding in Affiliated Ute Citizens v. United States, 406 U.S. 128 (1972) * * * .

* * *

V.

We conclude that upon the facts of this case defendants' conduct caused no injury to plaintiffs and the judgment of the district court must be reversed. It is undisputed that defendants did not purchase any shares of stock from plaintiffs, and that defendants' acts of trading in no way affected plaintiffs' decision to sell.

We are unable to agree with the observation of the district judge in *Shapiro* that " * * * it is the act of trading without disclosing material inside information which causes plaintiffs' injury * * * . Having breached that obligation [to abstain or disclose], the defendants are liable for plaintiffs' injuries." The flaw in this logic, we conclude, is that it assumes the very injury which it then declares compensable. It does so by presupposing that the duty to disclose is absolute, and that the plaintiff is injured when the information is denied him. The duty to disclose, however, is not an absolute one, but an alternative one, that of either disclosing or abstaining from trading. We conceive it to be the act of trading which essentially constitutes the violation of Rule 10b–5, for it is this which brings the illicit benefit to the insider, and it is this conduct which impairs the integrity of the market and which is the target of the rule. If the insider does not trade, he has an absolute right to keep material information secret. Investors must be prepared to accept the risk of trading in an open market without complete or always accurate information. Defendants' trading did not alter plaintiffs' expectations when they sold their stock, and in no way influenced plaintiffs' trading decision.

We hold, therefore, the defendants' act of trading with third persons was not causally connected with any claimed loss by plaintiffs who traded on the impersonal market and who were otherwise unaffected by the wrongful acts of the insider.

Likewise, we are not persuaded, as was the Second Circuit in its decision in *Shapiro,* supra, that Affiliated Ute Citizens v. United States, supra, mandates a "short, and * * * conclusive answer" to the contrary.

* * *

* * * It was shown in *Affiliated Ute* that the defendant bank employees had engaged in prior business dealings with the plaintiff Indians. They entered into a deliberate scheme to induce the plaintiffs to sell their stock without disclosure of material facts which would have influenced the decision to sell. The resulting sales were a direct result of the scheme. Thus it comes as no surprise that the Supreme Court concluded that "[U]nder the circumstances of this case," all that was necessary was that the information withheld be material in order to establish the requisite causation.

* * *

VI.

Neither do we believe that sound policy considerations support the result reached by the district court. * * *

The key issue, as we see it, is not whether the proscriptions of § 10(b) and Rule 10b–5 should encompass open market transactions, which they should, but whether the civil remedy must invariably be coextensive in its reach with the reach of the SEC, which under the Act, was designated by the Congress as the primary vehicle of its enforcement. We reject such a view where its application leads us inexorably to an unjust and unworkable result.[13] * * *

Where private civil actions under Rule 10b–5 have been employed in essentially face-to-face situations, the potential breadth of the action was usually contained. However, extension of the private remedy to impersonal market cases where plaintiffs have neither dealt with defendants nor been influenced in their trading decisions by any act of

---

[13] We specifically do not reach the question of availability of the remedy to open market situations where the insider trading with resultant price changes has in fact induced the plaintiffs to buy or sell to their injury. Here there was no proof that defendants' insider trading had any impact whatever upon the value of Old Line stock.

the defendants would present a situation wholly lacking in the natural limitations on damages present in cases dealing with face-to-face transactions. We think the potential liability of Bradford, Jr. in this case, noted earlier, is sufficiently illustrative of the dangers posed.[14]

* * *

In 1988, as part of the Insider Trading and Securities Fraud Enforcement Act, Congress adopted Exchange Act Section 20A, discussed in Section 13B. Legislative history cited with approval the Shapiro v. Merrill Lynch, Pierce, Fenner & Smith, Inc.,[15] opinion discussed in *Fridrich*.

III. DAMAGES AND PENALTIES IN THE CONTEXT OF INSIDER TRADING

As the preceding case indicates, courts have struggled with the requirement that private plaintiff's demonstrate causation in the context of open-market insider trading cases. Those courts who have resolved the causation issue in plaintiffs' favor also have been required to confront the calculation of damages.

Elkind v. Liggett & Myers, Inc.
United States Court of Appeals, Second Circuit, 1980.
635 F.2d 156.

■ Before MANSFIELD and NEWMAN, CIRCUIT JUDGES.

■ MANSFIELD, CIRCUIT JUDGE:

* * *

* * * The [district] court found * * * that on * * * July 17, 1972, officers of Liggett disclosed material inside information to individual financial analysts, leading to sale of Liggett stock by investors to whom this information was conveyed. Damages were computed on the basis of the difference between the price which members of the plaintiff class (uninformed buyers of Liggett stock between the time of the first tip and subsequent public disclosure) paid and what the stock sold for after the later disclosure. * * *

---

[14] Plaintiffs sold Old Line stock in the over-the-counter market in various lots on June 13, 14 and 15, 1972. Based upon the market data received in evidence at the trial, if all of the persons who had sold their shares of Old Line stock on those days alone had joined in the instant lawsuit, Bradford Jr.'s potential liability in damages would have totaled approximately $800,000. If a class action had been brought which included all investors who sold Old Line stock between April 21 and June 29, 1972, the damages could have totaled approximately $3,700,000. If the class had been further expanded to those selling up to November 20, 1972 (and the holding appealed from admits of no limitation short thereof), the damages would have run in excess of $7,000,000.00. As noted earlier, Bradford, Jr.'s profit from his illegal purchases, already disgorged in an SEC proceeding, amounted to about $13,000.

[15] 353 F.Supp. 264 (S.D.N.Y.1972), *aff'd*, 495 F.2d 228 (2d Cir.1974).

[The court of appeals agreed that the July 17 disclosure to financial analysts violated Rule 10b–5, leading the court to consider the damage issue.]

This case presents a question of measurement of damages which we have previously deferred, believing that damages are best addressed in a concrete setting. We ruled in [Shapiro v. Merrill Lynch, Pierce, Fenner & Smith, Inc., 495 F.2d 228 (2d Cir.1974),] that defendants selling on inside information would be liable to those who bought on the open market and sustained "substantial losses" during the period of insider trading.

* * *

[S]everal measures are possible. First, there is the traditional out-of-pocket measure used by the district court in this case. For several reasons this measure appears to be inappropriate. In the first place, * * * it is directed toward compensating a person for losses directly traceable to the defendant's fraud upon him. No such fraud or inducement may be attributed to a tipper or tippee trading on an impersonal market. Aside from this the measure poses serious proof problems that may often be insurmountable in a tippee-trading case. The "value" of the stock traded during the period of nondisclosure of the tipped information (i.e., the price at which the market would have valued the stock if there had been a disclosure) is hypothetical. Expert testimony regarding that "value" may, as the district court found in the present case, be entirely speculative. This has led some courts to conclude that the drop in price of the stock after actual disclosure and after allowing a period of time to elapse for the market to absorb the news may sometimes approximate the drop which would have occurred earlier had the tip been disclosed. The court below adopted this approach of using post-public disclosure market price as *nunc pro tunc* evidence of the "value" of the stock during the period of non-disclosure.

Whatever may be the reasonableness of the *nunc pro tunc* "value" method of calculating damages in other contexts, it has serious vulnerabilities here. It rests on the fundamental assumptions (1) that the tipped information is substantially the same as that later disclosed publicly, and (2) that one can determine how the market would have reacted to the public release of the tipped information at an earlier time by its reaction to that information at a later, proximate time. This theory depends on the parity of the "tip" and the "disclosure." When they differ, the basis of the damage calculation evaporates. One could not reasonably estimate how the public would have reacted to the news that the Titanic was near an iceberg from how it reacted to news that the ship had struck an iceberg and sunk. * * *

An equally compelling reason for rejecting the theory is its potential for imposition of Draconian, exorbitant damages, out of all proportion to the wrong committed, lining the pockets of all interim investors and their counsel at the expense of innocent corporate stockholders. Logic would compel application of the theory to a case where a tippee sells only 10 shares of a heavily traded stock (e.g., IBM), which then drops substantially when the tipped information is publicly disclosed. To hold the tipper and tippee liable for the losses suffered by every open market buyer of the stock as a result of the later decline in value of the stock after the news became public would be grossly unfair. While the securities laws do occasionally allow for potentially ruinous recovery,[16] we will not readily adopt a measure mandating "large judgments, payable in the last instance by innocent investors [here, Liggett shareholders], for the benefit of speculators and their lawyers," SEC v. Texas Gulf Sulphur Co., [401 F.2d 833, 867 (2d Cir.1968)] (Friendly, J., concurring), unless the statute so requires.

An alternative measure would be to permit recovery of damages caused by erosion of the market price of the security that is traceable to the tippee's wrongful trading, i.e., to compensate the uninformed investor for the loss in market value that he suffered as a direct result of the tippee's conduct. Under this measure an innocent trader who bought Liggett shares at or after a tippee sold on the basis of inside information would recover any decline in value of his shares caused by the tippee's trading. Assuming the impact of the tippee's trading on the market is measurable, this approach has the advantage of limiting the plaintiffs to the amount of damage actually caused in fact by the defendant's wrongdoing and avoiding windfall recoveries by investors at the expense of stockholders other than the tippee trader, which could happen in the present action against Liggett. The rationale is that if the market price is not affected by the tippee's trading, the uninformed investor is in the same position as he would have been had the insider abstained from trading. In such event the equilibrium of the market has not been disturbed and the outside investor has not been harmed by the informational imbalance. Only where the market has been contaminated by the wrongful conduct would damages be recoverable.

This causation-in-fact approach has some disadvantages. It allows no recovery for the tippee's violation of his duty to disclose the inside information before trading. Had he fulfilled this duty, others, including holders of the stock, could then have traded on an equal informational basis. Another disadvantage of such a measure lies in the difficult if not impossible burden it would impose on the uninformed trader of proving the time when and extent to which the integrity of the market was affected by the tippee's conduct. In some cases, such as * * * *Shapiro*, supra, the existence of very substantial trading by the tippee, coupled with a sharp change in market price over a short period, would provide the basis for measuring a market price movement attributable to the wrongful trading. On the other hand, in a case where there was only a modest amount of tippee trading in a heavy-volume market in the stock,

---

[16]   See, e.g., § 11 of the Securities Act of 1933 and §§ 9(e) and 18 of the Securities Exchange Act of 1934.

accompanied by other unrelated factors affecting the market price, it would be impossible as a practical matter to isolate such rise or decline in market price, if any, as was caused by the tippee's wrongful conduct. Moreover, even assuming market erosion caused by this trading to be provable and that the uninformed investor could show that it continued after his purchase, there remains the question of whether the plaintiff would not be precluded from recovery on the ground that any post-purchase decline in market price attributable to the tippee's trading would not be injury to him as a purchaser, i.e., "in connection with the purchase and sale of securities," but injury to him as a stockholder due to a breach of fiduciary duty by the company's officers, which is not actionable under § 10(b) of the 1934 Act or Rule 10b–5 promulgated thereunder. For these reasons, we reject this strict direct market-repercussion theory of damages.

A third alternative is (1) to allow any uninformed investor, where a reasonable investor would either have delayed his purchase or not purchased at all if he had had the benefit of the tipped information, to recover any post-purchase decline in market value of his shares up to a reasonable time after he learns of the tipped information or after there is a public disclosure of it but (2) limit his recovery to the amount gained by the tippee as a result of his selling at the earlier date rather than delaying his sale until the parties could trade on an equal informational basis. Under this measure if the tippee sold 5,000 shares at $50 per share on the basis of inside information and the stock thereafter declined to $40 per share within a reasonable time after public disclosure, an uninformed purchaser, buying shares during the interim (e.g., at $45 per share) would recover the difference between his purchase price and the amount at which he could have sold the shares on an equal informational basis (i.e., the market price within a reasonable time after public disclosure of the tip), subject to a limit of $50,000, which is the amount gained by the tippee as a result of his trading on the inside information rather than on an equal basis. Should the intervening buyers, because of the volume and price of their purchases, claim more than the tippee's gain, their recovery (limited to that gain) would be shared *pro rata*.

This third alternative, which may be described as the disgorgement measure, has in substance been recommended by the American Law Institute in its 1978 Proposed Draft of a Federal Securities Code, §§ 1603, 1703(b), 1708(b), 1711(j). It offers several advantages. To the extent that it makes the tipper and tippees liable up to the amount gained by their misconduct, it should deter tipping of inside information and tippee-trading. On the other hand, by limiting the total recovery to the tippee's gain, the measure bars windfall recoveries of exorbitant amounts bearing no relation to the seriousness of the misconduct. It also avoids the extraordinary difficulties faced in trying to prove traditional out-of-pocket damages based on the true "value" of the shares purchased or damages claimed by reason of market erosion attributable to tippee trading. A plaintiff would simply be required to prove (1) the time, amount, and price per share of his purchase, (2) that a reasonable investor would not have paid as high a price or made the purchase at all if he had had the information in the tippee's possession, and (3) the price to which the security had declined by the time he learned the tipped information or at a reasonable time after it became public, whichever event first occurred. He would then have a claim and, up to the limits of the tippee's gain, could recover the decline in market value of his shares before the information became public or known to him. In most cases the damages recoverable under the disgorgement measure would be roughly commensurate to the actual harm caused by the tippee's wrongful conduct. In a case where the tippee sold only a few shares, for instance, the likelihood of his conduct causing any substantial injury to intervening investors buying without benefit of his confidential information would be small. If, on the other hand, the tippee sold large amounts of stock, realizing substantial profits, the likelihood of injury to intervening uninformed purchasers would be greater and the amount of potential recovery thereby proportionately enlarged.

We recognize that there cannot be any perfect measure of damages caused by tippee-trading. The disgorgement measure, like others we have described, does have some disadvantages. It modifies the principle that ordinarily gain to the wrongdoer should not be a prerequisite to liability for violation of Rule 10b–5. It partially duplicates disgorgement remedies available in proceedings by the SEC or others. Under some market conditions such as where the market price is depressed by wholly unrelated causes, the tippee might be vulnerable to heavy damages, permitting some plaintiffs to recover undeserved windfalls. In some instances the total claims could exceed the wrongdoer's gain, limiting each claimant to a pro rata share of the gain. In other situations, after deducting the cost of recovery, including attorneys' fees, the remainder might be inadequate to make a class action worthwhile. However, as between the various alternatives we are persuaded, after weighing the pros and cons, that the disgorgement measure, despite some disadvantages, offers the most equitable resolution of the difficult problems created by conflicting interests.

In the present case the sole Rule 10b–5 violation was the tippee-trading of 1,800 Liggett shares on the afternoon of July 17, 1972. Since the actual preliminary Liggett earnings were released publicly at 2:15 P.M. on July 18 and were effectively disseminated in a Wall Street Journal article published on the morning of July 19, the only outside purchasers who might conceivably have been damaged by the insider-trading were those who bought Liggett shares between the afternoon of July 17 and the opening of the market on July 19. Thereafter all purchasers bought on an equal informational footing, and any outside purchaser who bought on July 17 and 18 was able to decide within a reasonable time after the July 18–19 publicity whether to hold or sell his shares in the light of the publicly-released news regarding Liggett's less favorable earnings.

The market price of Liggett stock opened on July 17, 1972, at $55P5/8P, and remained at substantially the same price on that date, closing at $55¹/₄. By the close of the market on July 18 the price declined to $52¹/₂ per share. Applying the disgorgement measure, any member of the plaintiff class who bought Liggett shares during the period from the afternoon of July 17 to the close of the market on July 18 and met the reasonable investor requirement would be entitled to claim a *pro rata* portion of the tippee's gain, based on the difference between their purchase price and the price to which the market price declined within a reasonable time after the morning of July 19. By the close of the market on July 19 the market price had declined to $46P3/8P per share. The total recovery thus would be limited to the gain realized by the tippee from the inside information, i.e., 1,800 shares multiplied by approximately $9.35 per share.

* * *

That the disgorgement measure of damages removes some of the teeth of Rule 10b–5 troubles many people. No doubt partially as a result of dissatisfaction with *Elkind,* Congress in 1984 amended the Exchange Act to provide civil penalties for insider trading. Exchange Act Section 21A now allows the Commission to seek, and a federal court to impose, such penalties, both on inside traders and on persons who control inside traders. The penalty is in the discretion of the court, but may be as high as three times the profit gained, or loss avoided, as a result of insider trading, except in the case of controlling persons, whose penalties can be as high as $1,425,000 regardless of profit gained or loss avoided (when read along with the Commission's Rule of Practice 1004, which relates to the adjustment of civil monetary penalties). The toughness of the penalty on controlling persons is mitigated, however, by the fact that, to be subject to a penalty, the Commission must show that the controlling person "knew or recklessly disregarded the fact that [the] controlled person was likely to engage in the * * * violations and failed to take appropriate steps to prevent [the violations]." In order to enhance the Commission's ability to uncover insider trading, Section 21A also provides for the payment of bounties, of up to 10 percent of the penalty, to persons who provide information that leads to the imposition of a penalty.

B. OTHER PROVISIONS IMPACTING LIABILITY FOR INSIDER TRADING

I. RULE 14e–3

As more fully dealt with in Chapter 11, the Commission is authorized to regulate non-deceptive acts relating to tender offers if that regulation is a "reasonably designed" method of preventing fraud or manipulation. It used that authority in 1980 to adopt Rule 14e–3. This rule generally makes it illegal to purchase or sell, or cause to be purchased or sold, securities that are or are to be the subject of a tender offer (or certain related securities) when a person "is in possession of material information relating to such tender offer which information he knows or has reason to know is nonpublic and which he knows or has reason to know has been acquired" from the tender offeror or the target, or from someone connected with either. The rule also makes it illegal for insiders to tip others with material information about tender offers. Rule 14e–3 may be violated without the existence of a related violation of a fiduciary or other such duty, as is required in a Rule 10b–5 case. Had Rule 14e–3 been in effect at the time of *Chiarella*, it presumably would have resolved the case, and not in Mr. Chiarella's favor. It was invoked, and its application upheld, in *O'Hagan*.

II. SECTION 20A

Section 20A presents an interesting, if not particularly useful, approach to insider trading. It creates an express private right against anyone violating the Exchange Act by purchasing or selling a security while in possession of material non-public information. It was adopted with much fanfare in 1988, as part of a Congressional "get-tough" campaign triggered by a wave of insider trading scandals. Notably, it does *not* say that purchasing or selling a security while in possession of material non-public information violates the Exchange Act. Instead, it in effect says that *if* such a purchase or sale violates the Exchange Act, Section 20A consequences attach. This piggy-back approach means that a complete analysis of whether a violation of some other provision (such as Rule 10b–5) logically must precede application of Section 20. Disgorgement (less any amounts required to be disgorged in a civil penalties action brought under Section 21A) is the measure of damages to be shared among anyone trading "contemporaneously" in the same class of shares traded by the violator. "Contemporaneously" is not defined, but clearly could encompass such a large group as to leave little incentive for any plaintiff to initiate litigation. Section 20A specifically provides that it is not intended as a substitute for any implied private right of action that might otherwise exist.

C. TRADING BY FEDERAL EMPLOYEES

As noted in Section 13A, the question of who is subject to the trading constraints of Rule 10b–5 is an interesting one. One issue that had percolated for years is whether those constraints properly applied, or should apply, to the securities transactions of government employees in possession of nonpublic information acquired in their official capacities. In April 2012, the Stop Trading on Congressional Knowledge ("STOCK") Act became law. The STOCK Act is intended, in part, to make it clear that Section 10(b) and Rule 10b–5 prohibit members and employees of Congress, as well as employees of the executive and judicial branches of government, from engaging in securities transactions while aware of material nonpublic information derived from federal employment. This was accomplished by an amendment to Section 21A (which otherwise deals with civil penalties for insider trading). The amendment provides that, for purposes of Section 10 and Rule 10b–5, federal government employees are in a position of trust and confidence owed to the government and the citizens of the United States with respect to all information they acquire in their official capacities

The STOCK Act contained several other provisions that do not affect the federal securities laws per se. Among other things, it required members of Congress and many others to publicly disclose securities and commodities futures transactions within 45 days (annual disclosure previously was the norm). The Act also called for disclosure of the terms of home mortgages and prohibited special access to initial public stock offerings. In April 2013, the Act's mandate that the called-for financial disclosures be available online was indefinitely suspended.

CHAPTER 14

LIABILITY FOR TRADING PROFITS: SECTION 16(b) AND THE SARBANES-OXLEY ACT OF 2002

SITUATION 14

As a result of discovery in connection with the shareholder suits, you and the plaintiffs' counsel learn that Tate and the two non-officer employees referred to in Situation 12 made a number of purchases and sales of Microtec common stock in the trading markets, both before and after the public announcement in early July of Microtec's decreased earnings and bad debt problems. For the sake of simplicity, assume they each made the following purchases and sales, acting independently:

January 1	100 purchased at	$10	July 1	500 sold at	$12
February 1	200 purchased at	10	August 1	200 sold at	10
March 1	100 purchased at	11	September 1	100 purchased at	7
April 1	100 purchased at	11	October 1	100 purchased at	7
May 1	100 purchased at	12	November 1	100 purchased at	7
June 1	100 purchased at	12	December 1	100 sold at	8

In considering this situation, refer to Exchange Act Section 16, in addition to the materials in this chapter.

A. LIABILITY FOR SHORT-SWING PROFITS

I. STATUTORY SCHEME

Exchange Act Section 16(b) is designed to minimize the unfair use of inside information. This area is also regulated by Rule 10b–5, but the two provisions are entirely different in their coverage. Rule 10b–5 is a fairly refined weapon aimed at discrete acts of wrongdoing. Section 16(b), on the other hand, is a spring gun that can hit the innocent as easily as the guilty. Under this section, profits made by insiders from transactions involving equity securities of publicly-held companies, when a purchase and a sale are less than six months apart, must be disgorged and paid to the issuer.

Before examining Section 16(b), it is helpful to discuss Section 16(a). This section requires beneficial owners of more than ten percent of any class of equity security (other than an exempted security) that is registered under the Exchange Act, and officers and directors of issuers of such securities, to file reports with the Commission and relevant securities exchanges concerning their holdings of all equity securities of such issuers. Section 16(a) sets the filing periods for initial reports to be filed upon becoming subject to the section (basically, at the same time a company registers an equity security under the Exchange Act or within 10 days of becoming a person listed in the section, unless the Commission provides for a shorter period). It also establishes the filing period for reports of changes in ownership—which now stands at within two business days after the change. Section 16(a), however, does give the Commission power to extend the two day reporting requirement when the requirement is not feasible, which the Commission has done to a very limited extent. Rule 16a–3 details the reporting requirements. The rule provides that initial reports of ownership are to be made on the Commission's Form 3, changes in ownership are to be reported on Form 4, and an annual report is to be made on Form 5. These are relatively short, fill-in-the-blanks forms.

Section 16(b) provides that: (1) any profit; (2) by any person subject to the reporting requirements of Section 16(a); (3) realized on any purchase and sale, or sale and purchase; (4) within any period of less than six months; (5) of any non-exempt equity security of an issuer that has an equity security registered under the Exchange Act, or of any security-based swap agreement involving any such equity security (6) "shall inure to and be recoverable by the issuer." An exception exists when the security was purchased in good faith in connection with a debt previously contracted. Under Section 16(b), an issuer may sue to recover these so-called short-swing profits, or any security holder of the issuer may sue derivatively to recover the profits when, after request, the issuer fails to bring suit within sixty days or when it fails diligently to prosecute a claim once filed.

Many questions concerning Section 16(b) are answered by the Commission's rules under Section 16, which are extensive and highly detailed. Rule 16b–3, dealing with transactions between an issuer and its officers and directors and exempting those transactions in particular circumstances, is of great practical utility in structuring employment compensation arrangements involving stock. The rules also provide exemptions from Section 16(b) in some specialized circumstances, such as those involving the disposition of securities in certain mergers or the withdrawal of securities from voting trusts. Some of the more interesting specialized situations are covered in Rules 16a–4, and 16b–6, which relate to so-called derivative securities. One important aspect of these specialized situations is that the grant of a derivative security, such as a stock option, generally is deemed to be a purchase of the underlying security, thus triggering (unless there is an applicable exemption) Section 16(b) short-swing trading liability if the purchase can be matched with an appropriate sale within less than six months.

Most general questions that arise under Section 16(b) can be grouped under one of five topics: (1) persons liable, (2) what constitutes a purchase or sale, (3) timing of purchases and sales, (4) who has standing to sue, and (5) calculation of profits. These topics will be discussed below. Before turning to these topics, it will be helpful to focus briefly on some basic points that are often confusing. First, unlike most provisions in the Exchange Act, Section 16(b) is not a criminal provision. It does not make short-swing trading illegal. Instead, the section merely provides that the profits from certain trades essentially belong to the issuer. Second, beneficial owners of exactly ten percent of a non-exempt equity security are not subject to the section, but only those who own in excess of ten percent. Third, a sale and purchase or purchase and sale (it does not matter which comes first) that fall exactly six months apart are not covered by the section either. The trades must be within less than six months of each other to be governed by Section 16(b). The rule of thumb is that, for matching purposes, the second trade must occur no later than two days prior to the sixth month anniversary of the first trade (*i.e.*, a trade on January 15 may be matched with one on July 13 of the same year, but not with on July 14). Finally, courts generally have taken the view that an insider's transactions in different types of equity securities issued by the same issuer cannot be matched to trigger short-swing profits. This latter point begs the question, of course, of whether securities that are only ostensibly different, but are in fact economic equivalents, might be treated differently. There is a smattering of case-law on this subject.[1]

II. PERSONS LIABLE

On the question of persons subject to Section 16(b), the statute speaks in terms of officers, directors, and greater than ten percent beneficial owners. As in so many areas of securities law, however, intricacies are buried beneath the surface.

a. TITLES

One interesting issue relates to titles. For most purposes, of course, a person's status as an officer or director of a corporation depends on whether he or she has been elected an officer or director in accordance with the requirements of state corporation law and the corporation's bylaws. In all but a rare case, a person so elected is given a traditional title that puts the public on notice of the person's status. Things are not so simple under Section 16(b).

---

[1]   *See, e.g.*, Gibbons v. Malone, 703 F.3d 595 (2d Cir. 2013) (Section 16(b) matching does not apply to two nonconvertible securities whose prices fluctuate relative to one another).

Two special definitions create complications:

Section 3(a)(7). The term "director" means any director of a corporation or any person performing similar functions with respect to any organization, whether incorporated or unincorporated.

Rule 16a–1(f). The term "officer" shall mean an issuer's president, principal financial officer, principal accounting officer (or, if there is no such accounting officer, the controller), any vice-president of the issuer in charge of a principal business unit, division or function (such as sales, administration or finance), any other officer who performs a policy-making function, or any other person who performs similar policy-making functions for the issuer. Officers of the issuer's parent(s) or subsidiaries shall be deemed officers of the issuer if they perform such policy-making functions for the issuer. [The rule goes on to cover the concept of "officer" in the context of trusts and limited partnerships.]

Although these definitions begin with the ordinary state law conceptions of directors and officers, they quickly diverge from these conceptions. Focusing only on corporations, it is easy to see that these definitions are broader than the state law concept because they include, with different wording and to a somewhat different degree, persons whose functions are similar to those performed by directors or named officers. At the same time, the Rule 16a–1 definition of "officer" is substantially narrower than the state law conception, because it includes persons who hold only certain positions or perform certain policy-making functions, while under the typical state corporation statute a corporation is free to create offices and bestow titles at will. A note to the rule gives some help on the question of what is included in the conception of "policy-making function." In general, the note indicates that the conception does not include functions that are not significant.

* * *

---

b.   DEPUTIZATION

"Deputization" is a legal concept that can be used to bring within the coverage of Section 16(b) a person or firm who, although not a director, officer, or greater than ten percent holder, has his, her, or its interest in a corporation represented by a person who sits on the board of directors. The concept began in 1952 with Learned Hand's concurring opinion in Rattner v. Lehman.[2] In that case, the investment banking firm of Lehman Brothers had made short-swing profits by trading in the stock of Consolidated Vultee Aircraft Corporation at a time when one of the

---

[2]   193 F.2d 564 (2d Cir.1952).

Lehman partners served as a director of that corporation. The question arose as to whether, under these facts alone, Lehman Brothers must disgorge the profits. Speaking to this question, Judge Hand said:

> [Section] 16(b) does not go so far; but I wish to say nothing as to whether, if a firm deputed a partner to represent its interests as a director on the board, the other partners would not be liable. True, they would not even then be formally "directors"; but I am not prepared to say that they could not be so considered; for some purposes the common law does treat a firm as a jural person.

Ten years later, the Supreme Court heard a Section 16(b) case involving the allegation of deputization, Blau v. Lehman,[3] that again had Lehman Brothers as a defendant. The complaint alleged that Lehman deputized one of its partners to represent its interests on the board of Tide Water Associated Oil Company and that the director "by reason of his special and inside knowledge of the affairs of Tide Water, advised and caused the defendants, Lehman Brothers, to purchase and sell 50,000 shares of * * * stock of Tide Water, realizing profits thereon." The district court found against the plaintiff on the issue of deputization and also determined that Lehman Brothers had traded solely on the basis of Tide Water's public announcements. Both the court of appeals and the Supreme Court affirmed, but in so doing, the Supreme Court put its imprimatur on the deputization theory:

> No doubt Lehman Brothers, though a partnership, could for purposes of § 16 be a "director" of Tide Water and function through a deputy, since § 3(a)(9) of the Act provides that " 'person' means * * * partnership" and § 3(a)(7) that " 'director' means any director of a corporation or any person performing similar functions * * * ." Consequently, Lehman Brothers would be a "director" of Tide Water, if as petitioner's complaint charged Lehman actually functioned as a director through [its partner], who had been deputized by Lehman to perform a director's duties not for himself but for Lehman. But the findings of the two courts below which we have accepted, preclude such a holding.

The most influential circuit court deputization case is the one that follows directly.

---

[3]   368 U.S. 403 (1962).

Feder v. Martin Marietta Corp.

United States Court of Appeals, Second Circuit, 1969.
406 F.2d 260.

■ Before WATERMAN, SMITH and HAYS, CIRCUIT JUDGES.

■ WATERMAN, CIRCUIT JUDGE:

Plaintiff-appellant, a stockholder of the Sperry Rand Corporation ("Sperry"), after having made the requisite demand upon Sperry which was not complied with, commenced this action pursuant to § 16(b) of the Securities Exchange Act of 1934 to recovery for Sperry "short-swing" profits realized upon Sperry stock purchases and sales by the Martin Marietta Corporation ("Martin"). Plaintiff alleged that George M. Bunker, the President and Chief Executive of Martin Marietta, was deputized by, or represented, Martin Marietta when he served as a member of the Sperry Rand Board of Directors and therefore during his membership Martin Marietta was a "director" of Sperry Rand within the meaning of Section 16(b). The United States District Court for the Southern District of New York, Cooper, J., sitting without a jury, finding no deputization, dismissed plaintiff's action. We hold to the contrary and reverse the judgment below.

* * *

Bunker served as a director of Sperry from April 29, 1963 to August 1, 1963, when he resigned. During the period December 14, 1962 through July 24, 1963, Martin Marietta accumulated 801,300 shares of Sperry stock of which 101,300 shares were purchased during Bunker's directorship. Between August 29, 1963 and September 6, 1963, Martin Marietta sold all of its Sperry stock. Plaintiff seeks to reach, on behalf of the Sperry Rand Corporation, the profits made by Martin Marietta from the 101,300 shares of stock acquired between April 29 and August 1, all of which, of course, were sold within six months after purchase.

The district court, in determining that Bunker was not a Martin deputy, made [a number of] findings of fact to support its decision * * * . * * * We assume all of [these] findings have a basis of fact in the evidence, but we find there was additional, more germane, uncontradicted evidence, overlooked or ignored by the district court, which we are firmly convinced require us to conclude that Martin Marietta was a "director" of Sperry Rand.

First and foremost is Bunker's testimony that as chief executive of Martin Marietta he was "ultimately responsible for the total operation of the corporation" including personal approval of all the firm's financial investments, and, in particular, all of Martin's purchases of Sperry stock. * * * Bunker's testimony revealed that while he was a Sperry director three Sperry officials had furnished him with information relating to the "short-range outlook" at Sperry, and, in addition, Bunker admitted discussing Sperry's affairs with two officials at Martin Marietta and participating in sessions when Martin's investment in Sperry was reviewed. Moreover, an unsigned document concededly originating from the Martin Marietta files, entitled "Notes on Exploratory Investment in Sperry Rand Corporation," describing the Sperry management, evaluating their abilities, and analyzing the merit of Sperry's forecasts for the future, further indicates that Martin Marietta may have benefited, or intended to benefit, from Bunker's association with Sperry Rand.

* * *

It appears to us that a person in Bunker's unique position could act as a deputy for Martin Marietta even in the absence of factors indicating an intention or belief on the part of both companies that he was so acting. We do not hold that, without more, Bunker's control over Martin Marietta, or the possibility that inside information was obtained or disclosed, mandates that Bunker was Martin's deputy. However, additional evidence detailed hereafter which indicates that the managements of Sperry Rand and of Martin Marietta intended that Bunker should act as Martin's deputy on the Sperry Board, and believed he was so acting, lends valuable support to our factual conclusion.

First, in Bunker's letter of resignation to General MacArthur, the Chairman of the Board of Directors of Sperry Rand, he stated:

> When I became a member of the Board in April, it appeared to your associates that the Martin Marietta ownership of a substantial number of shares of Sperry Rand should have representation on your Board. This representation does not seem to me really necessary and I prefer not to be involved in the affairs of Sperry Rand when there are so many other demands on my time * * * .

Martin Marietta urges that we should not read this letter to mean what it so clearly says. They would have us believe that this letter was so phrased because Bunker intended "to write a gentle letter of resignation to a great (but elderly) man whom he admired, in terms that he would understand." No matter how advanced in years the Chairman of the Sperry Board may have been, we are puzzled by defendant's contention that he, and only he, of all those on the Sperry Board, considered Bunker to be representing Martin's interests. Furthermore, if throughout Bunker's service, the Chairman of the Board misunderstood the purpose of Bunker's directorship, why Bunker upon resignation would want this misunderstanding perpetuated is even more perplexing. Certainly the more logical inference from the wording of Bunker's letter of resignation is the inference that Bunker served on the Sperry Board as a representative of Martin Marietta so as to protect Martin's investment in Sperry.

Second, the Board of Directors of Martin Marietta formally consented to and approved Bunker's directorship of Sperry prior to

Bunker's acceptance of the position. While Martin's organizational policy required that Bunker secure that Board's approval of any corporate directorship he were offered, the approval was not obtained until, significantly, the Board had been informed by Bunker that Martin had a 10 million dollar investment in Sperry stock at the time. Bunker testified that he "thought the Board would draw the inference that his presence on Sperry's Board would be to Martin's interest." * * * Surely such conduct by the Martin Board supports an inference that it deputized Bunker to represent its interests on Sperry's Board. * * *

Finally, Bunker's testimony clearly established that the Martin Marietta Corporation had representatives or deputies who served on the boards of other corporations. The only distinctions drawn by the court below to differentiate Bunker's Sperry relationship from the relationship to Martin Marietta of other Martin Marietta deputies on other corporate boards were that Bunker had no duty to report back to Martin what was going on at Sperry and there was a lesser degree of supervision over Bunker's actions than over the actions of the others. Otherwise Bunker was a typical Martin deputy. * * *

* * *

The Second Circuit has held that an entity deemed a director by virtue of deputization was entitled to take advantage of Rule 16b–3, providing an exemption for certain transactions between an issuer and its officers and/or directors.[4]

c.   BENEFICIAL OWNERSHIP

Under Section 16(b), an insider must disgorge "profits realized *by him* "(emphasis added). In the usual transaction, it is no trouble to determine the profits that have accrued to a particular owner. Sometimes, however, this is not the case. Take, for example, when shares are traded by a director's spouse or by an officer for the account of a minor child. Are any resulting profits "by" the insider? As will be discussed, the answer may be yes or no.

There have grown to be a number of court of appeals decisions of importance in this area. Two of these cases form an interesting pair. The first is Whiting v. Dow Chemical Co.[5] Whiting, a director of Dow Chemical Company, exercised an option to purchase more than $500,000 worth of Dow stock at approximately $24 per share. In the prior three month period, his wife had sold $1.6 million worth of Dow shares for $55–$56 a share. In the ensuing Section 16(b) litigation, the Second Circuit viewed the first question to be whether Whiting had been the beneficial

---

[4]   Roth v. Perseus LLC, 522 F.3d 242 (2d Cir.2008). In Huppe v. WPCS Int'l Inc., 670 F.3d 214, 219 (2d Cir. 2012), the court refused to by analogy extend the exemption to ten percent holders.

[5]   523 F.2d 680 (2d Cir.1975).

owner of his wife's shares. Whiting's and his wife's investment portfolios were kept separate, with at least general management of each in the hands of an investment banking firm. There was, however, "sufficient evidence to establish that the questioned transactions were part of a common plan, jointly managed by husband and wife." Moreover, focusing on the issue of the benefits that flowed to Whiting from his wife's Dow chemical investments, the court found that "there is hardly anything Mrs. Whiting gets out of the ownership that appellant does not share." In short, Whiting had been the beneficial owner of the Dow shares sold by his wife.

The court then focused on how to deal with the statutory mandate that an insider disgorge profits realized *by him*. As is characteristic of decisions under Section 16(b), the court determined to opt for maximum disgorgement and found that Whiting must personally be charged with all the profits on the transactions. In the interest of "prophylaxis," the Second Circuit rationalized its decision by asserting: "The whole profit is 'his' profit, 'realized by him' because the shares are 'his' by the statutory 'beneficial owner' concept as applied, and because he is a person in a position to obtain inside information."

Whittaker v. Whittaker Corp.,[6] decided by the Ninth Circuit in 1981, involved purchases and sales by a corporate director, who also served as chairman of the board of directors, for the account of his mother. Whittaker held his mother's power of attorney and, according to the district court, "exercised virtually complete control over his mother's affairs" and "felt free to utilize his mother's assets exactly as if they were his own." Accordingly, the Ninth Circuit found that Whittaker had been the beneficial owner of his mother's shares.

In rules passed after these cases were decided, the Commission set out detailed criteria for determining in various circumstances whether one is a "beneficial owner" of securities for the purposes of Section 16. In Rule 16a–1(a)(2), the Commission put its imprimatur on the *Whiting* and *Whittaker* type of analysis, indicating that, for determinations such as were necessary in those cases:[7]

> [The] term "beneficial owner" shall mean any person who, directly or indirectly, through any contract, arrangement, understanding, relationship or otherwise, has or shares a direct or indirect pecuniary interest in the equity securities, subject to the following * * * .

In the rule the Commission then provides that a pecuniary interest means "the opportunity, directly or indirectly, to profit or share in any profit derived from a transaction in the subject securities" and that the

---

6   639 F.2d 516 (9th Cir.1981).

7   Rule 16a–1 splits the issue of beneficial ownership into two distinct parts. Rule 16a–1(a)(1) handles the issue simply in the context of determining whether a person is a beneficial owner of more than ten percent of a class of equity security registered under the Exchange Act, and Rule 16–a–1(a)(2) handles the issue in all other contexts.

term "indirect pecuniary interest" in securities includes, among other possibilities, securities held by immediate family members who share the same home (with the proviso that "the presumption of such beneficial ownership may be rebutted").

Another interesting beneficial ownership issue arises under Section 16 when two or more people agree to act together in buying, holding, voting, or selling securities. The question is whether the group is considered the beneficial owner of the relevant securities held by members of the group. Rule 16a–1(a)(1) says that, solely for the purpose of determining who is a Section 16 "beneficial owner," that term means "any person who is deemed a beneficial owner pursuant to Section 13(d) of the Act and [its rules, with specialized exceptions]." The most helpful place to turn for further understanding is Rule 13d–5(b)(1). It provides that when a group agrees "to act together for the purpose of acquiring, holding, voting or disposing of equity securities of an issuer," the group is deemed to own beneficially all equity securities of that issuer that are beneficially owned by each member of the group.[8]

The Second Circuit interpreted these rules in Morales v. Quintel Entertainment, Inc.[9] This case involved the acquisition of Quintel stock, by the three shareholders of Psychic Reader's Network, under a sales agreement between the two corporations. One of the three shareholders ended up owning less than three percent of Quintel's stock, although the three together owned more than 10 percent. Thereafter the shareholder who owned less than three percent made a number of short-swing purchases and sales and was sued in a derivative action to recover profits he made on those trades. The district court granted summary judgment to the shareholder, but the Second Circuit used a straightforward reading of the Commission's rules and remanded for the district court to determine whether the three shareholders had agreed to act together for the purpose of acquiring, holding, or disposing of Quintel stock.

There are two additional and noteworthy Second Circuit opinions relating to beneficial ownership. First, in Huppe v. WPCS International Incorporated III QP,[10] the court held that limited partnerships that owned shares but that had delegated exclusive decision-making authority to their general partners nonetheless were the shares' beneficial owners. Then, in Mercer v. Gupta,[11] the court declined to extend the term "beneficial owner" to tippers who provide inside information, in exchange for payment, to another party who engages in the short-swing trading of shares.

---

[8]　The next part of the rule, subdivision (b)(2), then pulls from this aggregation of securities certain purchases from an issuer not involving any public offering.

[9]　249 F.3d 115 (2d Cir.2001).

[10]　670 F.3d 214 (2d Cir.2012).

[11]　No. 12–3393 (2d Cir., Apr. 5, 2013).

III. What Constitutes a Purchase or Sale?

Determining what constitutes a purchase or sale is easy in the usual context, but it is more difficult when unorthodox transactions are involved. In this regard, one case in particular is of the greatest importance. That case is Kern County Land Co. v. Occidental Petroleum Corp., which the Supreme Court decided in 1973:

Kern County Land Co. v. Occidental Petroleum Corp.

Supreme Court of the United States, 1973.
411 U.S. 582.

■ Mr. Justice White delivered the opinion of the Court.

* * * Unquestionably, one or more statutory purchases occur when one company, seeking to gain control of another, acquires more than 10% of the stock of the latter through a tender offer made to its shareholders. But is it a § 16(b) "sale" when the target of the tender offer defends itself by merging into a third company and the tender offeror then exchanges his stock for the stock of the surviving company and also grants an option to purchase the latter stock that is not exercisable within the statutory six-month period? This is the question before us in this case.

I

On May 8, 1967, after unsuccessfully seeking to merge with Kern County Land Co. (Old Kern), Occidental Petroleum Corp. (Occidental) announced an offer to expire on June 8, 1967, to purchase on a first-come, first-served basis 500,000 shares of Old Kern common stock at a price of $83.50 per share plus a brokerage commission of $1.50 per share. By May 10, 1967, 500,000 shares, more than 10% of the outstanding shares of Old Kern, had been tendered. On May 11, Occidental extended its offer to encompass an additional 500,000 shares. At the close of the tender offer, on June 8, 1967, Occidental owned 887,549 shares of Old Kern.

Immediately upon the announcement of Occidental's tender offer, the Old Kern management undertook to frustrate Occidental's takeover attempt [by various means]. * * * In addition, Old Kern undertook merger discussions with Tenneco, Inc. (Tenneco), and, on May 19, 1967, the Board of Directors of Old Kern announced that it had approved a merger proposal advanced by Tenneco. [In the merger, the] shareholders of Old Kern would receive a share of Tenneco cumulative convertible preference stock in exchange for each share of Old Kern common stock which they owned. * * *

* * * Realizing that, if the Old Kern-Tenneco merger were approved and successfully closed, Occidental would have to exchange its Old Kern shares for Tenneco stock and would be locked into a minority position in Tenneco, Occidental * * * negotiated an arrangement with Tenneco whereby Occidental granted Tenneco Corp., a subsidiary of Tenneco, an

option to purchase at $105 per share all of the Tenneco preference stock to which Occidental would be entitled in exchange for its Old Kern stock when and if the Old Kern-Tenneco merger was closed. The premium to secure the option, at $10 per share, totaled $8,866,230 and was to be paid immediately upon the signing of the option agreement. If the option were exercised, the premium was to be applied to the purchase price. By the terms of the option agreement, the option could not be exercised prior to December 9, 1967, a date six months and one day after expiration of Occidental's tender offer. On June 2, 1967, within six months of the acquisition by Occidental of more than 10% ownership of Old Kern, Occidental and Tenneco Corp. executed the option. * * *

The Old Kern-Tenneco merger plan was presented to and approved by Old Kern shareholders at their meeting on July 17, 1967. Occidental refrained from voting its Old Kern shares, but in a letter read at the meeting Occidental stated that it had determined prior to June 2 not to oppose the merger and that it did not consider the plan unfair or inequitable. Indeed, Occidental indicated that, had it been voting, it would have voted in favor of the merger.

* * *

The Old Kern-Tenneco merger transaction was closed on August 30. Old Kern shareholders thereupon became irrevocably entitled to receive Tenneco preference stock, share for share in exchange for their Old Kern stock. * * *

The option granted by Occidental on June 2, 1967, was exercised on December 11, 1967. Occidental, not having previously availed itself of its right, exchanged certificates representing 887,549 shares of Old Kern stock for a certificate representing a like number of shares of Tenneco preference stock. The certificate was then endorsed over to the optionee-purchaser, and in return $84,229,185 was credited to Occidental's accounts at various banks. Adding to this amount the $8,886,230 premium paid in June, Occidental received $93,905,415 for its Old Kern stock (including the 1,900 shares acquired prior to issuance of its tender offer). In addition, Occidental received dividends totaling $1,793,439.22. Occidental's total profit was $19,506,419.22 on the shares obtained through its tender offer.

On October 17, 1967, New Kern instituted a suit under § 16(b) against Occidental to recover the profits which Occidental had realized as a result of its dealings in Old Kern stock. The complaint alleged that the execution of the Occidental-Tenneco option on June 2, 1967, and the exchange of Old Kern shares for shares of Tenneco to which Occidental became entitled pursuant to the merger closed on August 30, 1967, were both "sales" within the coverage of § 16(b). Since both acts took place within six months of the date on which Occidental became the owner of more than 10% of the stock of Old Kern, New Kern asserted that § 16(b) required surrender of the profits realized by Occidental. New Kern eventually moved for summary judgment, and, on December 27, 1970, the District Court granted summary judgment in favor of New Kern. * * *

On appeal, the Court of Appeals reversed and ordered summary judgment entered in favor of Occidental. * * * We affirm.

II

* * *

Although traditional cash-for-stock transactions that result in a purchase and sale or a sale and purchase within the six-month, statutory period are clearly within the purview of § 16(b), the courts have wrestled with the question of inclusion or exclusion of certain "unorthodox" transactions. The statutory definitions of "purchase" and "sale" are broad and, at least arguably, reach many transactions not ordinarily deemed a sale or purchase. In deciding whether borderline transactions are within the reach of the statute, the courts have come to inquire whether the transaction may serve as a vehicle for the evil which Congress sought to prevent-the realization of short-swing profits based upon access to inside information-thereby endeavoring to implement congressional objectives without extending the reach of the statute beyond its intended limits. * * *

* * * We must decide * * * whether a "sale" within the ambit of the statute took place either when Occidental became irrevocably bound to exchange its shares of Old Kern for shares of Tenneco pursuant to the terms of the merger agreement between Old Kern and Tenneco or when Occidental gave an option to Tenneco to purchase from Occidental the Tenneco shares so acquired.

III

On August 30, 1967, the Old Kern-Tenneco merger agreement was signed, and Occidental became irrevocably entitled to exchange its shares of Old Kern stock for shares of Tenneco preference stock. Concededly, the transaction must be viewed as though Occidental had made the exchange on that day. But, even so, did the exchange involve a "sale" of Old Kern shares within the meaning of § 16(b)? We agree with the Court of Appeals that it did not, for we think it totally unrealistic to assume or infer from the facts before us that Occidental either had or was likely to have access to inside information, by reason of its ownership of more than 10% of the outstanding shares of Old Kern, so as to afford it an opportunity to reap speculative, short-swing profits from its disposition within six months of its tender-offer purchases.

* * *

It is also wide of the mark to assert that Occidental, as a sophisticated corporation knowledgeable in matters of corporate affairs and finance, knew that its tender offer would either succeed or would be met with a "defensive merger." If its takeover efforts failed, it is argued, Occidental knew it could sell its stock to the target company's merger partner at a substantial profit. Calculations of this sort, however, whether speculative or not and whether fair or unfair to other stockholders or to Old Kern, do not represent the kind of speculative abuse at which the statute is aimed, for they could not have been based on inside information obtained from substantial stockholdings that did not yet exist. * * *

* * *

The possibility that Occidental had, or had the opportunity to have, any confidential information about Old Kern * * * seems extremely remote. Occidental was, after all, a tender offeror, threatening to seize control of Old Kern, displace its management, and use the company for its own ends. * * *

There is, therefore, nothing in connection with Occidental's acquisition of Old Kern stock pursuant to its tender offer to indicate either the possibility of inside information being available to Occidental by virtue of its stock ownership or the potential for speculative abuse of such inside information by Occidental. Much the same can be said of the events leading to the exchange of Occidental's Old Kern stock for Tenneco preferred, which is one of the transactions that is sought to be classified a "sale" under § 16(b). The critical fact is that the exchange took place and was required pursuant to a merger between Old Kern and Tenneco. That merger was not engineered by Occidental but was sought by Old Kern to frustrate the attempts of Occidental to gain control of Old Kern. * * * The merger agreement was approved by a majority of the stockholders of Old Kern, excluding the votes to which Occidental was entitled by virtue of its ownership of Old Kern shares. Occidental, although registering its opinion that the merger would be beneficial to Old Kern shareholders, did not in fact vote at the stockholders' meeting at which merger approval was obtained. Under California law, its abstention was tantamount to a vote against approval of the merger. * * *

* * * We do not suggest that an exchange of stock pursuant to a merger may never result in § 16(b) liability. But the involuntary nature of Occidental's exchange, when coupled with the absence of the possibility of speculative abuse of inside information, convinces us that § 16(b) should not apply to transactions such as this one.

IV

Petitioner also claims that the Occidental-Tenneco option agreement should itself be considered a sale, either because it was the kind of transaction the statute was designed to prevent or because the agreement was an option in form but a sale in fact. But the mere execution of an option to sell is not generally regarded as a "sale." And we do not find in the execution of the Occidental-Tenneco option agreement a sufficient possibility for the speculative abuse of inside information with respect to Old Kern's affairs to warrant holding that the option agreement was itself a "sale" within the meaning of § 16(b).

The mutual advantages of the arrangement appear quite clear. As the District Court found, Occidental wanted to avoid the position of a minority stockholder with a huge investment in a company over which it had no control and in which it had not chosen to invest. On the other hand, Tenneco did not want a potentially troublesome minority stockholder that had just been vanquished in a fight for the control of Old Kern. Motivations like these do not smack of insider trading; and it is not clear to us, as it was not to the Court of Appeals, how the negotiation and execution of the option agreement gave Occidental any possible opportunity to trade on inside information it might have obtained from its position as a major stockholder of Old Kern. * * *

Neither does it appear that the option agreement, as drafted and executed by the parties, offered measurable possibilities for speculative abuse. What Occidental granted was a "call" option. Tenneco had the right to buy after six months, but Occidental could not force Tenneco to buy. * * * Thus, the option, by its very form, left Occidental with no choice but to sell if Tenneco exercised the option, which it was almost sure to do if the value of Tenneco stock remained relatively steady. On the other hand, it is difficult to perceive any speculative value to Occidental if the stock declined and Tenneco chose not to exercise its option.

* * *

Nor can we agree that we must reverse the Court of Appeals on the ground that the option agreement was in fact a sale because the premium paid was so large as to make the exercise of the option almost inevitable, particularly when coupled with Tenneco's desire to rid itself of a potentially troublesome stockholder. The argument has force, but resolution of the question is very much a matter of judgment, economic and otherwise, and the Court of Appeals rejected the argument. * * *

* * *

There are opinions that follow in the line of *Kern County,* but none is by the Supreme Court and none provides a conclusive test for determining when a court should engage in a subjective inquiry into the opportunity for speculative abuse that exists in a particular factual situation. What is clear is that such an inquiry likely will not occur in cases involving run-of-the-mill, straightforward purchases and sales, but may take place when a case involves transactions that: (1) are unorthodox and (2) are not viewed by a court as involving the real chance of speculative abuse.

An interesting twist in the issue of what constitutes a purchase or sale concerns so-called derivative securities. Not considering the exceptions, derivative securities are defined in Rule 16a–1(c) as "any option, warrant, convertible security, stock appreciation right, or similar right with an exercise or conversion privilege at a price related to an equity security, or similar securities with a value derived from the value of an equity security," so long as the exercise price is a fixed price. The twist is that, under Rule 16b–6, an increase or decrease in one's position in a derivative security is deemed to be a purchase or sale of the underlying equity security, so that, for example, the receipt of a stock option to buy a company's common stock is likely to be treated as a purchase of the common stock. A corollary is that the exercise or conversion of a derivative security generally is not considered to be a purchase of the underlying security. For the purposes of Section 16(b), then, the actual exercise of the usual stock option is a non-event. Courts have held that expiration of options[12] and pre-determined conversion price adjustments[13] also are non-events.

In the case of Analytical Surveys, Inc. v. Tonga Partners, L.P.,[14] the Second Circuit considered whether the exchange with the issuer of one promissory note convertible into equity for another such note with both fixed-price and floating-rate conversion components constituted a purchase of the second note. In ruling that it did (with respect to its fixed-price component), as well as that its subsequent conversion also was a purchase (with respect to the floating-rate component), the court rejected the defendants' arguments that (1) the events were "borderline" transactions eligible for exclusion under *Kern* and (2) that they qualified for the exception in 16(b) for securities purchased in good faith in connection with a debt previously contracted. Critical to the court's analysis was the fact that the new note extended the period during which inside information might play a role in the holder's decision-making.

IV. TIMING OF PURCHASES AND SALES

Section 16(b) contains the following provision on the issue of timing: "This subsection shall not be construed to cover any transaction where [a ten percent plus] beneficial owner was not such both at the time of the purchase and sale, or the sale and purchase * * * ." In general, this provision is clear enough. But the Supreme Court has decided two cases that deal with subtleties. These cases appear directly below.

Reliance Electric Co. v. Emerson Electric Co.

Supreme Court of the United States, 1972.
404 U.S. 418.

■ MR. JUSTICE STEWART delivered the opinion of the Court.

Section 16(b) of the Securities Exchange Act of 1934 provides, among other things, that a corporation may recover for itself the profits realized by an owner of more than 10% of its shares from a purchase and sale of its stock within any six-month period, provided that the owner held more

---

[12] Allaire Corp. v. Okumus, 433 F.3d 248 (2d Cir.2006).

[13] Morrison v. Madison Dearborn Capital Partners III, 389 F.Supp.2d 596 (D.Del.2005).

[14] 684 F.3d 36 (2d Cir.2012).

than 10% "both at the time of the purchase and sale." In this case, the respondent, the owner of 13.2% of a corporation's shares, disposed of its entire holdings in two sales, both of them within six months of purchase. The first sale reduced the respondent's holdings to 9.96%, and the second disposed of the remainder. The question presented is whether the profits derived from the second sale are recoverable by the Corporation under § 16(b). We hold that they are not.

I

On June 16, 1967, the respondent, Emerson Electric Co., acquired 13.2% of the outstanding common stock of Dodge Manufacturing Co., pursuant to a tender offer made in an unsuccessful attempt to take over Dodge. The purchase price for this stock was $63 per share. Shortly thereafter, the shareholders of Dodge approved a merger with the petitioner, Reliance Electric Co. Faced with the certain failure of any further attempt to take over Dodge, and with the prospect of being forced to exchange its Dodge shares for stock in the merged corporation in the near future, Emerson, following a plan outlined by its general counsel, decided to dispose of enough shares to bring its holdings below 10%, in order to immunize the disposal of the remainder of its shares from liability under § 16(b). Pursuant to counsel's recommendation, Emerson on August 28 sold 37,000 shares of Dodge common stock to a brokerage house at $68 per share. This sale reduced Emerson's holdings in Dodge to 9.96% of the outstanding common stock. The remaining shares were then sold to Dodge at $69 per share on September 11.

After a demand on it by Reliance for the profits realized on both sales, Emerson filed this action seeking a declaratory judgment as to its liability under § 16(b). * * *

* * * [T]he District Court held Emerson liable for the entire amount of its profits. The court found that Emerson's sales of Dodge stock were "effected pursuant to a single predetermined plan of disposition with the overall intent and purpose of avoiding Section 16(b) liability," and construed the term "time of * * * sale" to include "the entire period during which a series of related transactions take place pursuant to a plan by which a 10% beneficial owner disposes of his stock holdings".

On an interlocutory appeal * * * the Court of Appeals upheld the finding that Emerson "split" its sale of Dodge stock simply in order to avoid most of its potential liability under § 16(b), but it held this fact irrelevant under the statute so long as the two sales are "not legally tied to each other and [are] made at different times to different buyers * * * ." Accordingly, the Court of Appeals reversed the District Court's judgment as to Emerson's liability for its profits on the September 11 sale, and remanded for a determination of the amount of Emerson's liability on the August 28 sale. * * *

II

* * *

Among the "objective standards" contained in § 16(b) is the requirement that a 10% owner be such "both at the time of the purchase and sale * * * of the security involved." Read literally, this language clearly contemplates that a statutory insider might sell enough shares to bring his holdings below 10%, and later—but still within six months— sell additional shares free from liability under the statute. Indeed, commentators on the securities laws have recommended this exact procedure for a 10% owner who, like Emerson, wishes to dispose of his holdings within six months of their purchase.

Under the approach urged by Reliance, and adopted by the District Court, the apparent immunity of profits derived from Emerson's second sale is lost where the two sales, though independent in every other respect, are "interrelated parts of a single plan." But a "plan" to sell that is conceived within six months of purchase clearly would not fall within § 16(b) if the sale were made after the six months had expired, and we see no basis in the statute for a different result where the 10% requirement is involved rather than the six-month limitation.

* * *

The judgment is affirmed.

At least one district court case cautions that *Reliance Electric* should not be taken too far beyond its facts. In Reece Corp. v. Walco National Corp.,[15] the seller and the purchaser arranged to structure a bifurcated sales transaction to avoid Section 16(b) liability, obviously relying on *Reliance Electric*. The total shares to be sold amounted to 14.48 percent of an issuer's outstanding common stock. The parties entered into two separate sales agreements, signing and performing under the first agreement on one day and doing the same with the other agreement the next day. Partially to minimize profits on the first sale, which would inarguably come under Section 16(b), the parties set the price in this sale much lower than the average price for which the stock was to be sold in both transactions. Accordingly, they set the price for the shares involved in the second sale at higher than the average price. Although legally neither the purchaser nor the seller had to sign the second sales agreement after the completion of the first sale, the business realities were such that both parties wanted the second sale to follow the first as planned-the seller because of the high sales price in the second sale and the purchaser because of the inclusion in the second agreement of a covenant evidently much desired by it. In the ensuing Section 16(b) action, the district court refused to find that *Reliance Electric* protected the seller from disgorging profits on the second sale. After determining

---

[15] 565 F.Supp. 158 (S.D.N.Y.1983).

that the *Reliance Electric* holding "should be restricted closely to its facts," the court decided that "[t]he attempt to divide [the transaction] into two 'sales' was wholly artificial and contrived" and that there was, in substance, only one sale.

Foremost-McKesson, Inc. v.
Provident Securities Co.

Supreme Court of the United States, 1976.
423 U.S. 232.

■ MR. JUSTICE POWELL delivered the opinion of the Court.

This case presents an unresolved issue under § 16(b) of the Securities Exchange Act of 1934 (Act). * * * The question presented here is whether a person purchasing securities that put his holdings above the 10% level is a beneficial owner "at the time of the purchase" so that he must account for profits realized on a sale of those securities within six months. The United States Court of Appeals for the Ninth Circuit answered this question in the negative. We affirm.

I

Respondent, Provident Securities Co., was a personal holding company. In 1968 Provident decided tentatively to liquidate and dissolve, and it engaged an agent to find a purchaser for its assets. Petitioner, Foremost-McKesson, Inc., emerged as a potential purchaser * * * . * * *

* * * Provident and Foremost executed a purchase agreement * * * on September 25, 1969. The agreement provided that Foremost would buy two-thirds of Provident's assets for $4.25 million in cash and $49.75 million in Foremost convertible subordinated debentures. The agreement further provided that Foremost would register under the Securities Act of 1933 $25 million in principal amount of the debentures and would participate in an underwriting agreement by which those debentures would be sold to the public. At the closing on October 15, 1969, Foremost delivered to Provident the cash and a $40 million debenture which was subsequently exchanged for two debentures in the principal amounts of $25 million and $15 million. Foremost also delivered a $2.5 million debenture to an escrow agent on the closing date. On October 20 Foremost delivered to Provident a $7.25 million debenture representing the balance of the purchase price. These debentures were immediately convertible into more than 10% of Foremost's outstanding common stock.

On October 21 Provident, Foremost, and a group of underwriters executed an underwriting agreement to be closed on October 28. The agreement provided for sale to the underwriters of the $25 million debenture. On October 24 Provident distributed the $15 million and $7.25 million debentures to its stockholders, reducing the amount of Foremost common into which the company's holdings were convertible to less than 10%. On October 28 the closing under the underwriting agreement was accomplished. Provident thereafter distributed the cash proceeds of the debenture sale to its stockholders and dissolved.

Provident's holdings in Foremost debentures as of October 20 were large enough to make it a beneficial owner of Foremost within the meaning of § 16. Having acquired and disposed of these securities within six months, Provident faced the prospect of a suit by Foremost to recover any profits realized on the sale of the debenture to the underwriters. Provident therefore sued for a declaration that it was not liable to Foremost under § 16(b). The District Court granted summary judgment for Provident, and the Court of Appeals affirmed.

* * *

II

The meaning of the exemptive provision has been disputed since § 16(b) was first enacted. The discussion has focused on the application of the provision to a purchase-sale sequence, the principal disagreement being whether "at the time of the purchase" means "before the purchase" or "immediately after the purchase." The difference in construction is determinative of a beneficial owner's liability in cases such as Provident's where such owner sells within six months of purchase the securities the acquisition of which made him a beneficial owner. The commentators divided immediately over which construction Congress intended, and they remain divided. The Courts of Appeals also are in disagreement over the issue.

* * *

III

* * *

B

The exemptive provision, which applies only to beneficial owners and not to other statutory insiders, must have been included in § 16(b) for a purpose. Although the extensive legislative history of the Act is bereft of any explicit explanation of Congress' intent, the evolution of § 16(b) from its initial proposal through passage does shed significant light on the purpose of the exemptive provision.

* * *

Thomas G. Corcoran, a spokesman for S. 2693's drafters, explained § [16(b)] as forbidding an insider "to carry on any short-term specu[la]tions in the stock. He cannot, with his inside information get in and out of stock within six months." Hearings on H.R. 7852 and H.R. 8720 before the House Committee on Interstate and Foreign Commerce, 73d Cong., 2d Sess., 133 (1934). The Court of Appeals concluded that § [16(b)] of S. 2693 would have applied only to a beneficial owner who had that status before a purchase-sale sequence was initiated, and we agree. Foremost appears not to contest this point. The question thus becomes whether H.R. 8720's change in the language imposing liability and its addition of the exemptive provision were intended to change S. 2693's result in a purchase-sale sequence by a beneficial owner. We think the legislative history shows no such intent.

* * *

* * * We hold that, in a purchase-sale sequence, a beneficial owner must account for profits only if he was a beneficial owner "before the purchase."

IV

Additional considerations support our reading of the legislative history.

A

Section 16(b) imposes a strict prophylactic rule with respect to insider, short-swing trading. * * *

* * *

* * * Foremost recognizes the ambiguity of the exemptive provision, but argues that where "alternative constructions" of § 16(b)'s terms are available, we should choose the construction that best serves the statute's purposes. Foremost relies on statements generally to this effect in [Kern County Land Co. v. Occidental Petroleum Corp., 411 U.S. 582, 595 (1973)] and [Reliance Electric Co. v. Emerson Electric Co., 404 U.S. 418, 424 (1972)]. In neither of those cases, however, did the Court adopt the construction that would have imposed liability, thus recognizing that serving the congressional purpose does not require resolving every ambiguity in favor of liability under § 16(b). We reiterate that nothing suggests that the construction urged by Foremost would serve better to further congressional purposes. Indeed, the legislative history of § 16(b) indicates that by adding the exemptive provision Congress deliberately expressed a contrary choice. But even if the legislative record were more ambiguous, we would hesitate to adopt Foremost's construction. It is inappropriate to reach the harsh result of imposing § 16(b)'s liability without fault on the basis of unclear language. If Congress wishes to impose such liability, we must assume it will do so expressly or by unmistakable inference.

* * *

The holding in *Foremost-McKesson* has now been incorporated into Rule 16a–2(c).

The resolution of timing issues is somewhat different for officers and directors than for beneficial owners. As will be remembered, Section 16(b) provides that it does not "cover any transaction where [a ten percent plus] beneficial owner was not such both at the time of the purchase and sale, or the sale and purchase," but the statute is silent on timing issues in the case of officers and directors. The commission has filled the gap, however. In Rule 16a–2(a) it provides that transactions occurring before a person becomes an officer or director are not subject to Section 16 (except when an officer or director becomes subject to the section solely because his or her corporation has registered a class of equity securities under the Exchange Act). The story is different for transactions occurring after the termination of officer or director status. All such transactions are, under Rule 16a–2(b), subject to Section 16 if they can be matched, within the required six month period, with a purchase or sale that occurred when the person was an officer or director.

V. STANDING TO SUE AND THE STATUTE OF LIMITATIONS

On the subject of standing, Section 16(b) provides that a plaintiff must be the "owner of [a] security of the issuer" at the time suit is "instituted." In Gollust v. Mendell the Supreme Court decided an interesting issue concerning the meaning of that provision: Can a shareholder who has properly begun a Section 16 action maintain that action after the shareholder's stock has been exchanged for stock in the parent corporation as a result of a merger?

Gollust v. Mendell

Supreme Court of the United States, 1991.
501 U.S. 115.

■ JUSTICE SOUTER delivered the opinion of the Court.

* * *

* * * This case * * * requires us to address a plaintiff's standing under [Exchange Act] § 16(b) and, in particular, the requirements for continued standing after the institution of an action. We hold that a plaintiff, who properly "instituted [a § 16(b) action as] the owner of [a] security of the issuer," may continue to prosecute the action after his interest in the issuer is exchanged in a merger for stock in the issuer's new corporate parent.

I

In January 1987, respondent Ira L. Mendell filed a complaint under § 16(b) against petitioners in the United States District Court for the Southern District of New York, stating that he owned common stock in Viacom International, Inc. (International) and was suing on behalf of the corporation. He alleged that petitioners, a collection of limited partnerships, general partnerships, individual partners and corporations, "operated as a single unit" and were, for purposes of this litigation, a "single * * * beneficial owner of more than ten per centum of the common stock" of International. Respondent claimed that petitioners were liable to International under § 16(b) for approximately $11 million in profits earned by them from trading in International's common stock between July and October 1986. * * *

In June 1987, less than six months after respondent had filed his § 16(b) complaint, International was acquired by Arsenal Acquiring Corp., a shell corporation formed by Arsenal Holdings, Inc. (now named Viacom, Inc.) (Viacom) for the purpose of acquiring International. By the terms of the acquisition, Viacom's shell subsidiary was merged with International, which then became Viacom's wholly owned subsidiary and only asset. The stockholders of International received a combination of cash and stock in Viacom in exchange for their International stock.

As a result of the acquisition, respondent, who was a stockholder in International when he instituted this action, acquired stock in International's new parent corporation and sole stockholder, Viacom. Respondent amended his complaint to reflect the restructuring by claiming to prosecute the § 16(b) action on behalf of Viacom as well as International.

Following the merger, petitioners moved for summary judgment, arguing that respondent had lost standing to maintain the action when the exchange of stock and cash occurred, after which respondent no longer owned any security of International, the "issuer." The District Court held that § 16(b) actions "may be prosecuted only by the issuer itself or the holders of its securities," and granted the motion because respondent no longer owned any International stock. The court concluded that only Viacom, as International's sole security holder, could continue to prosecute this action against petitioners.

A divided Court of Appeals reversed. * * *

* * *

We granted certiorari * * * to determine whether a stockholder who has properly instituted a § 16(b) action to recover profits from a corporation's insiders may continue to prosecute that action after a merger involving the issuer results in exchanging the stockholder's interest in the issuer for stock in the issuer's new corporate parent.

II

A

* * *

* * * We begin with the text [of § 16(b)]. * * *

* * *

* * * The only textual restrictions on the standing of a party to bring suit under § 16(b) are that the plaintiff must be the "owner of [a] security" of the "issuer" at the time the suit is "instituted."

Although plaintiffs seeking to sue under the statute must own a "security," § 16(b) places no significant restriction on the type of security adequate to confer standing. * * * Nor is there any restriction in terms of either the number or percentage of shares, or the value of any other security, that must be held. In fact, the terms of the statute do not even require that the security owner have had an interest in the issuer at the time of the defendant's short-swing trading, and the courts to have addressed this issue have held that a subsequent purchaser of the issuer's securities has standing to sue for prior short-swing trading.

The second requirement for § 16(b) standing is that the plaintiff own a security of the "issuer" whose stock was traded by the insider defendant. An "issuer" of a security is defined under § 3(a)(8) of the 1934 Act as the corporation that actually issued the security, and does not include parent or subsidiary corporations. While this requirement is strict on its face, it is ostensibly subject to mitigation in the final requirement for § 16(b) standing, which is merely that the plaintiff own a security of the issuer at the time the § 16(b) action is "instituted." Today, as in 1934, the word "institute" is commonly understood to mean "inaugurate or commence; as to institute an action." Black's Law Dictionary 985–986 (3d ed. 1933) (citing cases). Congressional intent to adopt this common understanding is confirmed by Congress' use of the same word elsewhere to mean the commencement of an action. See, e.g., 8 U.S.C. § 1503(a) ("action * * * may be instituted only within five years after * * * final administrative denial"); 42 U.S.C. § 405(g) ("Any action instituted in accordance with this subsection shall survive notwithstanding any change in the person occupying the office of Secretary or any vacancy in such office").

The terms of § 16(b), read in context, thus provide standing of signal breadth, expressly limited only by conditions existing at the time an action is begun. Petitioners contend, however, that the statute should at least be read narrowly enough to require the plaintiff owning a "security" of the "issuer" at the time the action is "instituted" to maintain ownership of the issuer's security throughout the period of his participation in the litigation. But no such "continuous ownership requirement," is found in the text of the statute, nor does § 16(b)'s legislative history reveal any congressional intent to impose one.

This is not to say, of course, that a § 16(b) action could be maintained by someone who is subsequently divested of any interest in the outcome of the litigation. Congress clearly intended to put "a private-profit motive behind the uncovering of this kind of leakage of information, [by making] the stockholders [its] policemen." Hearings on H.R. 7852 and H.R. 8720 before the House Committee on Interstate and Foreign Commerce, 73d Cong., 2d Sess., 136 (1934) (testimony of Thomas G. Corcoran). The sparse legislative history on this question, which consists primarily of hearing testimony by one of the 1934 Act's drafters, merely confirms this conclusion.

Congress must, indeed, have assumed any plaintiff would maintain some continuing financial stake in the litigation for a further reason as well. For if a security holder were allowed to maintain a § 16(b) action after he had lost any financial interest in its outcome, there would be serious constitutional doubt whether that plaintiff could demonstrate the standing required by Article III's case or controversy limitation on federal court jurisdiction. * * *

Hence, we have no difficulty concluding that, in the enactment of § 16(b), Congress understood and intended that, throughout the period of his participation, a plaintiff authorized to sue insiders on behalf of an issuer would have some continuing financial interest in the outcome of the litigation, both for the sake of furthering the statute's remedial purposes by ensuring that enforcing parties maintain the incentive to litigate vigorously, and to avoid the serious constitutional question that would arise from a plaintiff's loss of all financial interest in the outcome of the litigation he had begun.

B

The conclusion that § 16(b) requires a plaintiff security holder to maintain some financial interest in the outcome of the litigation does not, however, tell us whether an adequate financial stake can be maintained when the plaintiff's interest in the issuer has been replaced by one in the issuer's new parent. We think it can be.

The modest financial stake in an issuer sufficient to bring suit is not necessarily greater than an interest in the original issuer represented by equity ownership in the issuer's parent corporation. A security holder eligible to institute suit will have no direct financial interest in the outcome of the litigation, since any recovery will inure only to the issuer's benefit. Yet the indirect interest derived through one share of stock is enough to confer standing, however slight the potential marginal increase in the value of the share. A bondholder's sufficient financial interest may be even more attenuated, since any recovery by the issuer will increase the value of the bond only because the issuer may become a slightly better credit risk.

Thus, it is difficult to see how such a bondholder plaintiff, for example, is likely to have a more significant stake in the outcome of a § 16(b) action than a stockholder in a company whose only asset is the issuer. Because such a bondholder's attenuated financial stake is nonetheless sufficient to satisfy the statute's initial standing requirements, the stake of a parent company stockholder like respondent should be enough to meet the requirements for continued standing, so long as that is consistent with the text of the statute. It is consistent, of course, and in light of the congressional policy of lenient standing, we will not read any further condition into the statute, beyond the requirement that a § 16(b) plaintiff maintain a financial interest in the outcome of the litigation sufficient to motivate its prosecution and avoid constitutional standing difficulties.

III

In this case, respondent has satisfied the statute's requirements. He owned a "security" of the "issuer" at the time he "instituted" this § 16(b) action. In the aftermath of International's restructuring, he retains a continuing financial interest in the outcome of the litigation derived from his stock in International's sole stockholder, Viacom, whose only asset is International. Through these relationships, respondent still stands to profit, albeit indirectly, if this action is successful, just as he would have done if his original shares had not been exchanged for stock in Viacom. Although a calculation of the values of the respective interests in International that respondent held as its stockholder and holds now as a Viacom stockholder is not before us, his financial interest is actually no less real than before the merger and apparently no more attenuated than the interest of a bondholder might be in a § 16(b) suit on an issuer's behalf.

The judgment of the Court of Appeals is, accordingly, affirmed.

An interesting, but unsuccessful, argument that a plaintiff shareholder suing under Section 16(b) must allege injury in fact in order to satisfy constitutional standing requirements was addressed by the Second Circuit in Donoghue v. Bulldog Investors General Partnership.[16] The court held that short-swing trading in an issuer's stock by a 10% beneficial owner causes injury to the issuer sufficient to confer constitutional standing on a shareholder suing on the issuer's behalf. The reasoning turned on the court's view that Section 16(b) created a right for an issuer to expect insiders to refrain from engaging in short-swing trading.

Somewhat related to the issue of standing is the question of whether the plaintiff has filed within the two-year period stated in the statute. In 2012, in the case of Credit Suisse Securities LLC v. Simmonds,[17] the Supreme Court split four to four on the issue of whether Section 16(b)'s two-year statute of limitations was subject to equitable tolling, but unanimously ruled that the limitations period begins to run on the date profit is realized—which is a literal reading of the statute.

VI. CALCULATION OF PROFITS

Section 16(b) provides no guidance on how to calculate profits. The leading case is Smolowe v. Delendo, decided by the Second Circuit in 1943.

---

[16]   696 F.3d 170 (2d Cir. 2012).

[17]   132 S.Ct. 1414 (2012).

Smolowe v. Delendo Corp.

United States Court of Appeals, Second Circuit, 1943.
136 F.2d 231.

■ Before SWAN, CHASE, and CLARK, CIRCUIT JUDGES.

■ CLARK, CIRCUIT JUDGE.

The issue on appeal is * * * the construction * * * of § 16(b) of the Securities Exchange Act of 1934, rendering directors, officers, and principal stockholders liable to their corporation for profits realized from security tradings within any six months' period. * * *

* * *

The controversy as to the construction of the statute involves * * * the method of computing "such profit." * * *

* * *

* * * [The defendants urge that] profits should be computed according to the established income tax rule which first looks to the identification of the stock certificate, and if that is not established, then applies the presumption which is hardly more than a rule of administrative convenience of "first in, first out." * * *

* * *

Defendants seek support for their position from the Senate hearings, where, in answer to Senator Barkley's comment, "All these transactions are a matter of record. It seems to me the simple way would be to charge him with the actual profit," [Thomas] Corcoran [, chief spokesman for the drafters and proponents of the Exchange Act,] responded: "It is the same provision you have in the income tax law. Unless you can prove the actual relationship between certificates, you take the highest price sold and the lowest price bought." This was an incorrect statement of the income tax law. The rule there is first in, first out, regardless of price, wherever the stock actually purchased and sold is not identifiable. But this does show the rule the proponents had in mind, even though its source is erroneously stated. Analysis will show that the income tax rules cannot apply without defeating the law almost completely. Under the basic rule of identifying the stock certificate, the large stockholder, who in most cases is also an officer or director, could speculate in long sales with impunity merely by reason of having a reserve of stock and upon carefully choosing his stock certificates for delivery upon his sales from this reserve. Moreover, his profits from any sale followed by a purchase would be practically untouchable, for the principle of identity admits of no gain without laboring proof of a subjective intent—always a nebulous issue— to effectuate the connected phases of this type of transaction. In consequence the statute would be substantially emasculated. We cannot ascribe to it a meaning so inconsistent with its declared purpose.

Once the principle of identity is rejected, its corollary, the first-in, first-out rule, is left at loose ends. At best it is a rule of convenience designed originally to hit marginal trading without shares in hand and supplementing the principle of identity. Its rationalization is the same as that for the identification rule, for which it operates as a presumptive principle; and it has no other support. If we reject one, we reject the other and for like reasons. Its application would render the large stockholder with a backlog of stock not immediately devoted to trading immune from the Act. Further, we should note that it does not fit the broad statutory language; a purchase followed immediately by a sale, albeit a transaction within the exact statutory language, would often be held immune from the statutory penalty because the purchase would be deemed by arbitrary rule to have been made at an earlier date; while a sale followed by purchase would never even be within the terms of the rule. We must look elsewhere for an answer to our problem of finding a reasonable and workable interpretation of the statute in the light of its admitted purpose.

Another possibility might be the striking of an average purchase price and an average sale price during the period, and using these as bases of computation. What this rule would do in concrete effect is to allow as offsets all losses made by such trading. This in effect the district court first planned to do * * * . But it corrected this in its supplemental opinion, properly pointing out that the statute provided for the recovery of "any" profit realized and obviously precluded a setting off of losses. Even had the statutory language been more uncertain, this rule seems one not to be favored in the light of the statutory purpose. Compared to other possible rules, it tends to stimulate more active trading by reducing the chance of penalty * * * . * * *

The statute is broadly remedial. Recovery runs not to the stockholder, but to the corporation. We must suppose that the statute was intended to be thoroughgoing, to squeeze all possible profits out of stock transactions, and thus to establish a standard so high as to prevent any conflict between the selfish interest of a fiduciary officer, director, or stockholder and the faithful performance of his duty. The only rule whereby all possible profits can be surely recovered is that of lowest price in, highest price out—within six months—as applied by the district court. We affirm it here, defendants having failed to suggest another more reasonable rule.

* * *

Although at first glance the profit calculation formulation of *Smolowe* seems simple enough, there are two aspects of profit calculation with which newcomers to Section 16(b) often have trouble. The first is that transactions are broken down into whatever components are necessary to effect a matching that maximizes profits—share by share if necessary. For example, one purchase of 100 shares will be matched with 100 sales of one share each if that leads to the greatest profits. Second, the matchings for a multi-share transaction that is broken into components can cover a period of just short of one year, not slightly less than six months. The only requirement is that, in each individual matching, the purchase and sale must be within six months of each other. For example, in the case of a 100 share sale on July 1, 50 shares involved in a matching could have been purchased on February 1 and 50 on November 1, even though February and November are more than six months apart.

B. BLACKOUT TRADING AND THE SARBANES-OXLEY ACT

Section 306 of Sarbanes-Oxley provides that, except as allowed by limited Commission rulemaking:

> [I]t shall be unlawful for any director or executive officer of an issuer of any equity security (other than an exempted security), directly or indirectly, to purchase, sell, or otherwise acquire or transfer any equity security of the issuer (other than an exempted security) during any blackout period with respect to such equity security if such director of officer acquires such equity security in connection with his or her service or employment as a director or executive officer.

"Blackout period" is defined in detail. Basically the definition relates to periods during which ordinary beneficiaries of pension plans may not trade an issuer's securities. The section also contains much detail with respect to, among other things, notices required to be given of blackout periods. One remedy provided by Section 306 is disgorgement of profits and, as in the case of Section 16(b), shareholders may sue to recover these profits, for the benefit of the issuer, in specified circumstances. In Exchange Act Release No. 34–47225 (Jan. 22, 2003), the Commission issued Regulation BTR, containing clarifying rules.

Note an extremely important difference between Section 306 and Exchange Act Section 16(b). Is not unlawful to engage in short-swing trading under Section 16(b)—the profits are merely to be disgorged to the issuer. Trading in violation of Section 306, on the other hand, is unlawful. Therefore, in addition to disgorgement, traders are subject to criminal sanctions as well as non-criminal actions by the Commission.

CHAPTER 15

MARKET MANIPULATION AND STABILIZATION

SITUATION 15

Assume you are back at the time of the Microtec public offering and that officers of Nielson Securities Co., the managing underwriter, inform Microtec that Nielson will stabilize the market price of Microtec's common stock during the period it is being distributed. This will be done by purchasing, at the public offering price, any shares that are offered for sale in the over-the-counter market.

Nielson officers also assure Microtec that after the offering Nielson intends to make a market in Microtec's common stock. Thereby, they say, Nielson will be able to support the price of the stock and prevent "wild swings" in its price.

Then assume you are at a time when the price of Microtec's stock is still near its low of $7, but that profits have increased to the point that Microtec has fairly substantial cash available for use in the business. Microtec's officers believe the stock price is substantially lower than it should be and that a good way to use Microtec's cash is to purchase Microtec shares from the public and hold them in treasury. This, they believe, will boost the stock's price.

In considering this situation, refer to the following, in addition to materials in this chapter: Exchange Act Sections 9, 10(b), and 15(c)(1) and (2), and Exchange Act Rule 10b–18 and Rule 104 of Regulation M.

A. MARKET MANIPULATION

The Exchange Act and its rules provide a comprehensive scheme for the regulation of activities that disrupt the free movement of securities prices in accordance with supply and demand. Because of an historical anomaly, Section 9 of the Act, which is entitled "Prohibition Against Manipulation of Security Prices," long dealt only with securities listed on securities exchanges. So as not to leave the manipulation of securities prices in the over-the-counter market unchecked, the federal courts pressed into service two general antifraud provisions, Securities Act Section 17(a) and Exchange Act Rule 10b–5. Exchange Act Sections 15(c)(1) and (2) also help prohibit manipulation in the over-the-counter market. Basically, the prohibitions against market manipulation ended up being the same irrespective of the market involved. The anomaly was addressed, however, in 2010, when Section 9 was amended to include not only securities not registered on an exchange but also security-based swaps (security-based swap agreements already were included).

Section 9 contains a number of prohibitions. The one at the heart of market manipulation is found in Section 9(a)(2), which makes it unlawful for any person:

> To effect, alone or with one or more other persons, a series of transactions in any security registered on a national securities exchange, any security not so registered, or in connection with any security-based swap or security-based swap agreement with respect to such security creating actual or apparent active trading in such security or raising or depressing the price of such security, for the purpose of inducing the purchase or sale of such security by others.

Although this prohibition relates to any person, and not only to those in the securities business, those in the securities business find the temptation of market manipulation closest at hand. The following case tells one of the more interesting stories of classic market manipulation by securities professionals.

SEC v. Resch-Cassin & Co.

United States District Court, Southern District of New York, 1973.
362 F.Supp. 964.

■ TENNEY, DISTRICT JUDGE.

Plaintiff, Securities and Exchange Commission (hereinafter the "Commission"), has applied for a permanent injunction enjoining Nagler-Weissman & Co., Inc. (hereinafter "Nagler-Weissman"), Robert Nagler (hereinafter "Nagler"), Adolph Weissman (hereinafter "Weissman") and Maxwell Forster (hereinafter "Forster") from further violations of the anti-fraud and anti-manipulation provisions of the Securities Act of 1933 (hereinafter "Securities Act") and the Securities Exchange Act of 1934 (hereinafter "Exchange Act"). The background of this litigation is the public offering of the stock of Africa, U.S.A., Inc. (hereinafter "Africa").

* * *

It appears that in the summer of 1970, Africa, a Delaware corporation located in Fillmore, California, registered 150,000 shares of its stock with the Commission for sale to the public at $10 per share on a "best efforts, all or none" basis. The underwriter for the offering was Resch-Cassin & Co., Inc. (hereinafter "Resch-Cassin"). * * * The principal inducement employed by Resch-Cassin in building interest in the stock focused on the anticipated after-market price. For example, Solon Patterson of the Alpha Fund of Atlanta, Georgia, which purchased 10,000 shares, was told both orally and in writing by defendant George Resch, Jr. (hereinafter "Resch") that the after-market price was expected to be well over $20 per share and [Alpha Fund] increased its order on the basis of this representation; Irby Bright, vice president of the First American National Bank in Nashville, Tennessee, which also purchased 10,000 shares, was told by defendant Michael Cassin (hereinafter "Cassin") that the after-market price would be at least $22 per share.

On Friday, October 23, 1970, trading commenced in Africa stock. Resch-Cassin, however, was having severe difficulty in completing the underwriting. * * *

It was, of course, crucial to Resch-Cassin that the after-market open at a premium in order to fulfill the promises made to Bright and Patterson and in order to induce purchasers * * * to buy the unsold portion of the issue. * * * In order to establish the price at the desired level, on Friday, October 23, 1970, Resch asked Peter Lewitin (hereinafter "Lewitin"), a trader at Smith, Jackson & Co., Inc. (hereinafter "Smith Jackson"), to trade the Africa stock, and Resch-Cassin gave Lewitin an order to buy 3,000 shares at $20 per share. As a result of this order, Lewitin made his "pink sheets"[1] market at $18 bid and $21 asked. At the same time other brokers were also trading in Africa stock. Among these were Mandelbaum Securities (hereinafter "Mandelbaum") and A.P. Montgomery & Co., Inc (hereinafter "Montgomery"). The trader at Mandelbaum, Jeffrey Greenstein (hereinafter "Greenstein"), learned about Africa stock from Lewitin and, after meeting with Resch and Cassin, decided to trade. At approximately noon on October 23, 1970, Greenstein received a call from Lewitin who informed him that the stock was "ready for trading" and that his market was $18–$21 by reason of the buy order for 3,000 shares at $20 referred to above. Lewitin also informed Greenstein that Greenstein could sell him at $19³/₄ any stock he was able to purchase. Therefore, Greenstein's opening quote for Africa was also $18–$21.

During the first day of trading, October 23, 1970, both Lewitin (Smith Jackson) and Greenstein (Mandelbaum) received only sell orders for Africa stock. As a result of large sell orders and lack of demand for Africa stock, they both continued to buy Africa stock, each time lowering their market, so that Lewitin quoted the stock as low as $14 bid, and Greenstein bought stock at as low as $14. Although Lewitin had limited experience he realized that there was something wrong with the way the stock was trading, and discontinued his efforts after only a half-hour or forty-five minutes, during which time the bid price had dropped from $18 to $14. * * * Since [his firm] was supplying most, if not all, of the demand for Africa stock, Lewitin's decision to stop trading the issue, together with the absence of any other demand, caused the market for the stock to

---

[1] Most brokers and dealers [at the time] subscribe[d] to the service of the National Quotation Bureau, Inc., a private organization which publishe[d] and circulate[d] each day among its subscribers loose-leaf sheets, "pink sheets", which contain quotations as to over-the-counter securities inserted for that day by subscribers. ["Pink sheets" is now an online publication by the OTC Market Group, the successor (after multiple name changes) to the National Quotation Bureau, Inc.]

collapse; by the close of the market on Friday, October 23, 1970, it was selling at the $11 level.

On Tuesday morning, October 27, 1970, the pink sheets reflected prices of $9$1/2$ to $11 and $9 to $12 with only two market-makers in the sheets. Unless Resch-Cassin wanted to abandon the Africa underwriting and return whatever funds had been raised to the subscribers, a trader had to be found who could establish and maintain the price of Africa stock at a sufficient premium to induce the public to purchase the unsold portion of the issue at the $10 offering price stated in the prospectus. Therefore, on either Monday, October 26, or Tuesday, October 27, Resch approached defendant Forster, the trader for Nagler-Weissman, and asked him if Nagler-Weissman would become a market-maker in the Africa stock [, and the firm agreed.]

Resch followed the same pattern he had with Smith Jackson by giving Nagler-Weissman a purchase order on October 27, 1970, this time for 1,000 shares of Africa stock for the account of Elsie Himes, a customer of Resch-Cassin. In fact, Mrs. Himes had ordered only 500 shares from Resch-Cassin. Resch-Cassin turned this customer order over to Nagler-Weissman and gave up the commission. With this order, Forster (Nagler-Weissman) could go into the market to buy Africa stock.

Starting at 1:14 P.M. on October 27, 1970, Forster made his first trade in Africa stock, purchasing 100 shares at $11 from Associated Investors. Following this transaction, he continued to buy the stock and between 1:16 P.M. and 1:50 P.M. he purchased 900 additional shares at prices ranging from $11$1/2$ to $16, the final price. Thus he moved the price from $11 to $16 in 34 minutes. All but 300 shares of the 1,000 were purchased from Montgomery, Forster always purchasing at the price offered by Montgomery without attempting to negotiate a better price. * * *

* * * On October 28, * * * Nagler-Weissman appeared for the first time in the pink sheets on Africa stock with a quote of $15–$17. * * * Although Nagler-Weissman's bid price for Africa stock was $15, the highest price it paid on this date was $14 a share. * * * despite the fact that Nagler-Weissman was the high bidder on October 28 and 29, it made no sales of Africa to anyone on these days. During the five trading days from October 30 through November 5, Nagler-Weissman was the high bidder on each day in the pink sheets on Africa stock, and on each day that it traded during that period the high price that it paid was below its quoted bid price.

* * *

Despite the "activity" created by Forster (Nagler-Weissman) there was, in fact, a lack of interest in purchasing Africa stock both by the public and by other broker-dealers throughout October, November and December, 1970. * * *

Yet, during this period the stock traded at a premium, never falling below the $10 offering price. * * *

* * *

[The sales to the public in the "best efforts, all or none," underwriting through Resch-Cassin were closed on November 23, 1970.] By December 14, the stock was trading at the $4 level.

* * *

Section 10(b) of the Exchange Act makes it unlawful for any person, by the use of interstate commerce or of the mails:

"To use or employ, in connection with the purchase or sale of any security registered on a national securities exchange or any security not so registered, *any* manipulative or deceptive device or contrivance. * * * " (Emphasis added.)

This prohibition with respect to manipulative activity is not confined to any particular kind of manipulation, but as more specifically defined in Rule 10b–5 is necessarily designed to outlaw every device "used to persuade the public that activity in a security is the reflection of a genuine demand instead of a mirage." 3 Loss, Securities Regulation, 1549–55 (2d ed. 1961). The Exchange Act does contain a section entitled "Manipulation of security prices", however, which defines "manipulation". This section, § 9(a)(2) of the Exchange Act, makes it unlawful to use the facility of a national securities exchange:

"To effect, alone or with one or more other persons, a series of transactions in any security registered on a national securities exchange *creating actual or apparent active trading in such security or raising or depressing the price of such security, for the purpose of inducing the purchase or sale of such security by others."* (Emphasis added.)

It is well settled that the manipulative activities expressly prohibited by § 9(a)(2) of the Exchange Act with respect to a listed security are also violations of § 17(a) of the Securities Act and § 10(b) of the Exchange Act when the same activities are conducted with respect to an over-the-counter security.

* * *

* * * There are various factors which characterize attempts by manipulators to raise the price of an over-the-counter security: (a) price leadership by the manipulator; (b) dominion and control of the market for the security; (c) reduction in the floating supply of the security; and (d) the collapse of the market for the security when the manipulator ceases his activity. * * *

* * *

All the classic elements of an over-the-counter manipulation are present in the instant case. The defendants presently before this Court engaged in a series of transactions in the common stock of Africa which created actual and apparent trading in, and raised the price of, that stock for the purpose of inducing its purchase by others. The apparent and actual trading was achieved with advancing pink sheet quotes, inducement of other brokers to enter quotes, and actual purchases. The price rise was effected by Nagler-Weissman's dominion and control of the market in the stock and total price leadership in both the sheets and actual purchase, as further evidenced by the virtual collapse of the market in the stock following the manipulation. The natural consequence of this course of conduct was to artificially stimulate the so-called market price of the stock while making it appear to be the product of the independent forces of supply and demand when, in reality, it was completely a creature of defendants' subterfuge. * * *

* * *

Unsurprisingly, the internet has created more-or-less endless opportunities for market manipulation. The Commission has, in recent years, brought charges against the perpetrators of a variety of schemes, including fraudulent tweeting, fraudulent chatboard posting, and engaging in high-speed algorithmic trading intended to influence a security's closing price. Section 10(b) and Rule 10b–5 are the most frequently cited sources of authority.

The Commission has long recognized that repurchases by issuers of their own securities involve the real possibility of market manipulation. But recognizing this problem has been one thing, and deciding what to do about it has been quite another. The following release first relates the Commission's years-long struggle over issuer repurchases and then outlines the Commission's current response to them: Rule 10b–18. Although in 2010 the Commission proposed[2] certain amendments modernizing and clarifying the rule the amendments have not yet been adopted. They would not, in any event, affect the description below.

Securities Exchange Act Release No. 19244

Securities and Exchange Commission, November 17, 1982.

PURCHASES OF CERTAIN EQUITY SECURITIES BY THE ISSUER

* * *

The Commission has considered on several occasions since 1967 the issue of whether to regulate an issuer's repurchases of its own securities. The predicates for this effort have been twofold: first, investors and particularly the issuer's shareholders should be able to rely on a market that is set by independent market forces and not influenced in any

---

[2]   Exchange Act Release 34–61414 (Jan. 25, 2010).

manipulative manner by the issuer or persons closely related to the issuer. Second, since the general language of the anti-manipulative provisions of the federal securities laws offers little guidance with respect to the scope of permissible issuer market behavior, certainty with respect to the potential liabilities for issuers engaged in repurchase programs has seemed desirable.

The most recent phase of this proceeding is proposed Rule 13e–2 which was published for public comment on October 17, 1980. This rule would have imposed disclosure requirements and substantive purchasing limitations on an issuer's repurchases of its common and preferred stock. * * *

The Commission has recognized that issuer repurchase programs are seldom undertaken with improper intent, may frequently be of substantial economic benefit to investors, and, that, in any event, undue restriction of these programs is not in the interest of investors, issuers, or the marketplace. Issuers generally engage in repurchase programs for legitimate business reasons and any rule in this area must not be overly intrusive. Accordingly, the Commission has endeavored to achieve an appropriate balance between the goals described above and the need to avoid complex and costly restrictions that impinge on the operation of issuer repurchase programs.

In light of these considerations, and based on the extensive public files developed in this proceeding, the Commission has determined that it is not necessary to adopt a mandatory rule to regulate issuer repurchases. * * * In lieu of direct regulation * * * , the Commission has determined that a safe harbor is the appropriate regulatory approach to offer guidance concerning the applicability of the anti-manipulative provisions of Rule 10b–5 and Section 9(a)(2) to issuer repurchase programs. New Rule 10b–18 reflects this determination.

The Commission wishes to stress, however, that the safe harbor is not mandatory nor the exclusive means of effecting issuer purchases without manipulating the market. As a safe harbor, new Rule 10b–18 will provide clarity and certainty for issuers and broker-dealers who assist issuers in their repurchase programs. If an issuer effects its repurchases in compliance with the conditions of the rule, it will avoid what might otherwise be substantial and unpredictable risks of liability under the general anti-manipulative provisions of the federal securities laws. * * *

* * * [T]he safe harbor is not the exclusive means by which issuers and their affiliated purchasers may effect purchases of the issuer's stock in the marketplace. Given the greatly varying characteristics of the markets for the stock of different issuers, there may be circumstances under which an issuer could effect repurchases outside of the guidelines that would not raise manipulative concerns. This is especially the case in the context of the uniform volume guidelines, which cannot easily reflect those varying market characteristics. * * *

* * *

There are, moreover, a number of Commission rules adopted to combat market manipulation: Regulation M contains several anti-manipulation rules. For instance, Rule 105, part of Regulation M, bars most short sellers who sell in a defined period immediately prior to the pricing of a public offering from purchasing shares during that public offering.

B. STABILIZATION

In light of the Exchange Act's strong general prohibition of market manipulation, it is interesting that one activity that is clearly manipulative—stabilization—is specifically allowed by the Exchange Act. The following release is the Commission's primary explanation of why this is so. Before turning to this release, however, it will be helpful to know what stabilization is and how it works. Essentially, stabilization is the purchasing in the trading markets of a security, by underwriters who are trying to distribute securities of the same class, for the purpose of preventing a decline in the market price of the security.

How stabilization works is most easily seen in the case of a class of securities that are already publicly traded when the issuer wants to sell additional securities of the same class in an offering registered under the Securities Act. As a practical matter, the underwriters must offer the new securities to the public at essentially the same price at which securities of the class were trading just prior to the time the registration statement became effective, that is, at the market price. More importantly, the underwriters have to pay the issuer a price that is just far enough below the market price to allow the underwriters a fair profit when the securities are sold at the market price.

The problem for the underwriters is that the market price might drop if the usual market forces of supply and demand were allowed free rein during the period when the underwriters are selling the new securities. If the market price were to drop, the underwriters could not sell their securities without lowering their offering price. In the long run, of course, underwriters would refuse to take the risks involved in this type of underwriting, at least without additional compensation. During the period underwriters are distributing an offering of securities, however, the forces of supply and demand are not allowed to run free. Rather, the underwriters are allowed, under Exchange Act Section 9(a)(6) and Rule 104 of Regulation M, to stabilize the market price for the class of securities they are selling.

Rule 104 is filled with detailed requirements and limitations. Basically, it allows underwriters to buy in the trading markets, at prices allowed by the Rule, any securities of the same class as those being underwritten. Typically stabilizing is maintained until the offering is completed. This process usually takes one or two days, but an offering sometimes drags on for much longer. It is important to remember that, during the entire time stabilizing goes on, the price of the securities that are stabilized is artificially maintained-that is, the price is manipulated.

Exchange Act Release No. 2446
Securities and Exchange Commission, March 18, 1940.

PEGGING, FIXING AND STABILIZING SECURITY PRICES

A. The Problem

Although the Securities Exchange Act contains a general prohibition against manipulating security prices up or down, it does not prohibit certain kinds of manipulation. Thus, Section 9(a)(6) permits the "pegging, fixing or stabilizing" of security prices, except to the extent that it may be "in contravention of such rules and regulations as the Commission may prescribe as necessary or appropriate in the public interest or for the protection of investors." * * *

* * *

C. Disadvantages of Stabilizing

* * * The oft-repeated and, in our opinion, wholly justified complaint against security stabilizing is that when the operation is ended and the "peg is pulled", the market price of the security frequently drops with ensuing loss to all who purchased it on the basis of an artificial, "pegged" market price. Insofar as stabilization prevents falling market prices and thus permits the issuance of securities at unjustifiably high prices, the practice must be regarded as an evil. * * *

* * *

[Also,] it should be noted that many people feel that stabilizing not only is fraudulent, but that its attendant evil of the over-pricing of security issues is inherent. They believe that *no* regulation short of complete prohibition can protect buyers against these dangers which arise from a deceptive and an artificial market. And they conclude that buyers should receive the ultimate protection of complete prohibition, regardless of the adverse effects which prohibition might have on the needs of industry for capital.

D. The Underwriter's Arguments in Justification of Stabilization

Without adopting the reasons frequently advanced to justify the widespread use of stabilizing in aid of security distributions we may restate the arguments as follows:

One argument runs that stabilization is warranted in order to offset the market "abnormalities" which result from the very fact of the offering. When a new or an additional issue of significant size is offered to the public a temporary glut of the market may often be the immediate result. * * * Therefore, the underwriters urge that stabilizing, although admittedly an artificial influence, is justified to neutralize a temporary condition of over-supply which itself may likewise be regarded as abnormal, and that temporary stabilizing controls, commensurate with the degree of the temporary abnormal disparity between supply and demand, are warranted to offset that unbalanced condition of the market.

Another argument is based upon the underwriter's view that it is appropriate and desirable for a seller to permit a buyer to return his securities if he so desires. * * * Dealers or underwriters in one section of the country may overestimate local demand just as investors may overestimate their own ability to carry a security. At the same time others may have been unable to fill their demand. It is consequently desirable, say the underwriters, that they should be permitted to repurchase and reallocate to others the securities of those who bought more than they can handle. * * *

The third argument is based upon the necessities of the situation. * * * Since underwriters today are primarily salesmen having only the limited capital of distributors, they claim that they cannot undertake long or even medium term commitments in order to insure the success of billions of dollars of security offerings. If an entire issue of securities is to be bought by such underwriters at a fixed price, it is said to be virtually necessary that those underwriters be able to protect themselves as well as the selling group dealers, against a "disorderly" open market during the resale of the issue to the public. This is said to follow because if the market price of a new issue sags even fractionally below the offering price, it cannot be sold at the offering price which was determined when the issuing corporation received its price for the issue. * * *

* * *

E.   The Economic Problem Presented by the Practice of Stabilization

* * *

This brings us to the crux of the problem viewed in its larger aspects; namely, the conflicting interests of two segments of the public as a whole. One part of the public, consisting of existing security holders, employees and others dependent upon the turning wheels of industry, has a direct interest in securing the financing of industry as cheaply and as effectively as possible. This other segment of the public, made up of purchasing investors, has an equally direct interest in obtaining appropriate investments at the cheapest possible prices. To both of these divisions of the investing public this Commission owes a duty. Furthermore, the Securities Exchange Act, while primarily directed towards the protection of investors, is also concerned with the protection of the nation's credit and banking structure and the health of its capital markets. Congress recognized the need for an adjustment between the interests of purchasing investors on the one hand and the needs of industry for capital funds on the other. Therefore, by section 9(a)(6) of the Securities

Exchange Act, it assigned to this Commission the duty of finding a reasonable middle ground between these two objectives which are by no means always easy to reconcile: (1) To guard the welfare of the multitude of direct individual investors against injury from stabilizing. (2) To guard against impeding the flow of individual savings into industrial expansion.

* * *

As indicated in Release No. 2446, stabilization can harm members of the trading public, who generally buy and sell securities on the assumption that prices are set in accordance with the law of supply and demand. For example, an investor who is contemplating the purchase of newly offered securities may check the current quotations for the security in the trading market and learn that it is trading at the public offering price. This investigation may provide false confidence that the market has valued the security at that price, particularly if it is done several days after the offering has begun, for if the offering has taken this long to complete, the new securities obviously are not being well received by the public. In this circumstance, the price likely will drop when the stabilizing bid is pulled, resulting in losses to anyone who bought in reliance on the apparent stability of the security's price in the market.

Because of the dangers of stabilization, the Commission requires (in Item 508(*l*)(1) of Regulation S–K) prospectus disclosures if an issuer knows or has reason to believe that the underwriters intend to stabilize. Still, the average investor checking market quotations has no easy way of telling whether stabilizing is currently going on.

Investors are not, however, the only ones who can suffer because of stabilization. The underwriters can fare even worse. Sometimes shareholders who own large amounts of securities wait to sell until a new offering is made, knowing that the underwriters will place a stabilizing bid. Then, as soon as stabilization begins, the shareholders start dumping their securities into the market. When this happens, the underwriters can end up buying a substantial amount of securities at the retail price.

CHAPTER 16

REGULATION OF THE SECURITIES BUSINESS

SITUATION 16

In the course of the lawsuits against Microtec, Nielson Securities Co., and others, Nielson officers have become impressed with your firm, and they have asked your firm to represent Nielson in connection with its broker-dealer business. This will involve giving advice on a continuing basis designed to prevent securities law violations. It will also involve representing Nielson in litigation.

This is a specialized area of securities law, and others in your firm will handle most of the work. Partners in your firm decide, however, that you may have some involvement with the client, and that you therefore need to familiarize yourself with the area.

In considering this situation, refer to Exchange Act Sections 3(a)(4), (5) and (80), 15, and 15A, in addition to the materials in this chapter.

A. REGULATION OF STOCK EXCHANGES AND FINRA

In its essence, Section 5 of the Exchange Act requires the registration of securities exchanges, unless the Commission allows an exemption from the Act's registration requirements. These requirements are detailed in Section 6 and its rules, which provide for the filing of an application on Exchange Act Form 1. Most of the requirements of Section 6 relate to the substance of rules that an exchange is required to adopt. For example, an exchange's rules must "assure a fair representation of its members in the selection of its directors and administration of its affairs," must be "designed to prevent fraudulent and manipulative acts and practices," and must "provide that * * * its members and persons associated with its members shall be appropriately disciplined for violation of the provisions of [the Exchange Act], the rules or regulations thereunder, or the rules of the exchange."

From the requirements for registration, it is easy to see that the drafters of the Exchange Act wanted registered exchanges to police themselves. Section 19 demonstrates the lengths to which this idea is taken. The section embodies a plan that involves self-regulation along with Commission oversight, which results in a high level of regulation and a minimum administrative burden on the Commission. As William O. Douglas described the Act's self-regulatory scheme, "[T]he exchanges take the leadership with Government playing a residual role.

Government [keeps] the shotgun, so to speak, behind the door, loaded, well oiled, cleaned, ready for use but with the hope it [will] never have to be used."[1]

Under Section 19, exchanges are required to file proposed rule changes with the Commission. After the Commission provides interested persons with the opportunity to be heard, it may either approve or disapprove a proposed rule change, or it may modify the change in any way it believes desirable. The Commission is also empowered to modify the rules of an exchange upon its own initiative. In addition, Section 19 uses the same scheme in the case of disciplinary actions against a person who is subject to an exchange's rules: exchanges make the initial decisions on discipline, but any final action by an exchange is subject to review by the Commission. Formal Commission action to override exchange-made decisions of any type is not common.

As originally drafted, the Exchange Act left the over-the-counter trading of securities generally unregulated. In 1938, however, Congress amended the Act to provide the same sort of self-regulatory scheme for this market as then existed for stock exchanges. The mechanism Congress chose was registration with the Commission of national securities associations and subjection of these associations to the Act's self-regulatory scheme.

Under Exchange Act Section 15(b)(8) and (9), brokers and dealers required to be registered under the act (as discussed in Section B of this Chapter) must be members of a registered securities association (regulated under Section 15A) if they wish to trade in the over-the-counter market, with very limited exceptions. For many years, all but a very small percentage of securities firms operating in that market were members of the National Association of Securities Dealers ("NASD"). In 2007 the NASD merged with the regulatory arm of the New York Stock Exchange, creating the Financial Industry Regulatory Authority ("FINRA"). Although the New York Stock Exchange subsequently withdrew, FINRA obviously exercises substantial clout. This is true notwithstanding Fiero v. Financial Industry Regulatory Authority, Inc.,[2] in which the Second Circuit indicated that FINRA's primary enforcement mechanisms are limited to revocation of registration and denial of reentry into the industry. The court specifically found that FINRA lacked the authority to bring court actions to collect disciplinary fines.

It probably is worth noting that until fairly recently there were somewhat clear distinctions (both legal and practical) between traditional securities exchanges (such as the New York Stock Exchange) and "over-the-counter" markets. The "over-the-counter" markets—notably Nasdaq (which was pioneered by the NASD)—led the way in adopting electronic technology. Traditional exchanges, however, now are

---

[1]   W. Douglas, Democracy and Finance 82 (1940).

[2]   660 F.3d 569 (2d Cir. 2011).

heavily reliant on electronic communication, and Nasdaq itself has registered as NASDAQ, a national exchange. Other electronic trading systems have developed in competition with the traditional exchanges; although historically regulated as broker-dealers, they now may choose to register either as broker-dealers or as exchanges.[3] Those registering as broker-dealers typically will be members of FINRA. Rule 15b9–1 does, however, exempt certain broker-dealers from FINRA registration if they do not trade on exchanges and trade primarily for their own accounts. Concerned that "high-frequency" or "algorithmic" traders conducting off-exchange trading were not subject to adequate oversight, the SEC has proposed revising the rule so as to relieve traders from FINRA registration only if their business is limited to an exchange of which they are a member.[4]

New to the landscape of financial intermediaries are "funding portals," defined in Exchange Act Section 3(a)(80). Pursuant to Section 4(a)(6) of the Securities Act, issuers may raise capital through exempt "crowdfunding" transactions (discussed in Chapter 5) facilitated either by these new entities or by brokers. Although funding portals are exempt from registering as brokers or dealers, they nonetheless must register with the Commission and become members of a registered national securities association (which may enforce against the funding portals only specifically tailored rules). To qualify as a funding portal, the entity must be acting as an intermediary solely in transactions pursuant to Securities Act Section 4(a)(6), must not offer investment advice or recommendations, and must not engage in solicitation (or compensate others for doing so) with respect to the securities offered or displayed on its website or portal. Funding portals also are prohibited from holding or otherwise handling investor funds. The discussion below relates to traditional broker-dealers and does not include funding portals.

B. REGULATION OF BROKERS AND DEALERS

I. BROKERS AND DEALERS, INCLUDING UNDERWRITERS

Exchange Act Section 15(a) makes it unlawful to operate as a broker or dealer, through the means or instrumentalities of interstate commerce or the mails, unless Exchange Act registration is accomplished or an exemption is provided by the Commission. Obviously, securities firms are subject to this registration requirement, but other parties may also be covered, sometimes without realizing it. The issue may arise because the Exchange Act's definitions of "broker" and "dealer" include more than just traditional securities firms:

---

[3]   Exchange Act Release No. 38,672 (May 23, 1997).

[4]   Exchange Act Release No. 34–74581 (Mar. 25, 2015).

Section 3(a)(4). The term "broker" means any person engaged in the business of effecting transactions in securities for the account of others.

Section 3(a)(5). The term "dealer" means any person engaged in the business of buying and selling securities for his own account, through a broker or otherwise, but does not include a bank, or any person insofar as he buys or sells securities for his own account, either individually or in some fiduciary capacity, but not as a part of a regular business.

As discussed in the preceding section, securities firms that operate as brokers or dealers are subject to regulation by FINRA and perhaps by one or more exchanges. In addition, brokers and dealers come under the direct application of a wide variety of Exchange Act provisions and rules. For example, Section 8 governs the lending of exchange-traded securities. Section 15(c)(1) and (2) prohibit a variety of manipulative, deceptive, or fraudulent conduct. Rule 15c2–8 requires the delivery of Securities Act prospectuses on written request of customers and in some other circumstances. Rule 15c3–1 requires brokers and dealers to maintain specified amounts of net capital. Section 17 and its rules mandate in detail the keeping of records and the filing with the Commission of reports.

Set out below is an important case describing the extent of the Commission's authority to regulate the conduct of brokers and dealers (including those engaging in underwriting public offerings).

Credit Suisse Securities, LLC v. Billing

Supreme Court of the United States, 2007.
551 U.S. 264.

■ JUSTICE BREYER delivered the opinion of the Court.

A group of buyers of newly issued securities have filed an antitrust lawsuit against underwriting firms that market and distribute those issues. The buyers claim that the underwriters unlawfully agreed with one another that they would not sell shares of a popular new issue to a buyer unless that buyer committed (1) to buy additional shares of that security later at escalating prices (a practice called "laddering"), (2) to pay unusually high commissions on subsequent security purchases from the underwriters, or (3) to purchase from the underwriters other less desirable securities (a practice called "tying"). The question before us is whether there is a "plain repugnancy" between these antitrust claims and the federal securities law. See Gordon v. New York Stock Exchange, Inc., 422 U.S. 659, 682 (1975) (quoting United States v. Philadelphia Nat. Bank, 374 U.S. 321, 350–351 (1963)). We conclude that there is. Consequently we must interpret the securities laws as implicitly precluding the application of the antitrust laws to the conduct alleged in this case. See 422 U.S., at 682, 689, 691 * * * .

I

A

The underwriting practices at issue take place during the course of an initial public offering (IPO) of shares in a company. An IPO presents an opportunity to raise capital for a new enterprise by selling shares to the investing public. A group of underwriters will typically form a syndicate to help market the shares. The syndicate will investigate and estimate likely market demand for the shares at various prices. It will then recommend to the firm a price and the number of shares it believes the firm should offer. Ultimately, the syndicate will promise to buy from the firm all the newly issued shares on a specified date at a fixed, agreed-upon price, which price the syndicate will then charge investors when it resells the shares. When the syndicate buys the shares from the issuing firm, however, the firm gives the syndicate a price discount, which amounts to the syndicate's commission. See generally L. Loss & J. Seligman, Fundamentals of Securities Regulation 66–72 (4th ed. 2001).

At the heart of the syndicate's IPO marketing activity lie its efforts to determine suitable initial share prices and quantities. At first, the syndicate makes a preliminary estimate that it submits in a registration statement to the Securities and Exchange Commission (SEC). It then conducts a "road show" during which syndicate underwriters and representatives of the offering firm meet potential investors and engage in a process that the industry calls "book building." During this time, the underwriters and firm representatives present information to investors about the company and the stock. And they attempt to gauge the strength of the investors' interest in purchasing the stock. For this purpose, underwriters might well ask the investors how their interest would vary depending upon price and the number of shares that are offered. They will learn, among other things, which investors might buy shares, in what quantities, at what prices, and for how long each is likely to hold purchased shares before selling them to others.

On the basis of this kind of information, the members of the underwriting syndicate work out final arrangements with the issuing firm, fixing the price per share and specifying the number of shares for which the underwriters will be jointly responsible. As we have said, after buying the shares at a discounted price, the syndicate resells the shares to investors at the fixed price, in effect earning its commission in the process.

* * *

II

A

Sometimes regulatory statutes explicitly state whether they preclude application of the antitrust laws. Compare, *e.g.*, Webb-Pomerene Act (expressly providing antitrust immunity) with § 601(b)(1) of the Telecommunications Act of 1996 (stating that antitrust laws remain applicable). * * * Where regulatory statutes are silent in respect to antitrust, however, courts must determine whether, and in what respects, they implicitly preclude application of the antitrust laws. Those determinations may vary from statute to statute, depending upon the relation between the antitrust laws and the regulatory program set forth in the particular statute, and the relation of the specific conduct at issue to both sets of laws. * * *

Three decisions from this Court specifically address the relation of securities law to antitrust law. In Silver v. New York Stock Exchange, 373 U.S. 341 (1963), the Court considered a dealer's claim that, by expelling him from the New York Stock Exchange, the Exchange had violated the antitrust prohibition against group "boycott[s]." 373 U.S., at 347. The Court wrote that, where possible, courts should "reconcil[e] the operation of both [*i.e.*, antitrust and securities] statutory schemes * * * rather than holding one completely ousted." *Id.*, at 357. It also set forth a standard, namely that "[r]epeal of the antitrust laws is to be regarded as implied only if necessary to make the Securities Exchange Act work, and even then only to the minimum extent necessary." *Ibid.* And it held that the securities law did *not* preclude application of the antitrust laws to the claimed boycott *insofar as the Exchange denied the expelled dealer a right to fair procedures. Id.*, at 359–360.

In reaching this conclusion, the Court noted that the SEC lacked jurisdiction under the securities law "to review particular instances of enforcement of exchange rules"; that "nothing [was] built into the regulatory scheme which performs the antitrust function of insuring" that rules that injure competition are nonetheless "justified as furthering" legitimate regulatory "ends"; that the expulsion "would clearly" violate "the Sherman Act unless justified by reference to the purposes of the Securities Exchange Act"; and that it could find *no such justifying purpose* where the Exchange took "anticompetitive collective action * * * *without according fair procedures." Id.*, at 357–358, 364 (emphasis added).

In *Gordon* the Court considered an antitrust complaint that essentially alleged "price fixing" among stockbrokers. It charged that members of the New York Stock Exchange had agreed to fix their commissions on sales under $500,000. And it sought damages and an injunction forbidding future agreements. 422 U.S., at 661, and n. 3. The lawsuit was filed at a time when regulatory attitudes toward fixed stockbroker commissions were changing. The fixed commissions challenged in the complaint were applied during a period when the SEC approved of the practice of fixing broker-commission rates. But Congress and the SEC had both subsequently disapproved for the future the fixing of some of those rates. See *id.*, at 690–691.

In deciding whether antitrust liability could lie, the Court repeated *Silver's* general standard in somewhat different terms: It said that an "implied repeal" of the antitrust laws would be found only "where there is a 'plain repugnancy' between the antitrust and regulatory provisions." 422 U.S., at 682 (quoting *Philadelphia Nat. Bank, supra,* at 350–351). It then held that the securities laws impliedly precluded application of the antitrust laws in the case at hand. The Court rested this conclusion on three sets of considerations. For one thing, the securities law "gave the SEC direct regulatory power over exchange rules and practices with respect to the fixing of reasonable rates of commission." 422 U.S., at 685 (internal quotation marks omitted). For another, the SEC had "taken an active role in review of proposed rate changes during the last 15 years," and had engaged in "continuing activity" in respect to the regulation of commission rates. *Ibid.* Finally, without antitrust immunity, "the exchanges and their members" would be subject to "conflicting standards." *Id.,* at 689.

This last consideration-the conflict-was complicated due to Congress', and the agency's, changing views about the validity of fixed commissions. As far as *the past* fixing of rates was concerned, the conflict was clear: The antitrust law had forbidden the very thing that the securities law had then permitted, namely an anticompetitive rate setting process. In respect to the future, however, the conflict was less apparent. That was because the SEC's new (congressionally authorized) prohibition of (certain) fixed rates would take effect in the near-term future. And after that time the SEC and the antitrust law would *both* likely prohibit some of the rate fixing to which the plaintiffs injunction would likely apply. See *id.,* at 690–691.

Despite the likely compatibility of the laws in the future, the Court nonetheless expressly found *conflict*. The conflict arose from the fact that the law permitted the SEC to supervise the competitive setting of rates and to *"reintroduc[e] * * * fixed rates,"id.,* at 691 (emphasis added), under certain conditions. The Court consequently wrote that "failure to imply repeal would render nugatory the legislative provision for regulatory agency supervision of exchange commission rates." *Ibid.* The upshot is that, in light of potential future conflict, the Court found that the securities law precluded antitrust liability even in respect to a practice that both antitrust law and securities law might forbid.

In United States v. National Association of Securities Dealers, Inc., 422 U.S. 694 (1975) *(NASD),* the Court considered a Department of Justice antitrust complaint claiming that mutual fund companies had agreed with securities broker-dealers (1) to fix "resale" prices, *i.e.,* the prices at which a broker-dealer would sell a mutual fund's shares to an investor or buy mutual fund shares from a fund investor (who wished to redeem the shares); (2) to fix other terms of sale including those related to when, how, to whom, and from whom the broker-dealers might sell and buy mutual fund shares; and (3) to forbid broker-dealers from freely selling to, and buying shares from, one another. See 422 U.S., at 700–703.

The Court again found "clear repugnancy," and it held that the securities law, by implication, precluded all parts of the antitrust claim. *Id.,* at 719. In reaching this conclusion, the Court found that antitrust law (*e.g.,* forbidding resale price maintenance) and securities law (*e.g.,* permitting resale price maintenance) were in conflict. In deciding that the latter trumped the former, the Court relied upon the same kinds of considerations it found determinative in *Gordon.* In respect to the last set of allegations (restricting a free market in mutual fund shares among brokers), the Court said that (1) the relevant securities law "enables [the SEC] to monitor the activities questioned"; (2) "the history of Commission regulations suggests no laxity in the exercise of this authority"; and hence (3) allowing an antitrust suit to proceed that is "so directly related to the SEC's responsibilities" would present "a substantial danger that [broker-dealers and other defendants] would be subjected to duplicative and inconsistent standards." See *NASD,* 422 U.S., at 734–735.

As to the other practices alleged in the complaint (concerning, *e.g.,* resale price maintenance), the Court emphasized that (1) the securities law "vested in the SEC final authority to determine whether and to what extent" the relevant practices "should be tolerated," *id.,* at 729; (2) although the SEC has not actively supervised the relevant practices, that is only because the statute "reflects a clear congressional determination that, subject to Commission oversight, mutual funds should be allowed to retain the initiative in dealing with the potentially adverse effects of disruptive trading practices," *id.,* at 727; and (3) the SEC has supervised the funds insofar as its "acceptance of fund-initiated restrictions for more than three decades * * * manifests an informed administrative judgment that the contractual restrictions * * * were appropriate means for combating the problems of the industry," *id.,* at 728. The Court added that, in these respects, the SEC had engaged in "precisely the kind of administrative oversight of private practices that Congress contemplated." *Ibid.*

* * *

This Court's prior decisions * * * make clear that, when a court decides whether securities law precludes antitrust law, it is deciding whether, given context and likely consequences, there is a "clear repugnancy" between the securities law and the antitrust complaint-or as we shall subsequently describe the matter, whether the two are "clearly incompatible." Moreover, *Gordon* and *NASD,* in finding sufficient incompatibility to warrant an implication of preclusion, have treated the following factors as critical: (1) the existence of regulatory authority under the securities law to supervise the activities in question; (2) evidence that the responsible regulatory entities exercise that authority; and (3) a resulting risk that the securities and antitrust laws, if both applicable, would produce conflicting guidance, requirements, duties, privileges, or standards of conduct. We also note (4) that in *Gordon* and *NA SD* the possible conflict affected practices that lie squarely within an area of financial market activity that the securities law seeks to regulate.

B

These principles, applied to the complaints before us, considerably narrow our legal task. For the parties cannot reasonably dispute the existence here of several of the conditions that this Court previously regarded as crucial to finding that the securities law impliedly precludes the application of the antitrust laws.

First, the activities in question here—the underwriters' efforts jointly to promote and to sell newly issued securities—is central to the proper functioning of well-regulated capital markets. The IPO process supports new firms that seek to raise capital; it helps to spread ownership of those firms broadly among investors; it directs capital flows in ways that better correspond to the public's demand for goods and services. Moreover, financial experts, including the securities regulators, consider the general kind of joint underwriting activity at issue in this case, including road shows and book-building efforts essential to the successful marketing of an IPO. * * * Thus, the antitrust complaints before us concern practices that lie at the very heart of the securities marketing enterprise.

Second, the law grants the SEC authority to supervise all of the activities here in question. Indeed, the SEC possesses considerable power to forbid, permit, encourage, discourage, tolerate, limit, and otherwise regulate virtually every aspect of the practices in which underwriters engage. See, *e.g.*, Securities Act §§ 2(a)(3), 10, 26 (granting SEC power to regulate the process of book-building, solicitations of "indications of interest," and communications between underwriting participants and their customers, including those that occur during road shows); Securities Exchange Act § 15(c)(2)(D) (granting SEC power to define and prevent through rules and regulations acts and practices that are fraudulent, deceptive, or manipulative) * * * . * * *

Third, the SEC has continuously exercised its legal authority to regulate conduct of the general kind now at issue. It has defined in detail, for example, what underwriters may and may not do and say during their road shows. * * * It has brought actions against underwriters who have violated these SEC regulations. * * *

The preceding considerations show that the first condition (legal regulatory authority), the second condition (exercise of that authority), and the fourth condition (heartland securities activity) that were present in *Gordon* and *NASD* are satisfied in this *case as* well. Unlike *Silver,* there is here no question of the existence of appropriate regulatory authority, nor is there doubt as to whether the regulators have exercised that authority. Rather, the question before us concerns the third condition: Is there a conflict that rises to the level of incompatibility? Is an antitrust suit such as this likely to prove practically incompatible with the SEC's administration of the Nation's securities laws?

III

A

Given the SEC's comprehensive authority to regulate IPO underwriting syndicates, its active and ongoing exercise of that authority, and the undisputed need for joint IPO underwriter activity, we do not read the complaints as attacking the bare existence of IPO underwriting syndicates or any of the joint activity that the SEC considers a necessary component of IPO-related syndicate activity. * * * Nor do we understand the complaints as questioning underwriter agreements to fix the levels of their commissions, whether or not the resulting price is "excessive." See *Gordon,* 422 U.S., at 688–689 (securities law conflicts with, and therefore precludes, antitrust attack on the fixing of commissions where SEC has not approved, but later *might* approve, the practice).

We nonetheless can read the complaints as attacking the *manner* in which the underwriters jointly seek to collect "excessive" commissions. The complaints attack underwriter efforts to collect commissions through certain practices (*i.e.,* laddering, tying, collecting excessive commissions in the form of later sales of the issued shares), which according to respondents the SEC itself has already disapproved and, in all likelihood, will not approve in the foreseeable future. In respect to this set of claims, they contend that there is no possible "conflict" since both securities law and antitrust law aim to prohibit the same undesirable activity. Without a conflict, they add, there is no "repugnance" or "incompatibility," and this Court may not imply that securities law precludes an antitrust suit.

B

We accept the premises of respondents' argument-that the SEC has full regulatory authority over these practices, that it has actively exercised that authority, but that the SEC has *disapproved* (and, for argument's sake, we assume that it will continue to disapprove) the conduct that the antitrust complaints attack. Nonetheless, we cannot accept respondents' conclusion. Rather, several considerations taken together lead us to find that, even on these prorespondent assumptions, securities law and antitrust law are clearly incompatible.

First, to permit antitrust actions such as the present one *still* threatens serious securities-related harm. For one thing, an unusually serious legal line-drawing problem remains unabated. In the present context only a fine, complex, detailed line separates activity that the SEC permits or encourages (for which respondents must concede antitrust immunity) from activity that the SEC must (and inevitably will) forbid (and which, on respondents' theory, should be open to antitrust attack).

For example, in respect to "laddering" the SEC forbids an underwriter to "solicit customers prior to the completion of the distribution regarding whether and at what price and in what quantity they intend to place immediate aftermarket orders for IPO stock[.]" * * * But at the same time the SEC permits, indeed encourages, underwriters (as part of the "book building" process) to "inquir[e] as to a customer's desired future position in the longer term (for example, three to six months), and the price or prices at which the customer might accumulate that position without reference to immediate aftermarket activity." * * *

It will often be difficult for someone who is not familiar with accepted syndicate practices to determine with confidence whether an underwriter has insisted that an investor buy more shares in the immediate aftermarket (forbidden), or has simply allocated more shares to an investor willing to purchase additional shares of that issue in the long run (permitted). And who but a securities expert could say whether the present SEC rules set forth a virtually permanent line, unlikely to change in ways that would permit the sorts of "laddering-like" conduct that it now seems to forbid? * * *

Similarly, in respect to "tying" and other efforts to obtain an increased commission from future sales, the SEC has sought to prohibit an underwriter "from demanding * * * an offer from their customers of any payment or other consideration [such as the purchase of a different security] in addition to the security's stated consideration." * * * But the SEC would permit a firm to "allocat[e] IPO shares to a customer because the customer has separately retained the firm for other services, when the customer has not paid excessive compensation in relation to those services." * * *

Under these standards, to distinguish what is forbidden from what is allowed requires an understanding of just when, in relation to services provided, a commission is "excessive," indeed, so "excessive" that it will remain *permanently* forbidden, see *Gordon,* 422 U.S., at 690–691. And who but the SEC itself could do so with confidence?

For another thing, evidence tending to show unlawful antitrust activity and evidence tending to show lawful securities marketing activity may overlap, or prove identical. Consider, for instance, a conversation between an underwriter and an investor about how long an investor intends to hold the new shares (and at what price), say a conversation that elicits comments concerning both the investor's short and longer term plans. That exchange might, as a plaintiff sees it, provide evidence of an underwriter's insistence upon "laddering" or, as a defendant sees it, provide evidence of a lawful effort to allocate shares to those who will hold them for a longer time. * * *

Further, antitrust plaintiffs may bring lawsuits throughout the Nation in dozens of different courts with different nonexpert judges and different nonexpert juries. In light of the nuanced nature of the evidentiary evaluations necessary to separate the permissible from the impermissible, it will prove difficult for those many different courts to reach consistent results. And, given the fact-related nature of many such evaluations, it will also prove difficult to assure that the different courts evaluate similar fact patterns consistently. The result is an unusually high risk that different courts will evaluate similar factual circumstances differently. See Hovenkamp, Antitrust Violations in Securities Markets, 28 J. Corp. L. 607, 629 (2003) ("Once regulation of an industry is entrusted to jury trials, the outcomes of antitrust proceedings will be inconsistent with one another * * * .").

Now consider these factors together-the fine securities-related lines separating the permissible from the impermissible; the need for securities-related expertise (particularly to determine whether an SEC rule is likely permanent); the overlapping evidence from which reasonable but contradictory inferences may be drawn; and the risk of inconsistent court results. Together these factors mean there is no practical way to confine antitrust suits so that they challenge only activity of the kind the investors seek to target, activity that is presently unlawful and will likely remain unlawful under the securities law. Rather, these factors suggest that antitrust courts are likely to make unusually serious mistakes in this respect. And the threat of antitrust mistakes, *i.e.*, results that stray outside the narrow bounds that plaintiffs seek to set, means that underwriters must act in ways that will avoid not simply conduct that the securities law forbids (and will likely continue to forbid), but also a wide range of joint conduct that the securities law permits or encourages (but which they fear could lead to an antitrust lawsuit and the risk of treble damages). And therein lies the problem.

This kind of problem exists to some degree in respect to other antitrust lawsuits. But here the factors we have mentioned make mistakes unusually likely (a matter relevant to Congress' determination of which institution should regulate a particular set of market activities). And the role that joint conduct plays in respect to the marketing of IPOs, along with the important role IPOs themselves play in relation to the effective functioning of capital markets, means that the securities-related costs of mistakes is unusually high. It is no wonder, then, that the SEC told the District Court (consistent with what the Government tells us here) that a "failure to hold that the alleged conduct was immunized would threaten to disrupt the full range of the Commission's ability to exercise its regulatory authority," adding that it would have a "chilling effect" on "lawful joint activities * * * of tremendous importance to the economy of the country."

We believe it fair to conclude that, where conduct at the core of the marketing of new securities is at issue; where securities regulators proceed with great care to distinguish the encouraged and permissible from the forbidden; where the threat of antitrust lawsuits, through error and disincentive, could seriously alter underwriter conduct in undesirable ways, to allow an antitrust lawsuit would threaten serious harm to the efficient functioning of the securities markets.

Second, any enforcement-related need for an antitrust lawsuit is unusually small. For one thing, the SEC actively enforces the rules and regulations that forbid the conduct in question. For another, as we have said, investors harmed by underwriters' unlawful practices may bring lawsuits and obtain damages under the securities law. * * * Finally, the SEC is itself required to take account of competitive considerations when it creates securities-related policy and embodies it in rules and regulations. And that fact makes it somewhat less necessary to rely upon antitrust actions to address anticompetitive behavior. See Securities Act § 2(b) (instructing the SEC to consider, "in addition to the protection of investors, whether the action will promote efficiency, competition, and capital formation"); Securities Exchange Act § 23(a)(2) (the SEC "shall consider among other matters the impact any such rule or regulation would have on competition"). * * *

In sum, an antitrust action in this context is accompanied by a substantial risk of injury to the securities markets and by a diminished need for antitrust enforcement to address anticompetitive conduct. Together these considerations indicate a serious conflict between, on the one hand, application of the antitrust laws and, on the other, proper enforcement of the securities law.

* * *

Although Congress has allowed the Commission substantial discretion in regulating broker-dealers, it still takes an active interest. Thus, Section 913 of the Dodd-Frank Act both added Section 15(k) of the Exchange Act, authorizing the Commission to adopt a uniform fiduciary standard for investment advisers, brokers, and dealers when providing personalized investment advice, and directed the Commission to conduct a study on the wisdom of such an adoption. The Commission is still in the process of collecting information relating to the costs and benefits of alternative standards of conduct.[5] Dodd-Frank also added other new subsections to Section 15 directing the Commission to facilitate certain disclosures to investors (including with respect to conflicts of interest) to be made by brokers, dealers, and investment advisers, and to consider the adoption of a variety of other rules. By contrast, the JOBS Act less deferentially contained provisions effectively, and in some cases outright, repealing some of the (specific) former limits on broker-dealer conduct imposed by FINRA and the Commission.

II. SPECIALIZED APPLICATIONS OF RULE 10b–5

Rule 10b–5 has a number of specialized applications in the regulation of brokers and dealers. The following cases will provide an

---

[5]   Exchange Act Release 34–69013 (Mar. 1, 2013); Statement of Chairman Jay Clayton (June 1, 2017) available at https://www.sec.gov/news/public-statement/statement-chairman-clayton-2017-05-31.

introduction to some of the more important issues involved in this regulation.

a.   FAIR DEALING

Chasins v. Smith, Barney & Co.

United States Court of Appeals, Second Circuit, 1970.
438 F.2d 1167.

■ Before SMITH, KAUFMAN and HAYS, CIRCUIT JUDGES.

■ J. JOSEPH SMITH, CIRCUIT JUDGE:

* * *

This is an appeal by Smith, Barney & Co., Inc., a stock brokerage firm [hereinafter "Smith, Barney"] from a judgment for damages on a determination * * * that Smith, Barney had violated [Rule] 10b–5, promulgated under the Securities Exchange Act, in not disclosing to appellee (Chasins) that it was making a market in the securities it sold Chasins in the over-the-counter market. * * * We find no error and affirm the judgment.

* * * At the time the four transactions in question in his appeal occurred, Chasins was the musical director of radio station WQXR in New York City and was the commentator on a musical program sponsored by Smith, Barney. According to Chasins it was due to this relationship that he opened his brokerage account with Smith, Barney by orally retaining it to act as his stockbroker. Smith, Barney acted in at least two capacities in these transactions, namely as Chasins' stockbroker and as principal, *i.e.*, the owner of the security being sold to Chasins. In all four transactions Smith, Barney sold the securities to Chasins in the over-the-counter market, and although it revealed in the confirmation slips that it was acting as principal and for its own account in selling to Chasins, Smith, Barney did not reveal that it was "making a market" in the securities involved as was the fact. Nor did Smith, Barney disclose how much it had paid for the securities sold as principal to Chasins or that it had acted as an "underwriter" as defined by the Securities Act of 1933 in connection with the distribution of securities of Welch Scientific Company and Howard Johnson Company, two of the companies whose securities Smith, Barney sold to Chasins.

Preceding the four sales of July and August, 1961, Smith, Barney sent Chasins a written analysis of his then current security holdings and its recommendations in regard to his objective of aggressive growth of his holdings. The recommendations included strong purchase recommendations for securities of Welch Scientific, Tex-Star Oil and Gas Corp., and Howard Johnson Company. Chasins and Thomas N. Delaney, Jr., an authorized agent of Smith, Barney had various telephone conversations prior to the transactions in question. Delaney testified that at least at the times of the four transactions in question Smith, Barney was "making a market" in those securities, *i.e.*, it was maintaining a position in the stocks on its own account by participating in over-the-counter trading in them; Smith, Barney's records indicated that at least from June 30, 1961, it had been trading in those stocks and had held positions in them during the times Chasins purchased the securities from it. There was no testimony that Chasins had any knowledge or notice that Smith, Barney was "making a market" in the securities of the three companies.

* * * Damages were awarded to Chasins in the amount of $18,616.64, with interest, which constituted the difference between the price at which Chasins purchased the securities from Smith, Barney and the price at which he later sold them (prior to discovering Smith, Barney's market making in the securities).

* * *

Smith, Barney's major contention in attacking the district court's finding * * * is that failure to disclose its "market making" role in the securities exchanged over the counter was not failure to disclose a material fact. * * *

Appellant * * * points to the fact that in over-the-counter trading, a market maker with an inventory in a stock is considered the best source of the security (the best available market); thus, the SEC has even punished a brokerage firm for not going directly to a firm with an inventory in a stock, *i.e.*, interposing another firm between them. However, the fact that dealing with a market maker should be considered by some desirable for some purposes does not mean that the failure to disclose Smith, Barney's market-making role is not under the circumstances of this case a failure to disclose a material fact. The question here is not whether Smith, Barney sold to Chasins at a fair price but whether disclosure of Smith, Barney's being a market maker in the Welch Scientific, Tex-Star Oil and Gas and Howard Johnson securities might have influenced Chasins' decision to buy the stock. * * * [T]he question of materiality becomes whether a reasonable man in Chasins' position might well have acted otherwise than to purchase if he had been informed of Smith, Barney's market making role in the three stocks in addition to the fact that Smith, Barney was the other principal in the transaction. The broker-dealer, Smith, Barney, had undertaken to make a written evaluation of Chasins' securities holdings and had strongly recommended sales of some of his holdings and purchases of these three stocks in which Smith, Barney was dealing as a principal.

Knowledge of the additional fact of market making by Smith, Barney in the three securities recommended could well influence the decision of a client in Chasins' position, depending on the broker-dealer's undertaking to analyze and advise, whether to follow its recommendation to buy the securities; disclosure of the fact would indicate the possibility of adverse interests which might be reflected in Smith, Barney's recommendations. Smith, Barney could well be caught in either a "short" position or a "long" position in a security, because of erroneous judgment of supply and demand at given levels. If over supplied, it may be to the interest of a market maker to attempt to unload the securities on his retail clients. Here, Smith, Barney's strong recommendations of the three securities Chasins purchased could have been motivated by its own market position rather than the intrinsic desirability of the securities for Chasins. An investor who is at least informed of the possibility of such adverse interests, due to his broker's market making in the securities recommended, can question the reasons for the recommendations. The investor, such as Chasins, must be permitted to evaluate overlapping motivations through appropriate disclosures, especially where one motivation is economic self-interest.

* * *

Subsequent cases, including Addeo v. Braver,[6] have relied on *Chasins* in holding that a broker-dealer's non-excessive commission on a recommended transaction was a material fact required to be disclosed. In a similar vein is SEC v. First Jersey Securities, Inc.[7] In that case, the Second Circuit accepted the argument that a broker-dealer controlling (although not "making") a market in particular stocks owed both selling and purchasing customers a duty to disclose that "the firm's manner of trading allowed it to fix the prices of the securities in a market largely unaffected by competition * * * ," and that charging the excessive mark-up facilitated by this non-disclosure was a violation of Sections 17(a) and 10(b) of the Exchange Act, as well as of Rule 10b–5.

In re Merrill Lynch, Pierce, Fenner & Smith, Inc.

Securities and Exchange Commission.
Exchange Act Release No. 14149 (November 9, 1977).

On June 22, 1973, the Commission instituted this proceeding and ordered a public hearing to determine whether Merrill Lynch, Pierce, Fenner & Smith Inc. ("Merrill Lynch"), two employees of its Securities Research Division and forty-seven of its account executives, willfully violated Section 17(a) of the Securities Act and Section 10(b) of the Securities Exchange Act ("Exchange Act") and Rule 10b–5 thereunder in connection with the recommendation and sale of the common stock of Scientific Control Corporation ("Scientific") to its customers during the period March 1, 1968 to November 21, 1969 ("relevant period") and whether Merrill Lynch and one of its employees failed reasonably to supervise its employees with a view to preventing violations of the anti-fraud provisions of the federal securities laws. * * *

---

6   956 F.Supp. 443 (S.D.N.Y.1997).

7   101 F.3d 1450 (2d Cir.1996).

* * *

Background

Scientific was a small Dallas based corporation engaged in the design, manufacture and sale of computers and data processing equipment. From the date of its incorporation on May 11, 1964 to the date of voluntary petition for an arrangement under Chapter XI of the Bankruptcy Act was filed on November 21, 1969, Scientific never enjoyed a profitable year.

Two offerings of Scientific's shares were made to the public through underwriting groups in which Merrill Lynch did not participate. * * *

* * *

Merrill Lynch Research

The Securities Research Division of Merrill Lynch maintained a recommendation regarding Scientific during the period from March 1, 1968 through November 10, 1969. That recommendation varied during the period as follows:

1.   March 1, 1968 through June 3, 1968—"Buy/Hold";

2.   June 4 through December 16, 1968—"Hold/Not O.K. to Exchange";

3.   December 17, 1968 through October 16, 1969—"Buy/Hold";

4.   October 16, 1969 through November 9, 1969—"Hold/O.K. to Exchange";

The recommendation "Buy/Hold" permitted account executives to solicit purchases of Scientific shares and to advise retention of shares already purchased. The recommendation "Hold/Not O.K. to Exchange," while not as affirmative a recommendation, permitted the account executives to solicit purchases and to advise retention or exchange of Scientific shares for those of another company. The recommendation "Hold/O.K. to Exchange," together with the text accompanying that recommendation as regards Scientific, advised against further purchases but permitted retention of already established positions.

During the entire period that Merrill Lynch maintained a recommendation, Scientific was accorded a quality classification of "speculative" and an investment characteristic of "growth." The texts of the Merrill Lynch recommendations further advised that an investment in Scientific was "highly speculative" and was appropriate only for accounts willing to assume high risks.

The research recommendations were available to Merrill Lynch's branch offices through a computer retrieval system known as the "QRQ." The QRQ system permitted interested account executives to retrieve current research recommendations at any time. In addition to the ratings ("Buy/Hold" etc.) set forth above, the QRQ opinions contained a brief text explaining the recommendation and financial data. Periodically, QRQ opinions, including the ratings and texts, were updated. In addition, Merrill Lynch issued "Wire Flashes" on Scientific which, similar to the QRQ's contained the research recommendations but also contained additional and more detailed explanatory material. Those wire flashes were issued on December 17, 1968, June 9, 1969 and October 16, 1969 and were directed to all account executives.

Respondent Pierce was primarily responsible for following Scientific and for formulating the research recommendations which were promulgated concerning Scientific. Pierce was, at all relevant times, the head of a group of analysts (informally called a "booth") following companies in the office equipment and machinery industries. * * *

During the period March 1, 1968 through November 9, 1969 Pierce met personally with representatives of management of Scientific on three occasions. During that same time period, Pierce also spoke with representatives of Scientific by telephone, and reviewed press releases issued by Scientific, the two prospectuses filed by Scientific in connection with its two public offerings of common stock on December 21, 1967 and October 31, 1968, annual reports, a proxy statement dated October 7, 1969 and company brochures. In addition, Pierce received information from an account executive in Dallas, Texas who knew some of the officers of Scientific.

While virtually all of the information which Pierce had concerning Scientific came either directly or indirectly from Scientific, the record of this proceeding supports the finding that Pierce did not subject this information to sufficiently critical evaluation and analysis. Accordingly, the recommendations on Scientific, both in the QRQ opinions and the Wire Flashes, often reflected an undue acceptance of management's statements and projections, many of which were either overly optimistic or simply untrue. These optimistic and misleading statements of management, to the extent that they were simply reiterated (in some instances, without attribution to management), rendered Merrill Lynch's recommendations inadequate and misleading.

As an example, the Wire Flash of December 17, 1968 simply repeated without qualification or attribution statements of management contained in Pierce's notes of a meeting with management held on December 4, 1968. Items in the Wire Flash that were taken almost verbatim from those notes include estimates of sales of $8–10 million in 1969 and earnings of $2.00 per share before taxes in 1970. In short, all Pierce did was reiterate the figures given him by John Baird ("Baird"), the President of Scientific. Such conduct was plainly insufficient under the circumstances.

* * *

In addition to placing undue reliance on management data, Pierce ignored certain developments, which can be characterized as "red flags" or "warning signals," and which should have suggested to him that management's optimistic statements were suspect and that Scientific's financial condition was worse than that represented. These developments included increasing slippage in management's projections of sales, earnings and product development; an increasing need for financing; and an unrealistically escalating backlog.

* * *

Applicable Legal Principles

In discharging its responsibility to oversee the selling practices of securities firms, the Commission has long held broker-dealers to high standards of honesty and fair dealing. The need for such high standards is based on the Commission's recognition of the potential for fraud and deception in the securities markets due to the unique and intangible nature of securities which Congress has characterized as "intricate merchandise."

When a broker-dealer recommends a security to its customer it represents that it has conducted a reasonable investigation of that security and that there exists a reasonable basis for the recommendation. In Hanly v. SEC, 415 F.2d 589 (1969), the Court of Appeals for the Second Circuit summarized the strict standards against which the actions of a salesman must be judged:

> He cannot recommend a security unless there is an adequate and reasonable basis for such recommendation. He must disclose facts which he knows and those which are reasonably ascertainable. By this recommendation he implies that a reasonable investigation has been made and that his recommendation rests on the conclusion based on such investigation. Where the salesman lacks essential information about a security, he should disclose this as well as the risks which arise from his lack of information. 415 F.2d 597.

The quantum of investigation will vary on the facts of each situation. To illustrate, it is clear that an unseasoned company such as Scientific requires a more thorough investigation than a well-established company. In no event will "blind reliance" upon a company's management alone be sufficient to constitute a reasonable investigation. All too frequently, the self interest of a company's management will color its presentation of the facts in a manner which vitiates the reliability of the information. A recommendation by a broker-dealer is perceived by a customer as (and it in fact should be) the product of independent and objective analysis can only be achieved when the scope of the investigation is extended beyond the company's management. The fact that Scientific's management disseminated inaccurate and misleading information to Pierce and others will not excuse Pierce's failure to conduct a reasonable investigation.

While the duty to go beyond the self-serving statements of management is present from the initiation of a recommendation, this duty is all the more compelling in the presence of "red flags" or "warning signal" [*sic*]. The receipt of information basis for a recommendation necessarily demands a detailed investigation. This is especially true when projections made by a company fail to materialize. Any credence previously given to such projections must be carefully re-evaluated with a jaundiced eye. And, when adverse information becomes known, it must be communicated to customers.

Further, we find that some of the information relied upon to form the basis of the Merrill Lynch recommendation which resulted in the purchase and sale of Scientific shares by customers was material non-public information. Such conduct is also violative of Section 10(b) of the Exchange Act and Rule 10b–5 thereunder.

Our conclusion that Merrill Lynch willfully violated the anti-fraud provisions of the securities laws in connection with the recommendation and sale of Scientific does not rest solely on Pierce's inadequate investigation of Scientific. We find that Merrill Lynch is also responsible for the false and misleading statements of twenty-eight of the forty-seven respondent account executives. This conduct is described in a subsequent portion of this opinion.

* * *

False and Misleading Statements of the Respondent Account Executives

According to the evidence adduced at the hearings the vast majority of Merrill Lynch's customers who purchased shares of Scientific had never heard of the company prior to being introduced to it by their account executive. Common to the testimony of investor witnesses was the fact that their account executives went beyond the Merrill Lynch research opinion by making optimistic representations, varying in nature and degree, which had no reasonable basis in fact and were false and misleading. These representations included statements regarding the future price of Scientific's shares, the comparability of Scientific's growth potential to established, highly successful and well capitalized companies, the likelihood that Scientific's shares would become listed on a national securities exchange, the soundness of an investment in Scientific and the quality of Scientific's management.

Most typical of the false and misleading statements made to various customers by the sanctioned account executives were representations concerning Scientific's future price. Customers testified that they were told at the time of their purchases that Scientific: would double in price in a short period of time; was expected to double its price within a year; had a very high potential to probably double its value in a very short period of time; should go up to $60 within six to nine months (at a time when its price was $30 per share); would possibly go to $40 or $50 per share within a year (at a time when its price was $30 per share); was selling at $32, had been as high as $60 and was expected to go back to that point within six months; should reach a price of $100; * * * and should not be sold until its price reached $100.

These statements about the future price of Scientific varied in terms of the specific price rise mentioned, the time period in which the rise would occur and the use of such qualifying words as would, should, could, probably, and expected. Nonetheless, these statements were predictions of specific and substantial price increases made without a reasonable basis.

We have consistently held that predictions of specific and substantial increases in the price of a speculative security of an unseasoned company are fraudulent and can not be justified. During the course of the hearings, the respondents frequently contended that if such statements about Scientific's future price were made they were not stated in terms of a guarantee but rather as being contingent upon the company attaining its sales and earnings projections. Even if we were to adopt that view of the evidence, it would matter little because predictions of substantial increases in price, under these circumstances, need not be presented in terms of a guarantee in order to be fraudulent. Further, couching such statements in terms of probability or possibility does not alter the character of the violation.

Almost as prevalent as the use of price predictions were comparisons of Scientific's potential growth to the growth experienced by established companies such as IBM; Scientific's potential for price appreciation was comparable to that of IBM; Scientific's stock was going to be like IBM's stock; and Scientific had the potential to be another IBM or Xerox.

These comparisons were totally unwarranted. In 1968 and 1969, Scientific had a weak and steadily deteriorating financial condition, it had never earned a profit, the company was unable to acquire capital needed to sustain its operations, it was unable to complete the development, manufacture and delivery of some of its products and it operated in the highly competitive environment of the computer industry which was already populated by several large successful companies. * * *

These comparisons of Scientific to IBM impliedly represented to potential investors that Scientific would enjoy a remarkable price appreciation similar to that experienced by IBM. Such comparisons were made without adequate factual support and are found to be willful violations of the anti-fraud provisions of the securities laws.

Several misrepresentations were made by various account executives regarding Scientific's future prospects for listing on a national securities exchange. Customers testified they were told that: Scientific would be listed on the New York or American Stock Exchange within a year; other customers testified that they were advised that there was a possibility Scientific could be listed on the New York or American Stock Exchange in the near future. * * *

Representations that Scientific's shares would, could or possibly could be listed on the New York or American Stock Exchange within a year or in the near future during 1968 and 1969 were made without reasonable basis. Scientific's history of losses precluded listing on either Exchange since both Exchanges required that a company have earnings for at least three consecutive years prior to listing. Having had no reasonable basis to support these statements regarding the listing of Scientific's shares, such statements are found to be false and misleading and violative of the anti-fraud provisions of the securities laws.

Interspersed among the various affirmative misrepresentations made in connection with the recommendation and sale of Scientific's shares to Merrill Lynch customers were omissions by the account executives to state material adverse facts regarding Scientific's true financial condition and the degree of risk involved in the purchase of the company's securities. For example, many customers testified that they were never told that Scientific had a history of losses or that the June 9, 1969 Wire Flash indicated Scientific estimated it would lose $1.55 million for fiscal year 1969. Further, numerous customers were not informed of the highly speculative nature of Scientific's shares or that Merrill Lynch only recommended the purchase of Scientific's shares to those accounts willing to assume major risks. These omissions, considered in the context of recommendations in which optimistic misstatements regarding Scientific were made, were false and misleading.

* * *

In addition to the misrepresentations and omissions which have been characterized heretofore in this opinion as being violative of the anti-fraud provisions of the securities laws, the record contains several instances of selling practices so inconsistent with a broker's responsibility of fair dealing that they can not escape our comment. As an example, one customer testified that she received a telephone call from her account executive while she was busy at work. The account executive recommended Scientific to her saying that it was "just fabulous" but that he had only "one hundred shares left." He pressed her for an immediate answer by telling her that he had someone else waiting to purchase these shares if she did not want them. The account executive also told her that Scientific was then selling at $33 but he was shooting for a $100 price. She purchased 75 shares of Scientific on May 19, 1969 based on her account executive's recommendation. Such high pressure sales tactics without affording the investor an opportunity to carefully consider even the basic facts are hardly conducive to informed investment decision making and have long been condemned by the Commission.

* * *

On March 9, 1969, The Dallas Times Herald published a feature article on Scientific entitled "Can Dallas Have Its Own IBM." A Merrill

Lynch account executive employed in the Dallas office ordered 250 to 500 photo offset copies of the article and mailed a substantial number of these copies to various Merrill Lynch account executives throughout the country. These account executives in turn reproduced the article, affixed a sticker identifying the firm and the individual account executive and mailed copies to customers. For the most part, the article was sent to customers to reassure them as to their investment in Scientific. In some instances, the article was used as a sales device.

The article by itself was misleading. Its title "Can Dallas Have Its Own IBM" appears to attach the glamour and prestige of IBM to Scientific. The substance of the article was overly optimistic and did nothing to dispel the implication of the title that Scientific may be another IBM. It contained self serving statements by Scientific's president concerning the company's projected sales, backlog of orders, products and the 20 per cent pre-tax profit margin for the computer industry. There was no mention of Scientific's history of losses or the highly speculative nature of the security. Moreover, there was a reference to the sale of the company's first $2.9 million 6700 time sharing computer system. The article stated that the company's president believed Scientific would market 100 of these time sharing systems during the next three years. At a price of $2.9 million per system the article suggested Scientific would have close to $300 million in sales over the next three years in addition to sales of their other computers. There was no reasonable basis in fact for such a projection.

The manner in which certain Merrill Lynch salesmen utilized this article leads us to conclude that this article was adopted by these Merrill Lynch account executives. These account executives had the responsibility to exercise reasonable care to ascertain whether statements made in the article had sufficient factual support. Had this article been properly reviewed it could have been easily discovered that the article contained inaccurate and hyperbolic statements which were misleading.

* * *

Public Interest

After consideration of the offer of settlement of Merrill Lynch wherein the firm offers: to accept the imposition of a censure; to pay a sum of up to $1,600,000 pursuant to the terms of its offer to compensate customers of Merrill Lynch who suffered losses resulting from transactions in Scientific; to undertake to review, and, where appropriate, adopt new or modified guidelines relating to its research and sales activities; and, to undertake to review and, where necessary, strengthen its Account Executive Training Programs, the Commission accepts Merrill Lynch's offer of settlement.

* * *

Twenty nine individual respondents have submitted offers of settlement wherein seven individuals offer to accept suspensions and twenty two individuals offer to accept censures. After consideration of these offers, the Commission has determined to accept them as being in the public interest. * * *

The Commission has also determined that it is appropriate and in the public interest to dismiss this proceeding against nineteen individual respondents. * * *

* * *

---

b.   CHURNING

Mihara v. Dean Witter & Co.

United States Court of Appeals, Ninth Circuit, 1980.
619 F.2d 814.

■ Before CHAMBERS and TANG, CIRCUIT JUDGES, and CAMPBELL, SENIOR DISTRICT JUDGE.

■ WILLIAM J. CAMPBELL, SENIOR DISTRICT JUDGE:

On April 26, 1974, Samuel Mihara filed this action in United States District Court for the Central District of California. * * * [P]laintiff alleges that the defendants, Dean Witter & Company and its account executive, George Gracis, engaged in excessive trading or "churning" in plaintiff's securities account * * *. Plaintiff sought relief under Section 10(b) of the Securities Exchange Act of 1934 and Rule 10b–5 promulgated thereunder * * *. * * *

* * *

On January 6, 1971, plaintiff Mihara opened a joint securities account with the Santa Monica office of Dean Witter. At that time Mihara was employed by the McDonnell-Douglas Corporation as a supervisory engineer. He was 38 years old and possessed a Bachelor of Science and Master's Degree in Engineering. * * *

* * *

Mihara invested $30,000 with Dean Witter. This money was to be invested according to Gracis' recommendations but subject to Mihara's approval.

The history of Mihara's investment account with Dean Witter & Company reflects speculative investments, numerous purchases and sales, and substantial reliance on the recommendations of Gracis. * * * From 1971 to 1973, Mihara's account lost considerable sums of money. Since many of the purchases were on margin, Mihara would often have to come up with additional funds as the equity in his account declined.

The final trading losses in the account totaled $46,464. This loss occurred during the period of January 1971 to May 1973.

Mihara first began to complain of the handling of his account when it showed a loss in April 1971. * * * In October of 1971, Mihara went to Mr. Cypherd, the office manager for the Santa Monica office of Dean Witter. Mihara complained to Cypherd about the handling of the account by Gracis. * * * As the value of Mihara's securities account continued to dwindle, he visited Cypherd on several occasions to complain further about Gracis. While Cypherd told Mihara he was "on top" of the account, the performance and handling of the account did not improve.

At about the same time that Mihara first contacted him, Cypherd was also made aware of substantial trading in the account by means of a Dean Witter Monthly Account Activity Analysis. This analysis was initiated by the Dean Witter computer whenever an account showed 15 or more trades in one month or commissions of $1,000 or more. * * *

In November 1973, Mihara went to the San Francisco office of Dean Witter and complained to Paul Dubow, the National Compliance Director for Dean Witter, Inc. * * * Apparently not satisfied with the results of that meeting, Mihara filed this suit in April 1974.

* * *

Plaintiff's expert, Mr. White, a former attorney with the Securities & Exchange Commission, testified at trial that the pattern of trading in the Mihara account reflected a pattern of churning. Plaintiff's Exhibit 20, Chart G, introduced at trial, indicated the following holding periods for Mihara's securities. In 1971, 50% of the securities were held for 15 days or less, 61% for 30 days or less, and approximately 76% were held for 60 days or less. Through June of 1973, 81.6% of the securities in the Mihara account were held for a period of 180 days or less. White also relied on the "turnover rate" in Mihara's account in reaching his conclusion. The turnover rate for a given period is arrived at by dividing the total dollar amount of stock purchases for a given period by the average monthly capital investment in the account. Plaintiff's Exhibit No. 20, Chart C, indicates that between January 1971 and July 1973, Mihara's average monthly investment of $36,653 was turned over approximately 14 times. On an annualized basis, Mihara's average capital monthly investment in 1971 of approximately $40,000 was turned over 9.3 times. His average capital investment in 1972 was $39,800 and that was turned over approximately 3.36 times. His average monthly capital investment for the first half of 1973 was $23,588 and that was turned over approximately .288 times. White testified that a substantial turnover in the early stages of the account followed by a significant decline in the turnover rate was typical of a churned account.

White also testified that the holding periods for securities in Mihara's account reflected a pattern of churning. He noted that churned accounts usually reflect significant turnover in the early stages, that is, a very short holding period for the securities purchased, followed by longer holding periods in the later stages of the account. Thus, the typical churned account is churned in the early stages of the account generating large commissions at the outset, followed by less trading and longer holding periods in the latter stages of the account, after significant commissions have been generated. Mihara's account reflects precisely that pattern. The cumulative total of commissions earned by Gracis was $12,672, the majority of which came in the early stages of the account.

In addition to the testimony of Mr. White that, in his expert opinion, Mihara's account had been "churned," plaintiff's expert witness McCuen also testified that in his opinion the securities purchased from Mihara's account were not suitable for Mihara's stated investment objectives. Mr. McCuen based his analysis in part on rankings found in reports in the "Value Line" investment service newsletter which rates those stocks poorly. Mr. McCuen noted that the securities in question were rated as high risk securities with below average financial strength.

* * *

* * * The jury * * * returned a verdict for the plaintiff.

* * * We affirm the judgment below in all respects.

When a securities broker engages in excessive trading in disregard of his customer's investment objectives for the purpose of generating commission business, the customer may hold the broker liable for churning in violation of Rule 10b–5. In order to establish a claim of churning, a plaintiff must show (1) that the trading in his account was excessive in light of his investment objectives; (2) that the broker in question exercised control over the trading in the account; and (3) that the broker acted with the intent to defraud or with the willful and reckless disregard for the interests of his client.

Whether trading is excessive is a question which must be examined in light of the investment objectives of the customer. While there is no clear line of demarcation, courts and commentators have suggested that an annual turnover rate of six reflects excessive trading. In Hecht v. Harris Upham & Company, 430 F.2d 1202, 1210 (9th Cir., 1970), this Court affirmed a finding of churning where an account had been turned over 8 to 11.5 times during a six-year ten-month period. In that case, 45% of the securities were held for less than six months, 67% were held for less than nine months, and 82% were held for less than a year. Under this Court's holding in *Hecht*, the evidence in the present case clearly supports a finding of excessive trading.

With regard to the second prerequisite, we believe that Gracis exercised sufficient control over Mihara's account in the present case to support a finding of churning. The account need not be a discretionary account whereby the broker executes each trade without the consent of the client. As the *Hecht* case indicates, the requisite degree of control is met when the client routinely follows the recommendations of the broker.

The present case, as in *Hecht*, reflects a pattern of *de facto* control by the broker.

The third requisite element of a 10b–5 violation-scienter-has also been established. The manner in which Mihara's account was handled reflects, at best, a reckless disregard for the client's investment concerns, and, at worst, an outright scheme to defraud plaintiff. * * *

* * *

c.   SUITABILITY

O'Connor v. R.F. Lafferty & Co., Inc.
United States Court of Appeals, Tenth Circuit, 1992.
965 F.2d 893.

■ Before BRORBY and MCWILLIAMS, CIRCUIT JUDGES, and ALLEY, DISTRICT JUDGE.

■ BRORBY, CIRCUIT JUDGE.

Plaintiff appeals the district court's grant of summary judgment disposing of her federal * * * securities law claims. * * *

I.   FACTS

In 1975, Carol M. O'Connor received a $200,000 property settlement from her divorce. She deposited this entire sum into an account with the investment firm of R.F. Lafferty & Company, Inc., to be handled by Roy Foulke. * * *

Ms. O'Connor gave Mr. Foulke and Lafferty complete discretion to handle her account. Mr. Foulke knew Ms. O'Connor was not an experienced investor. * * * Her husband or her father had always handled her finances. Ms. O'Connor informed Mr. Foulke the money she deposited represented virtually all of her assets. Ms. O'Connor also instructed Mr. Foulke she would need to rely on the $700 income generated from her deposit and the $800 maintenance payments from her ex-husband to meet her monthly living expenses. Ms. O'Connor also expected her account to generate sufficient income to cover the taxes on her alimony and on the account, the fees of her accountant and the servicing fees for her account. Mr. Foulke knew Ms. O'Connor relied on him to make all decisions concerning her securities account. Consequently, Mr. Foulke traded on Ms. O'Connor's account and notified her of the trading activity by sending a trade ticket within thirty-six hours and again at the end of the month in her statement.

In 1985, because of the success in Ms. O'Connor's investment account, her husband was relieved of his alimony obligation. Understandably, this event changed the nature of her financial plan.

From that point, Ms. O'Connor's account would have to generate $2,100 a month.

Ms. O'Connor first became concerned about the value of her account in February 1987. Ms. O'Connor contends that from 1982 through 1987 Mr. Foulke and Lafferty purchased several securities unsuitable for her investment objectives. Specifically, Ms. O'Connor objects to investments in oil and gas limited partnerships; units of stock and warrants in Patient Medical Systems Corporation; units of International Surgical and Pharmaceutical Corporation securities; units in Job Stores, Inc. securities; units in R.T. Acquisition Corporation securities; and units of Kerkoff Industries, Inc. securities. Ms. O'Connor requested a judgment for actual damages of $329,000 plus a reasonable rate of return on amounts unsuitably invested that earned no income.

In 1988, Ms. O'Connor directed Mr. Foulke to stop all trading on her account. She brought suit against Mr. Foulke and against Lafferty for the acts of Mr. Foulke as a controlling person and under the doctrine of respondeat superior asserting seven claims [, including] violation of § 10(b) of the 1934 Securities Exchange Act and Rule 10b–5 promulgated thereunder * * * .

* * *

II. ANALYSIS

A. Unsuitability

The district court granted Defendants' motion for summary judgment against Ms. O'Connor's § 10(b) and Rule 10b–5 claim. The court found the Defendants did not possess the requisite scienter or intent to defraud to sustain such a claim. The court also found that although the Defendants did invest in securities unsuitable for Ms. O'Connor's investment objectives, Ms. O'Connor could not demonstrate her justifiable reliance on the purchases where she had information the securities may be unsuitable and acted recklessly by failing to investigate. The court found persuasive deposition testimony by Ms. O'Connor where she admitted Mr. Foulke did not intend to defraud or hurt her. She further testified he did not willfully withhold information or lie to her.

* * *

Ms. O'Connor claims Defendants bought securities which were unsuitable for her investment needs. Federal courts recognize such a claim as a violation of § 10(b) and Rule 10b–5.

The unsuitability doctrine is premised on New York Stock Exchange Rule 405—Know Your Customer Rule and the National Association of Securities Dealers Rules of Fair Practice. Unsuitability claims can be analyzed as omission cases or fraudulent practices cases.

Some courts examining a § 10(b), Rule 10b–5 unsuitability claim have analyzed it simply as a misrepresentation or failure to disclose a material fact. In such a case, the broker has omitted telling the investor the recommendation is unsuitable for the investor's interests. The court may then use traditional laws concerning omission to examine the claim.

Under a misrepresentation or omission theory, a plaintiff can establish § 10(b), Rule 10b–5 liability by showing that in connection with the purchase or sale of a security—the broker made an untrue statement of a material fact, or failed to state a material fact, that in so doing, the broker acted knowingly with intent to deceive or defraud, and that plaintiff relied on the misrepresentations, and sustained damages as a proximate result of the misrepresentations.

In contrast, Ms. O'Connor asserts an unsuitability claim based on fraud by conduct. She does not assert Mr. Foulke omitted to tell her the stocks he purchased were unsuitable for her investment needs. Rather, she claims that his purchase of the stocks for her account acted as fraud upon her.

Fraud by conduct is a violation of Rule 10b–5(a) and (c) and is analogous to a churning claim. Churning is excessive trading on an account by a broker in light of the investor's objectives. This circuit has also recognized a violation of the NYSE Know Your Customer rule and the NASD Suitability Rule can be used to determine whether an account had been churned. See * * * Miley v. Oppenheimer & Co., Inc., 637 F.2d 318, 333 (5th Cir.1981). The *Miley* court acknowledged these rules are excellent tools to assess the *"reasonableness or excessiveness* of a broker's handling of an investor's account." (emphasis added). Thus, the rules are used to assess the quantity and quality of the broker's trading activity.

* * *

While the elements of a churning claim are well established, the elements of an unsuitability claim based on fraud are not. * * *

Because an unsuitability claim is so similar to a churning claim, we are persuaded the established "churning" elements can aid in our determination of the appropriate elements for an unsuitability cause of action. Today we adopt three elements to establish unsuitability based on fraud by conduct: The plaintiff must prove (1) the broker recommended (or in the case of a discretionary account purchased) securities which are unsuitable in light of the investor's objectives; (2) the broker recommended or purchased the securities with an intent to defraud or with reckless disregard for the investor's interests; and (3) the broker exercised control over the investor's account.

Whether the control element of a churning claim applies to its cousin the unsuitability claim has been an open question. We believe the control element is essential to satisfy the causation/reliance requirement of a § 10(b), Rule 10b–5 violation.

In this case, we conclude the scienter element is dispositive. Based on our review of the record we hold Ms. O'Connor has failed, as a matter of law, to establish the scienter requirement of an unsuitability claim and affirm the district court's summary judgment against Ms. O'Connor's § 10(b), Rule 10b–5 claim.

* * *

"Day trading" is a strategy for speculating on short-term changes in market price and generally involving buying and selling securities within a single day. FINRA Rule 2130 requires member firms promoting day-trading strategies to establish accounts for would-be day traders only upon "reasonable grounds for believing that the day-trading strategy is appropriate for the customer." As part of the required process, firms must either approve an account for day trading or obtain a written agreement that it will not be so used. Pursuant to Rule 2360, member firms promoting day-trading strategies also must provide non-institutional customers with risk-disclosure statements.

d.   NET CAPITAL, RECORDKEEPING, AND REPORTING REQUIREMENTS

In re Whitney & Co.

Securities and Exchange Commission, 1962.
40 S.E.C. 1100.

■ PER CURIAM:

These proceedings were instituted pursuant to Section 15(b) of the Securities Exchange Act of 1934 ("Act"), to determine whether to revoke the registration as a broker and dealer of Whitney & Company, Inc. ("registrant"), and whether, under Section 15A(b)(4) of the Act, Francis H. Mitchell, president of registrant, is a cause of an order of revocation if issued. Subsequent to the institution of these proceedings, registrant requested withdrawal of its registration.

* * *

Registrant, a Delaware corporation, became registered as a broker and dealer in September 1955. Registrant admits, and we find, that it had a net capital deficiency as computed under Rule * * * 15c3–1 of approximately $14,866 as of October 31, 1958, and $16,558 as of November 18, 1958, that between those dates registrant was in substantially the same capital position as it was on those dates, and that Mitchell, who was in full charge and control of all of registrant's activities, caused registrant to effect over-the-counter securities transactions during that period through the use of the mails and of the facilities of interstate commerce. * * * We conclude that registrant, aided and abetted by Mitchell, willfully violated the net capital requirements of Section 15(c)(3) of the Act and Rule 15c3–1 thereunder.

Registrant further failed to file a report of financial condition as of a date within the year 1958 as required by Rule * * * 17a–5 under Section

17(a) of the Act. Such a report was required to be filed within 45 days from the year's end, but no report was submitted until October 1959, after the institution of these proceedings. We find that registrant, aided and abetted by Mitchell, in this respect willfully violated Section 17(a) and Rule 17a–5.

The record also shows that as of October 30, and November 3, 1958, certain accounts in registrant's general ledger were not posted up to date. Accrued commissions and taxes payable were posted only to September 1, 1958, and accounts payable, prepaid expenses, and accounts receivable were posted to September 30, 1958. The unposted commissions aggregated $5,412 payable to some 50 salesmen and the other unposted liabilities totaled $5,034. Included in the latter amount was a note payable to a bank for $2,500, dated August 29, 1958, of which there was no record in registrant's books. We accordingly find that registrant, aided and abetted by Mitchell, willfully violated the record-keeping requirements of Section 17(a) and Rule * * * 17a–3 thereunder.

Respondents do not quarrel with the findings of willful violations of the Act, but urge that, since they are no longer in the securities business and registrant seeks to withdraw its registration, the public interest does not require revocation. They point out that by November 25, 1958, registrant's books were posted to November 18, and that by December 11, 1958, they had arranged for additional capital to be invested to correct the net capital deficiency. With respect to registrant's failure to file a timely financial report for 1958, respondents assert that submission of a certified report had appeared necessary in connection with other proceedings involving them and that the audit necessary for the report required by Rule 17a–5 was deferred in order to avoid the expense of two audits. They further argue that the fact that registrant had ceased doing business as a broker-dealer in November 1958, minimizes the seriousness of the reporting delay.

We have considered the factors urged in mitigation but have concluded that they do not warrant withdrawal of registration. Respondents were well aware of the provisions of our net capital rule. Registrant continued its securities business while its net capital was substantially below the amount required by Rule 15c3–1 and indeed, as the record shows, while it had a substantial deficit in net capital under that rule. Registrant's willful violation in this respect cannot be viewed lightly. As the Court of Appeals stated in Blaise D'Antoni & Associates, Inc. v. S.E.C., which upheld the revocation of registration based on net capital violations, "the net capital rule is one of the most important weapons in the Commission's arsenal to protect investors." Further, while Rule 17a–5 provides that application may be made for an extension of time for the filing of a report of financial condition in cases of undue hardship, registrant permitted the time for filing the required report to expire without requesting an extension despite the fact that Mitchell informed our staff on January 27, 1959, that a year-end audit was in process of preparation.

* * *

Under all the circumstances we conclude that it is in the public interest to revoke registrant's registration, and that Mitchell is a cause of such revocation.

* * *

---

e.   BOILER-ROOMS

Berko v. SEC

United States Court of Appeals, Second Circuit, 1963.
316 F.2d 137.

■ Before CLARK, FRIENDLY and MARSHALL, CIRCUIT JUDGES.

■ MARSHALL, CIRCUIT JUDGE.

This is a petition for review of an order of the Securities and Exchange Commission entered pursuant to a remand by this court of a former order of the Commission. The original petition sought review of a Commission order of February 6, 1961, which found that Irwin Berko, a salesman, was a cause of revocation of the broker and dealer registration of his employer, MacRobbins & Co., Inc.

* * * In its Findings and Opinion the Commission held, on the basis of the record, that MacRobbins & Co. and nine of its salesmen, including petitioner, had violated the anti-fraud provisions of Section 17(a) of the Securities Act of 1933; of Sections 10(b) and 15(c)(1) of the Securities Exchange Act of 1934; and of Rules 10b–5 and 15c1–2 thereunder, in the offer and sale of the stock of Sports Arenas, Inc., a Delaware corporation.

* * *

In its opinion * * * , the Commission reviews the applicable law and * * * emphasizes the evils inherent in "boiler-room" operations.[8] There

---

[8]   In its opinion on remand, the Commission sums up such operations as follows:

"These boiler-room operations, relying for the most part on oral representation, subject the requirements of fair dealing to their greatest test and the enforcement of the statutory prohibitions against fraud to grave difficulties. The assault on the investors' dollars is frequently initiated by sales brochures artfully contrived to avoid express falsehood; instead, nuances and implications are used in presenting information of a general nature to create an optimistic picture and to obscure, conceal or distort essential or material information concerning the specific security offered. This is soon followed by telephone solicitations by skilled salesmen recruited solely for their ability to execute effectively a 'hard sell' campaign. The optimistic picture presented by the brochures is heightened by oral projections of specific per share earnings, predictions of market price rises and other happy prospects wholly lacking an adequate basis. At no time is disclosure made of any known or reasonably ascertainable adverse information. Nor is any word of caution given as to the risks involved. When the conversation is completed and the transaction effected, the can be no question that MacRobbins was operating a "boiler-room" in plain violation of the statute and that there was ample evidence to support that portion of the order revoking its broker-dealer registration; indeed, the registrant had entered into a stipulation consenting to the revocation. MacRobbins had set up the operation for the principal and specialized purpose of selling a single stock, that of Sports Arenas, Inc. At least two brochures, both of which were properly found to be deceptive and misleading, were widely distributed through the mails. Ten salesmen were employed to make telephone calls to and receive telephone calls from prospective customers and to urge the purchase of Sports Arenas stock. A result was that more than 100,000 shares were sold between October 1957 and November 1958. The operation of MacRobbins was also characterized by a lack of knowledge or failure to disclose the true financial condition of Sports Arenas. * * *

* * *

The findings of the Commission are supported by substantial evidence and its order is based upon a fully permissible view of how best the "public interest" will be served. Berko worked in an office which was plainly established to be a "boiler-room" and which Berko knew to be a "boiler-room." He worked with two other salesmen in an office space having six telephones, as part of a sales operation which relied almost entirely upon long-distance telephone solicitation for its success. He studied, mailed out, and utilized brochures which he should have known and, on proper study, could have determined were deceptive and misleading. He did not know and hence was unable to tell prospective customers that Sports Arenas, Inc., was operating at a loss. Finally, although he sold some other stocks, Berko knew that Sports Arenas was the principal stock that MacRobbins was selling during the six-month period that he worked for the company.

These facts fully justified the Commission—in seeking to protect "the investing and usually naive public", Norris & Hirshberg, Inc. v. S.E.C., 85 U.S.App.D.C. 268, 177 F.2d 228, 233 (1949), and "those who lack business acumen," United States v. Monjar, 47 F.Supp. 421, 425 (D.Del.1942)—in holding Berko, a "boiler-room" salesman, chargeable with knowledge of the contents of the brochures and with responsibility for allowing customers to rely upon them. The Commission acted well within its mandate in concluding that the "public interest" requires that a salesman working out of a "boiler-room" be held to a higher duty to prospective customers than a salesman working out of a legitimate sales operation, and in concluding that a "boiler-room" salesman does not meet his obligation when he has no knowledge other than opinions and brochures furnished by the broker, "without any checking, investigation, or determination of the correctness of the same before putting them out to the public." S.E.C. v. Macon, 28 F.Supp. 127, 129 (D.Colo.1939). As the

---

customer is left with rosy expectations of gain without risk deliberately and dishonestly created by these high-pressure selling techniques."

Commission appropriately said in its opinion, "Whatever may be a salesman's obligation of inquiry, or his right to rely on information provided by his employer, where securities of an established issuer are being recommended to customers by a broker-dealer who is not engaged in misleading and deceptive high-pressure selling practices, * * * there can be little, if any, justification for a claim of reliance on literature furnished by an employer who is engaged in a fraudulent sales campaign." This is an entirely proper and indeed salutary principle for the Commission to employ in coping with the problems presented by "boiler-room" operations.

That Berko failed to meet the higher duty set forth in this principle has already been made clear. With knowledge of the wide circulation of the misleading brochures mailed by him and others to prospective customers and without adequate knowledge of the financial condition of Sports Arenas, Inc., including the fact disclosed by the nine and eleven months financial statements already available at the time of his conversation with Thurm, that it was operating at a loss, he sold the stock "to just about everybody." Moreover, at a time when the stock of Sports Arenas, Inc., was selling for $7 per share, he represented to Thurm that there was a good possibility that it would rise to as high as $15 per share within a year. No adequate basis existed, as Berko should have known, for such an optimistic representation. * * *

* * *

C. MARGIN REQUIREMENTS

Buying securities on excessive credit, or margin, was one of the problems that led to the stock market collapse that began in 1929. In many cases, customers who purchased securities used only a small percentage of their own money. As soon as security prices began to fall, large amounts of securities had to be dumped into a non-receptive market to prevent losses by those who had lent most of the money for the purchase of the securities. These sales then caused the market to fall even lower. The drafters of the Exchange Act were determined to prevent a recurrence of these conditions by establishing a system for regulating the amount of credit that can be used to purchase or carry securities.

The work of the drafters is found in Section 7 of the Exchange Act. It provides that, initially upon the passage of the Act in 1934, the amount of credit that may be used to purchase or carry a non-exempted equity security is not to be more than the higher of:

    (1) 55 per centum of the current market price of the security, or

(2) 100 per centum of the lowest market price of the security during the preceding thirty-six calendar months, but not more than 75 per centum of the current market price.

Congress realized that the amount of credit to be allowed, along with certain related matters, must be fine-tuned periodically. Therefore, in Section 7, Congress gave power over these issues to the Board of Governors of the Federal Reserve System (and made borrowing in violation of the Board's rules illegal). Since 1934 the Board has controlled margin requirements through a series of regulations and amendments to these regulations. Regulation T governs credit extended by brokers and dealers,[9] Regulation U covers the granting of credit by banks, and Regulation G handles lending by certain other persons. Regulation X contains rules governing borrowers. The current margin requirement under Regulation T for an initial investment is 50 percent.

Nothing in the authority granted to the Board of Governors of the Federal Reserve System prevents the entities or individuals regulated from imposing stricter margin requirements than those mandated by the applicable Regulation. For instance, FINRA (with the approval of the SEC) imposes somewhat stricter requirements on the accounts of "pattern day traders." For this purpose, "pattern day trading" generally is defined as the execution through a margin account of four intra-day purchases and sales within a period of five days.

D. REGULATION OF THE SECURITY-BASED SWAP INDUSTRY

In the Dodd-Frank Act of 2010, Congress sought to create a regulatory regime governing the market for swaps. The Commission was allocated responsibility for the part of the market known as "security-based swaps." In the words of the Commission, this means that the Commission regulates:

Dealers and major players in the security-based swap market;

Trading platforms and exchanges on which certain security-based swaps would be transacted;

Clearing agencies that generally step in the place of the original counterparties and effectively assume the risk should there be a default; and

Data repositories, which would collect data on security-based swaps as they are transacted by counterparties, make that information available to regulators, and disseminate data, such

---

[9]　It is worth noting that Exchange Act Rule 10b–16 requires brokers and dealers to make certain disclosures in connection with extensions of credit; changes in terms with less than thirty days notice are prohibited.

as the prices of security-based swap transactions, to the public.[10]

Although this is a specialized area generally beyond the scope of this book, it is worth noting that rules have been adopted for the registration and conduct of security-based swap dealers.[11] In addition, Regulation SBSR created a framework for regulatory reporting and disseminating security-based swap information. Other rules are still in progress.

---

[10] From "The Regulatory Regime for Security-Based Swaps," Securities and Exchange Commission (2013), available at www.sec.gov.

[11] These rules may be found at Rule 15Fb1–1, *et seq.*, and Rule 15Fh–1, *et seq.*

PART 4

SECURITIES LAW LITIGATION

CHAPTER 17

ISSUES FOR SECURITIES LITIGATORS

SITUATION 17

Your law firm has asked you to move, at least temporarily, from the corporate and securities department to the litigation department, where you are to work on securities matters traditionally handled by litigators. Looking toward this move, it is necessary that you become familiar with issues that are of special interest to litigators.

In considering this situation, refer to the following, in addition to the materials in this chapter: Securities Act Sections 8A, 9, 13, and 19–22, and Exchange Act Sections 20–22, 25, 27, and 27A.

A. COMMISSION'S INVESTIGATORY POWERS

The involvement of a securities litigator often begins at the point when a client learns it is the subject of an investigation by the Commission. So far as the Securities Act and the Exchange Act are concerned, the Commission's general powers in this respect derive from Securities Act Section 19 and Exchange Act Section 21, which give the Commission broad powers to conduct investigations into possible statutory violations. In addition, other sections of the securities laws give the Commission the power to hold hearings in specific circumstances. Examples are Securities Act Section 8A and Exchange Act Section 21C, which relate to cease-and-desist orders. The following case provides a good introduction to the general investigatory powers of the Commission.

SEC v. Jerry T. O'Brien, Inc.

Supreme Court of the United States, 1984.
467 U.S. 735.

■ JUSTICE MARSHALL delivered the opinion of the Court.

The Securities and Exchange Commission (SEC or Commission) has statutory authority to conduct non-public investigations into possible violations of the securities laws and, in the course thereof, to issue subpoenas to obtain relevant information. The question before us is whether the Commission must notify the "target" of such an investigation when it issues a subpoena to a third party.

I

This case represents one shard of a prolonged investigation by the SEC into the affairs of respondent Harry F. Magnuson and persons and firms with whom he has dealt. The investigation began in 1980, when the Commission's staff reported to the Commission that information in their possession tended to show that Magnuson and others had been trading in the stock of specified mining companies in a manner violative of the registration, reporting, and anti-fraud provisions of the Securities Act of 1933 and the Securities Exchange Act of 1934. In response, the Commission issued a Formal Order of Investigation[1] authorizing employees of its Seattle Regional Office to initiate a "private investigation" into the transactions in question and, if necessary, to subpoena testimony and documents "deemed relevant or material to the inquiry."

Acting on that authority, members of the Commission staff subpoenaed financial records in the possession of respondent Jerry T. O'Brien, Inc. (O'Brien), a broker-dealer firm, and respondent Pennaluna & Co. (Pennaluna). O'Brien voluntarily complied, but Pennaluna refused to disgorge the requested materials. Soon thereafter, in response to several inquiries by O'Brien's counsel, a member of the SEC staff informed O'Brien that it was a "subject" of the investigation.

O'Brien, Pennaluna, and their respective owners[2] promptly filed a suit in the District Court for the Eastern District of Washington, seeking to enjoin the Commission's investigation and to prevent Magnuson from complying with subpoenas that had been issued to him.[3] Magnuson filed a cross-claim, also seeking to block portions of the investigation. O'Brien then filed motions seeking authority to depose the Commission's officers and to conduct expedited discovery into the Commission's files.

The District Court denied respondents' discovery motions and soon thereafter dismissed their claims for injunctive relief. The principal ground for the court's decision was that respondents would have a full opportunity to assert their objections to the basis and scope of the SEC's investigation if and when the Commission instituted a subpoena enforcement action. The court did, however, rule that the Commission's

---

[1] A Formal Order of Investigation is issued by the Commission only after its staff has conducted a preliminary inquiry, in the course of which "no process is issued [nor] testimony compelled." 17 CFR § 202.5(a) (1983). The purposes of such an order seem to be to define the scope of the ensuing investigation and to establish limits within which the staff may resort to compulsory process. See H.R.Rep. No. 96–1321, pt. 1, p. 2 (1980).

[2] The relationships between O'Brien, Pennaluna, and their individual owners are not fully elucidated by the papers before us. Because, for the purposes of this litigation, the interests of all of these respondents are identical, hereinafter they will be referred to collectively as O'Brien, except when divergence in their treatment by the courts below requires that they be differentiated.

[3] The principal bases of O'Brien's suit were that the SEC's Formal Order of Investigation was defective, that the investigation did not have a valid purpose, that the Commission should have afforded the subjects of the investigation a chance to comment upon it, and that the issues around which the case revolved had been litigated and settled in another proceeding.

outstanding subpoenas met the requirements outlined in United States v. Powell, 379 U.S. 48 (1964), for determining whether an administrative summons is judicially enforceable. Specifically, the District Court held that the Commission had a legitimate purpose in issuing the subpoenas, that the requested information was relevant and was not already in the Commission's possession, and that the issuance of the subpoenas comported with pertinent procedural requirements.

Following the District Court's decision, the SEC issued several subpoenas to third parties. In response, Magnuson and O'Brien renewed their request to the District Court for injunctive relief, accompanying the request with a motion, pursuant to Rule 62(c) of the Federal Rules of Civil Procedure, for a stay pending appeal. For the first time, respondents expressly sought notice of the subpoenas issued by the Commission to third parties. Reasoning that respondents lacked standing to challenge voluntary compliance with subpoenas by third parties, and that, in any subsequent proceeding brought by the SEC, respondents could move to suppress evidence the Commission had obtained from third parties through abusive subpoenas, the District Court denied the requested relief.

A panel of the Court of Appeals for the Ninth Circuit affirmed the District Court's denial of injunctive relief with regard to the subpoenas directed at respondents themselves, agreeing with the lower court that respondents had an adequate remedy at law for challenging those subpoenas. However, the Court of Appeals reversed the District Court's denial of respondents' request for notice of subpoenas issued to third parties. In the Court of Appeals' view, "targets" of SEC investigations "have a right to be investigated consistently with the *Powell* standards." *Id.*, at 1068. To enable targets to enforce this right, the court held that they must be notified of subpoenas issued to others.

* * *

We granted certiorari because of the importance of the issue presented. We now reverse.

II

Congress has vested the SEC with broad authority to conduct investigations into possible violations of the federal securities laws and to demand production of evidence relevant to such investigations. *E.g.*, [Securities Act § 19(b), Exchange Act § 21(a), (b)]. Subpoenas issued by the Commission are not self-enforcing, and the recipients thereof are not subject to penalty for refusal to obey. But the Commission is authorized to bring suit in federal court to compel compliance with its process. *E.g.*, [Securities Act § 22(b), Exchange Act § 21(c)].

No provision in the complex of statutes governing the SEC's investigative power expressly obliges the Commission to notify the "target" of an investigation when it issues a subpoena to a third party. If such an obligation is to be imposed on the Commission, therefore, it must be derived from one of three sources: a constitutional provision; an understanding on the part of Congress, inferable from the structure of the securities laws, regarding how the SEC should conduct its inquiries; or the general standards governing judicial enforcement of administrative subpoenas enunciated in United States v. Powell, 379 U.S. 48 (1964), and its progeny. Examination of these three potential bases for the Court of Appeals' ruling leaves us unpersuaded that the notice requirement fashioned by that court is warranted.

A

Our prior cases foreclose any constitutional argument respondents might make in defense of the judgment below. The opinion of the Court in Hannah v. Larche, 363 U.S. 420 (1960), leaves no doubt that neither the Due Process Clause of the Fifth Amendment nor the Confrontation Clause of the Sixth Amendment is offended when a federal administrative agency, without notifying a person under investigation, uses its subpoena power to gather evidence adverse to him. The Due Process Clause is not implicated under such circumstances because an administrative investigation adjudicates no legal rights, and the Confrontation Clause does not come into play until the initiation of criminal proceedings. These principles plainly cover an inquiry by the SEC into possible violations of the securities laws.

It is also settled that a person inculpated by materials sought by a subpoena issued to a third party cannot seek shelter in the Self-Incrimination Clause of the Fifth Amendment. The rationale of this doctrine is that the Constitution proscribes only *compelled* self-incrimination, and, whatever may be the pressures exerted upon the person to whom a subpoena is directed, the subpoena surely does not "compel" anyone else to be a witness against himself. If the "target" of an investigation by the SEC has no Fifth Amendment right to challenge enforcement of a subpoena directed at a third party, he clearly can assert no derivative right to notice when the Commission issues such a subpoena.

Finally, respondents cannot invoke the Fourth Amendment in support of the Court of Appeals' decision. It is established that, when a person communicates information to a third party even on the understanding that the communication is confidential, he cannot object if the third party conveys that information or records thereof to law enforcement authorities. United States v. Miller, 425 U.S. 435, 443 (1976). Relying on that principle, the Court has held that a customer of a bank cannot challenge on Fourth Amendment grounds the admission into evidence in a criminal prosecution of financial records obtained by the Government from his bank pursuant to allegedly defective subpoenas, despite the fact that he was given no notice of the subpoenas. *Id.*, at 443, and n. 5. These rulings disable respondents from arguing that notice of subpoenas issued to third parties is necessary to allow a target to prevent an unconstitutional search or seizure of his papers.

B

The language and structure of the statutes administered by the Commission afford respondents no greater aid. The provisions vesting the SEC with the power to issue and seek enforcement of subpoenas are expansive. For example, § 19(b) of the Securities Act of 1933 empowers the SEC to conduct investigations "which, in the opinion of the Commission, are necessary and proper for the enforcement" of the Act and to "require the production of any books, papers, or other documents which the Commission deems relevant or material to the inquiry." Similarly, §§ 21(a) and 21(b) of the Securities Exchange Act of 1934 authorize the Commission to "make such investigations as it deems necessary to determine whether any person has violated, is violating, or is about to violate any provision of this chapter [or] the rules or regulations thereunder" and to demand to see any papers "the Commission deems relevant or material to the inquiry."

More generally, both statutes vest the SEC with "power to make such rules and regulations as may be necessary or appropriate to implement [their] provisions * * * ." [Securities Act § 19(a), Exchange Act § 23(a)(1).] Relying on this authority, the SEC has promulgated a variety of rules governing its investigations, one of which provides that, "[u]nless otherwise ordered by the Commission, all formal investigative proceedings shall be non-public." 17 CFR § 203.5 (1983). In other words, the Commission has formally adopted the policy of not routinely informing anyone, including targets, of the existence and progress of its investigations. To our knowledge, Congress has never questioned this exercise by the Commission of its statutory power. And, in another context, we have held that rulemaking authority comparable to that enjoyed by the SEC is broad enough to empower an agency to "establish standards for determining whether to conduct an investigation publicly or in private." FCC v. Schreiber, 381 U.S. 279, 292 (1965).

It appears, in short, that Congress intended to vest the SEC with considerable discretion in determining when and how to investigate possible violations of the statutes administered by the Commission. We discern no evidence that Congress wished or expected that the Commission would adopt any particular procedures for notifying "targets" of investigations when it sought information from third parties.

* * *

III

Nothing in this opinion should be construed to imply that it would be improper for the SEC to inform a target that it has issued a subpoena to someone else. But, for the reasons indicated above, we decline to curtail the Commission's discretion to determine when such notice would be appropriate and when it would not. * * *

* * *

B. STATUTES OF LIMITATION

I. PRIVATE RIGHTS OF ACTION

a. SECURITIES ACT OF 1933

Section 13 of the Securities Act contains that Act's provision on limitation of actions:

> Section 13. No action shall be maintained to enforce any liability created under section 11 or section 12(a)(2) unless brought within one year after the discovery of the untrue statement or the omission, or after such discovery should have been made by the exercise of reasonable diligence, or, if the action is to enforce a liability created under section 12(a)(1), unless brought within one year after the violation upon which it is based. In no event shall any such action be brought to enforce a liability created under section 11 or section 12(a)(1) more than three years after the security was bona fide offered to the public, or under section 12(a)(2) more than three years after the sale.

In June 2017, the Supreme Court held in California Public Employees' Retirement System v. ANZ Securities, Inc.,[4] that the three-year-from-offering limitations period was a statute of repose and was not subject to equitable tolling.

In the unlikely event a private right of action were to be implied under Section 17(a)(1) of the Securities Act, which relates to fraudulent conduct of various sorts, Section 804 of Sarbanes-Oxley would have an effect. Sarbanes-Oxley Section 804 amended 28 U.S.C. § 1658 to provide that, with respect to proceedings commenced on or after July 30, 2002:

> [A] private right of action that involves a claim of fraud, deceit, manipulation, or contrivance in contravention of a regulatory requirement concerning the securities laws . . . may be brought not later than the earlier of:
>
> (1) 2 years after the discovery of the facts constituting the violation; or
>
> (2) 5 years after such violation.

Note that Section 804 covers actions involving claims of "fraud," among other claims, such as for "deceit" and "manipulation." Though, as discussed at the beginning of Chapter 8BV, scienter is required only for actions under Section 17(a)(1), while negligence is all that is required under Sections 17(a)(2) and (3), Section 17(a)(3) uses the word "fraud." Plaintiffs' lawyers may claim that because of the use of the word "fraud"

---

[4]   137 S.Ct.2042 (2017).

in both Section 804 of Sarbanes-Oxley and in Section 17(a)(3), the statute of limitations for Section 17(a)(3) is the "two year from discovery/five year from occurrence" period of Sarbanes-Oxley.

b. EXCHANGE ACT OF 1934

Those sections of the Exchange Act expressly providing for civil liability contain their own provisions limiting actions. Thus, Section 9(f) (creating an express private right for manipulation) and Section 18(a) (creating an express private right for misrepresentations in Exchange Act filings) both state a "one year from discovery/three year from occurrence" rule similar to that contained in Section 13 of the Securities Act. Section 20A (creating an express private right for those trading contemporaneously with person violating the Exchange Act by insider trading) contains a "five year from last transaction" rule. Section 16(b) (establishing a right to recover on behalf of an issuer the profits from short-swing trading) provides for a limitation of two years after the date the profit in question was realized.

More generally, the "two year from discovery/five year from occurrence" limits imposed by Sarbanes-Oxley Section 804 now apply to proceedings brought under the Exchange Act. Those proceedings include those based on implied private rights of action under Section 10(b) and Rule 10b–5. In 2010, in Merck & Co. v. Reynolds,[5] the Supreme Court held that discovery occurs either when the plaintiff actually discovers the facts constituting the violation, or when a reasonably diligent plaintiff would have discovered those facts, whichever comes first. The facts constituting the violation include scienter; mere discovery that statements are inaccurate or incomplete will not suffice. The idea that "discovery" should be determined on the basis of inquiry notice (the point at which a plaintiff possesses enough information suggestive of wrongdoing that he should conduct further inquiry) specifically was rejected.

Lampf, Pleva, Lipkind, Prupis & Petigrown v. Gilbertson[6] is an earlier Supreme Court case that is instructive on the subject of equitable tolling in the context of a statute of limitations with an [x] number of years from discovery and [y] number of years from occurrence" structure. The Court had this to say:

> Finally, we address plaintiff-respondents' contention that, whatever limitations period is applicable to § 10(b) claims, that period must be subject to the doctrine of equitable tolling. Plaintiff-respondents note, correctly, that "[t]ime requirements in law suits * * * are customarily subject to 'equitable tolling.' " * * * . Thus, this Court has said that in the usual case, "where the party injured by the fraud remains in ignorance of it without

---

[5]   559 U.S. 633 (2010).

[6]   501 U.S. 350 (1991).

any fault or want of diligence or care on his part, the bar of the statute does not begin to run until the fraud is discovered, though there be no special circumstances or efforts on the part of the party committing the fraud to conceal it from the knowledge of the other party." Bailey v. Glover, 21 Wall. 342, 348 (1874). Notwithstanding this venerable principle, it is evident that the equitable tolling doctrine is a fundamentally inconsistent with the [x]-and-[y]-year structure.

The [x]-year period, by its terms, begins after discovery of the facts constituting the violation, making tolling unnecessary. The [y]-year limit is a period of repose inconsistent with tolling. * * * because the purpose of the [y]-year limitation is clearly to serve as a cutoff, we hold that tolling principles do not apply to that period.

This is, of course, consistent with the Court's recent decision in California Public Employees' Retirement System v. ANZ Securities, Inc., relating to Section 13 of the Securities Act. By contrast, in Credit Suisse Securities LLC v. Simmonds,[7] the Supreme Court remanded a Section 16(b) case to the lower courts for consideration of how "the usual rules of equitable tolling" would apply. Section 16(b)'s statute of limitations does not, of course have the structure discussed in *Lampf*.

II. CRIMINAL AND COMMISSION ACTIONS

In the case of criminal actions, the general statute of limitations for federal crimes applies. In 2013, the Supreme Court held in Gabelli v. SEC[8] that civil actions by the Commission seeking monetary penalties are governed by the five-year statute of limitations found in 28 U.S.C. § 2462 (covering federal civil penalties, fines, and forfeitures generally). The case below is an interesting follow-up.

Kokesh v. Securities and Exchange Commission

Supreme Court of the United States, 2017.
137 S.Ct. 1635.

■ JUSTICE SOTOMAYOR delivered the opinion of the Court.

A 5-year statute of limitations applies to any "action, suit or proceeding for the enforcement of any civil fine, penalty, or forfeiture, pecuniary or otherwise." 28 U.S.C. § 2462. This case presents the question whether § 2462 applies to claims for disgorgement imposed as a sanction for violating a federal securities law. The Court holds that it does. Disgorgement in the securities-enforcement context is a "penalty" within the meaning of § 2462, and so disgorgement actions must be commenced within five years of the date the claim accrues.

---

[7]   566 U.S. 221 (2012).

[8]   568 U.S. 442 (2013).

I

A

* * *

Initially, the only statutory remedy available to the SEC in an enforcement action was an injunction barring future violations of securities laws. See 1 T. Hazen, Law of Securities Regulation § 1:37 (7th ed., rev. 2016). In the absence of statutory authorization for monetary remedies, the Commission urged courts to order disgorgement as an exercise of their "inherent equity power to grant relief ancillary to an injunction." *SEC v. Texas Gulf Sulphur Co.,* 312 F.Supp. 77, 91 (S.D.N.Y.1970), aff'd in part and rev'd in part, 446 F.2d 1301 (C.A.2 1971). Generally, disgorgement is a form of "[r]estitution measured by the defendant's wrongful gain." Restatement (Third) of Restitution and Unjust Enrichment § 51, Comment *a,* p. 204 (2010) (Restatement (Third)). Disgorgement requires that the defendant give up "those gains . . . properly attributable to the defendant's interference with the claimant's legally protected rights." *Ibid.* Beginning in the 1970's, courts ordered disgorgement in SEC enforcement proceedings in order to "deprive . . . defendants of their profits in order to remove any monetary reward for violating" securities laws and to "protect the investing public by providing an effective deterrent to future violations." *Texas Gulf,* 312 F.Supp., at 92.

In 1990, as part of the Securities Enforcement Remedies and Penny Stock Reform Act, Congress authorized the Commission to seek monetary civil penalties. 104 Stat. 932, codified at 15 U.S.C. § 77t(d). The Act left the Commission with a full panoply of enforcement tools: It may promulgate rules, investigate violations of those rules and the securities laws generally, and seek monetary penalties and injunctive relief for those violations. In the years since the Act, however, the Commission has continued its practice of seeking disgorgement in enforcement proceedings.

This Court has already held that the 5-year statute of limitations set forth in 28 U.S.C. § 2462 applies when the Commission seeks statutory monetary penalties. See *Gabelli v. SEC,* 568 U.S. 442, 454 (2013). The question here is whether § 2462, which applies to any "action, suit or proceeding for the enforcement of any civil fine, penalty, or forfeiture, pecuniary or otherwise," also applies when the SEC seeks disgorgement.

B

Charles Kokesh owned two investment-adviser firms that provided investment advice to business-development companies. In late 2009, the Commission commenced an enforcement action in Federal District Court alleging that between 1995 and 2009, Kokesh, through his firms, misappropriated $34.9 million from four of those development companies. The Commission further alleged that, in order to conceal the misappropriation, Kokesh caused the filing of false and misleading SEC reports and proxy statements. The Commission sought civil monetary penalties, disgorgement, and an injunction barring Kokesh from violating securities laws in the future.

After a 5-day trial, a jury found that Kokesh's actions violated * * * the Securities Exchange Act of 1934. The District Court then turned to the task of imposing penalties sought by the Commission. As to the civil monetary penalties, the District Court determined that § 2462's 5-year limitations period precluded any penalties for misappropriation occurring prior to October 27, 2004—that is, five years prior to the date the Commission filed the complaint. The court ordered Kokesh to pay a civil penalty of $2,354,593, which represented "the amount of funds that [Kokesh] himself received during the limitations period." Regarding the Commission's request for a $34.9 million disgorgement judgment—$29.9 million of which resulted from violations outside the limitations period— the court agreed with the Commission that because disgorgement is not a "penalty" within the meaning of § 2462, no limitations period applied. The court therefore entered a disgorgement judgment in the amount of $34.9 million and ordered Kokesh to pay an additional $18.1 million in prejudgment interest.

The Court of Appeals for the Tenth Circuit affirmed. 834 F.3d 1158 (2016). It agreed with the District Court that disgorgement is not a penalty, and further found that disgorgement is not a forfeiture. *Id.*, at 1164–1167. The court thus concluded that the statute of limitations in § 2462 does not apply to SEC disgorgement claims.

This Court granted certiorari to resolve disagreement among the Circuits over whether disgorgement claims in SEC proceedings are subject to the 5-year limitations period of § 2462.[9]

II

Statutes of limitations "se[t] a fixed date when exposure to the specified Government enforcement efforts en[d]." *Gabelli,* 568 U.S., at 448. Such limits are " 'vital to the welfare of society' " and rest on the principle that " 'even wrongdoers are entitled to assume that their sins may be forgotten.' " *Id.,* at 449. The statute of limitations at issue here— 28 U.S.C. § 2462—finds its roots in a law enacted nearly two centuries ago. 568 U.S., at 445. In its current form, § 2462 establishes a 5-year limitations period for "an action, suit or proceeding for the enforcement of any civil fine, penalty, or forfeiture." This limitations period applies here if SEC disgorgement qualifies as either a fine, penalty, or forfeiture. We hold that SEC disgorgement constitutes a penalty.[10]

---

[9] Compare *SEC v. Graham,* 823 F.3d 1357, 1363 (C.A.11 2016) (holding that § 2462 applies to SEC disgorgement claims), with *Riordan v. SEC,* 627 F.3d 1230, 1234 (C.A.D.C. 2010) (holding that § 2462 does not apply to SEC disgorgement claims).

[10] Nothing in this opinion should be interpreted as an opinion on whether courts possess authority to order disgorgement in SEC enforcement proceedings or on whether courts have properly applied disgorgement principles in this context. The sole question presented in this

A

A "penalty" is a "punishment, whether corporal or pecuniary, imposed and enforced by the State, for a crime or offen[s]e against its laws." *Huntington v. Attrill,* 146 U.S. 657, 667 (1892). This definition gives rise to two principles. First, whether a sanction represents a penalty turns in part on "whether the wrong sought to be redressed is a wrong to the public, or a wrong to the individual." *Id.,* at 668. Although statutes creating private causes of action against wrongdoers may appear—or even be labeled—penal, in many cases "neither the liability imposed nor the remedy given is strictly penal." *Id.,* at 667. This is because "[p]enal laws, strictly and properly, are those imposing punishment for an offense committed against the State." *Ibid.* Second, a pecuniary sanction operates as a penalty only if it is sought "for the purpose of punishment, and to deter others from offending in like manner"—as opposed to compensating a victim for his loss. *Id.,* at 668.

The Court has applied these principles in construing the term "penalty." In *Brady v. Daly,* 175 U.S. 148 (1899), for example, a playwright sued a defendant in Federal Circuit Court under a statute providing that copyright infringers " 'shall be liable for damages * * * not less than one hundred dollars for the first [act of infringement], and fifty dollars for every subsequent performance, as to the court shall appear to be just.' " *Id.,* at 153. The defendant argued that the Circuit Court lacked jurisdiction on the ground that a separate statute vested district courts with exclusive jurisdiction over actions "to recover a penalty." *Id.,* at 152. To determine whether the statutory damages represented a penalty, this Court noted first that the statute provided "for a recovery of damages for an act which violates the rights of the plaintiff, and gives the right of action solely to him" rather than the public generally, and second, that "the whole recovery is given to the proprietor, and the statute does not provide for a recovery by any other person." *Id.,* at 154, 156. By providing a compensatory remedy for a private wrong, the Court held, the statute did not impose a "penalty." *Id.,* at 154.

Similarly, in construing the statutory ancestor of § 2462, the Court utilized the same principles. In *Meeker v. Lehigh Valley R. Co.,* 236 U.S. 412, 421–422 (1915), the Interstate Commerce Commission, a now-defunct federal agency charged with regulating railroads, ordered a railroad company to refund and pay damages to a shipping company for excessive shipping rates. The railroad company argued that the action was barred by [now 28 U.S.C. § 2462] * * * . The Court rejected that argument, reasoning that "the words 'penalty or forfeiture' in [the statute] refer to something imposed in a punitive way for an infraction of a public law." *Ibid.* A penalty, the Court held, does "not include a liability imposed [solely] for the purpose of redressing a private injury." *Ibid.* Because the liability imposed was compensatory and paid entirely to a

---

case is whether disgorgement, as applied in SEC enforcement actions, is subject to § 2462's limitations period.

private plaintiff, it was not a "penalty" within the meaning of the statute of limitations. *Ibid.*; see also *Gabelli,* 568 U.S., at 451–452 ("[P]enalties" in the context of § 2462 "go beyond compensation, are intended to punish, and label defendants wrongdoers").

B

Application of the foregoing principles readily demonstrates that SEC disgorgement constitutes a penalty within the meaning of § 2462.

First, SEC disgorgement is imposed by the courts as a consequence for violating what we described in *Meeker* as public laws. The violation for which the remedy is sought is committed against the United States rather than an aggrieved individual—this is why, for example, a securities-enforcement action may proceed even if victims do not support or are not parties to the prosecution. As the Government concedes, "[w]hen the SEC seeks disgorgement, it acts in the public interest, to remedy harm to the public at large, rather than standing in the shoes of particular injured parties." * * *

Second, SEC disgorgement is imposed for punitive purposes. In *Texas Gulf*—one of the first cases requiring disgorgement in SEC proceedings—the court emphasized the need "to deprive the defendants of their profits in order to . . . protect the investing public by providing an effective deterrent to future violations." 312 F.Supp., at 92. In the years since, it has become clear that deterrence is not simply an incidental effect of disgorgement. Rather, courts have consistently held that "[t]he primary purpose of disgorgement orders is to deter violations of the securities laws by depriving violators of their ill-gotten gains." *SEC v. Fischbach Corp.*, 133 F.3d 170, 175 (C.A.2 1997) * * * . Sanctions imposed for the purpose of deterring infractions of public laws are inherently punitive because "deterrence [is] not [a] legitimate nonpunitive governmental objectiv[e]." *Bell v. Wolfish,* 441 U.S. 520, 539, n. 20 (1979); see also *United States v. Bajakajian,* 524 U.S. 321, 329 (1998) ("Deterrence . . . has traditionally been viewed as a goal of punishment").

Finally, in many cases, SEC disgorgement is not compensatory. As courts and the Government have employed the remedy, disgorged profits are paid to the district court, and it is "within the court's discretion to determine how and to whom the money will be distributed." *Fischbach Corp.*, 133 F.3d, at 175. Courts have required disgorgement "regardless of whether the disgorged funds will be paid to such investors as restitution." *Id.*, at 176; see *id.*, at 175 ("Although disgorged funds may often go to compensate securities fraud victims for their losses, such compensation is a distinctly secondary goal"). Some disgorged funds are paid to victims; other funds are dispersed to the United States Treasury. See, *e.g., id.,* at 171 (affirming distribution of disgorged funds to Treasury where "no party before the court was entitled to the funds and . . . the persons who might have equitable claims were too dispersed for feasible identification and payment") * * * . Even though district courts may distribute the funds to the victims, they have not identified any statutory command that they do so. When an individual is made to pay a noncompensatory sanction to the Government as a consequence of a legal violation, the payment operates as a penalty. See *Porter v. Warner Holding Co.,* 328 U.S. 395, 402 (1946) (distinguishing between restitution paid to an aggrieved party and penalties paid to the Government).

SEC disgorgement thus bears all the hallmarks of a penalty: It is imposed as a consequence of violating a public law and it is intended to deter, not to compensate. The 5-year statute of limitations in § 2462 therefore applies when the SEC seeks disgorgement.

C

The Government's primary response to all of this is that SEC disgorgement is not punitive but "remedial" in that it "lessen[s] the effects of a violation" by " 'restor[ing] the status quo.' " As an initial matter, it is not clear that disgorgement, as courts have applied it in the SEC enforcement context, simply returns the defendant to the place he would have occupied had he not broken the law. SEC disgorgement sometimes exceeds the profits gained as a result of the violation. Thus, for example, "an insider trader may be ordered to disgorge not only the unlawful gains that accrue to the wrongdoer directly, but also the benefit that accrues to third parties whose gains can be attributed to the wrongdoer's conduct." *SEC v. Contorinis,* 743 F.3d 296, 302 (C.A.2 2014). Individuals who illegally provide confidential trading information have been forced to disgorge profits gained by individuals who received and traded based on that information—even though they never received any profits. *Ibid.* * * * And, as demonstrated by this case, SEC disgorgement sometimes is ordered without consideration of a defendant's expenses that reduced the amount of illegal profit. * * * In such cases, disgorgement does not simply restore the status quo; it leaves the defendant worse off. The justification for this practice given by the court below demonstrates that disgorgement in this context is a punitive, rather than a remedial, sanction: Disgorgement, that court explained, is intended not only to "prevent the wrongdoer's unjust enrichment" but also "to deter others' violations of the securities laws."

True, disgorgement serves compensatory goals in some cases; however, we have emphasized "the fact that sanctions frequently serve more than one purpose." *Austin v. United States,* 509 U.S. 602, 610 (1993). " 'A civil sanction that cannot fairly be said *solely* to serve a remedial purpose, but rather can only be explained as also serving either retributive or deterrent purposes, is punishment, as we have come to understand the term.' " Because disgorgement orders "go beyond compensation, are intended to punish, and label defendants wrongdoers" as a consequence of violating public laws, *Gabelli,* 568 U.S., at 451–452, they represent a penalty and thus fall within the 5-year statute of limitations of § 2462.

* * *

One of the most interesting things about the case, in the view of some commentators, is its footnote reserving the issue of whether the Commission has the authority to seek disgorgement in a court proceeding.

C. IN PARI DELICTO DEFENSE

In the securities law context, the *in pari delicto* defense most often comes up in a case involving Rule 10b–5. The classic example arises when plaintiff-customers sue a securities firm, alleging that they were cheated when they traded on information, provided by one of the securities firm's registered representatives, that was supposed to be inside information but was not. The securities firm then defends on the basis that, if the plaintiff's allegations are true, the plaintiff cannot prevail because he or she was *in pari delicto* with the registered representative. Courts of appeal had gone both ways on the question of the defense's applicability in this situation by the time the Supreme Court decided the following case in 1985.

Bateman Eichler, Hill Richards, Inc. v. Berner

Supreme Court of the United States, 1985.
472 U.S. 299.

■ JUSTICE BRENNAN delivered the opinion of the Court.

The question presented by this case is whether the common-law *in pari delicto* defense bars a private damages action under the federal securities laws against corporate insiders and broker-dealers who fraudulently induce investors to purchase securities by misrepresenting that they are conveying material non-public information about the issuer.

I

The respondent investors filed this action in the United States District Court for the Northern District of California, alleging that they incurred substantial trading losses as a result of a conspiracy between Charles Lazzaro, a registered securities broker employed by the petitioner Bateman Eichler, Hill Richards, Inc. (Bateman Eichler), and Leslie Neadeau, President of T.O.N.M. Oil & Gas Exploration Corporation (TONM), to induce them to purchase large quantities of TONM over-the-counter stock by divulging false and materially incomplete information about the company on the pretext that it was accurate inside information. Specifically, Lazzaro is alleged to have told the respondents that he personally knew TONM insiders and had learned, *inter alia*, that (a) "[v]ast amounts of gold had been discovered in Surinam, and TONM had options on thousands of acres in gold-producing regions of Surinam"; (b) the discovery was "not publicly known, but would subsequently be announced"; (c) TONM was currently engaged in negotiations with other companies to form a joint venture for mining the Surinamese gold; and (d) when this information was made public, "TONM stock, which was then selling from $1.50 to $3.00/share, would increase in value from $10 to $15/share within a short period of time, and * * * might increase to $100/share" within a year. Some of the respondents aver that they contacted Neadeau and inquired whether Lazzaro's tips were accurate; Neadeau stated that the information was "not public knowledge" and "would neither confirm nor deny those claims," but allegedly advised that "Lazzaro was a very trustworthy and a good man."

The respondents admitted in their complaint that they purchased TONM stock, much of it through Lazzaro, "on the premise that Lazzaro was privy to certain information not otherwise available to the general public." Their shares initially increased dramatically in price, but ultimately declined to substantially below the purchase price when the joint mining venture fell through.

Lazzaro and Neadeau are alleged to have made the representations set forth above knowing that the representations "were untrue and/or contained only half-truths, material omissions of fact and falsehoods," intending that the respondents would rely thereon, and for the purpose of "influenc[ing] and manipulat[ing] the price of TONM stock" so as "to profit themselves through the taking of commissions and secret profits." The respondents contended that this scheme violated, *inter alia,* § 10(b) of the Securities Exchange Act of 1934 and Securities and Exchange Commission (SEC) Rule 10b–5 promulgated thereunder. They sought capital losses and lost profits, punitive damages, and costs and attorney's fees.

* * *

II

The common-law defense at issue in this case derives from the Latin, *in pari delicto potior est condition defendentis*: "In a case of equal or mutual fault * * * the position of the [defending] party * * * is the better one." The defense is grounded on two premises: first, that courts should not lend their good offices to mediating disputes among wrongdoers; and second, that denying judicial relief to an admitted wrongdoer is an effective means of deterring illegality. In its classic formulation, the *in pari delicto* defense was narrowly limited to situations where the plaintiff truly bore at least substantially equal responsibility for his injury, because "in cases where both parties are in delicto, concurring in an illegal act, it does not always follow that they stand *in pari delicto*; for there may be, and often are, very different degrees in their guilt." 1 J. Story, Equity Jurisprudence 304–305 (13th ed. 1886) (Story). Thus there might be an "inequality of condition" between the parties, *id.,* at 305, or "a confidential relationship between th[em]" that determined their "relative standing" before a court, 3 J. Pomeroy, Equity Jurisprudence— 942a, p. 741 (5th ed. 1941) (Pomeroy). * * * Notwithstanding these traditional limitations, many courts have given the *in pari delicto* defense a broad application to bar actions where plaintiffs simply have been involved generally in "the same sort of wrongdoing" as defendants. Perma Life Mufflers, Inc. v. International Parts Corp., 392 U.S. [134, 138 (1968)].

In *Perma Life*, we emphasized "the inappropriateness of invoking broad common-law barriers to relief where a private suit serves important public purposes." * * * In separate opinions, five Justices agreed that the concept of "equal fault" should be narrowly defined in litigation arising under federal regulatory statutes. * * * The five Justices concluded, however, that where a plaintiff truly bore at least substantially equal responsibility for the violation, a defense based on such fault—whether or not denominated *in pari delicto*—should be recognized in antitrust litigation.

Bateman Eichler argues that *Perma Life*—with its emphasis on the importance of analyzing the effects that fault-based defenses would have on the enforcement of congressional goals—is of only marginal relevance to a private damages action under the federal securities laws. Specifically, Bateman Eichler observes that Congress *expressly* provided for private antitrust actions—thereby manifesting a "desire to go beyond the common law in the antitrust statute in order to provide substantial encouragement to private enforcement and to help deter anticompetitive conduct"—whereas private rights of action under § 10(b) of the Securities Exchange Act of 1934 are merely *implied* from that provision—thereby, apparently, supporting a broader application of the *in pari delicto* defense. * * *

We disagree. Nothing in *Perma Life* suggested that public policy implications should govern only where Congress expressly provides for private remedies; the classic formulation of the *in pari delicto* doctrine itself required a careful consideration of such implications before allowing the defense. Moreover, we repeatedly have emphasized that implied private actions provide "a most effective weapon in the enforcement" of the securities laws and are "a necessary supplement to Commission action." J.I. Case Co. v. Borak, 377 U.S. 426, 432 (1964). In addition, we have eschewed rigid common-law barriers in construing the securities laws. We therefore conclude that the views expressed in *Perma Life* apply with full force to implied causes of action under the federal securities laws. Accordingly, a private action for damages in these circumstances may be barred on the grounds of the plaintiff's own culpability only where (1) as a direct result of his own actions, the plaintiff bears at least substantially equal responsibility for the violations he seeks to redress, and (2) preclusion of suit would not significantly interfere with the effective enforcement of the securities laws and protection of the investing public.

A

The District Court and Court of Appeals proceeded on the assumption that the respondents had violated § 10(b) and Rule 10b–5—an assumption we accept for purposes of resolving the issue before us. Bateman Eichler contends that the respondents' *delictum* was substantially *par* to that of Lazzaro and Neadeau for two reasons. First, whereas many antitrust plaintiffs participate in illegal restraints of trade only "passively" or as the result of economic coercion, as was the case in *Perma Life*, the ordinary tippee acts *voluntarily* in choosing to trade on inside information. Second, § 10(b) and Rule 10b–5 apply literally to "any person" who violates their terms, and do not recognize gradations of culpability.

We agree that the typically voluntary nature of an investor's decision impermissibly to trade on an inside tip renders the investor more blameworthy than someone who is party to a contract solely by virtue of another's overweening bargaining power. We disagree, however, that an investor who engages in such trading is necessarily as blameworthy as a corporate insider or broker-dealer who discloses the information for personal gain. Notwithstanding the broad reach of § 10(b) and Rule 10b–5, there are important distinctions between the relative culpabilities of tippers, securities professionals, and tippees in these circumstances. The Court has made clear in recent Terms that a tippee's use of material non-public information does not violate § 10(b) and Rule 10b–5 unless the tippee owes a corresponding duty to disclose the information. Dirks v. SEC, 463 U.S. 646, 654–664 (1983); Chiarella v. United States, 445 U.S. 222, 230, n. 12 (1980). That duty typically is "derivative from * * * the insider's duty." Dirks v. SEC, *supra*, at 659; see also *id.*, at 664. In other words, "[t]he tippee's obligation has been viewed as arising from his role as a participant after the fact in the insider's breach of a fiduciary duty" toward corporate shareholders. Chiarella v. United States, *supra*, at 230, n. 12. In the context of insider trading, we do not believe that a person whose liability is solely derivative can be said to be as culpable as one whose breach of duty gave rise to that liability in the first place.

Moreover, insiders and broker-dealers who selectively disclose material non-public information commit a potentially broader range of violations than do tippees who trade on the basis of that information. A tippee trading on inside information will in many circumstances be guilty of fraud against individual shareholders, a violation for which the tipper shares responsibility. But the insider, in disclosing such information, also frequently breaches fiduciary duties toward the issuer itself. And in cases where the tipper intentionally conveys false or materially incomplete information to the tippee, the tipper commits an additional violation: fraud against the tippee. Such conduct is particularly egregious when committed by a securities professional, who owes a duty of honesty and fair dealing toward his clients. Absent other culpable actions by a tippee that can fairly be said to outweigh these violations by insiders and broker-dealers, we do not believe that the tippee properly can be characterized as being of substantially equal culpability as his tippers.

There is certainly no basis for concluding at this stage of this litigation that the respondents were *in pari delicto* with Lazzaro and Neadeau. The allegations are that Lazzaro and Neadeau masterminded this scheme to manipulate the market in TONM securities for their own personal benefit, and that they used the purchasing respondents as unwitting dupes to inflate the price of TONM stock. The respondents may well have violated the securities laws, and in any event we place no "stamp of approval" on their conduct. Chiarella v. United States, *supra*, at 238 (STEVENS, J., concurring). But accepting the facts set forth in the complaint as true—as we must in reviewing the District Court's dismissal on the pleadings—Lazzaro and Neadeau "awakened in [the respondents] a desire for wrongful gain that might otherwise have remained dormant, inspired in [their] mind[s] an unfounded idea that [they were] going to secure it, and then by fraud and false pretenses deprived [them] of [their] money," Stewart v. Wright, 147 F. 321, 328–329 (C.A.8), cert. denied, 203 U.S. 590 (1906)—actions that, if they occurred, were far more culpable under any reasonable view than the respondents' alleged conduct.

B

We also believe that denying the *in pari delicto* defense in such circumstances will best promote the primary objective of the federal securities laws—protection of the investing public and the national economy through the promotion of "a high standard of business ethics * * * in every facet of the securities industry." SEC v. Capital Gains Research Bureau, Inc., 375 U.S. 180, 186–187 (1963). Although a number of lower courts have reasoned that a broad rule of *caveat tippee* would better serve this goal, we believe the contrary position adopted by other courts represents the better view.

To begin with, barring private actions in cases such as this would inexorably result in a number of alleged fraudulent practices going undetected by the authorities and unremedied. * * *

Moreover, we believe that deterrence of insider trading most frequently will be maximized by bringing enforcement pressures to bear on the sources of such information—corporate insiders and broker-dealers. * * * In addition, corporate insiders and broker-dealers will in many circumstances be more responsive to the deterrent pressure of potential sanctions; they are more likely than ordinary investors to be advised by counsel and thereby to be informed fully of the "allowable limits on their conduct." Kuehnert v. Texstar Corp., *supra*, at 706 (Godbold, J., dissenting). Although situations might well arise in which the relative culpabilities of the tippee and his insider source merit a different mix of deterrent incentives, we therefore conclude that in tipper—tippee situations such as the one before us the factors discussed above preclude recognition of the *in pari delicto* defense.

* * *

_____

In Pinter v. Dahl, 486 U.S. 622 (1988), the Supreme Court extended the applicability of *Bateman Eichler* to suits involving Securities Act Section 12(a)(1), saying, in fact, that *Bateman Eichler* provides the appropriate test for allowance of the *in pari delicto* defense in a private action under any of the federal security laws. At the same time, however, the Court found "it necessary to circumscribe the scope of [the case's] application," noting:

> In our view, where the § [12(a)(1)] plaintiff is primarily an investor, precluding suit would interfere significantly with effective enforcement of the securities laws and frustrate the primary objective of the Securities Act. * * * Because the Act is specifically designed to protect investors, even where a plaintiff actively participates in the distribution of unregistered securities, his suit should not be barred where his promotional efforts are incidental to his role as an investor. Thus, the *in pari delicto* defense may defeat recovery in a § [12(a)(1)] action only where the plaintiff's role in the offering or sale of nonexempted, unregistered securities is more as a promoter than as an investor.

D. LIMITATIONS ON CONTRACTUAL RIGHTS, WAIVERS AND ARBITRABILITY

I. LIMITATIONS ON CONTRACTUAL RIGHTS

Securities Act Section 14 provides:

> Any condition, stipulation, or provision binding any person acquiring any security to waive compliance with any provision of [the Securities Act] or of the rules and regulations of the Commission shall be void.

And Section 29(a) of the Exchange Act is to the same effect:

> Any condition, stipulation, or provision binding any person to waive compliance with any provision of this [Act] or of any rule or regulation thereunder, or of any rule of a self-regulatory organization required thereby shall be void.

These provisions serve as the main limitations on the right of persons to contract with respect to matters covered by the Securities Act and the Exchange Act. The next case discusses the breadth of these limitations.

Kaiser-Frazer Corp. v. Otis & Co.

United States Court of Appeals, Second Circuit, 1952.
195 F.2d 838.

■ Before AUGUSTUS N. HAND and CLARK, CIRCUIT JUDGES, and BRENNAN, DISTRICT JUDGE.

■ AUGUSTUS N. HAND, CIRCUIT JUDGE.

On February 3, 1948, the plaintiff, Kaiser-Frazer Corporation, an automobile manufacturer, entered into a contract for the sale of 900,000 shares of its unissued common stock at $11.50 per share to Otis & Co., First California Company, and Allen & Co., securities underwriters, who in turn were to offer the stock for sale to the public at $13. per share. * * * The contract made the purchasers' obligation to accept the stock subject to [the condition that] the registration statement (including the prospectus) filed with the Securities & Exchange Commission pursuant to the Securities Act of 1933 was to comply with the Act and the Regulations of the SEC " * * * and neither the Registration Statement nor the Prospectus [were to] contain any untrue statement of a material fact nor omit to state any material fact required to be stated therein or necessary in order to make the statements therein not misleading * * * ." It is undisputed that the registration statement (including the prospectus) was filed with the SEC and became effective on February 3, 1948, the day the contract was signed. The contract set February 9, 1948 as the closing date, at which time Kaiser-Frazer was to have delivered the stock to the purchasers, and the latter were to have paid the purchase price. On the day of the closing, however, the representatives of Otis and First California [refused to accept the proffered stock] * * * . Shortly thereafter, Kaiser-Frazer initiated the present action against Otis in the District Court for the Southern District of New York. * * * The complaint * * * charged that Otis was guilty of a breach of contract for failing to accept and pay for 337,500 shares of stock and asked for damages in the total amount of $17,419,819 * * * .

The defendant's answer to the complaint set forth [as a defense] * * * that the registration statement contained false and misleading statements. After an extensive trial lasting six weeks, the district judge made findings of fact in favor of the plaintiff on substantially all of the points in issue, and entered judgment for the plaintiff in the amount of $3,120,743.51.

* * *

[The prospectus included in the registration statement featured a summary of consolidated sales and earnings showing profits for the year 1947, along with profits for the two months ended November 30, 1947 and for the quarter ended December 31, 1947.]

The [summary] contains no figure purporting to be the December 1947 profit as such; however, by subtracting the profit for the two months ending November 30, 1947 from the quarter ending December 31, 1947 profit, a figure of $4,009,383 is obtained which one would naturally assume to represent the profit of the Corporation for the single month of December 1947. * * * It is, however, sufficiently clear from the record that December earnings from the Corporation's operations were nowhere near that amount, but were rather in the neighborhood of $900,000. The difference in amount was due to the fact that a physical inventory was taken in the latter part of December 1947, at which time it was discovered that the Corporation had a much larger inventory than had been anticipated. The net amount of the adjustment that was made to reflect this fact was the sum of $3,371,155, which Kaiser-Frazer simply included under the final quarter's earnings in the summary. * * *

The district court found that the "summary of consolidated sales and earnings for the final quarter of the year 1947, set forth on page 7 of the prospectus, was computed in accordance with accepted accounting procedures," and that it was not misleading. With this conclusion we cannot agree. For, regardless of whether its accounting system was a sound one, Kaiser-Frazer stated its earnings in such a way as to represent that it had made a profit of about $4,000,000 in December 1947. This representation was $3,100,000 short of the truth. * * *

Kaiser-Frazer urges that since Otis had full knowledge of all the facts prior to the time it entered into the underwriting agreement, Otis cannot now rely on such facts as constituting a breach of warranty. Factually there is some support for Kaiser-Frazer's contention; the testimony at the trial indicates that representatives of Otis at least were informed of the actual December earnings and apparently took part in the preparation of the registration statement and the prospectus. But whatever the rules of estoppel or waiver may be in the case of an ordinary contract of sale, nevertheless it is clear that a contract which violates the laws of the United States and contravenes the public policy as expressed in those laws is unenforceable.[11] * * * This is so regardless of the equities as between the parties for " * * * the very meaning of public policy is the interest of others than the parties and that interest is not to be at the mercy of the defendant alone." Beasley v. Texas & Pacific Ry., 191 U.S. 492, 498. Any sale to the public by means of the prospectus involved here would have been a violation of the Securities Act of 1933 * * * . While it may be argued that the enforcement of the underwriting contract according to its terms would result only in the sale of the stock to Otis and that such a sale would not violate the Act, see [Securities Act § 4(1)],

---

[11] Further support of our holding may be found in § 14 of the Act of 1933, which provides as follows:

"Any condition, stipulation, or provision binding any person acquiring any security to waive compliance with any provision of this subchapter or of the rules and regulations of the Commission shall be void."

The broad language of this section may be construed to brush aside ordinary contract principles of estoppel and waiver that might otherwise apply to contracts for securities, including underwriting agreements.

we are satisfied that the contract was so closely related to the performance of acts forbidden by law as to be itself illegal. We cannot blind ourselves to the fact that the sale of this stock by Kaiser-Frazer, though, in so far as the particular contract was concerned, was a sale only to the underwriters, was but the initial step in the public offering of the securities which would necessarily follow. The prospectus, which has been found to have been misleading, formed an integral part of the contract and the public sale of the stock by the underwriter was to be made and could only have been made in reliance on that prospectus. We therefore conclude that the contract was unenforceable and that Kaiser-Frazer was not entitled to recover damages for Otis' breach thereof. * * *

* * *

II. WAIVER OF SECURITIES LAW RIGHTS

Section 14 of the Securities Act and Section 29 of the Exchange Act clearly provide that any attempted waiver of a right under the relevant Act is void. These provisions received substantial judicial scrutiny in the context of choice-of-law clauses included by Lloyd's of London in contracts with its investors.

The Society of Lloyd's, with its affiliates, operates a large insurance market in which individuals participate by becoming an underwriting Member, or "Name." Names invest in one or more syndicates managed by agents who attract underwriting business from brokers. As a condition of becoming a Name, one must sign an undertaking that (1) all rights and obligations of the parties shall be governed by and construed in accordance with the laws of England, and (2) the courts of England shall have exclusive jurisdiction over controversies arising out of membership in Lloyd's.

Following notoriously heavy losses for which Names incurred liability, hundreds of American Names attempted to bring claims in United States courts invoking the federal securities laws. A number of circuits[12] took the position that the Names' choice-of-law and choice-of-forum undertakings bar these claims, notwithstanding the anti-waiver provisions of the Securities Act and the Exchange Act. Of significance was the conclusion that English law provides reasonable recourse to the disappointed Names; the Circuit Courts generally have indicated that if available English remedies were not adequate substitutes for American law, the choice-of-law and choice-of-forum clauses would be subject to another level of scrutiny. The English remedies in question include

---

[12] Richards v. Lloyd's of London, 135 F.3d 1289 (9th Cir.1998); Haynsworth v. The Corporation, 121 F.3d 956 (5th Cir.1997); Allen v. Lloyd's of London, 94 F.3d 923 (4th Cir.1996); Shell v. R.W. Sturge Ltd., 55 F.3d 1227 (6th Cir.1995); Bonny v. Society of Lloyd's, 3 F.3d 156 (7th Cir.1993), cert. denied 510 U.S. 1113 (1994); Roby v. Corporation of Lloyd's, 996 F.2d 1353 (2d Cir.), cert. denied 510 U.S. 945 (1993); Riley v. Kingsley Underwriting Agencies Ltd., 969 F.2d 953 (10th Cir.), cert. denied, 506 U.S. 1021 (1992).

various actions for deceit and misrepresentation, most of which have somewhat more demanding causation and scienter requirements than remedies under the United States securities laws.

III. ARBITRABILITY OF SECURITIES LAW CLAIMS

a. JUDICIAL DEVELOPMENTS

Section 14 of the Securities Act has had one special application of far reaching consequences. In Wilko v. Swan,[13] the Supreme Court determined that a predispute agreement to arbitrate claims arising under the Securities Act could not be enforced. In reaching this decision, the Court first focused on the language in Section 14 declaring void any "provision binding any person * * * to waive compliance with any provision of [the Securities Act]" and then determined that the right of judicial trial and review of Securities Act claims was one of the rights declared in Section 14 not to be waivable.

Following *Wilko*, there was much uncertainty about whether, and in what circumstances, agreements to arbitrate claims under the Exchange Act could be enforced. This was a question of substantial importance, primarily since securities firms have long favored the arbitration of claims brought by customers against them, and many of these firms have systematically included in customer agreements a provision calling for the arbitration of disputes. Shearson/American Express, Inc. v. McMahon[14] laid to rest the main questions about the arbitrability of Exchange Act claims, and along with them the question of whether agreements to arbitrate RICO claims can be enforced. Two years later, in Rodriguez de Quijas v. Shearson/American Express, Inc., the Supreme Court overruled *Wilko*.

Rodriguez de Quijas v. Shearson/American Express, Inc.

Supreme Court of the United States, 1989.
490 U.S. 477.

■ JUSTICE KENNEDY delivered the opinion of the Court.

The question here is whether a predispute agreement to arbitrate claims under the Securities Act of 1933 is unenforceable, requiring resolution of the claims only in a judicial forum.

I

Petitioners are individuals who invested about $400,000 in securities. They signed a standard customer agreement with the broker, which included a clause stating that the parties agreed to settle any controversies "relating to [the] accounts" through binding arbitration

---

[13]   346 U.S. 427 (1953).
[14]   482 U.S. 220 (1987).

that complies with specified procedures. The agreement to arbitrate these controversies is unqualified, unless it is found to be unenforceable under federal or state law. The investments turned sour, and petitioners eventually sued respondent and its broker-agent in charge of the accounts, alleging that their money was lost in unauthorized and fraudulent transactions. In their complaint they pleaded various violations of federal and state law, including claims under § [12(a)(2)] of the Securities Act of 1933 and claims under three sections of the Securities Exchange Act of 1934.

The District Court ordered all the claims to be submitted to arbitration except for those raised under § [12(a)(2)] of the Securities Act. It held that the latter claims must proceed in the court action under our clear holding on the point in Wilko v. Swan, 346 U.S. 427 (1953). * * * The Court of Appeals reversed, concluding that the arbitration agreement is enforceable because this Court's subsequent decisions have reduced *Wilko* to "obsolescence." * * *

II

The *Wilko* case, decided in 1953, required the Court to determine whether an agreement to arbitrate future controversies constitutes a binding stipulation "to waive compliance with any provision" of the Securities Act, which is nullified by § 14 of the Act. The Court considered the language, purposes, and legislative history of the Securities Act and concluded that the agreement to arbitrate was void under § 14. But the decision was a difficult one in view of the competing legislative policy embodied in the Arbitration Act, which the Court described as "not easily reconcilable," and which strongly favors the enforcement of agreements to arbitrate as a means of securing "prompt, economical and adequate solution of controversies."

* * *

* * * The Court's characterization of the arbitration process in *Wilko* is pervaded by what Judge Jerome Frank called "the old judicial hostility to arbitration." Kulukundis Shipping Co. v. Amtorg Trading Corp., 126 F.2d 978, 985 (CA2 1942). That view has been steadily eroded over the years, beginning in the lower courts. The erosion intensified in our most recent decisions upholding agreements to arbitrate federal claims raised under the Securities Exchange Act of 1934, see Shearson/American Express Inc. v. McMahon, 482 U.S. 220 (1987), under the Racketeer Influenced and Corrupt Organizations (RICO) statutes, and under the antitrust laws. * * * To the extent that *Wilko* rested on suspicion of arbitration as a method of weakening the protections afforded in the substantive law to would-be complainants, it has fallen far out of step with our current strong endorsement of the federal statutes favoring this method of resolving disputes.

* * *

[I]n *McMahon* we stressed the strong language of the Arbitration Act, which declares as a matter of federal law that arbitration agreements "shall be valid, irrevocable, and enforceable, save upon such grounds as exist at law or in equity for the revocation of any contract." Under that statute, the party opposing arbitration carries the burden of showing that Congress intended in a separate statute to preclude a waiver of judicial remedies, or that such a waiver of judicial remedies inherently conflicts with the underlying purposes of that other statute. But as Justice Frankfurter said in dissent in *Wilko*, so it is true in this case: "There is nothing in the record before us, nor in the facts of which we can take judicial notice, to indicate that the arbitral system * * * would not afford the plaintiff the rights to which he is entitled." Petitioners have not carried their burden of showing that arbitration agreements are not enforceable under the Securities Act.

* * *

Shearson and *Rodriguez* provided the impetus for most securities firms to include in their client agreements a provision requiring the arbitration of disputes between the customer and the firm. These agreements typically choose New York as the state whose law is to govern the agreement, and under New York law only courts may award punitive damages. In Mastrobuono v. Shearson Lehman Hutton, Inc.,[15] the Supreme Court held that " * * * if contracting parties agree to include claims for punitive damages within the issues to be arbitrated, the FAA ensures that their agreement will be enforced according to its terms even if a rule of state law would otherwise exclude such claims from arbitration." * * * Under *Mastrobuono*, then, it did seem that a securities firm could include in a client agreement a provision that negates the possibility of punitive damages in arbitration, so long as the provision were sufficiently clear. Shortly after the decision was issued, however, the National Association of Securities Dealers, Inc., sent a Notice to Members stating that doing so would violate the NASD's Rules of Fair Practice.

Another important issue has been the question of who decides whether a party has agreed to arbitration, a court or an arbitrator. In First Options of Chicago, Inc. v. Kaplan,[16] the Kaplans had not personally signed an agreement calling for arbitration of disputes, although their controlled investment company had. When First Options of Chicago, Inc. tried to arbitrate its claims against the Kaplans for amounts unpaid by their company, the following opinion ensued:

---

[15]   514 U.S. 52 (1995).

[16]   514 U.S. 938 (1995).

First Options of Chicago, Inc. v. Kaplan

Supreme Court of the United States, 1995.
514 U.S. 938.

■ JUSTICE BREYER delivered the opinion of the Court.

In this case we consider * * * how courts should review certain matters under the federal Arbitration Act * * * .

* * *

When deciding whether the parties agreed to arbitrate a certain matter (including arbitrability), courts generally (though with a qualification we discuss below) should apply ordinary state-law principles that govern the formation of contracts. The relevant state law here, for example, would require the court to see whether the parties objectively revealed an intent to submit the arbitrability issue to arbitration.

This Court, however, has (as we just said) added an important qualification, applicable when courts decide whether a party has agreed that arbitrators should decide arbitrability: Courts should not assume that the parties agreed to arbitrate arbitrability unless there is "clea[r] and unmistakabl[e]" evidence that they did so. AT & T Technologies[, Inc. v. Communications Workers, 475 US. 643, 649 (1986)]. In this manner the law treats silence or ambiguity about the question "who (primarily) should decide arbitrability" differently from the way it treats silence or ambiguity about the question "whether a particular merits—related dispute is arbitrable because it is within the scope of a valid arbitration agreement"—for in respect to this latter question the law reverses the presumption.

But, this difference in treatment is understandable. The latter question arises when the parties have a contract that provides for arbitration of some issues. In such circumstances, the parties likely gave at least some thought to the scope of arbitration. And, given the law's permissive policies in respect to arbitration, one can understand why the law would insist upon clarity before concluding that the parties did not want to arbitrate a related matter. On the other hand, the former question—the "who (primarily) should decide arbitrability" question—is rather arcane. A party often might not focus upon that question or upon the significance of having arbitrators decide the scope of their own powers. And, given the principle that a party can be forced to arbitrate only those issues it specifically has agreed to submit to arbitration, one can understand why courts might hesitate to interpret silence or ambiguity on the "who should decide arbitrability" point as giving the arbitrators that power, for doing so might too often force unwilling parties to arbitrate a matter they reasonably would have thought a judge, not an arbitrator, would decide.

On the record before us, First Options cannot show that the Kaplans clearly agreed to have the arbitrators decide (*i.e.*, to arbitrate) the question of arbitrability. First Options relies on the Kaplans' filing with the arbitrators a written memorandum objecting to the arbitrators' jurisdiction. But merely arguing the arbitrability issue to an arbitrator does not indicate a clear willingness to arbitrate that issue, *i.e.*, a willingness to be effectively bound by the arbitrator's decision on that point. * * *

* * *

We conclude that, because the Kaplans did not clearly agree to submit the question of arbitrability to arbitration, the Court of Appeals was correct in finding that the arbitrability of the Kaplan/First Options dispute was subject to independent review by the courts.

* * *

———————

The trend in favor of upholding the arbitrability of claims was furthered in 2002, in the case of Howsam v. Dean Witter Reynolds, Inc.[17] In *Howsam*, pursuant to a standard arbitration clause, the client chose arbitration before the NASD, only to meet the argument that the claim was time-barred under the NASD's own rules. The Supreme Court determined that the applicability of the time-bar (that is, the timeliness of arbitration) presumptively is subject to arbitral rather than judicial jurisdiction. One of the keystones of the Court's reasoning was the parties' inferred intent, which would require an "arbitration-disfavoring presumption" to overcome.

b. LEGISLATIVE RESPONSE

In 2010, the Dodd-Frank Act manifested a somewhat different attitude toward arbitration than that exhibited by the Supreme Court. New Section 15(o) of the Exchange Act provides as follows:

> The Commission, by rule, may prohibit, or impose conditions or limitations on the use of, agreements that require customers or clients of any [broker or dealer] to arbitrate any future dispute between them arising under the Federal securities laws, the rules and regulations thereunder, or the rules of a self-regulatory organization if it finds that such prohibition, imposition of conditions, or limitations are in the public interest and for the protection of investors.

The Commission has not, however, moved to limit arbitration, although it has enhanced efforts to educate investors about the process.

---

[17] 537 U.S. 79 (2002).

Section 922 of Dodd-Frank went further in the context of whistleblower claims brought under the provisions of Sarbanes-Oxley. Mandatory pre-dispute arbitration of such claims is specifically banned.

E. PRIVATE SECURITIES LITIGATION REFORM ACT OF 1995 AND THE SECURITIES LITIGATION UNIFORM STANDARDS ACT OF 1998

In the Private Securities Litigation Reform Act of 1995, Congress made a number of changes to the civil procedure governing federal securities litigation (as well as several substantive changes to the securities laws referred to earlier in the book). The procedural changes are found primarily in Securities Act Section 27 and Exchange Act Section 21D, each entitled "Private Securities Litigation." Some of the more important changes made in these sections relate to:

- Appointment of the lead plaintiff;
- Appointment of lead counsel;
- Restrictions on attorneys' fees and expenses;
- Attorney conflict of interest;
- Disclosure of settlement terms;
- Stays of discovery by motions to dismiss; and
- Sanctions for abusive litigation.

In addition, procedural changes relating to motions are included in Securities Act Section 27A and Exchange Act Section 21E, each entitled "Application of Safe Harbor for Forward-Looking Statement." Exchange Act Section 15(c) was amended to prohibit referral fees, relating to securities litigation, to brokers and dealers and persons associated with them. Securities Act Section 20 and Exchange Act Section 21(d) were amended generally to prohibit the payment of attorneys' fees from funds disgorged as a result of actions brought by the Commission.[18]

The Private Securities Litigation Reform Act of 1995 also added Section 21D(b)(2) to the Exchange Act. It provides that a complaint seeking money damages under any provision of the Exchange Act requiring proof that the defendant acted with a particular state of mind must "state with particularity facts giving rise to a strong inference that the defendant acted with the required state of mind." This requirement (which, since 2010, has had a simplifying exception for actions against credit rating agencies) gave rise to a great deal of interpretive difficulty in the lower federal courts. The following case represents the Supreme Court's attempt to provide guidance in the area.

---

[18] Also, as discussed earlier in the book, Exchange Act Section 20 was amended to provide that the Commission may bring actions for aiding and abetting Exchange Act violations.

Tellabs, Inc. v. Makor Issues & Rights, Ltd.

Supreme Court of the United States, 2007.
551 U.S. 308.

■ JUSTICE GINSBURG delivered the opinion of the Court.

This Court has long recognized that meritorious private actions to enforce federal antifraud securities laws are an essential supplement to criminal prosecutions and civil enforcement actions brought, respectively, by the Department of Justice and the Securities and Exchange Commission (SEC). See, e.g., Dura Pharms., Inc. v. Broudo, 544 U.S. 336, 345 (2005); J I. Case Co. v. Borak, 377 U.S. 426 (1964). Private securities fraud actions, however, if not adequately contained, can be employed abusively to impose substantial costs on companies and individuals whose conduct conforms to the law. See Merrill Lynch, Pierce, Fenner & Smith Inc. v. Dabit, 547 U.S. 71, 81 (2006). As a check against abusive litigation by private parties, Congress enacted the Private Securities Litigation Reform Act of 1995 (PSLRA).

Exacting pleading requirements are among the control measures Congress included in the PSLRA. The Act requires plaintiffs to state with particularity both the facts constituting the alleged violation, and the facts evidencing scienter, *i.e.*, the defendant's intention "to deceive, manipulate, or defraud." Ernst & Ernst v. Hochfelder, 425 U.S. 185, 194 and n. 12 (1976). This case concerns the latter requirement. As set out in § 21D(b)(2) [added to the Securities Exchange Act by] the PSLRA, plaintiffs must "state with particularity facts giving rise to a strong inference that the defendant acted with the required state of mind."

Congress left the key term "strong inference" undefined, and Courts of Appeals have divided on its meaning. In the case before us, the Court of Appeals for the Seventh Circuit held that the "strong inference" standard would be met if the complaint "allege[d] facts from which, if true, a reasonable person could infer that the defendant acted with the required intent." 437 F.3d 588, 602 (2006). That formulation, we conclude, does not capture the stricter demand Congress sought to convey * * * . It does not suffice that a reasonable factfinder plausibly could infer from the complaint's allegations the requisite state of mind. Rather, to determine whether a complaint's scienter allegations can survive threshold inspection for sufficiency, a court governed by § 21D(b)(2) must engage in a comparative evaluation; it must consider, not only inferences urged by the plaintiff, as the Seventh Circuit did, but also competing inferences rationally drawn from the facts alleged. An inference of fraudulent intent may be plausible, yet less cogent than other, nonculpable explanations for the defendant's conduct. To qualify as "strong" within the intendment of [the section], we hold, an inference of scienter must be more than merely plausible or reasonable—it must be cogent and at least as compelling as any opposing inference of nonfraudulent intent.

Petitioner Tellabs, Inc., manufactures specialized equipment used in fiber optic networks. During the time period relevant to this case, petitioner Richard Notebaert was Tellabs' chief executive officer and president. Respondents (Shareholders) are persons who purchased Tellabs stock between December 11, 2000, and June 19, 2001. They accuse Tellabs and Notebaert (as well as several other Tellabs executives) of engaging in a scheme to deceive the investing public about the true value of Tellabs' stock.

Beginning on December 11, 2000, the Shareholders allege, Notebaert (and by imputation Tellabs) "falsely reassured public investors, in a series of statements * * * that Tellabs was continuing to enjoy strong demand for its products and earning record revenues," when, in fact, Notebaert knew the opposite was true. * * * [The Shareholders identified four specific untrue statements.] Based on Notebaert's sunny assessments, the Shareholders contend, market analysts recommended that investors buy Tellabs' stock.

* * *

The Court of Appeals recognized that the PSLRA "unequivocally raise[d] the bar for pleading scienter" by requiring plaintiffs to "plea[d] sufficient facts to create a strong inference of scienter." In evaluating whether that pleading standard is met, the Seventh Circuit said, "courts [should] examine all of the allegations in the complaint and then * * * decide whether collectively they establish such an inference. * * * [W]e will allow the complaint to survive," the court next and critically stated, "if it alleges facts from which, if true, a reasonable person could infer that the defendant acted with the required intent. * * * If a reasonable person could not draw such an inference from the alleged facts, the defendants are entitled to dismissal."

In adopting its standard for the survival of a complaint, the Seventh Circuit explicitly rejected a stiffer standard adopted by the Sixth Circuit, i.e., that "plaintiffs are entitled only to the most plausible of competing inferences." The Sixth Circuit's standard, the court observed, because it involved an assessment of competing inferences, "could potentially infringe upon plaintiffs' Seventh Amendment rights." We granted certiorari to resolve the disagreement among the Circuits on whether, and to what extent, a court must consider competing inferences in determining whether a securities fraud complaint gives rise to a "strong inference" of scienter.

* * *

II

In an ordinary civil action, the Federal Rules of Civil Procedure require only "a short and plain statement of the claim showing that the pleader is entitled to relief." Fed. Rule Civ. Proc. 8(a)(2). Although the rule encourages brevity, the complaint must say enough to give the defendant "fair notice of what the plaintiffs claim is and the grounds upon which it rests." Dura Pharms., Inc., 544 U.S., at 346 (internal quotation marks omitted). Prior to the enactment of the PSLRA, the sufficiency of a complaint for securities fraud was governed not by Rule 8, but by the heightened pleading standard set forth in Rule 9(b). * * * Rule 9(b) applies to "all averments of fraud or mistake"; it requires that "the circumstances constituting fraud * * * be stated with particularity" but provides that "[m]alice, intent, knowledge, and other condition of mind of a person, may be averred generally."

Courts of Appeals diverged on the character of the Rule 9(b) inquiry in § 10(b) cases * * * . * * * The Second Circuit's formulation was the most stringent. Securities fraud plaintiffs in that Circuit were required to "specifically plead those [facts] which they assert give rise to a *strong inference* that the defendants had" the requisite state of mind. Ross v. A. H. Robins Co., 607 F.2d 545, 558 (1979). * * *

Setting a uniform pleading standard for § 10(b) actions was among Congress' objectives when it enacted the PSLRA. Designed to curb perceived abuses of the § 10(b) private action—"nuisance filings, targeting of deep-pocket defendants, vexatious discovery requests and manipulation by class action lawyers," Dabit, 547 U.S., at 81 * * *—the PSLRA installed both substantive and procedural controls. Notably * * * Congress "impose[d] heightened pleading requirements in actions brought pursuant to § 10(b) and Rule 10b–5."

Under the PSLRA's heightened pleading instructions, any private securities complaint alleging that the defendant made a false or misleading statement must: (1) "specify each statement alleged to have been misleading [and] the reason or reasons why the statement is misleading," and (2) "state with particularity facts giving rise to a strong inference that the defendant acted with the required state of mind[.]" * * *

* * * While adopting the Second Circuit's "strong inference" standard, Congress did not codify that Circuit's case law interpreting the standard. * * * Our task is to prescribe a workable construction of the "strong inference" standard, a reading geared to the PSLRA's twin goals: to curb frivolous, lawyer-driven litigation, while preserving investors' ability to recover on meritorious claims.

III

A

We establish the following prescriptions: First, faced with a Rule 12(b)(6) motion to dismiss a § 10(b) action, courts must, as with any motion to dismiss for failure to plead a claim on which relief can be granted, accept all factual allegations in the complaint as true. * * *

Second, courts must consider the complaint in its entirety, as well as other sources courts ordinarily examine when ruling on Rule 12(b)(6) motions to dismiss, in particular, documents incorporated into the complaint by reference, and matters of which a court may take judicial notice. * * * The inquiry, as several Courts of Appeals have recognized, is whether all of the facts alleged, taken collectively, give rise to a strong inference of scienter, not whether any individual allegation, scrutinized in isolation, meets that standard. * * *

Third, in determining whether the pleaded facts give rise to a "strong" inference of scienter, the court must take into account plausible opposing inferences. The Seventh Circuit expressly declined to engage in such a comparative inquiry. A complaint could survive, that court said, as long as it "alleges facts from which, if true, a reasonable person could infer that the defendant acted with the required intent"; in other words, only "[I]f a reasonable person could not draw such an inference from the alleged facts" would the defendant prevail on a motion to dismiss. But in § 21D(b)(2), Congress did not merely require plaintiffs to "provide a factual basis for [their] scienter allegations," * * * *i.e.*, to allege facts from which an inference of scienter rationally could be drawn. Instead, Congress required plaintiffs to plead with particularity facts that give rise to a "strong"—*i.e.*, a powerful or cogent—inference. See American Heritage Dictionary 1717 (4th ed. 2000) (defining "strong" as "[p]ersuasive, effective, and cogent"); 16 Oxford English Dictionary 949 (2d ed. 1989) (defining "strong" as "[p]owerful to demonstrate or convince" (definition 1 6b)); cf. 7 *id.*, at 924 (defining "inference" as "a conclusion [drawn] from known or assumed facts or statements"; "reasoning from something known or assumed to something else which follows from it").

The strength of an inference cannot be decided in a vacuum. The inquiry is inherently comparative: How likely is it that one conclusion, as compared to others, follows from the underlying facts? To determine whether the plaintiff has alleged facts that give rise to the requisite "strong inference" of scienter, a court must consider plausible nonculpable explanations for the defendant's conduct, as well as inferences favoring the plaintiff. The inference that the defendant acted with scienter need not be irrefutable, *i.e.*, of the "smoking-gun" genre, or even the "most plausible of competing inferences," Fidel v. Farley, 392 F.3d 220, 227 (CA6 2004) * * * ." Recall in this regard that § 21D(b)'s pleading requirements are but one constraint among many the PSLRA installed to screen out frivolous suits, while allowing meritorious actions to move forward. Yet the inference of scienter must be more than merely "reasonable or" "permissible"—it must be cogent and compelling, thus strong in light of other explanations. A complaint will survive, we hold, only if a reasonable person would deem the inference of scienter cogent and at least as compelling as any opposing inference one could draw from the facts alleged.[19]

---

[19] Justice Scalia objects to this standard * * * . * * * [However,] an inference at least as likely as competing inferences can, in some cases, warrant recovery. See Summers v. Tice, 199 P.2d 1, 2–5 (Cal. 1948) (in bank) (plaintiff wounded by gunshot could recover from two defendants, even though the most he could prove was that each defendant was at least as likely to have injured him as the other) * * * . * * *

* * *

B

Tellabs contends that when competing inferences are considered, Notebaert's evident lack of pecuniary motive will be dispositive. The Shareholders, Tellabs stresses, did not allege that Notebaert sold any shares during the class period. * * * While it is true that motive can be a relevant consideration, and personal financial gain may weigh heavily in favor of a scienter inference, we agree with the Seventh Circuit that the absence of a motive allegation is not fatal. As earlier stated, allegations must be considered collectively; the significance that can be ascribed to an allegation of motive, or lack thereof, depends on the entirety of the complaint.

Tellabs also maintains that several of the Shareholders' allegations are too vague or ambiguous to contribute to a strong inference of scienter. * * * We agree that omissions and ambiguities count against inferring scienter, for plaintiffs must "state with particularity facts giving rise to a strong inference that the defendant acted with the required state of mind." We reiterate, however, that the court's job is not to scrutinize each allegation in isolation but to assess all the allegations holistically. In sum, the reviewing court must ask: When the allegations are accepted as true and taken collectively, would a reasonable person deem the inference of scienter at least as strong as any opposing inference?

IV

Accounting for its construction of § 21D(b)(2), the Seventh Circuit explained that the court "th[ought] it wis[e] to adopt an approach that [could not] be misunderstood as a usurpation of the jury's role." In our view, the Seventh Circuit's concern was undue. A court's comparative assessment of plausible inferences, while constantly assuming the plaintiffs allegations to be true, we think it plain, does not impinge upon the Seventh Amendment right to jury trial.

Congress, as creator of federal statutory claims, has power to prescribe what must be pleaded to state the claim, just as it has power to determine what must be proved to prevail on the merits. It is the federal lawmaker's prerogative, therefore, to allow, disallow, or shape the contours of—including the pleading and proof requirements for—10(b) private actions. * * *

* * *

While we reject the Seventh Circuit's approach to § 21D(b)(2), we do not decide whether, under the standard we have described, the Shareholders' allegations warrant "a strong inference that [Notebaert and Tellabs] acted with the required state of mind." * * *

* * *

■ JUSTICE SCALIA, concurring in the judgment.

I fail to see how an inference that is merely "at least as compelling as any opposing inference" can conceivably be called what the statute here at issue requires: a "strong inference." If a jade falcon were stolen from a room to which only A and B had access, could it possibly be said there was a "strong inference" that B was the thief? I think not, and I therefore think that the Court's test must fail. In my view, the test should be whether the inference of scienter (if any) is more plausible than the inference of innocence.

* * *

In order to avoid the limitations imposed by the Private Securities Litigation Reform Act of 1995, many lawyers began bringing class action suits in state courts. In response, Congress enacted the Securities Litigation Uniform Standards Act of 1998, which added Section 16 to the Securities Act and Section 28(f) to the Exchange Act. These sections cover most class actions involving securities fraud or problems with disclosure, and require such actions to be brought in federal court under federal law.

F. CLASS CERTIFICATION

Obviously, from the perspective of most plaintiff's attorneys, class litigation is more efficient (and lucrative) than bringing suit on behalf of individual clients. Set out below is a portion of a recent Supreme Court case discussing class certification in the securities context.

Amgen, Inc. et al v. Connecticut Retirement Plans and Trust Funds

Supreme Court of the United States, 2013.
568 U.S. 455.

■ JUSTICE GINSBURG delivered the Opinion of the Court.

This case involves a securities-fraud complaint filed by Connecticut Retirement Plans and Trust Funds (Connecticut Retirement) against biotechnology company Amgen Inc. and several of its officers (collectively, Amgen). Seeking class-action certification under Federal Rule of Civil Procedure 23, Connecticut Retirement invoked the "fraud-on-the-market" presumption endorsed by this Court in Basic Inc. v. Levinson, 485 U.S. 224 (1988), and recognized most recently in Erica P. John Fund, Inc. v. Halliburton Co., 563 U.S. [804] (2011). The fraud-on-the-market premise is that the price of a security traded in an efficient market will reflect all publicly available information about a company; accordingly, a buyer of the security may be presumed to have relied on that information in purchasing the security.

Amgen has conceded the efficiency of the market for the securities at issue and has not contested the public character of the allegedly fraudulent statements on which Connecticut Retirement's complaint is based. Nor does Amgen here dispute that Connecticut Retirement meets all of the class-action prerequisites stated in Rule 23(a): (1) the alleged class "is so numerous that joinder of all members is impracticable"; (2) "there are questions of law or fact common to the class"; (3) Connecticut Retirement's claims are "typical of the claims * * * of the class"; and (4) Connecticut Retirement will "fairly and adequately protect the interests of the class."

The issue presented concerns the requirement stated in Rule 23(b)(3) that "the questions of law or fact common to class members predominate over any questions affecting only individual members." Amgen contends that to meet the predominance requirement, Connecticut Retirement must do more than plausibly plead that Amgen's alleged misrepresentations and misleading omissions materially affected Amgen's stock price. According to Amgen, certification must be denied unless Connecticut Retirement proves materiality, for immaterial misrepresentations or omissions, by definition, would have no impact on Amgen's stock price in an efficient market.

While Connecticut Retirement certainly must prove materiality to prevail on the merits, we hold that such proof is not a prerequisite to class certification. Rule 23(b)(3) requires a showing that questions common to the class predominate, not that those questions will be answered, on the merits, in favor of the class. Because materiality is judged according to an objective standard, the materiality of Amgen's alleged misrepresentations and omissions is a question common to all members of the class Connecticut Retirement would represent. The alleged misrepresentations and omissions, whether material or immaterial, would be so equally for all investors composing the class. As vital, the plaintiff class's inability to prove materiality would not result in individual questions predominating. Instead, a failure of proof on the issue of materiality would end the case, given that materiality is an essential element of the class members' securities-fraud claims. As to materiality, therefore, the class is entirely cohesive: It will prevail or fail in unison. In no event will the individual circumstances of particular class members bear on the inquiry.

Essentially, Amgen, also the dissenters from today's decision, would have us put the cart before the horse. To gain certification under Rule 23(b)(3), Amgen and the dissenters urge, Connecticut Retirement must first establish that it will win the fray. But the office of a Rule 23(b)(3) certification ruling is not to adjudicate the case; rather, it is to select the "metho[d]" best suited to adjudication of the controversy "fairly and efficiently."

* * *

In Erica P. John Fund, Inc. v. Halliburton Co.,[20] referred to in *Amgen*, the Court determined that proof of loss causation was not necessary for class certification.

G. ATTORNEY-CLIENT AND WORK PRODUCT PRIVILEGES

As will be seen in the next case, questions about the attorney-client and work product privileges sometimes arise in atypical ways in the context of a securities law practice.

In re Subpoenas Duces Tecum

United States Court of Appeals, District of Columbia Circuit, 1984.
738 F.2d 1367.

■ Before WALD, MIKVA and DAVIS, CIRCUIT JUDGES.

■ DAVIS, CIRCUIT JUDGE:

Appellants challenge orders of the District Court granting appellees' motion to compel compliance with four subpoenas *duces tecum* on the grounds that the attorney-client and work product privileges had been waived by prior disclosure. We affirm.

I

Appellees, movants below, are seeking copies of documents which have been furnished by appellants, respondents below, to the Securities and Exchange Commission (SEC or Commission) and to a grand jury. The demand for those documents arose out of complaints filed by appellees as plaintiffs in Pennsylvania and transferred to the U.S. District Court for the Western District of Texas which involve (1) a class action brought against Tesoro Petroleum Corporation (Tesoro) and its officers and directors on behalf of Tesoro stockholders, and (2) a derivative action brought in Tesoro's name against its officers and directors. Plaintiffs allege in those complaints that defendants manipulated Tesoro stock in 1982 in order to remove enough stock from the public market to convert Tesoro from a public into a private corporation. The claim is that this contemplated corporate change was in part motivated by a desire to become free from public disclosure obligations, which obligations in turn might have caused disclosure of involvement by Tesoro in illegal payments to foreign officials before 1978. In the course of that Texas litigation, plaintiffs sought the papers now in question for use in connection with those suits. Because the documents are now in the possession, within the District of Columbia, of two law firms, Fulbright & Jaworski (Fulbright) and Vinson & Elkins (Vinson), subpoenas *duces tecum* were issued to those firms by the Clerk of the

---

[20] 131 S.Ct. 2179 (2011).

District Court, and, on their refusal to produce, a proceeding to enforce the subpoenas against them was begun in the court below.

Although neither law firm is a party to the law suits in Texas, their involvement here stems from the fact that the subpoenaed documents are the product of an investigation by Fulbright into Tesoro's alleged illegal payments to foreign officials. This came about as follows: After indications of improper corporate payments to officials, domestic and foreign, had become more frequent in the 1970's, the SEC established a "voluntary disclosure program," including independent investigations by the affected companies, and the agency made a general request to those companies to participate in the program. *In re Sealed Case*, 676 F.2d 793, 800–01 (D.C.Cir.1982). Following such a request to Tesoro, it hired Fulbright to perform a self-investigation on that subject and to help set up a special committee of independent directors to oversee it.[21] Tesoro disclosed the results of the investigation to the SEC under the "voluntary disclosure program." As stated by the District Court below, that program "promises wrongdoers more lenient treatment and the chance to avoid formal investigation and litigation in return for thorough self-investigation and complete disclosure of the results to the SEC."

Made available to the SEC, under that program, were a copy of the investigation's final report and several binders which contained pertinent corporate records and documents of Tesoro, as well as the notes of the lawyers taken during the course of their investigation. The SEC filed a civil complaint against Tesoro, following the agency's receipt and consideration of the documents, which was resolved by entry of a consent decree. The Commission also referred some aspects of Tesoro's circumstances to the Department of Justice, which then presented the matter to a grand jury, convened in October 1978 in the District of Columbia. Vinson represented Tesoro before the grand jury, and also is Tesoro's counsel in the Texas litigation. The grand jury obtained copies of the same documents through subpoenas served on the law firms.

After a hearing on the motion, the District Court ordered compliance, rejecting appellants' attorney-client and work product arguments. * * *

II

The questions before us are whether the District Court correctly determined that appellants' voluntary disclosure of the documents to the SEC effected waivers of attorney-client and work product privileges with respect to the documents now sought for discovery in the Texas suits. We deal with each privilege in turn.

---

[21] The special committee later retained Vinson to advise it with regard to certain legal matters arising in conjunction with the investigation.

A. Attorney-Client Privilege

Attorney-client communications ordinarily are privileged, and thus are protected from discovery by a party opponent under Fed.R.Civ.P. 26(b). By allowing confidentiality of the substance of client and lawyer discussions, the privilege is held by clients as a means of encouraging their candor in discussing their circumstances with their chosen legal representatives. The privilege, however, is not absolute. As stated by this court in Permian Corp. v. United States, 665 F.2d 1214, 1219 (D.C.Cir.1981) (quoting United States v. American Telephone & Telegraph, 642 F.2d 1285, 1299 (D.C.Cir.1980)), "[a]ny voluntary disclosure by the holder of such a privilege is inconsistent with the confidential relationship and thus waives the privilege." There was, of course, disclosure here but appellants maintain that, although Tesoro's disclosure to the SEC was voluntary, their waiver of the attorney-client privilege with respect to those disclosures was limited to the SEC. They contend that *Permian* is compatible with a theory which allows a "limited waiver" of the attorney-client privilege (excluding disclosures to government agencies) and cite authority from other courts supporting the correctness of that rule. We disagree, and hold that the District Court correctly interpreted and applied this court's precedent.

Contrary to appellants' assertion, the waiver theory explicated by the court in *Permian* is not limited to circumstances in which material that has been disclosed to one federal agency is sought by another federal agency. In *Permian*, Occidental Petroleum Corporation (Occidental) had allowed the SEC access to certain documents pursuant to an agreement by which Occidental attempted to retain its privileges. When the Department of Energy later sought access to some of the privileged materials, Occidental claimed that several of the documents were protected by the attorney-client privilege and that the prior disclosure to the SEC was a limited waiver of the privilege, *i.e.*, it was a waiver with respect to the SEC alone.

Rejecting the limited waiver argument, this court stated: "we are aware of no congressional directive or judicially recognized priority system that places a higher value on cooperation with the SEC than on cooperation with other regulatory agencies, including the Department of Energy." Appellants use this quotation to urge that the *Permian* court rejected the limited waiver theory only as between federal agencies. However, such a narrow reading of that case is an incorrect characterization of its reasoning and holding. There is no need to elaborate on this court's emphatic rejection of the limited waiver doctrine in a lengthy discussion in *Permian*, in which the court stated that

> The client cannot be permitted to pick and choose among his opponents, waiving the privilege for some and resurrecting the claim of confidentiality to obstruct others, or to invoke the privilege as to communications whose confidentiality he has

already compromised for his own benefit * * * . The attorney-client privilege is not designed for such tactical employment.

There is no meaningful distinction in the adventitious fact that only federal agencies were involved in *Permian*. For the purposes of the attorney-client privilege, there is nothing special about another federal agency in the role of potential adversary as compared to private party litigants acting as adversaries. Like Occidental in *Permian*, Tesoro willingly sacrificed its attorney-client confidentiality by voluntarily disclosing material in an effort to convince another entity, the SEC, that a formal investigation or enforcement action was not warranted. Having done so, appellants cannot now selectively assert protection of those same documents under the attorney-client privilege. A client cannot waive that privilege in circumstances where disclosure might be beneficial while maintaining it in other circumstances where nondisclosure would be beneficial. "We believe that the attorney-client privilege should be available only at the traditional price: a litigant who wishes to assert confidentiality must maintain genuine confidentiality". *Permian*, 665 F.2d at 1222. Having failed to maintain genuine confidentiality, appellants are precluded from properly relying on the attorney-client privilege.

B.   *Work Product Privilege*

The harder question concerns appellants' claim that the District Court erred in concluding that the disclosure effected an implied waiver of their work product privilege.

While the attorney-client privilege is intended to promote communication between attorney and client by protecting client confidences, the work product privilege is a broader protection, designed to balance the needs of the adversary system to promote an attorney's preparation in representing a client against society's general interest in revealing all true and material facts relevant to the resolution of a dispute. As this court stated in United States v. American Telephone & Telegraph, 642 F.2d 1285, 1299 (D.C.Cir.1980), *"the work product privilege does not exist to protect a confidential relationship, but rather to promote the adversary system by safeguarding the fruits of an attorney's trial preparation from the discovery attempts of an opponent * * * . A* disclosure made in the pursuit of such trial preparation, and not inconsistent with maintaining secrecy against opponents, should be allowed without waiver of the privilege." (Emphasis in original.)

Recently this court decided a work product case which called upon the court to discuss the legal considerations underlying waiver of that privilege in the context of the SEC's voluntary disclosure program, *In re Sealed Case*, 676 F.2d 793 (D.C.Cir.1982). *Sealed Case* involved resistance to a grand jury subpoena by a multinational corporation on work product grounds (among others) for its counsel's records which had been disclosed previously to the SEC in the voluntary disclosure program. This court affirmed the district court's determination that the corporation had waived its work product privilege:

> Company entered into an arrangement with the SEC under which, as a matter of both common sense and common knowledge, Company relinquished its right to prevent the government from examining whatever documents were necessary for a fair evaluation of the final report offered to its shareholders and the SEC. Just because Company was successful in hiding crucial documents from the SEC, we need not allow Company to withhold them from a grand jury investigating possible crimes uncovered during the SEC's investigation.

Sealed Case, 676 F.2d at 817.

Although the circumstances before us differ—this is a case involving private parties, not a grand jury investigation, and appellees here are seeking the documents which were disclosed to the SEC, not those which might have been successfully hidden—and though that opinion left open the precise case before us, the general reasoning of *Sealed Case* leads us to a similar conclusion here. As Judge Wright stated, "[t]he doctrine of implied waiver allows courts to retain some discretion to ensure that specific assertions of privilege are reasonably consistent with the purposes for which a privilege was created," and "[t]he question with respect to implied waiver is whether Wigmore's 'objective consideration' of fairness negates [the] assertion of privilege."[22] Obviously, the application of such a "fairness" standard is not without difficulty. However, because the underlying rationale of the work product privilege itself is also one of fairness, an analysis of whether that rationale maintains viability in particular circumstances involves of necessity the weighing of more abstract considerations within the context of those particulars.

Our present decision that there has been a waiver of the privilege rests on three main factors: (1) "the party claiming the privilege seeks to use it in a way that is not consistent with the purpose of the privilege," *Sealed Case*, 676 F.2d at 818; (2) appellants had no reasonable basis for believing that the disclosed materials would be kept confidential by the SEC; and (3) waiver of the privilege in these circumstances would not trench on any policy elements now inherent in this privilege. First, the advantage that the appellants seek from their attempt selectively to disclose their work product is greater "than the law must provide to maintain a healthy adversary system." *Id.* Fairness and consistency require that appellants not be allowed to gain the substantial advantages accruing to voluntary disclosure of work product to one adversary—the

---

[22] Wigmore stated that "Regard must be had * * * in every waiver * * * [to] the element of fairness and consistency." 8 J. Wigmore, Evidence § 2327 at 636 (J. McNaughton rev. 1961)).

SEC—while being able to maintain another advantage inherent in protecting that same work product from other adversaries. * * *

* * *

Second, appellants did not have any proper expectations of confidentiality which might mitigate the weight against them of such general considerations of fairness in the adversary process. Although we agree with appellants that not all voluntary disclosures effect a work product waiver, there is not here any "existence of common interests between transferor and transferee," United States v. AT & T, 642 F.2d 1285, 1299 (1980), which might establish a basis for expectations of confidentiality. Appellants contend, however, that such expectations were warranted because the materials were disclosed to the Commission pursuant to (1) SEC regulations which required their confidentiality and, (2) an understanding between Fulbright and the SEC that the materials would remain confidential.

There is a dispute between the parties whether the question of SEC regulations said to require confidentiality was raised below by appellants. We put aside this question because the regulations cited by appellants are not relevant to the circumstances before us. *See* 17 C.F.R. §§ 203.2, 230.122, 240.0–4 (1978). These regulations apply to formal SEC investigations—they afford no protection to documents previously disclosed under the voluntary disclosure program. Appellants maintain that "disclosure" of the materials did not occur until the formal investigation began—and thus the regulations do apply—because the SEC did not have physical possession of the materials until that time. But even before taking physical possession, the SEC unquestionably had full access to all of the documents and perused them. Contrary to appellants' argument, there is no significance to the distinction between full access and physical possession with respect to the issue of when disclosure took place. The materials were disclosed in full to the SEC prior to the institution of a formal investigation, and the regulations do not apply.

* * *

H. RACKETEER INFLUENCED AND CORRUPT ORGANIZATIONS ACT

The Racketeer Influenced and Corrupt Organizations Act (RICO), passed by Congress in 1970, allows private plaintiffs to recover treble damages when they are injured by certain "predicate offenses" relating to the conduct of an enterprise through a pattern of racketeering activity. This is in addition to the ability of federal prosecutors to seek prison terms of up to 20 years (and to freeze the defendant's assets before trial). After liberal invocation of RICO by private plaintiffs alleging fraud in the sale of securities (one of the listed predicate offenses), Congress in 1995 amended RICO to provide that, in a civil action, conduct that would be actionable as fraud in the purchase or sale of securities is not actionable under RICO, except against a person who has been criminally convicted in connection with the fraud. In the latter case, the statute of limitations begins to run on the date the conviction becomes final.

PART 5

SPECIAL RESPONSIBILITIES OF SECURITIES LAWYERS

CHAPTER 18

THE RESPONSIBILITIES OF SECURITIES LAWYERS: VARIOUS PERSPECTIVES

SITUATION 18

Assume that you are a junior attorney working on the Microtec initial public offering. Your firm has primary responsibility for drafting the registration statement. You seriously question the completeness and accuracy of some of the information that Microtec's representatives have provided. What are your obligations and those of your firm?

In considering this situation, refer to the following, in addition to the materials in this chapter: Securities Act Section 24 and Exchange Act Sections 4C and 32 and Part 205 of the Commission's rules.

A. SPECIAL POSITION OF SECURITIES LAWYERS

The environment in which securities lawyers practice is quite different from that of most other lawyers. This difference is largely the result of two distinguishing characteristics of securities law practice. First, it is often a securities lawyer who decides whether a particular securities transaction can proceed or, because of legal problems, must be cancelled. As a matter of common practice, for example, it is often true that unless a lawyer attests to the legality of a transaction by the delivery of an opinion, the parties to the transaction will not agree to proceed. Second, a securities lawyer typically does not merely advise clients on how to accomplish a transaction, but rather he or she is usually an active participant in the transaction.

The first of these characteristics, coupled with the knowledge that the Commission's own enforcement resources are wholly insufficient to police a significant fraction of securities transactions, has caused the Commission and others—in recent times many others—to advocate that a lawyer has a special responsibility to protect the public when working in the securities area. Proponents of expanded responsibility for securities lawyers sometimes liken the position of the securities lawyer to that of the certified public accountant, who long ago was held to have an overriding responsibility to the public, rather than merely to his or her clients. The second of these characteristics—active involvement by lawyers in securities transactions—sometimes insures that when the legality of a completed transaction is questioned, one or more securities lawyers will find themselves in the middle of the controversy, rather than somewhat comfortably on the sidelines.

The materials in this chapter point up well the distinguishing characteristics of securities law practice and the results that can flow from these characteristics.

The Emerging Responsibilities
of the Securities Lawyer

A.A. Sommer, Jr.*

Address to the Banking, Corporation and Business Law Section,
New York State Bar Association (January 24, 1974).**

* * *

Attorneys have since the earliest days of the federal securities laws been at the heart of the scheme that developed in response to those laws. While their formal participation mandated by the '33 and '34 Acts was limited * * *, the registration statement has always been a lawyer's document and with very, very rare exceptions the attorney has been the field marshall who coordinated the activities of others engaged in the registration process * * * . * * *

Counsel have been involved in many other ways with the federal securities laws. They are frequently called upon to give opinions with respect, principally, to the availability of exemptions from the requirements for registration and use of a statutory prospectus. None would deny the importance of these opinions: millions upon millions of dollars of securities have been put into the channels of commerce—not just sold once, but permanently into the trading markets—in reliance upon little more than the professional judgment of an attorney. * * *

Attorneys' opinions have played other roles as well. They are customarily rendered in connection with the closing of registered public offerings * * * . * * *

* * *

In a word, and the word is Professor Morgan Shipman's, the professional judgment of the attorney is often the "passkey" to securities transactions. If he gives an opinion that an exemption is available, securities get sold; if he doesn't give the opinion, they don't get sold. If he judges that certain information must be included in a registration statement, it gets included (unless the client seeks other counsel or the attorney crumbles under the weight of client pressure); if he concludes it need not be included, it doesn't get included.

---

*   Commissioner, Securities and Exchange Commission.

**   The Securities and Exchange Commission, as a matter of policy, disclaims responsibility for any private publication or speech by any of its members or employees. The views expressed here are my own and do not necessarily reflect the views of the Commission or of my fellow Commissioners.

* * *

We are consistently reminded that historically the attorney has been an advocate, that his professional ethics have over the years defined his function in those terms, that such a role includes unremitting loyalty to the interests of his client (short of engaging in or countenancing fraud). Whenever the effort is made to analogize the responsibilities of the attorney to those of the independent auditor, one is reminded that the federal securities law system conceives of the auditor as independent and defines his role specifically, whereas the attorney is not and cannot be independent in the same sense in which an auditor is independent. It has been asserted by very eminent counsel that, "The law, so far, [this was in 1969] is very clear. The lawyers' responsibility is exclusively to their own client." If this distinction is clear to lawyers, it is less clear to others. * * *

I would suggest that the security bar's *conception* of its role too sharply contrasts with the *reality* of its role in the securities process to escape notice and attention—and in such situations the reality eventually prevails. Lawyers are not paid in the amounts they are to put the representations of their clients in good English, or give opinions which assume a pure state of facts upon which any third year law student could confidently express an opinion.

We live in the age of the consumer. All of the old articles of faith which frustrated him in efforts to achieve equity have fallen or are falling: cognovit notes are repudiated in most places; the sale of installment paper no longer immunizes the paper purchaser from responsibility for the shoddiness of the merchandise; people pressured into purchases on their doorstep have time to think over their decision; the real costs of borrowing and purchases on installments must be disclosed. This pervading judicial and legislative concern for the interests of the consumer which has for forty years been present in large measure in the securities field (the securities laws may have been the first federal consumer legislation) is affecting and will affect increasingly the securities field—and those involved in it.

Consequently, I would suggest that all the old verities and truisms about attorneys and their roles are in question and in jeopardy—and, unless you are ineradicably dedicated to the preservation of the past, that is not all bad.

I would suggest that in securities matters (other than those where advocacy is clearly proper) the attorney will have to function in a manner more akin to that of the auditor than to that of the advocate. This means several things. It means he will have to exercise a measure of independence that is perhaps uncomfortable if he is also the close counselor of management in other matters, often including business decisions. It means he will have to be acutely cognizant of his responsibility to the public who engage in securities transactions that would never have come about were it not for his professional presence. It means he will have to adopt the healthy skepticism toward the representations of management which a good auditor must adopt. It means he will have to do the same thing the auditor does when confronted with an intransigent client—resign.

* * *

* * * How does this affect the traditional attorney-client privilege? Does it undermine the relationship of confidence between attorney and client that has been so important to the bar in doing its work? Must the attorney "welsh" on his client when he discerns an illegal direction to his activities? Must the attorney, in short, become another cop on the beat?

I would not suggest that the resolution of these problems is easy. The resolution will entail close study of the emerging case law, attention to the Code of Professional Responsibility, alertness to the demands of society upon the professionals it employs, and recognition of the pivotal role of counsel in the process by which securities are brought to market.

I would suggest that the bar will make a serious error if it seeks to defend itself against the emerging trends by reliance upon old shibboleths and axioms. Society will not stand for it * * * . Everyone has been shocked by the massive betrayal of public investors in recent years and inevitably the focus is upon the people and the process through which these debacles came about. This spotlight will, I predict, increasingly focus upon the role of attorney who is invariably a keeper of the stop and go signal.

* * *

I would urge that as lawyers we not be hesitant in representing our clients, but let us not be hesitant, either, in protecting those who rely, sometimes rather blindly, upon the protections of professional judgment. Corporate law lawyers are paid well, ultimately by society, for doing a professional job and assuming professional responsibility. Let us not, I urge, appear to society fearful and hesitant as we adapt to the emerging responsibilities of this age where consumer is king.

Statement of Policy Regarding Responsibilities and Liabilities of Lawyers in Advising with Respect to the Compliance by Clients with Laws Administered by the Securities and Exchange Commission

American Bar Association.
31 Business Lawyer 543 (1975).*

[T]he Committee on Counsel Responsibility and Liability of the Section of Corporation, Banking and Business Law of the American Bar Association has been examining the responsibilities and liabilities of

* Copyright © 1975 by the American Bar Association. All rights reserved. Reprinted with the permission of the American Bar Association and its Section of Business Law.

lawyers engaged in securities law matters. The Committee * * * prepared the following Statement of Policy * * *. The Statement of Policy was adopted by the ABA House of Delegates on August 12, 1975 pursuant to recommendation by the Council of the Section. * * *

* * *

AMERICAN BAR ASSOCIATION REPORT TO THE HOUSE OF DELEGATES SECTION OF CORPORATION, BANKING AND BUSINESS LAW RECOMMENDATION

The Section of Corporation, Banking and Business Law recommends adoption of the following resolution:

BE IT RESOLVED, that this Association adopts the following Statement of Policy regarding responsibilities and liabilities of lawyers in advising with respect to the compliance by clients with laws administered by the Securities and Exchange Commission ("SEC"):

1. The confidentiality of lawyer-client consultations and advice and the fiduciary loyalty of the lawyer to the client, as prescribed in the American Bar Association's Code of Professional Responsibility ("CPR"), are vital to the basic function of the lawyer as legal counselor because they enable and encourage clients to consult legal counsel freely, with assurance that counsel will respect the confidentiality of the client's communications and will advise independently and in the client's best interest without conflicting loyalties or obligations.

2. This vital confidentiality of consultation and advice would be destroyed or seriously impaired if it is accepted as a general principle that lawyers must inform the SEC or others regarding confidential information received by lawyers from their clients even though such action would not be permitted or required by the CPR. Any such compelled disclosure would seriously and adversely affect the lawyers' function as counselor, and may seriously and adversely affect the ability of lawyers as advocates to represent and defend their clients' interests.

3. In light of the foregoing considerations, it must be recognized that a lawyer cannot, consistently with his essential role as legal adviser, be regarded as a source of information concerning possible wrong-doing by clients. Accordingly, any principle of law which, except as permitted or required by the CPR, permits or obliges a lawyer to disclose to the SEC otherwise confidential information, should be established only by statute after full and careful consideration of the public interests involved, and should be resisted unless clearly mandated by law.

4. Lawyers have an obligation under the CPR to advise clients, to the best of their ability, concerning the need for or advisability of public disclosure of a broad range of events and circumstances, including the obligation of the client to make appropriate disclosures as required by various laws and regulations administered by the SEC. In appropriate circumstances, a lawyer may be permitted or required by the Disciplinary

Rules under the CPR to resign his engagement if his advice concerning disclosures is disregarded by the client and, if the conduct of a client clearly establishes his prospective commission of a crime or the past or prospective perpetration of a fraud in the course of the lawyer's representation, even to make the disclosures himself. However, the lawyer has neither the obligation nor the right to make disclosure when any reasonable doubt exists concerning the client's obligation of disclosure, i.e., the client's failure to meet his obligation is not clearly established, except to the extent that the lawyer should consider appropriate action, as required or permitted by the CPR, in cases where the lawyer's opinion is expected to be relied on by third parties and the opinion is discovered to be not correct, whether because it is based on erroneous information or otherwise.

5.   Fulfillment by attorneys of their obligations to clients under the CPR best serves the public interest of assisting and furthering clients' compliance with legal requirements. Efforts by the government to impose responsibility upon lawyers to assure the quality of their clients' compliance with the law or to compel lawyers to give advice resolving all doubts in favor of regulatory restrictions would evoke serious and far-reaching disruption in the role of the lawyer as counselor, which would be detrimental to the public, clients and the legal profession. In fulfillment of their responsibility to clients under the CPR, lawyers must be free to advise clients as to the full range of their legitimately available courses of action and the relative attendant risks involved. Furthermore, it is often desirable for the lawyer to point out those factors which may suggest a decision that is morally just as well as legally permissible. However, the decision as to the course to be taken should be made by the client. The client's actions should not be improperly narrowed through the insistence of an attorney who may, perhaps unconsciously, eliminate available choices from consideration because of his concern over possible personal risks if the position is taken which, though supportable, is subject to uncertainty or contrary to a known, but perhaps erroneous, position of the SEC or a questionable lower court decision. Public policy, we strongly believe, is best served by lawyers acting in conformance with their obligations to their clients and others as prescribed under the CPR. Accordingly, liability should not be imposed upon lawyers whose conduct is in conformance with the CPR.

* * *

The Attorney as Gatekeeper:
An Agenda for the SEC

John C. Coffee, Jr.
103 Columbia Law Review 1293 (2003).*

* * *

Today, the auditor certifies the firm's financial results, and under Sarbanes-Oxley, senior management certifies that the financial information in periodic reports filed with the SEC "fairly presents in all material respects" the firm's financial condition and results of operations. Even the securities analyst must now certify that its recommendations reflect the analyst's own personal views. Alone, the attorney escapes and need not certify in any way as to the accuracy of the client's disclosures. Yet, traditionally, the attorney is the field marshall of the disclosure process. More importantly, because the auditor's certificate covers only the financial statements that it reviews, no independent professional today expresses any view that the statements made in the textual portions of a Form 10–K or a registration statement are correct or have at least been subjected to a reasonable "due diligence" examination by the professional. Yet increasingly, the most important statements made by a corporate issuer are those set forth in its "Management's Discussion and Analysis of Financial Condition and Results of Operations" (MD & A). If after the Enron-era scandals we are concerned about the quality and reliability of the financial disclosures reaching the market, one of the most obvious, logical, and necessary steps would be to insert a gatekeeper into the disclosure process at exactly this stage and require some professional vetting of the issuer's textual statements.

Still, there remains a problem with this proposal that requires it to be downsized significantly. Put simply, what can the attorney reasonably be asked to certify? After all, the attorney has not audited the client; nor is a law firm organizationally or logistically equipped for any form of inquiry analogous to an audit. Nonetheless, a less onerous form of certification seems possible. Based on the opinions normally delivered by attorneys in registered offerings in the securities market, it would seem justifiable to ask the attorney principally responsible for preparing a disclosure document or report filed with the SEC to certify: (1) that such attorney believes the statements made in the document or report to be true and correct in all material respects; and (2) that such attorney is not aware of any additional material information whose disclosure is necessary in order to make the statements made, in the light of the circumstances under which they were made, not misleading.

In essence, this proposed certification simply tracks the language of Rule 10b–5. Far from intruding significantly into the marketplace, this obligation only generalizes existing practices in the private market.

---

*   Copyright © 2003 The Columbia Law Review; John C. Coffee, Jr. Reprinted with permission.

Today, in most public underwritten offerings, issuer's counsel delivers an opinion to the underwriters—sometimes called a "negative assurance" opinion—stating that it is not "aware" of any material information required to be disclosed that has not been disclosed. In this light, such a negative certification requirement would simply mandate for 1934 Act periodic filings what is already done by the private issuers in the primary market for 1933 Act disclosure documents. The marginal difference is that, in the case of periodic filings under the Securities Exchange Act, there is no private party in a position analogous to the underwriter who can demand such an opinion or certification from the attorney. SEC action would fill this void. The one respect in which this proposal does change current practice is that it would require that some attorney— whether inside or outside the corporation—assume responsibility for supervising the preparation of the disclosure document. Thus, it effectively requires the involvement of a gatekeeper and precludes internal corporate personnel from filing a Form 10–K or Form 10–Q without some review by counsel.

Beyond this structural value, such a requirement would have a profound symbolic and psychological effect on the bar because it would establish the attorney's obligations as a gatekeeper. Potentially, the SEC could go even further and require the certifying attorney responsible for the disclosure document to certify that the attorney believed adequate disclosure had been made "after making such inquiry that the attorney reasonably believed appropriate in the circumstance." This would integrate the certification requirement with the earlier discussed due diligence obligation. As here proposed, either in-house counsel or an outside attorney could provide such certification, but either would be subject to a due diligence obligation.

Admittedly, limits need to be recognized on what an attorney can certify. Because the attorney does not audit its client, the attorney should not be asked to certify the accuracy and completeness of all information disclosed in SEC filings. Thus, the proposal here made requires only a negative certification that the attorney had no reason to believe, and did not believe, that the information was materially false or misleading. Legally, such a certification would trigger "aiding and abetting" liability that the SEC could enforce if the attorney knew of the materially false or misleading information, and it could even trigger criminal liability under various federal statutes. But its primary effect is to mandate that an attorney serve as a gatekeeper for investors with respect to important disclosure documents.

Still other rules may be desirable, dealing with more specific problems. This discussion has not been intended to be exhaustive or to offer precise rules, but rather to advance a more general proposition: To the extent that the quality of disclosure declined in the 1990s, the most logical response is to identify a gatekeeper who can be asked to play a more active role in monitoring the issuer's disclosures. This is not a role that attorneys will want to play because it does impose costs on them, but it is a role they may be obliged to play because the social costs of allowing them to escape responsibility are even higher.

* * *

B. PRIMARY AND SECONDARY LIABILITY

Recall that many of the provisions of the federal securities laws imposing liability specify the parties against whom the provisions apply. For instance, liability under Sections 12(a)(1) and (2) of the Securities Act is imposed upon "sellers"; liability under Section 11 of that Act is imposed upon a specific list of prospective defendants. Although an attorney working on a deal conceivably could be a "seller" under the test of Pinter v. Dahl[1] (discussed in Chapter 8), it is clear that the Supreme Court did not think this generally would be the case. An attorney working on a Securities Act registration statement would not need to worry about Section 11 liability unless he or she was named in the registration statement as an expert (something that might happen in the case of a needed tax opinion).

The prospect of liability for attorneys as the result of Exchange Act Section 10(b) and Rule 10b–5 stood on an uncertain footing, especially after Central Bank of Denver, N.A. v. First Interstate Bank of Denver, N.A.[2] (discussed in Chapter 12) rejected liability to private plaintiffs for aiding and abetting violations of those provisions. Now, however, it appears that attorneys have little to fear in the context of private lawsuits alleging misstatements appearing in public documents. This is because, in Janus Capital Group, Inc. v. First Derivative Traders[3] (also discussed in Chapter 12), the Supreme Court held that attribution is critical in establishing "ultimate control" over, and thus primary liability for, any statement under Section 10(b) and Rule 10b–5. The extent of that ruling is explored in the following case.

ESG Capital Partners, LP v. Stratos

United States Court of Appeals, Ninth Circuit, 2016.
828 F.3d 1023.

■ PREGERSON, CIRCUIT JUDGE:

* * *

BACKGROUND

ESG Capital Partners, L.P. ("ESG Capital") was a group of investors formed to purchase pre-Initial Public Offering ("pre-IPO") Facebook

---

[1]   486 U.S. 622 (1988).

[2]   511 U.S. 164 (1994).

[3]   131 S.Ct. 2296 (2011).

shares. Timothy Burns ("managing agent Burns") was ESG Capital's managing agent. Managing agent Burns negotiated the purchase of pre-IPO Facebook stock with a man he believed to be "Ken Dennis." In fact, "Ken Dennis" was an alias for Troy Stratos, an alleged con artist.

Venable LLP is a law firm with nine offices throughout the country, including Los Angeles. Venable LLP represented "Dennis" (aka Stratos) in the Facebook deal, which is the subject of this securities fraud suit. One of the partners in Venable LLP's Los Angeles office, David Meyer ("attorney Meyer"), was "Dennis's" principal contact at Venable LLP throughout the Facebook deal. * * *

Attorney Meyer assisted Stratos in creating Soumaya Securities, LLC ("Soumaya Securities")—a company that Stratos could use to conduct business without detection. Attorney Meyer and Stratos named the company Soumaya Securities after billionaire Carlos Slim's late wife, Soumaya, and attorney Meyer told managing agent Burns that "Dennis" was affiliated with Slim. "Dennis" was not actually affiliated with Slim. And Soumaya Securities was not authorized to do business in California, had no bank accounts, and filed no tax returns.

Stratos, the alleged con artist, masqueraded as "Ken Dennis" in connection with all Soumaya Securities transactions, yet Soumaya Securities' operating documents, which attorney Meyer prepared, listed Stratos as Soumaya Securities' manager and sole member and "Kenneth Dennis" as its CEO. Attorney Meyer maintained a client trust account only for Stratos. As "Dennis," the CEO of Soumaya Securities, Stratos negotiated the sale of pre-IPO Facebook stocks to ESG Capital from March to April 2011.

Between February and November 2011, attorney Meyer met with Stratos 25 times in person and spoke to Stratos at least 100 times on the phone. Managing agent Burns had questions before confirming the deal and called attorney Meyer on April 18, 2011, to verify "Dennis's" representations. During their phone conversation, attorney Meyer informed managing agent Burns that "Dennis" was in contact with Facebook executives and had access to millions of Facebook shares. Attorney Meyer told managing agent Burns that "Dennis" "is who he says he is." In addition, attorney Meyer assured managing agent Burns that "Dennis" and Soumaya Securities were Slim's affiliates, that the sale was legitimate, that attorney Meyer represented "Dennis" and Soumaya Securities in the sale, and that attorney Meyer would provide deal documentation. ESG Capital pled that, without attorney Meyer's assurances, ESG Capital would not have gone through with the deal.

The day after the April 18 phone call, ESG Capital wired $2.8 million into Venable LLP's trust account as a deposit. Attorney Meyer called managing agent Burns to confirm receipt of the funds and that the "deal is on." That day, the entire $2.8 million was deposited into Stratos's personal client trust fund account, not to any account for Soumaya Securities. [Subsequent transfers brought the total transferred by ESG

Capital to $11.25 million.] Also that day, attorney Meyer had an all-day meeting with Stratos at Venable LLP's offices. ESG Capital pled that, had managing agent Burns known that the [funds] would not be held in trust pending the sale's completion, he would not have authorized attorney Meyer to release [them].

Throughout the negotiations, managing agent Burns communicated with "Dennis" through Stratos's * * * email address—the same email address that attorney Meyer used with Stratos. Attorney Meyer was copied on some of managing agent Burns's emails to "Dennis" at the email address that attorney Meyer knew belonged to Stratos. Venable LLP interacted with Stratos often while Stratos negotiated his deal with ESG Capital, and Venable LLP performed various nonlegal tasks for Stratos, such as purchasing office supplies and car insurance.

* * *

By December 22, 2011, ESG Capital still had not received the Facebook shares, and managing agent Burns threatened "Dennis" and attorney Meyer with legal action if its funds were not returned. In response, managing agent Burns received an email from Venable LLP's counsel, Stewart Webb, stating that "Venable received no such transfer and has no knowledge of the alleged transfer." Managing agent Burns responded by identifying each of ESG Capital's wire transfers made at Venable LLP's direction, along with the email address for "Dennis." Webb replied that the contact information managing agent Burns provided for "Dennis" was filed at Venable LLP under the name Troy Stratos, whom Venable LLP believed to be related to "Dennis." Webb told managing agent Burns that Venable LLP did not represent any party in the transactions between managing agent Burns and Soumaya Securities. Attorney Meyer was terminated by Venable LLP in 2012.

* * *

ESG Capital filed suit against Stratos and Venable LLP and attorney Meyer on March 6, 2013 * * * . * * * The district court * * * dismissed ESG Capital's first amended complaint ("FAC") with prejudice on August 15, 2013, denying leave to amend.

* * *

DISCUSSION

I.   ESG Capital's § 10(b) Federal Securities Fraud Claim

* * *

A.   Material Misrepresentations or Omissions

Venable LLP maintains that ESG Capital failed to plead that attorney Meyer made material misrepresentations or omissions. To make misrepresentations under § 10(b), attorney Meyer must be the "maker" of the statements. Janus Capital Grp., Inc. v. First Derivative Traders, 564 U.S. 135, 142–43 (2011). In addition, if an attorney has a duty to disclose, the attorney is liable for failing to provide truthful, nonmisleading information. Thompson [v. Paul], 547 F.3d [1055,] 1063 [(9th Cir. 2008)].

i.   Meyer was the Maker of the False Statements

"[T]he maker of a statement is the entity with authority over the content of the statement and whether and how to communicate it." *Janus Capital Grp.*, 564 U.S. at 144. Merely preparing or publishing another's statement does not make someone the "maker" of the statement, and attribution to another party generally indicates that the attributed party is the "maker." *Id.* at 142–43. In *Janus*, the Supreme Court considered whether an investment fund or its wholly owned subsidiary of investment advisers was the "maker" of false statements in its investment prospectus. The investment fund owned the subsidiary, but the two corporate entities were legally separate, with separate boards of trustees. *Id.* at 146–47. The investment fund had a statutory obligation under the SEC to file an investment prospectus. *Id.* at 147. The Supreme Court held that, although the investment advisers were significantly involved in preparing the prospectuses, their assistance was "subject to the ultimate control" of the investment fund. *Id.* at 148. The investment fund was thus the "maker" of the statements in its prospectus. *Id.*

ESG Capital alleged that attorney Meyer made multiple statements regarding the securities sale. The district court found that attorney Meyer did not make material misrepresentations or omissions, since "Meyer simply communicated Soumaya [Securities's] understanding of the deal, not his own." Attorney Meyer prefaced many of his emails with: "It is Soumaya's understanding * * * ." While it is true that attributing a statement to another party generally indicates that party as the "maker" of the statement, *see id.* at 142–43, we are not convinced that such a short, easy preface could shield a messenger from liability in all circumstances.

Even assuming that this disclaimer was sufficient to indicate that Soumaya Securities or Stratos was the "maker" of the statements in attorney Meyer's emails, attorney Meyer made other false statements directly to ESG Capital. Attorney Meyer told managing agent Burns that "he represented 'Ken Dennis' and Soumaya Securities in connection with pre-IPO Facebook transactions," that "Dennis" was affiliated with Slim, and that Dennis "is who he says he is." Yet Soumaya Securities was not affiliated with Slim, contrary to attorney Meyer's representations, and "Dennis" was not who he purported to be.

Attorney Meyer corresponded with Stratos at Stratos's email address—the same email address that Stratos used as "Ken Dennis" in its communications with ESG Capital. Attorney Meyer was copied on emails between ESG Capital and "Dennis" at this email address, so attorney Meyer must have known that ESG Capital believed it was communicating with "Ken Dennis" when it was actually emailing Troy Stratos. Finally, attorney Meyer told ESG Capital that its $2.8 million deposit would be released to Soumaya Securities, when in fact it was put into Stratos's personal client trust account.

Unlike the statements in the *Janus* investment prospectus, which were reasonably attributed to the investment fund, attorney Meyer made assurances to managing agent Burns on his own behalf. Attorney Meyer detailed his relationship to "Dennis" and made personal assurances regarding the Facebook deal and ESG Capital's deposit.

Not only did attorney Meyer make false statements to managing agent Burns, he also made material omissions when he failed to reveal that there was no Facebook deal; that Stratos, not Soumaya Securities, was Venable LLP's client; and that ESG Capital's $2.8 million deposit would be immediately dispersed to Stratos.

ii. Meyer Had a Duty to Disclose to ESG Capital

When attorneys have a duty to disclose information to third parties, they may be liable for misrepresentations under § 10(b). *Thompson*, 547 F.3d at 1061. In determining whether an attorney is liable under § 10(b), this court in *Thompson* surveyed other circuits' decisions, finding that attorneys may have a duty to nonclient third parties. *Id.* at 1061–63. In our survey of third party duties in *Thompson*, we took note of the Sixth Circuit's decision in Rubin v. Schottenstein, Zox & Dunn, 143 F.3d 263 (6th Cir.1998) (en banc). In *Rubin*, an attorney represented a company in connection with the sale of the company's debt and stock. *Thompson*, 547 F.3d at 1061–62 (citing *Rubin*, 143 F.3d at 266–68). The attorney assured a prospective investor that the company's stock was "fine," when the attorney knew that the company was actually in default on a loan, and the investment would have constituted further default. *Id.* The Sixth Circuit en banc panel held that the attorney had a duty to the investor, even though the investor was not his client. *Id.*

Applying *Rubin*'s logic, this court in *Thompson* ultimately articulated the following rule: "An attorney who undertakes to make representations to prospective purchasers of securities is under an obligation, imposed by Section 10(b), to tell the truth about those securities." *Id.* at 1063.

* * *

———

Although it was thought that the Court's reasoning in *Central Bank* disposed of all civil aiding and abetting liability under the federal securities laws, Congress has since amended both the Securities Act and the Exchange Act to provide for the Commission's ability to bring actions for aiding and abetting. Aiding and abetting liability may be imposed on the basis of either knowing or reckless conduct. This is an easier standard for the Commission to satisfy than the one applied in the case that follows (which was decided at a time at which the federal securities statutes themselves did not specifically address aiding and abetting).

SEC v. National Student Marketing Corp.

United States District Court, District of Columbia, 1978.
457 F.Supp. 682.

■ BARRINGTON D. PARKER, DISTRICT JUDGE:

This opinion covers the final act in a civil proceeding brought by the Securities and Exchange Commission (Commission or SEC) seeking injunctive sanctions against numerous defendants as a result of their participation in alleged securities laws violations relating to the National Student Marketing Corporation (NSMC) securities fraud scheme. The original defendants included the corporation and certain of its officers and directors; the accounting firm of Peat, Marwick, Mitchell & Co. (Peat Marwick) and two of its partners; several officers and directors of Interstate National Corporation (Interstate); the law firm of White & Case and one of its partners [, who represented NSMC]; and the law firm of Lord, Bissell & Brook (LBB) and two of its partners [, who represented Interstate]. The majority of these defendants are not now before the Court. As discovery progressed during the pre-trial stages of this litigation, NSMC and other principal defendants consented to the entry of final judgments of permanent injunction or otherwise reached a resolution of the charges against them. The only defendants remaining are Lord, Bissell & Brook; its two partners, Max E. Meyer and Louis F. Schauer; and Cameron Brown, a former president and director of Interstate, and presently a director of and consultant to NSMC.

The focal point of the Commission's charges against these defendants is the corporate merger of Interstate with NSMC on October 31, 1969. * * *

* * *

I. Background

A. *The Companies*

National Student Marketing Corporation * * * enjoyed early prosperity; it grew rapidly and experienced a steady increase in assets, sales and earnings. Its common stock, which was registered with the SEC and traded on the over-the-counter market, rose from an initial public offering of $6 per share in the spring of 1968 to a high of $144 per share in mid-December 1969. * * *

Interstate National Corporation * * * was an insurance holding company. Its principal assets were several wholly-owned subsidiary insurance companies. The company's common stock was traded on the over-the-counter market * * * . * * *

B. *The Merger Negotiations*

National Student Marketing Corporation developed a reputation for having a unique and successful marketing network for selling its own and other products to college and high school students. Commencing in 1969, it undertook a highly active program to acquire companies specializing in selling goods and services to students. It was in this connection that NSMC first approached representatives of Interstate [about a possible merger].

* * *

[A Merger Agreement ultimately was entered into, setting] forth fully the terms and conditions of [a proposed merger of Interstate into NSMC]. * * *

The Agreement * * * provided several conditions precedent to the obligations of the two corporations to consummate the merger. One required the receipt by NSMC of an opinion letter from Interstate's counsel LBB to the effect, *inter alia*, that Interstate had taken all actions and procedures required of it by law and that all transactions in connection with the merger had been duly and validly taken, to the best knowledge of counsel, in full compliance with applicable law; a similar opinion letter was required to be delivered from NSMC's counsel to Interstate. Another condition was the receipt by each company of a "comfort letter" from the other's independent public accountants [with respect to various accounting matters]. * * *

Finally, the Agreement specified that "[t]he transactions contemplated herein shall have been consummated on or before November 28, 1969."

Both NSMC and Interstate utilized proxy statements and notices of special stockholder meetings to secure shareholder approval of the proposed merger. Interstate's materials included a copy of the Merger Agreement and NSMC's Proxy Statement; the latter contained NSMC's financial statements for the fiscal year ended August 31, 1968, and the nine-month interim financial statement for the period ending May 31, 1969. * * *

* * *

C.   *The Closing and Receipt of the Comfort Letter*

The closing meeting for the merger was scheduled at 2 p.m. on Friday, October 31, at the New York offices of White & Case. * * *

Although Schauer had had an opportunity to review most of the merger documents at White & Case on the previous day, the comfort letter [of Peat Marwick, NSMC's accountants,] had not been delivered. When he arrived at White & Case on the morning of the merger, the letter was still not available, but he was informed by a representative of the firm that it was expected to arrive at any moment.

The meeting proceeded. When the letter had not arrived by approximately 2:15 p.m., Epley telephoned Peat Marwick's Washington office to inquire about it. Anthony M. Natelli, the partner in charge, thereupon dictated to Epley's secretary a letter which [outlined adjustments that would be necessary for fair and reasonable presentation of NSMC's unaudited consolidated financial statements.]

* * *

Epley delivered one copy of the typed letter to the conference room where the closing was taking place. Epley then returned to his office.

* * * Randell and Joy indicated that while NSMC disagreed with what they felt was a tightening up of its accounting practices, everything requested by Peat Marwick to "clean up" its books had been undertaken.

At the conclusion of this discussion, certain of the Interstate representatives, including at least Brown, Schauer and Meyer, conferred privately to consider their alternatives in light of the apparent nonconformity of the comfort letter with the requirements of the Merger Agreement. Although they considered the letter a serious matter and the adjustments as significant and important, they were nonetheless under some pressure to determine a course of action promptly since there was a 4 p.m. filing deadline if the closing were to be consummated as scheduled on October 31. Among the alternatives considered were: (1) delaying or postponing the closing, either to secure more information or to resolicit the shareholders with correct financials; (2) closing the merger; or (3) calling it off completely.

The consensus of the directors was that there was no need to delay the closing. The comfort letter contained all relevant information and in light of the explanations given by Randell and Joy, they already had sufficient information upon which to make a decision. Any delay * * * would make it impossible to resolicit shareholder approval before the merger upset date of November 28, 1969, and would cause either the complete abandonment of the merger or its renegotiation on terms possibly far less favorable to Interstate. The directors also recognized that delay or abandonment of the merger would result in a decline in the stock of both companies, thereby harming the shareholders and possibly subjecting the directors to lawsuits based on their failure to close the merger. The Interstate representatives decided to proceed with the closing. * * * When asked by Brown whether the closing could proceed on the basis of an unsigned comfort letter, Meyer responded that if a White & Case partner assured them that this was in fact the comfort letter and that a signed copy would be forthcoming from Peat Marwick, they could close. Epley gave this assurance. Meyer then announced that Interstate was prepared to proceed, [and] the closing was consummated * * * . * * *

Unknown to the Interstate group, several telephone conversations relating to the substance of the comfort letter occurred on the afternoon of the closing between Peat Marwick representatives and Epley. The accountants were concerned with the propriety of proceeding * * * . One such conversation occurred after Epley delivered the unsigned letter to the Interstate participants but before the merger had been consummated. At that time Epley was told that an additional paragraph would be added in order to characterize the adjustments. * * * Epley had the additional paragraph typed out, but failed to inform or disclose this change to Interstate. In a second conversation, after the closing was completed and the Interstate representatives had departed, Epley was informed of still another proposed addition, namely, a paragraph urging resolicitation of both companies' shareholders * * *. To this, he responded that the deal was closed and the letter was not needed. Peat Marwick nonetheless advised Epley that the letter would be delivered and that its counsel was considering whether further action should be taken by the firm.

* * *

At [a] meeting [following delivery of Peat Marwick's revised letter], the matter was fully discussed by the former Interstate principals. Of particular concern were the additional "break-even" and "resolicitation" paragraphs. * * *

On that afternoon, Schauer contacted Epley by telephone. Epley stated that he had not known of the additional paragraphs until after the closing. He added that in any case the additions did not expand upon the contents of the earlier unsigned letter; the "break-even" paragraph simply reflected the results of an arithmetic computation of the effects of the adjustments, and the "resolicitation" paragraph was gratuitous and a matter for lawyers, not accountants. * * *

* * *

Over the next several days the Interstate directors continued their discussion of the matter, consulting frequently with their counsel, Meyer and Schauer. As they viewed it, the available options were to attempt to undo the merger, either permanently or until the shareholders could be resolicited, or to leave things as they were. The attorneys indicated that rescission would be impractical, if not impossible, since Interstate no longer existed and NSMC had indicated that it would oppose any effort to undo the merger. Meanwhile, the market value of NSMC stock continued to increase, and the directors noted that any action on their part to undo the merger would most likely adversely affect its price. By the end of the week, the decision was made to abstain from any action. * * *

* * *

E. *Subsequent Events*

Following the acquisition of Interstate and several other companies NSMC stock rose steadily in price, reaching a peak in mid-December. However, in early 1970, after several newspaper and magazine articles appeared questioning NSMC's financial health, the value of the stock decreased drastically. Several private lawsuits were filed and the SEC initiated a wide-ranging investigation which led to the filing of this action.

II. THE PRESENT ACTION

[T]he Commission alleges that the defendants, both as principals and as aiders and abettors, violated § 10(b) of the 1934 Act, Rule 10b–5 promulgated thereunder, and § 17(a) of the 1933 Act, through their participation in the Interstate/NSMC merger and subsequent stock sales by Interstate principals, in each instance without disclosing the material information revealed by the Peat Marwick comfort letter.

* * *

Numerous charges, all of which appear to allege secondary liability, are leveled against the attorney defendants. Schauer is charged with "participating in the merger between Interstate and NSMC," apparently referring to his failure to interfere with the closing of the merger after receipt of the comfort letter. Such inaction, when alleged to facilitate a transaction, falls under the rubric of aiding and abetting. Both Schauer and Meyer are charged with issuing false opinions in connection with the merger and stock sales, thereby facilitating each transaction, and with acquiescence in the merger after learning the contents of the signed comfort letter. The Commission contends that the attorneys should have refused to issue the opinions in view of the adjustments revealed by the unsigned comfort letter, and after receipt of the signed version, they should have withdrawn their opinion with regard to the merger and demanded resolicitation of the Interstate shareholders. If the Interstate directors refused, the attorneys should have withdrawn from the representation and informed the shareholders or the Commission. * * * and finally, LBB is charged with vicarious liability for the actions of Meyer and Schauer with respect to the attorneys' activities on behalf of the firm.

Since any liability of the alleged aiders and abettors depends on a finding of a primary violation of the antifraud provisions, the Court will first address the issues relating to the Commission's charges against the principals. * * *

III. PAST VIOLATIONS

[Here the Court discusses the alleged violations of Brown and Meyer.]

[T]he Court finds that Brown and Meyer violated 10(b), Rule § 10b–5, and § 17(a) through their participation in the closing of the Interstate/NSMC merger * * * without first disclosing the material information contained in the unsigned comfort letter.

IV. AIDING AND ABETTING

The Court must now turn to the Commission's charges that the defendants aided and abetted these * * * violations of the antifraud provisions. The violations themselves establish the first element of aiding and abetting liability, namely that another person has committed a securities law violation. The remaining elements, though not set forth with any uniformity, are essentially that the alleged aider and abettor had a "general awareness that his role was part of an overall activity that is improper, and [that he] knowingly and substantially assisted the violation." SEC v. Coffey, [493 F.2d 1304, 1316 (6th Cir.1974)].

The Commission's allegations of aiding and abetting by the defendant seem to fall into [these] basic categories: (1) the failure of the attorney defendants to take any action to interfere in the consummation of the merger; (2) the issuance by the attorneys of an opinion with respect to the merger; [and] (3) the attorneys' subsequent failure to withdraw that opinion and inform the Interstate shareholders or the SEC of the inaccuracy of the nine-month financials * * * . The SEC's position is that the defendants acted or failed to act with an awareness of the fraudulent conduct by the principals, and thereby substantially assisted the two violations. The Court concurs with regard to the attorneys' failure to interfere with the closing, but must conclude that the remaining actions or inaction alleged to constitute aiding and abetting did not substantially facilitate * * * the merger * * * .

As noted, the first element of aiding and abetting liability has been established by the finding that Brown and Meyer committed primary violations of the securities laws. [The second element is that the alleged aider and abettor be generally aware of the fraudulent activity.] With the exception of LBB, which is charged with vicarious liability, each of the defendants was actually present at the closing of the merger when the comfort letter was delivered and the adjustments to the nine-month financials were revealed. Each was present at the Interstate caucus and the subsequent questioning of the NSMC representatives; each knew of the importance attributed to the adjustments by those present. They knew that the Interstate shareholders and the investing public were unaware of the adjustment and the inaccuracy of the financials. Despite the obvious materiality of the information, each knew that it had not been disclosed prior to the merger * * *. * * * the record amply demonstrates the "knowledge of the fraud, and not merely the undisclosed material facts," Hirsch v. du Pont, [553 F.2d 750, 759 (2d Cir.1977)], that is required to meet this element of secondary liability.

The final requirement for aiding and abetting liability is that the conduct provide knowing, substantial assistance to the violation. * * *

Upon receipt of the unsigned comfort letter, it became clear that the merger had been approved by the Interstate shareholders on the basis of materially misleading information. In view of the obvious materiality of the information, especially to attorneys learned in securities law, the attorneys' responsibilities to their corporate client required them to take steps to ensure that the information would be disclosed to the shareholders. However, it is unnecessary to determine the precise extent of their obligations here, since it is undisputed that they took no steps whatsoever to delay the closing pending disclosure to and resolicitation of the Interstate shareholders. But, at the very least, they were required to speak out at the closing concerning the obvious materiality of the information and the concomitant requirement that the merger not be closed until the adjustments were disclosed and approval of the merger was again obtained from the Interstate shareholders. Their silence was not only a breach of this duty to speak, but in addition lent the appearance of legitimacy to the closing. The combination of these factors clearly provided substantial assistance to the closing of the merger.

* * *

The Commission also asserts that the attorneys substantially assisted the merger violation through the issuance of an opinion that was false and misleading due to its omission of the receipt of the comfort letter and of the completion of the merger on the basis of the false and misleading nine-month financials. * * * Contrary to the implication made by the SEC, the opinion issued by the attorneys at the closing did not play a large part in the consummation of the merger. Instead, it was simply one of many conditions to the obligation of NSMC to complete the merger. It addressed a number of corporate formalities required of Interstate by the Merger Agreement, only a few of which could possibly involve compliance with the antifraud provisions of the securities laws. Moreover, the opinion was explicitly for the benefit of NSMC, which was already well aware of the adjustments contained in the comfort letter. Thus, this is not a case where an opinion of counsel addresses a specific issue and is undeniably relied on in completing the transaction. Under these circumstances, it is unreasonable to suggest that the opinion provided substantial assistance to the merger.

The SEC's contention with regard to counsel's alleged acquiescence in the merger transaction raises significant questions concerning the responsibility of counsel. The basis for the charge appears to be counsel's failure, after the merger, to withdraw their opinion, to demand resolicitation of the shareholders, to advise their clients concerning rights of rescission of the merger, and ultimately, to inform the Interstate shareholders or the SEC of the completion of the merger based on materially false and misleading financial statements. * * * Even if the attorneys' fiduciary responsibilities to the Interstate shareholders continued beyond the merger, the breach of such a duty would not have the requisite relationship to a securities transaction, since the merger had already been completed. It is equally obvious that such subsequent action or inaction by the attorneys could not substantially assist the merger.

* * *

Thus, the Court finds that the attorney defendants aided and abetted the violation of § 10(b), Rule 10b–5, and § 17(a) through their participation in the closing of the merger.

V. APPROPRIATENESS OF INJUNCTIVE RELIEF

* * * The crucial question [is] not whether a violation has occurred, but whether there exists a reasonable likelihood of future illegal conduct by the defendant * * * . * * *

* * *

The Commission has not demonstrated that the defendants engaged in the type of repeated and persistent misconduct which usually justifies the issuance of injunctive relief. Instead, it has shown violations which principally occurred within a period of a few hours at the closing of the merger in 1969. * * *

Further, it is difficult to characterize the violations presented here as either "willful, blatant, and often completely outrageous," SEC v. Manor Nursing Centers, Inc., 458 F.2d [1082, 1101 (2d Cir.1972)], or as the "garden variety fraud" urged by the Commission. There is no evidence to suggest that these defendants knew about the comfort letter adjustments prior to the receipt of the unsigned comfort letter at the closing; and after receiving the letter, the defendants were under some pressure to determine a course of action, either to proceed with the transactions as scheduled or to abort both the merger and stock sales. Although it has now been found that they unlawfully and with scienter decided to proceed, their actions in this regard hardly resemble the deliberate and well-planned fraudulent scheme frequently found in securities fraud cases.

Finally, the Commission asserts that an injunction is necessary because the professional occupations of the defendants provide significant opportunities for further involvement in securities transactions. * * * While the attorney defendants are more likely to be * * * involved [than is Brown], that fact is countered somewhat by their professional responsibilities as attorneys and officers of the court to conform their conduct to the dictates of the law. The Court is confident that they will take appropriate steps to ensure that their professional conduct in the future comports with the law.

After considering the "totality of circumstances" presented here, the Court concludes that the Securities and Exchange Commission has not fulfilled its statutory obligation to make a "proper showing" that injunctive relief is necessary to prevent further violations by these defendants. Accordingly, judgment will be entered for the defendants and the complaint will be dismissed.

In 1977 White & Case, Marion Jay Epley, III, and the Commission reached a settlement in *National Student Marketing*. Without admitting the allegations in the complaint, Epley consented to the entry of a permanent injunction against him and also agreed that, for 180 days, he would not practice before the Commission or advise clients with respect to matters involving securities registered under the federal securities laws. Also without admitting the Commission's allegations, White & Case agreed to adopt certain internal procedures in connection with its practice of securities law. No injunction was issued against the firm.

C. RULE 102(e), SECTION 4C AND PART 205

I. RULE 102(e)

a. IN RE CARTER

The following is a portion of an administrative proceeding seeking a practice bar based on aiding and abetting violations of the Exchange Act. It applies a more demanding standard than would now be applied if the Commission were to bring an action in court based on alleged aiding and abetting.

In re Carter

Securities and Exchange Commission.
Exchange Act Release No. 17597 (February 28, 1981).

William R. Carter and Charles J. Johnson, Jr., respondents, appeal from the initial decision of the Administrative Law Judge in this proceeding brought under Rule [102(e)] of the Commission's Rules of Practice.[4] In an opinion dated March 7, 1979, the Administrative Law Judge found that, in connection with their representation of National Telephone Company, Inc. [("National")] during the period from May 1974 to May 1975, Carter and Johnson willfully violated and willfully aided and abetted violations of Sections 10(b) and 13(a) of the Securities Exchange Act of 1934 (the "Exchange Act") and Rules 10b–5, 12b–20 and 13a–11 thereunder and that they engaged in unethical and improper professional conduct. In light of these findings, the Administrative Law Judge concluded that Carter and Johnson should be suspended from appearing or practicing before the Commission for periods of one year and nine months, respectively.

* * *

---

[4]   Rule 102(e) (until 1995, Rule 2(e)) provided in part:

    The Commission may deny, temporarily or permanently, the privilege of appearing or practicing before it in any way to any person who is found by the Commission after notice of and opportunity for hearing in the matter (i) not to possess the requisite qualifications to represent others, or (ii) to be lacking in character or integrity or to have engaged in unethical or improper professional conduct, or (iii) to have willfully aided and abetted the violation of any provision of the Federal securities laws, or the rules and regulations thereunder. [Eds.]

III. RESPONDENTS' CONDUCT

A.   National Telephone Company

* * * National * * * was founded in 1971 to lease sophisticated telephone equipment systems to commercial customers pursuant to long-term (5- to 10-year) leases. National enjoyed an impressive growth rate in its first three years * * * . * * *

* * *

In large measure, National was a prisoner of its own success. As is commonly the case with equipment leasing companies, the greater part of National's costs in connection with a new lease, including equipment marketing and installation expenses, was incurred well before rental payments commenced. Since rental payments were National's only significant source of revenues, the company's cash flow situation worsened with each new lease, and continued growth and operations could only be sustained through external financing. * * *

National's last successful effort to secure significant outside financing resulted in the execution, in May and June of 1974, of a $15 million credit agreement (the "Credit Agreement") with a group of five banks. * * * Unfortunately, funds available under the Credit Agreement * * * were not sufficient to finance National's expansion and operations * * * , and the pressure on National's cash flow continued.

National finally ran out of time in July of 1975, after being unable to secure sufficient external financing * * * . On July 2, 1975, National was forced to file a petition for an arrangement under * * * the Bankruptcy Act * * * .

On November 26, 1975, the Commission authorized a formal investigation into the facts and circumstances surrounding National's collapse in order to determine whether any violations of the federal securities laws had occurred. This investigation covered the involvement of respondents, as well as of their law firm.

* * *

B.   Respondents and Their Law Firm

[Carter and Johnson are partners in the New York City law firm of Brown, Wood, Ivey, Mitchell & Petty ("Brown, Wood"), which was counsel to National. In addition to his legal work for National, Johnson served as its secretary from July 1, 1974 to May 24, 1975.]

* * *

IV. AIDING AND ABETTING

Rule [102(e)(1)(iii)] provides that the Commission may deny, temporarily or permanently, the privilege of appearing or practicing before it to any person who is found by the Commission, after notice of and opportunity for hearing, to have *willfully violated*, or *willfully aided and abetted the violation* of, any provision of the federal securities laws or the rules and regulations thereunder.

* * *

C.   Aiding and Abetting

* * * Although "[t]he elements of an aiding and abetting claim have not yet crystallized into a set pattern,"[5] we have examined the decisions of the various circuits and conclude that certain legal principles are common to all the decisions.

In the context of the federal securities laws, these principles hold generally that one may be found to have aided and abetted a violation when the following three elements are present:

> 1.   there exists an independent securities law violation committed by some other party;

> 2.   the aider and abettor knowingly and substantially assisted the conduct that constitutes the violation; and

> 3.   the aider and abettor was aware or knew that his role was part of an activity that was improper or illegal.

[W]e have no difficulty in finding that National committed numerous substantial securities law violations. The second element—substantial assistance—is generally satisfied in the context of a securities lawyer performing professional duties, for he is inevitably deeply involved in his client's disclosure activities and often participates in the drafting of the documents, as was the case with Carter. And he does so knowing that he is participating in the preparation of disclosure documents—that is his job.

In this connection, we do not distinguish between the professional advice of a lawyer given orally or in writing and similar advice which is embodied in drafting documents to be filed with the Commission. Liability in these circumstances should not turn on such artificial distinctions, particularly in light of the almost limitless range of forms which legal advice may take. Moreover, the opposite approach, which would permit a lawyer to avoid or reduce his liability simply by avoiding participation in the drafting process, may well have the undesirable effect of reducing the quality of the disclosure by the many to protect against the defalcations of the few.

For these reasons, the crucial inquiry in a Rule [102(e)] proceeding against a lawyer inevitably tends to focus on the awareness or the intent element of the offense of aiding and abetting. It is that element which has been the source of the most disagreement among commentators and the courts. We do not seek to resolve that disagreement today. We do hold, however, that a finding of willful aiding and abetting within the meaning of Rule [102(e)(1)(iii)] requires a showing that respondents were

---

[5]   Woodward v. Metro Bank of Dallas, 522 F.2d 84, 94 (C.A.5 1975).

aware or knew that their role was part of an activity that was improper or illegal.

It is axiomatic that a lawyer will not be liable as an aider and abettor merely because his advice, followed by the client, is ultimately determined to be wrong. What is missing in that instance is a wrongful intent on the part of the lawyer. It is that element of intent which provides the basis for distinguishing between those professionals who may be appropriately considered as subjects of professional discipline and those who, acting in good faith, have merely made errors of judgment or have been careless.

Significant public benefits flow from the effective performance of the securities lawyer's role. The exercise of independent, careful and informed legal judgment on difficult issues is critical to the flow of material information to the securities markets. Moreover, we are aware of the difficulties and limitations attendant upon that role. In the course of rendering securities law advice, the lawyer is called upon to make difficult judgments, often under great pressure and in areas where the legal signposts are far apart and only faintly discernible.

If a securities lawyer is to bring his best independent judgment to bear on a disclosure problem, he must have the freedom to make innocent—or even, in certain cases, careless—mistakes without fear of legal liability or loss of the ability to practice before the Commission. Concern about his own liability may alter the balance of his judgment in one direction as surely as an unseemly obeisance to the wishes of his client can do so in the other. While one imbalance results in disclosure rather than concealment, neither is, in the end, truly in the public interest. Lawyers who are seen by their clients as being motivated by fears for their personal liability will not be consulted on difficult issues.

Although it is a close judgment, after careful review, we conclude that the available evidence is insufficient to establish that either respondent acted with sufficient knowledge and awareness or recklessness to satisfy the test for willful aiding and abetting liability. * * *

* * *

V. ETHICAL AND PROFESSIONAL RESPONSIBILITIES

A. The Findings of the Administrative Law Judge

The Administrative Law Judge found that both respondents "failed to carry out their professional responsibilities with respect to appropriate disclosure to all concerned, including stockholders, directors and the investing public * * * and thus knowingly engaged in unethical and improper professional conduct, as charged in the Order." In particular, he held that respondents' failure to advise National's board of directors of Hart's refusal to disclose adequately the company's perilous financial condition was itself a violation of ethical and professional standards referred to in Rule [102(e)(1)(ii)].

Respondents argue that the Commission has never promulgated standards of professional conduct for lawyers and that the Commission's application in hindsight of new standards would be fundamentally unfair. Moreover, even if it is permissible for the Commission to apply—without specific adoption or notice—generally recognized professional standards, they argue that no such standards applicable to respondents' conduct existed in 1974–75, nor do they exist today.

We agree that, in general, elemental notions of fairness dictate that the Commission should not establish new rules of conduct and impose them retroactively upon professionals who acted at the time without reason to believe that their conduct was unethical or improper. At the same time, however, we perceive no unfairness whatsoever in holding those professionals who practice before us to generally recognize norms of professional conduct, whether or not such norms had previously been explicitly adopted or endorsed by the Commission. To do so upsets no justifiable expectations, since the professional is already subject to those norms.

The ethical and professional responsibilities of lawyers who become aware that their client is engaging in violations of the securities laws have not been so firmly and unambiguously established that we believe all practicing lawyers can be held to an awareness of generally recognized norms. We also recognize that the Commission has never articulated or endorsed any such standards. That being the case, we reverse the Administrative Law Judge's findings under subparagraph (ii) of Rule [102(e)(1)] with respect to both respondents. Nevertheless, we believe that respondents' conduct raises serious questions about the obligations of securities lawyers, and the Commission is hereby giving notice of its interpretation of "unethical or improper professional conduct" as that term is used in Rule [102(e)(1)(ii)]. The Commission intends to issue a release soliciting comment from the public as to whether this interpretation should be expanded or modified.

* * *

The securities lawyer who is an active participant in a company's ongoing disclosure program will ordinarily draft and revise disclosure documents, comment on them and file them with the Commission. He is often involved on an intimate, day-to-day basis in the judgments that determine what will be disclosed and what will be withheld from the public markets. When a lawyer serving in such a capacity concludes that his client's disclosures are not adequate to comply with the law, and so advises his client, he is "aware," in a literal sense, of a continuing violation of the securities laws. On the other hand, the lawyer is only an adviser, and the final judgment—and, indeed, responsibility—as to what course of conduct is to be taken must lie with the client. Moreover, disclosure issues often present difficult choices between multiple shades of gray, and while a lawyer's judgment may be to draw the disclosure obligation more broadly than his client, both parties recognize the degree of uncertainty involved.

The problems of professional conduct that arise in this relationship are well-illustrated by the facts of this case. * * * Hart and Lurie were, in effect, pressing the company's lawyers hard for the minimum disclosure required by law. That fact alone is not an appropriate basis for a finding that a lawyer must resign or take some extraordinary action. Such a finding would inevitably drive a wedge between reporting companies and their outside lawyers; the more sophisticated members of management would soon realize that there is nothing to gain in consulting outside lawyers.

However, much more was involved in this case. * * * Any ambiguity in the situation plainly evaporated in late April and early May of 1975 when Hart first asked Johnson for a legal opinion flatly contrary to the express disclosure advice Johnson had given Hart only five days earlier, and when Lurie soon thereafter prohibited [an employee] from delivering a copy of the company's April 1975 Form 8–K to Brown, Wood.

These actions reveal a conscious desire on the part of National's management no longer to look to Brown, Wood for independent disclosure advice, but rather to embrace the firm within Hart's fraud and use it as a shield to avoid the pressures exerted by the banks toward disclosure. Such a role is a perversion of the normal lawyer-client relationship, and no lawyer may claim that, in these circumstances, he need do no more than stubbornly continue to suggest disclosure when he knows his suggestions are falling on deaf ears.

C. "Unethical or Improper Professional Conduct"

The Commission is of the view that a lawyer engages in "unethical or improper professional conduct" under the following circumstances: When a lawyer with significant responsibilities in the effectuation of a company's compliance with the disclosure requirements of the federal securities laws becomes aware that his client is engaged in a substantial and continuing failure to satisfy those disclosure requirements, his continued participation violates professional standards unless he takes prompt steps to end the client's noncompliance. The Commission has determined that this interpretation will be applicable only to conduct occurring after the date of this opinion.

We do not imply that a lawyer is obliged, at the risk of being held to have violated Rule [102(e)], to seek to correct every isolated disclosure action or inaction which he believes to be at variance with applicable disclosure standards, although there may be isolated disclosure failures that are so serious that their correction becomes a matter of primary professional concern. It is also clear, however, that a lawyer is not privileged to unthinkingly permit himself to be co-opted into an ongoing fraud and cast as a dupe or a shield for a wrongdoing client.

Initially, counselling accurate disclosure is sufficient, even if his advice is not accepted. But there comes a point at which a reasonable lawyer must conclude that his advice is not being followed, or even sought in good faith, and that his client is involved in a continuing course of violating the securities laws. At this critical juncture, the lawyer must take further, more affirmative steps in order to avoid the inference that he has been co-opted, willingly or unwillingly, into the scheme of nondisclosure.

The lawyer is in the best position to choose his next step. Resignation is one option, although we recognize that other considerations, including the protection of the client against foreseeable prejudice, must be taken into account in the case of withdrawal. A direct approach to the board of directors or one or more individual directors or officers may be appropriate; or he may choose to try to enlist the aid of other members of the firm's management. What is required, in short, is some prompt action that leads to the conclusion that the lawyer is engaged in efforts to correct the underlying problem, rather than having capitulated to the desires of a strong-willed, but misguided client.

Some have argued that resignation is the only permissible course when a client chooses not to comply with disclosure advice. We do not agree. * * * The lawyer's continued interaction with his client will ordinarily hold the greatest promise of corrective action. So long as a lawyer is acting in good faith and exerting reasonable efforts to prevent violations of the law by his client, his professional obligations have been met. In general, the best result is that which promotes the continued, strong-minded and independent participation by the lawyer.

We recognize, however, that the "best result" is not always obtainable, and that there may occur situations where the lawyer must conclude that the misconduct is so extreme or irretrievable, or the involvement of his client's management and board of directors in the misconduct is so thoroughgoing and pervasive that any action short of resignation would be futile. We would anticipate that cases where a lawyer has no choice but to resign would be rare and of an egregious nature.[6]

D. Conclusion

As noted above, because the Commission has never adopted or endorsed standards of professional conduct which would have applied to respondents' activities during the period here in question, and since generally accepted norms of professional conduct which existed outside

---

[6] This case does not involve, nor do we here deal with, the additional question of when a lawyer, aware of his client's intention to commit fraud or an illegal act, has a professional duty to disclose that fact either publicly or to an affected third party. Our interpretation today does not require such action at any point, although other existing standards of professional conduct might be so interpreted. * * *

the scope of Rule [102(e)] did not, during the relevant time period, unambiguously cover the situation in which respondents found themselves in 1974–75, no finding of unethical or unprofessional conduct would be appropriate. That being the case, we reverse the findings of the Administrative Law Judge under Rule [102(e)(1)(ii)]. In future proceedings of this nature, however, the Commission will apply the interpretation of subparagraph (ii) of Rule [102(e)(1)] set forth in this opinion.

* * *

b. RULE 102(e) DEVELOPMENTS FOLLOWING IN RE CARTER

In its decision in the *Carter* case, the Commission announced its intention to solicit public comment on its interpretation of "unethical or improper professional conduct." In Securities Act Release No. 6344 (September 21,1981), it did so. In this release the Commission indicated that it would, after consideration of submitted comments, issue a further release summarizing and analyzing the comments. It also announced that, based on the comments, it might or might not determine to expand or modify its interpretation. The ABA Section of Corporation, Banking and Business Law refused to comment on the Commission's interpretation (except briefly in a footnote), but rather in strong terms gave its opinion that the Commission lacked authority to establish ethical norms for the legal profession. It also indicated (i) that in light of existing professional codes of conduct, there was no demonstrated need for Commission action; (ii) that the establishment of ethical norms by the Commission would "open a floodgate" of regulation by other federal agencies, causing a number of problems; and (iii) that the relationship between lawyers and their corporate clients is not one well suited to Commission regulation.

The Commission never issued the further release promised in *Carter*. However, the Commission repeatedly signalled that it would not generally attempt to seek sanctions against lawyers for legal conduct permissible under established ethical rules.[7] (In other words, conduct sanctionable under Rule 102(e) must either be illegal or violate applicable professional rules—probably.)

Developments in the history of Rule 102(e) proceedings brought against accountants also are instructive. Consider the following case, decided in 1998.

---

[7] Greene, Lawyer Disciplinary Proceedings Before the Securities and Exchange Commission, 14 Sec.Reg.L.Rep. 168 (1982); Exchange Act Release No. 25893 (July 7, 1988).

Checkosky v. SEC

United States Court of Appeals, District of Columbia Circuit, 1998.

139 F.3d 221.

■ Before EDWARDS, CHIEF JUDGE, WILLIAMS and HENDERSON, CIRCUIT JUDGES.

■ WILLIAMS, CIRCUIT JUDGE:

Six years ago the Securities and Exchange Commission found that two accountants had engaged in "improper professional conduct" in violation of the Commission's Rule [102(e)(1)(ii)], 17 CFR § 201.102(e)(1)(ii). After review in this court we remanded the case to the Commission, holding that it had failed to adequately explain its interpretation of the rule. Checkosky v. SEC, 23 F.3d 452, 454 (D.C.Cir.1994) ("Checkosky I"). The Commission has evidently been unable to do so, voicing instead a multiplicity of inconsistent interpretations. In view of the Commission's inability to make any progress toward offering a single interpretation, and signs that the Commission is unlikely soon to make such progress, we are driven to the remedy reserved for rare cases of an agency's persistent failure to explain itself, and remand the case with instructions to dismiss the proceedings. See Greyhound Corp. v. ICC, 668 F.2d 1354 (D.C.Cir.1981).

* * *

Because the facts are recounted at length in the separate opinions of Judges Silberman and Randolph in Checkosky I, we supply only a brief summary. In the first half of the 1980s petitioners David Checkosky and Norman Aldrich, accountants at Coopers & Lybrand, performed a series of audits on behalf of Savin Corporation, a publicly traded company in the photocopier marketing business. During the years for which the audits were performed, Savin was trying (ultimately without success) to branch out into manufacturing by developing its own photocopier. Under generally accepted accounting principles ("GAAP"), costs of research and development must be expensed immediately rather than deferred. * * * [B]ut once R & D is complete, a company may defer so-called "start-up" costs, * * * treating them as a capital item, presumably to be depreciated in due course. After consulting with Checkosky, Savin decided to defer the escalating costs of its design effort by categorizing them as start-up costs. The Commission later found that in financial statements filed with it for periods between May 1, 1980, and December 31, 1984, Savin improperly deferred $37 million in research and development costs in this fashion. In all cases Checkosky and Aldrich had reported that Savin's statements conformed with GAAP and that their own audits had been conducted according to generally accepted auditing standards ("GAAS").

The Commission initiated disciplinary proceedings against Checkosky and Aldrich in 1987, charging that the two accountants had engaged in "improper professional conduct" in violation of Rule

[102(e)(1)(ii)]. * * * An administrative law judge suspended them for five years from "practicing before the Commission," a broad term that encompasses preparation of any document for filing with the Commission.[8] In 1992 the Commission affirmed the ALJ's finding that Checkosky and Aldrich had failed to observe GAAS and had improperly represented that Savin's financial statements complied with GAAP. In re David J. Checkosky & Norman A. Aldrich, 50 S.E.C. 1180 (1992). The Commission stated that "a mental awareness greater than negligence is not required" to state a violation of Rule [102(e)(1)(ii)], but "noted," as if in passing, that Checkosky and Aldrich's conduct "did in fact rise to the level of recklessness." Id. at 1197. The Commission thus affirmed the ALJ's finding that Checkosky and Aldrich violated Rule [102(e)(1)(ii)]. It reduced their suspension, however, from five years to two. Petitioners petitioned for review in this court on several grounds and we remanded to the Commission, holding that it had failed to adequately explain its interpretation and application of Rule [102(e)(1)(ii)]. Checkosky I, 23 F.3d at 454.

On January 21, 1997 the Commission issued an opinion on remand affirming the suspensions. In re David J. Checkosky & Norman A. Aldrich, 7 Fed.Sec.L.Rep. (CCH) Para. 74,386, at 63,421 (Jan. 21, 1997) ("1997 Op."). Checkosky and Aldrich again petitioned for review in this court, again claiming (among many other things) that the Commission had failed to articulate an intelligible standard for "improper professional conduct" under Rule [102(e)(1)(ii)]. Because we agree with this claim, we do not address the others.

* * *

In something of a tour de force, the Commission's 1997 opinion manages to both embrace and reject standards of (1) recklessness, (2) negligence and (3) strict liability—or so a careful (and intrepid) reader could find. * * * [A]fter devoting several pages to an attempt to demonstrate petitioners' recklessness, the opinion abruptly forswears any reliance on that concept as an element of improper professional conduct under Rule [102(e)(1)(ii)]: "We believe that Rule [102(e)(1)(ii)] does not mandate a particular mental state and that negligent actions by a professional may, under certain circumstances, constitute improper professional conduct." Id. at 63, 430.

On review the Commission adhered to the second of these positions, disavowing any suggestion that recklessness is necessary for a violation of Rule [102(e)(1)(ii)]. * * *

With recklessness out of the picture, negligence would seem to be the most obvious remaining candidate. But the 1997 opinion failed to adopt

---

[8] The regulations define "practicing before the Commission" to include "the preparation of any statement, opinion or other paper by any attorney, accountant, engineer or other professional or expert, filed with the Commission in any registration statement, notification, application, report or other document with the consent of such attorney, accountant, engineer or other professional or expert." 17 CFR § 201.102(f)(2).

an intelligible negligence standard. Instead, as we have already noted, it said only, "We believe that Rule [102(e)(1)(ii)] does not mandate a particular mental state and that negligent actions by a professional may, under certain circumstances, constitute improper professional conduct." 1997 Op. at 63,430 (emphasis added). Elementary administrative law norms of fair notice and reasoned decisionmaking demand that the Commission define those circumstances with some degree of specificity. It has not done so.

The only further definition the Commission offered was its observation that negligent deviations from GAAS or GAAP will be held to violate Rule [102(e)(1)(ii)] when they threaten the integrity of the Commission's processes. * * * This is fine as an identification of one of the main underlying purposes of Rule [102(e)], * * * but not as a standard for determining violations of the rule in disciplinary proceedings. Accountants and attorneys practicing in the securities field will draw little comfort from the knowledge that their missteps will escape sanction as long as they do not "threaten the integrity of the Commission's processes." It is simply impossible to know in advance what sorts of negligent errors will meet this "standard"; we can imagine both narrow and potentially all-embracing constructions.

Finally, the Commission's opinion leaves open the possibility that a "standard" revolving around perceived danger to future processes might not even require a showing of negligence:

> We wish to make clear, however, that the fact that GAAP and GAAS are professional standards against which we examine the conduct of accountants does not mean that every deviation from GAAP or GAAS is improper professional conduct warranting discipline under Rule [102(e)(1)(ii)]. Our processes are not necessarily threatened by innocent or even certain careless mistakes. At times, we have found improper professional conduct by accountants who engage in several deviations of [sic] GAAS or GAAP, or who deviated from GAAS or GAAP in more than one audit, or with more than one client. However, isolated failures may be so serious as to warrant discipline.

1997 Op. at 63,432 (footnotes omitted). In the space of four short sentences this passage achieves impressive feats of ambiguity. The first sentence does not clearly rule out the possibility that non-negligent deviations from GAAS and GAAP could violate Rule [102(e)(1)(ii)]. The second suggests by negative implication that some innocent, i.e., non-negligent, mistakes will be held to transgress the Rule. And the third and fourth explicitly reserve authority to penalize even an "isolated" deviation from GAAS or GAAP if "serious" enough, though as we have noted the relevant characteristics of seriousness are nowhere defined. * * *

* * * [T]he Commission's statements come close to a self-proclaimed license to charge and prove improper professional conduct whenever it

pleases, constrained only by its own discretion (combined, perhaps, with the standards of GAAS and GAAP).

In summary, the Commission's opinion yields no clear and coherent standard for violations of Rule [102(e)(1)(ii)]. Although we owe "substantial deference to an agency's interpretation of its own regulations," * * * we cannot defer to an agency when "we are at a loss to know what kind of standard it is applying or how it is applying that standard to this record." * * *

Of course the agency was in a bind. On the one hand, reliance on negligence had its perils. Judge Silberman had noted in Checkosky I that adoption of a negligence standard might be ultra vires; given that much of the substantive law enforced by the Commission requires a showing of scienter, use of a negligence standard to penalize professionals might be viewed as a back-door expansion of its regulatory oversight powers. See Checkosky I, 23 F.3d at 459 (Silberman, J.). * * * On the other hand a recklessness standard brought its own risks: there might not be substantial evidence to support a finding of reckless conduct. * * * Nevertheless the Commission had to make a choice. There is no justification for the government depriving citizens of the opportunity to practice their profession without revealing the standard they have been found to violate. * * *

When an agency utterly fails to provide a standard for its decision, it runs afoul of more than one provision of the Administrative Procedure Act. As Judge Silberman noted in the first appearance of this case before us, we have held on occasion that an "agency's failure to state its reasoning or to adopt an intelligible decisional standard is so glaring that we can declare with confidence that the agency action was arbitrary and capricious." Checkosky I, 23 F.3d at 463 (Silberman, J.). In addition, an agency violates the APA when it fails to include in its adjudicatory decision a meaningful "statement of findings and conclusions, and the reasons or basis therefor, on all the material issues of fact, law, or discretion presented on the record." 5 U.S.C. § 557(c)(3)(A). On at least these criteria, the Commission has defaulted.

* * *

* * * In view of the Commission's repeated failure to articulate a discernible standard for violations of Rule [102(e)(1)(ii)], the extraordinary duration of these proceedings, and the apparent unlikelihood of a clear resolution on remand, we conclude that it would be futile to allow the SEC a third "shot at the target." * * *

The case is remanded with instructions to dismiss the charge against petitioners.

* * *

The SEC subsequently adopted an amendment to Rule 102(e) defining "improper professional conduct" by persons licensed to practice as accountants. The definition includes intentional, knowing (including reckless) and, in some circumstances, negligent violation of applicable professional standards. It has been noted that members of the auditing profession have observed an uptick in Rule 102(e) enforcement activity.

II. Section 4C and Part 205

Section 602 of the Sarbanes-Oxley Act codified with minor changes the main part of Rule 102(e) as a new Section 4C of the Exchange Act. This new section relates to improper or unethical professional conduct, and other related problems, in the context of all federal securities laws. More importantly, Section 307 of Sarbanes-Oxley mandated the Commission to pass rules requiring minimum standards of professional conduct for securities lawyers representing issuers (which, under that Act's definition, essentially means Exchange Act reporting companies and companies that have filed a Securities Act registration statement). In Exchange Act Release No. 34B47276 (Jan. 29, 2003) the Commission issued the required rules, in a compendium entitled "Standards of Professional Conduct for Attorneys Appearing and Practicing Before the Commission in the Representation of an Issuer," and appearing at Part 205 of the Commission's rules. The rules are complex and go beyond the Section 307 mandate. Basically, they lay reporting and record-keeping obligations on both in-house and outside counsel in the case of material violations of the securities laws or fiduciary duties, or similar violations.

Rule 3 requires lawyers to report evidence of a material violation[9] by an issuer or by an officer, director, employee, or agent of an issuer. In most cases, the lawyer would report such a violation to the issuer's chief legal officer or to that officer and the chief executive officer. The chief legal officer then has the obligation to cause an inquiry into the allegation, and to report back to the lawyer who made the report of a possible violation. If the chief legal officer finds no violation, his or her response to the reporting lawyer must state the basis for the finding. If the chief legal officer finds a violation, he or she must advise the reporting attorney of his or her findings and the action he or she took relating to the violation. As an alternative to causing an inquiry into an allegation from a reporting attorney, the chief legal officer may refer the attorney's report to a qualified legal compliance committee of the board (these committees are discussed in the next paragraph).

If the reporting lawyer receives an appropriate response within a reasonable time, his or her obligations are complete. If the reporting lawyer does not receive an appropriate response within a reasonable

---

[9] "Evidence of a material violation" is defined in Rule 2(e) of the Standards of Professional Conduct. It "means credible evidence, based upon which it would be unreasonable, under the circumstances, for a prudent and competent attorney not to conclude that it is reasonably likely that a material violation has occurred, is ongoing, or is about to occur."

time, he or she must report the evidence of a material violation to the audit committee, another committee of independent directors, or to the full board of directions if the board has no committee consisting only of independent directors. Alternatively, the report may be made to a "qualified legal compliance committee" of independent directors, if the board has established such a committee. (The "qualified legal compliance committee" does not have to be a separate committee, but may be a board committee, such as the audit committee, that meets the Commission's requirements, which are set out in definitional form in Rule 2(k), and that is named as such.) If the reporting lawyer does not believe that the issuer has made an appropriate response, then his or her responsibility does not stop at receiving the report mentioned at the beginning of this paragraph. In such a situation, the lawyer must explain his or her reasons for such belief to the chief legal officer and the chief executive officer, and to directors to whom the lawyer may have reported the evidence of a material violation.

Rules 4 and 5 establish the responsibilities of subordinate lawyers and those who supervise them. Rule 6 details the manner in which the Commission will prosecute violations by lawyers. In this respect, it should be noted that, under Rule 6, lawyers who violate the Standards of Professional Conduct may be sanctioned by the Commission as if they had violated one of the federal securities laws. Rule 7 provides that nothing in the Standards of Professional Conduct creates a private right of action and that the Commission has exclusive authority to enforce compliance.

While the Commission was drafting these rules, there was speculation that perhaps the Commission would revisit *In re Carter* and fold in the standards of conduct set out there, changed as the Commission may have desired. This did not happen. There also was speculation that the Commission might revisit *National Student Marketing* and require lawyers always to inform the Commission if an issuer failed to take appropriate action after the lawyer had made the required reports to management of an issuer. Obviously, the Commission did not take this position. As originally proposed, the Commission's Standards of Professional Conduct required lawyers to make a "noisy withdrawal" when issuers failed to take appropriate actions with respect to a lawyer's report. This withdrawal would include disaffirming to the Commission any past tainted submissions. In response to massive opposition from lawyers, the Commission left the matter open for comment; it now is obvious that the Commission has set aside issuing further rules.

D. THE MODEL RULES OF PROFESSIONAL CONDUCT

Consider the following provisions of the ABA's Model Rules of Professional Conduct, revised in the aftermath of the events described immediately above.

RULE 1.6 CONFIDENTIALITY OF INFORMATION

(a) A lawyer shall not reveal information relating to representation of a client unless the client gives informed consent, the disclosure is impliedly authorized in order to carry out the representation, or the disclosure is permitted by paragraph (b).

(b) A lawyer may reveal information relating to the representation of a client to the extent the lawyer reasonably believes necessary:

(1) to prevent reasonably certain death or substantial bodily harm;

(2) to prevent the client from committing a crime or fraud that is reasonably certain to result in substantial injury to the financial interests or property of another and in furtherance of which the client has used or is using the lawyer's services;

(3) to prevent, mitigate or rectify substantial injury to the financial interests or property of another that is reasonably certain to result or has resulted from the client's commission or a crime or fraud in furtherance of which the client has used the lawyer's services; * * *

(6) to comply with other law or a court order; * * * .

(c) A lawyer shall make reasonable efforts to prevent the inadvertent or unauthorized disclosure of, or unauthorized access to, information relating to the representation of a client.

RULE 1.13 ORGANIZATION AS CLIENT

(a) A lawyer employed or retained by an organization represents the organization acting through its duly authorized constituents.

(b) If a lawyer for an organization knows that an officer, employee or other person associated with the organization is engaged in action, intends to act or refuses to act in a matter related to the representation that is a violation of a legal obligation to the organization, or a violation of law that reasonably might be imputed to the organization, and that is likely to result in substantial injury to the organization, then the lawyer shall proceed as is reasonably necessary in the best interest of the organization. Unless the lawyer reasonably believes that it is not necessary in the best interest of the organization to do so, the lawyer shall refer the matter to higher authority in the organization, including, if warranted by the circumstances, to the highest authority that can act on behalf of the organization as determined by applicable law.

(c) Except as provided in paragraph (d), if

(1) despite the lawyer's efforts in accordance with paragraph (b) the highest authority that can act on behalf of the organization insists upon or fails to address in a timely and appropriate manner an action or a refusal to act, that is clearly a violation of law, and

(2) the lawyer reasonably believes that the violation is reasonably certain to result in substantial injury to the corporation,

then the lawyer may reveal information relating to the representation whether or not Rule 1.6 permits such disclosure, but only if and to the extent the lawyer reasonably believes necessary to prevent substantial injury to the organization.

(d) Paragraph (c) shall not apply with respect to information relating to a lawyer's representation of an organization to investigate an alleged violation of law, or to defend the organization or an officer, employee or other constituent associated with the organization against a claim arising out of an alleged violation of law.

(e) A lawyer who reasonably believes that he or she has been discharged because of the lawyer's actions taken pursuant to paragraphs (b) or (c), or who withdraws under circumstances that require or permit the lawyer to take action under either of those paragraphs, shall proceed as the lawyer reasonably believes necessary to assure that the organization's highest authority is informed of the lawyer's discharge or withdrawal.

(f) In dealing with an organization's directors, officers, employees, members, shareholders or other constituents, a lawyer shall explain the identity of the client when the lawyer knows or reasonably should know that the organization's interests are adverse to those of the constituents with whom the lawyer is dealing.

(g) A lawyer representing an organization may also represent any of its directors, officers, employees, members, shareholders or other constituents, subject to the provisions of Rule 1.7 [on conflicts of interest]. If the organization's consent to the dual representation is required by Rule 1.7, the consent shall be given by an appropriate official of the organization other than the individual who is to be represented, or by the shareholders.

PART 6

STATE REGULATION OF SECURITIES

CHAPTER 19

STATE REGULATION OF SECURITIES

A. TRADITIONAL STATE SECURITIES REGULATION

SITUATION 19A

Assume you are back at the times of Microtec's public offering and the Microtec-Compuform merger and are considering the impact of state securities laws on the proposed transactions.

In considering this situation, refer to Securities Act Sections 16 and 18 and Exchange Act Section 28(f), in addition to the materials in this section.

I. PREEMPTION

Before reading the materials describing state regulation of securities offerings, it will be useful for you to realize that they are an accurate portrayal of that regulation, but that the sphere of state securities regulation itself was diminished in 1996. Before that time, Section 18 of the Securities Act provided that the Act did not preempt state securities regulation. In the National Securities Markets Improvement Act of 1996, Congress asserted partial preemption, thus reducing the jurisdiction of the states over securities regulation.

As amended, Section 18 designates a number of securities "covered securities" and provides that covered securities are exempt from state regulation with minor exception For general purposes, the most important covered securities are, in rough terms, securities of publicly held companies, securities that are offered or sold to "qualified purchasers" as defined by the Commission, securities offered or sold under a rule issued under Securities Act Section 4(a)(2) (the "private offering" exemption), and securities sold pursuant to Securities Act Section 4(a)(6) (the "crowdfunding" exemption).[1] The Commission has, by rule, provided that all offerees or purchasers in so-called "Tier II" offerings under Regulation A are "qualified purchasers." (Tier II offerings

---

[1] The National Securities Markets Improvement Act also added what is now Section 15(i) to the Exchange Act. This Section preempts most state broker-dealer regulation differing from the federal scheme. As amended, Section 15(i) now also preempts regulation of funding portals (although the state in which a funding portal has its principal place of business may exercise examination and enforcement authority with respect to requirements that do not differ from federal law). The National Securities Markets Improvement Act made a number of other changes, including changes in the allocation of authority over investment advisors (as to which Dodd-Frank also made changes).

under Regulation A are those between $20 million and $50 million in a twelve-month period.) An early challenge to the Commission's action brought by regulators in Montana and Massachusetts was rejected by the D.C. Circuit Court of Appeals.[2]

The states retain the power to impose certain notice requirements and charge fees, even in the case of the offerings described in Section 18. (There is, however, an exception for crowdfunding securities issued under Securities Act Section 4(a)(6). No state is permitted to charge fees with respect to those securities other than a state in which the issuer has its principal place of business and/or one in which the purchasers of a majority of the securities reside.) In addition, the states retain their ability to impose and enforce anti-fraud regulations (even in the case of crowdfunding securities), and state officials sometimes exercise their authority quite vigorously.

Federal dissatisfaction with a perceived upswing in private state court litigation subsequent to passage of the federal Private Securities Litigation Reform Act of 1995 led, in 1998, to the adoption of the Securities Litigation Uniform Standards Act ("SLUSA"). SLUSA added Sections 16(b)-(f) to the Securities Act and Section 28(f) to the Exchange Act. These sections deal with most class actions involving securities fraud or problems with disclosure, and require such actions to be brought in federal court under federal law.

The following case reveals the Supreme Court's expansive view of SLUSA.

Merrill Lynch, Pierce, Fenner & Smith, Inc. v. Dabit

Supreme Court of the United States, 2006.
547 U.S. 71.

■ JUSTICE STEVENS delivered the opinion of the Court.

Title I of the Securities Litigation Uniform Standards Act of 1998 (SLUSA) provides that "no covered class action" based on state law and alleging "a misrepresentation or omission of a material fact in connection with the purchase or sale of a covered security" "may be maintained in any State or Federal court by any private party." § 101(b) * * * . In this case the Second Circuit held that SLUSA only pre-empts state-law class-action claims brought by plaintiffs who have a private remedy under federal law. 395 F.3d 25 (2005). A few months later, the Seventh Circuit ruled to the contrary, holding that the statute also pre-empts state-law class-action claims for which federal law provides no private remedy. *Kircher* v. *Putnam Funds Trust*, 403 F.3d 478 (2005). The background, the text, and the purpose of SLUSA's pre-emption provision all support the broader interpretation adopted by the Seventh Circuit.

---

[2]   Lindeen v. SEC, 825 F.3d 646 (D.C.C.2016).

I

Petitioner Merrill Lynch, Pierce, Fenner & Smith, Inc. (Merrill Lynch), is an investment banking firm that offers research and brokerage services to investors. Suspicious that the firm's loyalties to its investment banking clients had produced biased investment advice, the New York attorney general in 2002 instituted a formal investigation into Merrill Lynch's practices. The investigation sparked a number of private securities fraud actions, this one among them.

Respondent, Shadi Dabit, is a former Merrill Lynch broker. He filed this class action * * * on behalf of himself and all other former or current brokers who, while employed by Merrill Lynch, purchased (for themselves and for their clients) certain stocks between December 1, 1999, and December 31, 2000. * * * Rather than rely on the federal securities laws, Dabit invoked the District Court's diversity jurisdiction and advanced his claims under Oklahoma state law.

The gist of Dabit's complaint was that Merrill Lynch breached the fiduciary duty and covenant of good faith and fair dealing it owed its brokers by disseminating misleading research and thereby manipulating stock prices. Dabit's theory was that Merrill Lynch used its misinformed brokers to enhance the prices of its investment banking clients' stocks: The research analysts, under management's direction, allegedly issued overly optimistic appraisals of the stocks' value; the brokers allegedly relied on the analysts' reports in advising their investor clients and in deciding whether or not to sell their own holdings; and the clients and brokers both continued to hold their stocks long beyond the point when, had the truth been known, they would have sold. * * *

* * *

* * * Merrill Lynch [moved] to dismiss Dabit's complaint. Senior Judge Milton Pollack granted the motion on the ground that the claims alleged fell "squarely within SLUSA's ambit." Ciccarelli v. Merrill Lynch & Co. (In re Merrill Lynch & Co. Research Reports Sec. Litig.), 2003 U.S. Dist. LEXIS 5999 * * * (Apr. 10, 2003).

The Court of Appeals for the Second Circuit, however, vacated the judgment and remanded for further proceedings. 395 F.3d at 51. It concluded that the claims asserted by holders did not allege fraud "in connection with the purchase or sale" of securities under SLUSA. Although the court agreed with Merrill Lynch that that phrase, as used in other federal securities laws, has been defined broadly by this Court, it held that Congress nonetheless intended a narrower meaning here—one that incorporates the "standing" limitation on private federal securities actions adopted in Blue Chip Stamps v. Manor Drug Stores, 421 U.S. 723 * * * (1975). Under the Second Circuit's analysis, fraud is only "in connection with the purchase or sale" of securities, as used in SLUSA, if it is alleged by a purchaser or seller of securities. Thus, to the extent that the complaint in this action alleged that brokers were fraudulently induced, not to sell or purchase, but to retain or delay selling their securities, it fell outside SLUSA's pre-emptive scope.

* * *

II

The magnitude of the federal interest in protecting the integrity and efficient operation of the market for nationally traded securities cannot be overstated. In response to the sudden and disastrous collapse in prices of listed stocks in 1929, and the Great Depression that followed, Congress enacted the Securities Act of 1933 (1933 Act) * * * and the Securities Exchange Act of 1934 (1934 Act) * * * . Since their enactment, these two statutes have anchored federal regulation of vital elements of our economy.

Securities and Exchange Commission (SEC) Rule 10b–5, * * * promulgated in 1942 pursuant to § 10(b) of the 1934 Act, * * * is an important part of that regulatory scheme. The Rule, like § 10(b) itself, broadly prohibits deception, misrepresentation, and fraud "in connection with the purchase or sale of any security." The SEC has express statutory authority to enforce the Rule. * * * Although no such authority is expressly granted to private individuals injured by securities fraud, in 1946 Judge Kirkpatrick of the United States District Court for the Eastern District of Pennsylvania, relying on "the general purpose" of the Rule, recognized an implied right of action thereunder. Kardon v. National Gypsum Co., 69 F. Supp. 512, 514. His holding was adopted by an "overwhelming consensus of the District Courts and Courts of Appeals," Blue Chip Stamps, 421 U.S., at 730 * * * and endorsed by this Court in Superintendent of Ins. of N. Y. v. Bankers Life & Casualty Co., 404 U.S. 6 * * * (1971).

* * *

By the time this Court first confronted the question, literally hundreds of lower court decisions had accepted "[the] conclusion that the plaintiff class for purposes of 10(b) and Rule 10b–5 private damages actions is limited to purchasers and sellers." Blue Chip Stamps, 421 U.S., at 731–732 * * * . Meanwhile, however, cases like Bankers Life & Casualty Co. had interpreted the coverage of the Rule more broadly to prohibit, for example, "deceptive practices *touching* [a victim's] sale of securities as an investor." 404 U.S., at 12–13 * * * (emphasis added) * * * . The "judicial oak which had grown from little more than a legislative acorn," as then-Justice Rehnquist described the rules governing private Rule 10b–5 actions, Blue Chip Stamps, 421 U.S., at 737, * * * had thus developed differently from the law defining what constituted a substantive violation of Rule 10b–5. Ultimately, the Court had to decide whether to permit private parties to sue for any violation of Rule 10b–5 that caused them harm, or instead to limit the private remedy to plaintiffs who were themselves purchasers or sellers.

Relying principally on "policy considerations" which the Court viewed as appropriate in explicating a judicially crafted remedy, *ibid.*, * * * the Court in Blue Chip Stamps chose to limit the private remedy. The main policy consideration tipping the scales in favor of precedent was the widespread recognition that "litigation under Rule 10b–5 presents a danger of vexatiousness different in degree and in kind from that which accompanies litigation in general." *Id.*, at 739 * * * . * * * the limitation of course had no application in Government enforcement actions brought pursuant to Rule 10b–5. See *id.*, at 751, n. 14 * * *

III

Policy considerations similar to those that supported the Court's decision in Blue Chip Stamps prompted Congress, in 1995, to adopt legislation targeted at perceived abuses of the class-action vehicle in litigation involving nationally traded securities. While acknowledging that private securities litigation was "an indispensable tool with which defrauded investors can recover their losses," the House Conference Report accompanying what would later be enacted as the Private Securities Litigation Reform Act of 1995 (Reform Act) * * * identified ways in which the class action device was being used to injure "the entire U.S. economy." H. R. Rep. No. 104–369, p. 31 (1995). According to the Report, nuisance filings, targeting of deep-pocket defendants, vexatious discovery requests, and "manipulation by class action lawyers of the clients whom they purportedly represent" had become rampant in recent years. Ibid. Proponents of the Reform Act argued that these abuses resulted in extortionate settlements, chilled any discussion of issuers' future prospects, and deterred qualified individuals from serving on boards of directors. Id., at 31–32.

Title I of the Reform Act, captioned "Reduction of Abusive Litigation," represents Congress' effort to curb these perceived abuses. Its provisions limit recoverable damages and attorney's fees, provide a "safe harbor" for forward-looking statements, impose new restrictions on the selection of (and compensation awarded to) lead plaintiffs, mandate imposition of sanctions for frivolous litigation, and authorize a stay of discovery pending resolution of any motion to dismiss. * * * Title I also imposes heightened pleading requirements in actions brought pursuant to § 10(b) and Rule 10b–5 * * * .

The effort to deter or at least quickly dispose of those suits whose nuisance value outweighs their merits placed special burdens on plaintiffs seeking to bring federal securities fraud class actions. But the effort also had an unintended consequence: It prompted at least some members of the plaintiffs' bar to avoid the federal forum altogether. Rather than face the obstacles set in their path by the Reform Act, plaintiffs and their representatives began bringing class actions under state law, often in state court. The evidence presented to Congress during a 1997 hearing to evaluate the effects of the Reform Act suggested that this phenomenon was a novel one; state-court litigation of class actions involving nationally traded securities had previously been rare. * * * to stem this "shift from Federal to State courts" and "prevent certain State private securities class action lawsuits alleging fraud from being used to frustrate the objectives of" the Reform Act, SLUSA §§ 2(2), (5), * * * Congress enacted SLUSA.

IV

The core provision of SLUSA reads as follows:

"CLASS ACTION LIMITATIONS.—No covered class action based upon the statutory or common law of any State or subdivision thereof may be maintained in any State or Federal court by any private party alleging—

> "(A) a misrepresentation or omission of a material fact in connection with the purchase or sale of a covered security; or

> "(B) that the defendant used or employed any manipulative or deceptive device or contrivance in connection with the purchase or sale of a covered security." * * *

A "covered class action" is a lawsuit in which damages are sought on behalf of more than 50 people. A "covered security" is one traded nationally and listed on a regulated national exchange. Respondent does not dispute that both the class and the securities at issue in this case are "covered" within the meaning of the statute, or that the complaint alleges misrepresentations and omissions of material facts. The only disputed issue is whether the alleged wrongdoing was "in connection with the purchase or sale" of securities.

Respondent urges that the operative language must be read narrowly to encompass (and therefore pre-empt) only those actions in which the purchaser-seller requirement of Blue Chip Stamps is met. Such, too, was the Second Circuit's view. But insofar as the argument assumes that the rule adopted in Blue Chip Stamps stems from the text of Rule 10b–5—specifically, the "in connection with" language, it must be rejected. * * * [T]his Court in Blue Chip Stamps relied chiefly, and candidly, on "policy considerations" * * * . The Blue Chip Stamps Court purported to define the scope of a private right of action under Rule 10b–5—not to define the words "in connection with the purchase or sale." * * * any ambiguity on that score had long been resolved by the time Congress enacted SLUSA. See United States v. O'Hagan, 521 U.S. 642, 656, 664 * * * (1997) * * * .

Moreover, when this Court *has* sought to give meaning to the phrase in the context of § 10(b) and Rule 10b–5, it has espoused a broad interpretation. A narrow construction would not, as a matter of first impression, have been unreasonable; one might have concluded that an alleged fraud is "in connection with" a purchase or sale of securities only when the plaintiff himself was defrauded into purchasing or selling particular securities. * * * [B]ut * * * [u]nder our precedents, it is enough that the fraud alleged "coincide" with a securities transaction—whether by the plaintiff or by someone else. See O'Hagan, 521 U.S., at 651 * * * . The requisite showing, in other words, is "deception 'in connection with the purchase or sale of any security,' not deception of an identifiable purchaser or seller." Id., at 658 * * * . Notably, this broader interpretation of the statutory language comports with the longstanding views of the SEC. * * *

Congress can hardly have been unaware of the broad construction adopted by both this Court and the SEC when it imported the key phrase—"in connection with the purchase or sale"—into SLUSA's core provision. And when "judicial interpretations have settled the meaning of an existing statutory provision, repetition of the same language in a new statute indicates, as a general matter, the intent to incorporate its * * * judicial interpretations as well." Bragdon v. Abbott, 524 U.S. 624, 645 * * * . Application of that presumption is particularly apt here; not only did Congress use the same words as are used in § 10(b) and Rule 10b–5, but it used them in a provision that appears in the same statute as § 10(b). Generally, "identical words used in different parts of the same statute are * * * presumed to have the same meaning." IBP, Inc. v. Alvarez, * * * 126 S. Ct. 514, 523, * * * (2005).

The presumption that Congress envisioned a broad construction follows not only from ordinary principles of statutory construction but also from the particular concerns that culminated in SLUSA's enactment. A narrow reading of the statute would undercut the effectiveness of the 1995 Reform Act and thus run contrary to SLUSA's stated purpose, viz., "to prevent certain State private securities class action lawsuits alleging fraud from being used to frustrate the objectives" of the 1995 Act. SLUSA § 2(5) * * * . As the Blue Chip Stamps Court observed, class actions brought by holders pose a special risk of vexatious litigation. * * * it would be odd, to say the least, if SLUSA exempted that particularly troublesome subset of class actions from its pre-emptive sweep. * * *

* * *

In concluding that SLUSA pre-empts state-law holder class-action claims of the kind alleged in Dabit's complaint, we do not lose sight of the general "presumption that Congress does not cavalierly pre-empt state-law causes of action." Medtronic, Inc. v. Lohr, 518 U.S. 470, 485 * * * (1996). But that presumption carries less force here than in other contexts because SLUSA does not actually pre-empt any state cause of action. It simply denies plaintiffs the right to use the class action device to vindicate certain claims. The Act does not deny any individual plaintiff, or indeed any group of fewer than 50 plaintiffs, the right to enforce any state-law cause of action that may exist.

Moreover, the tailored exceptions to SLUSA's pre-emptive command demonstrate that Congress did not by any means act "cavalierly" here. The statute carefully exempts from its operation certain class actions based on the law of the State in which the issuer of the covered security is incorporated, actions brought by a state agency or state pension plan, actions under contracts between issuers and indenture trustees, and derivative actions brought by shareholders on behalf of a corporation. * * * The existence of these carve-outs both evinces congressional sensitivity to state prerogatives in this field and makes it inappropriate for courts to create additional, implied exceptions.

Finally, federal law, not state law, has long been the principal vehicle for asserting class-action securities fraud claims. * * * More importantly, while state-law holder claims were theoretically available both before and after the decision in Blue Chip Stamps, the actual assertion of such claims by way of class action was virtually unheard of before SLUSA was enacted * * *. This is hardly a situation, then, in which a federal statute has eliminated a historically entrenched state-law remedy. * * *

V

The holder class action that respondent tried to plead, and that the Second Circuit envisioned, is distinguishable from a typical Rule 10b–5 class action in only one respect: It is brought by holders instead of purchasers or sellers. For purposes of SLUSA pre-emption, that distinction is irrelevant; the identity of the plaintiffs does not determine whether the complaint alleges fraud "in connection with the purchase or sale" of securities. The misconduct of which respondent complains here—fraudulent manipulation of stock prices—unquestionably qualifies as fraud "in connection with the purchase or sale" of securities * * *.

The judgment of the Court of Appeals for the Second Circuit is vacated, and the case is remanded for further proceedings consistent with this opinion.

As a follow-up, the Supreme Court held, in Kircher v. Putnam Funds Trust,[3] that a federal district court's order remanding a case to state court was not reviewable, even though it was mistaken under the standard set out in *Dabit*. Additional Supreme Court action in the area is expected in reaction to apparently divergent Circuit Court views of SLUSA's "in connection with" requirement.

There have been other interesting developments in the lower courts. For instance, the Third Circuit has determined that SLUSA does not require dismissal of an entire securities fraud class action when only some claims are precluded, notwithstanding SLUSA's definition of "covered class action" as "any single lawsuit" or "group of lawsuits."[4] The Ninth Circuit has held that state law claims for breach of contract and breach of the duty of good faith and fair dealing are not precluded by

---

[3]   547 U.S. 633 (2006).

[4]   White v. Lord Abbett & Co., LLC, 553 F.3d 248 (3d Cir.2009).

SLUSA unless such claims rest on misrepresentation or fraudulent omission.[5] The Sixth Circuit has ruled, however, that SLUSA does bar state breach of contract or fiduciary claims if any of the facts alleged in the complaint involve inadequate disclosure.[6]

II. STATE REGULATION OF SECURITIES OFFERINGS

The Uniform Securities Act, which is referred to in the following reading, was promulgated by the National Conference of Commissioners on Uniform State Laws in 1956 and revised in 1985. A majority of the states have adopted, at one time or another, some version or portion of the Uniform Securities Act—nonetheless leaving the significant diversity described. The Uniform Securities Act underwent sweeping revision in 2002[7] in order to respond to federal preemptive law, changes in technology and other developments. Eighteen states thus far have enacted the latest revisions.

Blue Sky Law and Practice: An Overview
Ronald M. Shapiro and Alan R. Sachs.
4 University of Baltimore Law Review 1 (1974).[*]

INTRODUCTION

[E]very state (as well as Puerto Rico and the District of Columbia) has enacted laws regulating the offer, sale and distribution of securities. From this background of numerous state laws emerges the chief characteristic of state regulation—diversity. * * *

* * *

TYPES OF STATE REGISTRATION FILING PROCEDURES

In those states that have enacted the Uniform Securities Act in some form, securities offerings registered with the SEC also must be registered by "coordination." In several states, registration material also may be filed in a manner equivalent to registration by "coordination," although the particular state securities law provision may describe its filing provision differently.

States that do not have registration by "coordination" usually provide for registration of offerings registered with the SEC by "notification" or "qualification." A statutory provision for filing by "qualification" or "notification" may require that a registration statement contain information in addition, or somewhat dissimilar, to the information required in a registration statement filed under the Act.

---

[5]   Freeman Investments LP v. Pacific Life Insurance Co., 704 F.3d 1110 (9th Cir. 2013).

[6]   Daniels v. Morgan Asset Management, Inc., 497 Fed.Appx. 548 (6th Cir. 2012).

[7]   The Uniform Securities Act of 2002 was again revised in 2005, but was not retitled.

[*]   Copyright 1974 by the University of Baltimore Law Review, Business Office: 1420 N. Charles Street, Baltimore, Maryland 21201. Reprinted with permission.

Notwithstanding the differences in the types of provisions under which an offering filed with the SEC is filed with the states, almost every state will accept a uniform application, entitled Form U–1, to register securities as an alternative to the state's own registration form.

* * *

DEGREES OF REVIEW OF REGISTRATION STATEMENT

State securities departments may review a registration statement filed in the manner described in one of three ways. First, some states, notably "disclosure" states, accord limited review to an offering filed under the state registration by "coordination" (or similar) provision. Such "limited" review normally involves checking the documents filed with the registration statement as to form rather than substance. Heavy reliance is placed by these states upon the SEC disclosure review. Letters of comment are not issued frequently. States which give a registration statement "limited" review often will inform counsel soon after the filing that it will be declared effective immediately upon SEC effectiveness.

Second, other states, most frequently those which have adopted special regulations or guidelines respecting certain kinds of offerings or certain kinds of issuers, will give a registration statement in-depth review. Securities officials in such states will perform the same function as the SEC staff and analyze the registration statement for full and fair disclosure. Furthermore, if their state has special guidelines applicable to the particular offering, they will also closely check compliance with such guidelines or regulations. The types of guidelines and special regulations which may be applicable to an in-depth review of a registration statement are discussed more fully below.

Third, a few states, which are frequently referred to as "fair, just and equitable" states because the state securities law requires the securities administrator to determine the fairness of the offering terms to investors, also give most offerings in-depth review. Even these states, however, may only subject an offering to limited scrutiny if the company is seasoned or, if for some other reason, the state administrator has reason to believe that there is no need to give the registration statement in-depth review.

* * *

As in the federal securities laws, there are a number of "securities" that, although offered and sold, are exempt from state securities registration. Such exemptions are usually premised upon extensive regulation of the particular issuers by other state, federal, or self-regulatory bodies. * * * [T]ypically exempt securities include those issued by state, federal and certain foreign governments; banks, savings and loan associations, trust companies, insurance companies, federal credit unions; certain utilities and common carriers; and non-profit organizations. Also typically excluded are commercial paper related to a current commercial transaction and investment contracts related to particular types of employee benefit plans. Each state statute should be carefully scrutinized as to the particular securities exempt from registration thereunder.

Predominant among the routes of non-registration are the so-called transactional exemptions. The transactional exemption from state registration most heavily relied upon is for a non-public distribution of securities. This so-called private offering exemption probably best points out the basic characteristic of state regulation—non-conformity. * * * "[P]rivate" or "limited" private offering exemptions * * * can be placed in four distinct categories. First are those which are based upon the concept contained in the Uniform Securities Act private offering provision, which limits the total number of permissible offerees of securities. Second, statutes in [some] states place restrictions upon the number of stockholders or other equity participants of entities which issue securities in reliance upon the exemption. This category of exemption can be very restrictive. Third, a few states limit one offering to a prescribed number of purchasers and a fixed maximum dollar amount. Furthermore, some states have adopted approaches similar to that set forth in SEC Rule [505 or 506]. * * * Finally, some states exempt only "isolated sales" of shares of the company that are held by the company or owner thereof. * * *

It is also significant that many states, like the SEC, integrate private or intrastate offerings with prior or subsequent private, intrastate, or public offerings. The result of the administrative integration of securities offerings usually means that one or more of them were made in violation of the registration provisions of the state securities law, resulting in a rescission offer to all purchasers, a possibility of the issuance of a temporary or permanent injunction, and potentially non-disclosed contingent liabilities in the registration statement for a public offering into which a private offering has been integrated. * * *

* * *

Marshall v. Harris

Supreme Court of Oregon, 1976.
276 Or. 447, 555 P.2d 756.

■ TONGUE, JUSTICE.

This is an action to recover money due and owing under a contract by which plaintiffs sold to defendant an interest in two racehorses and in their "earnings," in return for defendant's agreement to pay expenses involved in training and racing the horses. By affirmative defense and counterclaim, defendant contended that the contract was a "security" within the terms of the Oregon Securities Law, and that it had not been registered, as required by that statute, with the result that defendant was entitled to recover the money previously paid by him to plaintiffs under that contract.

The case was tried before the court, without a jury. The trial court held that the Oregon Securities Law did not apply to the facts of this case [and held for the plaintiffs].

The facts.

Plaintiffs own a ranch near Burns where they raise thoroughbred racehorses. * * *

In February 1973 plaintiffs' attorney suggested to them an arrangement under which he and three of his friends would pay the expenses for one of plaintiffs' horses in return for one-half of its winnings as a racehorse (i.e. a one-eighth interest to each of the four). An oral agreement was then made to that effect.

In May 1973 Mrs. Marshall was visited by Beverly Lewis, a long-time friend of hers, who was also interested in horses. During that visit they talked about plaintiffs' horses. In the course of that conversation Mrs. Marshall told her friend about the arrangement with plaintiffs' attorney and his three friends. Beverly Lewis then said that she had a friend, the defendant, who might also be interested in such an arrangement. Beverly Lewis then "mentioned this" to defendant, who said that he would like to talk to Mrs. Marshall. At that time defendant frequently went to the horse races and was considering buying a racehorse "outright."

Beverly Lewis then called Mrs. Marshall and arranged a meeting with defendant. At that meeting Mrs. Marshall explained the arrangement to defendant. They then discussed which horses were "available" and the cost of training and keeping the horses for racing. * * *

* * * Mr. Marshall suggested the names of the two horses that he thought were the "best." Defendant then decided to enter into an agreement under which he would pay for training, feeding and other expenses for those two horses until the end of 1974 in return for one-third interest in the horses and one-third of their racetrack "earnings" during 1973 and 1974. It was also understood that the horses were to be sent on to west coast tracks for racing. Plaintiffs expressly retained the right to control the "care" and "activities" of the horses. On June 18, 1973, a letter agreement confirming this understanding was prepared by plaintiffs' attorney and signed by plaintiffs and defendant. Defendant testified that Mrs. Marshall told him that the horses "would be running in October or November." This was denied by her.

In July the two horses were sent to California for training. Defendant paid the "bills" for the two horses until December 1, 1973, but not after that date. Both horses had been previously injured and neither raced in 1973.

* * *

The contract was an "investment contract" and the transaction was a "sale" of a "security."

ORS 59.015(13)(a) defines the term "security" for the purposes of the Oregon Securities Law to include an "investment contract." The most common definition of an "investment contract" is that adopted by the Supreme Court of the United States in Securities & Exchange Comm. v. W.J. Howey Co., 328 U.S. 293, 298–99 (1945) * * * .

* * * That test is satisfied in this case because it is clear from the facts that the defendant agreed to pay money to the plaintiffs with the expectation of deriving a profit to be created solely through the efforts of other persons. * * *

It is contended by the dissent that the sale of a fractional interest in a racehorse is not the sale of a "security" within the intended meaning of ORS 59.015(13)(a); that the "primary purpose of the Blue Sky Law is to * * * prevent * * * the sale of fraudulent and worthless corporate or quasi-corporate stocks and securities," and that "it is going to be a shock to a rancher" to learn that the sale of a "fractional interest in a horse or a registered bull" is subject to the provisions of that law.

While we may sympathize with these plaintiffs, such "shocks" are by no means uncommon to many in this day of constantly proliferating laws. * * *

* * *

—Exemption for "isolated transactions."

ORS 59.035 provides an exemption from registration of securities for:

> "(2) An isolated transaction not in the course of repeated and successive transactions in this state."

Plaintiffs contend that in the application of this exemption the court can consider only "transactions" relating to the two horses that were the subject of this agreement; that transactions relating to other horses cannot be considered, and that even if they could be properly considered plaintiffs had no "general purpose" because "here the buyer approached the vendor."

We have held that sales of stock to three, and perhaps even as few as two, different individuals may be "repeated and successive transactions," so as not to qualify within this exemption. We believe that the proper test to be applied in such a case is whether the sales in question are made "within a period of such reasonable time as to indicate that one general purpose actuates the vendor and that the sales promote the same aim and are not so detached and separated as to form no part of a single plan."

In this case it appears that in February 1973 plaintiffs sold a one-half interest in one horse to plaintiffs' attorney and three of his friends, with a one-eighth interest in that horse to each of the four of them, under substantially the same terms of agreement as those of the subsequent sale to defendant in June 1973 of an interest in two other horses—the sale which is the subject of this case. In addition, Mrs. Marshall discussed with [two others] at least the "possibility" of similar agreements with them relating to other horses at about the same time as the sale to defendant.

* * * [P]laintiffs did not sustain their burden to prove that the sale to defendant was exempt as an "isolated transaction not in the course of repeated and successive transactions in this state," within the meaning of ORS 59.035(2).

—Exemption as an "initial sale."

ORS 59.035(11) provides a further exemption for

"(11) The initial sale of any securities of a new organization by preorganization subscription or by subscription after organization but before the commencement of any business activity, if:

"(a) The number of persons solicited within this state does not exceed 25, and the number of persons purchasing the securities within or without this state does not exceed 10;

"(b) No commission or other remuneration is paid or given directly or indirectly in connection with the sale; and

"(c) The sale is not a part of an attempt to evade the provisions of the Oregon Securities Law."

Plaintiffs offered evidence sufficient to satisfy the requirements of subparagraphs (a), (b) and (c), but the question remains whether, as contended by plaintiffs, the sale to defendant was "the initial sale" of securities of a "new organization" by "subscription after organization but before the commencement of any business activity."

Again, plaintiffs contend that in deciding this question the transaction between plaintiffs and defendant involving two of plaintiffs' horses must be considered separately from the previous transactions with plaintiffs' attorney and his friends involving another horse. We believe, however, that in considering the exemption for an "initial sale," under the record in this case, as well as in considering the exemption for "isolated transactions," the transaction involving the sale to defendant of an interest in two horses cannot properly be separated from the prior transactions involving the sale to plaintiffs' attorney and his friends of an interest in one other horse. We find, after reviewing the record, that plaintiffs failed to sustain their burden to prove that for accounting or other business purposes these transactions were, in fact, treated as separate and distinct business "organization[s]" or entities. On the contrary, there was evidence that payment of bills for the expenses incurred by all three horses subject to these transactions were paid by plaintiffs by checks drawn on a single checking account. It also appears checks in payment for reimbursement of such expenses as received from defendant and also from plaintiffs' attorney for expenses incurred by the other horse were all deposited in this same account and that this was "the same account that [plaintiffs] operated the ranch with."

Plaintiffs also contend that even "if all of these transactions involving race horses are treated as a single business," the exemption still applies because "there had been no business activity by the race horses." We find, however, after reviewing the record, that although it is true that none of the three horses subject to these transactions had actually raced until October 1973, long after the sale by plaintiffs to defendant in June 1973, plaintiffs failed to sustain their burden to prove that this sale was made "before the commencement of any business activity." On the contrary, there was evidence that prior to June 1973 the horse subject to the transactions with plaintiffs' attorney and his friends had been sent to California for training in preparation for racing and that expenses for that purpose had been incurred prior to June 1973.

* * *

For all of these reasons, the judgment of the trial court must be reversed * * * .

* * *

Kreis v. Mates Investment Fund, Inc.

United States Court of Appeals, Eighth Circuit, 1973.
473 F.2d 1308.

■ Before BRIGHT and STEPHENSON, CIRCUIT JUDGES, and TALBOT SMITH, DISTRICT JUDGE.

■ PER CURIAM.

The matter before us is an action for rescission. The plaintiff, Fred P. Kreis, Jr. (hereafter "Kreis"), a citizen and resident of Missouri, bought shares of the defendant Mates Investment Fund, Inc. [, a corporation operating out of New York] (hereafter, the "Fund") [,] by mail, relying upon a glowing account thereof published in Barron's National Business and Financial Weekly in the issue dated June 3, 1968. Eventually Kreis became unhappy with his purchase. Hence this action.

The ground of rescission asserted was non-compliance by the Fund with the registration provisions of the Missouri Uniform Securities Act (hereafter the Act, or the "new" Act).

* * *

It was the holding of the District Court that, * * * although there was an offer by Kreis to buy the shares of the Fund * * * , there was no acceptance thereof in Missouri and hence that the Act does not apply to the purchase. * * *

* * *

The "new" Missouri Uniform Securities Act represents a substantial adoption of the Uniform Securities Act. The portion with which we are here principally concerned is a separate section dealing with what was aptly termed (by the draftsmen of the Uniform Act) to be the "bewildering state of affairs" in the case law governing transactions which crossed state lines. * * *

The Act provides in part as follows:

409.415 "Scope of the act and service of process

* * *

(d) For the purpose of this section, an offer to buy or to sell is accepted in this state when acceptance (1) is communicated to the offeror in this state and (2) has not previously been communicated to the offeror, orally or in writing, outside this state; and acceptance is communicated to the offeror in this state, whether or not either party is then present in this state, when the offeree directs it to the offeror in this state reasonably believing the offeror to be in this state and it is received at the place to which it is directed (or at any post office in this state in the case of a mailed acceptance)" [emphasis supplied].[8]

* * *

* * * In [this] subsection * * *, the stress is upon communication. Substantially, an offer is accepted here in Missouri when it is "communicated to the offeror in this state" (and has not theretofore been communicated outside the state). And it is "communicated to the offeror in this state" when the offeree directs it to him here and it is received where directed. At that point, for the purpose of the new Act, the offer has been accepted in Missouri.

* * *

In view of the stipulated fact that the only communication received by Kreis as to the action taken upon his offer, namely its acceptance in New York, was the written confirmation of the purchase, mailed by the Fund to Kreis, addressed to him, and received by him, at his home in Missouri, we hold that under the terms of Section 409.415(d) there was acceptance in this state. * * *

* * *

Reversed and remanded for further proceedings not inconsistent with this opinion.

---

8   Section 610 (d) of the Uniform Securities Act of 2002 is similar. [Eds.]

The following case shows how lawyers can find themselves liable under state securities laws if they do not carefully limit their involvement in their clients' securities transactions.

Johnson v. Colip

Supreme Court of Indiana, 1995.
658 N.E.2d 575.

■ SULLIVAN, JUSTICE.

This case requires us to explore the circumstances under which a securities lawyer who attends a meeting of prospective investors can be held to be an "agent" of the securities issuer as the term is defined in the Indiana Securities Act (the "Act"). [The defendant attorney, Gary Colip, incorporated and represented a corporation established to serve as general partner in several limited partnerships comprising interests in oil properties. He was also responsible for drafting the prospectus used to solicit investors in the partnerships.]

* * *

I

This case arises under the Indiana Securities Act, our state's contribution to the body of Blue Sky laws adopted by each state. Although not as well known as their federal counterparts, these statutes for the most part pre-date by many years the enactment of the first federal securities acts in 1933 and 1934 and in many cases provide more rigorous standards for the offer and sale of securities than does the federal regime. And in a time apparently characterized by federal retrenchment in this area, state regulation of securities may serve an increasingly important role both in protecting investors and assuring issuers of a level playing field when they compete for capital.

II

The Indiana Securities Act as in effect in December, 1983, the date of the conduct at issue in this case, provided a private cause of action against every "agent" of a seller or purchaser of securities "who materially aids in the sale or purchase * * * unless that person who is so liable sustains the burden of proof that he did not know, and in the exercise of reasonable care, could not have known of the existence of the facts by reason of which the liability is alleged to exist." Another section of our Securities Act defines the term "agent" to be:

> Any individual, other than a broker-dealer, who represents a broker-dealer or issuer in effecting or attempting to effect purchasers or sales of securities. A partner, officer, or director of a broker-dealer or issuer or a person occupying a similar status or performing similar functions is an agent only if he effects or attempts to effect a purchase or sale of securities in Indiana.

At issue is whether a genuine issue of material fact exists as to whether Colip was an agent of the other defendants and, if so, whether he "materially aided in the sale of securities herein" and was, therefore, liable to plaintiffs under the Act.

A

The provisions of the Act quoted above are based substantially upon § § 401(b) and 410 of the Uniform Securities Act of 1956. The comment to § 401 of the Uniform Act notes that whether a particular individual who represents an issuer is an "agent" depends "upon much the same factors which create an agency relationship at common law. That is to say, the question turns essentially on whether the individual has manifested a consent to the * * * issuer to act subject to his control." Indiana courts have long made the same inquiry to determine the existence of an agency relationship. Given the extensive amount of work that Colip performed for the corporation, we see little basis for granting Colip summary judgment if a common law agency relationship is all that is required to create an "agent" for purposes of the Act.

B

But while one must be a common law agent to be an "agent" under the Act, we perceive the Act as containing additional requirements as well. That is, whether Colip is an agency within the meaning of the Act turns on whether he effected or attempted to effect purchases or sales of securities.

* * *

In Baker v. Miles & Stockbridge, 95 Md.App. 145, 620 A.2d 356 (1993), the Maryland Court of Special Appeals conducted an extensive survey of the law in other jurisdictions in addressing this question. * * * resolution of this issue turned on whether the dealer-manager had presented sufficient facts to establish the existence of an agency relationship between the parties. [T]he Maryland court observed,

> Although the definition of "agent" in the state securities laws discussed above may vary to differing degrees from the definition [of agent in the Maryland Blue Sky Act], they each have one thing in common: they do not impose liability upon an attorney who merely provides legal services or prepares documents for his or her client. To impose liability, the attorney must do something more than act as legal counsel.

The court then held that "an attorney could conceivably be considered an agent if he or she represents a broker-dealer or issuer in effecting or attempting to effect the purchase or sale of securities." In order to be considered an agent, an attorney must

> act in a manner that goes beyond legal representation. The definition of "agent" in § 11–101(b) does not include attorneys who merely provide legal services, draft documents for use in

the purchase or sale of securities, or engage in their profession's traditional advisory functions. To rise to the level of "effecting" the purchase or sale of securities, the attorney must actively assist in offering securities for sale, solicit offers to buy, or actually perform the sale.

We agree * * * and hold that an attorney is an agent if his or her affirmative conduct or failure to act when reasonably expected to do so at a meeting of prospective investors made it more likely than not that the investors would purchase the securities than they would have been without such conduct or failure to act.

C

* * *

* * * [W]e are unable to infer with the same degree of certainty of the Court of Appeals that Colip's attendance at meetings of perspective investors constituted an attempt to effect the sale of securities. Certainly it may have done so and we believe that the determination as to whether or not it did constitutes an issue of fact inappropriate for resolution at summary judgment. For example, if when called upon at the meetings, Colip primarily reassured investors that risks about which they expressed concern were unlikely to materialize, such behavior made it more likely that not that the investors would purchase the securities and constituted an attempt to effect a purchase or sale. On the other hand, if Colip's principal function at the meeting was to either temper the exuberance of the principle promoters (a frequent reason why lawyers are asked to accompany "road shows" promoting new securities' offerings) or to discuss the technical aspects of the partnership agreement or its tax consequences with counsel for prospective investors (much as would occur in the negotiations in any reasonably sophisticated business transaction), we think these facts are not susceptible to the inference that an attempt to effect the purchase or sale of a security occurred. We hold that a genuine issue of material fact remains as to whether Colip's affirmative conduct or failure to act when reasonably expected to do so at a meeting with prospective investors made it more likely than not that the investors would purchase the securities and therefore constituted an attempt to effect the purchase or sale of the securities. Finally, we note that under [the Indiana Securities Act] Colip does have the opportunity to demonstrate to the finder of fact that he did not know, and in the exercise of reasonable care could not have known, of the existence of the facts by reason of which the liability is alleged to exist.

Conclusion

We reverse the grant of summary judgment in favor of Colip and remand this matter to the trial court for further proceedings consistent with this opinion.

* * *

B. STATE REGULATION OF CORPORATE TAKEOVERS

SITUATION 19B

Assume you are back at the time described in Situation 11, with Microtec planning a hostile tender offer to Compuform shareholders, and are considering the impact of state securities laws on the proposed tender offer.

In considering this situation, refer to Exchange Act Section 28, in addition to the materials in this section.

Beginning in 1968, with the passage by Congress of the Williams Act, states began passing their own statutes that regulate tender offers. Ultimately, over two-thirds of the states involved themselves in this exercise, almost universally by adopting provisions that in one way or another inhibit corporate takeovers. From the beginning, there have been questions about the constitutionality of these statutes. Largely because lower court cases became moot before the constitutional issues could be presented to the Supreme Court, it was many years before the Court had the opportunity to rule on these issues. In 1982, the Court finally got this opportunity, in Edgar v. Mite.[9] In a complicated plurality opinion, the Illinois Business Take-Over Act was found unconstitutional under the Supremacy and Commerce Clauses of the Federal Constitution.

Under the Illinois Act, any takeover offer for the shares of a target company was required to be registered with the Secretary of State. A target company was defined as a corporation or other issuer of securities of which shareholders located in Illinois own 10% of the class of equity securities subject to the offer, or for which any two of the following three conditions were met: the corporation had its principal executive office in Illinois, was organized under the laws of Illinois, or had at least 10% of its stated capital and paid-in surplus represented within the state. The registration process called for pre-announcement notification, provided an opportunity for a hearing at the request of a majority of a target company's outside directors or by Illinois shareholders who owned 10% of the class of securities subject to the offer, and required the Secretary of State to refuse registration to offers deemed unfair.

The Court in *MITE* found that the Illinois Act frustrated the objective of the Williams Act to create a "level playing field" for targets and acquirers. It also found that the Act directly regulated and prevented, unless its terms were satisfied, interstate tender offers which in turn would generate interstate transactions. Second, the burden the

---

[9]   457 U.S. 624 (1982).

Act imposed on interstate commerce was excessive in light of the local interests the Act purports to further.

After *MITE*, a number of states recast their statutes, or passed entirely new ones, in an attempt to avoid constitutional problems. The Supreme Court has spoken on the constitutionality of only one post-*MITE* statute. The case in which it did so appears directly below.

CTS Corp. v. Dynamics Corp. of America
Supreme Court of the United States, 1987.
481 U.S. 69.

■ JUSTICE POWELL delivered the opinion of the Court.

This case presents the questions whether the Control Share Acquisitions Chapter of the Indiana Business Corporation Law is preempted by the Williams Act, or violates the Commerce Clause of the Federal Constitution.

I

A

On March 4, 1986, the Governor of Indiana signed a revised Indiana Business Corporation Law. That law included the Control Share Acquisitions Chapter (Indiana Act or Act). Beginning on August 1, 1987, the Act will apply to any corporation incorporated in Indiana, unless the corporation amends its articles of incorporation or bylaws to opt out of the Act. * * * the Act applies only to "issuing public corporations." The term "corporation" includes only businesses incorporated in Indiana. An "issuing public corporation" is defined as:

"a corporation that has:

"(1) one hundred (100) or more shareholders;

"(2) its principal place of business, its principal office, or substantial assets within Indiana; and

"(3) either:

"(A) more than ten percent (10%) of its shareholders resident in Indiana;

"(B) more than ten percent (10%) of its shares owned by Indiana residents; or

"(C) ten thousand (10,000) shareholders resident in Indiana."

The Act focuses on the acquisition of "control shares" in an issuing public corporation. Under the Act, an entity acquires "control shares" whenever it acquires shares that, but for the operation of the Act, would bring its voting power in the corporation to or above any of three thresholds: 20%, 33 1/3%, or 50%. An entity that acquires control shares does not necessarily acquire voting rights. Rather, it gains those rights only "to the extent granted by resolution approved by the shareholders of the issuing public corporation." Section 9 requires a majority vote of all disinterested shareholders holding each class of stock for passage of such a resolution. The practical effect of this requirement is to condition acquisition of control of a corporation on approval of a majority of the pre-existing disinterested shareholders.

The shareholders decide whether to confer rights on the control shares at the next regularly scheduled meeting of the shareholders, or at a specially scheduled meeting. The acquiror can require management of the corporation to hold such a special meeting within 50 days if it files an "acquiring person statement," requests the meeting, and agrees to pay the expenses of the meeting. If the shareholders do not vote to restore voting rights to the shares, the corporation may redeem the control shares from the acquiror at fair market value, but it is not required to do so. Similarly, if the acquiror does not file an acquiring person statement with the corporation, the corporation may, if its bylaws or articles of incorporation so provide, redeem the shares at any time after 60 days after the acquiror's last acquisition.

B

On March 10, 1986, appellee Dynamics Corporation of America (Dynamics) owned 9.6% of the common stock of appellant CTS Corporation, an Indiana corporation. On that day, six days after the Act went into effect, Dynamics announced a tender offer for another million shares in CTS; purchase of those shares would have brought Dynamics' ownership interest in CTS to 27.5%. * * *

[Dynamics then sued in the United States District Court for the Northern District of Illinois, challenging the constitutionality of the Indiana Act on the grounds of federal pre-emption and unreasonable burden on interstate commerce. The District Court found the statute unconstitutional on both grounds, and the Seventh Circuit affirmed.]

II

The first question in this case is whether the Williams Act pre-empts the Indiana Act. * * *

* * *

B

The Indiana Act differs in major respects from the Illinois statute that the Court considered in Edgar v. MITE Corp., 457 U.S. 624 (1982). * * *

* * *

C

As the plurality opinion in *MITE* did not represent the views of a majority of the Court, we are not bound by its reasoning. We need not question that reasoning, however, because we believe the Indiana Act passes muster even under the broad interpretation of the Williams Act articulated by Justice WHITE in *MITE*. [T]he overriding concern of the *MITE* plurality was that the Illinois statute considered in that case operated to favor management against offerors, to the detriment of shareholders. By contrast, the statute now before the Court protects the independent shareholder against both of the contending parties. * * *

The Indiana Act operates on the assumption, implicit in the Williams Act, that independent shareholders faced with tender offers often are at a disadvantage. By allowing such shareholders to vote as a group, the Act protects them from the coercive aspects of some tender offers. If, for example, shareholders believe that a successful tender offer will be followed by a purchase of nontendering shares at a depressed price, individual shareholders may tender their shares—even if they doubt the tender offer is in the corporation's best interest—to protect themselves from being forced to sell their shares at a depressed price. * * * In such a situation under the Indiana Act, the shareholders as a group, acting in the corporation's best interest, could reject the offer, although individual shareholders might be inclined to accept it. The desire of the Indiana Legislature to protect shareholders of Indiana corporations from this type of coercive offer does not conflict with the Williams Act. Rather, it furthers the federal policy of investor protection.

In implementing its goal, the Indiana Act avoids the problems the plurality discussed in *MITE*. Unlike the *MITE* statute, the Indiana Act does not give either management or the offeror an advantage in communicating with the shareholders about the impending offer. The Act also does not impose an indefinite delay on tender offers. Nothing in the Act prohibits an offeror from consummating an offer on the 20th business day, the earliest day permitted under applicable federal regulations. Nor does the Act allow the state government to interpose its views of fairness between willing buyers and sellers of shares of the target company. Rather, the Act allows shareholders to evaluate the fairness of the offer collectively.

D

The Court of Appeals based its finding of pre-emption on its view that the practical effect of the Indiana Act is to delay consummation of tender offers until 50 days after the commencement of the offer. As did the Court of Appeals, Dynamics reasons that no rational offeror will purchase shares until it gains assurance that those shares will carry voting rights. Because it is possible that voting rights will not be conferred until a shareholder meeting 50 days after commencement of the offer, Dynamics concludes that the Act imposes a 50-day delay. This, it argues, conflicts with the shorter 20-business-day period established by the SEC as the minimum period for which a tender offer may be held open. We find the alleged conflict illusory.

The Act does not impose an absolute 50-day delay on tender offers, nor does it preclude an offeror from purchasing shares as soon as federal law permits. If the offeror fears an adverse shareholder vote under the Act, it can make a conditional tender offer, offering to accept shares on the condition that the shares receive voting rights within a certain period of time. * * *

Even assuming that the Indiana Act imposes some additional delay, nothing in *MITE* suggested that any delay imposed by state regulation, however short, would create a conflict with the Williams Act. The plurality argued only that the offeror should "be free to go forward without unreasonable delay." * * * [T]he Indiana Act provides that full voting rights will be vested—if this eventually is to occur—within 50 days after commencement of the offer. This period is within the 60-day maximum period Congress established for tender offers in [The Williams Act]. We cannot say that a delay within that congressionally determined period is unreasonable.

* * *

* * * Accordingly, we hold that the Williams Act does not pre-empt the Indiana Act.

III

As an alternative basis for its decision, the Court of Appeals held that the Act violates the Commerce Clause of the Federal Constitution. * * *

A

The principal objects of dormant Commerce Clause scrutiny are statutes that discriminate against interstate commerce. The Indiana Act is not such a statute. It has the same effects on tender offers whether or not the offeror is a domiciliary or resident of Indiana. * * *

* * * Because nothing in the Indiana Act imposes a greater burden on out-of-state offerors than it does on similarly situated Indiana offerors, we reject the contention that the Act discriminates against interstate commerce.

B

This Court's recent Commerce Clause cases also have invalidated statutes that adversely may affect interstate commerce by subjecting activities to inconsistent regulations. The Indiana Act poses no such problem. So long as each State regulates voting rights only in the corporations it has created, each corporation will be subject to the law of only one State. No principle of corporation law and practice is more firmly established than a State's authority to regulate domestic corporations, including the authority to define the voting rights of shareholders. Accordingly, we conclude that the Indiana Act does not create an impermissible risk of inconsistent regulation by different States.

C

The Court of Appeals did not find the Act unconstitutional for either of these threshold reasons. Rather, its decision rested on its view of the Act's potential to hinder tender offers. We think the Court of Appeals failed to appreciate the significance for Commerce Clause analysis of the fact that state regulation of corporate governance is regulation of entities whose very existence and attributes are a product of state law. * * * Every State in this country has enacted laws regulating corporate governance. By prohibiting certain transactions, and regulating others, such laws necessarily affect certain aspects of interstate commerce. This necessarily is true with respect to corporations with shareholders in States other than the State of incorporation. * * *

* * *

It thus is an accepted part of the business landscape in this country for States to create corporations, to prescribe their powers, and to define the rights that are acquired by purchasing their shares. A State has an interest in promoting stable relationships among parties involved in the corporations it charters, as well as in ensuring that investors in such corporations have an effective voice in corporate affairs.

There can be no doubt that the Act reflects these concerns. The primary purpose of the Act is to protect the shareholders of Indiana corporations. It does this by affording shareholders, when a takeover offer is made, an opportunity to decide collectively whether the resulting change in voting control of the corporation, as they perceive it, would be desirable. A change of management may have important effects on the shareholders' interests; it is well within the State's role as overseer of corporate governance to offer this opportunity. The autonomy provided by allowing shareholders collectively to determine whether the takeover is advantageous to their interests may be especially beneficial where a hostile tender offer may coerce shareholders into tendering their shares.

* * *

Dynamics argues in any event that the State has " 'no legitimate interest in protecting the nonresident shareholders.' " Dynamics relies heavily on the statement by the *MITE* Court that "[i]nsofar as the * * * law burdens out-of-state transactions, there is nothing to be weighed in the balance to sustain the law." But that comment was made in reference to an Illinois law that applied as well to out-of-state corporations as to in-state corporations. We agree that Indiana has no interest in protecting non-resident shareholders of nonresident corporations. But this Act applies only to corporations incorporated in Indiana. We reject the contention that Indiana has no interest in providing for the shareholders of its corporations the voting autonomy granted by the Act. Indiana has a substantial interest in preventing the corporate form from becoming a shield for unfair business dealing. Moreover, unlike the Illinois statute invalidated in *MITE*, the Indiana Act applies only to corporations that have a substantial number of shareholders in Indiana. Thus, every application of the Indiana Act will affect a substantial number of Indiana residents, whom Indiana indisputably has an interest in protecting.

* * *

IV

On its face, the Indiana Control Share Acquisitions Chapter evenhandedly determines the voting rights of shares of Indiana corporations. The Act does not conflict with the provisions or purposes of the Williams Act. To the limited extent that the Act affects interstate commerce, this is justified by the State's interests in defining the attributes of shares in its corporations and in protecting shareholders. Congress has never questioned the need for state regulation of these matters. Nor do we think such regulation offends the Constitution. Accordingly, we reverse the judgment of the Court of Appeals.

* * *

As was to be expected, after CTS a number a states copied the Indiana statute. Because so many publicly-held corporations are incorporated in Delaware but headquartered elsewhere, however, some states were pressured by Delaware corporations to pass an Indiana-type statute and to extend its application to them. One state that passed such a statute was Tennessee, whose Control Share Acquisition Act, adopted in 1988, was made applicable to foreign corporations that have their principal office and substantial assets in Tennessee. Within a few months, however, the Sixth Circuit found the Tennessee statute to violate the Commerce Clause insofar as it related to foreign corporations,[10] thus helping to dampen the hopes of corporations around the country that they would be able to get the benefits of a control share acquisition statute anywhere except in their state of incorporation.

Some states (including Delaware) have continued to adopt takeover legislation other than control share acquisition statutes, such as a so-called business combination act in which a controlling shareholder is prohibited in most circumstances from engaging in a merger or other business combination with a corporation it controls for a set number of years after obtaining control. Since CTS, the constitutionality of these other kinds of statutes has been tested only to a limited extent in the courts of appeals.

---

[10]   Tyson Foods, Inc. v. McReynolds, 865 F.2d 99 (6th Cir.1989).

PART 7

INTERNATIONAL ASPECTS OF SECURITIES LAW

CHAPTER 20

INTERNATIONAL REGULATION OF SECURITIES

SITUATION 20

Assume that several years after the Microtec-Compuform merger, the combined enterprise (still known as Microtec) finds itself in need of additional capital. Nielson Securities Co., the underwriter that assisted with Microtec's initial public offering, suggests that the cost of capital raised in an overseas offering could be significantly less than the cost of a domestic capital infusion. Microtec's managers are intrigued and would like to proceed with an offering of "eurosecurities."

Assume further that a German company, Computec, GMBH, is interested in placing its securities in the United States, and has contacted your firm for assistance.

In considering Microtec's situation, refer to Securities Act Rules 135E and 144A and Regulation S.

In considering Computec's situation, refer to the same Rules and Regulation, as well as Securities Act Section 22(a) and Forms F–1 and F–3, and Exchange Act Sections 12(g)(3) and 27, Rules 3a12–3(b) and 12g–3 and Form 20–F.

Capital cannot be jurisdictionally contained. Issuers realize the benefits of reaching out to foreign investors, just as investors realize the benefits of holding international portfolios. Development of round-the-clock trading venues, as well as means of virtually instantaneous communication and expeditious fund transfers, seem to suggest that national borders are artificial constructs without obvious relevance to issuers' capital needs or investors' hunger for profits. This portrayal does not, of course, comport with regulatory reality. The Securities Act and the Exchange Act do, in fact, reach some transactions and not others, just as do the regulations of foreign nations. Although the precise metes and bounds of coverage are problematic, some aspects are quite clear.

A. INTERNATIONALIZATION OF THE SECURITIES MARKETS

There are a number of reasons why American issuers conduct offshore offerings. Without a doubt, one of those reasons is that the burdens of foreign securities regulation are seen as significantly less than the burdens imposed by the United States. Ironically, foreign issuers also attempt to access American capital markets. These markets are sometimes claimed to be both broader and deeper than those of other countries—a state of affairs often attributed to the United States' tradition of a strong scheme of securities regulation.

Naturally, securities that are initially distributed in a different country may not stay there. Thus, foreign investors may buy securities of an American issuer in an initial distribution but may also purchase such securities on the United States trading markets. They may attempt to sell their holdings in a foreign trading market or on an American one. All of the same permutations may apply in the case of Americans acquiring and disposing of the securities of foreign issuers—and, for that matter, in the case of foreign investors dealing in the securities of issuers of non-American origin.

B. WHEN AND WHERE UNITED STATES LAWS APPLY

When must foreign persons comply with the provisions of the Securities Act or the Exchange Act? Are there circumstances in which United States persons need not comply with the Securities Act or the Exchange Act because their conduct has so little to do with the United States? An essential starting point in answering these questions is the definition of "interstate commerce." Under both the Securities Act and the Exchange Act, this term includes commerce or communication between any foreign country and any state.

I. BREADTH OF INTERSTATE COMMERCE

Because "interstate commerce" includes commerce with foreign countries, an argument can be made that any transaction with "one end" in the United States can be reached under the United States' securities laws. In fact, given the broad construction of "interstate commerce," a single telephone call involving one party in the United States might invoke the jurisdiction of American securities laws. Certainly, then, one should not be surprised to find that if a foreign issuer launches a public offering to United States investors, it must comply with the registration requirements of the Securities Act (and will be liable for any disclosure problems or fraud).

Suppose, however, that a United States issuer wishes to offer its securities exclusively to foreign investors. In a move not dictated by the language of the Securities Act, the Commission has taken the position that the purpose of the federal securities laws is to protect *American* investors, and that an offering that is carefully directed offshore and reasonably tailored to stay there need not be registered. This position is discussed in more detail later in this chapter. As an introductory matter, however, the Commission's view is sufficient to alert us that United States securities laws will not be extended to their utmost literal coverage. The considerations prompting this restraint include notions of international comity, as well as an interest in conserving the Commission's own enforcement resources.

II. IMPORTANCE OF CONTEXT

Let us return to the case of the foreign issuer raising capital from American investors. As a variation, suppose that the foreign issuer is not specifically targeting United States residents but simply makes no particular attempt to exclude them from its offering. Suppose, for instance, that such an issuer holds a press conference in its home country, in order to discuss its public offering plans. Reports of the conference are foreseeably circulated in the United States—perhaps because a few expatriates have subscriptions to newspapers (online or otherwise) from their former homeland. The breadth of the concept of an "offer," introduced in Chapter 3, would ordinarily suggest that the readers now resident in the United States are offerees. The United States offers would be integrated with the public offering in the issuer's home country, and it would appear that registration in the United States would be required. Or would it? Although, as we shall see, the answer is "probably not," we could get a different answer if we asked whether a United States purchaser could claim a remedy under the antifraud provisions of either the Securities Act or the Exchange Act.

In fact, coverage of the United States securities laws is interpreted most narrowly when the need for registration under one of the Acts is at issue, and most broadly when the question presented involves liability for violation of one of the antifraud provisions of either the Securities Act or the Exchange Act. From the standpoint of international comity, this is quite sensible. Presumably, no foreign nation will have a strong interest in preserving the ability of its nationals to engage in fraud, nor any strong aversion to having its nationals protected from the fraud of others. By contrast, foreign sovereigns may have their own schemes for registration and market regulation. Adding the requirements of the United States scheme might present outright conflicts and undue burdens on would-be securities transactions.

The difference in approach just described is well established, and in part has been exacerbated by the differing entities offering the relevant interpretations, as well as by the different purposes for which the interpretations have been offered. As noted above, the Commission has attempted to aid planners by defining the situations in which registration is and is not required. For predictable policy reasons, it has declined to take the most aggressive stance possible. The jurisdiction of the United States antifraud laws typically is determined by the federal courts, and is considered only after the alleged wrongdoing occurs. The following sections present separate analyses for United States registration requirements and for the rules relating to fraud.

C. UNITED STATES REGISTRATION REQUIREMENTS

It is clear that Congress initially intended to reach offerings of foreign securities in the United States. Such offerings were common and contributed to the losses suffered by American investors before passage of the primary United States securities legislation in 1933 and 1934. Given the breadth of the "interstate commerce" and "offer" concepts, however, the Acts could be construed to cover much more.

I. SECURITIES OFFERED ABROAD

a. REGULATION S

In 1964 the Commission issued Securities Act Release No. 4708,[1] announcing its belief that Section 5 of the Securities Act does not apply to offerings reasonably designed to "come to rest" outside of the United States. In the years that followed, numerous offerings by American and foreign issuers took place in reliance on the Release. These offerings were directed to foreign nationals and restricted in various ways preventing, for a period of time, resales to American investors.

In 1990 the Commission adopted (and in 1998 significantly amended) Regulation S to give additional guidance. Regulation S is a non-exclusive safe harbor from Securities Act registration for offers and sales taking place outside of the United States. Technically, it does not provide an exemption from registration. Rather, it expresses the Commission's view that registration for the protection of foreign investors is not within the principal purposes of the Securities Act.

Securities Act Release No. 6863
Securities and Exchange Commission, April 24, 1990.

OFFSHORE OFFERS AND SALES

* * *

* * * Regulation S as adopted includes two safe harbors. One safe harbor applies to offers and sales by issuers, securities professionals involved in the distribution process pursuant to contract, their respective affiliates, and persons acting on behalf of any of the foregoing (the "issuer safe harbor"), and the other applies to resales by persons other than the issuer, securities professionals involved in the distribution process pursuant to contract, their respective affiliates (except certain officers and directors), and persons acting on behalf of any of the foregoing (the "resale safe harbor"). An offer, sale or resale of securities that satisfies all conditions of the applicable safe harbor is deemed to be outside the United States within the meaning of the General Statement and thus not subject to the registration requirements of Section 5.

---

[1]   (July 9, 1964).

Two general conditions apply to the safe harbors. First, any offer or sale of securities must be made in an "offshore transaction," which requires that no offers be made to persons in the United States and that either: (i) the buyer is (or the seller reasonably believes that the buyer is) offshore at the time of the origination of the buy order, or (ii) for purposes of the issuer safe harbor, the sale is made in, on or through a physical trading floor of an established foreign securities exchange, or (iii) for purposes of the resale safe harbor, the sale is made in, on or through the facilities of a designated offshore securities market, and the transaction is not pre-arranged with a buyer in the United States. Second, in no event could "directed selling efforts" be made in the United States in connection with an offer or sale of securities made under a safe harbor. "Directed selling efforts" are activities undertaken for the purpose of, or that could reasonably be expected to result in, conditioning of the market in the United States for the securities being offered. Exceptions to the general conditions are made with respect to offers and sales to specified institutions not deemed U.S. persons, notwithstanding their presence in the United States.

The issuer safe harbor distinguishes three categories of securities offerings, based upon factors such as the nationality and reporting status of the issuer and the degree of U.S. market interest in the issuer's securities. The first category of offerings has been expanded from the Proposals and includes: securities offered in "overseas directed offerings," securities of foreign issuers in which there is no substantial U.S. market interest, securities backed by the full faith and credit of a foreign government, and securities issued pursuant to certain employee benefit plans. The term "overseas directed offerings" (which replaces "overseas domestic offerings" from the Reproposing Release) includes an offering of a foreign issuer's securities directed to any one foreign country, whether or not the issuer's home country, if such offering is conducted in accordance with local laws, offering practices and documentation. It also includes certain offerings of a domestic issuer's non-convertible debt securities, specified preferred stock and asset-backed securities denominated in the currency of a foreign country, which are directed to a single foreign country, and conducted in accordance with local laws, offering practices and documentation. The second category has been revised to include offerings of securities of U.S. reporting issuers and offerings of debt securities, asset-backed securities and specified preferred stock of foreign issuers with a substantial U.S. market interest. * * *

The issuer safe harbor requires implementation of procedural safeguards, which differ for each of the three categories, to ensure that the securities offered come to rest offshore. Offerings under the first category may be made offshore under the issuer safe harbor without any restrictions beyond the general conditions. Offerings made in reliance on the other two categories are subject to additional safeguards, such as restrictions on offer and sale to or for the account or benefit of U.S. persons.

The resale safe harbor has been expanded from the Proposals to allow reliance thereon by certain officers and directors of the issuer or distributors. In such a transaction, no remuneration other than customary broker's commissions may be paid. Otherwise, the resale safe harbor is adopted substantially as reproposed. Under the resale safe harbor, dealers and others receiving selling concessions, fees or other remuneration in connection with the offering (such as sub-underwriters) must comply with requirements designed to reinforce the applicable restriction on directed selling efforts in the United States and the offshore transaction requirement. * * *

The safe harbors are not exclusive and are not intended to create a presumption that any transaction failing to meet their terms is subject to Section 5. * * * Reliance on one of the safe harbors does not affect the availability of any exemption from the Securities Act registration requirements upon which a person may be able to rely.

Regulation S relates solely to the applicability of the registration requirements of Section 5 of the Securities Act. The Regulation does not limit in any way the scope or applicability of the antifraud or other provisions of the federal securities laws or provisions of state law relating to the offer and sale of securities.

* * *

Regulation S is composed of Securities Act Rules 901–905. The rules are quite detailed and make use of a number of defined terms. One important focus of the rules is preventing securities placed under their auspices by domestic issuers from "trickling back" into the United States under circumstances suggesting initial abuse of the rules. For instance, equity securities placed offshore by domestic issuers are subject to a one-year "distribution compliance period." During this period, no offers or sales may be made to United States persons, and issuers are required to restrict transfers accordingly. Other restrictions also apply: for instance, Rule 905 makes equity securities placed by domestic issuers under Regulation S "restricted securities" for purposes of resale under Rule 144, which is discussed in Chapter 7.

Pursuant to Regulation S's own terms, domestic offerings and offshore transactions qualifying under the regulation can occur contemporaneously. In other words, the regulation contains its own safe harbor from integration.

b.   CERTAIN PRESS COMMUNICATIONS

As part of the National Securities Markets Improvement Act of 1996, Congress directed the Commission to adopt rules clarifying the status of offshore press activities under the Securities Act. This action was stimulated by a concern that American journalists were being barred from press conferences, meetings, and receipt of press materials pertaining to proposed securities offerings and tender offers. The Commission obliged, responding in 1997 with new rules under both the Securities Act and the Exchange Act. These rules establish safe harbors for securities offerings by foreign issuers and selling security holders and for tender offers made by any bidder for a foreign private target.

The gist of Rule 135E under the Securities Act is that all press activity qualifying for a safe harbor must occur offshore, must be open to foreign journalists as well as American journalists, and must relate to an offering that will take place at least partially offshore. To qualify, a meeting must be in a foreign country (with no telephone or equivalent links to America) and written materials must be delivered on foreign soil. Written materials must bear appropriate legends and cannot be accompanied by any form of purchase order or coupon to indicate interest in the offering. Amended Rule 14d–1 under the Exchange Act states similar conditions for press activity that will not be deemed to launch a tender offer in the United States for the securities of a foreign issuer. Neither rule covers paid advertisements.

The safe harbors for press contacts are, of course, only with respect to filing and procedural matters and do not relate to the requirements of the United States laws prohibiting fraud.

c. "OFFSHORE" WEBSITES

Securities Act Release No. 33–7516

Securities and Exchange Commission, March 23, 1998.

STATEMENT OF THE COMMISSION REGARDING USE OF INTERNET WEB SITES TO OFFER SECURITIES, SOLICIT SECURITIES TRANSACTIONS OR ADVERTISE INVESTMENT SERVICES OFFSHORE

* * *

II. BACKGROUND

A. The Global Reach of the Internet

The development of the Internet presents numerous opportunities and benefits for consumers and investors throughout the world. It also presents significant challenges for regulators charged with protecting consumers and investors. Regulators in many countries are attempting to administer their respective laws to preserve important protections provided by their regulatory schemes without stifling the Internet's vast communications potential. * * * We share this goal in our administration of the U.S. securities laws. * * *

Information posted on Internet Web sites concerning securities and investments can be made readily available without regard to geographic and political boundaries. * * * Additionally, the interactive nature of the Internet makes it possible for investors to purchase electronically the securities or services offered. For these and other reasons, we believe that the use of the Internet by market participants and investors presents significant issues under the U.S. securities laws.

Although this release focuses on Internet Web sites, the Internet offers a variety of forms of communication. We distinguish between Web site postings and more targeted Internet communication methods. More targeted communication methods are comparable to traditional mail because the sender directs the information to a particular person, group or entity. These methods include e-mail and technology that allows mass e-mailing or "spamming." Information posted on a Web site, however, is not sent to any particular person, although it is available for anyone to search for and retrieve. * * * Offerors using those more targeted technologies must assume the responsibility of identifying when their offering materials are being sent to persons in the United States and must comply fully with the U.S. securities laws.

B.   Regulation of Offers

* * *

The posting of information on a Web site may constitute an offer of securities or investment services for purposes of the U.S. securities laws. * * * Our discussion of these issues will proceed on the assumption that the Web site contains information that constitutes an "offer" of securities or investment services under the U.S. securities laws. * * * Because anyone who has access to the Internet can obtain access to a Web site unless the Web site sponsor adopts special procedures to restrict access, the pertinent legal issue is whether those Web site postings are offers in the United States that must be registered.

III. OFFSHORE OFFERS AND SOLICITATIONS ON THE INTERNET

A.   General Approach

Some may argue that regulators could best protect investors by requiring registration or licensing for any Internet offer of securities or investment services that their residents could access. As a practical matter, however, the adoption of such an approach by securities regulators could preclude some of the most promising Internet applications by investors, issuers, and financial service providers.

The regulation of offers is a fundamental element of federal and some U.S. state securities regulatory schemes. Absent the transaction of business in the United States or with U.S. persons, however, our interest in regulating solicitation activity is less compelling. * * * We believe that our investor protection concerns are best addressed through the implementation by issuers and financial service providers of precautionary measures that are reasonably designed to ensure that offshore Internet offers are not targeted to persons in the United States or to U.S. persons. * * *

B. Procedures Reasonably Designed to Avoid Targeting the United States

When offerors implement adequate measures to prevent U.S. persons from participating in an offshore Internet offer, we would not view the offer as targeted at the United States and thus would not treat it as occurring in the United States for registration purposes. What constitutes adequate measures will depend on all the facts and circumstances of any particular situation. We generally would not consider an offshore Internet offer made by a non-U.S. offeror as targeted at the United States, however, if:

> The Web site includes a prominent disclaimer making it clear that the offer is directed only to countries other than the United States. For example, the Web site could state that the securities or services are not being offered in the United States or to U.S. persons, or it could specify those jurisdictions (other than the United States) in which the offer is being made; * * * and

> The Web site offeror implements procedures that are reasonably designed to guard against sales to U.S. persons in the offshore offering. For example, the offeror could ascertain the purchaser's residence by obtaining such information as mailing addresses or telephone numbers (or area code) prior to the sale. This measure will allow the offeror to avoid sending or delivering securities, offering materials, services or products to a person at a U.S. address or telephone number.

These procedures are not exclusive; other procedures that suffice to guard against sales to U.S. persons also can be used to demonstrate that the offer is not targeted at the United States. Regardless of the precautions adopted, however, we would view solicitations that appear by their content to be targeted at U.S. persons as made in the United States. Examples of this type of solicitation include purportedly offshore offers that emphasize the investor's ability to avoid U.S. income taxes on the investments. * * * We are concerned that the advice that we provide to assist those who attempt to comply with both the letter and spirit of the securities laws will be used by others as a pretext to violate those laws. Sham offshore offerings or procedures, or other schemes will not allow issuers or promoters to escape their registration obligations under the U.S. securities laws.

C. Effect of Attempts by U.S. Persons to Evade Restrictions

We recognize that U.S. persons may respond falsely to residence questions, disguise their country of residence by using non-resident addresses, or use other devices, such as offshore nominees, in order to participate in offshore offerings of securities or investment services. Thus, even if the foreign market participant has taken measures reasonably designed to guard against sales to U.S. persons, a U.S. person nevertheless could circumvent those measures.

In our view, if a U.S. person purchases securities or investment services notwithstanding adequate procedures reasonably designed to prevent the purchase, we would not view the Internet offer after the fact as having been targeted at the United States, absent indications that would put the issuer on notice that the purchaser was a U.S. person. This information might include (but is not limited to): receipt of payment drawn on a U.S. bank; provision of a U.S. taxpayer identification or social security number; or, statements by the purchaser indicating that, notwithstanding a foreign address, he or she is a U.S. resident. Confronted with such information, we would expect offerors to take steps to verify that the purchaser is not a U.S. person before selling to that person. * * * Additionally, if despite its use of measures that appear to be reasonably designed to prevent sales to U.S. persons, the offeror discovers that it has sold to U.S. persons, it may need to evaluate whether other measures may be necessary to provide reasonable assurance against future sales to U.S. persons.

* * *

IV. ADDITIONAL ISSUES UNDER THE SECURITIES ACT

* * *

B. Offshore Offerings by U.S. Issuers

Our approach to the use of Web sites to post offshore securities offerings distinguishes between domestic and foreign issuers. * * * for the following reasons, additional precautions are justified for Web sites operated by domestic issuers purporting not to make a public offering in the United States:

> The substantial contacts that a U.S. issuer has with the United States justifies our exercise of more extensive regulatory jurisdiction over its securities-related activities;

> There is a strong likelihood that securities of U.S. issuers initially offered and sold offshore will enter the U.S. trading markets; and

> U.S. issuers and investors have a much greater expectation that securities offerings by domestic issuers will be subject to the U.S. securities laws.

Our experience with abusive practices under Regulation S indicates that we should proceed cautiously when giving guidance to U.S. issuers in the area of unregistered offshore offerings. As a result, we would not consider a U.S. issuer using a Web site to make an unregistered offer to have implemented reasonable measures to prevent sales to U.S. persons unless, in addition to the general precautions discussed above in Section

III.B., the U.S. issuer implements password-type procedures that are reasonably designed to ensure that only non-U.S. persons can obtain access to the offer. * * * Under this procedure, persons seeking access to the Internet offer would have to demonstrate to the issuer or intermediary that they are not U.S. persons before obtaining the password for the site. * * *

* * *

d.   OUTSIDE THE SAFE HARBORS

Obviously, a cautious foreign issuer can plan an offering in reliance on Regulation S and conduct its press contacts in accordance with the applicable safe harbor rules. It is just as obvious that some foreign issuers will engage in what they believe are offerings having nothing to do with the United States and therefore will fail to consult its safe harbors, much less adhere to them. We should return, then, to the earlier example of the foreign issuer holding the foreign press conference, reports of which are received by expatriates in newspapers from their foreign home towns. Let us assume that there is some reason the conference does not qualify for a safe harbor—perhaps because written materials were distributed without appropriate legends.

The stance taken by courts in dealing with these matters may fairly be summarized as follows: "[I]n the absence of a strong American interest, there is 'no reason to extend jurisdiction to cases where the United States activities * * * are relatively small in comparison to those abroad.' "[2] This means, of course, that United States courts are called upon both to assess the presence and strength of American interests as well as to evaluate the balance of American and offshore activities. In doing so, they have identified and discussed a number of factors, including the presence of alternative regulatory schemes and the reasonable expectations of the person arguably required to comply with United States law.

II. SECURITIES OF FOREIGN ISSUERS OFFERED IN THE UNITED STATES

a.   EXEMPTIONS FROM SECURITIES ACT REGISTRATION

A foreign issuer planning an offering to United States nationals must register under the Securities Act or find an applicable exemption. The exemptions from registration largely are available without respect to the issuer's nationality. Regulation A, however, may be used only by domestic and Canadian issuers, and Rules 801 and 802 are available only to foreign issuers.

---

[2]   Plessey Company plc v. General Electric Company plc, 628 F.Supp. 477 (D.Del.1986).

Not infrequently, foreign issuers will place securities with American institutional investors under Section 4(a)(2) of the Securities Act (the "private offering" exemption discussed in chapter 6). They can, and often do, invoke the safe harbor of Rule 506 (also discussed in that chapter), which calls for restrictions on resales of the securities involved. The institutions acquiring the securities may rely on the resale provisions of Regulation S if they choose to attempt to dispose of the securities overseas. They may also sell pursuant to Rule 144A, the safe harbor for resales to institutional investors or new Section 4(a)(7), which permits resales to accredited investors. Rule 144, which deals generally with resales of restricted securities, also will be available when its terms are met.

Rules 801 and 802 were adopted by the Commission to facilitate rights offers, exchange offers and business combinations involving foreign private issuers. United States holders must own no more than ten percent of the securities subject to the transaction. To receive the benefit of the exemption, United States holders must be given equal treatment with foreign holders and any information provided to holders of the securities must be provided to United States holders in English. There are other technical requirements, including that the following legend must appear prominently on any informational document disseminated to United States holders:

> This [rights offering, exchange offer, or business combination] is made for the securities of a foreign company. The offer is subject to the disclosure requirements of a foreign country that are different from those of the United States. Financial statements included in the document, if any, have been prepared in accordance with foreign accounting standards that may not be comparable to the financial statements of United States companies.

b.   SECURITIES ACT REGISTRATION BY FOREIGN ISSUERS

If registration is required, a foreign issuer may use one of a specially designed series of forms. These forms are denominated "F–1" and "F–3," and generally parallel the "S–1" and "S–3" forms used by domestic issuers. The foreign issuer's financial statements either may be reconciled with U.S. generally accepted accounting principles or prepared in accordance with international financial reporting standards ("IFRS") published by the International Accounting Standards Board.[3] (Interestingly, although the Commission in 2008 issued a "roadmap" looking toward requiring IFRS-compliant financial statements from domestic filers, the effort has stalled.)[4] The Commission has entered into or is considering a number of multijurisdictional accords conforming the requirements for filings in multiple jurisdictions. For instance, specially

---

[3]   Securities Act Release No. 8,879 (Dec. 21, 2007).

[4]   Securities Act Release No. 8,902 (Nov. 14, 2008).

designated forms permit certain Canadian issuers to satisfy United States registration requirements with Canadian disclosure documents.

III. EXCHANGE ACT REGISTRATION AND REPORTING BY FOREIGN ISSUERS

In general, foreign issuers of securities traded on an exchange or quoted in an automated inter-dealer quotation system must register those securities under the Exchange Act using Form 20–F. Form 20–F calls for the same level of disclosure as Form F–1 under the Securities Act. Pursuant to Rule 3a12–3(b), the securities of foreign issuers registered under the Exchange Act are exempt from proxy regulation under Section 14, as well as short-swing trading regulation under Section 16.

Exchange Act Section 12(g)(1) now requires registration within 120 days of the last day of the first fiscal year in which an issuer (a) has total assets exceeding $10,000,000 and (b) a class of equity security "held of record" by *either* 2,000 or more persons *or* 500 or more unaccredited investors. In light of the practical difficulties of extraterritorial enforcement, Section 12(g)(3) gives the Commission authority to exempt the securities of foreign issuers from Section 12(g) "in the public interest and consistent with the protection of investors." Rule 12g–3–2 exempts a class of a foreign issuer's securities if that class has fewer than 300 holders resident in the United States. It also exempts a foreign issuer's securities if the issuer maintains a listing of its equity securities in their primary trading market outside the U.S. and electronically publishes certain disclosure documents in English. These exemptions do not address the requirement that an issuer register a security if it is traded on a U.S. national exchange (or, in the case of the second exemption, a security traded on the over-the-counter Bulletin Board).

Foreign issuers who have registered under the Exchange Act generally must comply with the requirements of the Sarbanes-Oxley Act of 2002 (although there have been a few concessions, such as tweaking the independent audit committee requirement to permit compliance with the laws of the issuer's home country). The perceived costs of compliance may discourage foreign issuers from entering United States markets and may have encouraged some foreign issuers to withdraw. To partially address this concern, the Commission has acted to ease Exchange Act deregistration by foreign issuers. The test focuses on whether the average daily trading volume of the securities to be deregistered has been no greater than five percent of the average volume on a worldwide basis during a twelve-month period (certain additional conditions apply).

IV. SPECIAL CASE OF AMERICAN DEPOSITARY RECEIPTS

It is difficult to consider the topic of foreign securities offered in the United States without encountering the subject of American Depositary

Receipts, or "ADRs." In recent years, ADRs have accounted for approximately 10 percent of the total value of the American public market in equity securities. In an ADR program, a United States bank agrees to act as depositary for a foreign issuer's securities. The bank issues ADRs, which are negotiable certificates representing ownership of some amount of the foreign issuer's securities, to American investors. The bank itself is the actual owner (typically through a foreign custodian) of the foreign issuer's securities. It receives dividends and passes them on in American dollars to the holders of the ADRs. It also forwards information and proxy materials received from the foreign issuer.

The Commission regards ADRs as securities issued by the United States bank maintaining the program, and it is the bank that must register them under the Securities Act. The amount of disclosure required depends on whether the ADR program is designed to raise capital for the foreign issuer or simply gives American investors access to securities that already have been issued. Exchange Act compliance, however, is a matter for the foreign issuer. Rule 12g–3, described in the preceding section, may excuse a foreign issuer whose ADRs are not traded on an exchange or automated quotation system from Exchange Act registration under Section 12(g). If the foreign issuer's ADRs are traded on an exchange or automated quotation system, the foreign issuer must file a full Form 20–F.

D. UNITED STATES ANTIFRAUD REQUIREMENTS

Federal courts do not define the international scope of the United States securities laws as coextensive with principles of international relations. In other words, they decline to assert the broadest application that might be tolerated by international law. Instead, they have sought to articulate the coverage of the federal securities laws in terms of (at least constructive) congressional intent. Still, where fraud is alleged, courts have interpreted the coverage of United States securities laws quite generously.

Until 2010, it was possible to distill the wisdom of many of the judicial precedents on application of United States antifraud provisions in terms of two tests. The first was the "conduct" test; the second was the "effects" test. The "conduct" test was based on a principle of foreign relations law stipulating that a country can assert jurisdiction over significant conduct within its territory, and was adopted to protect the integrity of American security markets from reputational inroads. As described by the Second Circuit in SEC v. Kasser,[5] the test prevented the United States from becoming "a Barbary Coast * * * harboring international securities 'pirates.'" The "effects" test was based on a perception that a primary congressional purpose in adopting the securities laws is to protect American investors.

---

[5]   548 F.2d 109 (2d Cir. 1977).

A great deal of the implied clarity of having two neatly labeled tests dissolved in application. For instance, is mailing documents into the United States conduct within the country or an effect within the country? More importantly, how much conduct and how much effect were enough to satisfy a judicial quest to comply with congressional intent? Courts generally assumed that could assert jurisdiction where either the "conduct" or "effect" approach so indicated. They also engaged in an "admixture" or "combination" approach.[6]

The Supreme Court case of Morrison v. National Australia Bank[7] was a game-changer—at least temporarily—as far as extraterritorial application of Exchange Act Section 10(b) and Rule 10b–5 is concerned. Courts applying the tests described above previously had viewed extraterritorial application of the two provisions as a question of subject matter jurisdiction. In *Morrison*, the Supreme Court declined to view the extraterritorial application of Section 10(b) and Rule 10b–5 as a question of subject matter jurisdiction, noting that pursuant to Section 27 of the Exchange Act, federal courts do have jurisdiction over all questions arising under the Act. Instead, it framed the inquiry exclusively as one of congressional intent with respect to which transactions Section 10(b) was to cover. Its answer appears below, along with the Court's discussion of the earlier jurisprudence in the area. The legislative response to *Morrison* follows.

Morrison v. National Australia Bank, Ltd.

Supreme Court of the United States, 2010.
561 U.S. 247.

■ JUSTICE SCALIA delivered the opinion of the Court.

We decide whether § 10(b) of the Securities Exchange Act of 1934 provides a cause of action to foreign plaintiffs suing foreign and American defendants for misconduct in connection with securities traded on foreign exchanges.

I

Respondent National Australia Bank Limited (National) was, during the relevant time, the largest bank in Australia. Its Ordinary Shares—what in America would be called "common stock"—are traded on the Australian Stock Exchange Limited and on other foreign securities exchanges, but not on any exchange in the United States. There are listed on the New York Stock Exchange, however, National's American Depositary Receipts (ADRs), which represent the right to receive a specified number of National's Ordinary Shares.

The complaint alleges the following facts, which we accept as true. In February 1998, National bought respondent HomeSide Lending, Inc.,

---

[6]　*See, e.g.*, Kauthar SDN BHD v. Sternberg, 149 F.3d 659 (7th Cir.1998).

[7]　130 S.Ct. 2869 (2010).

a mortgage servicing company headquartered in Florida. HomeSide's business was to receive fees for servicing mortgages (essentially the administrative tasks associated with collecting mortgage payments, * * *. The rights to receive those fees, so-called mortgage-servicing rights, can provide a valuable income stream. * * * How valuable each of the rights is depends, in part, on the likelihood that the mortgage to which it applies will be fully repaid before it is due, terminating the need for servicing. HomeSide calculated the present value of its mortgage-servicing rights by using valuation models designed to take this likelihood into account. It recorded the value of its assets, and the numbers appeared in National's financial statements.

From 1998 until 2001, National's annual reports and other public documents touted the success of HomeSide's business, and respondents Frank Cicutto (National's managing director and chief executive officer), Kevin Race (HomeSide's chief operating officer), and Hugh Harris (HomeSide's chief executive officer) did the same in public statements. But on July 5, 2001, National announced that it was writing down the value of HomeSide's assets by $450 million; and then again on September 3, by another $1.75 billion. The prices of both Ordinary Shares and ADRs slumped. After downplaying the July write-down, National explained the September write-down as the result of a failure to anticipate the lowering of prevailing interest rates (lower interest rates lead to more refinancings, i.e., more early repayments of mortgages), other mistaken assumptions in the financial models, and the loss of goodwill. According to the complaint, however, HomeSide, Race, Harris, and another HomeSide senior executive who is also a respondent here had manipulated HomeSide's financial models to make the rates of early repayment unrealistically low in order to cause the mortgage-servicing rights to appear more valuable than they really were. The complaint also alleges that National and Cicutto were aware of this deception by July 2000, but did nothing about it.

As relevant here, petitioners Russell Leslie Owen and Brian and Geraldine Silverlock, all Australians, purchased National's Ordinary Shares in 2000 and 2001, before the write-downs. They sued National, HomeSide, Cicutto, and the three HomeSide executives in the United States District Court for the Southern District of New York for alleged violations of §§ 10(b) and 20(a) of the Securities and Exchange Act of 1934, and SEC Rule 10b–5, promulgated pursuant to § 10(b). They sought to represent a class of foreign purchasers of National's Ordinary Shares during a specified period up to the September write-down.

Respondents moved to dismiss for lack of subject-matter jurisdiction under Federal Rule of Civil Procedure 12(b)(1) and for failure to state a claim under Rule 12(b)(6). The District Court granted the motion on the former ground, finding no jurisdiction because the acts in this country were, "at most, a link in the chain of an alleged overall securities fraud scheme that culminated abroad." * * * The Court of Appeals for the

Second Circuit affirmed on similar grounds. The acts performed in the United States did not "compris[e] the heart of the alleged fraud." * * * We granted certiorari * * * .

II

Before addressing the question presented, we must correct a threshold error in the Second Circuit's analysis. It considered the extraterritorial reach of § 10(b) to raise a question of subject-matter jurisdiction, wherefore it affirmed the District Court's dismissal under Rule 12(b)(1). * * * The Second Circuit is hardly alone in taking this position * * * .

But to ask what conduct § 10(b) reaches is to ask what conduct § 10(b) prohibits, which is a merits question. Subject-matter jurisdiction, by contrast, "refers to a tribunal's ' "power to hear a case." ' " [Quoting authority.] It presents an issue quite separate from the question whether the allegations the plaintiff makes entitle him to relief. * * * The District Court here had jurisdiction under [Exchange Act § 27] to adjudicate the question whether § 10(b) applies to National's conduct.

In view of this error, which the parties do not dispute, petitioners ask us to remand. We think that unnecessary. Since nothing in the analysis of the courts below turned on the mistake, a remand would only require a new Rule 12(b)(6) label for the same Rule 12(b)(1) conclusion. * * *

III

A

It is a "longstanding principle of American law 'that legislation of Congress, unless a contrary intent appears, is meant to apply only within the territorial jurisdiction of the United States.' " EEOC v. Arabian American Oil Co., 499 U.S. 244, 248 (1991) (Aramco) (quoting Foley Bros., Inc. v. Filardo, 336 U.S. 281, 285 (1949)). This principle represents a canon of construction, or a presumption about a statute's meaning, rather than a limit upon Congress's power to legislate * * * [and] rests on the perception that Congress ordinarily legislates with respect to domestic, not foreign matters. Smith v. United States, 507 U.S. 197, 204, n. 5 (1993). Thus, "unless there is the affirmative intention of the Congress clearly expressed" to give a statute extraterritorial effect, "we must presume it is primarily concerned with domestic conditions." Aramco, supra, at 248. The canon or presumption applies regardless of whether there is a risk of conflict between the American statute and a foreign law, see Sale v. Haitian Centers Council, Inc., 509 U.S. 155, 173–174 (1993). When a statute gives no clear indication of an extraterritorial application, it has none.

Despite this principle of interpretation, long and often recited in our opinions, the Second Circuit believed that, because the Exchange Act is silent as to the extraterritorial application of § 10(b), it was left to the court to "discern" whether Congress would have wanted the statute to apply. This disregard of the presumption against extraterritoriality did not originate with the Court of Appeals panel in this case. It has been repeated over many decades by various courts of appeals in determining the application of the Exchange Act, and § 10(b) in particular, to fraudulent schemes that involve conduct and effects abroad. That has produced a collection of tests for divining what Congress would have wanted, complex in formulation and unpredictable in application.

As of 1967, district courts at least in the Southern District of New York had consistently concluded that, by reason of the presumption against extraterritoriality, § 10(b) did not apply when the stock transactions underlying the violation occurred abroad. See Schoenbaum v. Firstbrook, 268 F.Supp. 385, 392 (1967) * * * . Schoenbaum involved the sale in Canada of the treasury shares of a Canadian corporation whose publicly traded shares (but not, of course, its treasury shares) were listed on both the American Stock Exchange and the Toronto Stock Exchange. Invoking the presumption against extraterritoriality, the court held that § 10(b) was inapplicable (though it incorrectly viewed the defect as jurisdictional). * * * The decision in Schoenbaum was reversed, however, by a Second Circuit opinion which held that "neither the usual presumption against extraterritorial application of legislation nor the specific language of [§]30(b) show Congressional intent to preclude application of the Exchange Act to transactions regarding stocks traded in the United States which are effected outside the United States * * * ." Schoenbaum, 405 F.2d, at 206. It sufficed to apply § 10(b) that, although the transactions in treasury shares took place in Canada, they affected the value of the common shares publicly traded in the United States. See id., at 208–209. Application of § 10(b), the Second Circuit found, was "necessary to protect American investors," id., at 206.

The Second Circuit took another step with Leasco Data Processing Equip. Corp. v. Maxwell, 468 F.2d 1326 (1972), which involved an American company that had been fraudulently induced to buy securities in England. There, unlike in Schoenbaum, some of the deceptive conduct had occurred in the United States but the corporation whose securities were traded (abroad) was not listed on any domestic exchange. Leasco said that the presumption against extraterritoriality apples only to matters over which the United States would not have prescriptive jurisdiction, 468 F.2d, at 1334. Congress had prescriptive jurisdiction to regulate the deceptive conduct in this country, the language of the Act could be read to cover that conduct, and the court concluded that "if Congress had thought about the point," it would have wanted § 10(b) to apply. Id., at 1334–1337.

With Schoenbaum and Leasco on the books, the Second Circuit had excised the presumption against extraterritoriality from the jurisprudence of § 10(b) and replaced it with the inquiry whether it would be reasonable (and hence what Congress would have wanted) to apply the statute to a given situation. As long as there was prescriptive jurisdiction to regulate, the Second Circuit explained, whether to apply § 10(b) even to "predominantly foreign" transactions became a matter of whether a court thought Congress "wished the precious resources of United States courts and law enforcement agencies to be devoted to them rather than leave the problem to foreign countries." Bersch v. Drexel Firestone, Inc., 519 F.2d 974, 985 (1975) * * * .

The Second Circuit had thus established that application of § 10(b) could be premised upon either some effect on American securities markets or investors (Schoenbaum) or significant conduct in the United States (Leasco). It later formalized these two applications into (1) an "effects test," "whether the wrongful conduct had a substantial effect in the United States or upon United States citizens," and (2) a "conduct test," "whether the wrongful conduct occurred in the United States." SEC v. Berger, 322 F.3d 187, 192–193 (C.A.2 2003). These became the north star of the Second Circuit's § 10(b) jurisprudence, pointing the way to what Congress would have wished. Indeed, the Second Circuit declined to keep its two tests distinct on the ground that "an admixture or combination of the two often gives a better picture of whether there is sufficient United States involvement to justify the exercise of jurisdiction by an American court." Itoba Ltd. v. Lep Group PLC, 54 F.3d 118, 122 (1995). The Second Circuit never put forward a textual or even extratextual basis for these tests. As early as Bersch, it confessed that "if we were asked to point to language in the statutes, or even in the legislative history, that compelled these conclusions, we would be unable to respond," 519 F.2d, at 993.

As they developed, these tests were not easy to administer. The conduct test was held to apply differently depending on whether the harmed investors were Americans or foreigners: When the alleged damages consisted of losses to American investors abroad, it was enough that acts "of material importance" performed in the United States "significantly contributed" to that result; whereas those acts must have "directly caused" the result when losses to foreigners abroad were at issue. See Bersch, 519 F.2d, at 993. And "merely preparatory activities in the United States" did not suffice "to trigger application of the securities laws for injury to foreigners located abroad." Id., at 992. This required the court to distinguish between mere preparation and using the United States as a "base" for fraudulent activities in other countries. * * * But merely satisfying the conduct test was sometimes insufficient without " 'some additional factor tipping the scales' " in favor of the application of American law. Interbrew v. Edperbrascan Corp., 23 F.Supp.2d 425, 432 (S.D.N.Y. 1998) * * * . District courts have noted the difficulty of applying such vague formulations. See, e.g., In re Alstom SA, 406 F.Supp.2d 346, 366–385 (S.D.N.Y.2005). There is no more damning indictment of the "conduct" and "effects" tests than the Second Circuit's own declaration that "the presence or absence of any single factor which was considered significant in other cases * * * is not necessarily dispositive in future cases." IIT v. Cornfeld, 619 F.2d 909, 918 (1980) (internal quotation marks omitted).

Other Circuits embraced the Second Circuit's approach, though not its precise application. Like the Second Circuit, they described their decisions regarding the extraterritorial application of § 10(b) as essentially resolving matters of policy. See, e.g., SEC v. Kasser, 548 F.2d 109, 116 (C.A.3 1977) * * *. While applying the same fundamental methodology of balancing interests and arriving at what seemed the best policy, they produced a proliferation of vaguely related variations on the "conduct" and "effects" tests. As described in a leading Seventh Circuit opinion: "Although the circuits * * * seem to agree that there are some transnational situations to which the antifraud provisions of the securities laws are applicable, agreement appears to end at that point." Id., at 665. * * *

At least one Court of Appeals has criticized this line of cases and the interpretive assumption that underlies it. In Zoelsch v. Arthur Andersen & Co., 824 F.2d 27, 32 (1987) (Bork, J.), the District of Columbia Circuit observed that rather than courts' "divining what 'Congress would have wished' if it had addressed the problem[, a] more natural inquiry might be what jurisdiction Congress in fact thought about and conferred." Although tempted to apply the presumption against extraterritoriality and be done with it, see id., at 31–32, that court deferred to the Second Circuit because of its "preeminence in the field of securities law," id., at 32. * * *

Commentators have criticized the unpredictable and inconsistent application of § 10(b) to transnational cases. * * * Some have challenged the premise underlying the Courts of Appeals' approach, namely that Congress did not consider the extraterritorial application of § 10(b) (thereby leaving it open to the courts, supposedly, to determine what Congress would have wanted). * * * Others, more fundamentally, have noted that using congressional silence as a justification for judge-made rules violates the traditional principle that silence means no extraterritorial application. * * *

The criticisms seem to us justified. The results of judicial-speculation-made-law—divining what Congress would have wanted if it had thought of the situation before the court—demonstrate the wisdom of the presumption against extraterritoriality. Rather than guess anew in each case, we apply the presumption in all cases, preserving a stable background against which Congress can legislate with predictable effects.

B

Rule 10b–5, the regulation under which petitioners have brought suit, was promulgated under § 10(b), and "does not extend beyond conduct encompassed by § 10(b)'s prohibition." United States v. O'Hagan,

521 U.S. 642, 651 (1997). Therefore, if § 10(b) is not extraterritorial, neither is Rule 10b–5.

On its face, § 10(b) contains nothing to suggest it applies abroad * * * . Petitioners and the Solicitor General contend, however, that three things indicate that § 10(b) or the Exchange Act in general has at least some extraterritorial application.

First, they point to the definition of "interstate commerce," a term used in § 10(b), which includes "trade, commerce, transportation, or communication * * * between any foreign country and any State." [Exchange Act § 3(a)(17).] But "we have repeatedly held that even statutes that contain broad language in their definitions of 'commerce' that expressly refer to 'foreign commerce' do not apply abroad." Aramco, 499 U.S., at 251. The general reference to foreign commerce in the definition of "interstate commerce" does not defeat the presumption against extraterritoriality.

Petitioners and the Solicitor General next point out that Congress, in describing the purposes of the Exchange Act, observed that the "prices established and offered in such transactions are generally disseminated and quoted throughout the United States and foreign countries." [Exchange Act § 2(2).] The antecedent of "such transactions," however, is found in the first sentence of the section, which declares that "transactions in securities as commonly conducted upon securities exchanges and over-the-counter markets are affected with a national public interest." § 2. Nothing suggests that this national public interest pertains to transactions conducted upon foreign exchanges and markets. The fleeting reference to the dissemination and quotation abroad of the prices of securities traded in domestic exchanges and markets cannot overcome the presumption against extraterritoriality.

Finally, there is § 30(b) of the Exchange Act, * * * which does mention the Act's extraterritorial application: "The provisions of [the Exchange Act] or of any rule or regulation thereunder shall not apply to any person insofar as he transacts a business in securities without the jurisdiction of the United States," unless he does so in violation of regulations promulgated by the Securities and Exchange Commission "to prevent * * * evasion of [the Act]." (The parties have pointed us to no regulation promulgated pursuant to § 30(b).) The Solicitor General argues that "[this] exemption would have no function if the Act did not apply in the first instance to securities transactions that occur abroad."

We are not convinced. In the first place, it would be odd for Congress to indicate the extraterritorial application of the whole Exchange Act by means of a provision imposing a condition precedent to its application abroad. And if the whole Act applied abroad, why would the Commission's enabling regulations be limited to those preventing "evasion" of the Act, rather than all those preventing "violation"? The provision seems to us directed at actions abroad that might conceal a domestic violation, or might cause what would otherwise be a domestic violation to escape on a technicality. At most, the Solicitor General's proposed inference is possible; but possible interpretations of statutory language do not override the presumption against extraterritoriality. See Aramco, supra, at 253.

The Solicitor General also fails to account for § 30(a), which reads in relevant part as follows:

> "It shall be unlawful for any broker or dealer . . . to make use of the mails or of any means or instrumentality of interstate commerce for the purpose of effecting on an exchange not within or subject to the jurisdiction of the United States, any transaction in any security the issuer of which is a resident of, or is organized under the laws of, or has its principal place of business in, a place within or subject to the jurisdiction of the United States, in contravention of such rules and regulations as the Commission may prescribe. * * * "

Subsection 30(a) contains what § 10(b) lacks: a clear statement of extraterritorial effect. Its explicit provision for a specific extraterritorial application would be quite superfluous if the rest of the Exchange Act already applied to transactions on foreign exchanges—and its limitation of that application to securities of domestic issuers would be inoperative. Even if that were not true, when a statute provides for some extraterritorial application, the presumption against extraterritoriality operates to limit that provision to its terms. See Microsoft Corp. v. AT & T Corp., 550 U.S. 437, 455–456 * * * (2007). No one claims that § 30(a) applies here.

The concurrence claims we have impermissibly narrowed the inquiry in evaluating whether a statute applies abroad, citing for that point the dissent in Aramco * * * . But we do not say, as the concurrence seems to think, that the presumption against extraterritoriality is a "clear statement rule," ibid., if by that is meant a requirement that a statute say "this law applies abroad." Assuredly context can be consulted as well. But whatever sources of statutory meaning one consults to give "the most faithful reading" of the text, * * * there is no clear indication of extraterritoriality here. * * *

In short, there is no affirmative indication in the Exchange Act that § 10(b) applies extraterritorially, and we therefore conclude that it does not.

IV

A

Petitioners argue that the conclusion that § 10(b) does not apply extraterritorially does not resolve this case. They contend that they seek no more than domestic application anyway, since Florida is where HomeSide and its senior executives engaged in the deceptive conduct of manipulating HomeSide's financial models; their complaint also alleged that Race and Hughes made misleading public statements there. This is less an answer to the presumption against extraterritorial application than it is an assertion—a quite valid assertion—that that presumption here (as often) is not self-evidently dispositive, but its application requires further analysis. For it is a rare case of prohibited extraterritorial application that lacks all contact with the territory of the United States. But the presumption against extraterritorial application would be a craven watchdog indeed if it retreated to its kennel whenever some domestic activity is involved in the case. The concurrence seems to imagine just such a timid sentinel, but our cases are to the contrary. In Aramco, for example, the Title VII plaintiff had been hired in Houston, and was an American citizen. * * * The Court concluded, however, that neither that territorial event nor that relationship was the "focus" of congressional concern, id., at 255, but rather domestic employment.

Applying the same mode of analysis here, we think that the focus of the Exchange Act is not upon the place where the deception originated, but upon purchases and sales of securities in the United States. Section 10(b) does not punish deceptive conduct, but only deceptive conduct "in connection with the purchase or sale of any security registered on a national securities exchange or any security not so registered." Those purchase-and-sale transactions are the objects of the statute's solicitude. It is those transactions that the statute seeks to "regulate," see Superintendent of Ins. of N.Y. v. Bankers Life & Casualty Co., 404 U.S. 6 (1971); it is parties or prospective parties to those transactions that the statute seeks to "protec[t]," id., at 10 * * * . And it is in our view only transactions in securities listed on domestic exchanges, and domestic transactions in other securities, to which § 10(b) applies.

The primacy of the domestic exchange is suggested by the very prologue of the Exchange Act, which sets forth as its object "[t]o provide for the regulation of securities exchanges * * * operating in interstate and foreign commerce and through the mails, to prevent inequitable and unfair practices on such exchanges * * * ." * * * We know of no one who thought that the Act was intended to "regulat[e]" foreign securities exchanges—or indeed who even believed that under established principles of international law Congress had the power to do so. The Act's registration requirements apply only to securities listed on national securities exchanges. Exchange Act § 12(a).

With regard to securities not registered on domestic exchanges, the exclusive focus on domestic purchases and sales is strongly confirmed by § 30(a) and (b), discussed earlier. The former extends the normal scope of the Exchange Act's prohibitions to acts effecting, in violation of rules prescribed by the Commission, a "transaction" in a United States security "on an exchange not within or subject to the jurisdiction of the United States." And the latter specifies that the Act does not apply to "any person insofar as he transacts a business in securities without the jurisdiction of the United States," unless he does so in violation of regulations promulgated by the Commission "to prevent evasion [of the Act]." Under both provisions it is the foreign location of the transaction that establishes (or reflects the presumption of) the Act's inapplicability, absent regulations by the Commission.

The same focus on domestic transactions is evident in the Securities Act of 1933, enacted by the same Congress as the Exchange Act, and forming part of the same comprehensive regulation of securities trading. * * * That legislation makes it unlawful to sell a security, through a prospectus or otherwise, making use of "any means or instruments of transportation or communication in interstate commerce or of the mails," unless a registration statement is in effect. [Securities Act § 5(a)(1).] The Commission has interpreted that requirement "not to include * * * sales that occur outside the United States." 17 CFR § 230.901 (2009).

Finally, we reject the notion that the Exchange Act reaches conduct in this country affecting exchanges or transactions abroad for the same reason that Aramco rejected overseas application of Title VII to all domestically concluded employment contracts or all employment contracts with American employers: The probability of incompatibility with the applicable laws of other countries is so obvious that if Congress intended such foreign application "it would have addressed the subject of conflicts with foreign laws and procedures." 499 U.S., at 256. Like the United States, foreign countries regulate their domestic securities exchanges and securities transactions occurring within their territorial jurisdiction. And the regulation of other countries often differs from ours as to what constitutes fraud, what disclosures must be made, what damages are recoverable, what discovery is available in litigation, what individual actions may be joined in a single suit, what attorney's fees are recoverable, and many other matters. * * * The Commonwealth of Australia, the United Kingdom of Great Britain and Northern Ireland, and the Republic of France have filed amicus briefs in this case. So have (separately or jointly) such international and foreign organizations as the International Chamber of Commerce, the Swiss Bankers Association, the Federation of German Industries, the French Business Confederation, the Institute of International Bankers, the European Banking Federation, the Australian Bankers' Association, and the Association Francaise des Entreprises Privées. They all complain of the interference with foreign securities regulation that application of § 10(b) abroad would produce, and urge the adoption of a clear test that will avoid that consequence. The transactional test we have adopted—whether the purchase or sale is made in the United States, or involves a security listed on a domestic exchange—meets that requirement.

B

The Solicitor General suggests a different test, which petitioners also endorse: "[A] transnational securities fraud violates [§]10(b) when the fraud involves significant conduct in the United States that is material to the fraud's success." * * * Neither the Solicitor General nor petitioners provide any textual support for this test. The Solicitor General sets forth a number of purposes such a test would serve: achieving a high standard of business ethics in the securities industry, ensuring honest securities markets and thereby promoting investor confidence, and preventing the United States from becoming a "Barbary Coast" for malefactors perpetrating frauds in foreign markets. * * * But it provides no textual support for the last of these purposes, or for the first two as applied to the foreign securities industry and securities markets abroad. It is our function to give the statute the effect its language suggests, however modest that may be; not to extend it to admirable purposes it might be used to achieve.

If, moreover, one is to be attracted by the desirable consequences of the "significant and material conduct" test, one should also be repulsed by its adverse consequences. While there is no reason to believe that the United States has become the Barbary Coast for those perpetrating frauds on foreign securities markets, some fear that it has become the Shangri-La of class-action litigation for lawyers representing those allegedly cheated in foreign securities markets. * * *

As case support for the "significant and material conduct" test, the Solicitor General relies primarily on Pasquantino v. United States, 544 U.S. 349 (2005). In that case we concluded that the wire-fraud statute, 18 U.S.C. § 1343 (2009 ed., Supp. II), was violated by defendants who ordered liquor over the phone from a store in Maryland with the intent to smuggle it into Canada and deprive the Canadian Government of revenue. * * * Section 1343 prohibits "any scheme or artifice to defraud,"—fraud simpliciter, without any requirement that it be "in connection with" any particular transaction or event. The Pasquantino Court said that the petitioners' "offense was complete the moment they executed the scheme inside the United States," and that it was "[t]his domestic element of petitioners' conduct [that] the Government is punishing." 544 U.S., at 371. Section 10(b), by contrast, punishes not all acts of deception, but only such acts "in connection with the purchase or sale of any security registered on a national securities exchange or any security not so registered." Not deception alone, but deception with respect to certain purchases or sales is necessary for a violation of the statute.

The Solicitor General points out that the "significant and material conduct" test is in accord with prevailing notions of international comity. If so, that proves that if the United States asserted prescriptive jurisdiction pursuant to the "significant and material conduct" test it would not violate customary international law; but it in no way tends to prove that that is what Congress has done.

Finally, the Solicitor General argues that the Commission has adopted an interpretation similar to the "significant and material conduct" test, and that we should defer to that. * * * We need "accept only those agency interpretations that are reasonable in light of the principles of construction courts normally employ." Aramco, 499 U.S., at 260, 111

S.Ct. 1227 (SCALIA, J., concurring in part and concurring in judgment). Since the Commission's interpretations relied on cases we disapprove, which ignored or discarded the presumption against extraterritoriality, we owe them no deference.

Section 10(b) reaches the use of a manipulative or deceptive device or contrivance only in connection with the purchase or sale of a security listed on an American stock exchange, and the purchase or sale of any other security in the United States. This case involves no securities listed on a domestic exchange, and all aspects of the purchases complained of by those petitioners who still have live claims occurred outside the United States. Petitioners have therefore failed to state a claim on which relief can be granted. We affirm the dismissal of petitioners' complaint on this ground.

* * *

The approach endorsed in *Morrison* has come to be known as the "transactional test." The case is subject to criticism for creating a number of ambiguities, including whether Section 10(b) and Rule 10b–5 should apply if a security cross-listed on both an American and foreign exchange were sold in a fraudulent overseas transaction.

Although *Morrison* involved a private plaintiff, the majority's logic seemed to extend to actions brought by the Commission and the Department of Justice as well. Less than a month after Morrison was decided, Congress passed the Dodd-Frank Act. It amended Section 27 of the Exchange Act to specify that U.S. federal courts have extraterritorial jurisdiction over actions brought by either the Commission or the United States involving allegations of fraud in violation of the Exchange Act and either "(1) conduct within the United States that constitutes significant steps in furtherance of the violation, even if the securities transaction occurs outside the United States and involves only foreign investors; or (2) conduct occurring outside the United States that has a foreseeable substantial effect within the United States." Similar provisions were adopted with respect to jurisdiction over actions under the Securities and Investment Advisors Acts. Dodd-Frank also directed the Commission to study whether the same approach should be taken for actions brought by private plaintiffs. The Commission released its report in 2012, noting various options and concluding that "[a]bsent legislation, lower federal courts in particular will likely be called upon to resolve myriad novel and difficult issues regarding the application of the new transactional test."

Ironically, given the Supreme Court's framing of extraterritorial applicability of Section 10(b) as something other than a question of subject matter jurisdiction, Section 27 as amended arguably does nothing to reverse *Morrison*'s holding with respect to transactional coverage; it merely confirms the Court's holding with respect to jurisdiction. Still, there is no doubt that Congress intended to restore what was generally the state of pre-*Morrison* law for government enforcement purposes, and the courts presumably will give effect to that intent.

E. OTHER REQUIREMENTS OF UNITED STATES LAW

Section 30(b) of the Exchange Act generally exempts from that Act's coverage any person transacting a business in securities outside the United States. Although Section 30(b) authorizes the Commission to regulate such persons, the Commission has declined to do so. Accordingly, foreign broker-dealers usually need not comply with the complicated regime to which domestic broker-dealers are subject.

This does not mean, however, that the other provisions of the Exchange Act do not apply to foreign persons. For instance, foreign security holders are required to file reports of their holdings as called for under Sections 13(d) and 16(a). Moreover, in Roth v. Fund of Funds,[8] the Second Circuit found a foreign mutual fund liable for short-swing trading profits under Section 16(b).

F. ENFORCEMENT MATTERS

The Commission does actively enforce the United States securities laws against foreign nationals. Its power to do so is, of course, subject to the difficulties of establishing subject matter and personal jurisdiction. According to Section 22(a) of the Securities Act and Section 27 of the Exchange Act, process may be served "wherever the defendant may be found." This breadth is limited by the due process requirement that the person to be charged must have good reason to know that his conduct will have an effect in the locale seeking jurisdiction.

As a practical matter, investigations involving foreign nationals can be hampered by foreign laws. In SEC v. Banca Della Svizzera Italiana, directly below, the court considered whether to compel a response to answer Commission interrogatories in a situation in which disclosure might subject the resisting party to criminal liability in its home country (under Swiss bank secrecy laws).

Securities and Exchange Commission v.
Banca Della Svizzera Italiana, et al.

United States District Court, Southern District of New York, 1981.
92 F.R.D. 111.

■ POLLACK, DISTRICT JUDGE:

[The SEC] moves this Court for an appropriate order pursuant to Fed.R.Civ.P. 37 for the failure and refusal of defendant, Banca Della Svizzera Italiana ("BSI") to provide the SEC with information relative to the identities of the principals for whom it purchased stock and stock

---

[8]   405 F.2d 421 (2d Cir.1968).

options on American exchanges in St. Joe Minerals Corporation ("St. Joe"), a New York corporation which produces natural resources.

The underlying law suit is an action by the SEC against the said defendant and unnamed others for an injunction and an accounting for violations of the insider trading provisions of the Securities Exchange Act of 1934, Sections 10(b) and 14(e), * * * and Rules 10b–5 and 14e–3 promulgated thereunder.

Jurisdiction over BSI exists by virtue of BSI's doing business here. There is evidence in the record that BSI operates in New York at 44 Wall Street through a subsidiary corporation. * * *

The issue posed to the Court is whether to compel a foreign party which transacted purchases on American securities exchanges to make discovery and answer interrogatories concerning its undisclosed principals where the acts of disclosure might subject that party to criminal liability in its home country. The Court has carefully balanced the interests at stake and considered the resisting party's professed good faith. It concludes that compelling the complete discovery demanded is not only justified in the instant case but required to preserve our vital national interest in maintaining the integrity of the securities markets against violations committed and/or aided and assisted by parties located abroad. Accordingly, an order should issue requiring full responses to the SEC's interrogatories.

The Facts

This action alleges insider trading on the part of BSI and its principals in the purchase and sale of call options for the common stock as well as the common stock itself of St. Joe. The options were traded through the Philadelphia Stock Exchange and the stock was traded on the New York Stock Exchange both of which are registered national exchanges. * * *

* * *

* * * [BSI's] transactions resulted in a virtually overnight profit just short of $2 million.

Promptly on noticing the undue activity in the options market, the SEC investigated and based on its findings brought this suit. The SEC contends that there is a strong probability that the purchasers were unlawfully using material non-public information which could only have been obtained or misappropriated from sources charged with a confidential duty not to disclose information prior to the public announcement of [a tender offer for St. Joe's shares].

* * *

The SEC endeavored by one or another procedural means, here and abroad, to obtain the identity of those who, along with the bank, were involved in the particular options purchases. No disclosure was forthcoming. Explanatory but uninformative letters so far as concerned the identity of the principals were received by the SEC from time to time. The SEC served formal interrogatories which were refined at the Court's suggestion to target the demanded disclosure in simplest terms. Conferences were held with the Court at which explanations were supplied and it was made clear at these that if need be an appropriate order enforceable by appropriate but, to the bank, unpalatable sanctions, might follow any continued impasse. Nonetheless, BSI declined to furnish the requested information voluntarily, adhering to its assertion of banking secrecy law. Eight months elapsed in the efforts to obtain the requisite disclosure by cooperative measures.

The bank regularly suggested, in the interim, a variety of alternative means by which the SEC might proceed to seek the disclosure. Some of these were doomed to failure in the opinion of the bank's own experts. It appeared to the Court that the proposals would only send the SEC on empty excursions, with little to show for them except more delay, more expense, more frustration, and possibly also, the inexorable operation of time bars against the claims by statutory limits for the assertion thereof. The proposed alternatives were not viable substitutes for direct discovery.

* * *

The Authorities and Commentators

1.　The Supreme Court's opinion in Societe

Any discussion of the issue posed here must begin with the Supreme Court's opinion in Societe Internationale Pour Participations Industrielles et Commerciales, S. A. v. Rogers, 357 U.S. 197 * * * (1958) which is the Court's latest decision on the subject. *Societe* holds that the good faith of the party resisting discovery is a key factor in the decision whether to impose sanctions when foreign law prohibits the requested disclosure.

In *Societe* a Swiss holding company was suing for the return of property seized by the Alien Property Custodian during World War II. The district court dismissed plaintiff's complaint as a sanction for its refusal to comply with the Court's order to produce bank records, despite a finding that the Swiss government had constructively seized the documents * * * and that plaintiff had shown good faith efforts to comply with the production order. * * * The Court of Appeals affirmed.

The Supreme Court reversed. It held that where plaintiff was prohibited by Swiss law from complying with the discovery order and there was no showing of bad faith, the sanction of dismissal without prejudice was not justified. The Court indicated that a party who had made deliberate use of foreign law to evade American law might be subject to sanctions.

* * *

Application of the Law to the Facts of this Case

BSI claims that it may be subject to criminal liability under Swiss penal and banking law if it discloses the requested information. However, this Court finds the factors in § 40 of the Restatement of Foreign Relations to tip decisively in favor of the SEC. Moreover, it holds BSI to be "in the position of one who deliberately courted legal impediments * * * and who thus cannot now be heard to assert its good faith after this expectation was realized." *Societe*, supra * * * . BSI acted in bad faith. It made deliberate use of Swiss nondisclosure law to evade in a commercial transaction for profit to it, the strictures of American securities law against insider trading. Whether acting solely as an agent or also as a principal (something which can only be clarified through disclosure of the requested information), BSI invaded American securities markets and profited in some measure thereby. * * * It cannot rely on Swiss nondisclosure law to shield this activity.

1.   The vital national interests at stake

The first of the § 40 factors is the vital national interest of each of the States. The strength of the United States interest in enforcing its securities laws to ensure the integrity of its financial markets cannot seriously be doubted. That interest is being continually thwarted by the use of foreign bank accounts. Congress, in enacting legislation on bank record-keeping, expressed its concern over the problem over a decade ago:

> Secret foreign bank accounts and secret foreign financial institutions have permitted a proliferation of "white collar" crime * * * (and) have allowed Americans and others to avoid the law and regulations concerning securities and exchanges. * * * The debilitating effects of the use of these secret institutions on Americans and the American economy are vast.

H.R.Rep.No. 975, 91 Cong., 2d Sess. 12, reprinted in (1970) U.S.Code Cong. & Admin.News 4394, 4397.

The evisceration of the United States interest in enforcing its securities laws continues up to the present. See, e.g., Wall Street Journal, Oct. 29, 1981, at 1, col. 5 ("some Wall Street sources believe the SEC faces an insurmountable problem: obtaining from foreign sources the information that often is necessary to identify violators").

The Swiss government, on the other hand, though made expressly aware of the litigation, has expressed no opposition. In response to BSI's lawyers inquiries, the incumbent Swiss Federal Attorney General, Rudolf Gerber, said only that a foreign court could not change the rule that disclosure required the consent of the one who imparted the secret and that BSI might thus be subject to prosecution. The Swiss government did not "confiscate" the Bank records to prevent violations of its law, as it did in *Societe*. NEITHER THE UNITED STATES NOR THE SWISS GOVERNMENT has suggested that discovery be halted. * * *

It is also of significance that the secrecy privilege, as even BSI's expert admits[,] * * * is one belonging to the bank customers and may be waived by them. It is not something required to protect the Swiss government itself or some other public interest. * * *

2.   Hardship considerations and the element of good faith

The second factor of § 40 of the Restatement of Foreign Relations is the extent and nature of the hardship that inconsistent enforcement actions would impose upon the party subject to both jurisdictions. It is true that BSI may be subject to fines and its officers to imprisonment under Swiss law. However, this Court notes that there is some flexibility in the application of that law. Not only may the particular bank involved obtain waivers from its customers to avoid prosecution, but Article 34 of the Swiss Penal Code contains a "State of Necessity" exception that relieves a person of criminal liability for acts committed to protect one's own good, including one's fortune, from an immediate danger if one is not responsible for the danger and one cannot be expected to give up one's good. * * *

Of course, given BSI's active part in the insider trading transactions alleged here, the Swiss government might well conclude—as this Court has—that BSI is responsible for the conflict it is in and that therefore the "State of Necessity" exception should not apply. However, that is certainly no cause for this Court to withhold its sanctions since the dilemma would be a result of BSI's bad faith. * * *

3.   The remaining § 40 factors

The last three of the § 40 Restatement of Foreign Relations Law factors—the place of performance, the nationality of the resisting party, and the extent to which enforcement can be expected to achieve compliance with the rule prescribed by that state—appear to be less important in this Circuit. It is significant nevertheless that they too tip in favor of the SEC. Performance may be said to occur here as well as in Switzerland since the actual answering of the interrogatories will presumably take place in the United States, where BSI's lawyers are. As for citizenship, it is true that BSI is a Swiss corporation. However, its transnational character, as evidenced by its large number of foreign affiliates, * * * and its New York "subsidiary" (so styled by it), render this Court less reluctant to order BSI to conform to our laws even where such an order may cause conflict with Swiss law. Last, with respect to enforcement, this Court believes that an appropriate formal order directing the demanded disclosure, to the extent that compliance has been incomplete, will serve as the requisite foundation for any further actions that may be needed in the form of sanctions and should serve to bring home the obligations a foreign entity undertakes when it conducts business on the American securities exchanges.

Conclusion

It would be a travesty of justice to permit a foreign company to invade American markets, violate American laws if they were indeed violated, withdraw profits and resist accountability for itself and its principals for the illegality by claiming their anonymity under foreign law.

———

In some instances, enforcement difficulties are eased by international treaty. For instance, the United States and Switzerland have a treaty calling for mutual assistance in the investigation of activity that is criminal in both countries. Such treaties are, of course, limited in their terms and subject to the constitutional constraint of approval by the United States Senate. More frequently, the Commission enters into non-binding Memoranda of Understanding, or "MOUs," with its counterparts in other countries. These MOUs typically call for inter-agency sharing of information.

The International Securities Enforcement Cooperation Act of 1990 gave the Commission a partial exemption from the United States Freedom of Information Act for information received from a foreign authority under an MOU. This legislation also permits the Commission to sanction securities professionals for activities illegal under foreign law. Moreover, the Commission generally is authorized (under the Securities Fraud Enforcement Act of 1988) to cooperate in foreign investigations, even where no violation of United States law has occurred.

INDEX

References are to Pages

SALE
Acquisitions, 188–192
Acts constituting, 69–72, 187–192
Prohibitions against, 44, 69
Rule 145 transactions, 189–192
Spin-offs, 187–196

SALE OF BUSINESS DOCTRINE,
    176–181

SARBANES-OXLEY ACT OF 2002,
    pp. 13, 28–29, 281–282, 341–342,
    346–349, 385–389, 468, 536–537,
    560, 575–577, 578, 607–609, 665–
    666, 671, 745–747

SCHEME LIABILITY, 512–523

SEASONED ISSUER, 41–42, 89

SEC AUTHORITY, EXTENT OF, 604–
    624

SECTION 16(b)
See Short-Swing Profits

SECURITIES ACT OF 1933
    Generally, 9–11
Background, 3

**SECURITIES AND EXCHANGE
    COMMISSION**
    Generally, 4–12
Cease-and-desist orders, 280, 414, 508,
    639
Exemptive authority, 198, 225, 354
Interpretations, 16–17
Investigation powers, 93, 639–643
No-action letters, 16–17
Organization of, 5–10
Pronouncements, 14–18
Quasi-judicial authority, 17
Refusal orders, 93
Releases, in general, 16–17
Rule 102(e) proceedings, 703–716
Rulemaking, 14–15
Rules, force of, 15
Stop orders, 104–105